PART 7

Research Writing

PART 8

Writing in the Disciplines

Glossary / Index
CULTURE LANGUAGE Guide

Inside the back cover:
Detailed Contents
Editing Symbols

g this book

...ook can answer your questions ...ng, grammar, research, and many other subjects. To find answers, you have many routes into the book:

Using a table of contents. The brief contents here shows the book's parts and chapters. The detailed contents inside the back cover shows each chapter's main headings as well.

Using a tabbed divider. On the back of each divider, a detailed outline directs you to the material covered in that part of the book.

Using the glossary. The "Glossary of Usage" (pp. 511–24) clarifies words that are commonly confused and misused.

Using the index. The index includes every term, concept, and problem word or expression in the book.

Using the "CULTURE LANGUAGE Guide." Just before the detailed contents at the back of the book, this guide indexes all the material for students using standard American English as a second language or second dialect.

Using the elements of the page. Each page of the handbook tells you where you are and what you can find there. (See the "Preface for Students," p. x, for sample pages with annotations that highlight the elements).

Using the eText or iPad version. Icons in the margins of this handbook link to a wide array of electronic resources available on the Pearson eText and iPad versions. (See p. xi for details on how to access an electronic version of the handbook.)

👁 Video tutorials illustrate key concepts in academic writing and research.

🔊 Audio podcasts answer common questions about grammar and punctuation.

📄 Student papers and sample documents provide examples of college, workplace, and public writing.

✳ Exercises offer opportunities for practice.

✔ Checklists from the handbook provide key information in a format that can be customized.

Why do you need this new edition?

This edition of *The Little, Brown Compact Handbook* differs from the previous edition in countless ways. Here are six that make the book indispensable:

1. Media-rich eText versions for *MyCompLab, MyWritingLab*, and the iPad ▪ **Video tutorials** illustrate key principles. ▪ **Podcasts** discuss common questions about grammar and usage. ▪ **Student papers and sample documents** provide models of common writing assignments. ▪ **Exercises** give opportunities for practice. ▪ **Checklists** from the handbook allow you to adapt key summaries for your own use. ▪ *MyCompLab* and *MyWritingLab* include additional resources on grammar, writing, and research.

2. More help with academic writing ▪ A chapter on **joining the academic community** provides tips for succeeding in face-to-face and online classes. ▪ Discussions of **genre** help you get started on college writing assignments. ▪ Discussions of **academic integrity** and **writing responsibly** throughout help you write successfully in an academic setting. ▪ **Four new sample papers** include a literacy narrative, a critique of a text, an argument, and a literary analysis. ▪ A **new chapter on essay exams** provides tips for writing under pressure and an annotated sample exam.

3. More help with research writing and documentation ▪ A revised chapter on **plagiarism** helps you recognize and avoid accidental plagiarism. ▪ Material on **evaluating online sources**—Web sites, social-networking sites, blogs, wikis, and multimedia—shows you how to distinguish between reliable and unreliable sources. ▪ Updated **annotated sample sources** illustrate how to find and format bibliographic information in articles and books and on Web sites.

4. More help with the writing process ▪ Coverage of **thesis** explains how to pose a thesis question and move from the question to a thesis statement. ▪ Coverage of **paragraphs** foregrounds relating paragraphs in an essay.

5. More help with visual and media literacy ▪ A new chapter on **presenting writing** helps you make choices when designing documents, using visuals and other media, and writing for the Web. ▪ Chapters on **critical reading and working with sources** explain how to analyze ads, graphs, and other visuals.

6. More help with grammar and usage ▪ New and revised CULTURE LANGUAGE notes provide added help if you are using standard American English as a second language or dialect. ▪ A revised chapter on **effective words** discusses and illustrates online dictionaries and thesauruses and gives tips for avoiding the shortcuts of online communication in academic writing.

MyCompLab®

Become a better writer and researcher—and get better grades in all your courses—with *MyCompLab*!

Writing, grammar, and research help are at your fingertips as you draft and revise.

Composing. This dynamic space for composing, revising, and editing is easy to use and is built to function like the most popular word-processing programs.

- Use the Writer's Toolkit to search for answers to your writing questions.
- View instructor, peer, and tutor comments on your work in one place.
- Store and manage all your work in one place.
- Access paper review help from experienced tutors through Pearson Tutor Services.

Access instruction, multimedia tutorials, and exercises in the Resources area to help you master skills and get a better grade.

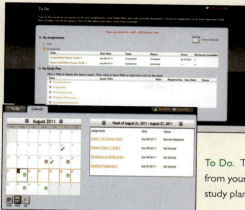

Manage all your written work and assignments online, in one easy-to-use place.

To Do. This area captures assignments and due dates from your instructor along with your personalized study plan.

Gradebook. This area shows writing and exercise scores. You can see how you are progressing toward a better grade!

Access the eText version

This book is available as an eText within *MyCompLab*. The eText is a convenient and powerful tool that you can use on any computer with an Internet connection or on your iPad® by downloading the Pearson eText app. You can search the eText by key term to find exactly what you need and can use the highlighting and note-taking features for studying. In addition, icons in the book's margins link to a wide array of electronic resources: video tutorials, podcasts, student papers, sample documents, exercises, and checklists.

Register for *MyCompLab* today!

Questions? Go to www.mycomplab.com/help.html and click "Student Support."

If this book did not come packaged with an access code to *MyCompLab,* you can purchase access online at **www.mycomplab.com/student-registration/index.html** or ask your bookstore to order an access card for you.

EIGHTH EDITION

The Little, Brown
Compact Handbook

Jane E. Aaron

Boston   Columbus   Indianapolis   New York   San Francisco
Upper Saddle River   Amsterdam   Cape Town   Dubai   London   Madrid   Milan
Munich   Paris   Montreal   Toronto   Delhi   Mexico City   São Paulo
Sydney   Hong Kong   Seoul   Singapore   Taipei   Tokyo

Executive Editor: Suzanne Phelps Chambers
Senior Development Editor: Anne Brunell Ehrenworth
Senior Supplements Editor: Donna Campion
Executive Digital Producer: Stefanie Snajder
Digital Editor: Sara Gordus
Digital Project Manager: Janell Lantana
Senior Marketing Manager: Thomas DeMarco
Production Manager: Bob Ginsberg
Project Coordination, Text Design, and Electronic Page Makeup:
    Cenveo Publisher Services/Nesbitt Graphics, Inc.
Cover Design Manager: John Callahan
Cover Designer: Kay Petronio
Cover Image: jocic/Shutterstock
Senior Manufacturing Buyer: Roy L. Pickering, Jr.
Printer and Binder: RR Donnelley & Sons Company/Crawfordsville
Cover Printer: Lehigh-Phoenix

Credits and acknowledgments for material borrowed from other sources
and reproduced, with permission, in this textbook appear on pages 525–26.

Library of Congress Cataloging-in-Publication Data

Aaron, Jane E.
  The Little, Brown compact handbook / Jane E. Aaron. — 8th ed.
    p. cm.
  ISBN 9780205236602
  1. English language—Grammar—Handbooks, manuals, etc. 2. English
language—Rhetoric—Handbooks, manuals, etc. I. Title. II. Title: Compact
handbook.

  PE1112.A23 2011
  808'.042--dc23

                              2011044538

10 9 8 7 6 5 4 3 2—DOC—14 13 12

ISBN 10: 0-205-23660-X
ISBN 13: 978-0-205-23660-2
www.pearsonhighered.com

Preface for Students

The Little, Brown Compact Handbook contains the basic information you'll need for writing in and out of school. Here you can find how to get ideas, use commas, craft an argument, find sources for research projects, cite sources, and write a résumé—all in a convenient, accessible package.

This book is mainly a reference for you to dip into as needs arise. You probably won't read the book all the way through, nor will you use everything it contains: you already know much of the content anyway, whether consciously or not. The trick is to figure out what you *don't* know—taking cues from your own writing experiences and the comments of others—and then to find the answers to your questions in these pages.

Using this book will not by itself make you a good writer; for that, you need to care about your work at every level, from finding a subject to spelling words. But learning how to use the handbook and its information can give you the means to write *what* you want in the *way* you want.

Reference aids

You have many ways to find what you need in the handbook:

- **Use a directory.** The brief contents inside the front cover displays all the book's parts and chapters. The more detailed contents inside the back cover provides each chapter's subheadings as well.
- **Use a tabbed divider.** At each tab, a detailed outline directs you to the material covered in that part of the book.
- **Use the glossary.** The "Glossary of Usage" (last tabbed divider) clarifies more than 275 words that are commonly confused and misused.
- **Use the index.** At the end of the book, the extensive index includes every term, concept, and problem word or expression mentioned in the book.
- **Use a list.** Two helpful aids fall inside the book's back cover: First, the "CULTURE LANGUAGE Guide" (just before "Contents") pulls together all the book's material for students who are using standard American English as a second language or a second dialect. And "Editing Symbols" (back cover flap) explains abbreviations often used to comment on papers.
- **Use the elements of the page.** As shown in the illustration on the next page, the handbook constantly tells you where you are and what you can find there.

The handbook's page elements

Running head (header) and page tab showing the topic being discussed on this page, its section code (**31a**), and its editing symbol (**pn agr**)

Icons for the eText linking to video tutorials, exercises, podcasts, student papers, sample documents, or checklists

Culture-language connection, a pointer for students using standard American English as a second language or a second dialect

Section heading, a main convention or topic labeled with the section code, 31a: chapter number (31) and section letter (a)

Examples, always indented, with underlining and annotations highlighting sentence elements and revisions

Key terms box, defining terms used on the page

Web box linking to the eText and *MyCompLab*

Summary or checklist box providing key information in accessible form

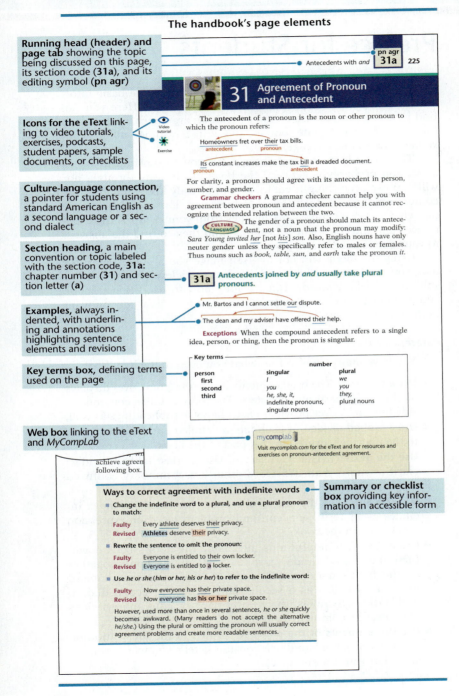

Antecedents with *and* **pn agr 31a** 225

31 Agreement of Pronoun and Antecedent

The **antecedent** of a pronoun is the noun or other pronoun to which the pronoun refers:

Homeowners fret over their tax bills.
antecedent   pronoun

Its constant increases make the tax bill a dreaded document.
pronoun   antecedent

For clarity, a pronoun should agree with its antecedent in person, number, and gender.

Grammar checkers A grammar checker cannot help you with agreement between pronoun and antecedent because it cannot recognize the intended relation between the two.

CULTURE LANGUAGE The gender of a pronoun should match its antecedent, not a noun that the pronoun may modify: *Sara Young invited her* [not *his*] son. Also, English nouns have only neuter gender unless they specifically refer to males or females. Thus nouns such as *book, table, sun,* and *earth* take the pronoun *it.*

31a **Antecedents joined by *and* usually take plural pronouns.**

Mr. Bartos and I cannot settle our dispute.

The dean and my adviser have offered their help.

Exceptions When the compound antecedent refers to a single idea, person, or thing, then the pronoun is singular.

Key terms

person	number singular	plural
first	I	we
second	you	you
third	he, she, it, indefinite pronouns, singular nouns	they, plural nouns

mycomplab Visit *mycomplab.com* for the eText and for resources and exercises on pronoun-antecedent agreement.

Ways to correct agreement with indefinite words

- Change the indefinite word to a plural, and use a plural pronoun to match:

  Faulty   Every athlete deserves their privacy.
  Revised Athletes deserve their privacy.

- Rewrite the sentence to omit the pronoun:

  Faulty   Everyone is entitled to their own locker.
  Revised Everyone is entitled to a locker.

- Use *he or she* (*him or her, his or her*) to refer to the indefinite word:

  Faulty   Now everyone has their private space.
  Revised Now everyone has his or her private space.

However, used more than once in several sentences, *he or she* quickly becomes awkward. (Many readers do not accept the alternative *he/she.*) Using the plural or omitting the pronoun will usually correct agreement problems and create more readable sentences.

Print and eText versions

The Little, Brown Compact Handbook is available as a print book and in several electronic versions:

- A Pearson eText provides the complete handbook and the electronic resources described below. The eText is accessible through *MyCompLab* and *MyWritingLab*, both interactive learning environments with abundant resources for writing. You can gain access to *MyCompLab* and *MyWritingLab* through your course instructor, with the purchase of a new copy of the handbook, or through an independent purchase at *mycomplab.com* or *mywritinglab.com*.

- A Pearson eText app for the iPad provides the complete handbook and the electronic resources described below.

- A subscription to the handbook as a *CourseSmart* e-textbook provides access to all of the handbook's content in a format that enables you to search the text, bookmark passages, integrate your notes, and print reading assignments that incorporate lecture notes. To subscribe, visit *coursesmart.com*.

eText resources

Icons in the handbook's margins link to a wealth of electronic resources:

- Nearly 150 video tutorials illustrate key concepts, offering tips and guidance on critical reading, evaluating sources, avoiding plagiarism, and many other topics.

- More than twenty-five audio podcasts discuss common questions about grammar, usage, punctuation, and mechanics.

- More than fifty student papers and sample documents illustrate the range of writing you'll do in composition classes, your other courses, the workplace, and the community.

- Exercises offer ample opportunities to sharpen your writing, grammar, and research skills.

- Editable checklists from the handbook allow you to adapt key summaries for your own use.

Preface for Instructors

The Little, Brown Compact Handbook provides writers with an accessible reference, one that helps them find what they need and then use what they find. Combining the authority of its parent, *The Little, Brown Handbook*, with a briefer and more convenient format, the *Compact Handbook* addresses writers of varying experience, in varying fields, answering common questions about the writing process, grammar and style, research writing, and more.

This new edition improves on the handbook's strengths as a clear, concise, and accessible reference, while keeping pace with rapid changes in writing and its teaching. In the context of the handbook's many reference functions, the following pages highlight as **New** the most significant additions and changes.

A guide to academic writing

The handbook gives students a solid foundation in the goals and requirements of college writing.

- **New** A new Chapter 8, "Joining the Academic Community," provides tips for succeeding in face-to-face and online classes and for writing responsibly in academic situations.
- **New** Key chapters stress academic integrity and avoiding plagiarism—the new Chapter 8 as well as Chapter 10 on academic writing and Chapter 53 on avoiding plagiarism. Other chapters throughout the handbook reinforce these important topics.
- **New** Common genres of academic writing receive emphasis in the context of the writing process, academic writing, and writing in the disciplines. Eleven examples of academic genres appear throughout the handbook. (See **2** pp. 95–96 for a list.)
- **New** Fresh examples of academic writing—a literacy narrative, a critique of a text, a proposal argument, and a literary argument—supplement the other sample papers and projects in the handbook.
- **New** Summarizing receives new emphasis in Chapter 9 on critical thinking and reading.
- Synthesis receives special emphasis wherever students might need help balancing their own and others' views, such as in responding to texts.
- **New** A chapter on essay exams gives helpful tips for writing under pressure and includes an annotated sample exam.
- Parts 7 and 8 give students a solid foundation in research writing and writing in the disciplines (literature, other humanities, social sciences, natural and applied sciences), along with exten-

sive coverage of documentation in MLA, Chicago, APA, and CSE styles.

A guide to research writing and documentation

With detailed advice, the handbook always attends closely to research writing and source citation. The discussion stresses using the library as Web gateway, managing information, evaluating and synthesizing sources, integrating source material, and avoiding plagiarism. The extensive coverage of four documentation styles—MLA, Chicago, APA, and CSE—reflects each style's latest version.

- **New** To help students develop their own perspectives on their research subjects, the text stresses asking questions, entering into dialog with sources, and presenting multiple views fairly and responsibly.
- **New** A sample entry from a student's annotated bibliography includes a source assessment, demonstrating an early step in evaluating sources.
- **New** Reflecting the varied ways that students may seek sources, the discussion of libraries' Web portals covers research guides and centralized search engines and also updates the material on databases.
- **New** An expanded discussion of evaluating Web sources—Web sites, social-networking sites, blogs, wikis, multimedia—helps students discern purposes and distinguish between reliable and unreliable sources.
- Case studies in source evaluation show the application of critical criteria to sample articles and Web documents.
- **New** The revised chapter on avoiding plagiarism and documenting sources gives more examples of deliberate and accidental plagiarism, new examples of material that must be cited, and updated advice about avoiding plagiarism with online sources.
- A research paper-in-progress on green consumerism follows a student through the research process and culminates in an annotated paper documented in MLA style.
- **New** Updated, annotated samples of key source types illustrate MLA and APA documentation, showing students how to find the bibliographical information needed to cite each type.
- For all documentation styles, color highlighting makes authors, titles, dates, and other citation elements easy to grasp.
- **New** Updated source lists in Part 8 provide reliable starting points for research in every discipline.

A guide to writing as a process

The handbook takes a practical approach to assessing the writing situation, generating ideas, developing the thesis statement, revising, and other elements of the writing process.

- **New** Genre joins subject, purpose, and audience as a key element of every writing situation, affecting content, format, and readers' expectations.
- **New** Expanded coverage of thesis now includes a detailed discussion of developing a thesis question and moving from the question to a thesis statement.
- **New** Chapter 6 on paragraphs opens with a discussion of relating paragraphs in the essay, expands on the discussion of coherence, and includes many new examples.
- **New** A comprehensive chapter on presenting writing covers designing print and electronic documents, creating and using visuals and other media in multimodal writing projects, and Web writing.

A guide to usage, grammar, and punctuation

The handbook's core reference material reliably and concisely explains basic concepts and common errors and provides hundreds of annotated examples from across the curriculum.

- **New** Part 3 on clarity and style includes many fresh examples, a discussion of online dictionaries and thesauruses, and advice on avoiding abbreviations, fragments, and other features of online communication.
- Summary and checklist boxes provide quick-reference help with color highlighting to distinguish sentence elements.

A guide to visual and media literacy

The handbook helps students process nonverbal information and use it effectively in their writing.

- **New** Chapter 7 on presenting writing and Chapter 51 on finding sources give practical tips for creating, selecting, and integrating visuals and multimedia into college writing projects.
- Thorough discussions of critically reading advertisements, graphs, and other visuals appear in Chapter 9 on critical reading, Chapter 11 on argument, and Chapter 52 on working with sources.
- Illustrations in several of the handbook's student papers show various ways to support written ideas with visual information.

A guide for culturally and linguistically diverse writers

At notes and sections labeled $\boxed{\text{CULTURE LANGUAGE}}$, the handbook provides extensive rhetorical and grammatical help for writers whose first language or dialect is not standard American English.

- Fully integrated coverage, instead of a separate section, means that students can find what they need without having to know which problems they do and don't share with native SAE speakers.

- " (CULTURE LANGUAGE) Guide," on pp. 580–81, orients students with advice on mastering SAE and pulls all the integrated coverage together in one place.
- **New** Many (CULTURE LANGUAGE) notes throughout the handbook use simpler language and add sentence-length examples. New notes cover oral presentations and plagiarism.

An accessible reference guide

The handbook is an open book for students, with a convenient lay-flat binding, tabbed dividers, and many internal features that help students navigate and use the content.

- A clean, uncluttered page design uses color and type clearly to distinguish parts of the book and elements of the pages.
- A brief table of contents inside the front cover provides an at-a-glance overview of the book, while a detailed table of contents appears inside the back cover.
- Color highlighting in boxes and on documentation models distinguishes important elements.
- A unique approach to terminology facilitates reference and reading. Headings in the text and tables of contents avoid or explain terms. And "Key terms" boxes in the text provide essential definitions, dramatically reducing cross-references and page flipping.
- An unusually accessible organization groups related problems so that students can easily find what they need.
- Cross-references give divider numbers in addition to page numbers, sending students directly to the appropriate tabbed section—for instance, "See **3** pp. 156–58."
- Annotations on both visual and verbal examples connect principles and illustrations.
- Dictionary-style headers in the index make it easy to find entries.
- A preface just for students details the book's reference aids, explains the page layout, and describes the print and e-textbook versions.

Two versions of the handbook

The handbook is available with a full complement of exercises built into the book. Otherwise identical to the book you're holding, *The Little, Brown Compact Handbook with Exercises* includes more than 140 sets of exercises on usage, grammar, punctuation, and mechanics as well as on rhetorical concerns such as thesis statements and paraphrasing. The exercises are in connected discourse, and their subjects come from across the academic curriculum.

Print and electronic formats

The eighth edition is available both in print and as an e-textbook in the following formats:

- **New** A Pearson eText provides the complete handbook and electronic resources on the *MyCompLab* and *MyWritingLab* Web sites (see below and opposite for more on the eText resources and the Web sites).

- **New** A Pearson eText app for the iPad provides the complete handbook and electronic resources (see below for more on the eText resources).

- A *CourseSmart* e-textbook, which is available by subscription at *coursesmart.com*, gives students access to all of the book's content in a format that enables them to search the text, bookmark passages, integrate their notes, and print reading assignments that incorporate lecture notes.

eText resources for students and instructors

New Icons in the handbook's margins link to a wide array of electronic resources:

- 👁 Nearly 150 video tutorials illustrate key concepts, offering tips and guidance on critical reading, evaluating sources, avoiding plagiarism, and many other topics.

- ((•‣ More than twenty-five audio podcasts discuss common questions about grammar, usage, punctuation, and mechanics.

- 📄 More than fifty student papers and sample documents illustrate the range of writing that students do in composition and other courses, the workplace, and the community.

- ✳ Exercises offer students ample opportunities to sharpen their writing, grammar, and research skills.

- ✔ Editable checklists from the handbook allow students to adapt key summaries for their own use.

Supplements

Pearson offers a variety of support materials to make teaching easier and to help students improve as writers. The following resources are geared specifically to *The Little, Brown Compact Handbook*. For more information on these and scores of additional supplements, visit *pearsonhighered.com* or contact your local Pearson sales representative.

- The Web site *MyCompLab* (*mycomplab.com*) integrates instruction, multimedia tutorials, and exercises for writing, grammar, and research with an online composing space and assessment tools. This seamless, flexible environment comes from extensive research in partnership with composition faculty and students across the country. It provides help for writers in the context of their writing, with functions for instructors' and peers' commentary. Special features include an e-portfolio, a bibliography tool, tutoring services, an assignment builder, and a gradebook and course-management organization created specifically for writing classes. In addition, *MyCompLab* includes the Pearson eText version of *The Little, Brown Compact Handbook* (see opposite).

■ The Web site *MyWritingLab* (*mywritinglab.com*) is a complete online-learning system with more than nine thousand exercises to help students become better writers. The exercises are progressive: within each skill module, students move from literal comprehension to critical application to use of skills in their own writing. The exercises cover grammar extensively and also extend to the writing process, paragraph development, essay development, and research. A thorough diagnostic test reveals students' individual needs, and an easy-to-use tracking system enables students and instructors to monitor all work done on the site. In addition, *MyWritingLab* includes the eText version of *The Little, Brown Compact Handbook* (see opposite).

■ *Exercises to Accompany The Little, Brown Compact Handbook* offers the same activities found in the exercise version of the handbook, all double-spaced so that students can work directly in the book. An answer key is available.

■ *Developmental Exercises to Accompany The Little, Brown Compact Handbook* provides activities in a workbook for developmental writers. An answer key is available.

■ *VangoNotes* are study guides in MP3 format that enable students to download handbook information into their own players and then listen to it whenever and wherever they wish. The notes include "need to know" tips for each handbook chapter, practice tests, audio flash cards for learning key concepts and terms, and a rapid review for exams. For more information, visit *VangoNotes.com*.

■ *Diagnostic and Editing Tests and Exercises* are cross-referenced to *The Little, Brown Compact Handbook* and are available both in print and online.

Acknowledgments

The Little, Brown Compact Handbook stays fresh and useful because instructors talk with Pearson's sales representatives and editors, answer questionnaires, write detailed reviews, and send me personal notes. For the eighth edition, I am especially grateful to the following instructors whose insights led to the improvements in this new edition: David L. Anderson, Butler County Community

College; Richard E. Baker, Adams State College; Mike Barrett, Moberly Area Community College; Sarah Kelly Burns, Virginia Western Community College; Lucia Cherciu, Dutchess Community College; Mary Connerty, Penn State Erie, the Behrend College; Dean Cooledge, University of Maryland Eastern Shore; Joseph Couch, Montgomery College; Margaret H. Davis, Spring Hill College; Mildred A. Duprey-Smith, College of Southern Nevada; Anthony Edgington, University of Toledo; Tarasa Gardner, Moberly Area Community College; Larry Giddings, Pikes Peak Community College; Barbara Goldstein, Hillsborough Community College; Andrew Green, University of Miami; Harold William Halbert, Montgomery County Community College; Jen Hazel, Owens Community College; Beth Kolp, Dutchess Community College; Jeraldine Kraver, University of Northern Colorado; Pat Leitch, Miami Dade College; Michael T. Lueker, Our Lady of the Lake University; Angie Macri, Pulaski Technical College; David MacWilliams, Adams State College; Victoria E. McLure, South Plains College; Marilee Motto, Owens Community College; and Neil Plakcy, Broward College.

In responding to the ideas of these thoughtful critics, I had the help of several creative people. Aaron McCullough, University of Michigan, guided me through the labyrinth of the contemporary library. Marilyn Hochman suggested improvements in the notes for students whose first language or dialect is not standard English. Sylvan Barnet, Tufts University, continued to lend his expertise in the chapter "Reading and Writing about Literature," which is adapted from his *Short Guide to Writing about Literature* and *Introduction to Literature* (with William Burto and William E. Cain). Ellen Kuhl provided creative, meticulous, and invaluable help with the material on research writing. And Carol Hollar-Zwick, sine qua non, served brilliantly as originator, sounding board, critic, coordinator, researcher, producer, and friend.

A superb publishing team helped to make this book. At Longman, editors Suzanne Phelps Chambers, Anne Brunell Ehrenworth, and Erin Reilly offered perceptive insights into instructors' and students' needs, while Laney Whitt responded to my many requests with efficiency and cheer. The production editor, Bob Ginsberg, helped resolve sometimes competing production goals in favor of quality and accuracy. Vernon Nahrgang copyedited the manuscript with unique precision and care. At Nesbitt Graphics, Jerilyn Bockorick made the book a pleasure to use, and Susan McIntyre performed her usual calm (and calming) miracles of scheduling and management to produce the book. I am grateful to all these collaborators.

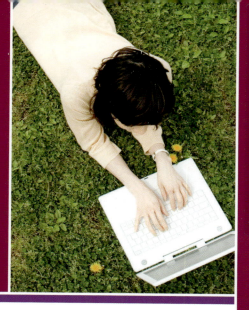

PART **1**

The Writing Process

The Writing Process

1 The Writing Situation

Like most writers (even very experienced ones), you may find writing sometimes easy but more often challenging, sometimes smooth but more often halting. Writing involves creation, and creation requires freedom, experimentation, and even missteps. Instead of proceeding in a straight line on a clear path, you might start writing without knowing what you have to say, circle back to explore a new idea, or keep going even though you're sure you'll have to rewrite later.

As uncertain as the writing process may be, you can bring some control to it by assessing your writing situation, particularly your subject, purpose, audience, and genre.

1a Assessing the writing situation

Any writing you do for others occurs in a context that both limits and clarifies your choices. You are communicating something about a particular subject to a particular audience of readers for a specific reason. You may be required to write in a particular genre. You may need to conduct research. You'll probably be up against a length requirement and a deadline. And you may be expected to present your work in a certain format and medium.

These are the elements of the **writing situation,** and analyzing them at the very start of a project can tell you much about how to proceed.

Exercise

Context

- **What is your writing for?** A course in school? Work? Something else? What do you know of the requirements for writing in this context?
- **What are the basic requirements of the writing task?** Consider length, deadline, subject, purpose, audience, and genre. What leeway do you have?
- **What medium will you use to present your writing?** Will you deliver it on paper, online, or orally? What does the presentation method require in preparation time, special skills, and use of technology?

Subject (pp. 5–6)

- **What does your writing assignment require you to write about?** If you don't have a specific assignment, what subjects might be appropriate for this situation?

mycomplab

Visit *mycomplab.com* for the eText and for resources and exercises on the writing situation.

- **What interests you about the subject?** What do you already know about it? What questions do you have about it?
- **What does the assignment require you to do with the subject?**

Purpose (pp. 6–7)

- **What aim does your assignment specify?** For instance, does it ask you to explain something or argue a point?
- **Why are you writing?**
- **What do you want your work to accomplish?** What effect do you intend it to have on readers?
- **How can you best achieve your purpose?**

Audience (pp. 7–8)

- **Who will read your writing?** Why will your readers be interested (or not) in your writing? How can you make your writing interesting to them?
- **What do your readers already know and think about your subject?** Do they have any characteristics—such as educational background, experience in your field, or political views—that could influence their reception of your writing?
- **How should you project yourself in your writing?** What role should you play in relation to readers, and what information should you give? How informal or formal should your writing be?
- **What do you want readers to do or think after they read your writing?**

Genre (pp. 8–9)

- **What genre, or type of writing, does the assignment call for?** Are you to write an analysis, a report, a proposal, or some other type? Or are you free to choose the genre in which to write?
- **What are the conventions of the genre you are using?** For example, readers might expect a claim supported by evidence, a solution to a defined problem, clear description, or easy-to-find information.

Research (7 pp. 311–68)

- **What kinds of evidence will best suit your subject, purpose, audience, and genre?** What combination of facts, examples, and expert opinions will support your ideas?
- **Does your assignment require research?** Will you need to consult sources of information or conduct other research, such as interviews, surveys, or experiments?
- **Even if research is not required, what additional information do you need to develop your subject?** How will you obtain it?
- **What style should you use to cite your sources?** (See **7** pp. 367–68 on source documentation in the academic disciplines.)

Deadline and length

- **When is the assignment due?** How will you apportion the work you have to do in the available time?
- **How long should your writing be?** If no length is assigned, what seems appropriate for your subject, purpose, and audience?

Presentation

- **What format or method of presentation does the assignment specify or imply?** For guidance in presenting academic writing, see pp. 53–58. See also **2** pp. 124–28 on oral presentations and pp. 128–37 on format in public writing.
- **How might you use headings, lists, illustrations, video, and other elements to achieve your purpose?** (See pp. 55–64.)

1b Finding your subject

A subject for writing has several basic requirements:

Video
tutorial

Exercise

- **It should be suitable for the assignment.**
- **It should be neither too general nor too limited for the assigned deadline and paper length.**
- **It should be something that interests you and that you are willing to learn more about.**

When you receive an assignment, study its wording and its implications about your writing situation to guide your choice of subject:

- **What's wanted from you?** Many writing assignments contain words such as *discuss, describe, analyze, report, interpret, explain, define, argue,* or *evaluate.* These words specify your approach to your subject, the kind of thinking expected, your general purpose, and even the form your writing should take. (See pp. 6–7.)
- **For whom are you writing?** Many assignments will specify or imply your readers, but sometimes you will have to figure out for yourself who your audience is and what it expects of you. (For more on analyzing your audience, see pp. 7–8.)
- **What kind of research is required?** An assignment may specify the kinds of sources you are expected to consult, and you can use such information to choose your subject. (If you are unsure whether research is required, check with your instructor.)
- **Does the subject need to be narrowed?** To do the subject justice in the length and time required, you'll often need to limit it. (See below.)

Answering questions about your assignment will help set some boundaries for your choice of subject. Then you can explore your own interests and experiences to narrow the subject so that you can cover it adequately within the space and time assigned. Federal aid to college students could be the subject of a book; the kinds of aid available or why the government should increase aid would be a more appropriate subject for a four-page paper due in a week. Here are some guidelines for narrowing broad subjects:

■ **Break your broad subject into as many specific subjects as you can think of.** Make a list.

■ **For each specific subject that interests you and fits the assignment, roughly sketch out the main ideas.** Consider how many paragraphs or pages of specific facts, examples, and other details you would need to pin those ideas down. This thinking should give you at least a vague idea of how much work you'd have to do and how long the resulting paper might be.

■ **Break a too-broad subject down further,** repeating the previous steps.

The Internet can also help you limit a general subject. Browse a directory such as *INFOMINE* (*infomine.ucr.edu*). As you pursue increasingly narrow categories, you may find a suitably limited topic.

1c Defining your purpose

Your **purpose** in writing is your chief reason for communicating something about your subject to a particular audience of readers. It is your answer to a potential reader's question, "So what?"

Most writing you do will have one of four main purposes:

Video
tutorial

■ **To entertain readers.**
■ **To express your feelings or ideas.**
■ **To explain something to readers (exposition).**
■ **To persuade readers to accept or act on your opinion (argument).**

These purposes often overlap in a single essay, but usually one predominates. And the dominant purpose will influence your slant on your subject, the details you choose, and even the words you use.

Many writing assignments narrow the purpose by using a signal word, such as the following:

■ **Report:** Survey, organize, and objectively present the available evidence on the subject.

■ **Summarize:** Concisely state the main points in a text, argument, theory, or other work.

■ **Discuss:** Examine the main points, competing views, or implications of the subject.

■ **Compare and contrast:** Explain the similarities and differences between two subjects. (See also pp. 48–49.)

■ **Define:** Specify the meaning of a term or a concept—distinctive characteristics, boundaries, and so on. (See also p. 47.)

- **Analyze:** Identify the elements of the subject, and discuss how they work together. (See also pp. 47–48 and **2** pp. 85–86.)
- **Interpret:** Infer the subject's meaning or implications.
- **Evaluate:** Judge the quality or significance of the subject, considering pros and cons. (See also **2** p. 87.)
- **Argue:** Take a position on the subject, and support your position with evidence. (See also **2** pp. 104–12.)

You can conceive of your purpose more specifically, too, in a way that incorporates your particular subject and the outcome you intend:

To explain the methods of an engineering study so that readers understand and accept your conclusions

To analyze how Annie Dillard's "Total Eclipse" builds to its climax so that readers appreciate the author's skill

To explain the steps in a new office procedure so that staffers will be able to follow it without difficulty

To argue against additional regulation of guns so that readers will perceive the disadvantages for themselves

1d Considering your audience

The readers likely to see your work—your **audience**—may influence your choice of subject and your definition of purpose. Your audience will certainly influence what you say about your subject and how you say it—for instance, how much background information you provide and whether you adopt a serious or a friendly tone.

For much academic and public writing, readers have specific needs and expectations. You still have many choices to make based on audience, but the options are somewhat defined. (See **2** pp. 93–101 and **8** pp. 375–97 on academic writing and **2** pp. 128–37 on public writing.) In other writing situations, the conventions are vaguer and the choices are more open. The following box contains questions that can help you define and make these choices.

Questions about audience

Identity and expectations

- **Who *are* my readers?**
- **What are my readers' expectations for the genre of my writing?** Do they expect features such as a particular organization and format, distinctive kinds of evidence, or a certain style of documenting sources?
- **What do I want readers to know or do after reading my work?** How should I make that clear to them?

Checklist

(continued)

Questions about audience
(continued)

■ **How should I project myself to my readers?** How formal or informal will they expect me to be? What role and tone should I assume?

Characteristics, knowledge, and attitudes

■ **What characteristics of readers are relevant for my subject and purpose?** For instance:

Age and sex
Occupation: students, professional colleagues, etc.
Social or economic role: subject-matter experts, voters, car buyers, potential employers, etc.
Economic or educational background
Ethnic background
Political, religious, or moral beliefs and values
Hobbies or activities

■ **How will the characteristics of readers influence their attitudes toward my subject?**
■ **What do readers already know and *not* know about my subject?** How much do I have to tell them? What aspects of my subject will be interesting and relevant to them?
■ **How should I handle any specialized terms?** Will readers know them? If not, should I define them?
■ **What ideas, arguments, or information might surprise, excite, or offend readers?** How should I handle these points?
■ **What misconceptions might readers have of my subject and/or my approach to it?** How can I dispel these misconceptions?

Uses and format

■ **What will readers do with my writing?** Should I expect them to read every word from the top, to scan for information, or to look for conclusions? Can I help readers by providing a summary, headings, illustrations, or other aids? (See pp. 53–69 on presenting writing.)

1e   Using genres

Writers use familiar **genres,** or types of writing, to express their ideas. You can recognize many genres: the poems and novels of literature, the résumé in business writing, the news article about a sporting event. In college you will be asked to write in a wide range of genres, such as analyses, lab reports, reviews, proposals, oral presentations, even blog posts.

Most simply, a genre is the conventional form that writing takes in a certain context. In academic writing, genre conventions help to further the aims of the disciplines; for instance, the features of a lab report emphasize the procedures, results, and conclusions that are important in scientific investigation. The conventions also help to improve communication because the writer knows what readers expect and readers can predict what they will encounter in the writing.

When you receive a writing assignment, be sure to understand any requirements relating to genre:

- ■ **Is a particular genre being assigned?** An assignment that asks you to write, say, an analysis, an argument, or a report has specified the genre for you to use.
- ■ **What are the conventions of the genre?** Your instructor and/or your textbook will probably outline the requirements for you. You can also learn about a genre by reading samples of it. Consult **2** pp. 95–96 for a list of the sample documents in this handbook.
- ■ **What flexibility do you have?** Within their conventions, most genres still allow plenty of room for your own approach and voice. Again, reading samples will show you much about your options.

2 Invention

Writers use a host of techniques to help invent or discover ideas and information about their subjects. **Whichever of the following techniques you use, do your work in writing, not just in your head.** Your ideas will then be retrievable, and the very act of writing will lead you to fresh insights.

Video tutorial

CULTURE LANGUAGE The discovery process encouraged here rewards rapid writing without a lot of thinking beforehand about what you will write or how. If your first language is not standard American English, you may find it helpful initially to do this exploratory writing in your native language or dialect and then to translate the worthwhile material for use in your drafts. This process can be productive, but it is extra work. You may want to try it at first and gradually move to composing in standard American English.

2a Keeping a journal

A **journal** is a diary of ideas kept on paper or on a computer. It gives you a place to record your responses, thoughts, and observations

Video tutorial

mycomplab

Visit *mycomplab.com* for the eText and for resources and exercises on invention.

about what you read, see, hear, or experience. It can also provide ideas for writing. Because you write for yourself, you can work out your ideas without the pressure of an audience "out there" who will evaluate logic or organization or correctness. If you write every day, even just for a few minutes, the routine will loosen your writing muscles and improve your confidence.

You can use a journal for varied purposes: perhaps to confide your feelings, explore your responses to movies and other media, practice certain kinds of writing (such as poems or news stories), pursue ideas from your course, or think critically about what you read. One student, Katy Moreno, used her journal for the last purpose. Her composition instructor had distributed "It's a Flat World, after All," an essay by Thomas L. Friedman about globalization and the job market. The instructor then gave the following assignment, calling for a response to reading:

> In "It's a Flat World, after All," Thomas L. Friedman describes today's global job market, focusing not on manufacturing jobs that have been "outsourced" to overseas workers but on jobs that require a college degree and are no longer immune to outsourcing. Friedman argues that keeping jobs in the United States requires that US students, parents, and educators improve math and science education. As a college student, how do you respond to this analysis of the global market for jobs? What do you think today's college students should be learning?

On first reading the essay, Moreno had found it convincing because Friedman's description of the job market matched her family's experience: her mother had lost her job when it was outsourced to India. After rereading the essay, however, Moreno was not persuaded that more math and science would necessarily improve students' opportunities and preserve their future jobs. She compared Friedman's advice with details she recalled from her mother's experience, and she began to develop a response by writing in her journal:

> Friedman is certainly right that more jobs than we realize are going overseas— that's what happened to Mom's job and we were shocked! But he gives only one way for students like me to compete—take more math and science. At first I thought he's totally right. But then I thought that what he said didn't really explain what happened to Mom—she had lots of math + science + tons of experience, but it was her salary, not better training, that caused her job to be outsourced. An overseas worker would do her job for less money. So she lost her job because of money + because she wasn't a manager. Caught in the middle. I want to major in computer science, but I don't think it's smart to try for the kind of job Mom had—at least not as long as it's so much cheaper for companies to hire workers overseas.

(Further examples of Moreno's writing appear in the next three chapters.)

CULTURE LANGUAGE A journal can be especially helpful if your first language is not standard American English. You can practice writing to improve your fluency, try out sentence patterns, and experiment with vocabulary words. Equally important, you can experiment with applying what you know from experience to what you read and observe.

2b Observing your surroundings

Sometimes you can find a good subject or good ideas by looking around you, not in the half-conscious way most of us move from place to place in our daily lives but deliberately, all senses alert. On a bus, for instance, are there certain types of passengers? What seems to be on the driver's mind? To get the most from observation, you should have a notepad and pen or a mobile device available for taking notes and making sketches. Back at your desk, study your notes and sketches for oddities or patterns that you'd like to explore further.

2c Freewriting

Writing into a subject

Many writers find subjects or discover ideas by **freewriting**: writing without stopping for a certain amount of time (say, ten minutes) or to a certain length (say, one page). The goal of freewriting is to generate ideas and information from *within* yourself by going around the part of your mind that doesn't want to write or can't think of anything to write. You let words themselves suggest other words. *What* you write is not important; that you *keep* writing is. Don't stop, even if that means repeating the same words until new words come. Don't go back to reread, don't censor ideas that seem off-track or repetitious, and above all don't stop to edit: grammar, punctuation, spelling, and the like are irrelevant at this stage.

Video tutorial

If you can dim or turn off your computer monitor, you can try **invisible writing** to keep moving forward while freewriting. As you type to a dark screen, the computer will record what you type but keep it from you and thus prevent you from tinkering with your prose. Invisible writing may feel uncomfortable at first, but it can free the mind for very creative results.

CULTURE LANGUAGE Invisible writing can be especially helpful if you are uneasy writing in standard American English and you tend to worry about errors while writing. The blank computer screen leaves you no choice but to explore ideas without regard for their expression. If you choose to write with the monitor on, concentrate on *what* you want to say, not *how* you're saying it.

Focused freewriting

Focused freewriting is more concentrated: you start with your subject and write about it without stopping for, say, fifteen minutes or one full page. As in all freewriting, you push to bypass mental blocks and self-consciousness, not debating what to say or editing what you've written. With focused freewriting, though, you let the physical act of writing take you into and around your subject.

An example of focused freewriting can be found in Katy Moreno's journal response to Thomas L. Friedman's "It's a Flat World, after All" on the previous page. Since she already had an idea about Friedman's essay, Moreno was able to start there and expand on the idea.

2d   Brainstorming

A method similar to freewriting is **brainstorming**—focusing intently on a subject for a fixed period (say, fifteen minutes), pushing yourself to list every idea and detail that comes to mind. Like freewriting, brainstorming requires turning off your internal editor so that you keep moving ahead. (The technique of invisible writing on a computer, described on the previous page, can help you move forward.)

Here is an example of brainstorming by a student, Johanna Abrams, on what a summer job can teach:

summer work teaches—
      how to look busy while doing nothing
      how to avoid the sun in summer
      seriously: discipline, budgeting money, value of money
which job? Burger King cashier? baby sitter? mail-room clerk?
mail room: how to sort mail into boxes: this is learning??
how to survive getting fired—humiliation, outrage
Mrs. King! the mail-room queen as learning experience
the shock of getting fired: what to tell parents, friends?
Mrs. K was so rigid—dumb procedures
initials instead of names on the mail boxes—confusion!
Mrs. K's anger, resentment: the disadvantages of being smarter than your boss
The odd thing about working in an office: a world with its own rules for how to act
what Mr. D said about the pecking order—big chick (Mrs. K) pecks on little
      chick (me)
a job can beat you down—make you be mean to other people

2e   Drawing

Like freewriting and brainstorming, the technique of **clustering**, or **idea mapping**, uses free association to produce rapid, unedited work. But it emphasizes the relations between ideas by combining writing and nonlinear drawing. Start with your topic at a center point and then radiate outward with ideas. Pursue related ideas in a branching structure until they seem exhausted. Then do the same with other ideas, continuously branching out or drawing arrows to show connections.

The example below shows how a student used clustering for ten minutes to expand on a subject he arrived at through freewriting: writing as a means of disguise.

Clustering or idea mapping

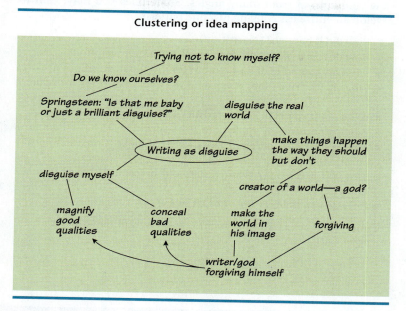

2f | Asking questions

Asking yourself a set of questions about your subject—and writing out the answers—can help you look at the subject objectively and see fresh possibilities in it.

1 | Journalist's questions

A journalist with a story to report poses a set of questions:

- Who was involved?
- What happened, and what were the results?
- When did it happen?
- Where did it happen?
- Why did it happen?
- How did it happen?

These questions can also be useful in probing an essay subject, especially when you are telling a story or examining causes and effects.

2 Questions about patterns

Student
paper

We think about and understand a vast range of subjects through patterns such as narration, classification, and comparison and contrast. Asking questions based on the patterns can help you view your subject from many angles. Sometimes you may want to develop an entire essay using just one pattern.

- **How did it happen?** (Narration)
- **How does it look, sound, feel, smell, taste?** (Description)
- **What are examples of it or reasons for it?** (Illustration or support)
- **What is it? What does it encompass, and what does it exclude?** (Definition)
- **What are its parts or characteristics?** (Division or analysis)
- **What groups or categories can it be sorted into?** (Classification)
- **How is it like, or different from, other things?** (Comparison and contrast)
- **Why did it happen? What results did or could it have?** (Cause-and-effect analysis)
- **How do you do it, or how does it work?** (Process analysis)

For more on these patterns, including paragraph-length examples, see pp. 45–49.

---

3 Thesis and Organization

Shaping your raw material helps you clear away unneeded ideas, spot possible gaps, and energize your subject. The two main operations in shaping material are focusing on a thesis (below) and organizing ideas (p. 18).

3a Conceiving a thesis statement

Your readers will expect your essay to be focused on and controlled by a main idea, or thesis. The thesis is the intellectual position you are taking on your topic. Often you will express the thesis in a one- or two-sentence **thesis statement** toward the beginning of your paper.

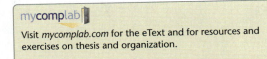
mycomplab
Visit *mycomplab.com* for the eText and for resources and exercises on thesis and organization.

As an expression of the thesis, the thesis statement serves three crucial functions and one optional one:

Functions of the thesis statement

■ **The thesis statement narrows your subject to a single, central idea** that you want readers to gain from your essay.
■ **It claims something specific and significant about your subject**, a claim that requires support.
■ **It conveys your purpose**—often explanatory or argumentative in college writing.
■ **It often concisely previews the arrangement of ideas**, in which case it can also help you organize your essay.

Video
tutorial

1 Formulating a thesis question

A thesis statement probably will not leap fully formed into your head. You can start on it by posing a **thesis question** to help you figure out your position, organize your ideas, start drafting, and stay on track.

Consider again Katy Moreno's assignment on p. 10:

. . . As a college student, how do you respond to [Friedman's] analysis of the global market for jobs? What do you think today's college students should be learning?

To respond to the assignment, Moreno reread Friedman's essay and her journal entry (p. 10). Then she wrote a question that could guide her thinking by connecting Friedman's essay and her experience of her mother's job loss:

How does my mother's job loss contradict Friedman's argument about technical training as key to success in the global job market?

2 Drafting a thesis statement

Drafting a thesis statement can occur at almost any time in the process of writing. Some instructors suggest that students develop a thesis statement when they have a good stock of ideas, to give a definite sense of direction. Other instructors suggest that students work with their thesis question at least through drafting, to keep their options open. And no matter when it's drafted, a thesis statement can change during the writing process, as the writer discovers ideas and expresses them in sentences.

Katy Moreno chose to try writing her thesis statement before drafting. Working from her thesis question (above), she wrote a sentence that named a topic and made a claim about it:

The outsourcing of my mother's job proves that Thomas L. Friedman's advice to improve students' technical training is too narrow.

Although Moreno later revised her thesis statement (see below), this draft statement gave her direction, and she used it in the first draft of her paper.

Following are more examples of thesis questions and answering thesis statements. Each statement consists of a topic and a claim. Notice how each statement also expresses purpose. Statements 1–2 are **explanatory**: the writers mainly want to explain something to readers. Statements 3–4 are **argumentative**: the authors mainly want to convince readers of something. Most of the thesis statements you write in college papers will be either explanatory or argumentative.

Thesis question	Explanatory thesis statement
1. Why did Abraham Lincoln delay in emancipating the slaves?	Lincoln delayed emancipating any slaves until 1863 because his primary goal was to restore and preserve the Union, with or without slavery. [**Topic:** Lincoln's delay. **Claim:** was caused by his goal of preserving the Union.]
2. What steps can prevent juvenile crime?	Juveniles can be diverted from crime by active learning programs, full-time sports, and intervention by mentors and role models. [**Topic:** juvenile crime. **Claim:** can be prevented in three ways.]

Thesis question	Argumentative thesis statement
3. Why should drivers' use of cell phones be banned?	Drivers' use of cell phones should be outlawed because people who talk and drive at the same time cause accidents. [**Topic:** drivers' use of cell phones. **Claim:** should be outlawed because it causes accidents.]
4. Which college students should be entitled to federal aid?	As an investment in its own economy, the federal government should provide a tuition grant to any college student who qualifies academically. [**Topic:** federal aid. **Claim:** should be provided to any college student who qualifies academically.]

CULTURE LANGUAGE In some cultures it is considered rude or unnecessary for a writer to state his or her main idea outright. When writing in standard American English for school or work, you can assume that readers expect a clear and early idea of what you think.

3 | Revising the thesis statement

You may have to write and rewrite a thesis statement before you come to a conclusion about your position. Katy Moreno used her draft thesis statement (previous page) in the first draft of her paper, but she saw that it put too little emphasis on her actual topic (*technical training*) and overstated her disagreement with Friedman (*proves . . . is too narrow*). After several revisions, her final thesis statement clarified the claim and said why the subject was significant:

> My mother's experience of having her job outsourced taught a lesson that Friedman overlooks: technical training by itself can be too narrow to produce the communicators and problem solvers needed by contemporary businesses.

As you draft and revise your thesis statement, ask the following questions:

Checklist for revising the thesis statement

- **How well does the subject of your statement capture the subject of your paper?**
- **What claim does your statement make about your subject?**
- **What is the significance of the claim?** How does it answer "So what?" and convey your purpose?
- **How can the claim be limited or made more specific?** Does it state a single idea and clarify the boundaries of the idea?
- **How unified is the statement?** How does each word and phrase contribute to a single idea?

✔ Checklist

✳ Exercise

Here are examples of thesis statements revised to meet these requirements:

Original	Revised
This new product brought in over $300,000 last year. [A statement of fact, not a claim about the product: what is significant about the product's success?]	This new product succeeded because of its innovative marketing campaign, including widespread press coverage, in-store entertainment, and a consumer newsletter.
People should not go on fad diets. [A vague statement that needs limiting with one or more reasons: what's wrong with fad diets?]	Fad diets can be dangerous when they deprive the body of essential nutrients or rely excessively on potentially harmful foods.
Televised sports are different from live sports. [A general statement that needs to be made more specific: how are they different, and why is the difference significant?]	Although television cannot transmit all the excitement of a live game, its close-ups and slow-motion replays reveal much about the players and the strategy of the game.
Cell phones can be convenient, but they can also be dangerous. [Not unified: how do the two parts of the sentence relate to each other?]	The convenience of cell phones does not justify the risks of driving while talking or texting.

3b   Organizing your ideas

Most essays share a basic pattern of introduction (states the subject), body (develops the subject), and conclusion (pulls the essay's ideas together). Introductions and conclusions are discussed on pp. 50–53. Within the body, every paragraph develops some aspect of the essay's main idea, or thesis. See pp. 34–35 for Katy Moreno's essay, with annotations highlighting the body's pattern of support for the thesis statement.

CULTURE LANGUAGE   If you are not used to reading and writing American academic prose, its pattern of introduction-body-conclusion and the organization schemes discussed on the next page may seem unfamiliar. For instance, instead of introductions that focus quickly on the topic and thesis, you may be used to openings that establish personal connections with readers. And instead of body paragraphs that stress general points and support those points with evidence, you may be used to general statements without support (because writers can assume that readers will supply the evidence themselves) or to evidence without explanation (because writers can assume that readers will infer the general points). When writing American academic prose, you need to take into account readers' expectations for directness and for the statement and support of general points.

1   The general and the specific

To organize material for an essay, you need to distinguish general and specific ideas and see the relations between ideas. General and specific refer to the number of instances or objects included in a group signified by a word. The following "ladder" illustrates a general-to-specific hierarchy:

Most general
↑ life form
  plant
  rose
↓ Uncle Dan's prize-winning American Beauty rose
Most specific

As you arrange your material, pick out the general ideas and then the specific points that support them. Set aside points that seem irrelevant to your key ideas. On a computer you can easily experiment with various arrangements of general ideas and supporting information: save your master list of ideas, duplicate it, and then use the Cut and Paste functions to move material around or (a little quicker) drag selected text to where you want it.

Student
paper

2 | Schemes for organizing essays

An essay's body paragraphs may be arranged in many ways that are familiar to readers. The choice depends on your subject, purpose, and audience.

- **Spatial:** In describing a person, place, or thing, move through space systematically from a starting point to other features—for instance, top to bottom, near to far, left to right.
- **Chronological:** In recounting a sequence of events, arrange the events as they actually occurred in time, first to last.
- **General to specific:** Begin with an overall discussion of the subject; then fill in details, facts, examples, and other support.
- **Specific to general:** First provide the support; then draw a conclusion from it.
- **Climactic:** Arrange ideas in order of increasing importance to your thesis or increasing interest to the reader.
- **Problem-solution:** First outline a problem that needs solving; then propose a solution.

3 | Outlines

It's not essential to craft a detailed outline before you begin drafting an essay; in fact, too detailed a plan could prevent you from discovering ideas while you draft. Still, even a rough scheme can show you patterns of general and specific, suggest proportions, and highlight gaps or overlaps in coverage.

There are several kinds of outlines, some more flexible than others.

Scratch or informal outline

A scratch or informal outline includes key general points in the order they will be covered. It may also list evidence for the points.

Here is Katy Moreno's scratch outline for her essay on the global job market:

Thesis statement

My mother's experience of having her job outsourced taught a lesson that Friedman overlooks: technical training by itself can be too narrow to produce the communicators and problem solvers needed by contemporary businesses.

Scratch outline

Mom's outsourcing experience
    Excellent tech skills
    Salary too high compared to overseas tech workers
    Lack of planning + communication skills, unlike managers who kept jobs
Well-rounded education to protect vs. outsourcing
    Tech training, as Friedman says
    Also, experience in communication, problem solving, other management
      skills

Tree diagram

In a tree diagram, ideas and details branch out in increasing specificity. Unlike more linear outlines, this diagram can be supplemented and extended indefinitely, so it is easy to alter. Johanna Abrams developed the following example from her brainstorming about a summer job (p. 12):

Thesis statement
Two months working in a large agency taught me that an office's pecking order should be respected.

Tree diagram

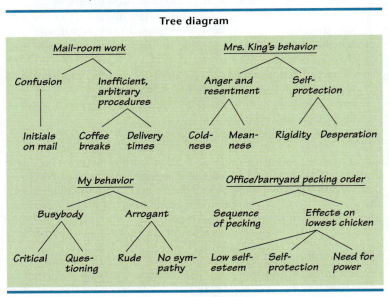

A tree diagram or other visual map can be especially useful for planning a project for the Web. The diagram can help you lay out the organization of your project and its links and then later can serve as a site map for your readers. (For more on writing for the Web, see pp. 64–69.)

Formal outline

A formal outline not only lays out main ideas and their support but also shows the relative importance of all the essay's elements. On the basis of her scratch outline (previous page), Katy Moreno prepared this formal outline for her essay on the global job market:

Video tutorial

Thesis statement
My mother's experience of having her job outsourced taught a lesson that Friedman overlooks: technical training by itself can be too narrow to

produce the communicators and problem solvers needed by contemporary businesses.

Formal outline

I. Summary of Friedman's article
  A. Reasons for outsourcing
    1. Improved technology and access
    2. Well-educated workers
    3. Productive workers
    4. Lower wages
  B. Need for improved technical training in US
II. Mother's experience
  A. Outsourcing of job
    1. Mother's education, experience, performance
    2. Employer's cost savings
  B. Retention of managers' jobs
    1. Planning skills
    2. Communication skills
III. Conclusions about ideal education
  A. Needs of US businesses
    1. Technical skills
    2. Management skills
      a. Communication
      b. Problem solving
      c. Versatility
  B. Personal goals
    1. Technical training
    2. English and history courses for management skills

This example illustrates several principles of outlining that can ensure completeness, balance, and clear relationships:

Video tutorial

- **All parts are systematically indented and labeled:** Roman numerals (I, II) for primary divisions; indented capital letters (A, B) for secondary divisions; further indented Arabic numerals (1, 2) for supporting examples. The next level down is indented further still and labeled with small letters: a, b.
- **The outline divides the material into several groups.** A long list of points at the same level should be broken up into groups.
- **Topics of equal generality appear in parallel headings,** with the same indention and numbering or lettering.
- **All subdivided headings break into at least two parts.** A topic cannot logically be divided into only one part.
- **All headings are expressed in parallel grammatical form**—in the example, as phrases using a noun plus modifiers. This is a topic outline; in a sentence outline all headings are expressed as full sentences (see **8** p. 449).

Note Because of its structure, a formal outline can be an excellent tool for analyzing a draft before revising it. See p. 26.

4 Unity and coherence

Two qualities of effective writing relate to organization: unity and coherence. When you perceive that someone's writing "flows well," you are probably appreciating these qualities.

To check an outline or draft for **unity**, ask these questions:

- **Is each section relevant to the main idea (thesis) of the essay?**
- **Within main sections, does each example or detail support the principal idea of that section?**

To check your outline or draft for **coherence**, ask the following questions:

- **Do the ideas follow a clear sequence?**
- **Are the parts of the essay logically connected?**
- **Are the connections clear and smooth?**

See also pp. 40–45 on unity and coherence in paragraphs.

4 Drafting

Video tutorial

Drafting is an occasion for exploration. Don't expect to transcribe solid thoughts into polished prose: solidity and polish will come with revision and editing. Instead, while drafting let the very act of writing help you find and form your meaning.

4a Starting to draft

Video tutorial

Beginning a draft sometimes takes courage, even for seasoned professionals. Procrastination may actually help if you let ideas for writing simmer at the same time. At some point, though, you'll have to face the blank paper or screen. The following techniques can help you begin:

- **Read over what you've already written**—notes, outlines, and so on—and immediately start your draft with whatever comes to mind.
- **Freewrite** (see p. 11).
- **Skip the opening and start in the middle.** Or write the conclusion.

---

mycomplab

Visit *mycomplab.com* for the eText and for resources and exercises on drafting.

- **Write a paragraph.** Explain what you think your essay will be about when you finish it.
- **Start writing the part that you understand best.** Using your outline, divide your work into chunks—say, one for the introduction, another for the first point, and so on. One of these chunks may call out to be written.

4b Maintaining momentum

Drafting requires momentum: the forward movement opens you to fresh ideas and connections. To keep moving while drafting, try one or more of these techniques.

Video
tutorial

- **Set aside enough time.** For a brief essay, a first draft is likely to take at least an hour or two.
- **Work in a quiet place.**
- **If you must stop working, write down what you expect to do next.** Then you can pick up where you stopped with minimal disruption.
- **Be as fluid as possible.** Spontaneity will allow your attitudes toward your subject to surface naturally in your sentences.
- **Keep going.** Skip over sticky spots; leave a blank if you can't find the right word; put alternative ideas or phrasings in brackets so that you can consider them later. If an idea pops out of nowhere but doesn't seem to fit in, quickly jot it down, or write it into the draft and bracket or boldface it for later attention.
- **Resist self-criticism.** Don't worry about your style, grammar, spelling, punctuation, and the like. Don't worry about what your readers will think. These are very important matters, but save them for revision.
- **Use your thesis statement and outline.** They can remind you of your planned purpose, organization, and content. However, if your writing leads you in a more interesting direction, follow.

If you write on a computer, frequently save the text you're drafting—at least every five or ten minutes and every time you leave the computer.

Video
tutorial

4c Examining a sample first draft

Katy Moreno's first-draft response to Thomas L. Friedman's "It's a Flat World, after All" appears on these pages. (The first two paragraphs include the page numbers in Friedman's article that Moreno summarized material from.) As part of her assignment, Moreno showed the draft to four classmates whose suggestions for revision appear in the margin. They used the Comment function of *Microsoft Word*, which allows users to add comments without inserting words into the document's text. (Notice that the class-mates ignore errors in grammar and punctuation, concentrating instead on larger issues such as thesis, clarity of ideas, and unity.)

Title?

In "It's a Flat World, after All," Thomas L. Friedman argues that, most US students are not preparing themselves as well as they should to compete in today's economy. Not like students in India, China, and other countries are (34-37). The outsourcing of my mother's job proves that Thomas L. Friedman's advice to improve students' technical training is too narrow.

> **Comment [Jared]:** Your mother's job being outsourced is interesting, but your introduction seems rushed.

> **Comment [Rabia]:** The end of your thesis statement is a little unclear—too narrow for what?

Friedman describes a "flat" world where recent technology like the Internet and wireless communication make it possible for college graduates all over the globe, in particular in India and China, to get jobs that once were gotten by graduates of US colleges and universities (37). He argues that US students need more math and science in order to compete (37).

> **Comment [Erin]:** Can you include the reasons Friedman gives for overseas students' success?

I came to college with first-hand knowledge of globalization and outsourcing. My mother, who worked for sixteen years in the field of information technology (IT), was laid off six months ago when the company she worked for decided to outsource much of its IT work to a company based in India. My mother majored in computer science, had sixteen years of experience, and her bosses always gave her good reviews. She never expected to be laid off and was surprised when she was. She wasn't laid off because of her background and performance. In fact, my mother had a very strong background in math and science and years of training and job experience. The reason was because her salary and benefits cost the company more than outsourcing her job did. Which hurt my family financially, as you can imagine.

> **Comment [Nathaniel]:** Tighten this paragraph to avoid repetition? Also, how does your mother's experience relate to Friedman and your thesis?

A number of well-paid people in the IT department where my mother worked, namely IT managers, were not laid off. As my mother explained at the time, they kept their jobs because they were better at planning and they communicated better, they were better writers and speakers than my mother.

> **Comment [Erin]:** What were the managers better at planning for?

Like my mother, I am more comfortable in front of a computer than I am in front of a group of people. I planned to major in computer science. Since my mother lost her job, though, I have decided to take courses in English and history too, where the classes will require me to do different kinds of work. When I enter the job market, my well-rounded education will make me a more attractive job candidate, and, will help me to be a versatile, productive employee.

> **Comment [Nathaniel]:** Can you be more specific about the kinds of work you'll need to do?

We know from our history that Americans have been innovative, hard-working people. We students have educational opportunities to compete in the global economy, but we must use our time in college wisely. As Thomas L. Friedman says, my classmates and I need to be ready for a rapidly changing future. We will have to work hard each day, which means being prepared for class, getting the best grades we can, and making the most of each class. Our futures depend on the decisions we make today.

> **Comment [Rabia]:** Can you work this point into your thesis?

> **Comment [Jared]:** Conclusion seems to go off in a new direction. Friedman mentions hard work, but it hasn't been your focus before.

> **Comment [Rabia]:** Don't forget your works cited.

5 Revising and Editing

During revision—literally "re-seeing"—you shift your focus outward from yourself and your subject toward your readers, concentrating on what will help them respond as you want. It's wise to revise in at least two stages, one devoted to fundamental meaning and structure (here called **revising**) and one devoted to word choice, grammar, punctuation, and other surface features (here called **editing**). Knowing that you will edit later gives you the freedom at first to look beyond the confines of the page or screen to the whole paper.

5a Revising the whole essay

To revise your writing, you have to read it critically, and that means you have to create some distance between your draft and yourself. One of the following techniques may help you to see your work objectively.

Video tutorial

Exercise

- ■ **Take a break after finishing the draft.** A few hours may be enough; a whole night or day is preferable.
- ■ **Ask someone to read and react to your draft.** If your instructor encourages collaboration among students, by all means take advantage of the opportunity to hear the responses of others. (See pp. 36–37 for more on collaboration.)

> **mycomplab**
>
> Visit *mycomplab.com* for the eText and for resources and exercises on revising and editing.

- **Read your draft in a new medium.** Typing a handwritten draft or printing out a word-processed draft can reveal weaknesses that you didn't see in the original.
- **Outline your draft.** Highlight the main points supporting the thesis, and convert these sentences to outline form. Then examine the outline you've made for logical order, gaps, and digressions. A formal outline can be especially illuminating because of its careful structure (see pp. 20–21).
- **Listen to your draft.** Read the draft out loud to yourself or a friend or classmate, record and listen to it, or have someone read the draft to you.
- **Ease the pressure.** Don't try to re-see everything in your draft at once. Use the checklist on the next page, making a separate pass through the draft for each item.

1 Revising on a word processor

Video tutorial

When you revise on a computer, take a few precautions to avoid losing your work and to keep track of your drafts:

- **Save your work every five to ten minutes.**
- **After doing any major work on a project, create a backup version of the file.**
- **Work on a copy of your latest draft.** Then the original will remain intact until you're truly finished with it. On the copy you can use your word processor's Track Changes function, which shows changes alongside the original text and allows you to accept or reject alterations later.
- **Save each draft under its own file name.** You may need to consult previous drafts for ideas or phrasings.

2 Titling your essay

Video tutorial

The revision stage is a good time to consider a title because attempting to sum up your essay in a phrase can focus your attention sharply on your topic, purpose, and audience. The title should tell the reader what your paper is about, but it should not restate the assignment or the thesis statement. Most titles fall into one of these categories:

- **A *descriptive title* announces the subject clearly and accurately.** Such a title is almost always appropriate and is usually expected for academic writing. Katy Moreno's final title—"Can We Compete? College Education for the Global Economy"—is an example.
- **A *suggestive title* hints at the subject to arouse curiosity.** Such a title is common in popular magazines and may be appropriate for writing that is somewhat informal. Moreno might have chosen a suggestive title such as "Training for the New World" or "Education for a Flat World" (echoing Thomas L. Friedman's title).

Checklist for revision

Checklist

Assignment

How have you responded to the assignment for this writing? Verify that your subject, purpose, and genre are appropriate for the requirements of the assignment.

Purpose

What is the purpose of your writing? Does it conform to the assignment? Is it consistent throughout the paper? (See pp. 6–7.)

Audience

How does the writing address the intended audience? How does it meet readers' likely expectations for your subject? Where might readers need more information?

Genre

How does your writing conform to the conventions of the genre you're writing in—features such as organization, kinds of evidence, language, and format?

Thesis

What is the thesis of your writing? Where does it become clear? How well do thesis and paper match: Does any part of the paper stray from the thesis? Does the paper fulfill the commitment of the thesis? (See pp. 14–17.)

Organization

What are the main points of the paper? (List them.) How well does each support the thesis? How effective is their arrangement for the paper's purpose? (See pp. 18–22.)

Development

How well do details, examples, and other evidence support each main point? Where, if at all, might readers find support skimpy or have trouble understanding the content? (See pp. 6–7, 45–49.)

Unity

What does each sentence and paragraph contribute to the thesis? Where, if at all, do digressions occur? Should they be cut, or can they be rewritten to support the thesis? (See pp. 22, 40.)

Coherence

How clearly and smoothly does the paper flow? Where does it seem rough or awkward? Can any transitions be improved? (See pp. 22, 40–45.)

Title, introduction, conclusion

How accurately and interestingly does the title reflect the essay's content? (See opposite.) How well does the introduction engage and focus readers' attention? (See pp. 50–51.) How effective is the conclusion in providing a sense of completion? (See pp. 51–53.)

For more information on essay titles, see **MLA** p. 447 (MLA format), **APA** p. 480 (APA format), and **6** pp. 301–02 (capitalizing words in a title).

5b | Examining a sample revision

Katy Moreno was satisfied with her first draft: she had her ideas down, and the arrangement seemed logical. Still, from the revision checklist she knew the draft needed work, and her classmates' comments (pp. 24–25) highlighted what she needed to focus on. Following is the first half of her revised draft, with marginal annotations highlighting the changes. Moreno used the Track Changes function on her word processor, so that deletions are crossed out and additions are in blue.

<table>
<tr><td>Descriptive title names topic and forecasts approach.</td><td>Can We Compete?
College Education for the Global Economy
~~Title?~~</td></tr>
<tr><td>Expanded introduction draws readers into Moreno's topic, clarifies her point of agreement with Friedman, and states her revised thesis.</td><td>Today's students cannot miss news stories about globalization of the economy and outsourcing of jobs, but are students aware of how these trends are affecting the job market? In "It's a Flat World, after All," Thomas L. Friedman argues that most US students are not preparing themselves as well as ~~they should to compete in today's economy. Not like~~ students in India, China, and other countries are to compete in today's economy, which requires hard-working, productive scientists and engineers (34-37). Friedman's argument speaks to me because my mother recently lost her job when it was outsourced to India. But her experience taught a lesson that Friedman overlooks: technical training by itself can be too narrow to produce the communicators and problem solvers needed by contemporary businesses. ~~The outsourcing of my mother's job proves that Thomas L. Friedman's advice to improve students' technical training is too narrow.~~</td></tr>
<tr><td>Expanded summary of Friedman's article specifies qualities of overseas workers.</td><td>Friedman describes a "flat" world where recent technology like the Internet and wireless communication makes it possible for college graduates all over the globe~~, in particular~~ to compete for high paying jobs that once belonged to graduates of US colleges and universities (34). He focuses on workers in India and China~~,~~ who graduate from college with excellent educations in math and science, who are eager for new opportunities, and who are willing to work exceptionally hard, often harder than their American counterparts and, for less money ~~to get jobs that once were gotten by graduates of US colleges and universities~~ (37). ~~He~~ Friedman argues that US students must be better prepared academically, especially in ~~need more~~ math and science, so that they can get and keep jobs that will otherwise go overseas ~~in order to compete~~ (37).</td></tr>
</table>

~~I came to college with first hand knowledge of globalization and~~ ~~outsourcing. My mother, who worked for sixteen years in the field of infor-~~ ~~mation technology (IT), was laid off six months ago when the company~~ ~~she worked for decided to outsource much of its IT work to a company~~ ~~based in India. My mother~~ At first glance, my mother's experience of losing her job might seem to support the argument of Friedman that better training in math and science is the key to competing in the global job market. Her experience, however, adds dimensions to the globalization story, which Friedman misses. First my mother had the kind of strong background in math and science that Friedman says, today's workers need. She majored in computer science, rose within the information technology (IT) department of a large company, ~~had sixteen years of experience,~~ and her bosses always gave her good performance reviews. Still, when her employer decided to outsource most of its IT work, my mother lost her job. ~~She never expected~~ ~~to be laid off and was surprised when she was. She wasn't laid off because~~ ~~of her background and performance. In fact, my mother had a very strong~~ ~~background in math and science and years of training and job experience.~~ The reason wasn't because her technical skills were inadequate. Instead, her salary and benefits cost the company more than outsourcing her job did. Until wages rise around the globe, jobs like my mother's will be vulnerable. No matter how well you are trained. ~~Which hurt my family finan-~~ ~~cially, as you can imagine.~~

> New opening sentences connect to introduction and thesis statement, restating points of agreement and disagreement with Friedman.

> Revisions condense long example of mother's experience.

> Paragraph's concluding sentences reinforce the point and connect to thesis statement.

5c Editing the revised draft

After you've revised your essay so that all the content is in place, then turn to the important work of removing any surface problems that could interfere with a reader's understanding or enjoyment of your ideas.

Exercise

1 Strategies for editing

Try these approaches to discover what needs editing:

- **Take a break.** Even fifteen minutes can clear your head.
- **Read the draft slowly, and read what you actually see.** Otherwise, you're likely to read what you intended to write but didn't. (If you have trouble slowing down, try reading your draft from back to front, sentence by sentence.)
- **Read as if you are encountering the draft for the first time.** Put yourself in the reader's place.
- **Have a classmate, friend, or relative read your work.** Make sure you understand and consider the reader's suggestions, even if eventually you decide not to take them.

- **Read the draft aloud or, even better, record it.** Listen for awkward rhythms, repetitive sentence patterns, and missing or clumsy transitions.
- **Learn from your own experience.** Keep a record of the problems that others have pointed out in your writing. When editing, check your work against this record.

In your editing, work first for clear and effective sentences that flow smoothly from one to the next. Then check your sentences for correctness. Use the questions in the checklist on the next page to guide your editing, referring to the page numbers in parentheses as needed.

2 A sample edited paragraph

The third paragraph of Katy Moreno's edited draft appears below. Among other changes, she tightened wording, improved parallelism (with *consistently received*), corrected several comma errors, and repaired the final sentence fragment.

> At first glance, my mother's experience of losing her job might seem to support the Friedman's argument of Friedman that better training in math and science is the key to competing in the global job market. However, Hher experience, however, adds dimensions to the globalization story, which that Friedman misses. First, my mother had the kind of strong background in math and science that Friedman says, today's workers need. She majored in computer science, rose within the information technology (IT) department of a large company, and consistently received her bosses always gave her good performance reviews. Still, when her employer decided to outsource most of its IT work, my mother lost her job. The reason wasn't becausethat her technical skills were inadequate. Instead, her salary and benefits cost the company more than outsourcing her job did. Until wages rise around the globe, jobs like my mother's will be vulnerable,. Nno matter how well you are a person is trained.

3 Editing on a computer

When you write on a word processor, consider these additional approaches to editing:

- **Don't rely on a spelling or grammar/style checker to find what needs editing.** See the discussion of these checkers on pp. 32–33.
- **If possible, edit a double-spaced paper copy.** Many people find it much harder to spot errors on a computer screen than on paper.
- **Use the Find command to locate and correct your common problems**—certain misspellings, overuse of *there is*, wordy phrases such as *the fact that*, and so on.
- **Resist overediting.** The ease of editing on a computer can lead to rewriting sentences over and over, stealing the life from your

Checklist for editing

Are my sentences clear?

Do my words and sentences mean what I Intend them to mean? Is anything confusing? Check especially for these:

Exact language (**3** pp. 161–68)
Parallelism (**3** pp. 149–51)
Clear modifiers (**4** pp. 240–45)
Clear reference of pronouns (**4** pp. 228–31)
Complete sentences (**4** pp. 245–48)
Sentences separated correctly (**4** pp. 249–52)

Are my sentences effective?

How well do words and sentences engage and hold readers' attention? Where does the writing seem wordy, choppy, or dull? Check especially for these:

Emphasis of main ideas (**3** pp. 141–48)
Smooth and informative transitions (pp. 44–45)
Variety in sentence length and structure (**3** pp. 151–54)
Appropriate language (**3** pp. 155–61)
Concise sentences (**3** pp. 169–74)

Do my sentences contain errors?

Where do surface errors interfere with the clarity and effectiveness of my sentences? Check especially for these:

- Spelling errors (**6** pp. 293–97)
- Sentence fragments (**4** pp. 245–48)
- Comma splices (**4** pp. 249–52)
- Verb errors
  Verb forms, especially -s and -ed endings, correct forms of irregular verbs, and appropriate helping verbs (**4** pp. 193–205)
  Verb tenses, especially consistency (**4** pp. 205–10)
  Agreement between subjects and verbs, especially when words come between them or the subject is *each, everyone,* or a similar word (**4** pp. 214–20)

- Pronoun errors
  Pronoun forms, especially subjective (*he, she, they, who*) vs. objective (*him, her, them, whom*) (**4** pp. 220–25)
  Agreement between pronouns and antecedents, especially when the antecedent contains *or* or the antecedent is *each, everyone, person,* or a similar word (**4** pp. 225–28)

- Punctuation errors
  Commas, especially with comma splices (**4** pp. 249–52) and with *and* or *but,* with introductory elements, with nonessential elements, and with series (**5** pp. 261–68)
  Apostrophes in possessives but not plural nouns (*Dave's/witches*) and in contractions but not possessive personal pronouns (*it's/its*) (**5** pp. 276–81)

Checklist

prose. If your grammar/style checker contributes to the temptation, consider turning it off.

■ **Take special care with additions and omissions.** Make sure you haven't omitted needed words or left in unneeded words.

Video tutorial

4 Working with spelling and grammar/style checkers

A spelling checker and grammar/style checker can be helpful *if* you work within their limitations. The programs miss many problems and may even flag items that are actually correct. Further, they know nothing of your purpose and your audience, so they cannot make important decisions about your writing. Always use these tools critically:

■ **Read your work yourself to ensure that it's clear and error-free.**
■ **Consider a checker's suggestions carefully, weighing each one against your intentions.** If you aren't sure whether to accept a checker's suggestion, consult a dictionary, writing handbook, or other source. Your version may be fine.

Using a spelling checker

Your word processor's spelling checker can be a great ally: it will flag words that are spelled incorrectly and will usually suggest alternative spellings that resemble what you've typed. However, this ally can also undermine you because of its limitations:

■ **The checker may flag a word that you've spelled correctly** just because the word does not appear in its dictionary.
■ **The checker may suggest incorrect alternatives.** In providing a list of alternative spellings for your word, the checker may highlight the one it considers most likely to be correct. For example, if you misspell *definitely* by typing *definately*, your checker may highlight *defiantly* as the correct option. You need to verify that the alternative suggested by the checker is actually what you intend before selecting it. Consult an online or printed dictionary when you aren't sure about the checker's recommendations.
■ **Most important, a spelling checker will not flag words that appear in its dictionary but you have misused.** The screen shot on the facing page shows a jingle that has circulated widely as a warning about spelling checkers.

Using a grammar/style checker

Grammar/style checkers can flag incorrect grammar or punctuation and wordy or awkward sentences. However, these programs can call your attention only to passages that *may* be faulty. They miss many errors because they are not yet capable of analyzing

Spelling checker

I have a spelling checker,
It came with my PC;
It plainly marks four my revue
Mistakes I cannot sea.
I've run this poem threw it,
I'm sure your please too no.
Its letter perfect in it's weigh,
My checker tolled me sew.

A spelling checker failed to catch any of the thirteen errors in this jingle. Can you spot them?

language in all its complexity. (For instance, they can't accurately distinguish a word's part of speech when there are different possibilities, as *light* can be a noun, a verb, or an adjective.) And they often question passages that don't need editing, such as an appropriate passive verb or a deliberate and emphatic use of repetition.

You can customize a grammar/style checker to suit your needs and habits as a writer. Most checkers allow you to specify whether to check grammar only or grammar and style. Some style checkers can be set to the level of writing you intend, such as formal, standard, and informal. (For academic writing choose formal.) You can also instruct the checker to flag specific grammar and style problems that tend to occur in your writing, such as mismatched subjects and verbs, apostrophes in plural nouns, overused passive voice, or a confusion between *its* and *it's*.

5d   Formatting and proofreading the final draft

After editing your essay, format and proofread it before you submit it to your instructor. Follow any required document format, such as MLA (**MLA** pp. 446–48) and APA (**APA** pp. 480–82). See also pp. 53–66 for help with document design.

Be sure to proofread the final essay several times to spot and correct errors. To increase the accuracy of your proofreading, you may need to experiment with ways to keep yourself from relaxing into the rhythm and the content of your prose. Here are a few tricks, including some used by professional proofreaders:

Video tutorial

- **Read printed copy,** even if you will eventually submit the paper electronically. Most people proofread more accurately when reading type on paper than when reading it on a computer screen. (At the same time, don't view the printed copy as error-free just because it's clean. Clean-looking copy may still harbor errors.)
- **Read the paper aloud,** very slowly, and distinctly pronounce exactly what you see.
- **Place a ruler under each line as you read it.**

- **Read "against copy,"** comparing your final draft one sentence at a time against the edited draft.
- **Ignore content.** To keep the content of your writing from distracting you, read the essay backward sentence by sentence. Or use your word processor to isolate each paragraph from its context by printing it on a separate page. (Of course, reassemble the paragraphs before submitting the paper.)

5e Examining a sample final draft

Katy Moreno's final essay appears on these pages, presented in MLA format except for page numbers. Comments in the margins point out key features of the essay's content.

Katy Moreno
Professor Lacourse
English 110
14 February 2011

Can We Compete?
College Education for the Global Economy

Descriptive title

Introduction

Today's students cannot miss news stories about globalization of the economy and outsourcing of jobs, but are students aware of how these trends are affecting the job market? In "It's a Flat World, after All,"

Summaries of Friedman cited with parenthetical page numbers using MLA style (**MLA** p. 403)

Thomas L. Friedman argues that most US students are not preparing themselves as well as students in India, China, and other countries to compete in today's economy, which requires hard-working, productive scientists and engineers (34-37). Friedman's argument speaks to me because my mother

Thesis statement: basic disagreement with Friedman

lost her job when it was outsourced to India. But her experience taught a lesson that Friedman overlooks: technical training by itself can be too narrow to produce the communicators and problem solvers needed by contemporary businesses.

Summary of Friedman's article

Friedman describes a "flat" world where recent technology like the Internet and wireless communication makes it possible for college graduates all over the globe to compete for high-paying jobs that once belonged to graduates of US colleges and universities (34). He focuses on workers in India and China who graduate from college with excellent educations in math and science, who are eager for new opportunities, and who are willing to work exceptionally hard, often harder than their American counterparts, and for less money (37). Friedman argues that US students must be better prepared academically, especially in math and science, so that they can get and keep jobs that will otherwise go overseas (37).

At first glance, my mother's experience of losing her job might seem to support Friedman's argument that better training in math and science is the key to competing in the global job market. However, her experience adds dimensions to the globalization story that Friedman misses. First, my mother had the kind of strong background in math and science that Friedman says today's workers need. She majored in computer science, rose within the information technology (IT) department of a large company, and consistently received good performance reviews. Still, when her employer decided to outsource most of its IT work, my mother lost her job. The reason wasn't that her technical skills were inadequate; instead, her salary and benefits cost the company more than outsourcing her job did. Until wages rise around the globe, jobs like my mother's will be vulnerable, no matter how well a person is trained.

The second dimension that Friedman misses is that a number of well-paid people in my mother's IT department, namely IT managers, were not laid off. As my mother explained at the time, they kept their jobs because they were experienced at figuring out the company's IT needs, planning for changes, researching and proposing solutions, and communicating in writing and speech—skills that her more narrow training and experience had missed. Friedman misses these skills by focusing only on technical training. Without the ability to solve problems creatively and to communicate, people with technical expertise alone may not have enough to save their jobs, as my mother learned.

Like my mother, I am more comfortable in front of a computer than I am in front of a group of people, and I had planned to major in computer science. Since my mother lost her job, however, I have decided to take courses in English and history as well. Classes in these subjects will require me to read broadly, think critically, research, and communicate ideas in writing—in short, to develop skills that make managers. When I enter the job market, my well-rounded education will make me a more attractive job candidate and will help me to become the kind of forward-thinking manager that US companies will always need to employ here in the US.

Many jobs that require a college degree are indeed going overseas, as Thomas L. Friedman says, and my classmates and I need to be ready for a rapidly changing future. But rather than focus only on math and science, we need to broaden our academic experiences so that the skills we develop make us not only employable but also indispensable.

Work Cited

Friedman, Thomas L. "It's a Flat World, after All." *New York Times Magazine* 3 Apr. 2005: 32-37. Print.

Margin annotations:

- Transition to disagreements with Friedman
- First disagreement with Friedman
- Examples to support first disagreement
- Example to qualify first disagreement
- Clarification of first disagreement
- Second disagreement with Friedman
- Explanation of second disagreement
- Conclusion summarizing both disagreements with Friedman
- Final point: business needs and author's personal goals
- Explanation of final point
- Conclusion recapping points of agreement and disagreement with Friedman and summarizing essay
- Work cited in MLA style (see **MLA** p. 411)

5f   Revising collaboratively

In many writing courses students work together on writing, most often commenting on each other's work to help with revision. This collaborative writing gives experience in reading written work critically and in reaching others through writing. Collaboration may occur face to face in small groups, via drafts and comments on paper, or online through a course-management system such as *Blackboard*, *Desire2Learn*, or *Moodle* or through a class blog, e-mail list, or wiki.

Whether you collaborate in person, on paper, or on a computer, you will be more comfortable and helpful and will benefit more from others' comments if you follow a few guidelines.

Commenting on others' writing

Video tutorial

- **Be sure you know what the writer is saying.** If necessary, summarize the paper to understand its content. (See **2** pp. 83–85.)
- **Address only your most significant concerns with the work.** Focus on the deep issues in other writers' drafts, especially early drafts: thesis, purpose, audience, organization, and support for the thesis. Use the revision checklist on p. 27 as a guide to what is significant. Unless you have other instructions, ignore mistakes in grammar, punctuation, and the like. (The temptation to focus on such errors may be especially strong if the writer is less experienced than you are with standard American English.) Emphasizing mistakes will contribute little to the writer's revision.
- **Remember that you are the reader, not the writer.** Don't edit sentences, add details, or otherwise assume responsibility for the paper.
- **Phrase your comments carefully.** Avoid misunderstandings by making sure comments are both clear and respectful. If you are responding on paper or online, not face to face with the writer, remember that the writer can't ask you for immediate clarification and can infer your attitudes only from your words, not from gestures, facial expressions, and tone of voice.
- **Be specific.** If something confuses you, say *why*. If you disagree with a conclusion, say *why*.
- **Be supportive as well as honest.** Tell the writer what you like about the paper. Word comments positively: instead of *This paragraph doesn't interest me,* say *You have an interesting detail here that I almost missed.* Question the writer in a way that emphasizes the effect of the work on you, the reader: *This paragraph confuses me because. . . .* And avoid measuring the work against a set of external standards: *This essay is poorly organized. Your thesis statement is inadequate.*
- **While reading, make your comments in writing.** Even if you will be delivering your comments in person later on, the written record will help you recall what you thought.

■ **Link comments to specific parts of a paper.** Especially if you are reading the paper on a computer, be clear about what in the paper each comment relates to. You can embed your comments directly into the paper, distinguishing them with highlighting or color, or you can use a word processor's Comment function.

Benefiting from comments on your writing

■ **Think of your readers as counselors or coaches.** They can help you see the virtues and flaws in your work and sharpen your awareness of readers' needs.

Video tutorial

■ **Read or listen to comments closely.**

■ **Know what the critic is saying.** If you need more information, ask for it, or consult the appropriate section of this handbook.

■ **Don't become defensive.** Letting comments offend you will only erect a barrier to improvement in your writing. As one writing teacher advises, "Leave your ego at the door."

■ **Revise your work in response to appropriate comments,** even if you are not required to do so. You will learn more from actually revising than from just thinking about it.

■ **Remember that you are the final authority on your work.** You should be open to suggestions, but you are free to decline advice when you think it is inappropriate.

■ **Keep track of both the strengths and the weaknesses others identify.** Then in later assignments you can build on your successes and give special attention to problem areas.

CULTURE LANGUAGE In some cultures writers do not expect criticism from readers, or readers do not expect to think and speak critically about what they read. If critical responses are uncommon in your native culture, collaboration may at first be uncomfortable for you. As a writer, think of a draft or even a final paper as more an exploration of ideas than the last word on your subject; then you may be more receptive to readers' suggestions. As a reader, allow yourself to approach a text skeptically, and know that your tactful questions and suggestions will usually be considered appropriate.

5g Preparing a writing portfolio

Your writing instructor may ask you to assemble samples of your writing into a portfolio, or folder, once or more during the course. Such a portfolio gives you a chance to consider all your writing over a period and to showcase your best work.

Although the requirements for portfolios vary, most instructors are looking for a range of writing that demonstrates your progress and strengths as a writer. You, in turn, see how you have advanced from one assignment to the next, as you've had time for new knowledge to sink in and time for practice. Instructors often allow students to revise papers before placing them in the portfolio, even if the papers were submitted earlier. In that case, every paper in the portfolio can benefit from all your learning.

An assignment to assemble a writing portfolio will probably also provide guidelines for what to include, how the portfolio will be evaluated, and how (or whether) it will be weighted for a grade. Be sure you understand the purpose of the portfolio and who will read it. For instance, if your composition instructor will be the only reader and his or her guidelines encourage you to show evidence of progress, you might include a paper that took big risks but never entirely succeeded. In contrast, if a committee of instructors will read your work and the guidelines urge you to demonstrate your competence as a writer, you might include only papers that did succeed.

Sample document

Unless the guidelines specify otherwise, provide error-free copies of your final drafts, label all your samples with your name, and assemble them all in a folder. Add a cover letter or memo that lists the samples, explains why you've included each one, and evaluates your progress as a writer. The self-evaluation involved should be a learning experience for you and will help your readers assess your development as a writer.

6 Paragraphs

Most written texts consist of **paragraphs:** groups of sentences set off by beginning indentions or sometimes by extra space. Paragraphs develop the main ideas that support the central idea, or thesis, of a piece of writing, and they break these supporting ideas into manageable chunks. For readers, paragraphs signal the movement between ideas and provide breathers from long stretches of text.

This chapter discusses relating the paragraphs within a piece of writing (next page) and the three qualities of an effective body paragraph: unity (p. 40), coherence (p. 40), and development (p. 45). In addition, the chapter discusses two special kinds of paragraphs: introductions and conclusions (pp. 50 and 51).

 Not all cultures share the paragraphing conventions of American academic writing. In some other languages, writing moves differently on the page from English—not left to right, but right to left or down rows from top to bottom. Even in languages that move as English does on the page, writers may

mycomplab

Visit *mycomplab.com* for the eText and for resources and exercises on paragraphs.

Checklist for revising paragraphs

- **Does each paragraph contribute to the essay as a whole?** Does each paragraph support the essay's central idea, or thesis? Does it relate to the paragraphs that come before and after it? (See below.)
- **Is each paragraph unified?** Does it adhere to one general idea that is either stated in a topic sentence or otherwise apparent? (See the next page.)
- **Is each paragraph coherent?** Do the sentences follow a clear sequence? Are the sentences linked as needed by parallelism, repetition or restatement, pronouns, consistency, and transitional expressions? (See the next page.)
- **Is each paragraph developed?** Is the general idea of the paragraph well supported with specific evidence such as details, facts, examples, and reasons? (See p. 45.)

Checklist

not use paragraphs at all. Or they may use paragraphs but not state the central ideas or provide transitional expressions to show readers how sentences relate. If your native language is not English and you have difficulty writing paragraphs, don't worry about paragraphing during drafting. Instead, during a separate step of revision, divide your text into parts that develop your main points and mark those parts with indentions.

6a Relating paragraphs in the essay

Paragraphs do not stand alone: they are key units of a larger piece of writing. Even if you draft a paragraph separately, it needs to connect to your central idea, or thesis—explaining it and deepening it. Together, paragraphs need to flow from one to the other so that readers easily grasp the points you are making and how each point contributes to the whole essay.

To see how effective body paragraphs work to help both writer and reader, look at the fourth paragraph of Katy Moreno's essay "Can We Compete?" from the previous chapter. Responding to an article by Thomas L. Friedman, Moreno is supporting her thesis that Friedman overlooks the need for technical employees to be good communicators and problem solvers.

The second dimension that Friedman misses is that a number of well-paid people in my mother's IT department, namely IT managers, were not laid off. As my mother explained at the time, they kept their jobs because they were experienced at figuring out the company's IT needs, planning for changes, researching and proposing solutions, and communicating in writing and speech—skills that her more narrow training and experience had missed. Friedman

New main point linking to previous paragraph and to thesis

Details to support new point

misses these skills by focusing only on technical training. Without the ability to solve problems creatively and to communicate, people with technical expertise alone may not have enough to save their jobs, as my mother learned.

> Concluding sentence summing up paragraph and linking to previous paragraph and to thesis

6b Maintaining paragraph unity

Video tutorial

Exercise

Just as readers expect paragraphs to relate clearly to an essay's thesis, they also generally expect each paragraph to be **unified**—that is, to develop a single idea. Often this idea is expressed in a **topic sentence**. For an example, look again at the paragraph above by Katy Moreno: the opening statement conveys Moreno's promise that she will explain something lacking in Friedman's argument, and the following sentences keep the promise. But what if Moreno had written this paragraph instead?

> The second dimension that Friedman misses is that a number of well-paid people in my mother's IT department, namely IT managers, were not laid off. As my mother explained at the time, they kept their jobs because they were experienced at figuring out the company's IT needs, planning for changes, researching and proposing solutions, and communicating in writing. Like my mother, these managers had families to support, so they were lucky to keep their jobs. Our family still struggles with the financial and emotional effects of my mother's unemployment.

> Topic sentence

> Details supporting sentence

> Digression

By wandering from the topic of why some managers kept their jobs, this paragraph fails to deliver on the commitment of its topic sentence. The paragraph is not unified.

A topic sentence need not always come first in the paragraph. For instance, it may come last, presenting your idea only after you have provided the evidence for it. Or it may not be stated at all, especially in narrative or descriptive writing in which the point becomes clear in the details. But always the idea should govern the paragraph's content as if it were standing guard at the opening.

6c Achieving paragraph coherence

Video tutorial

When a paragraph is **coherent**, readers can see how it holds together: the sentences seem to flow logically and smoothly into one another. Exactly the opposite happens with this paragraph:

> The ancient Egyptians were masters of preserving dead people's bodies by making mummies of them. Mummies several thousand years old have been discovered nearly intact. The skin, hair, teeth, finger- and toenails, and facial features of the mummies were evident. One can diagnose the diseases they suffered in life, such as smallpox, arthritis,

and nutritional deficiencies. The process was remarkably effective. Sometimes apparent were the fatal afflictions of the dead people: a middle-aged king died from a blow on the head, and polio killed a child king. Mummification consisted of removing the internal organs, applying natural preservatives inside and out, and then wrapping the body in layers of bandages.

The paragraph is hard to read. The sentences lurch instead of gliding from point to point.

The paragraph as it was actually written appears below. It is much clearer because the writer arranged information differently and also built links into his sentences so that they would flow smoothly:

- After stating the central idea in a topic sentence, the writer moves to two more specific explanations and illustrates the second with four sentences of examples.
- Words in green repeat or restate key terms or concepts.
- Words in orange link sentences and clarify relationships.
- Underlined phrases are in parallel grammatical form to reflect their parallel content.

> The ancient Egyptians were masters of preserving dead people's bodies by making mummies of them. Basically, mummification consisted of removing the internal organs, applying natural preservatives inside and out, and then wrapping the body in layers of bandages. And the process was remarkably effective. Indeed, mummies several thousand years old have been discovered nearly intact. Their skin, hair, teeth, finger- and toenails, and facial features are still evident. Their diseases in life, such as smallpox, arthritis, and nutritional deficiencies, are still diagnosable. Even their fatal afflictions are still apparent: a middle-aged king died from a blow on the head; a child king died from polio.

Topic sentence

Explanation

Specific examples

—Mitchell Rosenbaum (student),
"Lost Arts of the Egyptians"

1 Paragraph organization

A coherent paragraph organizes information so that readers can easily follow along. These are common paragraph schemes:

Video tutorial

- **General to specific:** Sentences downshift from more general statements to more specific ones. (See the paragraph by Rosenbaum above.)
- **Climactic:** Sentences increase in drama or interest, ending in a climax. (See the paragraph opposite about sleep.)
- **Spatial:** Sentences scan a person, place, or object from top to bottom, from side to side, or in some other way that approximates

the way people look at things. (See the paragraph by Woolf on p. 46.)

- **Chronological:** Sentences present events as they occurred in time, earlier to later. (See the paragraph by LaFrank on p. 44.)

2 Parallelism

Parallelism helps tie sentences together. In the next paragraph the underlined parallel structures link all sentences after the first one, and parallelism also appears within many of the sentences (as in *He served . . . , survived . . . , and earned* in sentence 8). The paragraph comes from a student's profile of President Ronald Reagan.

> Ronald Reagan holds a particularly interesting place in American history, combining successful careers in show business and in politics. After graduating from college in 1932, he worked as a radio sports announcer with an affinity for describing game details. He then launched a successful film career, starring in dozens of movies. After a stint in the US Army, he assumed the role of host for *General Electric Theater*, a weekly TV program that ran from 1953 to 1962. He first entered politics by supporting candidates and making speeches in the 1950s and early 1960s. He became governor of California in 1966 and served for eight years. He ran unsuccessfully for the US presidency in 1976 and then won the job in 1980, when he became the fortieth President. He served two terms, survived an assassination attempt, and earned a popularity that most politicians can only envy.
>
> —William Brooks (student), "Ronald Reagan, the Actor President"

3 Repetition and restatement

Repeating or restating key words helps make a paragraph coherent and also reminds readers what the topic is. In the following paragraph note the underlined repetition of *sleep* and the restatement of *adults*.

> Perhaps the simplest fact about sleep is that individual needs for it vary widely. Most adults sleep between seven and nine hours, but occasionally people turn up who need twelve hours or so, while some rare types can get by on three or four. Rarest of all are those legendary types who require almost no sleep at all; respected researchers have recently studied three such people. One of them—a healthy, happy woman in her seventies—sleeps about an hour every two or three days. The other two are men in early middle age, who get by on a few minutes a night. One of them complains about the daily fifteen minutes or so he's forced to "waste" in sleeping.
>
> —Lawrence A. Mayer, "The Confounding Enemy of Sleep"

Key term

parallelism The use of similar grammatical structures for similar elements of meaning within or among sentences: *The book caused a stir in the media and aroused debate in Congress.* (See also **3** pp. 149–51.)

4 Pronouns

Because pronouns refer to nouns, they can help relate sentences to each other. In the paragraph on the previous page by William Brooks, *he* works just this way by substituting for *Ronald Reagan*.

5 Consistency

Consistency (or the lack of it) occurs primarily in the person and number of nouns and pronouns and in the tense of verbs. Any inconsistencies not required by meaning will interfere with a reader's ability to follow the development of ideas.

Note the underlined inconsistencies in the next paragraphs:

Shifts in tense

In the Hopi religion, water <u>is</u> the driving force. Since the Hopi <u>lived</u> in the Arizona desert, they <u>needed</u> water urgently for drinking, cooking, and irrigating crops. Their complex beliefs <u>are</u> focused in part on gaining the assistance of supernatural forces in obtaining water. Many of the Hopi kachinas, or spirit essences, <u>were</u> directly concerned with clouds, rain, and snow.

Shifts in number

<u>Kachinas</u> represent the things and events of the real world, such as clouds, mischief, cornmeal, and even death. A <u>kachina</u> is not worshiped as a god but regarded as an interested friend. <u>They</u> visit the Hopi from December through July in the form of men who dress in kachina costumes and perform dances and other rituals.

Shifts in person

Unlike the man, the Hopi <u>woman</u> does not keep contact with kachinas through costumes and dancing. Instead, <u>one</u> receives a small likeness of a kachina, called a *tihu*, from the man impersonating the kachina. <u>You</u> are more likely to receive a tihu as a girl approaching marriage, though a child or older woman may receive one, too.

Grammar checkers A grammar checker cannot help you locate shifts in tense, number, or person among sentences. Shifts are sometimes necessary (as when tenses change to reflect actual differences

---

Key terms

pronoun A word that refers to and functions as a noun, such as *I, you, he, she, it, we, they*: *The bush had a beehive in <u>it</u>.* (See **4** p. 179.)

person The form of a pronoun that indicates whether the subject is speaking (first person: *I, we*), spoken to (second person: *you*), or spoken about (third person: *he, she, it, they*). All nouns are in the third person.

number The form of a noun, pronoun, or verb that indicates whether it is singular (one) or plural (more than one): *boy is, boys are.*

tense The form of a verb that indicates the time of its action, such as present (*I run*), past (*I ran*), or future (*I will run*). (See **4** p. 205.)

in time). Furthermore, a passage with needless shifts may still consist of sentences that are grammatically correct, as all the sentences are in the preceding examples.

6   Transitional expressions

Video
tutorial

Transitional expressions such as *therefore, in contrast,* or *meanwhile* can forge specific connections between sentences, as do the underlined expressions in this paragraph:

> Medical science has <u>thus</u> succeeded in identifying the hundreds of viruses that can cause the common cold. It has <u>also</u> discovered the most effective means of prevention. One person transmits the cold viruses to another most often by hand. <u>For instance</u>, an infected person covers his mouth to cough. He <u>then</u> picks up the telephone. <u>Half an hour later</u>, his daughter picks up the <u>same</u> telephone. <u>Immediately afterward</u>, she rubs her eyes. <u>Within a few days</u>, she, <u>too</u>, has a cold. <u>And thus</u> it spreads. To avoid colds, <u>therefore</u>, people should wash their hands often and keep their hands away from their faces.
> —Kathleen LaFrank (student), "Colds: Myth and Science"

Note that you can use transitional expressions to link paragraphs as well as sentences. In the first sentence of LaFrank's paragraph, the word *thus* signals that the sentence refers to an effect discussed in the preceding paragraph.

The following box lists many transitional expressions by the functions they perform.

Transitional expressions

Podcast

To add or show sequence
again, also, and, and then, besides, equally important, finally, first, further, furthermore, in addition, in the first place, last, moreover, next, second, still, too

To compare
also, in the same way, likewise, similarly

To contrast
although, and yet, but, but at the same time, despite, even so, even though, for all that, however, in contrast, in spite of, nevertheless, notwithstanding, on the contrary, on the other hand, regardless, still, though, yet

To give examples or intensify
after all, an illustration of, even, for example, for instance, indeed, in fact, it is true, of course, specifically, that is, to illustrate, truly

To indicate place
above, adjacent to, below, elsewhere, farther on, here, near, nearby, on the other side, opposite to, there, to the east, to the left

To indicate time

after a while, afterward, as long as, as soon as, at last, at length, at that time, before, earlier, eventually, formerly, immediately, in the meantime, in the past, later, meanwhile, now, shortly, simultaneously, since, so far, soon, subsequently, suddenly, then, thereafter, until, until now, when

To repeat, summarize, or conclude

all in all, altogether, as has been said, in brief, in conclusion, in other words, in particular, in short, in simpler terms, in summary, on the whole, that is, therefore, to put it differently, to summarize

To show cause or effect

accordingly, as a result, because, consequently, for this purpose, hence, otherwise, since, then, therefore, thereupon, thus, to this end

Note Draw carefully on this list because the expressions in each group are not interchangeable. For instance, *besides, finally,* and *second* may all be used to add information, but each has its own distinct meaning.

CULTURE LANGUAGE If transitional expressions are not common in your native language, you may be tempted to compensate when writing in English by adding them to the beginnings of most sentences. But such explicit transitions aren't needed everywhere, and in fact too many can be intrusive and awkward. When inserting transitional expressions, consider the reader's need for a signal: often the connection from sentence to sentence is already clear from the context or can be made clear by relating the content of sentences more closely (see **3** pp. 143–45). When you do need transitional expressions, try varying their positions in your sentences, as illustrated in the paragraph by LaFrank on the previous page.

6d   Developing paragraphs

An effective, well-developed paragraph always provides the specific information that readers need and expect in order to understand you and to stay interested in what you say. Paragraph length can be a rough gauge of development: anything much shorter than 100 to 150 words may leave readers with a sense of incompleteness.

To develop or shape an idea in a paragraph, one or more of the following patterns may help. (These patterns may also be used to develop entire essays. See p. 14.)

1   Narration

Narration retells a significant sequence of events, usually in the order of their occurrence (that is, chronologically). A narrator is

Video
tutorial

Student
paper

concerned not just with the sequence of events but also with their consequence, their importance to the whole.

> Jill's story is typical for "recruits" to religious cults. She was very lonely in college and appreciated the attention of the nice young men and women who lived in a house near campus. They persuaded her to share their meals and then to move in with them. Between intense bombardments of "love," they deprived her of sleep and sometimes threatened to throw her out. Jill became increasingly confused and dependent, losing touch with any reality besides the one in the group. She dropped out of school and refused to see or communicate with her family. Before long she, too, was preying on lonely college students.
>
> —Hillary Begas (student), "The Love Bombers"

2 | Description

Video
tutorial

Description details the sensory qualities of a person, scene, thing, or feeling, using concrete and specific words to convey a dominant mood, illustrate an idea, or achieve some other purpose.

Student
paper

> The sun struck straight upon the house, making the white walls glare between the dark windows. Their panes, woven thickly with green branches, held circles of impenetrable darkness. Sharp-edged wedges of light lay upon the window-sill and showed inside the room plates with blue rings, cups with curved handles, the bulge of a great bowl, the crisscross pattern in the rug, and the formidable corners and lines of cabinets and bookcases. Behind their conglomeration hung a zone of shadow in which might be a further shape to be disencumbered of shadow or still denser depths of darkness.
>
> —Virginia Woolf, *The Waves*

3 | Illustration or support

Video
tutorial

An idea may be developed with several specific examples, like those used by William Brooks on p. 42, or with a single extended example, as in the next paragraph:

Student
paper

> The experience is a familiar one to many emergency-room medics. A patient who has been pronounced dead and unexpectedly recovers later describes what happened to him during those moments—sometimes hours—when his body exhibited no signs of life. According to one repeated account, the patient feels himself rushing through a long, dark tunnel while noise rings in his ears. Suddenly, he finds himself outside his own body looking down with curious detachment at a medical team's efforts to resuscitate him. He hears what is said, notes what is happening but cannot communicate with anyone. Soon his attention is drawn to other presences in the room—spirits of dead relatives or friends—who communicate with him nonverbally. Gradually he is drawn to a vague "being of light." This being invites him to evaluate his life and shows him highlights of his past in panoramic vision. The patient longs to stay with the being of light but is reluctantly drawn back into his physical body and recovers.
>
> —Kenneth L. Woodward, "Life after Death?"

Sometimes you can develop a paragraph by providing your reasons for stating a general idea. For instance:

> There are three reasons, quite apart from scientific considerations, that mankind needs to travel in space. The first reason is the need for garbage disposal: we need to transfer industrial processes into space, so that the earth may remain a green and pleasant place for our grandchildren to live in. The second reason is the need to escape material impoverishment: the resources of this planet are finite, and we shall not forgo forever the abundant solar energy and minerals and living space that are spread out all around us. The third reason is our spiritual need for an open frontier: the ultimate purpose of space travel is to bring to humanity not only scientific discoveries and an occasional spectacular show on television but a real expansion of our spirit.
>
> —Freeman Dyson, "Disturbing the Universe"

4 Definition

Defining a complicated, abstract, or controversial term often requires extended explanation. The following definition comes from an essay asserting that "quality in product and effort has become a vanishing element of current civilization." Notice how the writer pins down meaning with examples and contrasts.

Video
tutorial

Student
paper

> In the hope of possibly reducing the hail of censure which is certain to greet this essay (I am thinking of going to Alaska or possibly Patagonia in the week it is published), let me say that quality, as I understand it, means investment of the best skill and effort possible to produce the finest and most admirable result possible. Its presence or absence in some degree characterizes every manmade object, service, skilled or unskilled labor—laying bricks, painting a picture, ironing shirts, practicing medicine, shoemaking, scholarship, writing a book. You do it well or you do it half-well. Materials are sound and durable or they are sleazy; method is painstaking or whatever is easiest. Quality is achieving or reaching for the highest standard as against being satisfied with the sloppy or fraudulent. It is honesty of purpose as against catering to cheap or sensational sentiment. It does not allow compromise with the second-rate.   —Barbara Tuchman, "The Decline of Quality"

5 Division or analysis

With division or analysis, you separate something into its elements—for instance, you might divide a newspaper into its sections. You may also approach the elements critically, interpreting their meaning and significance (see **2** pp. 85–87):

Video
tutorial

Student
paper

> The surface realism of the soap opera conjures up an illusion of "liveness." The domestic settings and easygoing rhythms encourage the viewer to believe that the drama, however ridiculous, is simply an extension of daily life. The conversation is so slow that some have called it "radio with pictures." (Advertisers have always assumed that busy housewives would listen, rather than watch.) Conversation is casual and

colloquial, as though one were eavesdropping on neighbors. There is plenty of time to "read" the character's face; close-ups establish intimacy. The sets are comfortably familiar: well-lit interiors of living rooms, restaurants, offices, and hospitals. Daytime soaps have little of the glamour of their prime-time relations. The viewer easily imagines that the conversation is taking place in real time.

—Ruth Rosen, "Search for Yesterday"

6 Classification

Video tutorial

Student paper

When you classify items, you sort them into groups. The classification allows you to see and explain the relations among the items. The following paragraph identifies three groups, or classes, of parents:

> In my experience, the parents who hire daytime sitters for their school-age children tend to fall into one of three groups. The first group includes parents who work and want someone to be at home when the children return from school. These parents are looking for an extension of themselves, someone who will give the care they would give if they were at home. The second group includes parents who may be home all day themselves but are too disorganized or too frazzled by their children's demands to handle child care alone. They are looking for an organizer and helpmate. The third and final group includes parents who do not want to be bothered by their children, whether they are home all day or not. Unlike the parents in the first two groups, who care for their children however they can, these parents seek a permanent substitute for themselves. —Nancy Whittle (student), "Modern Parenting"

7 Comparison and contrast

Video tutorial

Student paper

Comparison and contrast may be used separately or together to develop an idea. The following paragraph illustrates one of two common ways of organizing a comparison and contrast: **subject by subject,** first one subject and then the other.

> Consider the differences also in the behavior of rock and classical music audiences. At a rock concert, the audience members yell, whistle, sing along, and stamp their feet. They may even stand during the entire performance. The better the music, the more active they'll be. At a classical concert, in contrast, the better the performance, the more *still* the audience is. Members of the classical audience are so highly disciplined that they refrain from even clearing their throats or coughing. No matter what effect the powerful music has on their intellects and feelings, they sit on their hands.
> —Tony Nahm (student), "Rock and Roll Is Here to Stay"

The next paragraph illustrates the other common organization: **point by point,** with the two subjects discussed side by side and matched feature for feature.

> Arguing is often equated with fighting, but there are key differences between the two. Participants in an argument approach the subject to find common ground, or points on which both sides agree, while people

engaged in a fight usually approach the subject with an "us-versus-them" attitude. Participants in an argument are careful to use respectful, polite language, in contrast to the insults and worse that people in a fight use to get the better of their opponents. Finally, participants in an argument commonly have the goal of reaching a new understanding or larger truth about the subject they're debating, while those in a fight have winning as their only goal.

—Erica Ito (student),"Is an Argument Always a Fight?"

8 Cause-and-effect analysis

When you use analysis to explain why something happened or what did or may happen, then you are determining causes or effects. In the following paragraph the author looks at the cause of an effect—Japanese collectivism:

Video
tutorial

Student
paper

> The *shinkansen* or "bullet train" speeds across the rural areas of Japan giving a quick view of cluster after cluster of farmhouses surrounded by rice paddies. This particular pattern did not develop purely by chance, but as a consequence of the technology peculiar to the growing of rice, the staple of the Japanese diet. The growing of rice requires the construction and maintenance of an irrigation system, something that takes many hands to build. More importantly, the planting and the harvesting of rice can only be done efficiently with the cooperation of twenty or more people. The "bottom line" is that a single family working alone cannot produce enough rice to survive, but a dozen families working together can produce a surplus. Thus the Japanese have had to develop the capacity to work together in harmony, no matter what the forces of disagreement or social disintegration, in order to survive. —William Ouchi, *Theory Z*

9 Process analysis

When you analyze how to do something or how something works, you explain a process. The following example identifies a process, describes the equipment needed, and details the steps in the process:

Video
tutorial

Student
paper

> As a car owner, you waste money when you pay a mechanic to change the engine oil. The job is not difficult, even if you know little about cars. All you need is a wrench to remove the drain plug, a large, flat pan to collect the draining oil, plastic bottles to dispose of the used oil, and fresh oil. First, warm up the car's engine so that the oil will flow more easily. When the engine is warm, shut it off and remove its oil-filler cap (the owner's manual shows where this cap is). Then locate the drain plug under the engine (again consulting the owner's manual for its location) and place the flat pan under the plug. Remove the plug with the wrench, letting the oil flow into the pan. When the oil stops flowing, replace the plug and, at the engine's filler hole, add the amount and kind of fresh oil specified by the owner's manual. Pour the used oil into the plastic bottles and take it to a waste-oil collector, which any garage mechanic can recommend.

—Anthony Andreas (student), "Do-It-Yourself Car Care"

6e   Writing introductory and concluding paragraphs

1   Introductions

Video
tutorial

Exercise

An introduction draws readers from their world into yours.

■ **It focuses readers' attention on the topic and arouses their curiosity about what you have to say.**
■ **It specifies your subject and implies your attitude.**
■ **Often it includes your thesis statement.**
■ **It is concise and sincere.**

The box below gives options for focusing readers' attention.

Some strategies for introductions

Video
tutorial

■ Ask a question.
■ Relate an incident.
■ Use a vivid quotation.
■ Create a visual image that represents your subject.
■ Offer a surprising statistic or other fact.
■ Provide background.
■ State an opinion related to your thesis.

■ Outline the argument your thesis refutes.
■ Make a historical comparison or contrast.
■ Outline a problem or dilemma.
■ Define a word central to your subject.
■ In some business or technical writing, simply state your main idea.

CULTURE LANGUAGE These options for an introduction may not be what you are used to if your native language is not English. In other cultures readers may seek familiarity or reassurance from an author's introduction, or they may prefer an indirect approach to the subject. In academic and business English, however, writers and readers prefer concise, direct expression.

Effective openings

A very common introduction opens with a statement of the essay's general subject, clarifies or limits the subject in one or more sentences, and then asserts the point of the essay in the thesis statement (underlined in the following examples):

> Can your home or office computer make you sterile? Can it strike you blind or dumb? The answer is: probably not. Nevertheless, reports of side effects relating to computer use should be examined, especially in the area of birth defects, eye complaints, and postural difficulties. Although little conclusive evidence exists to establish a causal link between computer use and problems of this sort, the circumstantial evidence can be disturbing.
> —Thomas Hartmann,
> "How Dangerous Is Your Computer?"

> The Declaration of Independence is so widely regarded as a state-ment of American ideals that its origins in practical politics tend to be forgotten. Thomas Jefferson's draft was intensely debated and then revised in the Continental Congress. Jefferson was disappointed with the result. However, <u>a close reading of both the historical context and the re-visions themselves indicates that the Congress improved the document for its intended purpose.</u>
>
> —Ann Weiss (student), "The Editing of the Declaration of Independence"

In much public writing, it's more important to tell readers imme-diately what your point is than to try to engage them. This introduc-tion to a brief memo quickly outlines a problem and (in the thesis statement) suggests a way to solve it:

> Starting next month, the holiday rush and staff vacations will leave our department short-handed. <u>We need to hire two or perhaps three temporary keyboarders to maintain our schedules for the month.</u>

Additional effective introductions appear in sample papers else-where in this book: p. 34, **2** p. 102 and 116, **8** p. 384, and **MLA** p. 450.

Openings to avoid

When writing and revising your introduction, avoid approaches that are likely to bore or confuse readers:

Video
tutorial

- ■ **A vague generality or truth.** Don't extend your reach too wide with a line such as *Throughout human history . . .* or *In today's world. . . .* You may have needed a warm-up paragraph to start drafting, but your readers can do without it.

- ■ **A flat announcement.** Don't start with *The purpose of this essay is . . .* , *In this essay I will . . .* , or any similar presentation of your intention or topic.

- ■ **A reference to the essay's title.** Don't refer to the title of the essay in the first sentence—for example, *This is a big problem* or *This book is about the history of the guitar.*

- ■ **According to Webster. . . .** Don't start by citing a dictionary defi-nition. A definition can be an effective springboard to an essay, but this kind of lead-in has become dull with overuse.

- ■ **An apology.** Don't fault your opinion or your knowledge with *I'm not sure if I'm right, but I think . . .* , *I don't know much about this, but . . .* , or a similar line.

2 Conclusions

Your conclusion finishes off your essay and tells readers where you think you have brought them. It answers the question "So what?"

Video
tutorial

Effective conclusions

Usually set off in its own paragraph, the conclusion may con-sist of a single sentence or a group of sentences. It may take one or more of the approaches listed in the following box.

Video
tutorial

Some strategies for conclusions

- Recommend a course of action.
- Summarize the paper.
- Echo the approach of the introduction.
- Restate your thesis and reflect on its implications.
- Strike a note of hope or despair.

- Give a symbolic or powerful fact or other detail.
- Give an especially compelling example.
- Create an image that represents your subject.
- Use a quotation.

The following paragraph concludes the essay on the Declaration of Independence whose introduction appears on the previous page. The writer both summarizes her essay and echoes her introduction.

> The Declaration of Independence has come to be a statement of this nation's political philosophy, but that was not its purpose in 1776. Jefferson's passionate expression had to bow to the goals of the Congress as a whole to forge unity among the colonies and to win the support of foreign nations.
> —Ann Weiss (student), "The Editing of the Declaration of Independence"

In the next paragraph the author concludes an essay on environmental protection with a call for action:

> Until we get the answers, I think we had better keep on building power plants and growing food with the help of fertilizers and such insect-controlling chemicals as we now have. The risks are well known, thanks to the environmentalists. If they had not created a widespread public awareness of the ecological crisis, we wouldn't stand a chance. But such awareness by itself is not enough. Flaming manifestos and prophecies of doom are no longer much help, and a search for scapegoats can only make matters worse. The time for sensations and manifestos is about over. Now we need rigorous analysis, united effort and very hard work.
> —Peter F. Drucker, "How Best to Protect the Environment"

Conclusions to avoid

Video
tutorial

Several kinds of conclusions rarely work well:

- **A repeat of the introduction.** Don't simply replay your introduction. The conclusion should capture what the paragraphs of the body have added to the introduction.
- **A new direction.** Don't introduce a subject different from the one your essay has been about.
- **A sweeping generalization.** Don't conclude more than you reasonably can from the evidence you have presented. If your essay is about your frustrating experience trying to clear a parking ticket, you cannot reasonably conclude that *all* local police forces are too tied up in red tape to be of service to the people.

■ **An apology.** Don't cast doubt on your essay. Don't say, *Even though I'm no expert* or *This may not be convincing, but I believe it's true* or anything similar. Rather, to win your readers' confidence, display confidence.

7 Presenting Writing

Presenting your writing gives you a chance to display your hard work in the best possible light. Most of the time, this opportunity comes with challenges as well: to fulfill the requirements of the assignment, the conventions of the genre, and the expectations of your audience. This chapter will help you make decisions about designing papers effectively (below), incorporating visuals and other media (p. 58), and designing Web compositions (p. 64) and contributions to blogs and wikis (p. 68).

7a Designing academic writing

Many of the assignments you receive in college will require you to submit a written text either on paper or electronically—for instance, attached to an e-mail or uploaded to a course Web site. For such papers, the guidelines in this section will help you put your writing in an attractive, readable format. In addition, many academic style guides recommend specific formats. This book details two such formats:

■ **MLA style,** used in English, foreign languages, and some other humanities (**MLA** pp. 446–48).
■ **APA style,** used in the social sciences (**APA** pp. 480–82).

Other academic formats can be found in the style guides listed in **8** pp. 389, 393, and 397. Be sure to check with your instructor if you have any questions about the format he or she requires.

Some academic writing assignments will be purely digital, such as an autobiographical blog post or a Web site providing information about a service on your campus. Many of the following design guidelines apply to such projects as well, but they receive separate attention on pp. 64–69. If you are designing *PowerPoint* slides for an oral presentation, see **2** pp. 126–27.

Note When you write outside your college courses, your audience will have certain expectations for how your writing should look and read. Guidelines for such writing appear in Chapter 14.

1 Using principles of design

Most of the principles of design respond to the ways we read. White space, for instance, relieves our eyes and helps to lead us through a document. Groupings or lists show relationships. Visuals and color add variety and help to emphasize important elements.

The following sample document is the opening of a report for a marketing course. The page makes good use of white space, groups similar elements, uses bullets and fonts for emphasis, and successfully integrates and explains the photograph.

Sample marketing report

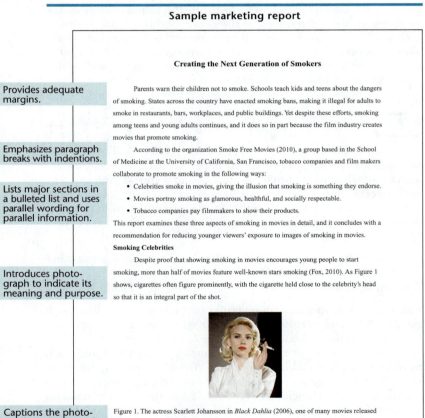

Creating the Next Generation of Smokers

Parents warn their children not to smoke. Schools teach kids and teens about the dangers of smoking. States across the country have enacted smoking bans, making it illegal for adults to smoke in restaurants, bars, workplaces, and public buildings. Yet despite these efforts, smoking among teens and young adults continues, and it does so in part because the film industry creates movies that promote smoking.

According to the organization Smoke Free Movies (2010), a group based in the School of Medicine at the University of California, San Francisco, tobacco companies and film makers collaborate to promote smoking in the following ways:

- Celebrities smoke in movies, giving the illusion that smoking is something they endorse.
- Movies portray smoking as glamorous, healthful, and socially respectable.
- Tobacco companies pay filmmakers to show their products.

This report examines these three aspects of smoking in movies in detail, and it concludes with a recommendation for reducing younger viewers' exposure to images of smoking in movies.

Smoking Celebrities

Despite proof that showing smoking in movies encourages young people to start smoking, more than half of movies feature well-known stars smoking (Fox, 2010). As Figure 1 shows, cigarettes often figure prominently, with the cigarette held close to the celebrity's head so that it is an integral part of the shot.

Figure 1. The actress Scarlett Johansson in *Black Dahlia* (2006), one of many movies released each year in which characters smoke. From *Daily Mail*, Associated Newspapers, 9 Mar. 2010.

Annotations (left margin):

- Provides adequate margins.
- Emphasizes paragraph breaks with indentions.
- Lists major sections in a bulleted list and uses parallel wording for parallel information.
- Introduces photograph to indicate its meaning and purpose.
- Captions the photograph so that it can be read independently from the text.

Exercise

As you design your own documents, follow the requirements of your assignment and think about your purpose, the expectations of your readers, and how readers will move through each document, on screen or on paper. Also consider the following general principles of design, noting how they overlap and support one another:

- **Conduct readers through the document.** Establish flow, a pattern for the eye to follow, with headings, lists, and other elements on the page or screen.
- **Use white space to ease crowding and focus readers' attention.** Provide ample margins, and give breathing room to headings, lists, and other elements. Even the space indicating paragraphs (an indention or a line of extra space) gives readers a break and reassures them that ideas are divided into manageable chunks.
- **Group information to show relationships.** Use headings (like those in this chapter) and lists (like the one you're reading) to convey the similarities and differences among parts of a document.
- **Standardize to create and fulfill expectations.** Help direct readers through your writing by, for instance, using the same size and color for all headings at the same level of importance. Standardizing also reduces clutter, making it easier for readers to determine the significance of the parts.
- **Emphasize important elements.** Establish hierarchies of information with type fonts and sizes, headings, indentions, color, boxes, and white space. In this book, for example, the importance of headings is clear from their size and color and from the presence of decorative elements, such as the box around 2 in the heading below.

2 Using elements of design in academic writing

Applying the preceding principles involves margins, line spacing, and type fonts and may involve highlighting, headings, lists, color, and illustrations. Many assignments will prescribe the format you should use. If you are addressing readers who have vision loss, consider as well the points in the box on p. 57.

Margins

Use margins at the top, bottom, and sides of a printed page to prevent pages from overwhelming readers with unpleasant crowding. Most academic documents use a one-inch margin on all sides.

Line spacing

Most text-heavy academic documents are double-spaced, with an initial indention for paragraphs, while most documents designed to be read on screen are single-spaced, with an extra line of space between paragraphs. Double or triple spacing sets off headings in both.

Type fonts and sizes

The readability of text derives partly from the type fonts (or faces) and their sizes. For academic and business documents, generally choose a standard font, as in these samples:

10-point Cambria   10-point Arial

12-point Cambria   12-point Arial

Fonts like Cambria and the one you're reading have **serifs**—the small lines finishing the letters, such as the downward strokes on the top of this T. Serif fonts are appropriate for formal writing and are easier for most people to read on paper. **Sans serif** fonts (*sans* means "without" in French), such as Arial above, are usually easier read on a screen and are clearer on paper for readers with some vision loss (see the next page). Generally avoid decorative fonts such as Comic Sans, *Freestyle Script*, and **Impact**.

The point size of a type font is not always a reliable guide to its actual size, but most standard fonts are readable in 10 or 12 points. If you are presenting your writing orally using *PowerPoint* slides, you will need to use a larger font. See **2** pp. 126–27 for tips on slide design.

Highlighting

Within a document's text, underlined, *italic*, and **boldface** can emphasize key words or sentences. In a printed paper, you may sometimes use boldface to give strong emphasis—for instance, to a term being defined. In Web documents, boldface and underlining are common to indicate links to media and other sites.

As a general rule, use highlighting selectively to complement your meaning, not merely to decorate your work. Many readers find type embellishments distracting.

Headings

Headings are signposts: they direct the reader's attention by focusing the eye on a document's most significant content. In digital projects, headings may be decorative as well as functional, capturing the reader's attention with large sizes, lots of white space, and unconventional fonts. In academic writing, however, headings are more purely functional. They break the text of a long document into discrete parts, create emphasis, and orient the reader.

When you use headings in academic writing, follow these guidelines:

- **Use one, two, or three levels of headings** depending on the needs of your material and the length of your document. Some level of heading every two or so pages will help keep readers on track.
- **Create an outline of your document to plan where headings should go.** Reserve the first level of heading for the main points

Considering readers with vision loss

If your audience may include readers who have low vision, problems with color perception, or difficulties processing visual information, adapt your design to meet these readers' needs:

Video
tutorial

- **Use large type fonts.** Most guidelines call for 14 points or larger.
- **Use standard type fonts.** Many people with low vision find it easier to read sans serif fonts such as Arial than serif fonts. Avoid decorative fonts with unusual flourishes, even in headings.
- **Avoid words in all-capital letters.**
- **Avoid relying on color alone to distinguish elements.** Label elements, and distinguish them by position or size.
- **Use red and green selectively.** To readers who are red-green color-blind, these colors will appear in shades of gray, yellow, or blue.
- **Use contrasting colors.** To make colors distinct, choose them from opposite sides of the color spectrum—violet and yellow, for instance, or orange and blue.
- **Use only light colors for tints behind type.** Make the type itself black or a very dark color.

(and sections). Use a second and perhaps a third level of heading to mark subsections of supporting information.

- **Keep headings as short as possible** while making them specific about the material that follows.
- **Word headings consistently**—for instance, all questions (*What Is the Scientific Method?*), all phrases with *-ing* words (*Understanding the Scientific Method*), or all phrases with nouns (*The Scientific Method*).
- **Indicate the relative importance of headings** with type size, positioning, and highlighting, such as capital letters or boldface.

First-Level Heading

Second-Level Heading

Third-Level Heading

Generally, you can use the same type font and size for headings as for the text.

- **Don't break a page immediately after a heading.** Push the heading to the next page.

Note Document format in psychology and some other social sciences requires a particular treatment of headings. See **8** pp. 481–82.

Lists

Lists give visual reinforcement to the relations between like items —for example, the steps in a process or the elements of a proposal. A list is easier to read than a paragraph, and it adds white space.

When wording a list, work for parallelism among items—for instance, all complete sentences or all phrases (see also **3** p. 151). Set the list with space above and below. Number the items, or mark them with bullets: centered dots or other devices, such as the squares used in the list below about color. On most word processors you can use the Format menu to create a list automatically.

Color

Web documents and other digital projects almost always use color, but conventional academic writing rarely uses color except in visuals. (Ask your instructor for his or her preferences.) If you do use color in an academic document, follow these guidelines:

- **Print text in black,** not red, blue, or another color.
- **Make sure that color headings are dark enough to be readable.**
- **Stick to the same color for all headings at the same level**—for instance, red for primary headings, black for secondary headings.
- **Use color for bullets, lines, and other nontext elements.** But use no more than a few colors to keep pages clean.
- **Use color to distinguish the parts of illustrations.** Use only as many colors as you need to make your illustration clear. (See below.)

See also the box on the previous page when using color for readers who have vision loss.

7b Using visuals and other media in multimodal writing

Exercise

Academic writing is often **multimodal**—that is, it includes more than one medium, whether text, charts, photographs, video, or audio. A simple multimodal paper involves just two media—mainly text with some illustrations embedded in the text. A paper submitted online might add links to audio or video files as well. This section provides guidelines for selecting and using such media in your writing. The next sections treat media in Web compositions and in blogs and wikis.

Caution Any visual or media file you include or link to in your writing requires the same detailed citation as a written source. See **7** pp. 360–68 for more on acknowledging sources.

1 Selecting visuals and other media

Video tutorial

Depending on your writing situation, you might use anything from a table to a bar chart to a video to support your writing. The following pages describe and illustrate the options.

Note The Web is an excellent resource for images, audio, and video (see **7** pp. 334–36). Your computer may include a program for creating tables, graphs, and other illustrations, or you can work with specialized software such as *Excel* (for graphs and charts) or *Adobe Illustrator* (for diagrams, maps, and the like). Use *PowerPoint* or a similar program for visuals in oral presentations (see **2** pp. 126–27).

Tables

Tables usually present raw data, making complex information accessible to readers. The data may show how variables relate to one another or how two or more groups contrast, as in the example below.

Table

Descriptive title falls above the table.	The layout of rows and columns is clear: headings align with their data, and numbers align vertically down columns.
Headings label horizontal rows and vertical columns.	

Table 1

Public- and private-school enrollment of US students age five and older, 2009

	Number of students	Percentage in public school	Percentage in private school
All students	74,603,000	85	15
Kindergarten through grade 8	39,179,000	88	12
Grades 9–12	16,332,000	92	8
College (undergraduate)	16,366,000	77	23
Graduate and professional school	2,737,000	50	50

Source: Data from *Digest of Education Statistics: 2009*; Natl. Center for Educ. Statistics, Apr. 2010; Web; 10 May 2011; table 2.

Pie charts

Pie charts show the relations among the parts of a whole. The whole totals 100 percent, and each pie slice is proportional in size to its share of the whole. Pie charts are appropriate when shares, not the underlying data, are the focus.

Pie chart

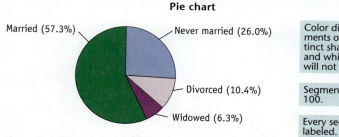

Married (57.3%)   Never married (26.0%)   Divorced (10.4%)   Widowed (6.3%)

Color distinguishes segments of the chart. Use distinct shades of gray, black, and white if your paper will not be read in color.
Segment percentages total 100.
Every segment is clearly labeled.
Caption below the chart explains it and credits the source.

Fig. 1. Marital status in 2008 of adults age eighteen and over. Data from *2010 Statistical Abstract*; US Census Bureau, Jan. 2009; Web; 26 Feb. 2011.

Bar charts

Bar charts compare groups or time periods on a measure such

as quantity or frequency. A bar chart is appropriate when relative size is important. A bar chart always starts with a zero point in the lower left corner so that the values on the vertical axis are clear.

Bar chart

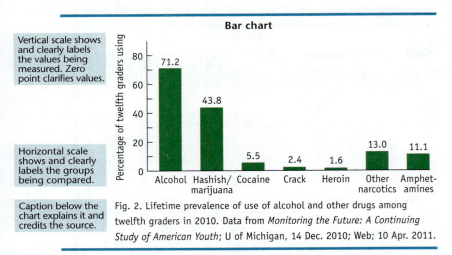

Vertical scale shows and clearly labels the values being measured. Zero point clarifies values.

Horizontal scale shows and clearly labels the groups being compared.

Caption below the chart explains it and credits the source.

Fig. 2. Lifetime prevalence of use of alcohol and other drugs among twelfth graders in 2010. Data from *Monitoring the Future: A Continuing Study of American Youth*; U of Michigan, 14 Dec. 2010; Web; 10 Apr. 2011.

Line graphs

Line graphs show change over time in one or more subjects. They are an economical and highly visual way to compare many points of data. A line graph always starts with a zero point in the lower left corner so that the values on the vertical axis are clear.

Line graph

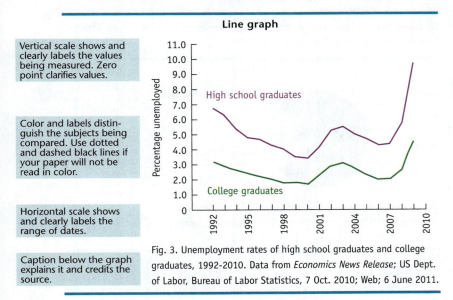

Vertical scale shows and clearly labels the values being measured. Zero point clarifies values.

Color and labels distinguish the subjects being compared. Use dotted and dashed black lines if your paper will not be read in color.

Horizontal scale shows and clearly labels the range of dates.

Caption below the graph explains it and credits the source.

Fig. 3. Unemployment rates of high school graduates and college graduates, 1992-2010. Data from *Economics News Release*; US Dept. of Labor, Bureau of Labor Statistics, 7 Oct. 2010; Web; 6 June 2011.

Diagrams

Diagrams show concepts visually, such as the structure of an organization, the way something works or looks, or the relations among subjects. Often, diagrams show what can't be described economically in words.

Diagram

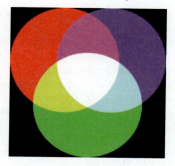

Diagram makes concept comprehensible.

Fig. 4. RGB color theory, applied to televisions and computer monitors, in which all possible colors and white are created from red, green, and blue. From "Color Theory"; *Wikipedia*; Wikimedia, 15 Mar. 2005; Web; 13 May 2011.

Caption below the diagram explains it and credits the source.

Images: Photographs, fine art, advertisements, and cartoons

Sometimes you may focus an entire paper on critically analyzing an image such as a painting or an advertisement. More often, you'll use images to support points you make in your papers or

Photograph

Photograph shows subject more economically and dramatically than words could.

Fig. 5. View of Saturn from the *Cassini* spacecraft, showing the planet and its rings. From *Cassini-Huygens: Mission to Saturn and Titan*; US Natl. Atmospheric and Space Administration, Jet Propulsion Laboratory, 24 Feb. 2005; Web; 26 June 2011.

Caption below the image explains it and credits the source.

presentations. You might clarify an informative astronomy report with a photograph of Saturn (see opposite), sharpen an analysis of a graphic novel by reproducing a frame or illustration, offer an advertisement from the 1950s as evidence for an assertion about an attitude of the time, or capture the crux of a political debate with a cartoon.

Video and audio

If you will present your writing digitally—for instance, as a Web page or blog—you may choose to emphasize or illustrate points in your writing with embedded or linked video and audio files. For example, you might explain a process with a video of how something works, support an interpretation of a play with a video of a scene from a performance, or illustrate a profile of a person by linking to an interview. The following screen shot shows a passage of text from an online paper that links to footage of the *I Have a Dream* speech delivered by Martin Luther King, Jr., in 1963.

Link to video file

King's speech uses inspirational techniques that are familiar in sermons. For example, in the final five minutes of the speech, King repeats "I have a dream" nine times and "let freedom ring" eleven times. In the video of the speech (http://www.youtube.com/watch?v=PbUtL_0vAJk), each repetition increases the power of the words and draws a stronger response from the audience.

2 Using visuals and other media effectively

An image or a video clip can attract readers' attention, but if it does no more it will amount to mere decoration or, worse, it will distract readers from the substance of your writing. Before using any visual or other media, consider whether it meets the requirements of your assignment, serves a purpose, and is appropriate for your audience.

Considering the requirements and limits of your writing situation

What do the type of writing you're doing and its format allow? Look through examples of similar writing to gauge the kinds of media, if any, that readers will expect. It matters, too, how you will present your work: a short animation sequence might be terrific in a

PowerPoint presentation or on the Web, but a printed document requires photographs, drawings, and other static means of explanation.

Making visuals and other media support your writing

Ensure that any visual you use relates directly to a point in your writing, adds to that point, and gives your audience something to think about. In an evaluation of an advertisement, the ad itself would support the claim you make about it. In a paper arguing for earthquake preparedness, a photograph could provide a visual record of earthquake damage and a chart could show levels of current preparedness.

The following two images supported a paper with this thesis: *By the mid-1960s, depictions of women in advertising reflected changing attitudes toward the traditional role of homemaker.*

Images as support

Visual examples support the thesis about changing attitudes toward women as homemakers.	Caption explains the visuals, tying them to the text of the paper and providing source information.

Fig. 1. An advertisement from 1945 (left) and a brochure illustration from 1965 (right) showing a change in the relationship between homemaking women and their appliances. Left: Hoover advertisement; 1945; print. Right: *Electric Ranges by Frigidaire*; 1965; print.

Integrating visuals and other media into your writing

Readers should understand why you are including visuals or other media in your writing and how they relate to the overall project:

- **In projects with embedded visuals, connect the visuals to your text.** When you include visuals in your writing, refer to them at the point(s) where readers will benefit from consulting them—for instance, "See fig. 2" or "See table 1." Number figures and tables separately (Fig. 1, Fig. 2, and so on; Table 1, Table 2, and so

Video
tutorial

Using visuals and other media responsibly

Visuals and other media require special care to avoid distortion and to ensure honest use of others' material.

- **Create and evaluate tables, charts, and graphs carefully.** Verify that the data you use are accurate and that the highlighted changes, relationships, or trends reflect reality. In a line graph, for instance, starting the vertical axis at zero puts the lines in context (see the sample on p. 60). See **2** pp. 114–15 on misrepresentations in visuals.
- **Be skeptical of images you find on the Web.** Altered photographs are posted and circulated widely on the Web. If a photograph seems inauthentic, check into its source or don't use it.
- **Provide a source note.** You must credit the source whenever you use someone else's data to create a visual, embed someone else's visual in your document, or link to someone else's media file. Each discipline has a slightly different style for such source notes: those in the illustrations on pp. 59–61 reflect MLA style. See also Chapters 58–61.
- **Obtain permission if it is required.** For projects that will reside on the Web, you may need to clear permission from the copyright holder of a visual or a media file. See **7** pp. 366–67 for a discussion of copyright and permission.

on). And always include a caption that explicitly ties the image to your text—so that readers don't have to puzzle out your intentions—and provides source information.

- **In online projects using audio or video, work the files or links into your text.** Your audience should know what you intend the media to show, whether you link to a photograph from a mainly text document or you integrate text, sound, still images, and video into a complex Web project. For instance, in the *I Have a Dream* sample on p. 62 the embedded link to footage of the speech invites readers to see and hear King for themselves.

7c Presenting writing on the Web

Many creators of Web-based projects upload files into existing forms that make design fairly easy. Even if you choose to use such software, you will still have to make choices about elements such as fonts, colors, layout, headings, and so on. The design guidelines for academic writing on pp. 53–58 can help you with such decisions, as can the following discussion of academic Web compositions such as a Web site or a multimodal project posted on a blog or wiki.

1 Conceiving a Web composition

Whether you are developing a Web site or preparing a digital composition to be posted on the Web, the following general guidelines will help you plan your project:

- **Consider how design can reflect your purpose and your sense of audience.** Type fonts and sizes, headings, visuals and other media, background colors, and other design elements can connect with readers and further the purpose of your writing.

- **Anticipate how readers will move within your composition.** A digital document with links to other pages, posts, Web sites, and media can disorient readers as they scroll up and down and pursue various links. Page length, links, menus, and other cues should work to keep readers oriented.

- **Imagine what readers may see on their screens.** Each reader's screen frames and organizes the experience of a Web composition. Screen space is limited, and it varies widely. Text and visual elements should be managed for maximum clarity and effectiveness on a variety of screens.

- **Integrate visuals, audio, and video into the text.** Web compositions will likely include visuals such as charts and photographs as well as video (such as animation or film clips) and audio (such as music or excerpts from interviews). Any visual or sound element should add essential information that can't be provided otherwise, and it should be well integrated with the rest of your composition. See pp. 62–64 for tips on using media effectively.

- **Acknowledge your sources.** It's easy to incorporate text, visuals, audio, and video from other sources into a Web composition, but you have the same obligation to cite your sources as you do in a printed document. (See **7** pp. 360–66 on citing sources.) Your Web composition is a form of publication, like a magazine or a book. Unless the material you are using explicitly allows copying without permission, you may need to seek the copyright holder's permission, just as print publishers do. (See **7** pp. 366–67 for more on copyright.)

Note If you anticipate that some of your readers may have visual, hearing, or reading disabilities, you'll need to consider their needs while designing Web sites. Some of these considerations are covered on p. 57, and others are fundamental to any effective Web-based design, as discussed in this section. In addition, avoid any content that relies exclusively on visuals or sound, instead supplementing such elements with text descriptions. At the same time, try to provide key concepts in words as well as in visuals and sound. For more on Web design for readers with disabilities, visit the American Council for the Blind at *acb.org/accessible-formats.html* and the World Wide Web Consortium at *www.w3.org/WAI*.

2 Creating a Web site

Traditional printed documents are intended to be read page by page in sequence. In contrast, Web sites are intended to be examined in whatever order readers choose as they follow links to pages within

Sample document

a site and to other sites. The diagram below shows a schematic Web site, with pages at different levels (orange and then blue squares) interconnecting with the home page and with one another.

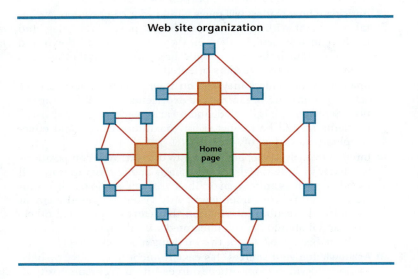

Web site organization

While reading Web sites, readers generally alternate between skimming pages for highlights and focusing intently on one section of text. To facilitate this kind of reading, you'll want to consider the guidelines on the facing page and also the site's structure and content, flow, and ease of navigation.

Structure and content

Sample document

Organize your Web site so that it efficiently arranges your content and also orients readers:

- **Sketch possible site plans before getting started.** A diagram like the one above can help you develop the major components of your project and create a logical space for each component.
- **Consider how menus can provide overviews of the organization as well as direct access to the linked content.** The Web site shown on the facing page includes a menu near the top of the page.
- **Treat the first few sentences of any page as a get-acquainted space for you and your readers.** In the sample Web site on the facing page, the text hooks readers with questions and orients them with general information.
- **Distill your text so that it includes only essential information.** Concise prose is essential in any writing situation, of course, but readers of Web sites expect to scan text quickly.

Web site home page

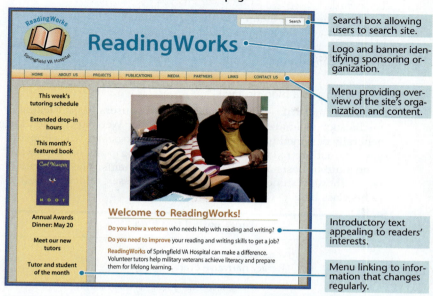

Search box allowing users to search site.

Logo and banner identifying sponsoring organization.

Menu providing overview of the site's organization and content.

Introductory text appealing to readers' interests.

Menu linking to information that changes regularly.

Flow

Take advantage of the Web's visual nature by thinking about how information will flow on each page:

- **Standardize elements of your design to create expectations in readers and to fulfill those expectations.** For instance, develop a uniform style for the main headings of pages, for headings within pages, and for menus.
- **Make scanning easy for readers.** Focus readers on crucial text by adding space around it. Add headings to break up text and to highlight content. Use lists to reinforce the parallel importance of items. (See pp. 54–58 for more on these and other design elements.)

Navigation

Provide a menu so that readers can navigate your Web site. Like the table of contents in a book, a menu lists the features of a site, giving its plan at a glance. By clicking on any item in the list, readers can go directly to a page that interests them.

Sample document

You can embed a menu at the top, side, or bottom of a page— or use more than one position. Menus at the top or side allow readers to move around the site without having to read the full home page. Menus at the bottom prevent readers from dead-ending—

that is, reaching a point where they can't easily move forward or backward.

In designing a menu, keep it simple: many different type fonts and colors will overwhelm readers instead of orienting them. And make your menus look the same from one page to the next so that readers recognize them easily.

3 Posting to a blog or a wiki

Blogs and wikis are Web sites that allow users to post text and media such as images and video. Unlike other Web sites, which are generally designed to provide information, blogs and wikis encourage interaction: readers can comment on blog posts or, on a wiki, contribute to posts and collaborate on documents. The illustration below shows a student's draft of a personal essay, which he posted to his class blog.

Paper posted to a blog

Descriptive title providing context for the post.

Standard font for readability.

Illustration supporting a point in the post.

Embedded link to another Web site.

FRIDAY, FEBRUARY 18, 2011

Literacy narrative draft

Comics: Telling Stories in Words and Art

For my seventh birthday, I received a Calvin and Hobbes comic book. I devoured the book, reading it cover to cover countless times, and was instantly attracted to how drawings and words worked together to tell very funny stories about the characters. I didn't always understand the vocabulary, the jokes, and references to the 1980s, but I laughed at what I did get: the funny arguments, crazy games, and hilarious schemes.

The summer after my birthday I began drawing my own comics. I created two characters modeled on Calvin and Hobbes—a boy named Timmy and his dog Snuffy. Over the next five years, I drew hundreds of comics about Timmy, Snuffy, and Timmy's family and friends. I drew the strip shown here, about one of Timmy's many mishaps, when I was ten. I have this strip and some of my other favorites posted on my personal blog: johnsdoodles @blogger.com.

Timmy experienced much of what I did over the next several years. He went on vacation to places I visited with my family, like New York and San Francisco. He visited aunts, uncles, and grandparents. He exasperated his parents, annoyed his sister, learned to play an instrument, and dreamed of being a pilot. He also did things I had not experienced: he once trained for the school marathon and came in third, dreamed of going to the prom like his sister, and slid down what seemed like a mile-long hill on a sled. Through Timmy, I used language and drawing to explore ideas, dreams, experiences, and feelings, all the time trying to make them funny.

Although I still draw and write, I left Timmy behind the summer I turned twelve. However, occasionally I look back at my Timmy comics and find it interesting to see how I used words and images to develop and display my sense of place in the world.

Posted by John Heywood at 4:23 PM.

You may create a blog or a wiki as an academic assignment, in which case you will need to make decisions about the appearance of the site as a whole. For most academic blog or wiki writing, however, you will post drafts of your papers and comment on your class-mates' work. You can compose and edit your text in your word processor and paste the text into the blog or wiki. At that point, you'll have the opportunity to write a descriptive title for your post, upload images and other media, and add links to other Web sites. You can also preview the post before making it public.

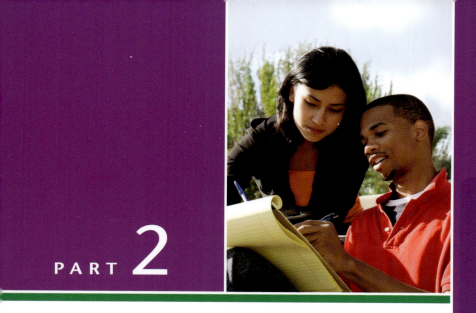

PART 2

Writing in and out of College

PART 2

Writing in and out of College

8 Joining the Academic Community

When you take college courses, you enter a community of teachers and students whose basic goal is to share and build knowledge about a subject, whether it is English, history, engineering, or something else. You participate in this community first by studying each subject, acquiring its vocabulary, and learning to express yourself in its ways. As you learn more about the subject, you contribute to the community and to its knowledge by asking questions and communicating your answers in writing. This active contribution to knowledge building is the core of academic work, and it depends on the integrity of everyone involved.

As you try to grasp the content of assigned reading and understand new concepts, academic knowledge building may at first seem out of reach. But developing the skills will be easier if you follow the advice in this chapter for engaging with course material, becoming an academic writer, developing academic integrity, and communicating with your instructor, your classmates, and other people at your school.

8a Getting the most from college courses

You will enjoy each course and learn more from it if you are an active, engaged member of the class. Follow the guidelines below to prepare for and contribute to your classes.

- **Participate in class.** Whether your class meets face to face or online, push aside other concerns so that you can listen attentively, ask questions, take notes, and add your voice to discussions. (See the box on the next page for special tips on taking online courses.)
- **Take notes.** Use the notes you take in class to integrate all the components of the course—your instructor's views and approach to the material, your own thoughts, and the assigned reading, even if you've already read it. When you're in class, record in your own words what you hear as completely as possible. Also try to sort out the main ideas from the secondary and supporting ones. If you miss something, leave space to insert it later. Review your notes shortly after class to reinforce learning.
- **Do assigned reading.** The assigned reading you do for college courses—such as textbooks, journal articles, essays, and works of

mycomplab

Visit *mycomplab.com* for the eText and for resources on participating in an academic community.

73

Video
tutorial

Taking online courses

The advice in this chapter and this entire handbook applies to courses taught face to face or online. But with online courses you'll work usually alone and often at your own pace. The following tips can help you succeed.

- **Study the syllabus.** The course outline will tell you the course goals, reading assignments, and writing assignments. Generally it will be your only reminder of what's expected.
- **Be disciplined.** Plan and stick to a regular study schedule so that you don't fall behind. When doing coursework, turn off distractions such as the cell phone, TV, and music player.
- **Participate.** If the course involves work with other students, take an active role. If you have questions or comments on the course material or wonder how you're doing in the course, ask the instructor.
- **Back up your work.** With all work and communication online, a computer crash could be disastrous. Routinely copy notes, drafts, and completed assignments to a flash drive, external hard drive, or online storage service such as Carbonite (*carbonite.com*).

literature—requires a greater focus on understanding and retention than does the reading you do for entertainment or for practical information. The following chapter describes an active process that will help you become an efficient and effective reader.

- **Be open to new perspectives.** College classes should not only add to what you know but also provoke reflection. You will get more out of the college experience if you are curious about new ideas and open to thinking about them.
- **Work with integrity.** All of your college work represents you to your instructor, your classmates, and the entire college community. Whether participating in class, taking an exam, or writing a paper, always show respect for others and for yourself with careful, honest work. See opposite for more on academic integrity.
- **Get help when you need it.** Most instructors hold weekly office hours, and many hold online office hours. In addition, most schools provide writing centers, tutoring centers, library tours, and other services.

8b Becoming an academic writer

As a college student you will probably do quite a lot of writing. Academic writing assignments vary, of course, depending on the discipline, the course, and the instructor. However, even within this variety you can orient yourself to each assignment by focusing on the following key goals. Each goal is discussed in more detail elsewhere in this book.

- **Know what the assignment requires.** Most assignments at least suggest a possible subject; they imply a purpose, audience, and genre (or type of writing); and they specify a length and a deadline. In that context, you refine your subject, your purpose, and your sense of audience as you proceed through the writing process, discussed in detail in **1** pp. 3–9.

- **Develop and organize your writing.** Most academic papers center on a main point, or thesis, and support the thesis with evidence. For more on developing a thesis and organizing a paper, see **1** pp. 14–22.

- **Synthesize your own and others' ideas.** College writing often involves researching and interacting with the works of other writers—being open to their ideas, responding to them, questioning them, comparing them, using them to answer questions. Such interaction requires you to read critically (the subject of the next chapter) and to synthesize, or integrate, others' ideas into your own. For more on synthesis, see pp. 86–87 and 93.

- **Use academic language.** Unless your instructor specifies otherwise, use formal, standard English, always avoiding the informalities of texting and online communication such as abbreviations and incomplete sentences. Academic language is discussed in detail on pp. 99–101 and in **3** pp. 155–61.

- **Revise and edit your writing.** College writing assignments require careful writing. Allow yourself enough time to revise and edit so that readers can see your main ideas, follow your train of thought, and make sense of your sentences. See **1** pp. 25–28 and 29–32 for discussions of revision and editing.

- **Acknowledge your sources.** As discussed below, academic writers build on the work of others by fully crediting borrowed ideas and information. Always record the publication information of any source you consult so that you can cite it if you use it in your writing.

8c Developing academic integrity

Academic integrity is the foundation of academic knowledge building. Trusting in one another's honesty allows students and scholars to examine and extend the work of other scholars, and it allows teachers to guide and assess the progress of their students.

As a student, you'll have opportunities to develop and demonstrate your integrity in class preparation and participation, in exams, and especially in writing. Many writing assignments will require you to consult sources such as journal articles, Web sites, and books. These works belong to their creators; you are free to borrow from them *if* you do so with integrity. That means representing the sources accurately, not misinterpreting or distorting what they say. It also means crediting the sources, not **plagiarizing**, or presenting sources' ideas and information as if you originated them. On most campuses, plagiarism is a punishable offense.

Plagiarism can be deliberate or accidental. Deliberate plagiarism is outright cheating: copying another writer's sentence and passing it off as your own, buying a paper from the Web, or getting someone else to write a paper for you. Accidental plagiarism is more common among students, often arising from careless or inexperienced handling of sources. For instance, you might cut and paste source information into your own ideas without clarifying who said what, or you might present a summary of a source without recognizing that parts of it are actually quoted. In these cases the plagiarism is unintentional, but it is still plagiarism.

You can build your integrity as a writer by working to develop your own ideas and by handling sources responsibly. The following tips can help. See also **7** pp. 360–68 for more on citing sources.

Gaining perspective

Consider your own knowledge and perspective on a subject before you start to research. This forethought will make it easier for you to recognize other authors' perspectives and to treat them fairly in your writing—whether or not you agree with them.

- **Before you consult sources, gauge what you already know and think about your subject.** Give yourself time to know your own mind before looking to others for information. Then you'll be able to reflect on how the sources reinforce, contradict, or expand what you already know.
- **Evaluate sources carefully.** Authors generally write from particular perspectives, and some are more overt about their biases than others. You needn't reject a source because it is biased; indeed, often you'll want to consider multiple perspectives. But you do need to recognize and weigh the writer's position. See **7** pp. 338–49 for a discussion of evaluating sources.
- **Treat sources fairly.** Represent an author's ideas and perspectives as they were originally presented, without misunderstanding or distortion. Be careful in paraphrasing and summarizing not to misrepresent the author's meaning. Be careful in editing quotations not to omit essential words.

Managing sources

You can avoid plagiarism by keeping close track of the sources you consult, the ideas that influence your thinking, and the words and sentences you borrow—and by carefully citing the sources in your writing. If these habits are unfamiliar, keep the following list handy.

- **Keep track of source information as you read.** Get in the habit of always recording publication information (the author, title, date, and so on) of any source you read as well as any ideas you glean from it. See the box in **7** p. 318 for a list of what to record.

■ **Be careful with quotations.** If you cut and paste a portion of an article, Web site, or other source into your document, put quotation marks around it so that you don't mix your words and the source's words accidentally. Check any quotation that you use in your own writing against the original source. For a more detailed discussion of how to quote sources, see **7** pp. 354–56.

■ **Use your own words in paraphrases and summaries.** A paraphrase or summary presents the ideas of a source but not in the exact words of the original and not in quotation marks. You will be less likely to use the source author's words (and thus plagiarize) if you look away from the source while you write down what you remember from it. Note, though, that you must still cite the source of a summary or paraphrase, just as you do with a quotation. For a more detailed discussion of how to summarize and paraphrase sources, see **7** pp. 353–54.

■ **Cite your sources.** As you draft, be conscious of when you're using source information and be conscientious about clearly marking where the borrowed material came from. In your final draft you'll use a particular style of citation within your text to refer to a detailed list of sources at the end. This book presents four such styles: MLA style for English and some other humanities (**MLA** pp. 402–48); APA style for the social sciences (**APA** pp. 461–82); Chicago style for history, philosophy, and some other humanities (**Chic** pp. 489–500); and CSE style for the natural and applied sciences (**CSE** pp. 501–07).

8d | Communicating in an academic setting

As a member of an academic community, you will not only write papers and projects but also write directly to instructors, classmates, and other people at your school via e-mail, course blogs, or course-management systems such as *Blackboard*, *Desire2Learn*, and *Moodle*. Though rarely as formal as assigned writing, this communication is also rarely as informal as what you might text a friend, post on *Twitter*, or comment on *Facebook*.

Even in a short e-mail, your message will receive a better hearing if you present yourself well and show respect for your reader(s). The message on the next page illustrates an appropriate mix of formality and informality when addressing an instructor.

Here are guidelines for such communication.

■ **Use the medium your instructor prefers.** Don't text, tweet, or use a social-networking site unless you're invited to do so.

■ **Use names.** In the body of your message, address your reader(s) by name if possible. Unless your teachers instruct otherwise,

E-mail message

Uses subject line to describe the content of the message.

Addresses instructor formally with title and last name.

Provides context for request.

Uses complete sentences and words.

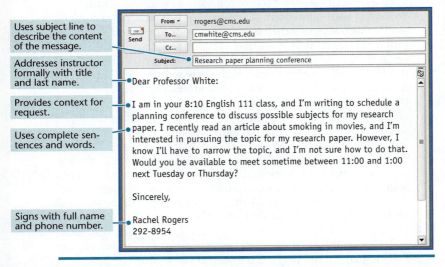

From ▾   rrogers@cms.edu
To...   cmwhite@cms.edu
Cc...
Subject: Research paper planning conference

Dear Professor White:

I am in your 8:10 English 111 class, and I'm writing to schedule a planning conference to discuss possible subjects for my research paper. I recently read an article about smoking in movies, and I'm interested in pursuing the topic for my research paper. However, I know I'll have to narrow the topic, and I'm not sure how to do that. Would you be available to meet sometime between 11:00 and 1:00 next Tuesday or Thursday?

Sincerely,

Rachel Rogers
292-8954

Signs with full name and phone number.

always address them formally, using *Professor, Dr., Ms.,* or *Mr.,* as appropriate, followed by the last name. Sign off with your own name and information on how to contact you.

■ **Pay attention to tone.** Don't use all capital letters, which SHOUT. And use irony or sarcasm only cautiously: in the absence of facial expressions, either one can lead to misunderstanding.

■ **Pay attention to correctness.** Especially when you write to instructors, avoid the shortcuts of texting and tweeting, such as incomplete sentences and abbreviations (*u* for *you, r* for *are,* and so on). (See also p. 99 for a discussion of academic language.) Proofread for errors in grammar, punctuation, and spelling.

■ **Send messages only to the people who need them.** As a general rule, avoid sending messages to many recipients at once—all the students in a course, say—unless what you have to say applies to all of them. Before you hit Reply All in response to a message, ensure that "all" want to see the response.

■ **Guard your own and others' privacy.** Online tools allow us to broadcast hurtful information about others—and allow others to do the same to us. Before you post a message about yourself or someone else, consider whether it's worthwhile and who will see it, not only now but in the future. When forwarding messages, make sure not to pass on previous private messages by mistake.

■ **Don't write anything that you wouldn't say face to face or wouldn't write in a printed letter.** Electronic messages can be saved and forwarded and can be retrieved in disputes over grades and other matters.

9 Critical Thinking and Reading

Video tutorial

Throughout college and beyond, you will be expected to think, read, and write critically. **Critical** here does not mean "negative" but "skeptical," "exacting," "creative," "curious." You already operate critically every day as you figure out why things happen to you or what your experiences mean. This chapter introduces more formal methods for reading texts critically (below), summarizing (p. 83) developing a critical response (p. 85), and viewing images critically (p. 87).

Note Critical thinking plays a large role in research writing. See **7** pp. 338–49 on evaluating print and online sources and **7** pp. 350–51 on synthesizing sources.

9a Using techniques of critical reading

Video tutorial

In college and work, much of your critical thinking will focus on written texts (a short story, a journal article, a blog) or on visual objects (a photograph, a chart, a film). Like all subjects worthy of critical consideration, such works operate on at least three levels: (1) what the creator actually says or shows, (2) what the creator does not say or show explicitly but builds into the work (intentionally or not), and (3) what you think. Discovering each level of the work involves a number of reading techniques that are discussed in this chapter.

CULTURE • LANGUAGE The idea of reading critically may require you to make some adjustments if readers in your native culture tend to seek understanding or agreement more than engagement from what they read. Readers of English use texts for all kinds of reasons, including pleasure, reinforcement, and information. But they also read questioningly, to uncover the author's motives (*What are this author's biases?*), test their own ideas (*Can I support my point of view as well as this author supports hers?*), and arrive at new knowledge (*Why is the author's evidence so persuasive?*).

1 Previewing the material

Video tutorial

When you're reading a work of literature, such as a short story or a poem, it's often best just to plunge right in. But for critical reading of other works, it's worthwhile to skim before reading word for word, forming expectations and even some preliminary questions. The preview will make your reading more informed and fruitful.

■ **Gauge length and level.** Is the material brief and straightforward so that you can read it in one sitting, or will it require more time?

- **Check the facts of publication.** Does the date of publication suggest currency or datedness? Does the publisher or publication specialize in scholarly articles, popular books, or something else? For a Web publication, who or what sponsors the site—an individual? a nonprofit organization? a government body? a college or university?

- **Look for content cues.** What do the title, introduction, headings, illustrations, conclusion, and other features tell you about the topic, the author's approach, and the main ideas?

- **Learn about the author.** Does a biography tell you about the author's publications, interests, biases, and reputation in the field? If there is no biography, what can you gather about the author from his or her words? Use a Web search to trace unfamiliar authors.

- **Consider your preliminary response.** What do you already know about the topic? What questions do you have about either the topic or the author's approach to it? What biases of your own—for instance, curiosity, boredom, or an outlook similar or opposed to the author—might influence your reading of the work?

Following is an essay by Thomas Sowell, an economist who writes on economics, politics, and education. The essay was first published in the 1990s, but the debate over student loans has hardly subsided. Since Sowell wrote, the number of college graduates with loan debt has increased by a third and the average amount they owe has almost tripled. Preview the essay using the guidelines in the preceding list, and then read it until you think you understand what the author is saying. Note your questions and reactions in writing.

Student Loans

1 The first lesson of economics is scarcity: There is never enough of anything to fully satisfy all those who want it.

2 The first lesson of politics is to disregard the first lesson of economics. When politicians discover some group that is being vocal about not having as much as they want, the "solution" is to give them more. Where do politicians get this "more"? They rob Peter to pay Paul.

3 After a while, of course, they discover that Peter doesn't have enough. Bursting with compassion, politicians rush to the rescue. Needless to say, they do not admit that robbing Peter to pay Paul was a dumb idea in the first place. On the contrary, they now rob Tom, Dick, and Harry to help Peter.

4 The latest chapter in this long-running saga is that politicians have now suddenly discovered that many college students graduate heavily in debt. To politicians it follows, as the night follows the day, that the government should come to their rescue with the taxpayers' money.

5 How big is this crushing burden of college students' debt that we hear so much about from politicians and media deep thinkers? For those students who graduate from public colleges owing money, the debt averages a little under $7000. For those who graduate from private colleges owing money, the average debt is a little under $9000.

Buying a very modestly priced automobile involves more debt than 6 that. And a car loan has to be paid off faster than the ten years that college graduates get to repay their student loans. Moreover, you have to keep buying cars every several years, while one college education lasts a lifetime.

College graduates of course earn higher incomes than other peo- 7 ple. Why, then, should we panic at the thought that they have to repay loans for the education which gave them their opportunities? Even graduates with relatively modest incomes pay less than 10 percent of their annual salary on the first loan the first year—with declining percentages in future years, as their pay increases.

Political hysteria and media hype may focus on the low-income 8 student with a huge debt. That is where you get your heart-rending stories—even if they are not all that typical. In reality, the soaring student loans of the past decade have resulted from allowing high-income people to borrow under government programs.

Before 1978, college loans were available through government pro- 9 grams only to students whose family income was below some cut-off level. That cut-off level was about double the national average income, but at least it kept out the Rockefellers and the Vanderbilts. But, in an era of "compassion," Congress took off even those limits.

That opened the floodgates. No matter how rich you were, it still 10 paid to borrow money through the government at low interest rates. The money you had set aside for your children's education could be invested somewhere else, at higher interest rates. Then, when the student loan became due, parents could pay it off with the money they had set aside—pocketing the difference in interest rates.

To politicians and the media, however, the rapidly growing loans 11 showed what a great "need" there was. The fact that many students welshed when time came to repay their loans showed how "crushing" their burden of debt must be. In reality, those who welsh typically have smaller loans, but have dropped out of college before finishing. People who are irresponsible in one way are often irresponsible in other ways.

No small amount of the deterioration of college standards has been 12 due to the increasingly easy availability of college to people who are not very serious about getting an education. College is not a bad place to hang out for a few years, if you have nothing better to do, and if someone else is paying for it. Its costs are staggering, but the taxpayers carry much of that burden, not only for state universities and city colleges, but also to an increasing extent even for "private" institutions.

Numerous government subsidies and loan programs make it possible 13 for many people to use vast amounts of society's resources at low cost to themselves. Whether in money terms or in real terms, federal aid to higher education has increased several hundred percent since 1970. That has enabled colleges to raise their tuition by leaps and bounds and enabled professors to be paid more and more for doing less and less teaching.

Naturally all these beneficiaries are going to create hype and hysteria 14 to keep more of the taxpayers' money coming in. But we would be fools to keep on writing blank checks for them.

When you weigh the cost of things, in economics that's called 15 "trade-offs." In politics, it's called "mean-spirited." Apparently, if we just took a different attitude, scarcity would go away.

—Thomas Sowell

2 Reading

Reading is itself more than a one-step process. You want to understand the first level on which the text operates—what the author actually says—and begin to form your impressions.

First reading

The first time through new material, read as steadily and smoothly as possible, trying to get the gist of what the author is saying.

- **Read in a place where you can concentrate.** Choose a quiet environment away from distractions such as music or talking.
- **Give yourself time.** Rushing yourself or worrying about something else you have to do will prevent you from grasping what you read.
- **Try to enjoy the work.** Seek connections between it and what you already know. Appreciate new information, interesting relationships, forceful writing, humor, good examples.
- **Make notes sparingly during this first reading.** Mark major stumbling blocks—such as a paragraph you don't understand—so that you can try to resolve them before rereading.

CULTURE LANGUAGE If English is not your first language and you come across unfamiliar words, don't stop and look up every one. You will be distracted from an overall understanding of the text. Instead, try to guess the meanings of the unfamiliar words by using context clues, such as examples and synonyms of the words. Be sure to circle the words and look them up later. You may want to keep a vocabulary log of the words, their definitions, and the sentences in which they appeared.

Rereading

After the first reading, plan on at least one other. This time read *slowly*. Your main concern should be to grasp the content and how it is constructed. That means rereading a paragraph if you didn't get the point or using a dictionary to look up words you don't know.

Use your pen, pencil, or keyboard freely to highlight and distill the text:

- **Distinguish main ideas from supporting ideas.** Look for the central idea (the thesis), for the main idea of each paragraph or section, and for the evidence supporting ideas.
- **Learn key terms.** Understand both their meanings and their applications.
- **Identify the connections among ideas.** Be sure you see why the author moves from point A to point B to point C and how those points relate to support the central idea. It often helps to outline the text or to summarize it (see opposite).

- **Distinguish between facts and opinions.** Especially when reading an argument, tease apart the facts from the author's opinions that may or may not be based on facts. (See p. 106 for more on facts and opinions.)
- **Add your own comments.** In the margins or separately, note links to other readings or to class discussions, questions to explore further, possible topics for your writing, points you find especially strong or weak.

An example of critical reading

The following sample shows how a student, Charlene Robinson, approached "Student Loans." After her first reading, Robinson went through Sowell's text more slowly and added her comments and questions. Here are the first four paragraphs with her annotations:

> The first lesson of economics is scarcity: There is never enough of anything to fully satisfy all those who want it.

fact

> The first lesson of politics is to disregard the first lesson of economics. When politicians discover some group that is being vocal about not having as much as they want, the "solution" is to give them more. Where do politicians get this "more"? They rob Peter to pay Paul.

opinion—basic contradiction between economics and politics

← *biblical reference?*

> After a while, of course, they discover that Peter doesn't have enough. Bursting with compassion, politicians rush to the rescue. Needless to say, they do not admit that robbing Peter to pay Paul was a dumb idea in the first place. On the contrary, they now rob Tom, Dick, and Harry to help Peter.

ironic and dismissive language

> The latest chapter in this long-running saga is that politicians have now suddenly discovered that many college students graduate heavily in debt. To politicians it follows, as the night follows the day, that the government should come to their rescue with the taxpayers' money.

politicians = fools? or irresponsible?

9b Summarizing

A good way to master the content of a text and to see its strengths and weaknesses is to **summarize** it: distill it to its main points, in your own words. The following box gives a method of summarizing:

Video tutorial

Writing a summary

- **Understand the meaning.** Look up words or concepts you don't know so that you understand the author's sentences and how they relate to one another.
- **Understand the organization.** Work through the text to identify its sections—single paragraphs or groups of paragraphs focused on a single topic. To understand how parts of a work relate to one another, try drawing a tree diagram or creating an outline (**1** pp. 19–21).

Video tutorial

(continued)

Writing a summary
(continued)

- **Distill each section.** Write a one- or two-sentence summary of each section you identify. Focus on the main point of the section, omitting examples, facts, and other supporting evidence.
- **State the main idea.** Write a sentence or two capturing the author's central idea.
- **Support the main idea.** Write a full paragraph (or more, if needed) that begins with the central idea and supports it with the sentences that summarize sections of the work. The paragraph should concisely and accurately state the thrust of the entire work.
- *Use your own words.* By writing, you re-create the meaning of the work in a way that makes sense for you. You also avoid plagiarism.
- *Cite the source.* If you use a summary in writing that you do for others, always acknowledge the source.

Summarizing even a passage of text can be tricky. Here we'll look at attempts to summarize the following material from an introductory biology textbook.

Original text

As astronomers study newly discovered planets orbiting distant stars, they hope to find evidence of water on these far-off celestial bodies, for water is the substance that makes possible life as we know it here on Earth. All organisms familiar to us are made mostly of water and live in an environment dominated by water. They require water more than any other substance. Human beings, for example, can survive for quite a few weeks without food, but only a week or so without water. Molecules of water participate in many chemical reactions necessary to sustain life. Most cells are surrounded by water, and cells themselves are about 70–95% water. Three-quarters of Earth's surface is submerged in water. Although most of this water is in liquid form, water is also present on Earth as ice and vapor. Water is the only common substance to exist in the natural environment in all three physical states of matter: solid, liquid, and gas.

—Neil A. Campbell and Jane B. Reece, *Biology*

The first attempt to summarize the passage accurately restates ideas in the original, but it does not pare the passage to its essence:

Draft summary

Astronomers look for water in outer space because life depends on it. It is the most common substance on Earth and in living cells, and it can be a liquid, a solid (ice), or a gas (vapor).

The work of astronomers and the three physical states of water add color and texture to the original, but they are asides to the key concept that water sustains life because of its role in life. The following revision narrows the summary to this concept:

Revised summary

Water is the most essential support for life, the dominant substance on Earth and in living cells and a component of life-sustaining chemical processes.

When Charlene Robinson summarized Thomas Sowell's "Student Loans," she first drafted this sentence about paragraphs 1–4:

Draft summary

As much as politicians would like to satisfy voters by giving them everything they ask for, the government cannot afford a student loan program.

Reading the sentence and Sowell's paragraphs, Robinson saw that this draft misread the text by asserting that the government cannot afford student loans. She realized that Sowell's point is more complicated than that and rewrote her summary:

Revised summary

As their support of the government's student loan program illustrates, politicians ignore the economic reality that using resources to benefit one group (students in debt) involves taking the resources from another group (taxpayers).

Caution Using your own words when writing a summary not only helps you understand the meaning but also constitutes the first step in avoiding plagiarism. The second step is to cite the source when you use the summary in something written for others. See **7** pp. 360–68.

Note Do not count on the AutoSummarize function on your word processor for summarizing texts that you may have copied onto your computer. The summaries are rarely accurate, and you will not gain the experience of interacting with the texts on your own.

9c Developing a critical response

Once you've grasped the content of what you're reading—what the author says—then you can turn to understanding what the author does not say outright but suggests or implies or even lets slip. At this stage you are concerned with the purpose or intention of the author and with how he or she carries it out.

Critical thinking and reading consist of four overlapping operations: analyzing, interpreting, synthesizing, and (often) evaluating.

Video
tutorial

1 Analyzing

Analysis is the separation of something into its parts or elements, the better to understand it. To see these elements in what you are reading, begin with a question that reflects your purpose in analyzing the text: why you're curious about it or what you're trying to make out of it. This question will serve as a kind of lens that highlights some features and not others.

Analyzing Thomas Sowell's "Student Loans" (pp. 80–81), you might ask one of these questions:

Questions for analysis	Elements
What is Sowell's attitude toward politicians?	References to politicians: content, words, tone
How does Sowell support his assertions about the loan program's costs?	Support: evidence, such as statistics and examples

2 Interpreting

Identifying the elements of something is only a start: you also need to interpret the meaning or significance of the elements and of the whole. Interpretation usually requires you to infer the author's **assumptions**—opinions or beliefs about what is or what could or should be. (*Infer* means to draw a conclusion based on evidence.)

Assumptions are pervasive: we all adhere to certain values, beliefs, and opinions. But assumptions are not always stated outright. Speakers and writers may judge that their audience already understands and accepts their assumptions; they may not even be aware of their assumptions; or they may deliberately refrain from stating their assumptions for fear that the audience will disagree. That is why your job as a critical thinker is to interpret what the assumptions are.

Thomas Sowell's "Student Loans" is based on certain assumptions, some obvious, some not. Analyzing Sowell's attitude toward politicians requires focusing on the statements about them. They "disregard the first lesson of economics" (paragraph 2), which implies that they ignore important principles (knowing that Sowell is an economist himself makes this a reasonable assumption). Politicians also "rob Peter to pay Paul," are "[b]ursting with compassion," "do not admit . . . a dumb idea," are characters in a "long-running saga," and arrive at the solution of spending taxes "as the night follows the day"—that is, inevitably (paragraphs 2–4). From these statements and others, we can infer the following:

> Sowell assumes that politicians become compassionate when a cause is loud and popular, not necessarily just, and they act irresponsibly by trying to solve the problem with other people's (taxpayers') money.

3 Synthesizing

Video tutorial

If you stopped at analysis and interpretation, critical thinking and reading might leave you with a pile of elements and possible meanings but no vision of the whole. With **synthesis** you make connections among parts *or* among wholes. You use your perspective—your knowledge and beliefs—to create a new whole by drawing conclusions about relationships and implications.

A key component of academic reading and writing, synthesis receives attention in the next chapter (pp. 97–98) and then in the context of research writing (see **7** pp. 350–51). Sometimes you'll respond directly to a text, as in the following statement about Thomas Sowell's essay "Student Loans," which connects Sowell's assumptions about politicians to a larger idea also implied by the essay:

> Sowell's view that politicians are irresponsible with taxpayers' money reflects his overall opinion that the laws of economics, not politics, should drive government.

Often synthesis will take you outside the text to its surroundings. The following questions can help you investigate the context of a work:

- **How does the work compare with works by others?** For instance, how have other writers responded to Sowell's views on student loans?
- **How does the work fit into the context of other works by the same author or group?** How do Sowell's views on student loans typify, or not, the author's other writing on politics and economics?
- **What cultural, economic, or political forces influence the work?** What other examples might Sowell have given to illustrate his view that economics, not politics, should determine government spending?
- **What historical forces influence the work?** How has the indebtedness of college students changed over the past four decades?

4 Evaluating

Critical reading and writing often end at synthesis: you form and explain your understanding of what the work says and doesn't say. If you are also expected to **evaluate** the work, however, you will go further to judge its quality and significance. You may be evaluating a source you've discovered in research (see **7** pp. 338–49), or you may be completing an assignment to state and defend a judgment, such as *Thomas Sowell does not summon the evidence to support his case*. You can read Charlene Robinson's critical response to Thomas Sowell's "Student Loans"on pp. 102–04.

Video
tutorial

Evaluation takes a certain amount of confidence. You may think that you lack the expertise to cast judgment on another's work, especially if the work is difficult or the author well known. True, the more informed you are, the better a critical reader you are. But conscientious reading and analysis will give you the internal authority to judge a work *as it stands* and *as it seems to you*, against your own unique bundle of experiences, observations, and attitudes.

Video
tutorial

9d Viewing visuals critically

Every day we are bombarded with visuals—pictures on billboards, commercials on television, graphs and charts in newspapers and textbooks, to name just a few examples. Most visuals slide by without our noticing them, or so we think. But visuals, sometimes even more than text, can influence us covertly. Their creators have purposes, some worthy, some not, and understanding those purposes requires critical reading. The method parallels that in the previous section for reading text critically: preview, read for comprehension, analyze, interpret, synthesize, and (often) evaluate.

1 Previewing a visual

Your first step in exploring a visual is to form initial impressions of its origin and purpose and to note its distinctive features. This previewing process is like the one for previewing a text (pp. 79–80):

- **What do you see?** What is most striking about the visual? What is its subject? What is the gist of any text or symbols? What is the overall effect of the visual?
- **What are the facts of publication?** Where did you first see the visual? Was it created especially for that location or for others as well? What can you tell about when the visual was created?
- **What do you know about the person or group that created the visual?** For instance, was the creator an artist, scholar, news organization, or corporation? What seems to have been the creator's purpose?
- **What is your preliminary response?** What about the visual interests, confuses, or disturbs you? Are the form, style, and subject familiar or unfamiliar? How might your knowledge, experiences, and values influence your reception of the visual?

If possible, print a copy of the visual or scan it into your reading journal, and write comments in the visual's margins or separately.

2 Reading a visual

Reading a visual requires the same level of concentration as reading a text. Try to answer the following questions about the visual. If some answers aren't clear at this point, skip the question until later.

- **What is the purpose?** Is the visual mainly explanatory, conveying information, or is it argumentative, trying to convince readers of something or to persuade them to act? What information or point of view does it seem intended to get across?
- **Who is the intended audience?** What does the source of the visual, including its publication facts, tell about the creator's expectations for readers' knowledge, interests, and attitudes? What do the features of the visual itself add to your impression?
- **What do any words or symbols add?** Whether located on the visual or outside it (such as in a caption), do words or symbols add information, focus your attention, or alter your impression?
- **What action, change, people, places, or things are shown?** Does

the visual tell a story? Do its characters or other features tap into your knowledge, or are they unfamiliar?

■ **What is the form of the visual?** Is it a photograph, advertisement, painting, graph, diagram, cartoon, or something else? How do its content and apparent purpose and audience relate to its form?

The illustration below shows the notes that a student, Matthew Greene, made on an advertisement for *BoostUp.org*.

Annotation of an advertisement

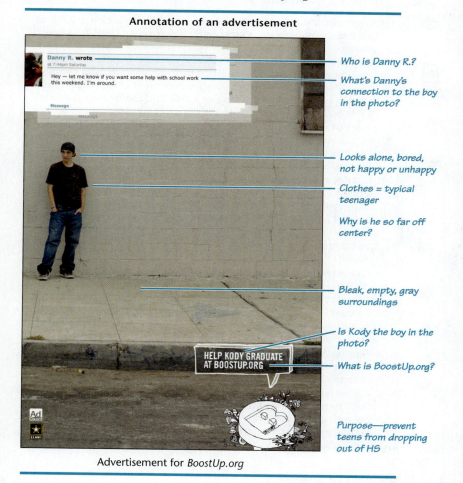

Advertisement for *BoostUp.org*

3 **Analyzing a visual**

Elements for analysis

As when analyzing a written work, you analyze a visual by identifying its elements. The visual elements you might consider appear

Sample document

in the following box. Keep in mind that a visual is a *composition* whose every element likely reflects a deliberate effort to communicate. Still, few visuals include all the elements, and you can narrow the list further by posing a question about the visual you are reading, as discussed after the box.

Video tutorial

Sample document

Elements of visuals

■ **Emphasis:** Most visuals pull your eyes to certain features: a graph line moving sharply upward, a provocative figure, bright color, thick lines, and so on. The cropping of a photograph or the date range in a chart will also reflect what the visual's creator considers important.

■ **Narration:** Most visuals tell stories, whether in a sequence (a TV commercial or a graph showing changes over time) or at a single moment (a photograph, a painting, or a pie chart). Sometimes dialog or a title or caption contributes to the story.

■ **Point of view:** The creator of the visual influences responses by taking account of both the viewer's physical relation to the subject—for instance, whether it is seen head-on or from above—and the viewer's assumed attitude toward the subject.

■ **Arrangement:** Patterns among colors or forms, figures in the foreground and background, and elements that are juxtaposed or set apart contribute to the visual's meaning and effect.

■ **Color:** Colors can direct the viewer's attention and convey the creator's attitude toward the subject. Color may also suggest a mood, an era, a cultural connection, or another frame in which to view the visual.

■ **Characterization:** The figures and objects in a visual have certain qualities—sympathetic or not, desirable or not, and so on. Their characteristics reflect the roles they play in the visual's story.

■ **Context:** The source of a visual or the background in a visual affects its meaning, whether it is a graph from a scholarly journal or a photo of a car on a sunny beach.

■ **Tension:** Visuals often communicate a problem or seize attention with features that seem wrong, such as misspelled or misaligned words, distorted figures, or controversial relations between characters.

■ **Allusions:** An **allusion** is a reference to something the audience is likely to recognize and respond to. Examples include a cultural symbol such as a dollar sign, a mythological figure such as a unicorn, or a familiar movie character such as Darth Vader from *Star Wars*.

Question for analysis

You can focus your analysis of elements by framing your main interest in the visual as a question. Matthew Greene posed this question about the *BoostUp.org* ad: *Does the ad move readers to learn more about* BoostUp.org *and how they can help teens to graduate?* The question led Greene to focus on certain elements of the ad:

Elements of the ad	Responses
Emphasis	The grayness and the placement of Kody at the far left put primary emphasis on the boy's isolation. Danny R.'s message, breaking up the gray, receives secondary emphasis.
Narration	The taped-on message suggests a story and connection between Kody and Danny R. Danny R. might be a friend, relative, or mentor. Based on the direct appeal in the word bubble, it appears that Danny R. is trying to help Kody graduate by offering to help him with schoolwork.
Arrangement	The ad places Danny R. and Kody together on the left side of the page, with Danny's message a bright spot on the dull landscape. The appeal to help Kody graduate is subtle and set on its own—the last thing readers look at. It also pulls the elements together so that the ad makes sense.
Color	The lack of color in most of the photo emphasizes Kody's isolation. The whiteness of Danny R.'s message relieves the grayness, like a ray of hope.

Sample Web pages for analysis

The screen shots on the next page are from *AIDS Clock*, an interactive Web site sponsored by the United Nations Population Fund (*www.unfpa.org/aids_clock*). The top image is the home page, displaying a traditional world map. The bottom image appears when viewers click on "Resize the map": now each country's size reflects the number of its people who live with HIV, the virus that causes AIDS. (For example, South Africa grows while the United States shrinks.) The large blue number at the top changes every twelve seconds to give the total number of people living with HIV in the world. Try to answer the questions in the annotations above the screen shots.

4 | Interpreting a visual

The strategies for interpreting a visual parallel those for interpreting a written text (p. 86). In this process you look more deeply at the elements, considering them in relation to the likely assumptions and intentions of the visual's creator. You aim to draw reasonable inferences about *why* the visual looks as it does, such as this inference about the *BoostUp.org* advertisement on p. 89:

> The creators of the *BoostUp.org* ad assume that readers want students to graduate from high school.

This statement is supported by the ad's text: the word bubble connecting to the *BoostUp.org* logo specifically says, "Help Kody graduate at BoostUp.org."

Elements of Web pages

Emphasis and color: What elements on these pages draw your attention? How does color distinguish and emphasize elements?

Narration: What story do the two Web pages tell? What does each map contribute to the story? What does the blue number contribute? (Notice that the number changes from the first screen to the second.)

Arrangement: What does the arrangement of elements on the pages contribute to the story being told?

Tension: How do you respond to the distorted map in the second image? What does the distortion contribute to your view of the Web site's effectiveness?

Context: How does knowing the Web site's sponsoring organization, the United Nations Population Fund, affect your response to these images?

AIDS Clock Web pages, 2011

5 Synthesizing ideas about a visual

As discussed on pp. 86–87, with synthesis you take analysis and interpretation a step further to consider how a work's elements and underlying assumptions relate and what the overall message is. You may also expand your synthesis to view the whole visual in a larger context: How does the work fit into the context of other works? What cultural, economic, political, or historical forces influence the work?

Placing a visual in its context often requires research. For instance, to learn more about the assumptions underlying the *BoostUp.org* advertisement and the goals of the larger ad campaign, Matthew Greene visited the Web sites of *BoostUp.org* and the Ad Council, one of the ad's sponsors. The following entry from his reading journal synthesizes this research and his own ideas about the ad:

> The *BoostUp.org* magazine ad that features Kody is part of a larger campaign designed to raise public awareness about high school dropouts and encourage pubic support to help teens stay in school. Sponsored by the US Army and the nonprofit Ad Council, *BoostUp.org* profiles high school seniors who are at risk of dropping out and asks individuals to write the students personal messages of support. Ads like "Kody" are the first point of contact between the public and the teens, but they don't by themselves actually help the teens. For that, readers need to visit *BoostUp.org*. Thus the ad's elements work together like pieces of a puzzle, with the solution to be found only on the Web site.

6 Evaluating a visual

If your critical reading moves on to evaluation, you'll form judgments about the quality and significance of the visual: Is the message of the visual accurate and fair, or is it distorted and biased? Can you support, refute, or extend the message? Does the visual achieve its apparent purpose, and is the purpose worthwhile? How does the visual affect you?

Student
paper

10 Academic Writing

The academic disciplines differ widely in their subjects and approaches, but they all share the common goal of building knowledge through questioning, research, and communication. The differences among disciplines lie mainly in the kinds of questions asked, the kinds of research done to find the answers, and the genres, or types of writing, used to communicate the answers, such as case studies, research reports, literary analyses, and reviews of others' writings.

mycomplab

Visit *mycomplab.com* for the eText and for resources and exercises on academic writing.

Exercise

Both a discipline's concerns and the kind of writing create an academic writing situation, which in turn shapes your choice of subject, definition of purpose, conception of audience, use of genre, choice of structure and content, and even use of language. This chapter introduces academic writing situations in general. See **8** (Chapters 55–57) for the particular goals and expectations of writing about literature and in other humanities, the social sciences, and the natural and applied sciences.

10a Determining purpose, audience, and genre

Like any writing, academic writing occurs in a particular situation created by your assignment and by your subject, purpose, audience, and genre. The assignment and subject will be different for each project, but some generalizations can be made about the other elements. (If you haven't already done so, read **1** pp. 3–9 on writing situations and their elements.)

1 Purpose

For most academic writing, your general purpose will be mainly explanatory or mainly argumentative. That is, you will aim to clarify your subject by analyzing, describing, or reporting on it so that readers understand it as you do; or you will aim to gain readers' agreement with a debatable idea about the subject. (See **1** pp. 6–7 for more on general purposes and pp. 104–19 for more on argument.)

Your specific purpose—including your subject and how you hope readers will respond—depends on the genre, the kind of writing that you're doing. (See the facing page.) For instance, in a literature review for a biology class, you want readers to understand the research area you're covering, the recent contributions made by researchers, the issues needing further research, and the sources you consulted. Not coincidentally, these topics correspond to the major sections of a literature review. In following the standard format, you both help to define your purpose and begin to meet the discipline's (and thus your instructor's) expectations.

Your specific purpose will be more complex as well. You take a course to learn about a subject and the ways experts think about it. Your writing, in return, contributes to the discipline through the knowledge you uncover and the lens of your perspective. At the same time, as a student you want to demonstrate your competence with research, evidence, format, and other requirements of the discipline.

2 Audience

Many academic writing assignments will specify or assume an educated audience or an academic audience. Such readers look for writing that is clear, balanced, well organized, and well reasoned. Other assignments will specify or assume an audience of experts on your subject, readers who look in addition for writing that meets the subject's requirements for claims and evidence, organization, language, format, and other qualities.

Much of your academic writing will have only one reader besides you: the instructor of the course for which you are writing. Instructors fill two main roles as readers:

- **They represent the audience you are addressing.** They may actually be members of the audience, as when you address academic readers or subject experts. Or they may imagine themselves as members of your audience—reading, for instance, as if they sat on the city council. In either case, they're interested in how effectively you write for the audience.
- **They serve as coaches,** guiding you toward achieving the goals of the course and, more broadly, toward the academic aims of building and communicating knowledge.

Like everyone else, instructors have preferences and peeves, but you'll waste time and energy trying to anticipate them. Do attend to written and spoken directions for assignments, of course. But otherwise view your instructors as representatives of the community you are writing for. Their responses will be guided by the community's aims and expectations and by a desire to teach you about them.

3 Genre

Many academic writing assignments will suggest the genre in which you are to write—the kind of writing and/or the format. Sometimes the genre is prescribed, such as the literature review mentioned earlier, with its standard content and format. Other assignments imply the genre, such as those that ask you to analyze, explain, compare, or argue. In these cases your responses would most likely be conventional academic essays—introduction, thesis statement, supporting paragraphs, conclusion—with additional features for analyzing and comparing subjects, explaining them, or arguing about them.

Whether genre is specified or implied in your assignment, you are being asked to demonstrate your ability to write competently in that genre. If it is unfamiliar to you, take time to learn its features and conventions. This book contains examples of the following genres. Studying these samples along with the surrounding explanations and annotations will give you a good sense of how other writers have worked within genre conventions.

Personal response to a text (**1** p. 34)
Informative Web site (**1** p. 67)
Personal narrative posted to a blog (**1** p. 68)

In addition, common assignments in literature, other humanities, the social sciences, and the natural and applied sciences are described in **8** pp. 381, 387, 390–91, and 394, respectively. And Chapter 14 contains examples of genres used in public writing: complaint letter, application letter and résumé, memo, report, flyer, and newsletter.

10b Writing in response to texts

Student
paper

Academic knowledge building depends on reading, analyzing, and expanding on the work of others. Thus many academic writing assignments require you to respond to one or more texts—not only to written products such as short stories and journal articles but also to visual communications such as images, charts, films, and advertisements. As you form a response to a text, you synthesize, or integrate, its ideas and information with yours to come to your own conclusions. As you write your response, you support your ideas about the text by citing evidence from it.

Note A common academic assignment, the research paper, expects you to consult and respond to multiple texts in order to support and extend your ideas. See **7** (Chapters 50–54). This section focuses on responding directly to a single text, but the skills involved apply to research writing as well.

1 Deciding how to respond

When an assignment asks you to respond directly to a text, you might take one of the following approaches. (Note that the word *author* refers to a photographer, painter, or other creator as well as to a writer.)

- **Agree with and extend the author's ideas,** exploring related ideas and providing additional examples.
- **Agree with the author on some points but disagree on others.**
- **Disagree with the author on one or more main points.**
- **Explain how the author achieves a particular effect,** such as evoking a historical period or balancing opposing views.
- **Analyze the overall effectiveness of a text**—for example, how well a writer supports a thesis with convincing evidence or whether an advertisement succeeds in its unstated purpose.

2 | Forming a response

You will likely have an immediate response to at least some of the texts you analyze: you may agree or disagree strongly with what the author is saying. But for some other responses, you may need time and thought to determine what the author is saying and what you think about it.

Whatever your assignment, your first task is to examine the text thoroughly so that you're sure you understand what the author says outright and also assumes or implies. You can use the process of critical reading described in the previous chapter to take notes on the text, summarize it, and develop a critical response. Then, as you write, use the following tips to convey your response to readers.

Responding to a text

- **Make sure your writing has a point**—a central idea, or thesis, that focuses your response. (For more on developing a thesis, see **1** pp. 14–17.)
- **Include a very brief summary if readers may be unfamiliar with your subject.** But remember that your job is not just to report what the text says or what a visual shows; it is to *respond* to the work from your own critical perspective. (For more on summary, see pp. 83–85.)
- **Center each paragraph on an idea of your own that supports your thesis.** Generally, state the idea outright, in your own voice.
- **Support the paragraph idea with evidence from the text**—quotations, paraphrases, details, and examples.
- **Conclude each paragraph with your interpretation of the evidence.** As a general rule, avoid ending paragraphs with source evidence; instead, end with at least a sentence that explains what the evidence shows.

Video
tutorial

---

3 | Emphasizing synthesis in your response

Following the suggestions in the preceding box will lead you to show readers the synthesis you achieved by thinking critically about the text. That is, you integrate your perspective with that of the author in order to support a conclusion of your own about the work.

A key to synthesis is deciding how to present evidence from your reading and observation in your writing. Especially when you are writing about a relatively unfamiliar subject, you may be tempted to let a text or other source do the talking for you through extensive summary or quotations. However, readers of your academic writing will expect to see you managing ideas and information to make your points. Thus a typical paragraph of text-based writing should open with your own idea, give evidence from the text, and conclude with your interpretation of the evidence. You can see this pattern in the following paragraph from an essay that appears later in this chapter.

Writer's idea

Evidence and interpretation

The most fundamental and most debatable assumption underlying Sowell's essay is that higher education is a kind of commodity that not everyone is entitled to. In order to diminish the importance of graduates' average debt from education loans, Sowell claims that a car loan will probably be higher (131). This comparison between education and an automobile implies that the two are somehow equal as products and that an affordable higher education is no more a right than a new car is. Sowell also condemns the "irresponsible" students who drop out of school and "the increasingly easy availability of college to people who are not very serious about getting an education" (132). But he overlooks the value of encouraging education, including the education of those who don't finish college or who aren't scholars. For many in the United States, education has a greater value than that of a mere commodity like a car. And even from an economic perspective such as Sowell's, the cost to society of an uneducated public needs to be taken into account. By failing to give education its due, Sowell undermines his argument at its core.

Writer's conclusion

Note Effective synthesis requires careful handling of evidence from the text (quotations and paraphrases) so that it meshes smoothly into your sentences yet is clearly distinct from your own ideas. See **7** pp. 356–59 on integrating borrowed material.

10c Choosing structure and content

Many academic writing assignments will at least imply how you should organize your paper and even how you should develop your ideas. As with the literature review mentioned earlier, the required genre will break into discrete parts, each with its own requirements for content.

For most academic assignments, the broad aims of building and exchanging knowledge determine features that are common across disciplines. Follow these general guidelines for your academic writing, supplementing them as indicated with others elsewhere in this book:

- **Develop a main point for your writing.** Depending on the genre, the main point may be a claim or thesis, a summary of findings, or a conclusion based on primary research that you have conducted, such as an experiment, observation, a survey, or an interview. For more on thesis statements, see **1** pp. 14–17.
- **Support the main point with evidence,** drawn usually from reading, personal experience, or primary research. The kinds of evidence will depend on the discipline you're writing in and the type

of paper you're doing. For more on evidence in the disciplines, see **8** pp. 381 (literature), 386–87 (other humanities), 389–90 (social sciences), and 393–94 (natural and applied sciences).

- **Synthesize.** Put your sources to work for you by thinking critically about them. Integrate them into your own perspective using your own voice. For more on synthesis, see pp. 97–98 and **7** pp. 350–51 in the discussion of research writing.

- **Acknowledge sources fully, including online sources.** *Not* acknowledging sources undermines the knowledge-sharing foundation of academic writing and constitutes plagiarism, which can be punishable (see **7** pp. 360–66). For lists of disciplines' documentation guides, see **8** pp. 389, 393, and 397. For documentation guidelines and samples, see **MLA** pp. 402–46 (English and some other humanities), **APA** pp. 461–79 (social sciences), **Chic** pp. 489–500 (history, philosophy, and other humanities), and **CSE** pp. 501–07 (natural and applied sciences).

- **Organize clearly within the framework of the type of writing you're doing.** Develop your ideas as simply and directly as your purpose and content allow. Clearly relate sentences, paragraphs, and sections so that readers always know where they are in the paper's development.

CULTURE LANGUAGE These features are not universal. In some cultures, for instance, academic writers may be indirect or may not have to acknowledge well-known sources. Recognizing such differences between practices in your native culture and in the United States can help you adapt to US academic writing.

10d Using academic language

American academic writing relies on a dialect called standard American English. The dialect is also used in business, the professions, government, the media, and other sites of social and economic power where people of diverse backgrounds must communicate with one another. It is "standard" not because it is better than other forms of English, but because it is accepted as the common language, much as the dollar bill is accepted as the common currency.

Video tutorial

In writing, standard American English varies a great deal, from the formality of an academic research report to the more relaxed language of this handbook to informal e-mails between coworkers in a company. Even in academic writing, standard American English allows much room for the writer's own tone and voice, as the following passages on the same topic show:

More formal

Responsibility for the widespread problem of obesity among Americans depends on the person or group describing the problem and proposing a

Drawn-out phrasing, such as *widespread problem of obesity among Americans*.

More complicated sentence structures, such as *take strong issue with the food industry, citing food manufacturers and fast-food chains that create and advertise.* . . .

More formal vocabulary: *responsibility, children, television.*

solution. Some people believe the cause lies with individuals who make poor eating choices for themselves and parents who feed unhealthy foods to their children. Others take strong issue with the food industry, citing food manufacturers and fast-food chains that create and advertise food that is high in sugar, fat, and sodium. Still others place responsibility on American society as a whole for preferring a sedentary lifestyle centered on screen-based activities such as watching television and using computers for video games and social interaction.

Less formal

More informal phrasing, such as *obesity epidemic.*

Less complicated sentence structures, such as *demonize food manufacturers and fast-food chains for creating and advertising.* . . .

More informal vocabulary: *blame, kids, TV.*

Who or what is to blame for the obesity epidemic depends on who is talking and what they want to do about the problem. Some people blame eaters for making bad choices and parents for feeding their kids unhealthy foods. Others demonize food manufacturers and fast-food chains for creating and advertising sugary, fatty, and sodium-loaded food. Still others point to Americans generally for spending too much time in front of screens watching TV, playing video games, or going on *Facebook.*

As different as they are, both examples illustrate several common features of academic language:

- **It follows the conventions of standard American English for grammar and usage.** These conventions are described in guides to the dialect, such as this handbook.
- **It uses a standard vocabulary,** not one that only some groups understand, such as slang, an ethnic or regional dialect, or another language. (See **3** pp. 155–57 for more on specialized vocabularies.)
- **It does *not* use the informalities of everyday speech, texting, and instant messaging.** These informalities include incomplete sentences, slang, no capital letters, and shortened spellings (*u* for *you, b4* for *before, thru* for *through,* and so on). (See **3** p. 156 for more on these forms.)
- **It generally uses the third person (*he, she, it, they*).** The first person *I* is sometimes appropriate to express personal opinions, but academic writers tend to avoid it and make conclusions speak for themselves. The first-person *we* can connect with readers and invite them to think along, but, again, many academic writers avoid it. The second-person *you* is appropriate only in addressing readers directly (as in this handbook), and even then it may seem condescending or too chummy. Definitely avoid using or implying *you* in conversational expressions such as *You know what I mean* and *Don't take this the wrong way.*

■ **It is authoritative and neutral.** In the examples on the facing page, the writers express themselves confidently, not timidly (as in *Explaining the causes of obesity requires the reader's patience because . . .*). They also refrain from hostility (*The food industry's callous attitude toward health . . .*) and enthusiasm (*The food industry's clever and appealing advertisements . . .*).

At first, the diverse demands of academic writing may leave you groping for an appropriate voice. In an effort to sound fresh and confident, you may write too casually, as if speaking to friends or family:

Too casual

Getting the truth about the obesity epidemic in the US requires some heavy lifting. It turns out that everyone else is to blame for the problem—big eaters, reckless corporations, and all those Americans who think it's OK to be a couch potato.

In an effort to sound "academic," you may produce wordy and awkward sentences:

Wordy and awkward

The responsibility for the problem of widespread obesity among Americans depends on the manner of defining the problem and the proposals for its solution. In some discussions, the cause of obesity is thought to be individuals who are unable or unwilling to make healthy choices in their own diets and parents who similarly make unhealthy choices for their children. [The passive voice in this example—*cause . . . is thought to be* instead of *people blame*—adds to its wordiness and indirection. See **4** pp. 212–14 for more on verb voice.]

A cure for writing too informally or too stiffly is to read academic writing so that the language and style become familiar and to edit your writing (see **1** pp. 29–32).

(CULTURE LANGUAGE) If your first language is not English or is an English dialect besides standard American, you know well the power of communicating with others who share your language. Learning to write standard American English in no way requires you to abandon your first language. Like most multilingual people, you are probably already adept at switching between languages as the situation demands—speaking one way with your relatives, say, and another way with an employer. As you practice academic writing, you'll develop the same flexibility with it.

10e A sample critical response

The following essay illustrates a common academic assignment, a critical response to, or **critique** of, a text. In the essay, Charlene Robinson responds to Thomas Sowell's essay "Student Loans" (pp. 80–81). Robinson arrived at her response, an argument, through the process of critical reading outlined in the previous chapter and then by gathering and organizing her ideas, developing a thesis about Sowell's text that synthesized his ideas and hers, and drafting and revising until she believed she had supported her thesis with sufficient evidence from her own experience and from Sowell's text.

Robinson did not assume that her readers would see the same things in Sowell's essay or share her views, so her essay offers evidence of Sowell's ideas in the form of direct quotations, summaries, and paraphrases (restatements in her own words). Robinson documents these borrowings from Sowell using the style of the Modern Language Association (MLA): the numbers in parentheses are page numbers in the book containing Sowell's essay, listed at the end as a work cited. (See **MLA** pp. 402–48 for more on MLA style.)

Note Critical writing is *not* summarizing. Robinson summarized Sowell's text to clarify it for herself (p. 85), and she briefly summarizes Sowell's argument in her introduction. But her critical writing goes well beyond summary to bring her perspective to Sowell's work.

Weighing the Costs

Introduction	In the essay "Student Loans," the economist Thomas Sowell challenges the US government's student-loan program for three main reasons: a scarce resource (taxpayers' money) goes to many undeserving students, a high number of recipients fail to repay their loans, and the easy availability of money has led to both lower academic standards and higher college tuitions. Sowell wants his readers to "weigh the costs of things" (133) in order to see, as he does, that the loan program should not receive so much government funding. Sowell wrote his essay in the 1990s, but the argument he makes is still heard frequently today and is worth examining. Does Sowell provide the evidence of cost and other problems to lead the reader to agree with his argument? The answer is no, because hard evidence is less common than debatable and unsupported assumptions about students, scarcity, and the value of education.
Summary of Sowell's essay	
Robinson's critical question	
Thesis statement	
First main point	Sowell's portrait of student-loan recipients is questionable. It is based on averages, some statistical and some not, but averages are often deceptive. For example, Sowell cites college graduates' low average debt of $7,000 to $9,000 (131) without giving the full range of statistics or acknowledging that when he was writing many students' debt was much higher. (Today the average debt itself is much higher.) Similarly, Sowell dismisses "heart-rending stories" of "the low-income student with a huge debt" as "not at all typical" (132), yet he invents his own exaggerated version of the typical loan recipient: an affluent slacker ("Rockefellers" and "Vanderbilts") for whom college is a "place
Evidence for first point: paraphrases and quotations from Sowell's text	

to hang out for a few years" sponging off the government, while his or her parents clear a profit from making use of the loan program (132). Although such students (and parents) may well exist, are they really typical? Sowell does not offer any data one way or the other—for instance, how many loan recipients come from each income group, what percentage of loan funds go to each group, how many loan recipients receive significant help from their parents, and how many receive none. Together, Sowell's statements and omissions cast doubt on the argument that students don't need or deserve the loans.

Another set of assumptions in the essay has to do with "scarcity": "There is never enough of anything to fully satisfy all those who want it," Sowell says (131). This statement appeals to readers' common sense, but the "lesson" of scarcity does not necessarily apply to the student-loan program. Sowell omits many important figures needed to prove that the nation's resources are too scarce to support the program, such as the total cost of the program, its percentage of the total education budget and the total federal budget, and its cost compared to the cost of defense, Medicare, and other expensive programs. Moreover, Sowell does not mention the interest paid by loan recipients, even though the interest must offset some of the costs of running the program and covering unpaid loans. Thus his argument that there isn't enough money to run the student loan program is unconvincing.

The most fundamental and most debatable assumption underlying Sowell's essay is that higher education is a kind of commodity that not everyone is entitled to. In order to diminish the importance of graduates' average debt from education loans, Sowell claims that a car loan will probably be higher (131). This comparison between education and an automobile implies that the two are somehow equal as products and that an affordable higher education is no more a right than a new car is. Sowell also condemns the "irresponsible" students who drop out of school and "the increasingly easy availability of college to people who are not very serious about getting an education" (132). But he overlooks the value of encouraging education, including the education of those who don't finish college or who aren't scholars. For many in the United States, education has a greater value than that of a mere commodity like a car. And even from an economic perspective such as Sowell's, the cost to society of an uneducated public needs to be taken into account. By failing to give education its due, Sowell undermines his argument at its core.

Sowell writes with conviction, and his concerns are valid: high taxes, waste, unfairness, declining educational standards, obtrusive

---

Evidence for first point: Sowell's omissions

Conclusion of first point: Robinson's interpretation

Transition to second main point

Second main point

Evidence for second point: Sowell's omissions

Conclusion of second point: Robinson's interpretation

Third main point

Evidence for third point: paraphrases and quotations from Sowell's text

Evidence for third point: Sowell's omissions

Conclusion of third point: Robinson's interpretation

Conclusion

government. However, the essay's flaws make it unlikely that Sowell could convince readers who do not already agree with him. He does not support his portrait of the typical loan recipient, he fails to demonstrate a lack of resources for the loan program, and he neglects the special nature of education compared to other services and products. Sowell may have the evidence to back up his assumptions, but by omitting it he himself does not truly weigh the costs of the loan program.

Work Cited

Sowell, Thomas. "Student Loans." *Is Reality Optional? and Other Essays.* Stanford: Hoover, 1993. 131-33. Print.

—Charlene Robinson (student)

11 Argument

Argument is writing that attempts to solve a problem, open readers' minds to an opinion, change readers' opinions, or move readers to action. Using various techniques, you engage readers to find common ground and narrow the distance between your views and theirs.

CULTURE LANGUAGE The ways of conceiving and writing arguments described here may be initially uncomfortable to you if your native culture approaches such writing differently. In some cultures, for example, a writer is expected to begin indirectly, to avoid asserting his or her opinion outright, to rely for evidence on appeals to tradition, or to establish a compromise rather than argue a position. In American academic and business settings, writers aim for a well-articulated opinion, evidence gathered from many sources, and a direct and concise argument for the opinion.

11a Understanding and using the elements of argument

An argument has four main elements: subject, claims, evidence, and assumptions. (The last three are adapted from the work of the British philosopher Stephen Toulmin.)

1 The subject

Video
tutorial

An argument starts with a subject and often with a view of the subject as well—that is, an idea that makes you want to write about the subject. (If you don't have a subject or you aren't sure what you think, see **1** pp. 9–14 for some invention techniques.) Your subject should meet several requirements:

- **It can be disputed:** reasonable people can disagree over it.
- **It *will* be disputed:** it is controversial.
- **It is narrow enough to research and argue in the space and time available.**

Exercise

On the flip side of these requirements are several kinds of subjects that will not work as the starting place of argument: indisputable facts, such as the functions of the human liver; personal preferences or beliefs, such as a moral commitment to vegetarianism; and ideas that few would disagree with, such as the virtues of a secure home.

2 Claims

Claims are statements that require support. In an argument you develop your subject into a central claim or thesis, asserted outright in a thesis statement (see **1** pp. 14–17). This central claim is what the argument is about.

A thesis statement is always an **opinion**—that is, a judgment based on facts and arguable on the basis of facts. It may be one of the following:

- **A claim about past or present reality:**

  In both its space and its equipment, the college's chemistry lab is outdated.

  Academic cheating increases with students' economic insecurity.

- **A claim of value:**

  The new room fees are unjustified given the condition of the dormitories.

  Computer music pirates undermine the system that encourages the very creation of music.

- **A recommendation for a course of action,** often a solution to a perceived problem:

  The college's outdated chemistry lab should be replaced incrementally over the next five years.

  Schools and businesses can help to resolve the region's traffic congestion by implementing car pools and rewarding participants.

The backbone of an argument consists of specific claims that support the thesis statement. These may also be statements of opinion, or they may fall into one of two other categories:

- **Statements of *fact*,** including facts that are generally known or are verifiable (such as the cost of tuition at your school) and those that can be inferred from verifiable facts (such as the monetary value of a college education).
- **Statements of *belief*,** or convictions based on personal faith or values, such as *The primary goal of government should be to*

provide equality of opportunity for all. Although seemingly argu-able, a statement of belief is not based on facts and so cannot be contested on the basis of facts.

3 Evidence

Video tutorial

Evidence demonstrates the validity of your claims. The evi-dence to support the claim that the school needs a new chemistry lab might include the present lab's age, an inventory of facilities and equipment, and the testimony of chemistry professors.

There are several kinds of evidence:

Exercise

- **Facts,** statements whose truth can be verified or inferred: *Poland is slightly smaller than New Mexico.*
- **Statistics,** facts expressed as numbers: *Of those polled, 22% pre-fer a flat tax.*
- **Examples,** specific instances of the point being made: *Many groups, such as the elderly and people with disabilities, would ben-efit from this policy.*
- **Expert opinions,** the judgments formed by authorities on the ba-sis of their own examination of the facts: *Affirmative action is necessary to right past injustices, a point argued by Howard Glick-stein, a past director of the US Commission on Civil Rights.*
- **Appeals to readers' beliefs or needs,** statements that ask readers to accept a claim in part because it states something they already ac-cept as true without evidence: *The shabby, antiquated chemistry lab shames the school, making it seem a second-rate institution.*

Video tutorial

Evidence must be reliable to be convincing. Ask these questions about your evidence:

- **Is it accurate**—trustworthy, exact, and undistorted?
- **Is it relevant**—authoritative, pertinent, and current?
- **Is it representative**—true to its context, neither under- nor over-representing any element of the sample it's drawn from?
- **Is it adequate**—plentiful and specific?

4 Assumptions

Video tutorial

An **assumption** is an opinion, a principle, or a belief that ties evidence to claims: the assumption explains why a particular piece of evidence is relevant to a particular claim. For instance:

> **Claim:** The college needs a new chemistry laboratory.
> **Evidence** (in part): The testimony of chemistry professors.
> **Assumption:** Chemistry professors are the most capable of evaluating the present lab's quality.

Video tutorial

Assumptions are not flaws in arguments but necessities: we all acquire beliefs and opinions that shape our views of the world. Interpreting a work's assumptions is a significant part of critical reading and viewing (see pp. 86 and 91), and recognizing your own assumptions is a significant part of argument. If your readers do not share your assumptions or if they perceive that you are not forthright about your biases, they will be less receptive to your argument.

11b Writing reasonably

Reasonableness is essential if an argument is to establish common ground between you and your readers. Readers expect logical thinking, appropriate appeals, fairness toward the opposition, and, combining all of these, writing that is free of fallacies.

1 Logical thinking

The thesis of your argument is a conclusion you reach by reasoning about evidence. Two processes of reasoning, induction and deduction, are familiar to you even if you don't know their names.

Video tutorial

Induction

When you're about to buy a used car, you consult friends, relatives, and consumer guides before deciding what kind of car to buy. Using **induction,** or **inductive reasoning,** you make specific observations about cars (your evidence) and you induce, or infer, a **generalization** that Car X is most reliable. The generalization is a claim supported by your observations.

You might also use inductive reasoning in a term paper on print advertising:

Evidence: Advertisements in newspapers and magazines.
Evidence: Comments by advertisers and publishers.
Evidence: Data on the effectiveness of advertising.
Generalization or claim: Print is the most cost-effective medium for advertising.

Reasoning inductively, you connect your evidence to your generalization by assuming that what is true in one set of circumstances (the evidence you examine) is also true in a similar set of circumstances (evidence you do not examine). With induction you create new knowledge out of old.

The more evidence you accumulate, the more probable it is that your generalization is true. Note, however, that absolute certainty is not possible. At some point you must *assume* that your evidence justifies your generalization, for yourself and your readers. Most errors in inductive reasoning involve oversimplifying either the evidence or the generalization. See pp. 109–11 on fallacies.

Deduction

You use **deduction,** or **deductive reasoning,** when you proceed from your generalization that Car X is the most reliable used car to your own specific circumstances (you want to buy a used car) to the conclusion that you should buy Car X. In deduction your assumption is a generalization, principle, or belief that you think is true. It links the evidence (new information) to the claim (the conclusion you draw). With deduction you apply old information to new.

Say that you want the school administration to postpone new room fees for one dormitory. You can base your argument on a deductive **syllogism**:

> **Premise:** The administration should not raise fees on dorm rooms in poor condition. [A generalization or belief that you assume to be true.]
> **Premise:** The rooms in Polk Hall are in poor condition. [New information: a specific case of the first premise.]
> **Conclusion:** The administration should not raise fees on the rooms in Polk Hall. [Your claim.]

As long as the premises of a syllogism are true, the conclusion derives logically and certainly from them. Errors in constructing syllogisms lie behind many of the fallacies discussed on pp. 109–11.

2 | Rational, emotional, and ethical appeals

In most arguments you will combine **rational appeals** to readers' capacities for logical reasoning with **emotional appeals** to readers' beliefs and feelings. The following example illustrates both: the second sentence makes a rational appeal (to the logic of financial gain), and the third sentence makes an emotional appeal (to the sense of fairness and open-mindedness).

> Advertising should show more people who are physically challenged. The millions of Americans with disabilities have considerable buying power, yet so far advertisers have made no attempt to tap that power. Further, by keeping people with disabilities out of the mainstream depicted in ads, advertisers encourage widespread prejudice against disability, prejudice that frightens and demeans those who hold it.

For an emotional appeal to be successful, it must be appropriate for the audience and the argument:

- **It must not misjudge readers' actual feelings.**
- **It must not raise emotional issues that are irrelevant to the claims and the evidence.** See the next two pages on specific inappropriate appeals, such as bandwagon and ad hominem.

A third kind of approach to readers, the **ethical appeal,** is the sense you give of being a competent, fair person who is worth heeding. A rational appeal and an appropriate emotional appeal contribute to your ethical appeal, and so does your acknowledging opposing views (see opposite). An argument that is concisely written and correct in grammar, spelling, and other matters will underscore your competence. In addition, a sincere and even tone will assure readers that you are a balanced person who wants to reason with them.

A sincere and even tone need not exclude language with emotional appeal—words such as *frightens* and *demeans* at the end of the example above about advertising. But avoid certain forms of expression that will mark you as unfair:

- **Insulting words,** such as *idiotic* or *fascist.*
- **Biased language,** such as *fags* or *broads* (see **3** pp. 158–61).
- **Sarcasm,** such as the phrase *What a brilliant idea* to indicate contempt for the idea and its originator.
- **Exclamation points!** They'll make you sound shrill!

3 Acknowledgment of opposing views

A good test of your fairness in argument is how you handle possible objections. Assuming your thesis is indeed arguable, then others can marshal their own evidence to support a different view or views. By dealing squarely with those opposing views, you show yourself to be honest and fair. You strengthen your ethical appeal and thus your entire argument.

Before or while you draft your essay, list for yourself all the opposing views you can think of. You'll find them in your research, by talking to friends and classmates, and by critically thinking about your own ideas. You can also look for a range of views in an online discussion that deals with your subject. Two places to start are the *Yahoo!* archive of discussion groups at *groups.yahoo.com* and the *Google* blog directory at *blogsearch.google.com*.

A common way to handle opposing views is to state them, refute those you can, grant the validity of others, and demonstrate why, despite their validity, the opposing views are less compelling than your own. A somewhat different approach, developed by the psychologist Carl Rogers, emphasizes the search for common ground. In a **Rogerian argument** you start by showing that you understand readers' views and by establishing points on which you and readers agree and disagree. Creating a connection in this way can be especially helpful when you expect readers to resist your argument, because the connection encourages them to hear you out as you develop your claims.

4 Fallacies

Fallacies—errors in argument—either evade the issue of the argument or treat the argument as if it were much simpler than it is.

Exercise

Evasions

An effective argument squarely faces the central issue or question it addresses. An ineffective argument may dodge the issue in one of the following ways:

- **Begging the question:** treating an opinion that is open to question as if it were already proved or disproved.

The college library's expenses should be reduced by cutting subscriptions to useless periodicals. [Begged questions: Are some of the library's periodicals useless? Useless to whom?]

■ **Non sequitur** (Latin: "It does not follow"): linking two or more ideas that in fact have no logical connection. Usually the problem is an unstated assumption that links the ideas but is false.

She uses a wheelchair, so she must be unhappy. [Unstated assumption: People who use wheelchairs are unhappy.]

■ **Red herring:** introducing an irrelevant issue intended to distract readers from the relevant issues.

A campus speech code is essential to protect students, who already have enough problems coping with rising tuition. [Tuition costs and speech codes are different subjects. What protections do students need that a speech code will provide?]

■ **Appeal to readers' fear or pity:** substituting emotions for reasoning.

She should not have to pay taxes because she is an aged widow with no friends or relatives. [Appeals to people's pity. Should age and loneliness, rather than income, determine a person's tax obligation?]

■ **Bandwagon:** inviting readers to accept a claim because everyone else does.

As everyone knows, marijuana use leads to heroin addiction. [What is the evidence?]

■ **Ad hominem** (Latin: "to the man"): attacking the qualities of the people holding an opposing view rather than the substance of the view itself.

One of the scientists has been treated for emotional problems, so his pessimism about nuclear waste merits no attention. [Do the scientist's previous emotional problems invalidate his current views?]

Oversimplifications

In a vain attempt to create something neatly convincing, an ineffective argument may conceal or ignore complexities in one of the following ways:

■ **Hasty generalization:** making a claim on the basis of inadequate evidence.

It is disturbing that several of the youths who shot up schools were users of violent video games. Obviously, these games can breed violence, and they should be banned. [A few cases do not establish the relation between the games and violent behavior. Most youths who play violent video games do not behave violently.]

■ **Sweeping generalization:** making an insupportable statement. Many sweeping generalizations are **absolute statements** involving words such as *all, always, never,* and *no one* that allow

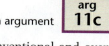

no exceptions. Others are **stereotypes,** conventional and over-simplified characterizations of a group of people:

People who live in cities are unfriendly.
Californians are fad-crazy.
Women are emotional.
Men can't express their feelings.

(See also **3** pp. 158–61 on sexist and other biased language.)

■ **Reductive fallacy:** oversimplifying (reducing) the relation between causes and effects.

Poverty causes crime. [If so, then why do people who are not poor commit crimes? And why aren't all poor people criminals?]

■ **Post hoc fallacy** (from Latin, *post hoc, ergo propter hoc*: "after this, therefore because of this"): assuming that because *A* preceded *B*, then *A* must have caused *B*.

The town council erred in permitting the adult bookstore to open, for shortly afterward two women were assaulted. [It cannot be assumed without evidence that the women's assailants visited or were influenced by the bookstore.]

■ **Either/or fallacy:** assuming that a complicated question has only two answers, one good and one bad, both good, or both bad.

Either we permit mandatory drug testing in the workplace or productivity will continue to decline. [Productivity is not necessarily dependent on drug testing.]

11c Organizing an argument

All arguments include the same parts:

Student
paper

■ The *introduction* **establishes the significance of the subject and provides background.** The introduction may run a paragraph or two, and it generally includes the thesis statement. However, if you think your readers may have difficulty accepting your thesis statement before they see at least some support for it, then it may come later in the paper. (See **1** pp. 50–51 for more on introductions.)

■ The *body* **states and develops the claims supporting the thesis.** In one or more paragraphs, the body develops each claim with clearly relevant evidence. See the next page for more on organizing the body.

■ The *response to opposing views* details and addresses those views, either demonstrating your argument's greater strengths or conceding the opponents' points. See the next page for more on organizing this response.

■ The *conclusion* **completes the argument,** restating the thesis, summarizing the supporting claims, and making a final appeal to readers. (See **1** pp. 51–53 for more on conclusions.)

Video
tutorial

The structure of the body and the response to opposing views depends on your subject, purpose, audience, and form of reasoning. Here are several possible arrangements:

A common scheme

Claim 1 and evidence
Claim 2 and evidence
Claim X and evidence
Response to opposing views

A variation

Claim 1 and evidence
Response to opposing views
Claim 2 and evidence
Response to opposing views
Claim X and evidence
Response to opposing views

The Rogerian scheme

Common ground and concession
   to opposing views
Claim 1 and evidence
Claim 2 and evidence
Claim X and evidence

The problem-solution scheme

The problem: claims and evidence
The solution: claims and evidence
Response to opposing views

11d Using visual arguments

Arguments can be visual as well as verbal. Advertisements often provide the most vivid and memorable examples of visual arguments, but writers in almost every field—from medicine to music, from physics to physical education—support their claims with images. The main elements of written arguments discussed on pp. 105–07—claims, evidence, and assumptions—appear also in visual arguments.

Caution Any visual you include in a paper requires the same detailed citation as a written source. If you plan to publish your argument online, you will also need to seek permission from the author. See 7 pp. 360–67 on citing sources and obtaining permission.

1 Claims

Sample
document

The claims in a visual may be made by composition as well as by content, with or without accompanying words. For instance:

Visual A photograph framing hundreds of chickens crammed into small cages, resembling familiar images of World War II concentration camps.

Claim Commercial poultry-raising practices are cruel and unethical.

Visual A chart with dramatically contrasting bars that represent the optimism, stress, and heart disease reported by people before and after they participated in a program of daily walking.

Claim Daily exercise leads to a healthier and happier life.

The advertisement on the next page is one in the "Army Strong" series that the United States Army runs for recruitment. The ad makes several claims both in the photograph and in the text.

Claims in a visual

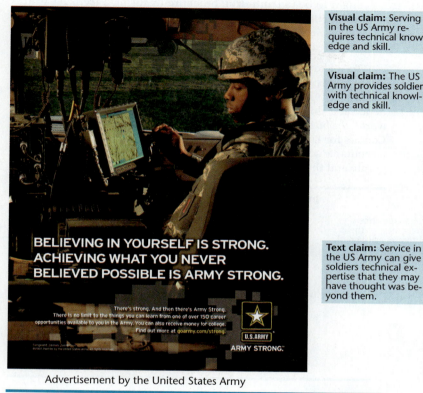

Visual claim: Serving in the US Army requires technical knowledge and skill.

Visual claim: The US Army provides soldiers with technical knowledge and skill.

BELIEVING IN YOURSELF IS STRONG.
ACHIEVING WHAT YOU NEVER
BELIEVED POSSIBLE IS ARMY STRONG.

There's strong. And then there's Army Strong.
There is no limit to the things you can learn from one of over 150 career opportunities available to you in the Army. You can also receive money for college. Find out more at goarmy.com/strong.

U.S.ARMY
ARMY STRONG.

Text claim: Service in the US Army can give soldiers technical expertise that they may have thought was beyond them.

Advertisement by the United States Army

2 Evidence

The kinds of evidence offered by visuals parallel those found in written arguments:

Sample document

- **Facts:** You might provide facts in the form of data, as in a graph showing a five-year rise in oil prices or in the text of the US Army advertisement promising "one of over 150 career opportunities." Or you might draw an inference from data, as the army ad does by stating that the army provides "money for college."
- **Examples:** Most often, you'll use examples to focus on an instance of your argument's claims. In the army ad, the soldier using technical equipment is an example supporting the claim that the army gives soldiers technical training.
- **Expert opinions:** You might present a chart from an expert showing a trend in unemployment among high school and college graduates.

■ **Appeals to beliefs or needs:** You might depict how things clearly ought to be (an anti-drug brochure featuring a teenager who is confidently refusing peer pressure) or, in contrast, show how things clearly should not be (a Web site for an anti-hunger campaign featuring images of emaciated children).

To make a visual work hard as evidence, be sure it relates directly to a point in your argument and that it accurately represents the subject. The graph below appears to provide good visual evidence for this claim: *Already among the highest in the developed world, the birthrate of US teens is on the rise.* The data come from the Centers for Disease Control and Prevention (CDC), a US agency and a reputable source. But the data are incomplete, so the claim is inaccurate and the graph is misleading.

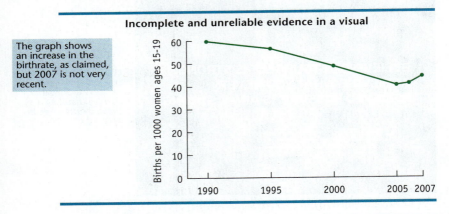

Incomplete and unreliable evidence in a visual

The graph shows an increase in the birthrate, as claimed, but 2007 is not very recent.

In fact, later data show that the birthrate resumed its downward trend in 2008. The graph below uses more recent data to support a modified claim: *Still among the highest in the developed world, the birthrate of US teens has fallen almost every year since 1990.*

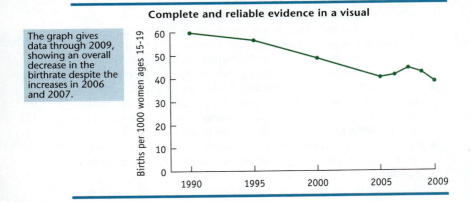

Complete and reliable evidence in a visual

The graph gives data through 2009, showing an overall decrease in the birthrate despite the increases in 2006 and 2007.

For more on using visuals and other media in your writing, see **1** pp. 58–64.

3 Assumptions

Like a written argument, a visual argument is based on assumptions—your ideas about the relation between evidence and claims (p. 106). Look again at the US Army ad on p. 113. The advertiser seems to have assumed that a strictly factual claim about the benefits of joining the army would not attract as many recruits as a photograph and text that together claim opportunities for training, education, and life change. With the photograph of the soldier, comfortable among technical equipment, the advertiser seems also to be appealing to young men and women who are interested in technical training.

Sample document

As in written arguments, the assumptions in a visual argument must be appropriate for your readers if the argument is to succeed with them. The army ad originally appeared in magazines with young adult readers, an audience that might be interested in the possibility of training and life change. But to readers uninterested in technical training, the photograph's emphasis on using equipment might actually undermine the ad's effectiveness.

4 Appeals

Visuals can help to strengthen the rational, emotional, and ethical appeals of your written argument (pp. 108–09):

- **Visuals can contribute evidence,** as long as they come from reliable sources, present information accurately and fairly, and relate clearly to the argument's claims.
- **Visuals can appeal to a host of ideas and emotions,** including patriotism, curiosity, moral values, sympathy, and anger. Any such appeal should correctly gauge readers' beliefs and feelings, and it should be clearly relevant to the argument.
- **Visuals can show that you are a competent, fair, and trustworthy source of information,** largely through their relevance, reliability, and sensitivity to readers' needs and feelings.

To see how appeals can work in visuals, look at the billboard from the Ad Council on the next page. The visual illustrates this claim: *Public-service advertisers try to discourage young drivers from drinking by addressing them directly and depicting the risks.*

5 Recognizing fallacies

When making a visual argument, you'll need to guard against all the fallacies discussed on pp. 109–11. Here we'll focus on specific visual examples. The first, which appears in the army ad on p. 113, is snob appeal: inviting readers to be like someone they admire. The soldier is clearly comfortable and competent with the equipment,

Appeals in a visual

Rational appeal: Backs up the writer's claim with text that uses slang to address young drivers and a photograph that shows the results of drunk driving.

Emotional appeal: Dramatically illustrates the attempt to discourage young drivers from drinking.

Ethical appeal: Conveys the writer's competence through the appropriateness of the visual for the point being made.

and the ad appeals to the reader's wish to be someone who is equally as capable and fulfilled. If you join the US Army, the ad says subtly, you too may become strong. The ad does have some substance in its specific and verifiable claim of "over 150 career opportunities" and "money for college," but the soldier in quiet command of his equipment makes a stronger claim.

Another example of a visual fallacy is the hasty generalization, a claim that is based on too little evidence or that misrepresents the facts. The first graph on p. 114 illustrates this fallacy: in omitting recent data that undercut the writer's claim, the graph misrepresents the facts.

11e Examining a sample argument

The following essay by Aimee Lee, a student, illustrates the principles discussed in this chapter. As you read the essay, notice especially the structure, the relation of claims and supporting evidence (including illustrations), the kinds of appeals Lee makes, and the ways she addresses opposing views.

Awareness, Prevention, Support:

A Proposal to Reduce Cyberbullying

Introduction: identification of the problem

My roommate and I sat in front of her computer staring at the vicious message under her picture. She quickly removed the tag that identified her, but the comments already posted on the photo proved that the damage was done. While she slept, my roommate had become the victim of a cyberbully. She had joined an increasing number of college students who are targeted in texts, e-mails, social-networking sites, and other Web sites that broadcast photographs, videos, and comments. My roommate's experience alerted me that our campus needs a program aimed at awareness and prevention of cyberbullying and support for its victims.

Although schoolyard bullying typically ends with high school graduation, cyberbullying continues in college. According to data gathered by researchers at the Massachusetts Aggression Reduction Center (MARC) of Bridgewater State College, cyberbullying behavior decreases when students enter college, but it does not cease. Examining the experiences of first-year students, the researchers found that 8% of college freshmen had been cyberbullied at college and 3% admitted to having cyberbullied another student (Englander, Mills, and McCoy 217-18). In a survey of fifty-two freshmen, I found further evidence of cyberbullying on this campus. I asked two questions: (1) Have you been involved in cyberbullying as a victim, a bully, or both? (2) If you answered "no" to the first question, do you know anyone who has been involved in cyberbullying as a victim, a bully, or both? While a large majority of the students I surveyed (74%) have not been touched by cyberbullying, a significant number (26%) have been involved personally or know someone who has, as shown in fig. 1. Taken together, the evidence demonstrates that cyberbullying is significant in colleges and specifically on our campus.

Uninvolved (74%)

Involved as victim or as cyberbully (11%)

Knows someone involved as victim or as cyberbully (15%)

Fig. 1. Involvement in cyberbullying among fifty-two first-year students.

The proposed "Stop Cyberbullying" program aims to reduce the behavior through a month-long campaign of awareness, prevention, and support modeled on the college's "Alcohol Awareness Month" program. The program can raise awareness of cyberbullying by explaining what cyberbullying is and by informing students about the college's code of conduct, which prohibits cyberbullying behavior but which few people read. The program can work to prevent cyberbullying by appealing to students to treat those around them respectfully. And, with the participation of the

Thesis statement: proposal for a solution to the problem

Evidence of the problem: published research

Evidence of the problem: student's own research

Pie chart showing results of student's research

Explanation of proposed solution: goals of the program

counseling department, the program can provide support for victims, their friends, and others involved in the behavior.

If adopted, the program can use online and print media to get the message out to the entire college community. For instance, an extensive brochure distributed to first-year students and available through the counseling center can describe cyberbullying and how it violates the college's code of conduct, give strategies for avoiding it, and provide resources for help. During the month-long campaign, flyers posted on campus (see fig. 2) can also raise awareness of the problem, and brief postings to the college's Web site, *Facebook* page, and *Twitter* feed can reach students who take online and hybrid classes as well as those in traditional classes.

Explanation of proposed solution: specific actions

Have YOU been a victim of cyberbullying?
Have you read something about yourself that made you feel embarrassed, intimidated, or just bad?

Are YOU a cyberbully? Have you sent a message or posted something that you knew would make someone feel embarrassed, intimidated, or just bad?

Do YOU know someone who is being cyberbullied or who is bullying someone else?

Together WE can BREAK the cycle:
• **Wait before you post!** Think about who may read it and how they might respond.
• **Be informed about our campus code of conduct** and what it says about cyberbullying.
• **Get help if you need it.** The counseling office is available to help you cope with or stop cyberbullying.

You can help stop cyberbullying
www.mrcc.edu/cyberbullying

STOP

Visual evidence of program publicity

Fig. 2. Sample flyer for proposed "Stop Cyberbullying" program.

Anticipation of objection: code of conduct does enough

Because this college already has a code of conduct in place and because the state has recently enacted anti-bullying legislation that includes cyberbullying, some students and administrators may contend that enough is being done to deal with the problem. To the administration's credit, the code of conduct contains specific language about online behavior, but promises of punishment for proven allegations do not address several aspects of the problem.

Response to objection: anonymity of cyberbullies

First, cyberbullies are sometimes anonymous. To accuse another student of cyberbullying, the victim needs to know the identity of the bully. While postings on *Facebook* are attached to real names, most college gossip sites are anonymous. On such sites, a cyberbully can post photographs, videos, and aggressive messages under the cover of anonymity.

Second, even when the identities of cyberbullies are known, the bullying is often invisible to those in a position to take action against it. According to Ikuku Aoyama and Tony L. Talbert at Baylor University, cyberbullying occurs frequently in groups of people who know each other and who attack and retaliate: students are rarely "pure bullies" or "pure victims" but instead are often part of a "bully-victim group" (qtd. in Laster). Moreover, even if students want to separate from bullying groups, Englander, Mills, and McCoy found that they probably will not report cyberbullying incidents to authorities because students generally believe that administrators are unlikely to do anything about cyberbullying (221). Thus counselors and administrators who may be interested in helping students to cope are often unaware of the problem.

Response to objection: invisibility of the problem

Third, conduct codes rarely affect cyberbullying. While some cyberbullying has resulted in tragedy, many aggressive incidents do not rise to the level of punishable offenses ("Cyberbullying"). More often they consist of a humiliating photograph or a mean message—hurtful, to be sure, but not necessarily in violation of the law or the code of conduct. Indeed, the hurdles to getting recourse through official channels are fairly high.

Response to objection: conduct codes ineffective

Given its hidden nature and the inability of punitive measures to stop it, cyberbullying needs another approach—namely, a program that teaches students to recognize and regulate their own behavior and provides help when they find themselves in a difficult situation. This program will not heal the wound suffered by my roommate, nor will it prevent all cyberbullying. But if adopted, the program will demonstrate to the college community that the administration is aware of the problem, eager to prevent it, and willing to commit resources to support students who are affected by it.

Conclusion

[New page.]

Works Cited

"Cyberbullying Goes to College." *Bostonia*. Boston U, Spring 2009. Web. 18 Feb. 2011.

Englander, Elizabeth, Elizabeth Mills, and Meghan McCoy. "Cyberbullying and Information Exposure: User-Generated Content in Post-Secondary Education." *Violence and Society in the Twenty-First Century*. Spec. issue of *International Journal of Contemporary Sociology* 46.2 (2009): 213-30. Web. 21 Feb. 2011.

Laster, Jill. "Two Scholars Examine Cyberbullying among College Students." *Chronicle of Higher Education*. Chronicle of Higher Education, June 2010. Web. 18 Feb. 2011.

Works cited in MLA style

—Aimee Lee (student)

12 Essay Exams

In writing an essay for an examination, you summarize or analyze a topic, usually in several paragraphs or more and usually within a time limit. An essay question not only tests your knowledge of a subject (as short-answer and objective questions do) but also tests your ability to think critically about what you have learned. If you have not already done so, read Chapter 9 on critical thinking and reading.

12a Preparing for an essay examination

To do well on an essay exam, you will need to understand the course content, not only the facts but also the interpretation of them and the relations between them.

- **Take careful lecture notes.**
- **Thoughtfully, critically read the assigned texts or articles.**
- **Review regularly.** Give the material time to sink in and stimulate your thinking.
- **Create summaries.** Recast others' ideas in your own words, and extract the meaning from notes and texts. (See pp. 83–85 for instructions on summarizing.)
- **Prepare notes or outlines to reorganize the course material around key topics or issues.** One technique is to create and answer likely essay questions. For instance, in a business course you might focus on the advantages and disadvantages of several approaches to management. In a short-story course you might locate a theme running through all the stories you have read by a certain author or from a certain period. In a psychology course you might outline various theorists' views of what causes a disorder such as schizophrenia. Working through such topics can help you anticipate questions, master the material, and allocate your time during the actual exam.

12b Planning your time and your answer

When you first receive an examination, take a few minutes to get your bearings and plan an approach. The time will not be wasted.

- **Read the exam all the way through at least once.** Don't start answering any questions until you've seen them all.

■ **Weigh the questions.** Determine which questions seem most important, which ones are going to be most difficult for you, and approximately how much time you'll need for each question. (Your instructor may help by assigning a point value to each question as a guide to its importance or by suggesting an amount of time for you to spend on each question.)

Planning continues when you turn to an individual essay question. Resist the temptation to rush right into an answer without some planning, for a few minutes can save you time later and help you produce a stronger essay.

■ **Read the question at least twice.** You will be more likely to stick to the question and answer it fully.

■ **Examine the words in the question and consider their implications.** Look especially for words such as *describe, define, explain, summarize, analyze, evaluate*, and *interpret*, each of which requires a different kind of response. Here, for example, is an essay question whose key term is *explain*:

Video tutorial

Question
Given humans' natural and historical curiosity about themselves, why did a scientific discipline of anthropology not arise until the 20th century? Explain, citing specific details.

See **1** pp. 45–49 for discussions of many of the terms likely to appear in essay questions.

■ **Make a brief outline of the main ideas you want to cover.** Use the back of the exam sheet or booklet for scratch paper. In the brief outline below, a student planned her answer to the anthropology question above.

Outline
1. Unscientific motivations behind 19th-c anthro.
   Imperialist/colonialist govts.
   Practical goals
   Nonobjective and unscientific (Herodotus, Cushing)
2. 19th-c ethnocentricity (vs. cultural relativism)
3. 19th-c anthro. = object collecting
   20th-c shift from museum to univ.
   Anthro. becomes acad. disc. and professional (Boas, Malinowski)

■ **Write a thesis statement for your essay that responds directly to the question and represents your view of the topic.** (If you are unsure of how to write a thesis statement, see **1** pp. 14–17.) Include key phrases that you can expand with supporting evidence for your view. The thesis statement of the student whose outline appears above concisely previews a three-part answer to the sample question:

Exercise

Thesis statement

Anthropology did not emerge as a scientific discipline until the 20th century because of the practical and political motivations behind 19th-century ethnographic studies, the ethnocentric bias of Western researchers, and a conception of culture that was strictly material.

12c Starting the essay

An essay exam does not require a smooth and inviting opening. Instead, begin by stating your thesis immediately and giving an overview of the rest of your essay. Such a capsule version of your answer tells your reader (and grader) generally how much command you have and also how you plan to develop your answer. It also gets you off to a good start.

12d Developing the essay

Sample document

Develop your essay as you would develop any piece of sound academic writing:

- **Observe the methods, terms, or other special requirements of the discipline in which you are writing.**
- **Support your thesis statement with solid generalizations,** each one perhaps the topic sentence of a paragraph.
- **Support each generalization with specific, relevant evidence.**

Sample document

If you observe a few *don't*s as well, your essay will have more substance:

- **Avoid filling out the essay by repeating yourself.**
- **Avoid other kinds of wordiness that pad and confuse,** whether intentionally or not. (See **3** pp. 169–74.)
- **Avoid resorting to purely subjective feelings.** Keep focused on analysis, or whatever is asked of you. (It may help to abolish the word *I* from the essay.)

The following essay illustrates a successful answer to the sample essay question on the preceding page about anthropology. It was written in the allotted time of forty minutes. Marginal comments on the essay highlight its effective elements.

Introduction stating thesis	Anthropology did not emerge as a scientific discipline until the 20th century because of the practical and political motivations behind 19th-century ethnographic studies, the ethnocentric bias of Western researchers, and a conception of culture that was strictly material.
Direct answer to question and preview of three-part response	
First main point: practical aims	Before the 20th century, ethnographic studies were almost always used for practical goals. The study of human culture can be

traced back at least as far as Herodotus's investigations of the Mediterranean peoples. Herodotus was like many pre-20th-century "anthropologists" in that he was employed by a government that needed information about its neighbors, just as the colonial nations in the 19th century needed information about their newly conquered subjects. The early politically motivated ethnographic studies that the colonial nations sponsored tended to be isolated projects, and they aimed less to advance general knowledge than to solve a specific problem. Frank Hamilton Cushing, who was employed by the American government to study the Zuni tribe of New Mexico, and who is considered one of the pioneers of anthropology, didn't even publish his findings. The political and practical aims of anthropologists and the nature of their research prevented their work from being a scholarly discipline in its own right.

> Example

> Example

Anthropologists of the 19th century also fell short of the standards of objectivity needed for truly scientific study. This partly had to do with anthropologists' close connection to imperialist governments. But even independent researchers were hampered by the prevailing assumption that Western cultures were inherently superior. While the modern anthropologist believes that a culture must be studied in terms of its own values, early ethnographers were ethnocentric: they judged "primitive" cultures by their own "civilized" values. "Primitive" peoples were seen as uninteresting in their own right. The reasons to study them, ultimately, were to satisfy curiosity, to exploit them, or to prove their inferiority. There was even some debate as to whether so-called savage peoples were human.

> Second main point: ethnocentricity

Finally, the 19th century tended to conceive of culture in narrow, material terms, often reducing it to a collection of artifacts. When not working for a government, early ethnographers usually worked for a museum. The enormous collections of exotica still found in many museums today are the legacy of this 19th-century object-oriented conception of anthropology, which ignored the myths, symbols, and rituals the objects related to. It was only when the museum tradition was broadened to include all aspects of a culture that anthropology could come into existence as a scientific discipline. When anthropologists like Franz Boas and Bronislaw Malinowski began to publish their findings for others to read and criticize and began to move from the museum to the university, the discipline gained stature and momentum.

> Third main point (with transition *Finally*): focus on objects

> Examples

In brief, anthropology required a whole series of ideological shifts to become modern. Once it broke free of its purely practical bent, the cultural prejudices of its practitioners, and the narrow conception that limited it to a collection of objects, anthropology could grow into a science.

> Conclusion, restating thesis supported by essay

12e Rereading the essay

The time limit on an essay examination does not allow for the careful rethinking and revision you would give an essay or research paper. You need to write clearly and concisely the first time. But try to leave yourself a few minutes after finishing the entire exam for rereading the essay (or essays) and doing touch-ups.

- **Correct mistakes:** illegible passages, misspellings, grammatical errors, and accidental omissions.
- **Verify that your thesis is accurate**—that it is, in fact, what you ended up writing about.
- **Ensure that you have supported all your generalizations.** Cross out irrelevant ideas and details, and add any information that now seems important. (Write on another page, if necessary, keying the addition to the page on which it belongs.)

13　Oral Presentations

Effective speakers use organization, voice, and other techniques to help their audiences follow and appreciate their presentations.

13a　Organizing the presentation

Give your oral presentation a recognizable shape so that listeners can see how ideas and details relate to each other.

The introduction

The beginning of an oral presentation should try to accomplish three goals:

- **Gain the audience's attention and interest.** Begin with a question, an unusual example or statistic, or a short, relevant story.
- **Put yourself in the speech.** Demonstrate your expertise, experience, or concern to gain the interest and trust of your audience.
- **Introduce and preview your topic and purpose.** By the time your introduction is over, listeners should know what your subject is and the direction you'll take to develop your ideas.

Your introduction should prepare your audience for your main points but not give them away. Think of it as a sneak preview of your speech, not the place for an apology such as *I wish I'd had more time to prepare . . .* or a dull statement such as *My speech is about. . . .*

mycomplab

Visit *mycomplab.com* for the eText and for resources and exercises on oral presentations.

Supporting material

Just as you do when writing, you should use facts, statistics, examples, and expert opinions to support the main points of your oral presentation. In addition, you can make your points more memorable with vivid description, well-chosen quotations, true or fictional stories, and analogies.

The conclusion

You want your conclusion to be clear, of course, but you also want it to be memorable. Remind listeners of how your topic and main idea connect to their needs and interests. If your speech was motivational, tap an emotion that matches your message. If your speech was informational, give some tips on how to remember important details.

13b Delivering the presentation

Methods of delivery

You can deliver an oral presentation in several ways:

- **Impromptu, without preparation:** Make a presentation without planning what you will say. Impromptu speaking requires confidence and excellent general preparation.
- **Extemporaneously:** Prepare notes to glance at but not read from. This method allows you to look and sound natural while ensuring that you don't forget anything.
- **Speaking from a text:** Read aloud from a written presentation. You won't lose your way, but you may lose your audience. Avoid reading for an entire presentation.
- **Speaking from memory:** Deliver a prepared presentation without notes. You can look at your audience every minute, but the stress of retrieving the next words may make you seem tense and unresponsive.

Vocal delivery

The sound of your voice will influence how listeners receive you. Rehearse your presentation several times until you are confident that you are speaking loudly, slowly, and clearly enough for your audience to understand you.

Physical delivery

You are more than your spoken words when you make an oral presentation. If you are able, stand up to deliver your presentation, turning your body toward one side of the room and then the other, stepping out from behind any lectern or desk, and gesturing as appropriate. Above all, make eye contact with your audience as you speak. Looking directly in your listeners' eyes conveys your honesty, your confidence, and your control of the material.

CULTURE LANGUAGE Eye contact is customary in the United States, both in conversation and in oral presentation. Listeners expect it and may perceive a speaker who doesn't make eye contact as evasive or insincere.

Visual aids

Sample document

You can supplement an oral presentation with visual aids such as posters, models, slides, or videos.

■ **Use visual aids to underscore your points.** Short lists of key ideas, illustrations such as graphs or photographs, and objects such as models can make your presentation more interesting and memorable. But use visual aids judiciously: a battery of illustrations or objects will bury your message rather than amplify it.

■ **Match visual aids and setting.** An audience of five people may be able to see a photograph and share a chart; an audience of a hundred will need projected images.

■ **Coordinate visual aids with your message.** Time each visual to reinforce a point you're making. Tell listeners what they're looking at. Give them enough viewing time so that they don't mind turning their attention back to you.

■ **Show visual aids only while they're needed.** To regain your audience's attention, remove or turn off any aid as soon as you have finished with it.

Many speakers use *PowerPoint* or other software to project main points, key images, video, or other elements. To use *PowerPoint* or other software effectively, follow the guidelines with the samples on the facing page and also these tips:

■ **Don't put your whole presentation on screen.** Select key points and distill them to as few words as possible. Use slides as quick, easy-to-remember summaries or ways to present examples. For a twenty-minute presentation, plan to use approximately ten slides.

■ **Use a simple design.** Avoid turning your presentation into a show about the software's many capabilities.

■ **Make text readable.** The type should be easy to see for viewers in the back of the room, whether the lights are on or not.

■ **Use a consistent design.** For optimal flow through the presentation, each slide should be formatted similarly.

■ **Add relevant images and media.** *PowerPoint* allows you to play images, audio, and video as part of your presentation. Before you add them, however, be sure each has a point so that you don't overload the presentation with bells and whistles. See **1** pp. 58–64 on choosing and using visuals and other media.

■ **Review all your slides before the presentation.** Using the Slide Sorter mode, go through the slides to be sure they are complete, consistent, and easy to read.

PowerPoint slides

Making a Difference?	First slide, introducing the project and presentation.
A Service-Learning Project at ReadingWorks	
Springfield Veterans Administration Hospital	Simple, consistent slide design focusing viewers' attention on information, not *PowerPoint* features.
Jessica Cho	
Nathan Hall	
Alex Ramirez	
SPRING 2011	

Semester goals

- Research adult literacy.
- Tutor military veterans.
- Keep a journal.
- Collaborate on documents for ReadingWorks.
- Report experiences and findings.

Later slide, including a title and brief, bulleted points to be explained by the speaker.

Photographs reinforcing the project's activities.

■ **During the presentation, don't talk to the computer or the projection.** Move away from both and face the audience.

Practice

Take time to rehearse your presentation out loud, with the notes you will be using. Gauge your performance by making an audio- or videotape of yourself or by practicing in front of a mirror. Practicing out loud will also tell you if your presentation is running too long or too short.

If you plan to use visual aids, you'll need to practice with them, too. Your goal is to eliminate hitches (upside-down slides, missing charts) and to weave the visuals seamlessly into your presentation.

Stage fright

Many people report that speaking in front of an audience is their number-one fear. Even many experienced and polished speakers have some anxiety about delivering an oral presentation, but they use this nervous energy to their advantage, letting it propel them into working hard on each presentation. Several techniques can help you reduce anxiety:

- **Use simple relaxation exercises.** Deep breathing or tensing and relaxing your stomach muscles can ease some of the physical symptoms of speech anxiety—stomachache, rapid heartbeat, and shaky hands, legs, and voice.
- **Think positively.** Instead of worrying about the mistakes you might make, concentrate on how well you've prepared and practiced your presentation and how significant your ideas are.
- **Don't avoid opportunities to speak in public.** Practice and experience build speaking skills and offer the best insurance for success.

14 Public Writing

Writing outside of school, such as for business or for community work, resembles academic writing in many ways. It usually involves the same basic writing process, discussed in **1** pp. 3–34: assessing the writing situation, developing what you want to say, freely working out your meaning in a draft, and revising and editing so that your writing will achieve your purpose with readers. It often involves research, as discussed in **7** pp. 311–68. And it involves the standards of conciseness, appropriate and exact language, and correct grammar and usage discussed in **3** through **6**.

Exercise

But public writing has its own conventions, too. They vary widely, depending on what you're writing and why, whether it's a proposal for your job or a flyer for a community group. This chapter covers several types of public writing: business letters and résumés (opposite); memos, reports, and proposals (p. 132); and flyers and newsletters for community work (p. 135).

CULTURE LANGUAGE Public writing in the United States, especially in business, favors efficiency and may seem abrupt or impolite compared with such writing in your native culture. For instance, a business letter elsewhere may be expected to begin with polite questions about the addressee or with compliments for the addressee's company, whereas US business letters are expected to get right to the point.

mycomplab

Visit *mycomplab.com* for the eText and for resources and exercises on public writing.

14a Writing business letters and résumés

When you write for business, you are addressing busy people who want to see quickly why you are writing and how they should respond to you. Follow these general guidelines:

Sample
document

- **State your purpose right at the start.**
- **Be straightforward, clear, concise, objective, and courteous.**
- **Observe conventions of grammar and usage,** which make your writing clear and impress your reader with your care.

1 Business letter format

For any business letter, use either unlined white paper measuring $8\frac{1}{2}" \times 11"$ or what is called letterhead stationery with your address at the top of the sheet. Print the letter single-spaced (with double spacing between elements) on only one side of a sheet.

A common business-letter form is illustrated on the next page:

- **The** *return-address heading* **gives your address and the date.** Do not include your name. If you are using stationery with a printed heading, you need only give the date.
- **The** *inside address* **shows the name, title, and complete address of the person you are writing to.**
- **The** *salutation* **greets the addressee.** Whenever possible, address your letter to a specific person. (Contact the company or department to ask whom to address.) If you can't find a person's name, then use a job title (*Dear Human Resources Manager, Dear Customer Service Manager*) or use a general salutation (*Dear Smythe Shoes*). Use *Ms.* as the title for a woman when she has no other title, when you don't know how she prefers to be addressed, or when you know that she prefers *Ms.*
- **The** *body* **contains the substance.** Instead of indenting the first line of each paragraph, double-space between paragraphs.
- **The** *close* **should reflect the level of formality in the salutation:** *Respectfully, Cordially, Yours truly,* and *Sincerely* are more formal closes; *Regards* and *Best wishes* are less formal.
- **The** *signature* **has two parts:** your name typed four lines below the close, and your handwritten signature in the space between. Give your name as you would sign checks and other documents.
- **Include any additional information below the signature,** such as *Enc.* (indicating an enclosure with the letter) or *cc: Margaret Zusky* (indicating that a copy is being sent to the person named).

Use an envelope that will accommodate the letter once it is folded horizontally in thirds. The envelope should show your name and address in the upper left corner and the addressee's name, title,

Business letter (job application)

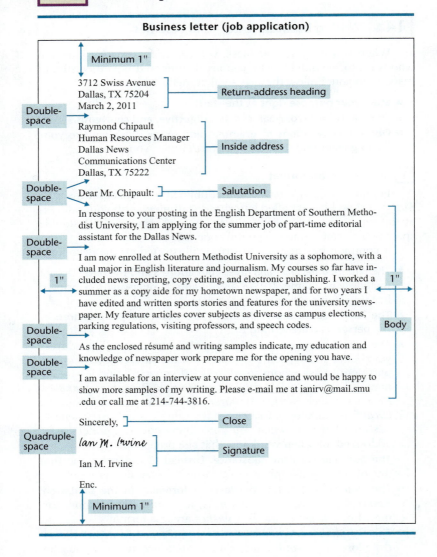

Minimum 1"

3712 Swiss Avenue
Dallas, TX 75204 ⎤ — Return-address heading
March 2, 2011 ⎦

Double-space

Raymond Chipault ⎤
Human Resources Manager |
Dallas News ⎬— Inside address
Communications Center |
Dallas, TX 75222 ⎦

Double-space

Dear Mr. Chipault: ⎤— Salutation

In response to your posting in the English Department of Southern Methodist University, I am applying for the summer job of part-time editorial
assistant for the Dallas News.

Double-space

I am now enrolled at Southern Methodist University as a sophomore, with a
dual major in English literature and journalism. My courses so far have included news reporting, copy editing, and electronic publishing. I worked a
summer as a copy aide for my hometown newspaper, and for two years I
have edited and written sports stories and features for the university newspaper. My feature articles cover subjects as diverse as campus elections,
parking regulations, visiting professors, and speech codes.

1"   1"

Body

Double-space

As the enclosed résumé and writing samples indicate, my education and
knowledge of newspaper work prepare me for the opening you have.

Double-space

I am available for an interview at your convenience and would be happy to
show more samples of my writing. Please e-mail me at ianirv@mail.smu
.edu or call me at 214-744-3816.

Sincerely, ⎤— Close

Quadruple-space

Ian M. Irvine ⎤— Signature
Ian M. Irvine ⎦

Enc.

Minimum 1"

and address in the center. For easy machine reading, the United States
Postal Service recommends all capital letters and no punctuation
(spaces separate the elements on a line), as in this address:

RAYMOND CHIPAULT
HUMAN RESOURCES MANAGER
DALLAS NEWS
COMMUNICATIONS CENTER
DALLAS TX 75222-0188

Sample
document

2 Job-application letter

The sample on the facing page illustrates the key features of a job-application letter:

- **Interpret your résumé for the particular job.** Don't detail your entire résumé, reciting your job history. Instead, highlight and reshape only the relevant parts.
- **Announce at the outset what job you seek and how you heard about it.**
- **Include any special reason you have for applying,** such as a specific career goal.
- **Summarize your qualifications for this particular job,** including relevant facts about education and employment history and emphasizing notable accomplishments. Mention that additional information appears in an accompanying résumé.
- **Describe your availability.** At the end of the letter, mention that you are free for an interview at the convenience of the addressee, or specify when you will be available (for instance, when your current job or classes leave you free, or when you could travel to the employer's city).

3 Résumé

Sample
document

The résumé that accompanies a job application should provide information in table format that allows a potential employer to evaluate your qualifications. The résumé should include your name and address, the position you seek, your education and employment history, any special skills or awards, and how to obtain your references. Fit all the information on one uncrowded page unless your education and experience are extensive. The sample on p. 132 gives guidelines for a résumé that you submit in print.

Employers may need an electronic version of your résumé so that they can add it to a computerized database of applicants. The employers may scan your printed résumé to convert it to an electronic file, which they can then store in an appropriate database, or they may request that you embed your résumé in an e-mail message. To produce a scannable or electronic résumé, follow the guidelines below and consult the sample on p. 133.

- **Keep the design simple for accurate scanning or electronic transmittal.** Avoid images, unusual type, more than one column, vertical or horizontal lines, italics, and underlining.
- **Use concise, specific words to describe your skills and experience.** The employer's computer may use keywords (often nouns) to identify the résumés of suitable job candidates, and you want to ensure that your résumé includes the appropriate keywords. Name your specific skills—for example, the computer programs you can operate—and write concretely with words like

Résumé (print)

Name and contact information	**Ian M. Irvine**	3712 Swiss Avenue Dallas, TX 75204 214-744-3816 ianirv@mail.smu.edu

Desired position stated simply and clearly

Position desired — Part-time editorial assistant.

Education before work experience for most college students

Education — *Southern Methodist University*, 2009 to present.
Current standing: sophomore.
Major: English literature and journalism.
Journalism courses: news reporting, copy editing, electronic publishing, communication arts, broadcast journalism.

Abilene (Texas) Senior High School, 2005-09.
Graduated with academic, college-preparatory degree.

Headings marking sections, set off with space and highlighting

Employment history — 2009 to present. Reporter, *Daily Campus*, student newspaper of Southern Methodist University.
Write regular coverage of baseball, track, and soccer teams.
Write feature stories on campus policies and events. Edit sports news, campus listings, features.

Conventional use of capital letters: yes for proper nouns and after periods; no for job titles, course names, department names, and so on

Summer 2010. Copy aide, *Abilene Reporter-News*.
Assisted reporters with copy routing and research.

Summer 2009. Painter, Longhorn Painters, Abilene.
Prepared and painted exteriors and interiors of houses.

Special skills — Fluent in Spanish.
Proficient in Internet research and word processing.

Standard, consistent type font

References — Available on request:

Placement Office
Southern Methodist University
Dallas, TX 75275

manager (not *person with responsibility for*) and *reporter* (not *staff member who reports*). Look for likely keywords in the employer's description of the job you seek.

14b Writing memos, reports, and proposals

1 Memos

Sample document

Business memos address people within the same organization. Most memos deal briefly with a specific topic, such as an answer to a question or an evaluation.

Résumé (scannable or electronic)

Ian M. Irvine
3712 Swiss Avenue
Dallas, TX 75204
214-744-3816
ianirv@mail.smu.edu

KEYWORDS: Editor, editorial assistant, publishing, electronic publishing.

OBJECTIVE
Part-time editorial assistant.

EDUCATION
Southern Methodist University, 2009 to present.
Major: English literature and journalism.
Journalism courses: news reporting, copy editing, electronic publishing, communication arts, broadcast journalism.

Abilene (Texas) Senior High School, 2005-09.
Academic, college preparatory degree.

EMPLOYMENT HISTORY
Reporter, Daily Campus, Southern Methodist University, 2009 to present.
Writer of articles for student newspaper on sports teams, campus policies, and local events. Editor of sports news, campus listings, and features.

Copy aide, Abilene Reporter-News, Abilene, summer 2010.
Assistant to reporters, routing copy and doing research.

Painter, Longhorn Painters, Abilene, summer 2009.
Preparation and painting of exteriors and interiors of houses.

SPECIAL SKILLS
Fluent in Spanish.
Proficient in Internet research and word processing.

REFERENCES
Available on request:
Placement Office
Southern Methodist University
Dallas, TX 75275

Annotations (right margin):

- Accurate keywords, allowing the employer to place the résumé into an appropriate database
- Simple design, avoiding unusual type, italics, multiple columns, decorative lines, and images
- Standard font easily read by scanners
- Every line aligning at left margin

The content of a memo comes quickly to the point and disposes of it efficiently. State your reason for writing in the first sentence. Devote the first paragraph to a concise presentation of your answer, conclusion, or evaluation. In the rest of the memo explain your reasoning or evidence. Use headings or lists as appropriate to highlight key information.

Memos are usually sent as e-mails or as word-processing documents attached to e-mails. See the sample on the next page, and consult the guidelines on pp. 77–78 for using e-mail and other electronic communication.

Memo

Names of addressee and people receiving copies

Subject description providing context for the memo

Body paragraphs single-spaced with double spacing between them; paragraphs not indented

Numbered list distilling and emphasizing key points

Writer's electronic signature giving contact information

From ▾   pphillips@bigelow.com
To...   Aileen Rosen
Cc...   Larry Mendes; James MacGregor
Subject: 2011 sales of Quick Wax in Territory 12

Since it was introduced in January 2011, Quick Wax has been unsuccessful in Territory 12 and has not affected the sales of our Easy Shine. Discussions with customers and my own analysis of Quick Wax suggest three reasons for its failure to compete with our product.

1. Quick Wax has not received the promotion necessary for a new product. Advertising has been sporadic and has not developed a clear, consistent image for the product. In addition, the Quick Wax representative in Territory 12 is new and inexperienced. He is not known to customers, and his sales pitch (which I once overheard) is weak. As far as I can tell, his efforts are not supported by his home office.

2. When Quick Wax does make it to the store shelves, buyers do not choose it over our product. Though priced competitively with Easy Shine, Quick Wax is poorly packaged. The container seems smaller than ours, though in fact it holds the same eight ounces. The lettering on the package (red on blue) is difficult to read, in contrast to the Easy Shine package.

3. Our special purchase offers and my increased efforts to serve existing customers have had the intended effect of keeping customers satisfied with our product and reducing their inclination to stock something new.

Patricia Phillips
Sales Representative
Bigelow Wax Company
pphillips@bigelow.com
960-556-5565

2 │ Reports and proposals

Sample document

Sample document

Reports and proposals are text-heavy documents, sometimes lengthy, that convey information such as the results of research, a plan for action, or a recommendation for change. As with other business correspondence, you will prepare a report or proposal for a specific purpose, and you will be addressing interested but busy readers.

Reports and proposals usually divide into sections. The sections vary depending on the purpose of the document, but usually they include an overview or summary, which tells the reader what the document is about; a statement of the problem or need, which justifies the report or proposal; a statement of the plan or solution, which responds to the need or problem; and a recommendation or evaluation. Consider the following guidelines as you prepare a report or proposal:

■ **Do your research.** To write a successful report or proposal, you must be well informed. Be alert to where you have enough information or where you don't.

■ **Focus on the purpose of each section.** Stick to the point of each section, saying only what you need to say, even if you have

Report

Canada Geese at ABC Institute: An Environmental Problem

Summary

The flock of Canada geese on and around ABC Institute's grounds has grown dramatically in recent years to become a nuisance and an environmental problem. This report reviews the problem, considers possible solutions, and proposes that ABC Institute and the US Fish and Wildlife Service cooperate to reduce the flock by humane means.

The Problem

Canada geese began living at Taylor Lake next to ABC Institute when they were relocated there in 1985 by the state game department. As a nonmigratory flock, the geese are present year-round, with the highest population each year occurring in early spring. In recent years the flock has grown dramatically. The Audubon Society's annual Christmas bird census shows a thirty-fold increase from the 37 geese counted in 1986 to the 1125 counted in 2010.

The principal environmental problem caused by the geese is pollution of grass and water by defecation. Geese droppings cover the ABC Institute's grounds as well as the park's picnicking areas. The runoff from these droppings into Taylor Lake has substantially affected the quality of the lake's water, so that local authorities have twice (2009 and 2010) issued warnings against swimming.

Possible Solutions

The goose overpopulation and resulting environmental problems have several possible solutions:

- Harass the geese with dogs and audiovisual effects (light and noise) so that the geese choose to leave. This solution is inhumane to the geese and unpleasant for human neighbors.
- Feed the geese a chemical that will weaken the shells of their eggs and thus reduce growth of the flock. This solution is inhumane to the geese and also impractical, because geese are long-lived.
- Kill adult geese. This solution is, obviously, inhumane to the geese.
- Thin the goose population by trapping and removing many geese (perhaps 600) to areas less populated by humans, such as wildlife preserves.

Though costly (see figures below), the last solution is the most humane. It would be harmless to the geese, provided that sizable netted enclosures are used for traps. [Discussion of solution and "Recommendations" section follow.]

Descriptive title conveying report's contents

Standard format: summary, statement of the problem, solutions, and (not shown) recommendations

Major sections delineated by headings

Formal tone, appropriate to a business-writing situation

Single spacing with double spacing between paragraphs and around the list

Bulleted list emphasizing alternative solutions

additional information. Each section should accomplish its purpose and contribute to the whole.

- **Follow an appropriate format.** In many businesses, reports and proposals have specific formatting requirements. If you are unsure about the requirements, ask your supervisor.

14c Writing for community work

At some point in your life, you're likely to volunteer for a community organization such as a soup kitchen, a daycare center, or a literacy program. Many college courses involve service learning, in

Student paper

which you do such volunteer work, write about the experience for your course, and write *for* the organization you're helping.

The writing you do for a community group may range from flyers to grant proposals. Two guidelines will help you prepare effective projects like the ones here, for a literacy program.

- **Craft each document for its purpose and audience.** You are trying to achieve a specific aim with your readers, and the approach and tone you use will influence their responses. If, for example, you are writing letters to local businesses to raise funds for a homeless shelter, bring to mind the people who will read your

Flyer

Large type and color focusing a distant reader's attention on important information: what's happening, when, where, and who is invited

White space drawing viewers' eyes to main message and creating flow among elements

Color highlighting key information

Less important information set in smaller type

FIRST ANNUAL AWARDS DINNER

ReadingWorks
Springfield VA Hospital

WHEN
Friday night
May 20
7:30 to 10:30

WHERE
Suite 42
Springfield VA Hospital

WHO
Students, tutors, and their families are invited to join us for an evening of food and music as we celebrate their efforts and accomplishments.

For information
contact ReadingWorks
209-556-1212

ReadingWorks of Springfield Veterans Administration Hospital
111 South Springdale Drive
Springfield, MI 45078

letter. How can you best persuade those readers to donate money?

■ **Expect to work with others.** Much public writing is the work of more than one person. Even if you draft the document on your own, others will review the content, tone, and design. Such collaboration is rewarding, but it sometimes requires patience and goodwill. See **1** pp. 36–37 for advice on collaborating.

Newsletter

ReadingWorks

Springfield Veterans Administration Hospital   SUMMER 2011

From the director

Can you help? With more and more learners in the ReadingWorks program, we need more and more tutors. You may know people who would be interested in participating in the program, if only they knew about it.

Those of you who have been tutoring VA patients in reading and writing know both the great need you fulfill and the great benefits you bring to the students. New tutors need no special skills—we'll provide the training—only patience and an interest in helping others.

We've scheduled an orientation meeting for Friday, September 9, at 6:30 PM. Please come and bring a friend who is willing to contribute a couple of hours a week to our work.

Thanks,
Kate Goodman

FIRST ANNUAL AWARDS DINNER

A festive night for students and tutors

The first annual Reading-Works Awards Dinner on May 20 was a great success. Springfield's own Golden Fork provided tasty food and Amber Allen supplied lively music. The students decorated Suite 42 on the theme of books and reading. In all, 127 people attended.

The highlight of the night was the awards ceremony. Nine students, recommended by their tutors, received certificates recognizing their efforts and special accomplishments in learning to read and write:

Ramon Berva
Edward Byar
David Dunbar
Tony Garnier
Chris Guigni
Akili Haynes
Josh Livingston
Alex Obeld
B. J. Resnansky

In addition, nine tutors received certificates commemorating five years of service to ReadingWorks:

Anita Crumpton
Felix Cruz-Rivera
Bette Elgen

Kayleah Bortoluzzi
Harriotte Henderson
Ben Obiso
Meggie Puente
Max Smith
Sara Villante

Congratulations to all!

PTSD: New Guidelines

Most of us are working with veterans who have been diagnosed with post-traumatic stress disorder. Because this disorder is often complicated by alcoholism, depression, anxiety, and other problems, the National Center for PTSD has issued some guidelines for helping PTSD patients in ways that reduce their stress.

● The hospital must know your tutoring schedule, and you need to sign in and out before and after each tutoring session.

● To protect patients' privacy, meet them only in designated visiting and tutoring areas, never in their rooms.

● Treat patients with dignity and respect, even when (as sometimes happens) they grow frustrated and angry. Seek help from a nurse or orderly if you need it.

Annotations (right margin):

Multicolumn format allowing room for headings, articles, and other elements on a single page

Two-column heading emphasizing the main article

Elements helping readers skim for highlights: spacing, varied font sizes, lines, and a bulleted list

Color focusing readers' attention on banner, headlines, and table of contents

Lively but uncluttered overall appearance

Box in the first column highlighting table of contents

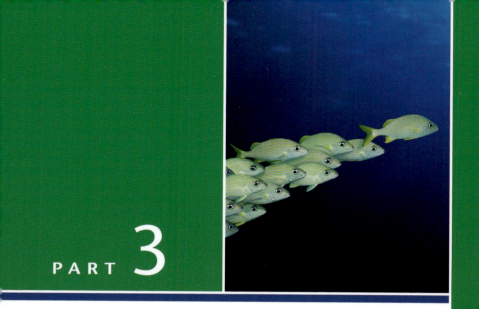

PART 3

Clarity and Style

Clarity and Style

15 Emphasis

Video tutorial

When you speak, your tone of voice, facial expressions, and even hand gestures work with your words and sentences to convey your meaning. When you write, your words and sentences must do that work alone. To write exactly what you mean, edit to emphasize the main ideas in your sentences by attending to your subjects and verbs (below), using sentence beginnings and endings (p. 143), co-ordinating equally important ideas (p. 145), and subordinating less important ideas (p. 147). In addition, emphatic writing is concise writing, the subject of Chapter 20.

Grammar checkers A grammar checker may spot some problems with emphasis, such as nouns made from verbs, passive voice, wordy phrases, and long sentences that may also be flabby and unemphatic. However, no checker can help you determine whether the important ideas in your sentences receive appropriate emphasis.

15a Using subjects and verbs effectively

Exercise

The heart of every sentence is its subject, which usually names the actor, and its predicate verb, which usually specifies the subject's action: *Children* [subject] *grow* [verb]. When these elements do not identify the key actor and action in the sentence, readers must find that information elsewhere and the sentence may be wordy and unemphatic.

In the following sentences, the subjects and verbs are underlined.

> **Unemphatic** The intention of the company was to expand its workforce. A proposal was also made to diversify the backgrounds and abilities of employees.

These sentences are unemphatic because their key ideas do not appear in their subjects and verbs. In the revision below, the sentences are not only clearer but more concise.

> **Revised** The company intended to expand its workforce. It also proposed to diversify the backgrounds and abilities of employees.

Key terms

subject Who or what a sentence is about: *Biologists often study animals.* (See **4** pp. 184–85.)

predicate The part of a sentence containing a verb that asserts something about the subject: *Biologists often study animals.* (See **4** pp. 184–85.)

---

mycomplab

Visit *mycomplab.com* for the eText and for resources and exercises on emphasis.

The constructions discussed below and opposite usually drain meaning from a sentence's subject and verb.

Nouns made from verbs

Nouns made from verbs can obscure the key actions of sentences and add words. These nouns include *intention* (from *intend*), *proposal* (from *propose*), *decision* (from *decide*), *expectation* (from *expect*), and *inclusion* (from *include*).

Unemphatic	After the company made a decision to hire more workers with disabilities, its next step was the construction of wheelchair ramps and other facilities.
Revised	After the company decided to hire more workers with disabilities, it next constructed wheelchair ramps and other facilities.

Weak verbs

Weak verbs, such as *made* and *was* in the unemphatic sentence above, tend to stall sentences just where they should be moving and often bury key actions:

Unemphatic	The company is now the leader among businesses in complying with the 1990 disabilities act. Its officers make frequent speeches on the act to business groups.
Revised	The company now leads other businesses in complying with the 1990 disabilities act. Its officers frequently speak on the act to business groups.

Forms of *be, have,* and *make* are often weak, but don't try to eliminate every use of them: *be* and *have* are essential as helping verbs (*is going, has written*); *be* links subjects and words describing them (*Planes are noisy*); and *have* and *make* have independent meanings (among them "possess" and "force," respectively). But do consider replacing forms of *be, have,* and *make* when one of the words following the verb could be made into a strong verb itself, as in the following examples.

Unemphatic	**Emphatic**
was influential	influenced
is a glorification	glorifies
have a preference	prefer
had the appearance	appeared, seemed
made a claim	claimed

Key terms

noun A word that names a person, thing, quality, place, or idea: *student, desk, happiness, city, democracy.* (See **4** pp. 178–79.)

helping verb A verb used with another verb to convey time, obligation, and other meanings: *was drilling, would have been drilling.* (See **4** p. 181.)

Passive voice

Verbs in the passive voice state actions received by, not performed by, their subjects. Thus the passive de-emphasizes the true actor of the sentence, sometimes omitting it entirely. Generally, prefer the active voice, in which the subject performs the action. (See also **4** pp. 212–14 for help with editing the passive voice.)

Unemphatic	The 1990 law is seen by most businesses as fair, but the costs of complying have sometimes been objected to.
Revised	Most businesses see the 1990 law as fair, but some have objected to the costs of complying.

15b Using sentence beginnings and endings

Readers automatically seek a writer's principal meaning in the main clause of a sentence—essentially, in the subject that names the actor and in the verb that usually specifies the action (see p. 141). Thus you can help readers understand the meaning you intend by controlling the information in your subjects and the relation of the main clause to any modifiers attached to it.

Old and new information

Generally, readers expect the beginning of a sentence to contain information that they already know or that you have already introduced. They then look to the ending for new information. In the unemphatic passage below, the second and third sentences both begin with new topics, while the old topics appear at the ends of the sentences. The pattern of the passage is A→B. C→B. D→A.

Unemphatic   Education (A) often means controversy (B) these days, with rising costs and constant complaints about its inadequacies. But the value (C) of schooling should not be obscured by the controversy (B). The single best means (D) of economic advancement, despite its shortcomings, remains education (A).

Key terms

passive voice The verb form when the subject names the *receiver* of the verb's action: *The house was destroyed by the tornado.*

active voice The verb form when the subject names the *performer* of the verb's action: *The tornado destroyed the house.*

main clause A word group that can stand alone as a sentence, containing a subject and a predicate and not beginning with a subordinating word: *The books were expensive.* (See **4** p. 191.)

modifier A word or word group that describes another word or word group: *sweet candy, running in the park.* (See **4** pp. 181–82 and 191.)

In the more emphatic revision, the old information begins each sentence and the new information ends the sentence. The passage follows the pattern A→B. B→C. A→D.

Revised $\overset{A}{\underline{\text{Education}}}$ often means $\overset{B}{\underline{\text{controversy}}}$ these days, with rising costs and constant complaints about its inadequacies. But the $\overset{B}{\underline{\text{controversy}}}$ should not obscure the $\overset{C}{\underline{\text{value}}}$ of schooling. $\overset{A}{\underline{\text{Education}}}$ remains, despite its shortcomings, the single best $\overset{D}{\underline{\text{means}}}$ of economic advancement.

Cumulative and periodic sentences

You can call attention to information by placing it first or last in a sentence, reserving the middle for incidentals:

Unemphatic   Education remains the single best means of economic advancement, despite its shortcomings. [Emphasizes shortcomings.]

Revised   Despite its shortcomings, education remains the single best means of economic advancement. [Emphasizes advancement more than shortcomings.]

Revised   Education remains, despite its shortcomings, the single best means of economic advancement. [De-emphasizes shortcomings.]

A sentence that adds modifiers to the main clause is called **cumulative** because it accumulates information as it proceeds:

Cumulative   Education has no equal in opening minds, instilling values, and creating opportunities.

Cumulative   Most of the Great American Desert is made up of bare rock, rugged cliffs, mesas, canyons, mountains, separated from one another by broad flat basins covered with sun-baked mud and alkali, supporting a sparse and measured growth of sagebrush or creosote or saltbush, depending on location and elevation.

—Edward Abbey

The opposite kind of sentence, called **periodic,** saves the main clause until just before the end (the period) of the sentence. Everything before the main clause points toward it:

Periodic   In opening minds, instilling values, and creating opportunities, education has no equal.

Periodic   With people from all over the world—Korean doctors, Jamaican cricket players, Vietnamese engineers, Haitian cabdrivers, Chinese grocers, Indian restaurant owners—the American mosaic is continually changing.

The periodic sentence creates suspense by reserving important information for the end. But readers should already have an idea of the subject of the sentence—because it was mentioned in the preceding sentence—so that they know what the opening modifiers describe.

15c Using coordination

Use **coordination** to show that two or more elements in a sentence are equally important in meaning and thus to clarify the relationship between them:

Ways to coordinate information in sentences

■ **Link main clauses with a comma and a coordinating conjunction:** *and, but, or, nor, for, so, yet.*

Independence Hall in Philadelphia is faithfully restored**,** but many years ago it was in bad shape.

■ **Relate main clauses with a semicolon alone or a semicolon and a conjunctive adverb:** *however, indeed, thus,* etc.

The building was standing**;** however, it suffered from neglect.

■ **Within clauses, link words and phrases with a coordinating conjunction:** *and, but, or, nor.*

The people and officials of the nation were indifferent to Independence Hall or took it for granted.

■ **Link main clauses, words, or phrases with a correlative conjunction:** *both . . . and, not only . . . but also,* etc.

People not only took the building for granted but also neglected its upkeep.

Grammar checkers A grammar checker may spot some errors in punctuating coordinated elements, and it can usually flag long sentences that may contain excessive coordination. But otherwise a checker can provide little help with coordination because it cannot recognize the relations among ideas in sentences.

┌ **Key terms** ───────────────
coordinating conjunctions *And, but, or, nor,* and sometimes *for, so, yet.* (See **4** p. 183.)
conjunctive adverbs Modifiers that describe the relation of the ideas in two clauses, such as *hence, however, indeed,* and *thus.* (See **4** p. 252.)
correlative conjunctions Pairs of connecting words, such as *both . . . and, either . . . or, not only . . . but also.* (See **4** p. 183.)

1 Coordinating to relate equal ideas

Coordination shows the equality between elements, as illustrated by the examples in the box on the preceding page. At the same time that it clarifies meaning, it can also help smooth choppy sentences:

Choppy sentences
We should not rely so heavily on oil. Coal and uranium are also overused. We have a substantial energy resource in the moving waters of our rivers. Smaller streams add to the total volume of water. The resource renews itself. Oil and coal are irreplaceable. Uranium is also irreplaceable. The cost of water does not increase much over time. The costs of coal, oil, and uranium rise dramatically.

The following revision groups coal, oil, and uranium and clearly opposes them to water (the connecting words are underlined):

Ideas coordinated
We should not rely so heavily on oil, coal, and uranium, for we have a substantial energy resource in the moving waters of our rivers and streams. Oil, coal, and uranium are irreplaceable and thus subject to dramatic cost increases; water, however, is self-renewing and more stable in cost.

2 Coordinating effectively

Exercise

Use coordination only to express the *equality* of ideas or details. A string of coordinated elements—especially main clauses—implies that all points are equally important:

Excessive coordination
The weeks leading up to the resignation of President Nixon were eventful, and the Supreme Court and the Congress closed in on him, and the Senate Judiciary Committee voted to begin impeachment proceedings, and finally the President resigned on August 9, 1974.

Such a passage needs editing to stress the important points (underlined below) and to de-emphasize the less important information:

Revised
The weeks leading up to the resignation of President Nixon were eventful, as the Supreme Court and the Congress closed in on him and the Senate Judiciary Committee voted to begin impeachment proceedings. Finally, the President resigned on August 9, 1974.

Even within a single sentence, coordination should express a logical equality between ideas:

Faulty
John Stuart Mill was a nineteenth-century utilitarian, and he believed that actions should be judged by their usefulness or by the happiness they cause. [The two clauses are not separate and equal: the second expands on the first by explaining what a utilitarian such as Mill believed.]

Revised John Stuart Mill, <u>a nineteenth-century utilitarian</u>, believed that actions should be judged by their usefulness or by the happiness they cause.

15d Using subordination

Exercise

Use **subordination** to indicate that some elements in a sentence are less important than others for your meaning. Usually, the main idea appears in the main clause, and supporting details appear in subordinate structures:

Ways to subordinate information in sentences

- **Use a subordinate clause beginning with a subordinating word:** *who* (*whom*), *that, which, although, because, if,* etc.

  Although some citizens had tried to rescue Independence Hall, they had not gained substantial public support.

  The first strong step was taken by the federal government, which made the building a national monument.

- **Use a phrase.**

  Like most national monuments, Independence Hall is protected by the National Park Service.

  Protecting many popular tourist sites, the service is a highly visible government agency.

- **Use a short modifier.**

  At the red brick Independence Hall, park rangers give guided tours and protect the irreplaceable building from vandalism.

Grammar checkers A grammar checker may spot some errors in punctuating subordinated elements, and it can usually flag long sentences that may contain excessive subordination. But otherwise a checker can provide little help with subordination because it cannot recognize the relations among ideas in sentences.

1 Subordinating to emphasize main ideas

A string of main clauses can make everything in a passage seem equally important.

Key terms

subordinate clause A word group that contains a subject and verb, begins with a subordinating word such as *because* or *who,* and is not a question: *Words can do damage <u>when they hurt feelings</u>.* (See **4** p. 191.)

phrase A word group that lacks a subject or predicate or both: *Words can do damage <u>by hurting feelings</u>.* (See **4** p. 188.)

| String of main clauses | Computer prices have dropped, and production costs have dropped more slowly, and computer manufacturers have had to struggle, for their profits have been shrinking. |

Emphasis comes from keeping the truly important information in the main clause (underlined) and subordinating the less important details:

| Revised | Because production costs have dropped more slowly than prices, <u>computer manufacturers have had to struggle with shrinking profits</u>. |

2 Subordinating effectively

Use subordination only for the less important information in a sentence.

| Faulty | Ms. Angelo was in her first year of teaching, although she was a better instructor than others with many years of experience. |

The preceding sentence suggests that Angelo's inexperience is the main idea, whereas the writer intended to stress her skill *despite* her inexperience. Reducing the inexperience to a subordinate clause and elevating the skill to the main clause (underlined) gives appropriate emphasis:

| Revised | Although Ms. Angelo was in her first year of teaching, <u>she was a better instructor than others with many years of experience</u>. |

Subordination loses its power to emphasize when too much loosely related detail crowds into one long, meandering sentence:

| Overloaded | The boats that were moored at the dock when the hurricane, which was one of the worst in three decades, struck were ripped from their moorings, because the owners had not been adequately prepared, since the weather service had predicted that the storm would blow out to sea, which they do at this time of year. |

The revision stresses important information in the main clauses (underlined):

| Revised | <u>Struck by one of the worst hurricanes in three decades, the boats at the dock were ripped from their moorings</u>. <u>The owners were unprepared</u> because the weather service had said that hurricanes at this time of year blow out to sea. |

16 Parallelism

Parallelism gives similar grammatical form to sentence elements that have similar function and importance.

Video tutorial

The air is dirtied by factories belching smoke
                    and
                    cars spewing exhaust.

In the preceding example the two underlined phrases have the same function and importance (both specify sources of air pollution), so they also have the same grammatical construction. Parallelism makes form follow meaning.

Grammar checkers A grammar checker cannot recognize faulty parallelism because it cannot recognize the relations among ideas.

✳ Exercise

16a Using parallelism with *and, but, or, nor, yet*

The coordinating conjunctions *and, or, nor,* and *yet* always signal a need for parallelism.

The industrial base was shifting and shrinking. [Parallel words.]

Politicians rarely acknowledged the problem or proposed alternatives. [Parallel phrases.]

Industrial workers were understandably disturbed that they were losing their jobs and that no one seemed to care. [Parallel clauses.]

When sentence elements linked by coordinating conjunctions are not parallel in structure, the sentence is awkward and distracting:

Nonparallel The reasons steel companies kept losing money were that their plants were inefficient, high labor costs, and foreign competition was increasing.

Revised The reasons steel companies kept losing money were inefficient plants, high labor costs, and increasing foreign competition.

Nonparallel Success was difficult even for efficient companies because of the shift away from all manufacturing in the United States and the fact that steel production was shifting toward emerging nations.

Key term

coordinating conjunctions Words that connect elements of the same kind and importance: *and, but, or, nor,* and sometimes *for, so, yet.* (See 4 p. 183.)
---

mycomplab

Visit *mycomplab.com* for the eText and for resources and exercises on parallelism.

149

Revised	Success was difficult even for efficient companies because of the shift away from all manufacturing in the United States and toward steel production in emerging nations.

All the words required by idiom or grammar must be stated in compound constructions (see also p. 168):

Faulty	Given training, workers can acquire the skills and interest in other jobs. [Idiom dictates different prepositions with *skills* and *interest*.]
Revised	Given training, workers can acquire the skills for and interest in other jobs.

16b Using parallelism with *both . . . and, not . . . but,* or another correlative conjunction

Correlative conjunctions stress equality and balance between elements. Parallelism confirms the equality.

It is not a tax bill but a tax relief bill, providing relief not for the needy but for the greedy.   —Franklin Delano Roosevelt

With correlative conjunctions, the element after the second connector must match the element after the first connector:

Nonparallel	Huck Finn learns not only that human beings have an enormous capacity for folly but also enormous dignity. [The first element includes *that human beings have*; the second element does not.]
Revised	Huck Finn learns that human beings have not only an enormous capacity for folly but also enormous dignity. [Repositioning *that human beings have* makes the two elements parallel.]

16c Using parallelism in comparisons

Parallelism confirms the likeness or difference between two elements being compared using *than* or *as*:

Nonparallel	Huck Finn proves less a bad boy than to be an independent spirit. In the end he is every bit as determined in rejecting help as he is to leave for "the territory."
Revised	Huck Finn proves less a bad boy than an independent spirit. In the end he is every bit as determined to reject help as he is to leave for "the territory."

(See also 4 pp. 234–35 on making comparisons logical.)

> **Key term**
>
> **correlative conjunctions** Pairs of words that connect elements of the same kind and importance, such as *but . . . and, either . . . or, neither . . . nor, not . . . but, not only . . . but also.* (See 4 p. 183.)

16d Using parallelism with lists, headings, and outlines

The items in a list or outline are coordinate and should be parallel. Parallelism is essential in a formal topic outline and in the headings that divide a paper into sections. (See **1** pp. 20–21 and 56–57 for more on outlines and headings.)

Nonparallel	Revised
Changes in Renaissance England	Changes in Renaissance England
1. Extension of trade routes	1. Extension of trade routes
2. Merchant class became more powerful	2. Increased power of the merchant class
3. The death of feudalism	3. Death of feudalism
4. Upsurging of the arts	4. Upsurge of the arts
5. Religious quarrels began	5. Rise of religious quarrels

17 Variety and Details

Writing that's interesting as well as clear has at least two features: the sentences vary in length and structure, and they are well textured with details.

Grammar checkers Some grammar checkers will flag long sentences, and you can check for appropriate variety in a series of such sentences. But generally these programs cannot help you see where variety may be needed because they cannot recognize the relative importance and complexity of your ideas.

17a Varying sentence length

In most contemporary writing, sentences tend to vary from about ten to about forty words. When sentences are all at one extreme or the other, readers may have difficulty focusing on main ideas and seeing the relations among them.

- **Long sentences.** If most of your sentences contain thirty-five words or more, your main ideas may not stand out from the details that support them. Break some of the long sentences into shorter, simpler ones.
- **Short sentences.** If most of your sentences contain fewer than ten or fifteen words, all your ideas may seem equally important

mycomplab

Visit *mycomplab.com* for the eText and for resources and exercises on variety and details.

and the links between them may not be clear. Try combining sentences with coordination (p. 145) and subordination (p. 147) to show relationships and stress main ideas over supporting information.

17b Varying sentence structure

Video tutorial

A passage will be monotonous if all its sentences follow the same pattern, like soldiers marching in a parade. Try the following techniques for varying structure.

1 Subordination

A string of main clauses in simple or compound sentences can be especially plodding.

Monotonous   The moon is now drifting away from the earth. It moves away at the rate of about one inch a year. This movement is lengthening our days. They increase a thousandth of a second every century. Forty-seven of our present days will someday make up a month. We might eventually lose the moon altogether. Such great planetary movement rightly concerns astronomers, but it need not worry us. It will take 50 million years.

Enliven such writing—and make the main ideas stand out—by expressing the less important information in subordinate clauses and phrases. In the revision below, underlining indicates subordinate structures that used to be main clauses:

Revised   The moon is now drifting away from the earth <u>about one inch a year</u>. <u>At a thousandth of a second every century</u>, this movement is lengthening our days. Forty-seven of our present days will someday make up a month, <u>if we don't eventually lose the moon altogether</u>. Such great planetary movement rightly concerns astronomers, but it need not worry us. It will take 50 million years.

> ┌─ **Key terms** ────────────────────────────────────
>
> **main clause** A word group that can stand alone as a sentence because it contains a subject and a predicate and does not begin with a subordinating word: *Tourism is an industry. It brings in over $2 billion a year.* (See **4** p. 191.)
>
> **subordinate clause** A word group that contains a subject and predicate, begins with a subordinating word such as *because* or *who,* and is not a question: *Tourism is an industry that brings in over $2 billion a year*. (See **4** p. 191.)
>
> **phrase** A word group that lacks a subject or predicate or both: *Tourism is an industry valued at over $2 billion a year*. (See **4** p. 188.)

2 | Sentence combining

As the preceding example shows, subordinating to achieve variety often involves combining short, choppy sentences into longer units that link related information and stress main ideas. Here is another unvaried passage:

> **Monotonous** Astronomy may seem a remote science. It may seem to have little to do with people's daily lives. Many astronomers find otherwise. They see their science as soothing. It gives perspective to everyday routines and problems.

Combining five sentences into one, the following revision is both clearer and easier to read. Underlining highlights the changes.

> **Revised** Astronomy may seem a remote science having little to do with people's daily lives, but many astronomers find their science soothing because it gives perspective to everyday routines and problems.

3 | Varied sentence beginnings

An English sentence often begins with its subject, which generally captures old information from a preceding sentence (see p. 143):

> The defendant's lawyer was determined to break the prosecution's witness. He relentlessly cross-examined the stubborn witness for a week.

However, an unbroken sequence of sentences beginning with the subject quickly becomes monotonous:

> **Monotonous** The defendant's lawyer was determined to break the prosecution's witness. He relentlessly cross-examined the witness for a week. The witness had expected to be dismissed within an hour and was visibly irritated. She did not cooperate. She was reprimanded by the judge.

Beginning some of these sentences with other expressions improves readability and clarity:

> **Revised** The defendant's lawyer was determined to break the prosecution's witness. For a week he relentlessly cross-examined the witness. Expecting to be dismissed within an hour, the witness was visibly irritated. She did not cooperate. Indeed, she was reprimanded by the judge.

The underlined expressions represent the most common choices for varying sentence beginnings:

- **Adverb modifiers,** such as *For a week* (modifies the verb *cross-examined*).

Key term

adverb A word or word group that describes a verb, an adjective, another adverb, or a whole sentence: *dressed sharply, clearly unhappy, soaring from the mountain.* (See **4** p. 181.)

- **Adjective modifiers,** such as *Expecting to be dismissed within an hour* (modifies *witness*).
- **Transitional expressions,** such as *Indeed*. (See **1** pp. 44–45 for a list.)

CULTURE LANGUAGE In standard American English, placing some negative adverb modifiers at the beginning of a sentence requires you to use the word order of a question, in which the verb or a part of it precedes the subject. These modifiers include *never, rarely, seldom,* and adverb phrases beginning in *no, not since,* and *not until.*

	adverb	subject	verb phrase

Faulty Seldom a witness has held the stand so long.

	adverb	helping verb	subject	main verb

Revised Seldom has a witness held the stand so long.

4 **Varied word order**

Occasionally you can vary a sentence and emphasize it at the same time by inverting the usual order of parts:

A dozen witnesses testified for the prosecution, and the defense attorney barely questioned eleven of them. The twelfth, however, he grilled. [Normal word order: *He grilled the twelfth, however.*]

Inverted sentences used without need are artificial. Use them only when emphasis demands.

17c **Adding details**

Relevant details such as facts and examples create the texture and life that keep readers awake and help them grasp your meaning. For instance:

Flat Constructed after World War II, Levittown, New York, consisted of thousands of houses in two basic styles. Over the decades, residents have altered the houses so dramatically that the original styles are often unrecognizable.

Detailed Constructed on potato fields after World War II, Levittown, New York, consisted of more than seventeen thousand houses in Cape Cod and ranch styles. Over the decades, residents have added expansive front porches, punched dormer windows through roofs, converted garages to sun porches, and otherwise altered the houses so dramatically that the original styles are often unrecognizable.

Key term

adjective A word or word group that describes a noun or pronoun: *sweet smile, certain someone*. (See **4** p. 181.)

Note The details in the revised passage work because they relate to the writer's point and make that point clearer. Details that don't support and clarify your point will likely distract or annoy readers.

18 Appropriate and Exact Language

The clarity and effectiveness of your writing will depend greatly on the use of language that is appropriate for your writing situation (below) and that expresses your meaning exactly (p. 161).

18a Choosing appropriate language

Video tutorial

Appropriate language suits your writing situation—your subject, purpose, and audience. In most college and career writing you should rely on what's called **standard American English,** the dialect of English normally expected and used in school, business, the professions, government, and the communications media. (For more on its role in academic writing, see **2** pp. 99–101.)

Exercise

The vocabulary of written standard English is huge, allowing you to express an infinite range of ideas and feelings. However, it does exclude words that only some groups of people use, understand, or find inoffensive. It also excludes words and expressions that are commonly spoken but are too imprecise for writing. Whenever you doubt a word's status, consult a dictionary (see p. 162). A label such as *nonstandard, slang,* or *colloquial* tells you that the word is not generally appropriate in academic or business writing.

Grammar checkers A grammar checker can often be set to flag potentially inappropriate words, such as nonstandard dialect, slang, colloquialisms, and gender-specific terms (*manmade, mailman*). However, the checker can flag only words listed in its dictionary of questionable words. For example, a checker flagged *businessman* as potentially sexist in A *successful businessman puts clients first,* but the checker did not flag *his* in A *successful businessperson listens to his clients.* If you use a checker, you'll still need to judge whether your words are appropriate for your writing situation.

1 Nonstandard dialect (CULTURE LANGUAGE)

Like many countries, the United States includes scores of regional, social, and ethnic groups with their own distinct **dialects,** or versions of English. Standard American English is one of those dialects, and so are African American Vernacular English, Appalachian English, Creole, and the English of coastal Maine. All the dialects of English share many features, but each also has its own vocabulary, pronunciation, and grammar.

If you speak a dialect of English besides standard American English, be careful about using your dialect in situations where standard English is the norm, such as in academic or business writing. Dialects are not wrong in themselves, but forms imported from one dialect into another may still be perceived as unclear or incorrect. When you know standard English is expected in your writing, edit to eliminate expressions in your dialect that you know (or have been told) differ from standard English. These expressions may include *theirselves, hisn,* and others labeled *nonstandard* by a dictionary. They may also include the verb forms discussed in **4** pp. 196–202. For help identifying and editing nonstandard language, see the "(CULTURE LANGUAGE) Guide" just before the back endpapers of this book.

Your participation in the community of standard English does not require you to abandon your own dialect. You may want to use it in writing you do for yourself, such as journals and drafts, which should be composed as freely as possible. You may want to quote it in an academic paper, as when reporting conversation in dialect. And, of course, you will want to use it with others who speak it.

2 Shortcuts of online communication

Rapid communication by e-mail and text or instant messaging encourages some informalities that are inappropriate for academic writing. If you use these media frequently, you may need to proofread your academic papers especially to identify and revise errors such as the following:

- **Sentence fragments.** Make sure every sentence has a subject and a predicate. Avoid fragments such as *Observing the results* or *After the meeting.* (See **4** pp. 245–48.)
- **Missing punctuation.** Between and within sentences, use standard punctuation marks. Check especially for missing commas within sentences and missing apostrophes in possessives and contractions. (See **5** pp. 261–70 and 278–81.)
- **Missing capital letters.** Use capital letters at the beginnings of sentences, for proper nouns and adjectives, and in titles. (See **6** pp. 299–302.)
- **Nonstandard abbreviations and spellings.** Avoid forms such as *2* for *to* or *too, b4* for *before, bc* for *because, ur* for *you are* or *you're,* and + or & for *and.* (See **6** pp. 293–97 and 305–06.)

3 Slang

Slang is the language used by a group, such as musicians or computer programmers, to reflect common experiences and to make technical references efficient. The following example is from an essay on the slang of "skaters" (skateboarders):

> Curtis slashed ultra-punk crunchers on his longboard, while the Rube-man flailed his usual Gumbyness on tweaked frontsides and lofty fakie ollies.
> —Miles Orkin, "Mucho Slingage by the Pool"

Among those who understand it, slang may be vivid and forceful. It often occurs in dialog, and an occasional slang expression can enliven an informal essay. But most slang is too flippant and imprecise for effective communication, and it is generally inappropriate for college or business writing. Notice the gain in seriousness and precision achieved in the following revision:

| Slang | Many students start out <u>pretty together</u> but then <u>get weird</u>. |
| Revised | Many students start out <u>with clear goals</u> but then <u>lose their direction</u>. |

4 Colloquial language

Colloquial language is the everyday spoken language, including expressions such as *go crazy, do the dirty work,* and *get along.*

When you write informally, colloquial language may be appropriate to achieve the casual, relaxed effect of conversation. An occasional colloquial word dropped into otherwise more formal writing can also help you achieve a desired emphasis. But most colloquial language is not precise enough for college or career writing. In such writing you should generally avoid any words and expressions labeled *informal* or *colloquial* in your dictionary.

| Colloquial | According to a Native American myth, the Great Creator <u>had a dog hanging around with him</u> when he created the earth. |
| Revised | According to a Native American myth, the Great Creator <u>was accompanied by a dog</u> when he created the earth. |

Note See also 2 pp. 99–101 for a discussion of formal and informal language in academic writing.

5 Technical words

All disciplines and professions rely on specialized language that allows the members to communicate precisely and efficiently with each other. Chemists, for instance, have their *phosphatides,* and literary critics have their *motifs* and *subtexts.* Without explanation, technical words are meaningless to nonspecialists. When you are writing for nonspecialists, avoid unnecessary technical terms and carefully define terms you must use.

6 Indirect and pretentious writing

Small, plain, and direct words are almost always preferable to big, showy, or evasive words. Take special care to avoid euphemisms, double talk, and pretentious writing.

A **euphemism** is a presumably inoffensive word that a writer or speaker substitutes for a word deemed potentially offensive or too blunt, such as *passed away* for *died* or *misspeak* for *lie*. Use euphemisms only when you know that blunt, truthful words would needlessly hurt or offend members of your audience.

A kind of euphemism that deliberately evades the truth is **double talk** (also called **doublespeak** or **weasel words**): language intended to confuse or to be misunderstood. Today double talk is unfortunately common in politics and advertising—the *revenue enhancement* that is really a tax, the *peace-keeping function* that is really war making, the *biodegradable* bags that last decades. Double talk has no place in honest writing.

Euphemism and sometimes double talk seem to keep company with **pretentious writing,** fancy language that is more elaborate than its subject requires. Choose your words for their exactness and economy. The big, ornate word may be tempting, but pass it up. Your readers will be grateful.

> **Pretentious** Hardly a day goes by without a new revelation about the devastation of the natural world, and to a significant extent our dependence on the internal combustion engine is the culprit. Respected scientific minds coalesce around the argument that carbon dioxide emissions, such as those from automobiles imbibing gasoline, are responsible for a gradual escalation in temperatures on the planet earth.
>
> **Revised** Much of the frequent bad news about the environment can be blamed on the internal combustion engine. Respected scientists argue that carbon dioxide emissions, such as those from gas-powered cars, are warming the earth.

7 | Sexist and other biased language

Video tutorial

Even when we do not mean it to, our language can reflect and perpetuate hurtful prejudices toward groups of people. Such biased language can be obvious—words such as *nigger, honky, mick, kike, fag, dyke,* and *broad.* But it can also be subtle, generalizing about groups in ways that may be familiar but that are also inaccurate or unfair.

Exercise

Biased language reflects poorly on the user, not on the person or persons whom it mischaracterizes or insults. Unbiased language does not submit to false generalizations. It treats people respectfully as individuals and labels groups as they wish to be labeled.

Stereotypes of race, ethnicity, religion, age, and other characteristics

A **stereotype** is a generalization based on poor evidence, a kind of formula for understanding and judging people simply because of their membership in a group:

Men are uncommunicative.
Women are emotional.
Liberals want to raise taxes.
Conservatives are affluent.

At best, stereotypes betray a noncritical writer, one who is not thinking beyond notions received from others. In your writing, be alert for statements that characterize whole groups of people:

Stereotype   Elderly drivers should have their licenses limited to daytime driving only. [Asserts that all elderly people are poor night drivers.]

Revised   Drivers with impaired night vision should have their licenses limited to daytime driving only.

Some stereotypes have become part of the language, but they are still potentially offensive:

Stereotype   The administrators are too blind to see the need for a new gymnasium. [Equates vision loss and lack of understanding.]

Revised   The administrators do not understand the need for a new gymnasium.

Sexist language

Among the most subtle and persistent biased language is that expressing narrow ideas about men's and women's roles, position, and value in society. Like other stereotypes, this **sexist language** can wound or irritate readers, and it indicates the writer's thoughtlessness or unfairness. The following box suggests some ways of eliminating sexist language.

Eliminating sexist language

■ **Avoid demeaning and patronizing language:**

Sexist   Dr. Keith Kim and Lydia Hawkins coauthored the article.

Revised   Dr. Keith Kim and Dr. Lydia Hawkins coauthored the article.

Revised   Keith Kim and Lydia Hawkins coauthored the article.

Sexist   Ladies are entering almost every occupation formerly filled by men.

Revised   Women are entering almost every occupation formerly filled by men.

■ **Avoid occupational or social stereotypes:**

Sexist   The considerate doctor commends a nurse when she provides his patients with good care.

Revised   The considerate doctor commends a nurse who provides good care for patients.

(continued)

Podcast

Eliminating sexist language
(continued)

Sexist   The grocery shopper should save her coupons.
Revised   Grocery shoppers should save their coupons.

■ **Avoid referring needlessly to gender:**

Sexist   Marie Curie, a woman chemist, discovered radium.
Revised   Marie Curie, a chemist, discovered radium.

Sexist   The patients were tended by a male nurse.
Revised   The patients were tended by a nurse.

However, don't overcorrect by avoiding appropriate references to gender: *Pregnant women* [not *people*] *should avoid drinking alcohol and smoking.*

■ **Avoid using *man* or words containing *man* to refer to all human beings.** Here are a few alternatives:

businessman	businessperson
chairman	chair, chairperson
congressman	congressperson, legislator
craftsman	craftsperson, artisan
layman	layperson
mailman	letter carrier, mail carrier
mankind	humankind, humanity, human beings, humans
manmade	handmade, manufactured, synthetic, artificial
manpower	personnel, human resources
policeman	police officer
salesman	salesperson

Sexist   Man has not reached the limits of social justice.
Revised   Humankind [or Humanity] has not reached the limits of social justice.

Sexist   The furniture consists of manmade materials.
Revised   The furniture consists of synthetic materials.

■ **Avoid the generic *he*,** the male pronoun used to refer to both genders. (See also **4** pp. 227–28.)

Sexist   The newborn child explores his world.
Revised   Newborn children explore their world. [Use the plural for the pronoun and the word it refers to.]
Revised   The newborn child explores the world. [Avoid the pronoun altogether.]
Revised   The newborn child explores his or her world. [Substitute male and female pronouns.]

Use the last option sparingly—only once in a group of sentences and only to stress the singular individual.

CULTURE
LANGUAGE   Forms of address vary widely from culture to culture. In some cultures, for instance, one shows respect by referring to all older women as if they were married, using the equivalent of *Mrs.* Usage in the United States is changing toward making no assumptions about marital status, rank, or other characteristics—for instance, addressing a woman as *Ms.* unless she is known to prefer *Mrs.* or *Miss.*

Appropriate labels

We often need to label groups: *swimmers, politicians, mothers, Christians, Westerners, students.* But labels can be shorthand stereotypes, slighting the person labeled and ignoring the preferences of the group members themselves. Although sometimes dismissed as "political correctness," showing sensitivity about labels hurts no one and helps gain your readers' trust and respect.

- **Avoid labels that (intentionally or not) insult the person or group you refer to.** A person with emotional problems is not a *mental patient.* A person with cancer is not a *cancer victim.* A person using a wheelchair is not *wheelchair-bound.*

- **Use names for racial, ethnic, and other groups that reflect the preferences of each group's members,** or at least many of them. Examples of current preferences include *African American* or *black* and *people with disabilities* (rather than *the disabled* or *the handicapped*). But labels change often. To learn how a group's members wish to be labeled, ask them directly, attend to usage in reputable periodicals, or check a recent dictionary.

- **Identify a person's group only when it is relevant to the point you're making.** Consider the context of the label: Is it a necessary piece of information? If not, don't use it.

A helpful reference for appropriate labels is *Guidelines for Bias-Free Writing,* by Marilyn Schwartz and the Task Force on Bias-Free Language of the Association of American University Presses.

18b Choosing exact language

To write clearly and effectively, you will want to find the words that fit your meaning exactly and convey your attitude precisely.

Grammar checkers A grammar checker can provide some help with inexact language. For instance, you can set it to flag commonly confused words (such as *affect/effect* and *continuous/continual*), misused prepositions in idioms (such as *accuse for* instead of *accuse of*), and clichés. But a checker can't help you at all with inappropriate connotation, excessive abstraction, or other problems discussed in this section.

Video tutorial

1 Word meanings and synonyms

For writing exactly, a dictionary is essential and a thesaurus can be helpful.

Dictionaries

Video tutorial

A dictionary defines words and provides pronunciation, grammatical functions, etymology (word history), and other information. The following sample is from *Merriam-Webster's Collegiate Dictionary*.

Print dictionary entry

Spelling and word division — Pronunciation

reck·on \'re-kən\ *vb* **reck·oned; reck·on·ing** \'re-kə-niŋ, 'rek-niŋ\ [ME *rekenen*, fr. OE *-recenian* (as in *gerecenian* to narrate); akin to OE *reccan*] *vt* (13c) **1 a :** COUNT ⟨~ the days till Christmas⟩ **b :** ESTI-MATE, COMPUTE ⟨~ the height of a building⟩ **c :** to determine by refer-ence to a fixed basis ⟨the existence of the U.S. is ~*ed* from the Decla-ration of Independence⟩ **2 :** to regard or think of as: CONSIDER **3** *chiefly dial* : THINK, SUPPOSE ⟨I ~ I've outlived my time —Ellen Glas-gow⟩ ~ *vi* **1 :** to settle accounts **2 :** to make a calculation **3 a :** JUDGE **b** *chiefly dial* : SUPPOSE, THINK **4 :** to accept something as certain ⟨ place reliance ⟨I ~ on your promise to help⟩ — **reckon with :** to take into consideration — **reckon without :** to fail to consider : IGNORE

Etymology

Meanings

Quotation and source

Idioms

Grammatical functions and forms — Label — Synonym

This sample is from a print dictionary, but Merriam-Webster and others provide online dictionaries that give the same informa-tion in less abbreviated form and also allow you to hear how a word is pronounced. Here is part of the entry for *reckon* from *Merriam-Webster Online* (*merriam-webster.com*):

Partial online dictionary entry

reck·on 🔊 *verb* \'re-kən\

reck·oned | reck·on·ing 🔊

Definition of RECKON ⋯⋯⋯⋯⋯⋯⋯⋯

transitive verb

1 a : COUNT ⟨*reckon* the days till Christmas⟩

   b : ESTIMATE, COMPUTE ⟨*reckon* the height of a building⟩

   c : to determine by reference to a fixed basis ⟨the existence of the United States is *reckoned* from the Declaration of Independence⟩

2 : to regard or think of as : CONSIDER

3 *chiefly dialect* : THINK, SUPPOSE ⟨I *reckon* I've outlived my time — Ellen Glasgow⟩

Other useful online sites are *Dictionary.com* (*dictionary.com*) and *The Free Dictionary* (*thefreedictionary.com*), which provide entries from several dictionaries at once.

If you prefer a print dictionary, good ones, in addition to *Merriam Webster's Collegiate*, include *American Heritage College Dictionary*, *Random House Webster's College Dictionary*, and *Webster's New World College Dictionary*. Some of these books come with CD versions.

CULTURE LANGUAGE If English is not your native language, you probably should have a dictionary prepared especially for students using English as a second language (ESL). Such a dictionary contains special information on prepositions, count versus noncount nouns, and many other matters. The following are reliable print ESL dictionaries, each with an online version at the URL in parentheses: *Longman Dictionary of Contemporary English (ldoceonline.com), Oxford Advanced Learner's Dictionary (oxfordadvancedlearnersdictionary.com), Merriam-Webster Advanced Learner's English Dictionary (learnersdictionary.com).*

Thesauruses

To find a word with the exact shade of meaning you intend, you may want to consult a thesaurus, or collection of **synonyms**—words with approximately the same meaning. A print or online thesaurus lists most imaginable synonyms for thousands of words. For instance, on the site *Thesaurus.com*, the word *reckon* has nearly fifty synonyms, including *account, evaluate,* and *judge.*

Because a thesaurus aims to open up possibilities, its lists of synonyms include approximate as well as precise matches. The thesaurus does not define synonyms or distinguish among them, however, so you need a dictionary to discover exact meanings. In general, don't use a word from a thesaurus—even one you like the sound of —until you are sure of its appropriateness for your meaning.

2 The right word for your meaning

All words have one or more basic meanings, called **denotations**—the meanings listed in the dictionary, without reference to emotional associations. If readers are to understand you, you must use words according to their established meanings.

- **Consult a dictionary whenever you are unsure of a word's meaning.**
- **Distinguish between similar-sounding words that have widely different denotations:**

Inexact   Older people often suffer infirmaries [places for the sick].
Exact   Older people often suffer infirmities [disabilities].

Some words, called **homonyms,** sound exactly alike but differ in meaning: for example, *principal/principle* and *rain/reign/rein.* (See **6** pp. 293–94 for a list of commonly confused homonyms.)

■ **Distinguish between words with related but distinct meanings:**

Inexact   Television commercials <u>continuously</u> [unceasingly] interrupt programming.

Exact   Television commercials <u>continually</u> [regularly] interrupt programming.

In addition to their emotion-free meanings, many words carry related meanings that evoke specific feelings. These **connotations** can shape readers' responses and are thus a powerful tool for writers. The following word pairs have related denotations but very different connotations:

pride: sense of self-worth
vanity: excessive regard for oneself

firm: steady, unchanging, unyielding
stubborn: unreasonable, bullheaded

enthusiasm: excitement
mania: excessive interest or desire

A dictionary can help you track down words with the exact connotations you want. Besides providing meanings, your dictionary may also distinguish synonyms to guide your choices. A thesaurus can help if you use it carefully, as discussed on the previous page.

3   Concrete and specific words

Clear, exact writing balances abstract and general words, which outline ideas and objects, with concrete and specific words, which sharpen and solidify.

■ **Abstract words** name ideas: *beauty, inflation, management, culture, liberal.* **Concrete words** name qualities and things we can know by our five senses of sight, hearing, touch, taste, and smell: *sleek, humming, rough, salty, musty.*

■ **General words** name classes or groups of things, such as *birds, weather,* and *buildings,* and include all the varieties of the class. **Specific words** limit a general class, such as *buildings,* by naming a variety, such as *skyscraper, Victorian courthouse,* or *hut.*

Abstract and general words are useful in the broad statements that set the course for your writing.

The wild horse in America has a <u>romantic</u> history.

Relations between the sexes today are more <u>relaxed</u> than they were in the past.

But such statements need development with concrete and specific detail. Detail can turn a vague sentence into an exact one:

Vague   The size of his hands made his smallness real. [How big were his hands? How small was he?]

Exact Not until I saw his delicate, doll-like hands did I realize that he stood a full head shorter than most other men.

Note You can use your computer's Find function to help you find and revise abstract and general words that you tend to overuse. Examples of such words include *nice, interesting, things, very, good, a lot, a little,* and *some.*

4 Idioms

Idioms are expressions in any language that do not fit the rules for meaning or grammar—for instance, *put up with, plug away at, make off with.*

Idioms that involve prepositions can be especially confusing for both native and nonnative speakers of English. Some idioms with prepositions are listed in the following box. (More appear in **4** pp. 204–05.)

Video tutorial

Idioms with prepositions

Exercise

abide by a rule
    in a place or state
according to
accords with
accuse of a crime
accustomed to
adapt from a source
    to a situation
afraid of
agree on a plan as a group
    to someone else's plan
    with a person
angry with
aware of
based on
belong in or on a place
    to a group
capable of
certain of
charge for a purchase
    with a crime
concur in an opinion
    with a person
contend for a principle
    with a person
dependent on

differ about or over a question
    from in some quality
    with a person
disappointed by or in a person
    in or with a thing
familiar with
identical with or to
impatient for a raise
    with a person
independent of
infer from
inferior to
involved in a task
    with a person
oblivious of or to one's surroundings
    of something forgotten
occupied by a person
    in study
    with a thing
opposed to
part from a person
    with a possession
prior to
proud of
related to

(continued)

Idioms with prepositions
(continued)

rewarded by the judge
        for something done
        with a gift
similar to
sorry about an error
        for a person

superior to
wait at a place
        for a train, a person
        in a room
        on a customer

CULTURE LANGUAGE If you are learning standard American English, you may find its prepositions difficult; their meanings can shift depending on context, and they have many idiomatic uses. In mastering the prepositions of standard English, you probably can't avoid memorization. But you can help yourself by memorizing related groups, such as *at/in/on* and *for/since*.

At, *in*, or *on* in expressions of time

- Use *at* before actual clock time: *at 8:30*.
- Use *in* before a month, year, century, or period: *in April, in 2012, in the twenty-first century, in the next month.*
- Use *on* before a day or date: *on Tuesday, on August 3, on Labor Day.*

At, *in*, or *on* in expressions of place

- Use *at* before a specific place or address: *at the school, at 511 Iris Street.*
- Use *in* before a place with limits or before a city, state, country, or continent: *in the house, in a box, in Oklahoma City, in China, in Asia.*
- Use *on* to mean "supported by" or "touching the surface of": *on the table, on Iris Street, on page 150.*

For or *since* in expressions of time

- Use *for* before a period of time: *for an hour, for two years.*
- Use *since* before a specific point in time: *since 1999, since Friday.*

A dictionary of English as a second language is the best source for the meanings of prepositions; see the suggestions on p. 163.

5 Figurative language

Figurative language (or a **figure of speech**) departs from the literal meanings of words, usually by comparing very different ideas or objects:

Literal   As I try to write, I can think of nothing to say.
Figurative   As I try to write, my mind is a slab of black slate.

Imaginatively and carefully used, figurative language can capture meaning more precisely and emotionally than literal language. Here is a figure of speech at work in technical writing (paraphrasing the physicist Edward Andrade):

> The molecules in a liquid move continuously like couples on an over-crowded dance floor, jostling each other.

The two most common figures of speech are the simile and the metaphor. Both compare two things of different classes, often one abstract and the other concrete. A **simile** makes the comparison explicit and usually begins with *like* or *as*:

> Whenever we grow, we tend to feel it, as a young seed must feel the weight and inertia of the earth when it seeks to break out of its shell on its way to becoming a plant.
> —Alice Walker

A **metaphor** claims that the two things are identical, omitting such words as *like* and *as*:

> A school is a hopper into which children are heaved while they are young and tender; therein they are pressed into certain standard shapes and covered from head to heels with official rubber stamps.
> —H. L. Mencken

To be successful, figurative language must be fresh and unstrained, calling attention not to itself but to the writer's meaning. Be especially wary of mixed metaphors, which combine two or more incompatible figures:

Mixed   Various thorny problems that we try to sweep under the rug continue to bob up all the same.

Improved   Various thorny problems that we try to weed out continue to thrive all the same.

6   Trite expressions

Trite expressions, or **clichés,** are phrases so old and so often repeated that they have become stale. They include the following:

add insult to injury	let bygones be bygones
better late than never	live like a king [or queen]
easier said than done	moving experience
face the music	a needle in a haystack
few and far between	point with pride
green with envy	pride and joy
hard as a rock	ripe old age
heavy as lead	rude awakening
hit the nail on the head	shoulder the burden
hour of need	shoulder to cry on
in the final analysis	smart as a whip
ladder of success	sneaking suspicion

stand in awe	tough as nails
strong as an ox	tried and true
thin as a rail	wise as an owl

To edit clichés, listen to your writing for any expressions that you have heard or used before. You can also supplement your efforts with a style checker, which may include a cliché detector. When you find a cliché, substitute fresh words of your own or restate the idea in plain language.

19 Completeness

The most serious kind of incomplete sentence is the grammatical fragment (see **4** pp. 245–48). But sentences are also incomplete when they omit one or more words needed for clarity.

Grammar checkers A grammar checker will not flag most kinds of incomplete sentences discussed in this chapter.

19a Writing complete compounds

You may omit words from a compound construction when the omission will not confuse readers:

> Environmentalists have hopes for alternative fuels and [for] public transportation.

> Some cars will run on electricity and some [will run] on hydrogen.

Exercise

Such omissions are possible only when the words omitted are common to all the parts of a compound construction. When the parts differ in any way, all words must be included in all parts:

> One new car <u>gets</u> eighty miles per gallon; some old cars <u>get</u> as little as five miles per gallon. [One verb is singular, the other plural.]

> Environmentalists believe <u>in</u> and work <u>for</u> fuel conservation. [Idiom requires different prepositions with *believe* and *work*.]

Key term

compound construction Two or more elements (words, phrases, clauses) that are equal in importance and that function as a unit: *Rain fell, and streams overflowed* (clauses); *dogs and cats* (words).

---

mycomp**lab**

Visit *mycomplab.com* for the eText and for resources and exercises on complete sentences.

19b Adding needed words

In haste or carelessness, do not omit small words that are needed for clarity:

Incomplete Regular payroll deductions are a type painless savings. You hardly notice missing amounts, and after period of years the contributions can add a large total.

Revised Regular payroll deductions are a type of painless savings. You hardly notice the missing amounts, and after a period of years the contributions can add up to a large total.

Attentive proofreading is the only insurance against this kind of omission. *Proofread all your papers carefully.* See **1** pp. 33–34 for tips.

CULTURE LANGUAGE If your native language or dialect is not standard American English, you may have difficulty knowing when to use the English articles *a, an,* and *the.* For guidelines see **4** pp. 237–38.

20 Conciseness

Concise writing makes every word count. Conciseness is not the same as mere brevity: detail and originality should not be cut with needless words. Rather, the length of an expression should be appropriate to the thought.

You may find yourself writing wordily when you are unsure of your subject or when your thoughts are tangled. It's fine, even necessary, to grope while drafting. But you should straighten out your ideas and eliminate wordiness during revision and editing.

Grammar checkers A grammar checker will identify at least some wordy structures, such as repeated words, weak verbs, passive voice, and *there is* and *it is* constructions. But a checker can't identify all potentially wordy structures, nor can it tell you whether a structure is appropriate for your ideas.

CULTURE LANGUAGE As you'll see in this chapter's examples, wordiness is not a problem of incorrect grammar. A sentence may be perfectly grammatical but still contain unneeded words that make it unclear or awkward.

mycomplab

Visit *mycomplab.com* for the eText and for resources and exercises on conciseness.

Video
tutorial

Ways to achieve conciseness

Wordy (87 words)

The highly pressured <u>nature</u> of critical-care nursing is <u>due to the fact that</u> the patients have life-threatening illnesses. Critical-care nurses must <u>have possession of</u> steady nerves to <u>care for patients who are critically ill and very sick.</u> The nurses must also have posses- sion of interpersonal skills. They must also have medical skills. <u>It is considered by most health-care professionals</u> that these nurses are essential if <u>there is to be improvement of patients</u> who are now in critical care from that status to the status of intermediate care.

— Focus on subject and verb, and cut or shorten empty words and phrases.

— Avoid nouns made from verbs.

— Cut unneeded repetition.

— Combine sentences.

— Change passive voice to active voice.

— Revise *there is* construc- tions.

— Cut unneeded repeti- tion, and reduce clauses and phrases.

Concise (37 words)

Critical-care nursing is highly pressured because the patients have life- threatening illnesses. Critical-care nurses must possess steady nerves and interpersonal and medical skills. Most health-care professionals consider these nurses essential if patients are to improve to intermediate care.

20a Focusing on the subject and verb

Exercise

Using the subjects and verbs of your sentences for the key ac- tors and actions will reduce words and emphasize important ideas. (See pp. 141–43 for more on this topic.)

Wordy The <u>reason</u> why most of the country shifts to daylight time <u>is</u> that summer days are much longer than winter days.

Concise Most of the <u>country</u> <u>shifts</u> to daylight time because summer days are much longer than winter days.

Focusing on subjects and verbs will also help you avoid several other causes of wordiness discussed further on pp. 142–43:

Nouns made from verbs

Wordy The <u>occurrence</u> of the winter solstice, the shortest day of the year, <u>is</u> an event occurring about December 22.

Concise The winter <u>solstice</u>, the shortest day of the year, <u>occurs</u> about December 22.

Weak verbs

Wordy The earth's axis <u>has</u> a tilt as the planet <u>is</u> in orbit around the sun so that the northern and southern hemispheres <u>are</u> alter- nately in alignment toward the sun.

Concise   The earth's axis <u>tilts</u> as the planet <u>orbits</u> the sun so that the northern and southern hemispheres alternately <u>align</u> toward the sun.

Passive voice

Wordy   During its winter the northern hemisphere <u>is tilted</u> farthest away from the sun, so the nights <u>are made</u> longer and the days <u>are made</u> shorter.

Concise   During its winter the northern hemisphere <u>tilts</u> away from the sun, which <u>makes</u> the nights longer and the days shorter.

See also **4** pp. 213–14 on changing the passive voice to the active voice, as in the example above.

20b Cutting empty words

Empty words walk in place, gaining little or nothing in meaning. Many can be cut entirely. The following are just a few examples:

Exercise

all things considered	in a manner of speaking
as far as I'm concerned	in my opinion
for all intents and purposes	last but not least
for the most part	more or less

Other empty words can also be cut, usually along with some of the words around them:

area	element	kind	situation
aspect	factor	manner	thing
case	field	nature	type

Still others can be reduced from several words to a single word:

For	Substitute
at all times	always
at the present time	now, yet
because of the fact that	because
due to the fact that	because
for the purpose of	for
in order to	to
in the event that	if
in the final analysis	finally

Cutting or reducing such words and phrases will make your writing move faster and work harder.

Key terms

passive voice The verb form when the subject names the *receiver* of the verb's action: *The house <u>was destroyed</u> by the tornado.* (See **4** p. 213.)

active voice The verb form when the subject names the *performer* of the verb's action: *The tornado <u>destroyed</u> the house.* (See **4** p. 213.)

con
20e Conciseness

Wordy	In my opinion, the council's proposal to improve the city center is inadequate, all things considered.
Concise	The council's proposal to improve the city center is inadequate.

20c Cutting unneeded repetition

Video
tutorial

Unnecessary repetition weakens sentences:

Wordy	Many unskilled workers without training in a particular job are unemployed and do not have any work.
Concise	Many unskilled workers are unemployed.

Be especially alert to phrases that say the same thing twice. In the examples below, the unneeded words are underlined:

circle around	important [basic] essentials
consensus of opinion	puzzling in nature
cooperate together	repeat again
final completion	return again
frank and honest exchange	square [round] in shape
the future to come	surrounding circumstances

CULTURE LANGUAGE The preceding phrases are redundant because the main word already implies the underlined word or words. A dictionary will tell you what meanings a word implies. *Assassinate*, for instance, means "murder someone well known," so the following sentence is redundant: *Julius Caesar was assassinated and killed*.

20d Reducing modifiers

Modifiers can be expanded or contracted depending on the emphasis you want to achieve. When editing sentences, consider whether any modifiers can be reduced without loss of emphasis or clarity.

Wordy	The weight-loss industry faces new competition from lipolysis, which is a cosmetic procedure that is relatively noninvasive.
Concise	The weight-loss industry faces new competition from lipolysis, a relatively noninvasive cosmetic procedure.

20e Revising *there is* or *it is*

You can postpone the sentence subject with the words *there* and *it*: *There are three points made in the text. It was not fair that only*

Key term

modifier A word or word group that limits or qualifies another word: *slippery* road, cars *with tire chains*.
---

seniors could vote. These **expletive constructions** can be useful to emphasize the subject (as when introducing it for the first time) or to indicate a change in direction. But often they just add words and weaken sentences:

<table>
<tr><td>Wordy</td><td>There is a completely noninvasive laser treatment that makes people thinner by rupturing fat cells and releasing the fat into the spaces between cells. It is the expectation of some doctors that the procedure will replace liposuction.</td></tr>
<tr><td>Concise</td><td>A completely noninvasive laser treatment makes people thinner by rupturing fat cells and releasing the fat into the spaces between cells. Some doctors expect that the procedure will replace liposuction.</td></tr>
</table>

CULTURE LANGUAGE When you must use an expletive construction, be careful to include *there* or *it*. Only commands and some questions can begin with verbs.

20f Combining sentences

Video tutorial

Often the information in two or more sentences can be combined into one tight sentence.

<table>
<tr><td>Wordy</td><td>People who receive fat-releasing laser treatments can lose inches from their waists. They can also lose inches from their hips and thighs. They do not lose weight. The released fat remains in their bodies.</td></tr>
<tr><td>Concise</td><td>People who receive fat-releasing laser treatment can lose inches from their waists, hips, and thighs; but they do not lose weight because the released fat remains in their bodies.</td></tr>
</table>

20g Rewriting jargon

Jargon can refer to the special vocabulary of any discipline or profession (see p. 157). But it has also come to describe vague, inflated language that is overcomplicated, even incomprehensible. When it comes from government or business, we call it **bureaucratese.**

<table>
<tr><td>Jargon</td><td>The necessity for individuals to become separate entities in their own right may impel children to engage in open rebelliousness against parental authority or against sibling influence, with resultant bewilderment of those being rebelled against.</td></tr>
<tr><td>Translation</td><td>Children's natural desire to become themselves may make them rebel against bewildered parents or siblings.</td></tr>
</table>

PART 4

Sentence Parts and Patterns

PART 4

Sentence Parts and Patterns

176

Basic Grammar

Grammar describes how language works, and understanding it can help you create clear and accurate sentences. This section explains the kinds of words in sentences (Chapter 21) and how to build basic sentences (22), expand them (23), and classify them (24).

Grammar checkers A grammar checker can both offer assistance and cause problems as you compose sentences. Look for the cautions and tips for using a checker in this and the next part of this book. For more information about grammar checkers, see **1** pp. 32–33.

21 Parts of Speech

Video
tutorial

Exercise

All English words fall into eight groups, called **parts of speech**: nouns, pronouns, verbs, adjectives, adverbs, prepositions, conjunctions, and interjections.

Note In different sentences a word may serve as different parts of speech. For example:

The government sent <u>aid</u> to the city. [*Aid* is a noun.]
Governments <u>aid</u> citizens. [*Aid* is a verb.]

The *function* of a word in a sentence always determines its part of speech in that sentence.

21a Recognizing nouns

Video
tutorial

Nouns name. They may name a person (*Helen Mirren, Barack Obama, astronaut*), a thing (*chair, book, Mt. Rainier*), a quality (*pain, mystery, simplicity*), a place (*city, Washington, ocean, Red Sea*), or an idea (*reality, peace, success*).

The forms of nouns depend partly on where they fit in certain groups. As the following examples indicate, the same noun may appear in more than one group.

- A *common noun* names a general class of things and does not begin with a capital letter: *earthquake, citizen, earth, fortitude, army.*
- A *proper noun* names a specific person, place, or thing and begins with a capital letter: *Angelina Jolie, Washington Monument, El Paso, US Congress.*

mycomplab

Visit *mycomplab.com* for the eText and for resources and exercises on the parts of speech.

- A *count noun* names a thing considered countable in English. Most count nouns add -*s* or -*es* to distinguish between singular (one) and plural (more than one): *citizen, citizens; city, cities*. Some count nouns form irregular plurals: *woman, women; child, children.*

- A *noncount noun* names things or qualities that aren't considered countable in English: *earth, sugar, chaos, fortitude.* Noncount nouns do not form plurals.

- A *collective noun* is singular in form but names a group: *army, family, herd, US Congress.*

In addition, most nouns form the **possessive** by adding -'*s* to show ownership (*Nadia's books, citizen's rights*), source (*Auden's poems*), and some other relationships.

21b Recognizing pronouns

Most **pronouns** substitute for nouns and function in sentences as nouns do: *Susanne Ling enlisted in the Air Force when she graduated.* Pronouns fall into groups depending on their form or function:

- A *personal pronoun* refers to a specific individual or to individuals: *I, you, he, she, it, we,* and *they.*

- An *indefinite pronoun* does not refer to a specific noun: *anyone, everything, no one, somebody,* and so on. *No one came. Nothing moves. Everybody speaks.*

- A *relative pronoun* relates a group of words to a noun or another pronoun: *who, whoever, which, that. Everyone who attended received a prize. The book that won is a novel.*

- An *interrogative pronoun* introduces a question: *who, whom, whose, which, what. What song is that? Who will contribute?*

- A *demonstrative pronoun* identifies or points to a noun: *this, these, that, those,* and so on. *Those berries are ripe. This is the site.*

- An *intensive pronoun* emphasizes a noun or another pronoun: *myself, himself, itself, themselves,* and so on. *I myself asked that question. The price itself is in doubt.*

- A *reflexive pronoun* indicates that the sentence subject also receives the action of the verb: *myself, himself, itself, themselves,* and so on. *He perjured himself. They injured themselves.*

The personal pronouns *I, he, she, we,* and *they* and the relative pronouns *who* and *whoever* change form depending on their function in the sentence. (See Chapter 30.)

21c Recognizing verbs

Verbs express an action (*bring, change, grow, consider*), an occurrence (*become, happen, occur*), or a state of being (*be, seem, remain*).

1 Forms of verbs

Verbs have five distinctive forms. If the form can change as described here, the word is a verb:

- **The *plain form* is the dictionary form of the verb.** When the subject is a plural noun or the pronoun *I*, *we*, *you*, or *they*, the plain form indicates action that occurs in the present, occurs habitually, or is generally true.

  A few artists live in town today.
  They hold classes downtown.

- **The *-s form* ends in *-s* or *-es*.** When the subject is a singular noun, a pronoun such as *everyone*, or the personal pronoun *he*, *she*, or *it*, the *-s* form indicates action that occurs in the present, occurs habitually, or is generally true.

  The artist lives in town today.
  She holds classes downtown.

- **The *past-tense form* indicates that the action of the verb occurred before now.** It usually adds *-d* or *-ed* to the plain form, although most irregular verbs create it in different ways (see pp. 193–95).

  Many artists lived in town before this year.
  They held classes downtown. [Irregular verb.]

- **The *past participle* is usually the same as the past-tense form, except in most irregular verbs.** It combines with forms of *have* or *be* (*has climbed*, *was created*), or by itself it modifies nouns and pronouns (*the sliced apples*).

  Artists have lived in town for decades.
  They have held classes downtown. [Irregular verb.]

- **The *present participle* adds *-ing* to the verb's plain form.** It combines with forms of *be* (*is buying*), modifies nouns and pronouns (*the boiling water*), or functions as a noun (*Running exhausts me*).

  A few artists are living in town today.
  They are holding classes downtown.

The verb *be* has eight forms rather than the five forms of most other verbs:

Plain form	be		
Present participle	being		
Past participle	been		
	I	*he, she, it*	*we, you, they*
Present tense	am	is	are
Past tense	was	was	were

2 | Helping verbs

Some verb forms combine with **helping verbs** to indicate time, possibility, obligation, necessity, and other kinds of meaning: *can run*, *was sleeping*, *had been* working. In these **verb phrases** *run*, *sleeping*, and *working* are **main verbs**—they carry the principal meaning.

Verb phrase

Helping   *Main*

Artists <u>can</u>   <u>train</u> others to draw.

The techniques <u>have</u>   <u>changed</u> little.

The most common helping verbs are listed in the box below. See pp. 198–202 for more on helping verbs.

Common helping verbs

Forms of *be*: be, am, is, are, was, were, been, being
Forms of *have*: have, has, had, having
Forms of *do*: do, does, did

be able to	could	may	ought to	used to
be supposed to	had better	might	shall	will
can	have to	must	should	would

21d | Recognizing adjectives and adverbs

Adjectives describe or modify nouns and pronouns. They specify which one, what quality, or how many.

old   city   generous   one   two   pears

adjective   noun   adjective   pronoun   adjective   noun

Adverbs describe or modify verbs, adjectives, other adverbs, and whole groups of words. They specify when, where, how, and to what extent.

nearly destroyed   too quickly

adverb   verb   adverb   adverb

very   generous   Unfortunately, taxes will rise.

adverb   adjective   adverb   word group

An *-ly* ending often signals an adverb, but not always: *friendly* is an adjective; *never* and *not* are adverbs. The only way to tell whether a word is an adjective or an adverb is to determine what it modifies.

Adjectives and adverbs appear in three forms: **positive** (*green, angrily*), **comparative** (*greener, more angrily*), and **superlative** (*greenest, most angrily*).

See Chapter 33 for more on adjectives and adverbs.

21e Recognizing connecting words: Prepositions and conjunctions

Connecting words are mostly small words that link parts of sentences. They never change form.

1 Prepositions

Prepositions form nouns or pronouns (plus any modifiers) into word groups called **prepositional phrases**: *about love, down the stairs*. These phrases usually serve as modifiers in sentences, as in *The plants trailed down the stairs*. (See p. 189.)

Common prepositions

about	before	except for	of	throughout
above	behind	excepting	off	till
according to	below	for	on	to
across	beneath	from	onto	toward
after	beside	in	on top of	under
against	between	in addition to	out	underneath
along	beyond	inside	out of	unlike
along with	by	inside of	outside	until
among	concerning	in spite of	over	up
around	despite	instead of	past	upon
as	down	into	regarding	up to
aside from	due to	like	round	with
at	during	near	since	within
because of	except	next to	through	without

CULTURE LANGUAGE The meanings and uses of English prepositions can be difficult to master. See **3** pp. 165–66 for a discussion of prepositions in idioms. See pp. 204–05 for two-word verbs that include prepositions, such as *look after* and *look up*.

2 Subordinating conjunctions

Subordinating conjunctions form sentences into word groups called **subordinate clauses,** such as *when the meeting ended* or *that she knew*. These clauses serve as parts of sentences: *Everyone was relieved when the meeting ended. She said that she knew.* (See p. 191.)

Common subordinating conjunctions

after	even if	rather than	until
although	even though	since	when
as	if	so that	whenever
as if	if only	than	where
as long as	in order that	that	whereas
as though	now that	though	wherever
because	once	till	whether
before	provided	unless	while

CULTURE LANGUAGE Learning the meanings of subordinating conjunctions can help you to express your ideas clearly. Note that each one conveys its meaning on its own. It does not need help from another function word, such as the coordinating conjunction *and, but, for,* or *so:*

Faulty Even though the parents are illiterate, but their children may read well. [*Even though* and *but* have the same meaning, so both are not needed.]

Revised Even though the parents are illiterate, their children may read well.

3 Coordinating and correlative conjunctions

Coordinating and correlative conjunctions connect words or word groups of the same kind, such as nouns or sentences.

Coordinating conjunctions consist of a single word:

Coordinating conjunctions

and	nor	for	yet
but	or	so	

Biofeedback or simple relaxation can relieve headaches.
Relaxation works well, and it is inexpensive.

Correlative conjunctions are combinations of coordinating conjunctions and other words:

Common correlative conjunctions

both . . . and	neither . . . nor
not only . . . but also	whether . . . or
not . . . but	as . . . as
either . . . or	

Both biofeedback and relaxation can relieve headaches.

The headache sufferer learns not only to recognize the causes of head-aches but also to control those causes.

21f Recognizing interjections

Interjections express feeling or command attention. They are rarely used in academic or business writing.

Oh, the meeting went fine.
They won seven thousand dollars! Wow!

22 The Sentence

The **sentence** is the basic unit of expression. It is grammatically complete and independent: it does not serve as an adjective, adverb, or other single part of speech.

22a Recognizing subjects and predicates

Video tutorial

Most sentences make statements. First the **subject** names something; then the **predicate** makes an assertion about the subject or describes an action by the subject.

Subject	Predicate
Art	thrives.

Exercise

The **simple subject** consists of one or more nouns or pronouns, whereas the **complete subject** also includes any modifiers. The **simple predicate** consists of one or more verbs, whereas the **complete predicate** adds any words needed to complete the meaning of the verb plus any modifiers.

Sometimes, as in the short example *Art thrives,* the simple and complete subject and predicate are the same. More often, they are different:

Subject	Predicate
complete / simple	complete / simple
Some contemporary art	stirs controversy.
complete / simple	complete / simple
Congress and the media	discuss and dispute its value.

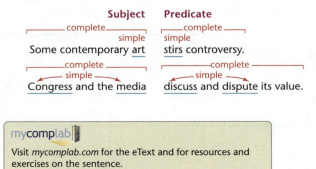

mycomplab

Visit *mycomplab.com* for the eText and for resources and exercises on the sentence.

In the last example on the facing page, the simple subject and simple predicate are both **compound**: in each, two words joined by a coordinating conjunction (*and*) serve the same function.

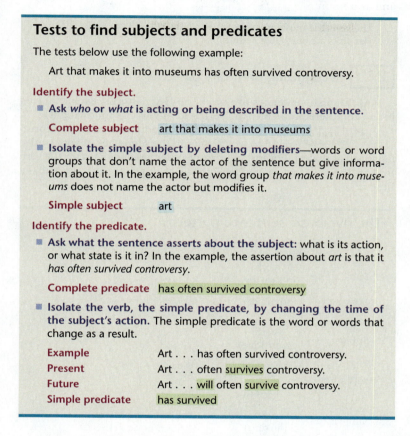

Tests to find subjects and predicates

The tests below use the following example:

Art that makes it into museums has often survived controversy.

Identify the subject.

■ Ask *who* or *what* is acting or being described in the sentence.

Complete subject art that makes it into museums

■ **Isolate the simple subject by deleting modifiers**—words or word groups that don't name the actor of the sentence but give information about it. In the example, the word group *that makes it into museums* does not name the actor but modifies it.

Simple subject art

Identify the predicate.

■ **Ask what the sentence asserts about the subject:** what is its action, or what state is it in? In the example, the assertion about *art* is that it *has often survived controversy.*

Complete predicate has often survived controversy

■ **Isolate the verb, the simple predicate, by changing the time of the subject's action.** The simple predicate is the word or words that change as a result.

Example	Art . . . has often survived controversy.
Present	Art . . . often survives controversy.
Future	Art . . . will often survive controversy.
Simple predicate	has survived

Note If a sentence contains a word group such as *that makes it into museums* or *because viewers agree about its quality,* you may be tempted to mark the subject and verb in the word group as the subject and verb of the sentence. But these word groups are subordinate clauses, made into modifiers by the words they begin with: *that* and *because.* See pp. 191–92 for more on subordinate clauses.

CULTURE LANGUAGE The subject of a sentence in standard American English may be a noun (*art*) or a pronoun that refers to the noun (*it*), but not both. (See p. 255.)

Faulty	Art it can stir controversy.
Revised	Art can stir controversy.
Revised	It can stir controversy.

When identifying the subject and the predicate of a sentence, be aware that some English words can serve as both nouns and verbs. For example, *visits* in the following sentences functions as a verb and as a noun:

> She visits the museum every Saturday. [Verb.]
> Her visits are enjoyable. [Noun.]

22b Recognizing predicate patterns

✳ Exercise

All English sentences are based on five patterns, each differing in the complete predicate (the verb and any words following it).

CULTURE LANGUAGE Word order in English sentences may not correspond to word order in the sentences of your native language or dialect. For instance, some other languages prefer the verb first in the sentence, whereas English strongly prefers the subject first.

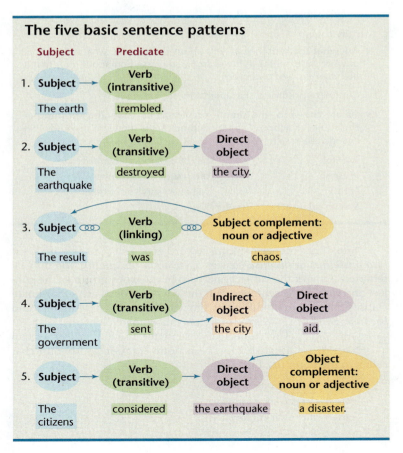

The five basic sentence patterns

Subject | Predicate

1. Subject → Verb (intransitive)
   The earth | trembled.

2. Subject → Verb (transitive) → Direct object
   The earthquake | destroyed | the city.

3. Subject ⚬⚬ Verb (linking) ⚬⚬ Subject complement: noun or adjective
   The result | was | chaos.

4. Subject → Verb (transitive) | Indirect object → Direct object
   The government | sent | the city | aid.

5. Subject → Verb (transitive) → Direct object | Object complement: noun or adjective
   The citizens | considered | the earthquake | a disaster.

Pattern 1: The earth trembled.

In the simplest pattern the predicate consists only of an **intransitive verb,** a verb that does not require a following word to complete its meaning.

Subject	Predicate
	Intransitive verb
The earth	trembled.
The hospital	may close.

Pattern 2: The earthquake destroyed the city.

In pattern 2 the verb is followed by a **direct object**, a noun or pronoun that identifies who or what receives the action of the verb. A verb that requires a direct object to complete its meaning is called **transitive.**

Subject	Predicate	
	Transitive verb	*Direct object*
The earthquake	destroyed	the city.
Education	opens	doors.

CULTURE LANGUAGE   Only transitive verbs may be used in the passive voice: *The city was destroyed by the earthquake.* Your dictionary says whether a verb is transitive or intransitive, often with an abbreviation such as *tr.* or *intr.* Some verbs (*begin, learn, read, write,* and others) can be both transitive and intransitive.

Pattern 3: The result was chaos.

In pattern 3 the verb is followed by a **subject complement,** a word that renames or describes the subject. A verb in this pattern is called a **linking verb** because it links its subject to the description following. The linking verbs include *be, seem, appear, become, grow, remain, stay, prove, feel, look, smell, sound,* and *taste.* Subject complements are usually nouns or adjectives.

Subject	Predicate	
	Linking verb	*Subject complement*
The result	was	chaos. [Noun.]
The man	became	an accountant. [Noun.]
The car	seems	expensive. [Adjective.]

Pattern 4: The government sent the city aid.

In pattern 4 the verb is followed by a direct object and an **indirect object,** a word identifying to or for whom the action of the

---

Key term

passive voice The verb form when the subject names the receiver of the verb's action: *The door was opened.* (See p. 213.)

verb is performed. The direct object and indirect object refer to different things, people, or places.

Subject	Predicate		
	Transitive verb	*Indirect object*	*Direct object*
The government	sent	the city	aid.
One company	offered	its employees	bonuses.

A number of verbs can take indirect objects, including *send* and *offer* (preceding examples) and *allow, bring, buy, deny, find, get, give, leave, make, pay, read, sell, show, teach,* and *write.*

 With some verbs that express action done to or for someone, the indirect object must be turned into a phrase beginning with *to* or *for*. In addition, the phrase must come after the direct object. The verbs that require these changes include *admit, announce, demonstrate, explain, introduce, mention, prove, recommend, say,* and *suggest.*

	indirect object direct object
Faulty	The manual explains <u>workers</u> the new <u>procedure</u>.
	direct object *to* phrase
Revised	The manual explains the new <u>procedure</u> <u>to workers</u>.

Pattern 5: The citizens considered the earthquake a disaster.

In pattern 5 the verb is followed by a direct object and an **object complement**, a word that renames or describes the direct object. Object complements may be nouns or adjectives.

Subject	Predicate		
	Transitive verb	*Direct object*	*Object complement*
The citizens	considered	the earthquake	a disaster.
Success	makes	some people	nervous.

23   Phrases and Subordinate Clauses

Most sentences contain word groups that serve as adjectives, adverbs, or nouns and thus cannot stand alone as sentences.

- A *phrase* lacks either a subject or a predicate or both: *fearing an accident*; *in a panic.*
- A *subordinate clause* contains a subject and a predicate but begins with a subordinating word: *when prices rise*; *whoever laughs.*

23a Recognizing phrases

1 Prepositional phrases

A **prepositional phrase** consists of a preposition plus a noun, a pronoun, or a word group serving as a noun, called the **object of the preposition.** A list of prepositions appears on p. 182.

(see p. 182)

🎙️ Podcast

Preposition	Object
of	spaghetti
on	the surface
with	great satisfaction
upon	entering the room
from	where you are standing

Prepositional phrases usually function as adjectives or adverbs.

Exercise

Life on a raft was an opportunity for adventure.
  adjective phrase   *adjective phrase*

Huck Finn rode the raft by choice.
                    adverb phrase

With his companion, Jim, Huck met many types of people.
    adverb phrase   *adjective phrase*

2 Verbal phrases

Certain forms of verbs, called **verbals,** can serve as modifiers or nouns. Often these verbals appear with their own modifiers and objects in **verbal phrases.**

🌼 Exercise

Note Verbals cannot serve as verbs in sentences. *The sun rises over the dump* is a sentence; *The sun rising over the dump* is a sentence fragment. (See p. 246.)

Participial phrases

Present participles end in *-ing*: *living, walking.* **Past participles** usually end in *-d* or *-ed*: *lived, walked.* **Participial phrases** are made from participles plus modifiers and objects. Participles and participial phrases serve as adjectives.

Strolling shoppers fill the malls.
adjective

They make selections determined by personal taste.
                      adjective phrase

Note With irregular verbs, the past participle may have a different ending—for instance, *hidden funds.* (See pp. 193–95.)

CULTURE LANGUAGE The present and past participles of verbs that express feelings have different meanings. The present participle modifies the thing that causes the feeling: *It was a* *boring lecture*. The past participle modifies the thing that experiences the feeling: *The bored students slept*. See pp. 235–36.

Gerund phrases

A **gerund** is the *-ing* form of a verb when it serves as a noun. Gerunds and gerund phrases can do whatever nouns can do.

sentence
┌── subject ──┐
Shopping satisfies personal needs.

noun
┌── object of preposition ──┐
Malls are good at creating such needs.
noun phrase

Infinitive phrases

An **infinitive** is the plain form of a verb plus *to*: *to hide*. Infinitives and infinitive phrases serve as adjectives, adverbs, or nouns.

sentence
┌──── subject ────┐   ┌──── subject complement ────┐
To design a mall is to create an artificial environment.
noun phrase   noun phrase

Malls are designed to make shoppers feel safe.
adverb phrase

The environment supports the impulse to shop.
adjective

CULTURE LANGUAGE Infinitives and gerunds may follow some verbs and not others and may differ in meaning after a verb: *The cowboy stopped to sing* (he stopped to do the activity). *The cowboy stopped singing* (he finished the activity). (See pp. 202–04.)

3 Absolute phrases

An **absolute phrase** consists of a noun or pronoun and a participle, plus any modifiers. It modifies the entire rest of the sentence it appears in.

┌──── absolute phrase ────┐
Their own place established, many ethnic groups are making way for new arrivals.

Unlike a participial phrase (p. 189), an absolute phrase always contains a noun that serves as a subject.

participial
┌── phrase ──┐
Learning English, many immigrants discover American culture.

┌──── absolute phrase ────┐
Immigrants having learned English, their opportunities widen.

4 Appositive phrases

An **appositive** is usually a noun that renames another noun. An appositive phrase includes modifiers as well.

Exercise

~appositive phrase¬
Bizen ware, a dark stoneware, is produced in Japan.

Appositives and appositive phrases sometimes begin with *that is, such as, for example,* or *in other words.*

————— appositive phrase —————
Bizen ware is used in the Japanese tea ceremony, that is, the Zen Buddhist observance that links meditation and art.

23b Recognizing subordinate clauses

A **clause** is any group of words that contains both a subject and a predicate. There are two kinds of clauses, and the distinction between them is important.

- A *main clause* makes a complete statement and can stand alone as a sentence: *The sky darkened.*
- A *subordinate clause* is just like a main clause *except* that it begins with a subordinating word: *when the sky darkened*; *whoever calls.* The subordinating word reduces the clause from a complete statement to a single part of speech: an adjective, adverb, or noun. Use subordinate clauses to support the ideas in main clauses, as described in **3** pp. 147–48.

Exercise

Note A subordinate clause punctuated as a sentence is a sentence fragment. (See p. 247.)

Adjective clauses

An **adjective clause** modifies a noun or pronoun. It usually begins with the relative pronoun *who, whom, whose, which,* or *that.* The relative pronoun is the subject or object of the clause it begins. The clause ordinarily falls immediately after the word it modifies.

~adjective clause¬
Parents who cannot read may have bad memories of school.

————— adjective clause —————
One school, which is open year-round, helps parents learn to read.

Adverb clauses

An **adverb clause** modifies a verb, an adjective, another adverb, or a whole word group. It always begins with a subordinating conjunction, such as *although, because, if,* or *when* (see p. 183 for a list).

————— adverb clause —————
The school began teaching parents when adult illiteracy gained national attention.

————— adverb clause ————— ~main clause—
Because it was directed at people who could not read, advertising had to be inventive.

Noun clauses

A **noun clause** replaces a noun in a sentence and serves as a subject, object, or complement. It begins with *that, what, whatever, who, whom, whoever, whomever, when, where, whether, why,* or *how*.

└─────── sentence subject ───────┘
Whether the program would succeed depended on door-to-door advertising. noun clause

└─────── object of verb ───────┘
Teachers explained in person how the program would work.
noun clause

24 Sentence Types

Video tutorial

The four basic sentence structures vary in the number of main and subordinate clauses. Each structure gives different emphasis to the main and supporting information in a sentence.

Exercise

24a Recognizing simple sentences

A **simple sentence** consists of a single main clause and no subordinate clause.

┌─────── main clause ───────┐
Last summer was unusually hot.

┌──────────────── main clause ────────────────┐
The summer made many farmers leave the area for good or reduced them to bare existence.

24b Recognizing compound sentences

A **compound sentence** consists of two or more main clauses and no subordinate clause.

┌── main clause──┐ ┌──── main clause ────┐
Last July was hot, but August was even hotter.

┌──────── main clause ────────┐ ┌──────── main clause ────────┐
The hot sun scorched the earth, and the lack of rain killed many crops.

24c Recognizing complex sentences

A **complex sentence** consists of one main clause and one or more subordinate clauses.

mycomplab

Visit *mycomplab.com* for the eText and for resources and exercises on sentence types.

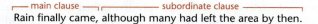

— main clause — subordinate clause —
Rain finally came, although many had left the area by then.

main clause — subordinate clause —
Those who remained were able to start anew because the government
subordinate clause

came to their aid.

24d Recognizing compound-complex sentences

A **compound-complex sentence** has the characteristics of both the compound sentence (two or more main clauses) and the complex sentence (at least one subordinate clause).

— subordinate clause — main clause —
When government aid finally came, many people had already been reduced
— main clause —
to poverty and others had been forced to move.

──────Verbs──────

Verbs express actions, conditions, and states of being. The basic uses and forms of verbs are described on pp. 179–81. This section explains and solves the most common problems with verbs' forms (Chapter 25), tenses (26), mood (27), and voice (28) and shows how to make verbs match their subjects (29).

25 Verb Forms

25a Use the correct forms of *sing/sang/sung* and other irregular verbs.

Most verbs are **regular**: they form their past tense and past participle by adding *-d* or *-ed* to the plain form.

Video tutorial

Plain form	Past tense	Past participle
live	lived	lived
act	acted	acted

mycomplab

Visit *mycomplab.com* for the eText and for resources and exercises on verb forms.

Video
tutorial

Exercise

About two hundred English verbs are **irregular**: they form their past tense and past participle in some irregular way. Check a dictionary under the verb's plain form if you have any doubt about its other forms. If the verb is irregular, the dictionary will list the plain form, the past tense, and the past participle in that order (*go, went, gone*). If the dictionary gives only two forms (as in *think, thought*), then the past tense and the past participle are the same.

Common irregular verbs

Plain form	Past tense	Past participle
be	was, were	been
become	became	become
begin	began	begun
bid	bid	bid
bite	bit	bitten, bit
blow	blew	blown
break	broke	broken
bring	brought	brought
burst	burst	burst
buy	bought	bought
catch	caught	caught
choose	chose	chosen
come	came	come
cut	cut	cut
dive	dived, dove	dived
do	did	done
dream	dreamed, dreamt	dreamed, dreamt
drink	drank	drunk
drive	drove	driven
eat	ate	eaten
fall	fell	fallen
find	found	found
flee	fled	fled
fly	flew	flown
forget	forgot	forgotten, forgot
freeze	froze	frozen
get	got	got, gotten
give	gave	given
go	went	gone
grow	grew	grown

Key terms

plain form The dictionary form of the verb: *I walk. You forget*. (See p. 180.)

past-tense form The verb form indicating action that occurred in the past: *I walked. You forgot*. (See p. 180.)

past participle The verb form used with *have, has,* or *had*: *I have walked*. It may serve as a modifier: *It is a forgotten book*. (See p. 180.)

Plain form	Past tense	Past participle
hang (suspend)	hung	hung
have	had	had
hear	heard	heard
hide	hid	hidden
hold	held	held
keep	kept	kept
know	knew	known
lead	led	led
leave	left	left
lend	lent	lent
let	let	let
lose	lost	lost
pay	paid	paid
ride	rode	ridden
ring	rang	rung
run	ran	run
say	said	said
see	saw	seen
shake	shook	shaken
sing	sang, sung	sung
sink	sank, sunk	sunk
sleep	slept	slept
slide	slid	slid
speak	spoke	spoken
spring	sprang, sprung	sprung
stand	stood	stood
steal	stole	stolen
swim	swam	swum
swing	swung	swung
take	took	taken
tear	tore	torn
throw	threw	thrown
wear	wore	worn
write	wrote	written

Grammar checkers A grammar checker may not flag incorrect forms of irregular verbs. For example, a checker flagged *The runner stealed second base* (*stole* is correct) but not *The runner had steal second base* (*stolen* is correct). When in doubt about the forms of irregular verbs, refer to the preceding list or consult a dictionary.

CULTURE LANGUAGE Some English dialects use verb forms that differ from those of standard American English: for instance, *drug* for *dragged*, *growed* for *grew*, *come* for *came*, or *went* for *gone*. In situations requiring standard American English, use the forms in the list here or in a dictionary.

Faulty   They have went to the movies.
Revised   They have gone to the movies.

25b Distinguish between *sit* and *set, lie* and *lay,* and *rise* and *raise.*

Podcast

The forms of *sit* and *set, lie* and *lay,* and *rise* and *raise* are easy to confuse.

Plain form	Past tense	Past participle
sit	sat	sat
set	set	set
lie	lay	lain
lay	laid	laid
rise	rose	risen
raise	raised	raised

In each of these confusing pairs, one verb is intransitive (it does not take an object) and one is transitive (it does take an object). (See p. 187 for more on this distinction.)

Intransitive

The patients lie in their beds. [*Lie* means "recline" and takes no object.]

Visitors sit with them. [*Sit* means "be seated" or "be located" and takes no object.]

Patients' temperatures rise. [*Rise* means "increase" or "get up" and takes no object.]

Transitive

Orderlies lay the dinner trays on tables. [*Lay* means "place" and takes an object, here *trays.*]

Orderlies set the trays down. [*Set* means "place" and takes an object, here *trays.*]

Nursing aides raise the shades. [*Raise* means "lift" or "bring up" and takes an object, here *shades.*]

25c Use the *-s* and *-ed* forms of the verb when they are required.

CULTURE LANGUAGE

Exercise

Speakers of some English dialects and nonnative speakers of English sometimes omit the *-s* and *-ed* verb endings when they are required in standard American English.

Note If you tend to omit these endings in writing, practice pronouncing them when speaking or when reading correct verbs aloud, such as those in the examples here. The spoken practice can help you remember the endings in writing.

Grammar checkers A grammar checker will flag many omitted *-s* and *-ed* endings from verbs, as in *he ask* and *was ask.* But it will miss many omissions, too.

1 **Required -s ending**

Use the -s form of a verb when *both* of these situations hold:

- **The subject is a singular noun (*woman*), an indefinite pronoun (*everyone*), or *he, she,* or *it.*** These subjects are **third person,** used when someone or something is being spoken about.
- **The verb's action occurs in the present.**

> The letter asks [not ask] for a quick response.
> Delay costs [not cost] money.
> It wastes [not waste] time.
> Everyone hopes [not hope] for a good outcome.

Be especially careful with the -s forms of *be* (*is*), *have* (*has*), and *do* (*does, doesn't*). These forms should always be used to indicate present time with third-person singular subjects.

> The company is [not be] late in responding.
> It has [not have] problems.
> It doesn't [not don't] have the needed data.
> The contract does [not do] depend on the response.

In addition, *be* has the -s form *was* in the past tense with *I* and third-person singular subjects:

> The company was [not were] in trouble before.

Except for the past tense *I was,* the pronouns *I* and *you* and all plural subjects do *not* take the -s form of verbs:

> I am [not is] a student.
> You are [not is] also a student.
> They are [not is] students, too.

2 **Required -ed or -d ending**

The -ed or -d verb form is required in *any* of these situations:

- **The verb's action occurred in the past:**

> The company asked [not ask] for more time.

- **The verb form functions as a modifier:**

> The data concerned [not concern] should be retrievable.

- **The verb form combines with a form of *be* or *have*:**

> The company is supposed [not suppose] to be the best.
> It has developed [not develop] an excellent reputation.

Watch especially for a needed -ed or -d ending when it isn't pronounced clearly in speech, as in *asked, discussed, mixed, supposed, walked,* and *used.*

Use helping verbs with main verbs appropriately.

✳
Exercise

Helping verbs combine with main verbs in verb phrases: *The line should have been cut. Who was calling?*

Grammar checkers   A grammar checker often spots omitted helping verbs and incorrect main verbs with helping verbs, but sometimes it does not. A checker flagged *Many been fortunate* and *She working* but overlooked other errors, such as *The conference will be occurred.*

1   Required helping verbs

Standard American English requires helping verbs in certain situations:

■ **The main verb ends in *-ing*:**

Researchers are conducting fieldwork all over the world. [Not Researchers conducting. . . .]

■ **The main verb is *been* or *be*:**

Many have been fortunate in their discoveries. [Not Many been. . . .]
Some could be real-life Indiana Joneses. [Not Some be. . . .]

■ **The main verb is a past participle,** such as *talked, thrown,* or *begun.*

Their discoveries were covered in newspapers and magazines. [Not Their discoveries covered. . . .]

The researchers have given interviews on TV. [Not The researchers given. . . .]

The omission of a helping verb may create an incomplete sentence, or **sentence fragment**, because a present participle (*conducting*), an irregular past participle (*been*), or the plain form *be* cannot stand alone as the only verb in a sentence (see p. 246). To work as sentence verbs, these verb forms need helping verbs.

2   Combination of helping verb + main verb

Helping verbs and main verbs combine into verb phrases in specific ways.

┌─ **Key terms** ───

helping verb A word such as *can, may, be, have,* or *do* that forms a verb phrase with another verb to show time, permission, and other meanings. (See p. 181.)

main verb The verb that carries the principal meaning in a verb phrase: *has walked, could be happening.* (See p. 181.)

verb phrase A helping verb plus a main verb: *will be singing, would speak.* (See p. 181.)

└───

Note The main verb in a verb phrase (the one carrying the main meaning) does not change to show a change in subject or time: *she has <u>sung</u>, you had <u>sung</u>.* Only the helping verb may change.

Form of *be* + present participle

The **progressive tenses** indicate action in progress. Create them with *be, am, is, are, was, were,* or *been* followed by the main verb's present participle:

She is <u>working</u> on a new book.

Be and *been* always require additional helping verbs to form progressive tenses:

can	might	should			have	
could	must	will	}	be working	has	} been working
may	shall	would			had	

When forming the progressive tenses, be sure to use the *-ing* form of the main verb.

Faulty   Her ideas are <u>grow</u> more complex. She is <u>developed</u> a new approach to ethics.

Revised   Her ideas are <u>growing</u> more complex. She is <u>developing</u> a new approach to ethics.

Form of *be* + past participle

The **passive voice** of the verb indicates that the subject *receives* the action of the verb. Create the passive voice with a form of *be* (*be, am, is, are, was, were, being,* or *been*) followed by the main verb's past participle:

Her latest book <u>was completed</u> in four months.

Be, being, and *been* always require additional helping verbs to form the passive voice:

have			am	was		
has	}	been completed	is	were	}	being completed
had			are			

will <u>be</u> completed

Key terms

present participle The *-ing* form of a verb: *flying, playing.* (See p. 180.)

progressive tenses Verb tenses expressing action in progress—for instance, *I am flying. I was flying. I will be flying.* (See p. 208.)

past participle The *-d* or *-ed* form of a regular verb: *hedged, walked.* Most irregular verbs have distinctive past participles: *eaten, swum.* (See p. 180.)

passive voice The verb form when the subject names the receiver of the verb's action: *An essay <u>was written</u> by every student.* (See p. 213.)

Always use the main verb's past participle for the passive voice:

Faulty   Her next book will be <u>publish</u> soon.
Revised   Her next book will be <u>published</u> soon.

Note Only transitive verbs may form the passive voice:

Faulty   A philosophy conference <u>will be occurred</u> in the same week.
[*Occur* is not a transitive verb.]
Revised   A philosophy conference <u>will occur</u> in the same week.

See pp. 213–14 for advice on when to use and when to avoid the passive voice.

Forms of *have*

Four forms of *have* serve as helping verbs: *have, has, had, having.* One of these forms plus the main verb's past participle creates one of the **perfect tenses,** those expressing action completed before another specific time or action:

Some students <u>have complained</u> about the laboratory.
Others <u>had complained</u> before.

Will and other helping verbs sometimes accompany forms of *have* in the perfect tenses:

Several more students <u>will have complained</u> by the end of the week.

Forms of *do*

Do, does, and *did* have three uses as helping verbs, always with the plain form of the main verb:

- **To pose a question:** *How <u>did</u> the trial <u>end</u>?*
- **To emphasize the main verb:** *It <u>did end</u> eventually.*
- **To negate the main verb, along with *not* or *never*:** *The judge <u>did not withdraw</u>.*

Be sure to use the main verb's plain form with any form of *do*:

Faulty   The judge did <u>remained</u> in court.
Revised   The judge did <u>remain</u> in court.

Modals

The modal helping verbs include *can, may, should, would,* and several two- and three-word combinations, such as *have to* and *be*

Key terms

transitive verb A verb that requires an object to complete its meaning: *Everyone <u>wrote</u> an essay (essay* is the object of *wrote).* (See p. 187.)

perfect tenses Verb tenses expressing an action completed before another specific time or action: *We have eaten. We had eaten. We will have eaten.* (See p. 207.)

able to. (See p. 181 for a list of helping verbs.) Use the plain form of the main verb with a modal unless the modal combines with another helping verb (usually *have*):

Faulty   The equipment <u>can detects</u> small vibrations. It <u>should have detect</u> the change.

Revised   The equipment <u>can detect</u> small vibrations. It <u>should have detected</u> the change.

Modals convey various meanings, with these being most common:

■ **Ability:** *can, could, be able to*

The equipment <u>can detect</u> small vibrations. [Present.]

The equipment <u>could detect</u> small vibrations. [Past.]

The equipment <u>is able to detect</u> small vibrations. [Present. Past: *was able to.* Future: *will be able to.*]

■ **Possibility:** *could, may, might; could/may/might have* + past participle

The equipment <u>could fail</u>. [Present.]
The equipment <u>may fail</u>. [Present or future.]
The equipment <u>might fail</u>. [Present or future.]
The equipment <u>may have failed</u>. [Past.]

■ **Necessity or obligation:** *must, have to, be supposed to*

The lab <u>must purchase</u> a backup. [Present or future.]
The lab <u>has to purchase</u> a backup. [Present or future. Past: *had to.*]
The lab <u>will have to purchase</u> a backup. [Future.]
The lab <u>is supposed to purchase</u> a backup. [Present. Past: *was supposed to.*]

■ **Permission:** *may, can, could*

The lab <u>may spend</u> the money. [Present or future.]
The lab <u>can spend</u> the money. [Present or future.]
The lab <u>could spend</u> the money. [Present or future, more tentative.]
The lab <u>could have spent</u> the money. [Past.]

■ **Intention:** *will, shall, would*

The lab <u>will spend</u> the money. [Future.]

Shall we <u>offer</u> advice? [Future. Use *shall* for questions requesting opinion or consent.]

We <u>would have offered</u> advice. [Past.]

■ **Request:** *could, can, would*

<u>Could</u> [or <u>Can</u> or <u>Would</u>] you please <u>obtain</u> a bid? [Present or future.]

■ **Advisability:** *should, had better, ought to; should have* + past participle

You should obtain three bids. [Present or future.]
You had better obtain three bids. [Present or future.]
You ought to obtain three bids. [Present or future.]
You should have obtained three bids. [Past.]

- **Past habit:** *would, used to*

In years past we would obtain five bids.
We used to obtain five bids.

25e Use a gerund or an infinitive after a verb as appropriate.

Nonnative speakers of English may find it difficult to see whether a gerund or an infinitive should follow a verb. Gerunds and infinitives may follow certain verbs but not others. Sometimes the use of a gerund or an infinitive with the same verb changes the meaning.

Grammar checkers A grammar checker will spot some but not all errors in matching gerunds or infinitives with verbs. For example, a checker failed to flag *I practice to swim* and *I promise helping out*. Use the lists given here and a dictionary of English as a second language to determine whether an infinitive or a gerund is appropriate. (See **3** p. 163 for a list of ESL dictionaries.)

1 Either gerund or infinitive

A gerund or an infinitive may come after the following verbs with no significant difference in meaning.

begin	continue	intend	prefer
can't bear	hate	like	start
can't stand	hesitate	love	

The pump began working.
The pump began to work.

2 Meaning change with gerund or infinitive

With four verbs, a gerund has quite a different meaning from an infinitive:

forget	stop
remember	try

The engineer stopped eating. [He no longer ate.]
The engineer stopped to eat. [He stopped in order to eat.]

Key terms

gerund The *-ing* form of the verb used as a noun: *Smoking* is unhealthful. (See p. 190.)

infinitive The plain form of the verb usually preceded by *to: to smoke.* An infinitive may serve as an adjective, adverb, or noun. (See p. 190.)

3 Gerund, not infinitive

Do not use an infinitive after these verbs:

admit	discuss	mind	recollect
adore	dislike	miss	resent
appreciate	enjoy	postpone	resist
avoid	escape	practice	risk
consider	finish	put off	suggest
deny	imagine	quit	tolerate
detest	keep	recall	understand

Faulty   He finished <u>to eat</u> lunch.
Revised   He finished <u>eating</u> lunch.

4 Infinitive, not gerund

Do not use a gerund after these verbs:

agree	claim	manage	promise
appear	consent	mean	refuse
arrange	decide	offer	say
ask	expect	plan	wait
assent	have	prepare	want
beg	hope	pretend	wish

Faulty   He decided <u>checking</u> the pump.
Revised   He decided <u>to check</u> the pump.

5 Noun or pronoun + infinitive

Some verbs may be followed by an infinitive alone or by a noun or pronoun and an infinitive. The presence of a noun or pronoun changes the meaning.

ask	dare	need	wish
beg	expect	promise	would like
choose	help	want	

He expected <u>to watch</u>.
He expected <u>his workers</u> <u>to watch</u>.

Some verbs *must* be followed by a noun or pronoun before an infinitive:

advise	encourage	oblige	require
allow	forbid	order	teach
cause	force	permit	tell
challenge	hire	persuade	train
command	instruct	remind	urge
convince	invite	request	warn

He instructed <u>his workers</u> <u>to watch</u>.

Do not use *to* before the infinitive when it follows one of these verbs and a noun or pronoun:

feel	hear	make ("force")	watch
have	let	see	

He let his workers <u>learn</u> by observation.

25f Use the appropriate particles with two-word verbs.

Exercise

Standard American English includes some verbs that consist of two words: the verb itself and a **particle**, a preposition or adverb that affects the meaning of the verb.

<u>Look up</u> the answer. [Research the answer.]
<u>Look over</u> the answer. [Examine the answer.]

The meanings of these two-word verbs are often quite different from the meanings of the individual words that make them up. (There are some three-word verbs, too, such as *run out of.*) A dictionary of English as a second language will define two-word verbs and say whether the verbs may be separated in a sentence, as explained below and opposite. (See **3** p. 163 for a list of ESL dictionaries.) A grammar checker will recognize few if any misuses of two-word verbs.

Note Many two-word verbs are more common in speech than in more formal academic or business writing. For formal writing, consider using *research* instead of *look up, examine* or *inspect* instead of *look over.*

1 Inseparable two-word verbs

Verbs and particles that may not be separated by any other words include the following:

catch on	go over	play around	stay away
come across	grow up	run into	stay up
get along	keep on	run out of	take care of
give in	look into	speak up	turn up at

Faulty   Children <u>grow</u> quickly <u>up</u>.
Revised   Children <u>grow up</u> quickly.

Key terms

preposition A word such as *about, for,* or *to* that takes a noun or pronoun as its object: *at the house, in the woods.* (See p. 182 for a list of prepositions.)

adverb A word that modifies a verb, adjective, other adverb, or whole word group. (See p. 181.)
---

2 Separable two-word verbs

Most two-word verbs that take direct objects may be separated by the object.

Parents <u>help out</u> their children.
Parents <u>help</u> their children <u>out</u>.

If the direct object is a pronoun, the pronoun *must* separate the verb from the particle.

Faulty   Parents <u>help out</u> them.
Revised   Parents <u>help</u> them <u>out</u>.

The separable two-word verbs include the following:

bring up	give up	point out	throw out
call off	hand in	put away	try on
call up	hand out	put back	try out
drop off	help out	put off	turn down
fill out	leave out	put on	turn off
fill up	look over	take off	turn on
find out	look up	take out	turn up
give away	make up	take over	wrap up
give back	pick up	throw away	wake up

26 Verb Tenses

Tense shows the time of a verb's action. The box on the next page illustrates the tense forms for a regular verb. (Irregular verbs have different past-tense and past-participle forms. See the box on pp. 194–95.)

Grammar checkers   A grammar checker can provide little help with incorrect verb tenses and tense sequences because correctness usually depends on meaning.

Video tutorial

CULTURE LANGUAGE   In standard American English, a verb conveys time and sequence through its form. In some other languages and English dialects, various markers besides verb form may indicate the time of a verb. For instance, in African American Vernacular English, *I be attending class on Tuesday* means that the speaker attends class every Tuesday. But to someone who doesn't know the dialect, the sentence could mean last Tuesday, this Tuesday,

mycomplab

Visit *mycomplab.com* for the eText and for resources and exercises on verb tenses.

Video
tutorial

Exercise

Tenses of a regular verb (active voice)

Present Action that is occurring now, occurs habitually, or is generally true

Simple present Plain form or -s form	**Present progressive** Am, is, or are plus -ing form
I walk. You/we/they walk. He/she/it walks.	I am walking. You/we/they are walking. He/she/it is walking.

Past Action that occurred before now

Simple past Past-tense form (-d or -ed)	**Past progressive** Was or were plus -ing form
I/he/she/it walked. You/we/they walked.	I/he/she/it was walking. You/we/they were walking.

Future Action that will occur in the future

Simple future Will plus plain form	**Future progressive** Will be plus -ing form
I/you/he/she/it/we/they will walk.	I/you/he/she/it/we/they will be walking.

Present perfect Action that began in the past and is linked to the present

Present perfect Have or has plus past participle (-d or -ed)	**Present perfect progressive** Have been or has been plus -ing form
I/you/we/they have walked. He/she/it has walked.	I/you/we/they have been walking. He/she/it has been walking.

Past perfect Action that was completed before another past action

Past perfect Had plus past participle (-d or -ed)	**Past perfect progressive** Had been plus -ing form
I/you/he/she/it/we/they had walked.	I/you/he/she/it/we/they had been walking.

Future perfect Action that will be completed before another future action

Future perfect Will have plus past participle (-d or -ed)	**Future perfect progressive** Will have been plus -ing form
I/you/he/she/it/we/they will have walked.	I/you/he/she/it/we/they will have been walking.

or every Tuesday. In standard American English, the intended meaning is indicated by verb tense:

> I attended class on Tuesday. [Past tense indicates *last* Tuesday.]
> I will attend class on Tuesday. [Future tense indicates *next* Tuesday.]
> I attend class on Tuesday. [Present tense indicates habitual action, *every* Tuesday.]

26a Observe the special uses of the present tense (*sing*).

The present tense has several distinctive uses.

Action occurring now
She understands the problem.
We define the problem differently.

Habitual or recurring action
Banks regularly undergo audits.
The audits monitor the banks' activities.

A general truth
The mills of the gods grind slowly.
The earth is round.

Discussion of literature, film, and so on
Huckleberry Finn has adventures we all envy.
In that article the author examines several causes of crime.

Future time
Next week we draft a new budget.
Funding ends in less than a year.

(The present tense shows future time with expressions like those in the examples above: *next week, in less than a year.*)

26b Observe the uses of the perfect tenses (*have/had/will have sung*).

The **perfect tenses** consist of a form of *have* plus the verb's past participle (*closed, hidden*). They indicate an action completed before another specific time or action. The present perfect tense also indicates action begun in the past and continued into the present.

present perfect
The dancer has performed here only once. [The action is completed at the time of the statement.]

present perfect
Critics have written about the performance ever since. [The action began in the past and continues now.]

past perfect
The dancer had trained in Asia before his performance. [The action was completed before another past action.]

future perfect
He will have danced here again by the end of the year. [The action begins now or in the future and will be completed by a specific time in the future.]

CULTURE LANGUAGE With the present perfect tense, the words *since* and *for* are followed by different information. After *since*, give a specific point in time: *The play has run since 1989.* After *for*, give a span of time: *It has run for decades.*

26c Observe the uses of the progressive tenses (*is/was/will be singing*).

The **progressive tenses** indicate continuing (therefore progressive) action. In standard American English the progressive tenses consist of a form of *be* plus the verb's *-ing* form (present participle). (The words *be* and *been* must be combined with other helping verbs. See p. 199.)

present progressive
The team is improving.

past progressive
Last year the team was losing.

future progressive
The owners will be watching for signs of improvement.

present perfect progressive
Sports writers have been expecting an upturn.

past perfect progressive
New players had been performing well.

future perfect progressive
If the season goes badly, fans will have been watching their team lose for ten straight years.

Note Verbs that express unchanging conditions (especially mental states) rather than physical actions do not usually appear in the progressive tenses. These verbs include *adore, appear, believe, belong, care, hate, have, hear, know, like, love, mean, need, own, prefer, remember, see, sound, taste, think, understand,* and *want*.

Faulty   She is wanting to study ethics.
Revised   She wants to study ethics.

26d Keep tenses consistent.

Exercise

Within a sentence, the tenses of verbs and verb forms need not be identical as long as they reflect actual changes in time: *Ramon will graduate from college thirty years after his father arrived in America.* But needless shifts in tense will confuse or distract readers:

Inconsistent tense	Immediately after Booth shot Lincoln, Major Rathbone threw himself upon the assassin. But Booth pulls a knife and plunges it into the major's arm.
Revised	Immediately after Booth shot Lincoln, Major Rathbone threw himself upon the assassin. But Booth pulled a knife and plunged it into the major's arm.
Inconsistent tense	The main character in the novel suffers psychologically because he has a clubfoot, but he eventually triumphed over his disability.

Revised   The main character in the novel <u>suffers</u> psychologically because he <u>has</u> a clubfoot, but he eventually <u>triumphs</u> over his disability. [Use the present tense to discuss the content of literature, film, and so on.]

26e   Use the appropriate sequence of verb tenses.

The **sequence of tenses** is the relation between the verb tense in a main clause and the verb tense in a subordinate clause. The tenses should change when necessary to reflect changes in actual or relative time. The main difficulties with tense sequence are discussed on these pages.

Exercise

1   Past or past perfect tense in main clause

When the verb in the main clause is in the past or past perfect tense, the verb in the subordinate clause must also be past or past perfect:

> main clause: subordinate clause:
>   past   past

The researchers <u>discovered</u> that people <u>varied</u> widely in their knowledge of public events.

> main clause: subordinate clause:
>   past   past perfect

The variation <u>occurred</u> because respondents <u>had been born</u> in different decades.

> main clause: subordinate clause:
> past perfect   past

None of them <u>had been born</u> when Dwight Eisenhower <u>was</u> President.

Exception   Always use the present tense for a general truth, such as *The earth is round*:

> main clause: subordinate clause:
>   past   present

Most <u>understood</u> that popular Presidents <u>are</u> not necessarily good Presidents.

2   Conditional sentences

A **conditional sentence** states a factual relation between cause and effect, makes a prediction, or speculates about what might happen. Such a sentence usually contains a subordinate clause beginning with *if*, *when*, or *unless* and a main clause stating the result. The three kinds of conditional sentences use distinctive verbs.

Key terms

main clause A word group that can stand alone as a sentence because it contains a subject and a predicate and does not begin with a subordinating word. *Books are valuable.* (See p. 191.)

subordinate clause A word group that contains a subject and a predicate, begins with a subordinating word such as *because* or *who,* and is not a question: *Books are valuable <u>when they enlighten</u>.* (See p. 191.)

Factual relation

Statements linking factual causes and effects use matched tenses in the subordinate and main clauses:

subordinate clause:
present main clause:
present

When a voter <u>casts</u> a ballot, he or she <u>has</u> complete privacy.

subordinate clause:
past main clause:
past

When voters <u>registered</u> in some states, they <u>had</u> to pay a poll tax.

Prediction

Predictions generally use the present tense in the subordinate clause and the future tense in the main clause:

subordinate clause:
present main clause:
future

Unless citizens <u>regain</u> faith in politics, they <u>will</u> not <u>vote</u>.

Sometimes the verb in the main clause consists of *may, can, should,* or *might* plus the verb's plain form: *If citizens <u>regain</u> faith, they <u>may vote</u>.*

Speculation

The verbs in speculations depend on whether the linked events are possible or impossible. For possible events in the present, use the past tense in the subordinate clause and *would, could,* or *might* plus the verb's plain form in the main clause:

subordinate clause:
past main clause:
would + verb

If voters <u>had</u> more confidence, they <u>would vote</u> more often.

Use *were* instead of *was* in the subordinate clause, even when the subject is *I, he, she, it,* or a singular noun. (See pp. 211–12 for more on this distinctive verb form.)

subordinate clause:
past main clause:
would + verb

If the voter <u>were</u> more confident, he or she <u>would vote</u> more often.

For impossible events in the present—events that are contrary to fact—use the same forms as above (including the distinctive *were* when applicable):

subordinate clause:
past main clause:
might + verb

If Lincoln <u>were</u> alive, he <u>might inspire</u> confidence.

For impossible events in the past, use the past perfect tense in the subordinate clause and *would, could,* or *might* plus the present perfect tense in the main clause:

subordinate clause:
past perfect main clause:
might + present perfect

If Lincoln <u>had lived</u> past the Civil War, he <u>might have helped</u> stabilize the country.

27 Verb Mood

Mood in grammar is a verb form that indicates the writer's or speaker's attitude toward what he or she is saying. The **indicative mood** states a fact or opinion or asks a question: *The theater needs help.* The **imperative mood** expresses a command or gives a direction. It omits the subject of the sentence, *you*: *Help the theater.*

The **subjunctive mood** is trickier and requires distinctive verb forms described below and on the next page.

Grammar checkers A grammar checker may spot some errors in the subjunctive mood, but it may miss others. For example, a checker flagged *I wish I was home* (should be *were home*) but not *If I were home, I will not leave* (should be *would not leave*).

| 27a | **Use the subjunctive verb forms appropriately, as in *I wish I were*.** |

The subjunctive mood expresses a suggestion, requirement, or desire, or it states a condition that is contrary to fact (that is, imaginary or hypothetical).

Exercise

■ **Verbs such as *ask, insist, urge, require, recommend,* and *suggest* indicate request or requirement.** They often precede a subordinate clause beginning with *that* and containing the substance of the request or requirement. For all subjects, the verb in the *that* clause is the plain form:

plain form

Rules require that every donation <u>be</u> mailed.

■ **Contrary-to-fact clauses state imaginary or hypothetical conditions. They usually begin with *if* or *unless,* or they follow *wish.*** For present contrary-to-fact clauses, use the verb's past-tense form (for *be,* use the past-tense form *were*):

past   past

If the theater <u>were</u> in better shape and <u>had</u> more money, its future would be assured.

Key terms

plain form The dictionary form of a verb: *buy, make, run, talk*. (See p. 180.)

past-tense form The *-d* or *-ed* form of a regular verb (*lived, walked*). Most irregular verbs create the form in other ways (see pp. 193–95).

---

mycomplab

Visit *mycomplab.com* for the eText and for resources and exercises on verb mood.

past

I wish I <u>were</u> able to donate money.

For past contrary-to-fact clauses, use *had* plus the verb's past participle:

past perfect

The theater would be better funded if it <u>had been</u> better managed.

Note Do not use the helping verb *would* or *could* in a contrary-to-fact clause beginning with *if*:

| Not | Many people would have helped if they <u>would have</u> known. |
| But | Many people would have helped if they <u>had</u> known. |

See also p. 210 on verb tenses in sentences like these.

27b | Keep mood consistent.

Shifts in mood within a sentence or among related sentences can be confusing. Such shifts occur most frequently in directions.

| Inconsistent mood | Cook the mixture slowly, and <u>you should stir</u> it until the sugar is dissolved. [Mood shifts from imperative to indicative.] |
| Revised | <u>Cook</u> the mixture slowly, and <u>stir</u> it until the sugar is dissolved. [Consistently imperative.] |

28 Verb Voice

Video tutorial

The **voice** of a verb tells whether the subject of the sentence performs the action (**active**) or is acted upon (**passive**). The actor in a passive sentence may be named in a prepositional phrase (as in *Rents are controlled <u>by the city</u>*), or the actor may be omitted (as in *Rents are controlled*).

> **Key term**
> **past participle** For a regular verb, the same as the past-tense form, ending in *-d* or *-ed*. Most irregular verbs create the form in other ways (see pp. 193–95).

mycomplab

Visit *mycomplab.com* for the eText and for resources and exercises on verb voice.

Active and passive voice

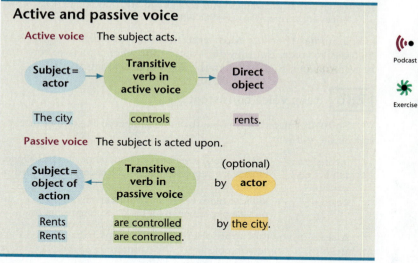

Active voice The subject acts.

Subject = actor → Transitive verb in active voice → Direct object

The city   controls   rents.

Passive voice The subject is acted upon.

Subject = object of action ← Transitive verb in passive voice   (optional) by actor

Rents   are controlled   by the city.
Rents   are controlled.

CULTURE LANGUAGE A passive verb always consists of a form of *be* plus the past participle of the main verb: *Rents are controlled. People were inspired.* Other helping verbs must also be used with the words *be, being,* and *been: Rents will be controlled. Rents are being controlled. Rents have been controlled. People would have been inspired.* Only a transitive verb (one that takes an object) may be used in the passive voice. (See p. 187.)

28a   **Generally, prefer the active voice. Use the passive voice when the actor is unknown or unimportant.**

The active voice is usually clearer, more concise, and more forthright than the passive voice.

Weak passive   The library is used by both students and teachers, and the plan to expand it has been praised by many.

Strong active   Both students and teachers use the library, and many have praised the plan to expand it.

The passive voice is useful in two situations: when the actor is unknown and when the actor is unimportant or less important than the object of the action.

The Internet was established in 1969 by the US Department of Defense. The network has been extended internationally to governments, universities, corporations, and private individuals. [In the first sentence the writer wishes to stress the Internet rather than the Department of Defense. In the second sentence the actor is unknown or too complicated to name.]

After the solution had been cooled to 10°C, the acid was added. [The person who cooled and added, perhaps the writer, is less important than the facts that the solution was cooled and acid was added. Passive sentences are common in scientific writing.]

Grammar checkers Most grammar checkers can be set to spot the passive voice. But they can't determine when a passive verb may be appropriate, such as when the actor is unknown.

28b Keep voice consistent.

Shifts in voice that involve shifts in subject are usually unnecessary and confusing.

Inconsistent subject and voice	Internet <u>blogs</u> <u>cover</u> an enormous range of topics. Opportunities for people to discuss pet issues <u>are provided</u> on these sites.
Revised	Internet <u>blogs</u> <u>cover</u> an enormous range of topics and <u>provide</u> opportunities for people to discuss pet issues.

A shift in voice is appropriate when it helps focus the reader's attention on a single subject, as in *The candidate <u>campaigned</u> vigorously and <u>was nominated</u> on the first ballot.*

29 Agreement of Subject and Verb

Video tutorial

A subject and its verb should agree in number and person.

More <u>Japanese Americans</u> <u>live</u> in Hawaii and California than elsewhere.
subject · · · · · verb

Video tutorial

<u>Daniel Inouye</u> <u>was</u> the first Japanese American in Congress.
subject · · · · verb

Exercise

Most problems of subject-verb agreement arise when endings are omitted from subjects or verbs or when the relation between sentence parts is uncertain.

Key terms

		number	
		singular	**plural**
person		I eat.	We eat.
first		You eat.	You eat.
second		He/she/it eats.	They eat.
third		The bird eats.	Birds eat.

---

mycomplab

Visit *mycomplab.com* for the eText and for resources and exercises on subject-verb agreement.

Grammar checkers A grammar checker will catch many simple errors in subject-verb agreement, such as *Addie and John is late*, and some more complicated errors, such as *Is Margaret and Tom going with us?* (should be *are* in both cases). But a checker failed to flag *The old group has gone their separate ways* (should be *have*) and offered a wrong correction for *The old group have gone their separate ways*, which is already correct.

29a The *-s* and *-es* endings work differently for nouns and verbs.

An *-s* or *-es* ending does opposite things to nouns and verbs: it usually makes a noun *plural*, but it always makes a present-tense verb *singular*. Thus a singular-noun subject will not end in *-s*, but its verb will. A plural-noun subject will end in *-s*, but its verb will not. Between them, subject and verb use only one *-s* ending.

Exercise

Singular subject	Plural subject
The boy plays.	The boys play.
The bird soars.	The birds soar.

The only exceptions to these rules involve the nouns that form irregular plurals, such as *child/children, woman/women*. The irregular plural still requires a plural verb: *The children play. The women read*.

CULTURE LANGUAGE If your first language or dialect is not standard American English, subject-verb agreement may be difficult, especially for the following reasons:

■ **Some English dialects omit the *-s* ending for singular verbs or use the *-s* ending for plural verbs.**

Nonstandard	The voter resist change.
Standard	The voter resists change.
Standard	The voters resist change.

The verb *be* changes spelling for singular and plural in both present and past tense. (See also p. 180.)

Nonstandard	Taxes is high. They was raised just last year.
Standard	Taxes are high. They were raised just last year.

Have also has a distinctive *-s* form, *has*:

Nonstandard	The new tax have little chance of passing.
Standard	The new tax has little chance of passing.

■ **Some other languages change all parts of verb phrases to match their subjects.** In English verb phrases, however, only the helping verbs *be, have,* and *do* change for different subjects. The modal helping verbs—*can, may, should, will*, and others—do not change:

Nonstandard   The tax mays pass next year.
Standard   The tax may pass next year.

The main verb in a verb phrase also does not change for different subjects:

Nonstandard   The tax may passes next year.
Standard   The tax may pass next year.

29b Subject and verb should agree even when other words come between them.

Podcast

The survival of hibernating frogs in freezing temperatures is [not are] fascinating.

A chemical reaction inside the cells of the frogs stops [not stop] the formation of ice crystals.

Note Phrases beginning with *as well as, together with, along with,* and *in addition to* do not change a singular subject to plural:

The president, together with the deans, has [not have] agreed.

29c Subjects joined by *and* usually take plural verbs.

Video
tutorial

Frost and Roethke were contemporaries.

Exceptions When the parts of the subject form a single idea or refer to a single person or thing, they take a singular verb:

Avocado and bean sprouts is a California sandwich.

When a compound subject is preceded by the adjective *each* or *every*, the verb is usually singular:

Each man, woman, and child has a right to be heard.

29d When parts of a subject are joined by *or* or *nor*, the verb agrees with the nearer part.

Either the painter or the carpenter knows the cost.

The cabinets or the bookcases are too costly.

When one part of the subject is singular and the other plural, avoid awkwardness by placing the plural part closer to the verb so that the verb is plural:

Awkward   Neither the owners nor the contractor agrees.

Revised   Neither the contractor nor the owners agree.

29e | With *everyone* and other indefinite pronouns, use a singular or plural verb as appropriate.

Most indefinite pronouns are singular in meaning (they refer to a single unspecified person or thing), and they take a singular verb:

Exercise

Something smells.   Neither is right.

Four indefinite pronouns are always plural in meaning: *both, few, many, several.*

Both are correct.   Several were invited.

Six indefinite pronouns may be either singular or plural in meaning: *all, any, more, most, none, some.* The verb with one of these pronouns depends on what the pronoun refers to:

All of the money is reserved for emergencies. [*All* refers to *money.*]

All of the funds are reserved for emergencies. [*All* refers to *funds.*]

None may be singular even when referring to a plural word, especially to emphasize the meaning "not one": *None* [*Not one*] of the *animals has a home.*

((•● Podcast

CULTURE LANGUAGE   See p. 239 for the distinction between *few* ("not many") and *a few* ("some").

29f | Collective nouns such as *team* take singular or plural verbs depending on meaning.

Use a singular verb with a collective noun when the group acts as a unit.

((•● Podcast

Key term

indefinite pronoun A pronoun that does not refer to a specific person or thing:

Singular			*Singular or plural*	*Plural*
anybody	everyone	nothing	all	both
anyone	everything	one	any	few
anything	much	somebody	more	many
each	neither	someone	most	several
either	nobody	something	none	
everybody	no one		some	

The team has won five of the last six meets.

But when the group's members act separately, not together, use a plural verb:

The old team have gone their separate ways.

If a combination such as *team have* seems awkward, reword the sentence: *The members of the old team have gone their separate ways.*

The collective noun *number* may be singular or plural. Preceded by *a*, it is plural; preceded by *the*, it is singular:

A number of people are in debt.

The number of people in debt is very large.

CULTURE LANGUAGE Some noncount nouns (nouns that don't form plurals) are collective nouns because they name groups: for instance, *furniture, mail, equipment, military.* These noncount nouns usually take singular verbs: *Mail arrives daily.* But some of these nouns take plural verbs, including *clergy, military, police,* and any collective noun that comes from an adjective, such as *the poor, the rich, the elderly.* If you mean one representative of the group, use a singular noun such as *police officer* or *poor person.*

29g *Who, which,* and *that* take verbs that agree with their antecedents.

When used as subjects, *who, which,* and *that* refer to another word in the sentence, called the **antecedent.** The verb agrees with the antecedent:

Mayor Garber ought to listen to the people who work for her.

Bardini is the only aide who has her ear.

Agreement problems often occur with *who* and *that* when the sentence includes *one of the* or *the only one of the*:

Bardini is one of the aides who work unpaid. [Of the aides who work unpaid, Bardini is one.]

Bardini is the only one of the aides who knows the community. [Of the aides, only one, Bardini, knows the community.]

CULTURE LANGUAGE In phrases with *one of the,* be sure the noun is plural: *He is one of the aides* [not *aide*] *who volunteer.*

Key term

collective noun A noun with singular form that names a group of individuals or things—for instance, *army, audience, committee, crowd, family.*

29h *News* and other singular nouns ending in *-s* take singular verbs.

Singular nouns ending in *-s* include *athletics, economics, mathematics, measles, mumps, news, physics, politics,* and *statistics,* as well as place names such as *Athens, Wales,* and *United States.*

> After so long a wait, the news has to be good.

> Statistics is required of psychology majors.

A few of these words also take plural verbs, but only when they describe individual items rather than whole bodies of activity or knowledge: *The statistics prove him wrong.*

Measurements and figures ending in *-s* may also be singular when the quantity they refer to is a unit:

> Three years is a long time to wait.

> Three-fourths of the library consists of reference books.

29i The verb agrees with the subject even when it precedes the subject.

The verb precedes the subject mainly in questions and in constructions beginning with *there* or *here* and a form of *be*:

> Is voting a right or a privilege?

> Are a right and a privilege the same thing?

> There are differences between them.

29j *Is, are,* and other linking verbs agree with their subjects, not subject complements.

Make a linking verb agree with its subject, usually the first element in the sentence, not with the noun or pronoun serving as a subject complement.

> The child's sole support is her court-appointed guardians.

> Her court-appointed guardians are the child's sole support.

Key terms

linking verb A verb that connects or equates the subject and subject complement: for example, *seem, become, appear, grow,* and forms of *be.* (See p. 187.)

subject complement A word that describes or renames the subject: *They became chemists.* (See p. 187.)

29k Use singular verbs with titles and with words being defined.

Hakada Associates is a new firm.

Dream Days remains a favorite book.

Folks is a down-home word for *people.*

Pronouns

Pronouns—words such as *she* and *who* that refer to nouns—merit special care because all their meaning comes from the other words they refer to. This section discusses pronoun case (Chapter 30), matching pronouns and the words they refer to (31), and making sure pronouns refer to the right nouns (32).

30 Pronoun Case

👁 Video tutorial

✳ Exercise

Case is the form of a noun or pronoun that shows the reader how it functions in a sentence.

■ **The subjective case** indicates that the word is a subject or subject complement.

■ **The objective case** indicates that the word is an object of a verb or preposition.

Key terms

subject Who or what a sentence is about: *Biologists often study animals. They often work in laboratories.* (See pp. 184–85.)

subject complement A word or words that rename or describe the sentence subject: *The best biologists are she and Scoggins.* (See p. 187.)

object of verb The receiver of the verb's action (**direct object**): *Many biologists study animals. The animals teach them.* Or the person or thing the action is performed for (**indirect object**): *Some biologists give animals homes. The animals give them pleasure.* (See pp. 187–88.)

object of preposition The word linked by *with, for,* or another preposition to the rest of the sentence: *Many biologists work in a laboratory. For them the lab often provides a second home.* (See p. 189.)

■ **The possessive case** indicates that the word owns or is the source of a noun in the sentence.

Nouns change form only to show possession: *teacher's* (see **5** pp. 278–80). Most of the pronouns listed below change more often.

Subjective	Objective	Possessive
I	me	my, mine
you	you	your, yours
he	him	his
she	her	her, hers
it	it	its
we	us	our, ours
you	you	your, yours
they	them	their, theirs
who	whom	whose
whoever	whomever	—

Video tutorial

Grammar checkers A grammar checker may flag some problems with pronoun case, but it will also miss a lot. For instance, one checker spotted the error in *We asked whom would come* (should be *who*), but it overlooked *We dreaded them coming* (should be *their*).

CULTURE LANGUAGE In standard American English, *-self* pronouns do not change form to show function. Their only forms are *myself, yourself, himself, herself, itself, ourselves, yourselves, themselves.* Avoid nonstandard forms such as *hisself, ourself,* and *theirselves.*

Faulty He bought hisself a new laptop.
Revised He bought himself a new laptop.

30a **Distinguish between compound subjects and compound objects: *she and I* vs. *her and me*.**

Compound subjects or objects—those consisting of two or more nouns or pronouns—have the same case forms as they would if one noun or pronoun stood alone:

compound
subject
She and Novick discussed the proposal.

compound
object
The proposal disappointed her and him.

Podcast

If you are in doubt about the correct form, try this test:

A test for case forms in compound constructions

1. **Identify a compound construction** (one connected by *and, but, or, nor*).

   [He, Him] and [I, me] won the prize.
   The prize went to [he, him] and [I, me].

(continued)

Video tutorial

Podcast

> ## A test for case forms in compound constructions
> *(continued)*
>
> 2. **Write a separate sentence for each part of the compound:**
>
>   [He, Him] won the prize. [I, Me] won the prize.
>   The prize went to [he, him]. The prize went to [I, me].
>
> 3. **Choose the pronouns that sound correct.**
>
>   He won the prize. I won the prize. [Subjective.]
>   The prize went to him. The prize went to me. [Objective.]
>
> 4. **Put the separate sentences back together.**
>
>   He and I won the prize.
>   The prize went to him and me.

30b   Use the subjective case for subject complements: *It was she.*

After a linking verb, a pronoun renaming the subject (a subject complement) should be in the subjective case:

subject complement

The ones who care most are she and Novick.

subject
complement

It was they whom the mayor appointed.

If this construction sounds stilted to you, use the more natural order: *She and Novick are the ones who care most. The mayor appointed them.*

30c   The use of *who* vs. *whom* depends on the pronoun's function in its clause.

Podcast

Use *who* where you would use *he* or *she*—all ending in vowels. Use *whom* where you would use *him* or *her*—all ending in consonants.

1 Questions

Exercise

At the beginning of a question, use *who* for a subject and *whom* for an object:

subject ↴
Who wrote the policy?   object ↰
Whom does it affect?

To find the correct case of *who* in a question, use the following test.

Key term

linking verb A verb, such as a form of *be,* that connects a subject and a word that renames or describes the subject (subject complement): *They are biologists.* (See p. 187.)

1. **Pose the question:**

   [Who, Whom] makes that decision?
   [Who, Whom] does one ask?

2. **Answer the question, using a personal pronoun.** Choose the pronoun that sounds correct, and note its case:

   [She, Her] makes that decision. She makes that decision. [Subjective.]
   One asks [she, her]. One asks her. [Objective.]

3. **Use the same case (*who or whom*) in the question:**

   Who makes that decision? [Subjective.]
   Whom does one ask? [Objective.]

 Subordinate clauses

In a subordinate clause, use *who* or *whoever* for a subject, *whom* or *whomever* for an object.

   subject ⟶
   Give old clothes to whoever needs them.

   object ⟵
   I don't know whom the mayor appointed.

To determine which form to use, try the following test:

1. **Locate the subordinate clause:**

   Few people know [who, whom] they should ask.
   They are unsure [who, whom] makes the decision.

2. **Rewrite the subordinate clause as a separate sentence, substituting a personal pronoun for *who, whom.*** Choose the pronoun that sounds correct, and note its case:

   They should ask [she, her]. They should ask her. [Objective.]
   [She, her] makes the decision. She makes the decision. [Subjective.]

3. **Use the same case (*who or whom*) in the subordinate clause:**

   Few people know whom they should ask. [Objective.]
   They are unsure who makes the decision. [Subjective.]

Note Don't let expressions such as *I think* and *she says* mislead you into using *whom* rather than *who* for the subject of a clause.

   subject ⟶
   He is the one who I think is best qualified.

To choose between *who* and *whom* in such constructions, delete the

┌─ **Key term** ─────────────────────────────────────
subordinate clause A word group that contains a subject and a predicate and also begins with a subordinating word, such as *who, whom,* or *because.* (See p. 191.)
└──

interrupting phrase so that you can see the true relation between parts: *He is the one who is best qualified.*

30d   Use the appropriate case in other constructions.

1   *We* or *us* with a noun

The choice of *we* or *us* before a noun depends on the use of the noun:

object of
preposition

Freezing weather is welcomed by us skaters.

subject

We skaters welcome freezing weather.

2   Pronoun in an appositive

In an appositive the case of a pronoun depends on the function of the word the appositive describes or identifies:

appositive
identifies object

The class elected two representatives, DeShawn and me.

appositive
identifies subject

Two representatives, DeShawn and I, were elected.

3   Pronoun after *than* or *as*

When a pronoun follows *than* or *as* in a comparison, the case of the pronoun indicates what words may have been omitted. A subjective pronoun must be the subject of the omitted verb:

subject

Some critics like Glass more than he [does].

An objective pronoun must be the object of the omitted verb:

object

Some critics like Glass more than [they like] him.

4   Subject and object of infinitive

Both the object *and* the subject of an infinitive are in the objective case:

subject
of infinitive

The school asked him to speak.

object
of infinitive

Students chose to invite him.

Key terms

appositive   A noun or noun substitute that renames another noun immediately before it. (See p. 190.)

infinitive   The plain form of the verb plus *to*: *to run*. (See p. 190.)

5 | Case before a gerund

Ordinarily, use the possessive form of a pronoun or noun immediately before a gerund:

The coach disapproved of their lifting weights.

The coach's disapproving was a surprise.

31 | Agreement of Pronoun and Antecedent

The **antecedent** of a pronoun is the noun or other pronoun to which the pronoun refers:

Homeowners fret over their tax bills.
antecedent   pronoun

Its constant increases make the tax bill a dreaded document.
pronoun   antecedent

Video tutorial

Exercise

For clarity, a pronoun should agree with its antecedent in person, number, and gender.

Grammar checkers A grammar checker cannot help you with agreement between pronoun and antecedent because it cannot recognize the intended relation between the two.

CULTURE LANGUAGE The gender of a pronoun should match its antecedent, not a noun that the pronoun may modify: *Sara Young invited her* [not *his*] *son.* Also, English nouns have only neuter gender unless they specifically refer to males or females. Thus nouns such as *book, table, sun,* and *earth* take the pronoun *it*: *I am reading a new book. It is inspiring.*

Key terms

gerund The *-ing* form of a verb used as a noun: *Running is fun.* (See p. 190.)

	number	
person	**singular**	**plural**
first	*I*	*we*
second	*you*	*you*
third	*he, she, it,*	*they,*
	indefinite pronouns,	plural nouns
	singular nouns	
gender		
masculine	*he,* nouns naming males	
feminine	*she,* nouns naming females	
neuter	*it,* all other nouns	

Video
tutorial

31a **Antecedents joined by *and* usually take plural pronouns.**

Mr. Bartos and I cannot settle our dispute.

The dean and my adviser have offered their help.

Exceptions When the compound antecedent refers to a single idea, person, or thing, then the pronoun is singular:

My friend and adviser offered her help.

When the compound antecedent follows *each* or *every*, the pronoun is singular:

Every girl and woman took her seat.

31b **When parts of an antecedent are joined by *or* or *nor*, the pronoun agrees with the nearer part.**

Tenants or owners must present their grievances.

Either the tenant or the owner will have her way.

When one subject is plural and the other singular, the sentence will be awkward unless you put the plural subject second.

Awkward   Neither the tenants nor the owner has yet made her case.

Revised   Neither the owner nor the tenants have yet made their case.

31c **With *everyone, person,* and other indefinite words, use a singular or plural pronoun as appropriate.**

Indefinite words—indefinite pronouns and generic nouns—do not refer to any specific person or thing. Most indefinite pronouns

---

Key terms

indefinite pronoun A pronoun that does not refer to a specific person or thing:

Singular			Singular or plural	Plural
anybody	everyone	nothing	all	both
anyone	everything	one	any	few
anything	much	somebody	more	many
each	neither	someone	most	several
either	nobody	something	none	
everybody	no one		some	

generic noun A singular noun such as *person* or *student* when it refers to a typical member of a group, not to a particular individual.

and all generic nouns are singular in meaning. When they serve as antecedents, they take singular pronouns:

Each of the animal shelters in the region has <u>its</u> population of homeless pets.
indefinite pronoun

Every worker in our shelter cares for <u>his or her</u> favorite animal.
generic noun

Four indefinite pronouns are plural in meaning: *both, few, many, several*. As antecedents, they take plural pronouns:

Many of the animals show affection for <u>their</u> caretakers.

Six indefinite pronouns may be singular or plural in meaning: *all, any, more, most, none, some*. As antecedents, they take singular pronouns if they refer to singular words, plural pronouns if they refer to plural words:

Most of the shelter's equipment was donated by <u>its</u> original owner. [*Most* refers to *equipment*.]

Most of the veterinarians donate <u>their</u> time. [*Most* refers to *veterinarians*.]

None may be singular even when referring to a plural word, especially to emphasize the meaning "not one": *None* [*Not one*] *of the shelters has increased its capacity.*

Most agreement problems arise with the singular indefinite words. We often use these words to mean "many" or "all" rather than "one" and then refer to them with plural pronouns, as in *Everyone has <u>their</u> own locker.* Often, too, we mean indefinite words to include both masculine and feminine genders and thus resort to *they* instead of the **generic** *he*—the masculine pronoun referring to both genders, as in *Everyone deserves <u>his</u> privacy.* (For more on the generic *he*, which many readers view as sexist, see **3** p. 160.) To achieve agreement in such cases, you have the options listed in the following box.

Ways to correct agreement with indefinite words

■ **Change the indefinite word to a plural, and use a plural pronoun to match:**

Faulty	Every athlete deserves <u>their</u> privacy.
Revised	**Athletes** deserve <u>their</u> privacy.

■ **Rewrite the sentence to omit the pronoun:**

Faulty	Everyone is entitled to <u>their</u> own locker.
Revised	Everyone is entitled to **a** locker.

(continued)

Ways to correct agreement with indefinite words
(continued)

■ Use *he or she* (*him or her, his or her*) to refer to the indefinite word:

| **Faulty** | Now everyone has their private space. |
| **Revised** | Now everyone has **his or her** private space. |

However, used more than once in several sentences, *he or she* quickly becomes awkward. (Many readers do not accept the alternative *he/she*.) Using the plural or omitting the pronoun will usually correct agreement problems and create more readable sentences.

31d Collective nouns such as *team* take singular or plural pronouns depending on meaning.

Use a singular pronoun with a collective noun when referring to the group as a unit:

The committee voted to disband itself.

When referring to the individual members of the group, use a plural pronoun:

The old team have gone their separate ways.

If *team have . . . their* seems awkward, reword the sentence: *The members of the old team have gone their separate ways*.

CULTURE LANGUAGE In standard American English, collective nouns that are noncount nouns (they don't form plurals) usually take singular pronouns: *The mail sits in its own basket*. A few noncount nouns take plural pronouns, including *clergy, military, police, the rich,* and *the poor*: *The police support their unions*.

32 Reference of Pronoun to Antecedent

Video tutorial

A **pronoun** should refer clearly to its **antecedent**, the noun it substitutes for. Otherwise, readers will have difficulty grasping the pronoun's meaning.

> **Key term**
>
> **collective noun** A noun with singular form that names a group of individuals or things—for instance, *army, audience, committee, crowd, family, group, team*.

mycomplab

Visit *mycomplab.com* for the eText and for resources and exercises on pronoun reference.

Grammar checkers A grammar checker cannot recognize unclear pronoun reference. For instance, a checker did not flag any of the confusing examples on this page and the next.

CULTURE LANGUAGE In standard American English, a pronoun needs a clear antecedent nearby, but don't use both a pronoun and its antecedent as the subject of the same clause: *Jim* [not *Jim he*] *told Mark to go alone.* (See also p. 255.)

32a Make a pronoun refer clearly to one antecedent.

When either of two nouns can be a pronoun's antecedent, the reference will not be clear.

Video tutorial

Confusing   Emily Dickinson is sometimes compared with Jane Austen, 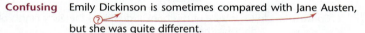 but she was quite different.

Revise such a sentence in one of two ways:

■ **Replace the pronoun with the appropriate noun.**

Clear   Emily Dickinson is sometimes compared with Jane Austen, but Dickinson [or Austen] was quite different.

Exercise

■ **Avoid repetition by rewriting the sentence.** If you use the pronoun, make sure it has only one possible antecedent.

Clear   Despite occasional comparison, Emily Dickinson and Jane Austen were quite different.

Clear   Though sometimes compared with her, Emily Dickinson was quite different from Jane Austen.

32b Place a pronoun close enough to its antecedent to ensure clarity.

A clause beginning with *who, which,* or *that* should generally fall immediately after the word to which it refers.

Confusing   Jody found a lamp in the attic that her aunt had used.

Clear   In the attic Jody found a lamp that her aunt had used.

32c Make a pronoun refer to a specific antecedent, not an implied one.

A pronoun should refer to a specific, stated noun or other pronoun so that readers understand its meaning.

Exercise

1 Vague *this, that, which,* or *it*

This, that, which, or *it* should refer to a specific noun, not to a whole word group expressing an idea or situation.

Confusing   The British knew little of the American countryside, and they had no experience with the colonists' guerrilla tactics. This gave the colonists an advantage.

Clear   The British knew little of the American countryside, and they had no experience with the colonists' guerrilla tactics. This ignorance and inexperience gave the colonists an advantage.

2 Indefinite antecedents with *it* and *they*

It and *they* should have definite noun antecedents. Rewrite the sentence if the antecedent is missing.

Confusing   In Chapter 4 of this book it describes the early flights of the Wright brothers.

Clear   Chapter 4 of this book describes the early flights of the Wright brothers.

Confusing   Even in reality TV shows, they present a false picture of life.

Clear   Even reality TV shows present a false picture of life.

Clear   Even in reality TV shows, the producers present a false picture of life.

3 Implied nouns

A noun may be implied in some other word or phrase, as *happiness* is implied in *happy*, *driver* is implied in *drive*, and *mother* is implied in *mother's*. But a pronoun cannot refer clearly to an implied noun, only to a specific, stated one.

Confusing   In Cohen's report she made claims that led to a lawsuit.

Clear   In her report Cohen made claims that led to a lawsuit.

Confusing   Her reports on psychological development generally go unnoticed outside it.

Clear   Her reports on psychological development generally go unnoticed outside the field.

32d Use *you* only to mean "you, the reader."

You should clearly mean "you, the reader." The context must be appropriate for such a meaning:

Inappropriate   In the fourteenth century you had to struggle simply to survive.

Revised   In the fourteenth century one [or a person] had to struggle simply to survive.

Writers sometimes drift into *you* because *one, a person,* or a similar indefinite word can be difficult to sustain. Sentence after sentence, the indefinite word may sound stuffy, and it requires *he* or *he or she* for pronoun-antecedent agreement (see pp. 226–28). To avoid these problems, try using plural nouns and pronouns:

Original	In the fourteenth century <u>one</u> had to struggle simply to survive.
Revised	In the fourteenth century <u>people</u> had to struggle simply to survive.

32e Keep pronouns consistent.

Within a sentence or a group of related sentences, pronouns should be consistent. Partly, consistency comes from making pronouns and their antecedents agree (see Chapter 31). In addition, the pronouns within a passage should match each other.

Inconsistent pronouns	<u>One</u> finds when reading that <u>your</u> concentration improves with practice, so that <u>I</u> now comprehend more in less time.
Revised	<u>I</u> find when reading that <u>my</u> concentration improves with practice, so that <u>I</u> now comprehend more in less time.

Modifiers

Modifiers describe or limit other words in a sentence. They are adjectives, adverbs, or word groups serving as adjectives or adverbs. This section shows how to solve problems in the forms of modifiers (Chapter 33) and in their relation to the rest of the sentence (34).

33 Adjectives and Adverbs

Adjectives modify nouns (*happy child*) and pronouns (*special someone*). **Adverbs** modify verbs (*almost see*), adjectives (*very happy*), other adverbs (*not very*), and whole word groups (*Otherwise, I'll go*). The only way to tell whether a modifier should be an adjective or an adverb is to determine its function in the sentence.

Video tutorial

Exercise

Grammar checkers A grammar checker will spot some but not all problems with misused adjectives and adverbs. For instance, a checker flagged *Some children suffer bad* and *James did not see nothing*. But it did not flag *Educating children good should be everyone's focus*.

CULTURE LANGUAGE In standard American English, an adjective does not change along with the noun it modifies to show plural number: *square* [not *squares*] *spaces*. Only nouns form plurals.

33a Use adjectives only to modify nouns and pronouns.

Video tutorial

Do not use adjectives instead of adverbs to modify verbs, adverbs, or other adjectives:

Faulty   Educating children <u>good</u> should be everyone's focus.

Revised   Educating children <u>well</u> should be everyone's focus.

Faulty   Some children suffer <u>bad</u>.

Revised   Some children suffer <u>badly</u>.

CULTURE LANGUAGE Choosing between *not* and *no* can be a challenge. *Not* is an adverb, so it makes a verb or an adjective negative:

They do <u>not</u> learn. They are <u>not</u> happy. They have <u>not</u> been in class.

(See p. 243 for where to place *not* in relation to verbs and adjectives.) *No* is an adjective, so it makes a noun negative:

<u>No</u> child likes to fail. <u>No</u> good school fails children.

Place *no* before the noun or any other modifier.

33b Use an adjective after a linking verb to modify the subject. Use an adverb to modify a verb.

Some verbs may or may not be linking verbs, depending on their meaning in the sentence. When the word after the verb modifies the subject, the verb is linking and the word should be an adjective: *He looked <u>happy</u>*. When the word modifies the verb, however, it should be an adverb: *He looked <u>carefully</u>*.

Key term

linking verb A verb that connects a subject and a word that describes the subject—for instance, *sound, feel, appear,* and forms of *be.* (See p. 187.)

Two word pairs are especially tricky. One is *bad* and *badly*:

The weather grew bad.
 linking adjective
 verb

She felt bad.
 linking adjective
 verb

Flowers grow badly in such soil.
 verb adverb

The other pair is *good* and *well*. *Good* serves only as an adjective. *Well* may serve as an adverb with a host of meanings or as an adjective meaning only "fit" or "healthy."

Decker trained well.
 verb adverb

She felt well.
 linking adjective
 verb

Her health was good.
 linking adjective
 verb

Podcast

33c | **Use the comparative and superlative forms of adjectives and adverbs appropriately.**

Adjectives and adverbs can show degrees of quality or amount with the endings *-er* and *-est* or with the words *more* and *most* or *less* and *least*. Most modifiers have the three forms shown in the following chart:

Exercise

Positive The basic form listed in the dictionary	**Comparative** A greater or lesser degree of the quality	**Superlative** The greatest or least degree of the quality
Adjectives		
red	redder	reddest
awful	more/less awful	most/least awful
Adverbs		
soon	sooner	soonest
quickly	more/less quickly	most/least quickly

If sound alone does not tell you whether to use *-er/-est* or *more/most*, consult a dictionary. If the endings can be used, the dictionary will list them. Otherwise, use *more* or *most*.

1 | Irregular adjectives and adverbs

Irregular modifiers change the spelling of their positive form to show comparative and superlative degrees.

Positive	Comparative	Superlative
Adjectives		
good	better	best
bad	worse	worst
little	littler, less	littlest, least
many		
some }	more	most
much		

Positive	Comparative	Superlative
Adverbs		
well	better	best
badly	worse	worst

2 Double comparisons

A double comparative or double superlative combines the *-er* or *-est* ending with the word *more* or *most*. It is redundant.

> Chang was the wisest [not most wisest] person in town.
> He was smarter [not more smarter] than anyone else.

3 Logical comparisons

Absolute modifiers

Some adjectives and adverbs cannot logically be compared—for instance, *perfect, unique, dead, impossible, infinite*. These absolute words can be preceded by adverbs like *nearly* or *almost* that mean "approaching," but they cannot logically be modified by *more* or *most* (as in *most perfect*).

Not	He was the most unique teacher we had.
But	He was a unique teacher.

Completeness

To be logical, a comparison must also be complete in the following ways:

- **The comparison must state a relation fully enough for clarity.**

Unclear	Carmakers worry about their industry more than environmentalists.
Clear	Carmakers worry about their industry more than environmentalists do.
Clear	Carmakers worry about their industry more than they worry about environmentalists.

- **The items being compared should in fact be comparable.**

Illogical	The cost of a hybrid car can be greater than a gasoline-powered car. [Illogically compares a cost and a car.]
Revised	The cost of a hybrid car can be greater than the cost of [or that of] a gasoline-powered car.

See also **3** p. 150 on parallelism with comparisons.

Any versus *any other*

Use *any other* when comparing something with others in the same group. Use *any* when comparing something with others in a different group.

Illogical	Los Angeles is larger than <u>any</u> city in California. [Since Los Angeles is itself a city in California, the sentence seems to say that Los Angeles is larger than itself.]
Revised	Los Angeles is larger than <u>any other</u> city in California.
Illogical	Los Angeles is larger than <u>any other</u> city in Canada. [The cities in Canada constitute a group to which Los Angeles does not belong.]
Revised	Los Angeles is larger than <u>any</u> city in Canada.

33d Watch for double negatives.

Video tutorial

Exercise

In a **double negative** two negative words such as *no, not, none, neither, barely, hardly,* or *scarcely* cancel each other out. Some double negatives are intentional: for instance, *She was <u>not unhappy</u>* indicates with understatement that she was indeed happy. But most double negatives say the opposite of what is intended: *Jenny did <u>not feel nothing</u>* asserts that Jenny felt other than nothing, or something. For the opposite meaning, one of the negatives must be eliminated (*She felt <u>nothing</u>*) or one of them must be changed to a positive (*She did not feel <u>anything</u>*).

Faulty	The IRS <u>cannot hardly</u> audit all tax returns. <u>None</u> of its audits <u>never</u> touch many cheaters.
Revised	The IRS <u>cannot</u> audit all tax returns. Its audits <u>never</u> touch many cheaters.

33e Distinguish between present and past participles as adjectives.

Exercise

Both present participles and past participles may serve as adjectives: *a <u>burning</u> building, a <u>burned</u> building.* As in the examples, the two participles usually differ in the time they indicate.

But some present and past participles—those derived from verbs expressing feeling—can have altogether different meanings. The present participle modifies something that causes the feeling: *That was a <u>frightening</u> storm* (the storm frightens). The past participle modifies something that experiences the feeling: *They quieted the <u>frightened</u> horses* (the horses feel fright).

Key terms

present participle The *-ing* form of a verb: *flying, writing, eating, swimming.* (See p. 180.)

past participle The *-d* or *-ed* form of a regular verb: *slipped, walked.* Most irregular verbs have distinctive past participles, such as *eaten* or *swum.* (See p. 180.)

The following participles are among those likely to be confused:

amazing/amazed	fascinating/fascinated
amusing/amused	frightening/frightened
annoying/annoyed	frustrating/frustrated
astonishing/astonished	interesting/interested
boring/bored	pleasing/pleased
confusing/confused	satisfying/satisfied
depressing/depressed	shocking/shocked
embarrassing/embarrassed	surprising/surprised
exciting/excited	tiring/tired
exhausting/exhausted	worrying/worried

33f Use *a, an, the,* and other determiners appropriately.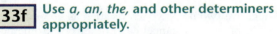

Determiners are special kinds of adjectives that mark nouns because they always precede nouns. Some common determiners are *a, an,* and *the* (called **articles**) and *my, their, whose, this, these, those, one, some,* and *any.*

Native speakers of standard American English can rely on their intuition when using determiners, but speakers of other languages and dialects often have difficulty with them. In standard American English, the use of determiners depends on the context they appear in and the kind of noun they precede:

- A *proper noun* **names a particular person, place, or thing and begins with a capital letter:** *February, Joe Allen, Red River.* Most proper nouns are not preceded by determiners.
- A *count noun* **names something that is countable in English and can form a plural:** *girl/girls, apple/apples, child/children.* A singular count noun is always preceded by a determiner; a plural count noun sometimes is.
- A *noncount noun* **names something not usually considered countable in English, and so it does not form a plural.** A noncount noun is sometimes preceded by a determiner. Here is a sample of noncount nouns, sorted into groups by meaning:

Abstractions: confidence, democracy, education, equality, evidence, health, information, intelligence, knowledge, luxury, peace, pollution, research, success, supervision, truth, wealth, work

Food and drink: bread, broccoli, candy, cereal, flour, meat, milk, salt, water, wine

Emotions: anger, comfort, courage, happiness, hate, joy, love, respect, satisfaction

Natural events and substances: air, blood, dirt, gasoline, gold, hair, heat, ice, oil, oxygen, rain, silver, smoke, weather, wood

Groups: clergy, clothing, equipment, furniture, garbage, jewelry, junk, legislation, machinery, mail, military, money, police, vocabulary

Fields of study: architecture, accounting, biology, business, chemistry, engineering, literature, psychology, science

A dictionary of English as a second language will tell you whether a noun is a count noun, a noncount noun, or both. (See **3** p. 163 for recommended dictionaries.)

Note Many nouns are sometimes count nouns and sometimes noncount nouns:

> The library has a room for readers. [*Room* is a count noun meaning "walled area."]
>
> The library has room for reading. [*Room* is a noncount noun meaning "space."]

Grammar checkers Partly because the same noun may fall into different groups, a grammar checker is an unreliable guide to missing or misused articles and other determiners. For instance, a checker flagged the omitted *a* before *Scientist* in *Scientist developed new processes*; it did not flag the omitted *a* before *new* in *A scientist developed new process*; and it mistakenly flagged the correctly omitted article *the* before *Vegetation* in *Vegetation suffers from drought.*

1 *A, an,* and *the*

With singular count nouns

A or *an* precedes a singular count noun when the reader does not already know its identity, usually because you have not mentioned it before:

Exercise

> A scientist in our chemistry department developed a process to strengthen metals. [*Scientist* and *process* are being introduced for the first time.]

The precedes a singular count noun that has a specific identity for the reader, for one of the following reasons:

- **You have mentioned the noun before:**

> A scientist in our chemistry department developed a process to strengthen metals. The scientist patented the process. [*Scientist* and *process* were identified in the preceding sentence.]

- **You identify the noun immediately before or after you state it:**

> The most productive laboratory is the research center in the chemistry department. [*Most productive* identifies *laboratory. In the chemistry department* identifies *research center.* And *chemistry department* is a shared facility—see the next page.]

- **The noun names something unique—the only one in existence:**

> The sun rises in the east. [*Sun* and *east* are unique.]

■ **The noun names an institution or facility that is shared by the community of readers:**

Many men and women aspire to the presidency. [*Presidency* is a shared institution.]

The cell phone has changed business communication. [*Cell phone* is a shared facility.]

The is not used before a singular noun that names a general category:

Wordsworth's poetry shows his love of nature [not the nature].
General Sherman said that war is hell. [*War* names a general category.]
The war in Iraq left many wounded. [*War* names a specific war.]

With plural count nouns

A or *an* never precedes a plural noun. *The* does not precede a plural noun that names a general category. *The* does precede a plural noun that names specific representatives of a category.

Men and women are different. [*Men* and *women* name general categories.]

The women formed a team. [*Women* refers to specific people.]

With noncount nouns

A or *an* never precedes a noncount noun. *The* does precede a noncount noun that names specific representatives of a general category.

Vegetation suffers from drought. [*Vegetation* names a general category.]
The vegetation in the park withered or died. [*Vegetation* refers to specific plants.]

With proper nouns

A or *an* never precedes a proper noun. *The* generally does not precede proper nouns.

Garcia lives in Boulder.

There are exceptions, however. For instance, we generally use *the* before plural proper nouns (*the Murphys, the Boston Celtics*) and before the names of groups and organizations (*the Department of Justice, the Sierra Club*), ships (*the Lusitania*), oceans (*the Pacific*), mountain ranges (*the Alps*), regions (*the Middle East*), rivers (*the Mississippi*), and some countries (*the United States, the Netherlands*).

2 Other determiners

The uses of English determiners besides articles also depend on context and kind of noun. The following determiners may be used as indicated with singular count nouns, plural count nouns, or non-count nouns.

With any kind of noun (singular count, plural count, noncount)

my, our, your, his, her, its, their, possessive nouns (*boy's, boys'*)
whose, which(ever), what(ever)
some, any, the other
no

<u>Their</u> account is overdrawn. [Singular count.]
<u>Their</u> funds are low. [Plural count.]
<u>Their</u> money is running out. [Noncount.]

Only with singular nouns (count and noncount)

this, that

<u>This</u> account has some money. [Count.]
<u>That</u> information may help. [Noncount.]

Only with noncount nouns and plural count nouns

most, enough, other, such, all, all of the, a lot of

<u>Most</u> funds are committed. [Plural count.]
<u>Most</u> money is needed elsewhere. [Noncount.]

Only with singular count nouns

one, every, each, either, neither, another

<u>One</u> car must be sold. [Singular count.]

Only with plural count nouns

these, those
both, many, few, a few, fewer, fewest, several
two, three, and so forth

<u>Two</u> cars are unnecessary. [Plural count.]

Note *Few* means "not many" or "not enough." *A few* means "some" or "a small but sufficient quantity."

<u>Few</u> committee members came to the meeting.
<u>A few</u> members can keep the committee going.

Do not use *much* with a plural count noun.

<u>Many</u> [not <u>Much</u>] members want to help.

Only with noncount nouns

much, more, little, a little, less, least, a large amount of

<u>Less</u> luxury is in order. [Noncount.]

Note *Little* means "not many" or "not enough." *A little* means "some" or "a small but sufficient quantity."

Little time remains before the conference.
The members need a little help from their colleagues.

Do not use *many* with a noncount noun.

Much [not Many] work remains.

34 Misplaced and Dangling Modifiers

Video tutorial

The arrangement of words in a sentence is an important clue to their relationships. Modifiers will be unclear if readers can't connect them to the words they modify.

Grammar checkers A grammar checker cannot recognize most problems with modifiers. For instance, a checker failed to flag the misplaced modifiers in *Gasoline high prices affect usually car sales* or the dangling modifier in *The vandalism was visible passing the building.*

34a Reposition misplaced modifiers.

Podcast

A **misplaced modifier** falls in the wrong place in a sentence. It is usually awkward or confusing. It may even be unintentionally funny.

1 Clear placement

Exercise

Readers tend to link a modifier to the nearest word it could modify—usually the nearest noun. Any other placement can link the modifier to the wrong word.

Confusing	He served steak to the men on paper plates.
Clear	He served the men steak on paper plates.
Confusing	According to the police, many dogs are killed by automobiles and trucks roaming unleashed.
Clear	According to the police, many dogs roaming unleashed are killed by automobiles and trucks.

2 *Only* and other limiting modifiers

Limiting modifiers include *almost, even, exactly, hardly, just, merely, nearly, only, scarcely,* and *simply.* For clarity place such a modifier immediately before the word or word group you intend it to limit.

Unclear	The archaeologist only found the skull on her last dig.
Clear	The archaeologist found only the skull on her last dig.
Clear	The archaeologist found the skull only on her last dig.

3 Adverbs with grammatical units

Adverbs can often move around in sentences, but some will be awkward if they interrupt certain grammatical units:

Exercise

■ **A long adverb stops the flow from subject to verb.**

subject ⌐—— adverb ——⌐ verb
Awkward The city, after the hurricane, began massive rebuilding.

⌐—— adverb ——⌐ subject verb
Revised After the hurricane, the city began massive rebuilding.

■ **Any adverb is awkward between a verb and its direct object.**

⌐— verb —⌐ adverb object
Awkward The hurricane had damaged badly many homes in the city.

⌐— verb —⌐ object
Revised The hurricane had badly damaged many homes in the city.
adverb

■ **A *split infinitive*—an adverb placed between *to* and the verb—annoys many readers.**

infinitive
Awkward The weather service expected temperatures to not rise.

infinitive
Revised The weather service expected temperatures not to rise.

A split infinitive may sometimes be natural and preferable, though it may still bother some readers.

⌐— infinitive —⌐
Several US industries expect to more than triple their use of robots.

┌─ **Key terms** ──
adverb A word or word group that describes a verb, adjective, other adverb, or whole word group, specifying how, when, where, or to what extent: *quickly see, solid like a boulder.*

direct object The receiver of the verb's action: *The car hit a tree.* (See p. 187.)

infinitive A verb form consisting of *to* plus the verb's plain (or dictionary) form: *to produce, to enjoy.* (See p. 190.)

In the preceding example, the split infinitive is more economical than the alternatives, such as *Several US industries expect to increase their use of robots by more than three times.*

- **A long adverb is usually awkward inside a verb phrase.**

Awkward People who have osteoporosis can, by increasing their daily intake of calcium and vitamin D, improve their bone density.

Revised By increasing their daily intake of calcium and vitamin D, people who have osteoporosis can improve their bone density.

CULTURE LANGUAGE In a question, place a one-word adverb immediately after the subject:

Will spacecraft ever be able to leave the solar system?

4 Other adverb positions **CULTURE LANGUAGE**

Placements of a few adverbs can be difficult for nonnative speakers of English:

- **Adverbs of frequency** include *always, never, occasionally, often, rarely, seldom, sometimes,* and *usually.* They generally appear at the beginning of a sentence, before a one-word verb, or after a helping verb.

Robots have sometimes put humans out of work.

Sometimes robots have put humans out of work.

Adverbs of frequency always follow the verb *be.*

Robots are often helpful to workers.

Robots are seldom useful around the house.

When *rarely, seldom,* or another negative adverb of frequency begins a sentence, the normal subject-verb order changes. (See also **3** p. 154.)

Rarely are robots simple machines.

Key term

verb phrase A verb consisting of a helping verb and a main verb that carries the principal meaning: *will have begun, can see.* (See p. 181.)

■ **Adverbs of degree** include *absolutely, almost, certainly, completely, definitely, especially, extremely, hardly,* and *only.* They fall just before the word modified (an adjective, another adverb, sometimes a verb).

adverb   adjective
Robots have been especially useful in making cars.

■ **Adverbs of manner** include *badly, beautifully, openly, sweetly, tightly, well,* and others that describe how something is done. They usually fall after the verb.

verb   adverb
Robots work smoothly on assembly lines.

■ **The adverb** *not* changes position depending on what it modifies. When it modifies a verb, place it after the helping verb (or the first helping verb if more than one).

helping   main
verb   verb
Robots do not think.

When *not* modifies another adverb or an adjective, place it before the other modifier.

adjective
Robots are not sleek machines.

5 Order of adjectives (CULTURE LANGUAGE)

English follows distinctive rules for arranging two or three adjectives before a noun. (A string of more than three adjectives before a noun is rare.) The rules arrange adjectives by type and by meaning, as shown in the following chart:

Determiner	Opinion	Size or shape	Color	Origin	Material	Noun used as adjective	Noun
many						state	**laws**
	lovely		green	Thai			**birds**
a	fine			German			**camera**
this		square			wooden		**table**
all						business	**reports**
the			blue		litmus		**paper**

See **5** p. 268 on punctuating adjectives before a noun.

┌─ **Key term** ─────────────────────────────
adjective A word that describes a noun or pronoun, specifying which one, what quality, or how many: *good one, three cars.* (See p. 181.)

34b Connect dangling modifiers to their sentences.

A **dangling modifier** does not sensibly modify anything in its sentence.

Dangling Passing the building, the vandalism became visible. ⟶ ⑦

Dangling modifiers usually introduce sentences, contain a verb form, and imply but do not name a subject. In the example above, the implied subject is the someone or something passing the building. Readers assume that this implied subject is the same as the subject of the sentence (*vandalism* in the example), but vandalism does not pass buildings. The modifier "dangles" because it does not connect sensibly to the rest of the sentence. Here is another example:

Dangling Although intact, graffiti covered every inch of the walls and windows. [The walls and windows, not the graffiti, were intact.] ⟶ ⑦

To revise a dangling modifier, you have to recast the sentence it appears in. (Revising just by moving the modifier will leave it dangling: *The vandalism became visible passing the building.*) Choose a revision method depending on what you want to emphasize in the sentence.

- **Rewrite the dangling modifier as a complete clause with its own stated subject and verb.** Readers can accept that the new subject and the sentence subject are different.

Dangling Passing the building, the vandalism became visible. ⟶ ⑦

Identifying and revising dangling modifiers

Exercise

- **Find a subject.** If the modifier lacks a subject of its own (e.g., *when in diapers*), identify what it describes.
- **Connect the subject and modifier.** Verify that what the modifier describes is in fact the subject of the main clause. If it is not, the modifier is probably dangling:

┌── modifier ──┐   subject
Dangling When in diapers, my mother remarried.

- **Revise as needed.** Revise a dangling modifier (*a*) by recasting it with a subject of its own or (*b*) by changing the subject of the main clause:

Revision *a* When I was in diapers, my mother remarried.
Revision *b* When in diapers, I attended my mother's second wedding.

Revised As we passed the building, the vandalism became visible.

- **Change the subject of the sentence to a word the modifier properly describes.**

Dangling Trying to understand the causes, vandalism has been extensively studied.

Revised Trying to understand the causes, researchers have extensively studied vandalism.

Sentence Faults

A word group punctuated as a sentence will confuse or annoy readers if it lacks needed parts, has too many parts, or has parts that don't fit together.

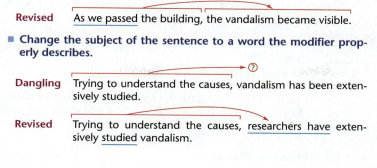

35 Sentence Fragments

A **sentence fragment** is part of a sentence that is set off as if it were a whole sentence by an initial capital letter and a final period or other end punctuation. Although writers occasionally use fragments deliberately and effectively (see p. 248), readers perceive most fragments as serious errors.

Video tutorial

Exercise

Complete sentence versus sentence fragment

A complete sentence or main clause
1. contains a subject and a predicate verb (The wind blows)
2. and is not a subordinate clause (beginning with a word such as *because* or *who*).

A sentence fragment
1. lacks a predicate verb (*The wind blowing*),
2. or lacks a subject (*And blows*),
3. or is a subordinate clause not attached to a complete sentence (*Because the wind blows*).

---

mycomplab

Visit *mycomplab.com* for the eText and for resources and exercises on sentence fragments.

Grammar checkers A grammar checker can spot many but not all sentence fragments, and it may flag sentences that are actually commands, such as *Continue reading*.

35a Test your sentences for completeness.

Video tutorial

A word group that is punctuated as a sentence should pass *all three* of the following tests. If it does not, it is a fragment and needs revision.

Test 1: Find the predicate verb.

Look for a verb that can serve as the predicate of a sentence. Some fragments lack any verb at all.

Fragment	Uncountable numbers of sites on the Web.
Revised	Uncountable numbers of sites make up the Web.

Other fragments may include a verb form but not a **finite verb**— that is, a verb that changes form as indicated below. A verbal does not change; it cannot serve as a predicate verb without the aid of a helping verb.

	Finite verbs in complete sentences	Verbals in sentence fragments
Singular	The network grows.	The network growing.
Plural	Networks grow.	Networks growing.
Present	The network grows.	
Past	The network grew.	The network growing.
Future	The network will grow.	

CULTURE LANGUAGE Some languages allow forms of *be* to be omitted as helping verbs or linking verbs. But English requires stating forms of *be,* as shown in the following revised example.

Fragments	The network growing. It much larger than anticipated.
Revised	The network is growing. It is much larger than anticipated.

Key terms

predicate The part of a sentence containing a verb that asserts something about the subject: *Ducks swim.* (See pp. 184–85.)

verbal A verb form that can serve as a noun, a modifier, or a part of a sentence verb, but not alone as the only verb of a sentence: *drawing, to draw, drawn.* (See p. 189.)

helping verb A verb such as *is, were, have, might,* and *could* that combines with various verb forms to indicate time and other kinds of meaning: for instance, *were drawing, might draw.* (See p. 181.)

Test 2: Find the subject.

The subject of the sentence will usually come before the verb. If there is no subject, the word group is probably a fragment:

| Fragment | And has enormous popular appeal. |
| Revised | And <u>the Web</u> has enormous popular appeal. |

In one kind of complete sentence, a command, the subject *you* is understood: [*You*] *Try this recipe.*

CULTURE LANGUAGE Some languages allow the omission of the sentence subject, especially when it is a pronoun. But in English, except in commands, the subject is always stated:

| Fragment | Web commerce has exploded. Has hurt traditional stores. |
| Revised | Web commerce has exploded. <u>It</u> has hurt traditional stores. |

Test 3: Make sure the clause is not subordinate.

A subordinate clause usually begins with a subordinating word, such as one of the following:

Subordinating conjunctions			Relative pronouns	
after	once	until	that	who/whom
although	since	when	which	whoever/whomever
as	than	where		whose
because	that	whereas		
if	unless	while		

Subordinate clauses serve as parts of sentences (as nouns or modifiers), not as whole sentences:

Fragment	When the government devised the Internet.
Revised	The government devised the Internet.
Revised	When the government devised the Internet, <u>no expansive computer network existed</u>.

| Fragment | The reason that the government devised the Internet. |
| Revised | The reason that the government devised the Internet <u>was to link departments and defense contractors</u>. |

Note Questions beginning with *how, what, when, where, which, who, whom, whose,* and *why* are not sentence fragments: *Who was responsible? When did it happen?*

Key terms

subject The part of a sentence that names who or what performs the action or makes the assertion of the predicate: *Ducks swim.* (See pp. 184–85.)

subordinate clause A word group that contains a subject and a predicate, begins with a subordinating word such as *because* or *who,* and is not a question: *Ducks can swim <u>when they are young</u>.* A subordinate clause may serve as a modifier or as a noun. (See p. 191.)

35b | Revise sentence fragments.

Video tutorial

Almost all sentence fragments can be corrected in one of the two ways shown in the following box. The choice depends on the importance of the information in the fragment and thus how much you want to stress it.

Revision of sentence fragments

Option 1

Rewrite the fragment as a complete sentence. This revision gives the information in the fragment the same importance as that in other complete sentences.

Fragment	A major improvement in public health occurred with the widespread use of vaccines. Which protected children against life-threatening diseases.
Revised	A major improvement in public health occurred with the widespread use of vaccines. They protected children against life-threatening diseases.

Two main clauses may be separated by a semicolon instead of a period (see **5** p. 273).

Option 2

Combine the fragment with a main clause. This revision subordinates the information in the fragment to the information in the main clause.

Fragment	The polio vaccine eradicated the disease from most of the globe. The first vaccine to be used widely.
Revised	The polio vaccine, the first to be used widely, eradicated the disease from most of the globe.

35c | Be aware of the acceptable uses of incomplete sentences.

Podcast

A few word groups lacking the usual subject-predicate combination are incomplete sentences, but they are not fragments because they conform to the expectations of most readers. They include commands (*Move along. Shut the window.*); exclamations (*Oh no!*); questions and answers (*Where next? To Kansas.*); and descriptions in employment résumés (*Weekly volunteer in soup kitchen.*)

Experienced writers sometimes use sentence fragments when they want to achieve a special effect. Such fragments appear more in informal than in formal writing. Unless you are experienced and thoroughly secure in your own writing, you should avoid all fragments and concentrate on writing clear, well-formed sentences.

When two main clauses fall in a row, readers need a signal that one main clause is ending and another is beginning. The four ways to provide this signal appear in the box on the next page.

Two problems in punctuating main clauses fail to signal the break between main clauses. One is the **comma splice,** in which the clauses are joined (or spliced) *only* with a comma:

Video tutorial

Comma splice   The ship was huge, its mast stood eighty feet high.

Video tutorial

The other is the **fused sentence** (or **run-on sentence**), in which no punctuation or conjunction appears between the clauses.

Exercise

Fused sentence   The ship was huge its mast stood eighty feet high.

Grammar checkers   A grammar checker can detect many comma splices, but it will miss most fused sentences. A checker may also question sentences that are actually correct, such as *Money being tighter now than before, we need to spend carefully*.

CULTURE LANGUAGE   In standard American English, a sentence may not include more than one main clause unless the clauses are separated by a comma and a coordinating conjunction or by a semicolon. If your native language does not have such a rule or has accustomed you to writing long sentences, you may need to edit your English writing especially for comma splices and fused sentences.

36a   Separate main clauses not joined by *and, but,* or another coordinating conjunction.

If your readers point out comma splices or fused sentences in your writing, you're not creating enough separation between main clauses in your sentences. Punctuate consecutive main clauses in the following ways.

Video tutorial

Separate sentences

Make the clauses into separate sentences when the ideas expressed are only loosely related.

┌─ **Key term** ───

main clause A word group that can stand alone as a sentence because it contains a subject and a predicate and does not begin with a subordinating word: *A dictionary is essential.*
└──

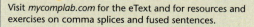

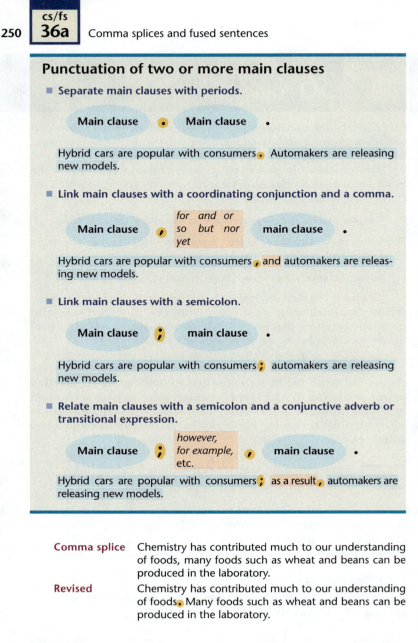

Punctuation of two or more main clauses

- **Separate main clauses with periods.**

  Main clause **.** Main clause **.**

  Hybrid cars are popular with consumers. Automakers are releasing new models.

- **Link main clauses with a coordinating conjunction and a comma.**

  Main clause **,** *for and or so but nor yet* main clause **.**

  Hybrid cars are popular with consumers, and automakers are releasing new models.

- **Link main clauses with a semicolon.**

  Main clause **;** main clause **.**

  Hybrid cars are popular with consumers; automakers are releasing new models.

- **Relate main clauses with a semicolon and a conjunctive adverb or transitional expression.**

  Main clause **;** *however, for example, etc.* **,** main clause **.**

  Hybrid cars are popular with consumers; as a result, automakers are releasing new models.

Comma splice	Chemistry has contributed much to our understanding of foods, many foods such as wheat and beans can be produced in the laboratory.
Revised	Chemistry has contributed much to our understanding of foods. Many foods such as wheat and beans can be produced in the laboratory.

Key terms

coordinating conjunction *And, but, or, nor, for, so, yet.* (See p. 183.)

conjunctive adverb A modifier that describes the relation of the ideas in two clauses, such as *consequently, however, indeed, moreover,* and *therefore.* (See p. 252.)

Coordinating conjunction

Insert a coordinating conjunction in a comma splice when the ideas in the main clauses are closely related and equally important:

| Comma splice | Some laboratory-grown foods taste good, they are nutritious. |
| Revised | Some laboratory-grown foods taste good, <u>and</u> they are nutritious. |

In a fused sentence insert a comma and a coordinating conjunction:

| Fused sentence | Chemists have made much progress they still have a way to go. |
| Revised | Chemists have made much progress, <u>but</u> they still have a way to go. |

Semicolon

Insert a semicolon between clauses if the relation between the ideas is very close and obvious without a conjunction:

| Comma splice | Good taste is rare in laboratory-grown vegetables, they are usually bland. |
| Revised | Good taste is rare in laboratory-grown vegetables; they are usually bland. |

Subordination

When one idea is less important than the other, express the less important idea in a subordinate clause:

| Comma splice | The vitamins are adequate, the flavor is poor. |
| Revised | <u>Although</u> the vitamins are adequate, the flavor is poor. |

36b　Separate main clauses related by *however, for example,* and so on.

Two groups of words describe how one main clause relates to another: **conjunctive adverbs** and other **transitional expressions.** See the list of these words on the next page. (See also **1** pp. 44–45 for a longer list of transitional expressions.)

When two main clauses are related by a conjunctive adverb or another transitional expression, they must be separated by a period or by a semicolon. The adverb or expression is also generally set off by a comma or commas.

Key term

subordinate clause A word group that contains a subject and a predicate, begins with a subordinating word such as *because* or *who,* and is not a question: *Ducks can swim <u>when they are young</u>.* A subordinate clause may serve as a modifier or as a noun. (See p. 191.)

Common conjunctive adverbs and transitional expressions

accordingly	for instance	instead	otherwise
anyway	further	in the meantime	similarly
as a result	furthermore	in the past	still
at last	hence	likewise	that is
besides	however	meanwhile	then
certainly	incidentally	moreover	thereafter
consequently	in contrast	nevertheless	therefore
even so	indeed	nonetheless	thus
finally	in fact	now	undoubtedly
for all that	in other words	of course	until now
for example	in short	on the contrary	

Comma splice Healthcare costs are higher in the United States than in many other countries, consequently health insurance is also more costly.

Revised Healthcare costs are higher in the United States than in many other countries. Consequently, health insurance is also more costly.

Revised Healthcare costs are higher in the United States than in many other countries; consequently, health insurance is also more costly.

Conjunctive adverbs and transitional expressions are different from coordinating conjunctions (*and, but,* and so on) and subordinating conjunctions (*although, because,* and so on):

- **Unlike conjunctions, conjunctive adverbs and transitional expressions do not join two clauses into a grammatical unit.** They merely describe the way two clauses relate in meaning.
- **Unlike conjunctions, conjunctive adverbs and transitional expressions can be moved within a clause.** No matter where in the clause an adverb or expression falls, though, the clause must be separated from another main clause by a period or semicolon:

Healthcare costs are higher is the United States than in many other countries; health insurance, consequently, is also more costly.

37 Mixed Sentences

A **mixed sentence** contains parts that do not fit together. The misfit may be in meaning or in grammar.

Grammar checkers A grammar checker may recognize a simple mixed construction such as *reason is because,* but it will fail to flag most mixed sentences.

37a Match subjects and predicates in meaning.

In a sentence with mixed meaning, the subject is said to do or be something illogical. Such a mixture is sometimes called **faulty predication** because the predicate conflicts with the subject.

1 Illogical equation with *be*

When a form of *be* connects a subject and a word that describes the subject (a complement), the subject and complement must be logically related:

Mixed   A compromise between the city and the country would be the ideal place to live.

Revised   A community that offered the best qualities of both city and country would be the ideal place to live.

2 *Is when, is where*

Definitions require nouns on both sides of *be.* Clauses that define and begin with *when* or *where* are common in speech but should be avoided in writing:

Mixed   An examination is when you are tested on what you know.

Revised   An examination is a test of what you know.

Key terms

subject The part of a sentence that names who or what performs the action or makes the assertion of the predicate: *Geese fly.* (See pp. 184–85.)

predicate The part of a sentence containing a verb that asserts something about the subject: *Geese fly.* (See pp. 184–85.)

---

mycomplab

Visit *mycomplab.com* for the eText and for resources on mixed sentences.

3 *Reason is because*

The commonly heard construction *reason is because* is redundant since *because* means "for the reason that":

Mixed   The <u>reason</u> the temple requests donations <u>is because</u> the school needs expansion.

Revised   The <u>reason</u> the temple requests donations <u>is that</u> the school needs expansion.

Revised   The temple requests donations <u>because</u> the school needs expansion.

4 Other mixed meanings

Faulty predications are not confined to sentences with *be*:

Mixed   The u͟se of emission controls w͟as created to reduce air pollution.

Revised   Emission <u>controls</u> <u>were created</u> to reduce air pollution.

37b Untangle sentences that are mixed in grammar.

Exercise

Many mixed sentences start with one grammatical plan or construction but end with a different one:

        ⌐——— modifier (prepositional phrase) ————⌐ verb
Mixed   By paying more attention to impressions than facts leads us to misjudge others.

        ⌐——— modifier (prepositional phrase)———⌐ subject
Revised   By paying more attention to impressions than facts, <u>we</u>
            verb
        <u>misjudge</u> others.

Constructions that use *Just because* clauses as subjects are common in speech but should be avoided in writing:

        ⌐— modifier (subordinate clause)—⌐⌐— verb —⌐
Mixed   Just because no one is watching doesn't mean we have license to break the law.

        ⌐— modifier (subordinate clause)—⌐ subject + verb
Revised   Even when no one is watching, <u>we don't have</u> license to break the law.

A mixed sentence is especially likely when you are working on a computer and connect parts of two sentences or rewrite half a sentence but not the other half. A mixed sentence may also occur when you don't make the subject and predicate verb carry the principal meaning. (See **3** p. 141.)

37c State parts of sentences, such as subjects, only once.

In some languages other than English, certain parts of sentences may be repeated. These include the subject in any kind of clause or an object or adverb in an adjective clause. In English, however, these parts are stated only once in a clause.

1 Repetition of subject

You may be tempted to restate a subject as a pronoun before the verb. But the subject needs stating only once in its clause:

Faulty	The liquid it reached a temperature of 110°C.
Revised	The liquid reached a temperature of 110°C.

Faulty	Gases in the liquid they escaped.
Revised	Gases in the liquid escaped.

2 Repetition in an adjective clause

Adjective clauses begin with *who, whom, whose, which, that, where,* and *when.* The beginning word replaces another word: the subject (*He is the person who called*), an object of a verb or preposition (*He is the person whom I mentioned*), or a preposition and pronoun (*He knows the office where [in which] the conference will occur*).

Do not state the word being replaced in an adjective clause:

Faulty	The technician whom the test depended on her was burned. [*Whom* should replace *her.*]
Revised	The technician whom the test depended on was burned.

Adjective clauses beginning with *where* or *when* do not need an adverb such as *there* or *then*:

Faulty	Gases escaped at a moment when the technician was unprepared then.
Revised	Gases escaped at a moment when the technician was unprepared.

Note *Whom, which,* and similar words are sometimes omitted but are still understood by the reader. Thus the word being replaced should not be stated.

Faulty	Accidents rarely happen to technicians the lab has trained them. [*Whom* is understood: . . . *technicians whom the lab has trained.*]
Revised	Accidents rarely happen to technicians the lab has trained.

Punctuation

PART 5

Punctuation

38 End Punctuation

End a sentence with one of three punctuation marks: a period (.), a question mark (?), or an exclamation point (!).

Grammar checkers A grammar checker may flag missing question marks after direct questions or incorrect combinations of marks (such as a question mark and a period at the end of a sentence), but it cannot do much else.

Video tutorial

Exercise

38a Use a period after most sentences and with some abbreviations.

1 Statements, mild commands, and indirect questions

Statement

The airline went bankrupt.   It no longer flies.

Mild command

Think of the possibilities.   Please consider others.

Indirect question

An **indirect question** reports what someone asked but not in the exact form or words of the original question:

The judge asked why I had been driving with my lights off.
No one asked how we got home.

CULTURE LANGUAGE In standard American English, the reporting verb in an indirect question (for example, *asked* or *said*) usually precedes a clause that contains a subject and verb in normal order, not question order: *The reporter asked why the negotiations failed* [not *why did the negotiations fail*].

2 Abbreviations

Use periods with abbreviations that consist of or end in small letters. Otherwise, omit periods from abbreviations.

Dr.	Mr., Mrs.	e.g.	Feb.	ft.
St.	Ms.	i.e.	p.	a.m., p.m.
PhD	BC, BCE	USA	IBM	AM, PM
BA	AD, CE	US	USMC	AIDS

Note When a sentence ends in an abbreviation with a period, don't add a second period: *My first class is at 8 a.m.*

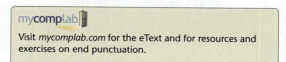

38b Use a question mark after a direct question and sometimes to indicate doubt.

1 Direct questions

Who will follow her**?**
What is the difference between these two people**?**

After indirect questions, use a period: *We wondered who would follow her.* (See the preceding page.)

Questions in a series are each followed by a question mark:

The officer asked how many times the suspect had been arrested. Three times**?** Four times**?** More than that**?**

Note Do not combine question marks with other question marks, periods, commas, or other punctuation.

2 Doubt

A question mark within parentheses can indicate doubt about a number or date.

The Greek philosopher Socrates was born in 470 (**?**) BC and died in 399 BC from drinking poison. [Socrates's birthdate is not known for sure.]

Use sentence structure and words, not a question mark, to express sarcasm or irony.

Not Stern's friendliness (?) bothered Crane.
But Stern's insincerity bothered Crane.

38c Use an exclamation point after an emphatic statement, interjection, or command.

No**!** We must not lose this election**!**
Come here immediately**!**

Follow mild interjections and commands with commas or periods, as appropriate: *Oh, call whenever you can.*

Note Do not combine exclamation points with periods, commas, or other punctuation marks. And use exclamation points sparingly, even in informal writing. Overused, they'll fail to impress readers, and they may make you sound overemotional.

┌─ **Key term** ──────────────────────────────────
interjection A word that expresses feeling or commands attention, either alone or within a sentence: *Oh! Hey! Wow!*
└──

39 The Comma

The comma (,) is the most common punctuation mark inside sentences. Its main uses are shown in the box on the next page.

Video
tutorial

Grammar checkers A grammar checker will ignore many comma errors. For example, a checker failed to catch the missing commas in *We cooked lasagna_spinach_and apple pie* and the misused commas in *The trip was short but, the weather was perfect.*

39a Use a comma before *and, but,* or another coordinating conjunction linking main clauses.

When a coordinating conjunction links words or phrases, do not use a comma: *Dugain plays_and sings Irish_and English folk songs.* However, *do* use a comma when a coordinating conjunction joins main clauses, as in the next examples.

Exercise

Caffeine can keep coffee drinkers alert, and it may elevate their mood.

Caffeine was once thought to be safe, but now researchers warn of harmful effects.

Coffee drinkers may suffer sleeplessness, for the drug acts as a stimulant.

Note The comma goes *before,* not after, a coordinating conjunction that links main clauses: *Caffeine increases heart rate, and it* [not *and, it*] *constricts blood vessels.*

Exception Some writers omit the comma between main clauses that are very short and closely related in meaning: *Caffeine helps but it also hurts.* If you are in doubt about whether to use the comma in such a sentence, use it. It will always be correct.

39b Use a comma to set off most introductory elements.

An **introductory element** begins a sentence and modifies a word or words in the main clause. It is usually followed by a comma.

Exercise

Key terms

coordinating conjunctions *And, but, or, nor,* and sometimes *for, so, yet.* (See **4** p. 183.)

main clause A word group that can stand alone as a sentence because it contains a subject and a predicate and does not begin with a subordinating word: *Water freezes at temperatures below 32°F.* (See **4** p. 191.)

---

mycomplab

Visit *mycomplab.com* for the eText and for resources and exercises on the comma.

Video
tutorial

Principal uses of the comma

■ **Separate main clauses linked by a coordinating conjunction** (previous page):

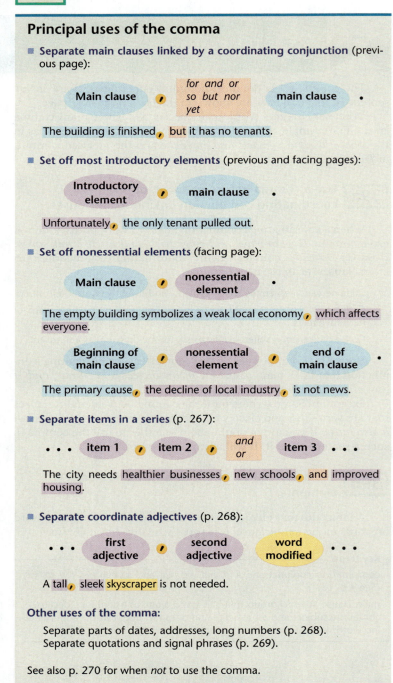

Main clause　,　*for and or*
so but nor
yet　main clause　.

The building is finished, but it has no tenants.

■ **Set off most introductory elements** (previous and facing pages):

Introductory
element　,　main clause　.

Unfortunately, the only tenant pulled out.

■ **Set off nonessential elements** (facing page):

Main clause　,　nonessential
element　.

The empty building symbolizes a weak local economy, which affects everyone.

Beginning of
main clause　,　nonessential
element　,　end of
main clause　.

The primary cause, the decline of local industry, is not news.

■ **Separate items in a series** (p. 267):

. . .　item 1　,　item 2　,　*and*
or　item 3　. . .

The city needs healthier businesses, new schools, and improved housing.

■ **Separate coordinate adjectives** (p. 268):

. . .　first
adjective　,　second
adjective　word
modified　. . .

A tall, sleek skyscraper is not needed.

Other uses of the comma:

Separate parts of dates, addresses, long numbers (p. 268).
Separate quotations and signal phrases (p. 269).

See also p. 270 for when *not* to use the comma.

Subordinate clause

Even when identical twins are raised apart, they grow up very like each other.

Verbal or verbal phrase

Explaining the similarity, some researchers claim that one's genes are one's destiny.

Concerned, other researchers deny the claim.

Prepositional phrase

In a debate that has lasted centuries, scientists use identical twins to argue for or against genetic destiny.

Transitional expression

Of course, scientists can now look directly at the genes themselves to answer questions.

You may omit the comma after a short subordinate clause or prepositional phrase if its omission does not create confusion: *When snow falls the city collapses. By the year 2000 the world population had topped 6 billion*. You may also omit the comma after some transitional expressions when they start sentences: *Thus the debate continues* (see p. 267). However, in both situations the comma is never wrong.

Note Take care to distinguish *-ing* words used as modifiers from *-ing* words used as subjects. The former almost always take a comma; the latter never do.

┌────── modifier ──────┐   subject   verb

Studying identical twins, geneticists learn about inheritance.

┌────── subject ──────┐   verb

Studying identical twins helps geneticists learn about inheritance.

39c   Use a comma or commas to set off nonessential elements.

Commas around part of a sentence often signal that the element is not necessary to the meaning. This **nonessential element**

Exercise

Key terms

subordinate clause A word group that contains a subject and a predicate, begins with a subordinating word such as *because* or *who,* and is not a question: *When water freezes, crystals form.* (See **4** p. 191.)

verbal A verb form used as an adjective, adverb, or noun. A verbal plus any object or modifier is a **verbal phrase**: *frozen water, ready to freeze, rapid freezing.* (See **4** p. 189.)

prepositional phrase A word group consisting of a preposition, such as *for* or *in,* followed by a noun or pronoun plus any modifiers: *in a jar, with a spoon.* (See **4** p. 189.)

transitional expression A word or phrase that shows the relationship between sentences: *for example, however, in fact, of course.* (See **1** pp. 44–45.)

may modify or rename the word it refers to, but it does not limit the word to a particular individual or group. The meaning of the word would still be clear if the element were deleted:

Nonessential element

The company, which is located in Oklahoma, has a good reputation.

(Because it does not restrict meaning, a nonessential element is also called a **nonrestrictive element**.)

In contrast, an **essential** (or **restrictive**) **element** *does* limit the word it refers to: the element cannot be omitted without leaving the meaning too general. Because it is essential, such an element is *not* set off with a comma or commas.

Essential element

The company rewards employees who work hard.

Omitting *who work hard* would distort the meaning: the company doesn't necessarily reward *all* employees, only the hardworking ones.

The same element in the same sentence may be essential or nonessential depending on your meaning and the context:

Essential

Not all the bands were equally well received, however. The band playing old music held the audience's attention. The other groups created much less excitement. [*Playing old music* identifies a particular band.]

Nonessential

A new band called Fats made its debut on Saturday night. The band, playing old music, held the audience's attention. If this performance is typical, the group has a bright future. [*Playing old music* adds information about a band already named.]

Note When a nonessential element falls in the middle of a sentence, be sure to set it off with a pair of commas, one *before* and one *after* the element.

1 Nonessential phrases and clauses

Most nonessential phrases and subordinate clauses function as adjectives or, less commonly, as adverbs. In each of the following examples, the underlined words could be omitted with no loss of clarity.

Key terms

phrase A word group lacking a subject or a verb or both: *in Duluth, carrying water.* (See **4** p. 188.)

subordinate clause A word group that contains a subject and a predicate, begins with a subordinating word such as *who* or *although,* and is not a question: *Samson, who is thirty, coaches in Utah.* (See **4** p. 191.)

A test for nonessential and essential elements

1. **Identify the element:**

   Hai Nguyen <u>who emigrated from Vietnam</u> lives in Dallas.
   Those <u>who emigrated with him</u> live elsewhere.

2. **Remove the element.** Does the fundamental meaning of the sentence change?

   Hai Nguyen lives in Dallas. *No.*
   Those live elsewhere. *Yes.* [Who are *Those*?]

3. **If** *no,* **the element is** *nonessential* **and** *should* **be set off with punctuation:**

   Hai Nguyen, who emigrated from Vietnam, lives in Dallas.

   If *yes,* **the element is** *essential* **and should** *not* **be set off with punctuation:**

   Those who emigrated with him live elsewhere.

Elizabeth Blackwell was the first woman to graduate from an American medical school, <u>in 1849</u>. [Phrase.]

She was a medical pioneer, <u>helping to found the first medical college for women</u>. [Phrase.]

She taught at the school, <u>which was affiliated with the New York Infirmary</u>. [Adjective clause.]

Blackwell, <u>who published books and papers on medicine</u>, practiced pediatrics and gynecology. [Adjective clause.]

She moved to England in 1869, <u>when she was forty-eight</u>. [Adverb clause.]

Note Use *that* only in an essential clause, never in a nonessential clause:

Faulty The tree, <u>that</u> is 120 years old, shades the house.
Revised The tree, <u>which</u> is 120 years old, shades the house.

Many writers reserve *which* for nonessential clauses.

2 Nonessential appositives

A nonessential appositive merely adds information about the word it refers to.

Toni Morrison's fifth novel, *Beloved,* won the Pulitzer Prize in 1988. [The word *fifth* identifies the novel, while the title adds a detail.]

Key term

appositive A noun that renames another noun immediately before it: *His wife, <u>Kyra Sedgwick</u>, is also an actor.* (See **4** p. 190.)

In contrast, an essential appositive limits or defines the word it refers to:

> Morrison's novel *The Bluest Eye* is about an African American girl who longs for blue eyes. [Morrison has written more than one novel, so the title is essential to identify the intended one.]

3 Other nonessential elements

Like nonessential modifiers or appositives, many other elements contribute to texture, tone, or overall clarity but are not essential to the meaning. Unlike nonessential modifiers or appositives, these other nonessential elements generally do not refer to any specific word in the sentence.

Note Use a pair of commas—one before, one after—when any of these elements falls in the middle of a sentence.

Absolute phrases

Household recycling having succeeded, the city now wants to extend the program to businesses.

Many businesses, their profits already squeezed, resist recycling.

Parenthetical and transitional expressions

Generally, set off parenthetical and transitional expressions with commas:

> The world's most celebrated holiday is, perhaps surprisingly, New Year's Day. [Parenthetical expression.]

> Interestingly, Americans have relatively few holidays. [Parenthetical expression.]

> US workers, for example, receive fewer holidays than European workers do. [Transitional expression.]

(Dashes and parentheses may also set off parenthetical expressions. See pp. 286–87.)

When a transitional expression links main clauses, precede it with a semicolon and follow it with a comma (see p. 273):

> European workers often have long paid vacations; indeed, they may receive a full month after just a few years with a company.

Key terms

absolute phrase A phrase modifying a whole main clause and consisting of a participle and its subject: *Their homework completed, the children watched TV.* (See **4** p. 190.)

parenthetical expression An explanatory or supplemental word or phrase, such as *all things considered, to be frank,* or a brief example or fact. (See p. 287.)

transitional expression A word or phrase that shows the relationship between sentences: *for example, however, in fact, of course.* (See **1** pp. 44–45.)

Exception The conjunctions *and* and *but,* sometimes used as transitional expressions, are never followed by commas (see p. 261). Usage varies with some other transitional expressions, depending on the expression and the writer's judgment. Many writers omit commas with expressions that we read without pauses, such as *also, hence, next, now, then,* and *thus.* The same applies to *therefore* and *instead* when they fall inside or at the ends of clauses.

US workers therefore put in more work days. But the days themselves may be shorter.

Then the total hours worked would come out roughly the same.

Phrases of contrast

The substance, not the style, is important.

Substance, unlike style, cannot be faked.

Tag questions

They don't stop to consider others, do they?

Jones should be allowed to vote, shouldn't he?

Yes* and *no

Yes, the editorial did have a point.

No, that can never be.

Words of direct address

Cody, please bring me the newspaper.

With all due respect, sir, I will not.

Mild interjections

Well, you will never know who did it.

Oh, they forgot all about the baby.

39d Use commas between items in a series.

A **series** consists of three or more items of equal importance. The items may be words, phrases, or clauses.

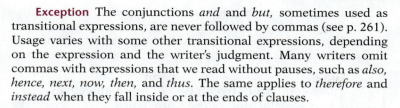
Podcast

Anna Spingle married at the age of seventeen, had three children by twenty-one, and divorced at twenty-two.

She worked as a cook, a baby-sitter, and a crossing guard.

Key terms

tag question A question at the end of a statement, consisting of a pronoun, a helping verb, and sometimes *not*: *It isn't wet, is it*?

interjection A word that expresses feeling or commands attention: *Oh, must we?*

Some writers omit the comma before the coordinating conjunction in a series (*Breakfast consisted of coffee, eggs and kippers*). But the final comma is never wrong, and it always helps the reader see the last two items as separate.

39e Use commas between two or more adjectives that equally modify the same word.

Podcast

Exercise

Adjectives that equally modify the same word—**coordinate adjectives**—may be separated either by *and* or by a comma.

Spingle's scratched and dented car is old, but it gets her to work.
She has dreams of a sleek, shiny car.

Adjectives are not coordinate—and should not be separated by commas—when the one nearer the noun is more closely related to the noun in meaning.

Spingle's children work at various part-time jobs.
They all expect to go to a nearby community college.

Tests for commas with adjectives

1. **Identify the adjectives.**

   She was a faithful sincere friend.
   They are dedicated medical students.

2. **Can the adjectives be reversed without changing meaning?**

   She was a sincere faithful friend. *Yes.*
   They are medical dedicated students. *No.*

3. **Can the word *and* be sensibly inserted between the adjectives?**

   She was a faithful and sincere friend. *Yes.*
   They are dedicated and medical students. *No.*

4. **If *yes* to both questions, the adjectives *are* coordinate and *should* be separated by a comma.**

   She was a faithful, sincere friend.

   If *no* to both questions, the adjectives are *not* coordinate and should *not* be separated by a comma.

   They are dedicated medical students.

39f Use commas in dates, addresses, place names, and long numbers.

Within a sentence, any date, address, or place name that contains a comma should also end with a comma.

Dates

July 4, 1776, is the date the Declaration was signed.

The bombing of Pearl Harbor on Sunday, December 7, 1941, prompted American entry into World War II.

Do not use commas between the parts of a date in inverted order (*15 December 1992*) or in dates consisting of a month or season and a year (*December 1941*).

Addresses and place names

Use the address 220 Cornell Road, Woodside, California 94062, for all correspondence. [Do not use a comma between a state name and a zip code.]

Columbus, Ohio, is the location of Ohio State University.

Long numbers

Use the comma to separate the figures in long numbers into groups of three, counting from the right. With numbers of four digits, the comma is optional.

The new assembly plant cost $7,525,000.

A kilometer is 3,281 feet [*or* 3281 feet].

CULTURE LANGUAGE Usage in standard American English differs from that in some other languages and dialects, which use a period, not a comma, to separate the figures in long numbers.

39g Use commas with quotations according to standard practice.

Exercise

The words *she said, he writes,* and so on identify the source of a quotation. These **signal phrases** should be separated from the quotation by punctuation, usually a comma or commas.

"Knowledge is power," writes Francis Bacon.

"The shore has a dual nature," observes Rachel Carson, "changing with the swing of the tides." [The signal phrase interrupts the quotation at a comma and thus ends with a comma.]

Exceptions Do not use commas with signal phrases in the following situations:

- ■ **Use a semicolon or a period after a signal phrase that interupts a quotation between main clauses.** The choice depends on the punctuation of the original:

  Not   "That part of my life was over," she wrote, "his words had sealed it shut."

  But   "That part of my life was over," she wrote. "His words had sealed it shut." [*She wrote* interrupts the quotation at a period.]

  Or   "That part of my life was over," she wrote; "his words had sealed it shut." [*She wrote* interrupts the quotation at a semicolon.]

- Omit a comma when a signal phrase follows a quotation ending in an exclamation point or a question mark:

   "Claude**!**" Mrs. Harrison called.
   "Why must I come home**?**" he asked.

- Use a colon when a complete sentence introduces a quotation:

   Her statement was clear**:** "I will not resign."

- Omit commas when a quotation is integrated into your sentence structure, including a quotation introduced by *that*:

   James Baldwin insists that "one must never, in one's life, accept . . . in-justices as commonplace."

   Baldwin thought that the violence of a riot "had been devised as a corrective" to his own violence.

- Omit commas with a quoted title unless it is a nonessential appositive:

   The Beatles recorded "She Loves You" in 1963.
   The Beatles' first huge US hit**,** "She Loves You**,**" appeared in 1963.

39h Delete commas where they are not required.

Exercise

Commas can make sentences choppy and even confusing if they are used more often than needed.

1 No comma between subject and verb, verb and object, or preposition and object

Not   The returning soldiers, received a warm welcome. [Separated subject and verb.]

But   The returning soldiers received a warm welcome.

Not   They had chosen, to fight for their country despite, the risks. [Separated verb *chosen* and its object; separated preposition *despite* and its object.]

But   They had chosen to fight for their country despite the risks.

2 No comma in most compound constructions

Compound constructions consisting of two elements almost never require a comma. The only exception is the sentence consist-

---

Key terms

nonessential appositive A word or words that rename an immediately preceding noun but do not limit or define the noun: *The author's first story, "Biloxi," won a prize.* (See pp. 265–66.)

compound construction Two or more words, phrases, or clauses connected by a coordinating conjunction, usually *and, but, or, nor*: *man and woman, old or young, leaking oil and spewing steam.*

ing of two main clauses linked by a coordinating conjunction: *The computer failed, but employees kept working* (see p. 261).

```
                        ┌───────── compound subject ─────────┐
Not   Banks, and other financial institutions have helped older people
              ┌──────── compound object of preposition ────────┐
      with money management, and investment.

But   Banks and other financial institutions have helped older people
      with money management and investment.

                              ┌──────── compound predicate ────────┐
Not   One bank created special accounts for older people, and held
      ┌─compound object of verb─┐
      classes, and workshops.

But   One bank created special accounts for older people and held
      classes and workshops.
```

3 | No comma after a conjunction

Not   Parents of adolescents notice increased conflict at puberty, and, they complain of bickering.

But   Parents of adolescents notice increased conflict at puberty, and they complain of bickering.

Not   Although, other primates leave the family at adolescence, humans do not.

But   Although other primates leave the family at adolescence, humans do not.

4 | No commas around essential elements

Not   Hawthorne's work, *The Scarlet Letter*, was the first major American novel. [The title is essential to distinguish the novel from the rest of Hawthorne's work.]

But   Hawthorne's work *The Scarlet Letter* was the first major American novel.

Not   The symbols, that Hawthorne uses, have influenced other novelists. [The clause identifies which symbols have been influential.]

But   The symbols that Hawthorne uses have influenced other novelists.

Key terms

conjunction A connecting word such as a **coordinating conjunction** (*and, but, or,* and so on) or a **subordinating conjunction** (*although, because, when,* and so on). (See 4 p. 183.)

essential element Limits the word it refers to and thus can't be omitted without leaving the meaning too general. (See pp. 264–65.)

Not	Published in 1850, *The Scarlet Letter* still resonates today, because of its theme of secret sin.
But	Published in 1850, *The Scarlet Letter* still resonates today because of its theme of secret sin. [The adverb clause is essential to explain why the novel resonates.]

Note Like the *because* clause in the preceding example, most adverb clauses are essential because they describe conditions necessary to the main clause.

5 **No commas around a series**

Commas separate the items *within* a series (pp. 267–68) but do not separate the series from the rest of the sentence.

Not	The skills of, hunting, herding, and agriculture, sustained the Native Americans.
But	The skills of hunting, herding, and agriculture sustained the Native Americans.

6 **No comma before an indirect quotation**

Not	The report concluded, that dieting could be more dangerous than overeating.
But	The report concluded that dieting could be more dangerous than overeating.

40 The Semicolon

Video tutorial

The semicolon (;) separates equal and balanced sentence elements—usually main clauses and occasionally items in series.

Grammar checkers A grammar checker can spot a few errors in the use of semicolons. For example, a checker suggested using a semicolon after *perfect* in *The set was perfect, the director had planned every detail,* thus correcting a comma splice. But it missed the incorrect semicolon in *The set was perfect; deserted streets, dark houses, and gloomy mist* (a colon would be correct).

Key term

adverb clause A word group that contains a subject and a predicate, begins with a subordinating conjunction such as *if* or *because,* and modifies a verb, adverb, adjective, or whole word group. (See **4** p. 191.)
---

mycomplab

Visit *mycomplab.com* for the eText and for resources and exercises on the semicolon.

40a Use a semicolon between main clauses not joined by *and, but*, or another coordinating conjunction.

When no coordinating conjunction links two main clauses, the clauses should be separated by a semicolon.

A new ulcer drug arrived on the market with a mixed reputation; doctors find that the drug works but worry about its side effects.

The side effects are not minor; some leave the patient quite uncomfortable or even ill.

Note This rule prevents the errors known as comma splices and fused sentences. (See **4** pp. 249–52.)

40b Use a semicolon between main clauses related by *however, for example*, and so on.

When a conjunctive adverb or another transitional expression relates two main clauses in a single sentence, the clauses should be separated with a semicolon:

An American immigrant, Levi Strauss, invented blue jeans in the 1860s; eventually, his product clothed working men throughout the West.

The position of the semicolon between main clauses never changes, but the conjunctive adverb or transitional expression may move around in the second clause. Wherever the adverb or expression falls, it is usually set off with a comma or commas. (See p. 266.)

Blue jeans have become fashionable all over the world; however, the American originators still wear more jeans than anyone else.

Blue jeans have become fashionable all over the world; the American originators, however, still wear more jeans than anyone else.

Blue jeans have become fashionable all over the world; the American originators still wear more jeans than anyone else, however.

Key terms

main clause A word group that can stand alone as a sentence because it contains a subject and a predicate and does not begin with a subordinating word: *Parks help cities breathe.* (See **4** p. 191.)

coordinating conjunctions *And, but, or, nor,* and sometimes *for, so, yet.*

conjunctive adverb A modifier that describes the relation of the ideas in two clauses, such as *consequently, hence, however, indeed, instead, nonetheless, otherwise, still, then, therefore, thus.* (See **4** p. 252.)

transitional expression A word or phrase that shows the relationship between ideas. Transitional expressions include conjunctive adverbs as well as *in fact, of course,* and many other words and phrases. (See **1** pp. 44–45.)

Distinguishing the semicolon and the colon

Semicolon

The semicolon separates elements of *equal* importance, almost always complete main clauses.

Few enrolling students know exactly what they want from the school; most hope generally for a managerial career.

Colon

The colon is a mark of introduction that separates elements of *unequal* importance, such as statements and explanations or introductions and quotations. The first element must be a complete main clause; the second element need not be. (See pp. 275–76.)

The business school caters to working students: it offers special evening courses in business writing, finance, and management.

The school has one goal: to train students to be responsible, competent businesspeople.

Note The semicolons in the preceding sentences about jeans prevent the error known as a comma splice. (See **4** pp. 249–52.)

40c Use semicolons between main clauses or series items containing commas.

Normally, commas separate main clauses linked by coordinating conjunctions (*and, but, or, nor*) and separate items in a series. But when the clauses or series items contain commas, a semicolon between them makes the sentence easier to read.

> Lewis and Clark led the men of their party with consummate skill, inspiring and encouraging them, doctoring and caring for them; and they kept voluminous journals.   —Page Smith

> The custody case involved Amy Dalton, the child; Ellen and Mark Dalton, the parents; and Ruth and Hal Blum, the grandparents.

40d Delete or replace unneeded semicolons.

Podcast

Too many semicolons can make writing choppy. And semicolons are often misused in certain constructions that call for other punctuation or no punctuation.

1 No semicolon between a main clause and a subordinate clause or phrase

The semicolon does not separate unequal parts, such as main clauses and subordinate clauses or phrases.

Not Pygmies are in danger of extinction; because of encroaching development.

But Pygmies are in danger of extinction because of encroaching development.

Not According to African authorities; only about 35,000 Pygmies exist today.

But According to African authorities, only about 35,000 Pygmies exist today.

2 No semicolon before a series or explanation

Colons and dashes, not semicolons, introduce series, explanations, and so forth. (See below and p. 285.)

Podcast

Not Teachers have heard all sorts of reasons why students do poorly; psychological problems, family illness, too much work, too little time.

But Teachers have heard all sorts of reasons why students do poorly: psychological problems, family illness, too much work, too little time.

41 The Colon

The colon (:) is mainly a mark of introduction: it signals that the words following will explain or amplify. The colon also has several conventional uses, such as in expressions of time.

Video tutorial

Grammar checkers Many grammar checkers cannot recognize missing or misused colons and instead simply ignore them.

41a Use a colon to introduce a concluding explanation, a series, an appositive, and some quotations.

As an introducer, a colon is always preceded by a complete main clause. It may or may not be followed by a main clause. This is one way the colon differs from the semicolon, which generally separates main clauses only. (See the box opposite.)

> ┌─ **Key term** ─────────────────────────────
> **main clause** A word group that can stand alone as a sentence because it contains a subject and a predicate and does not begin with a subordinating word: *Soul food is a varied cuisine.* (See **4** p. 191.)

mycomplab

Visit *mycomplab.com* for the eText and for resources and exercises on the colon.

Explanation

Soul food has a deceptively simple definition: the ethnic cooking of African Americans.

Sometimes a concluding explanation is preceded by *the following* or *as follows* and a colon:

A more precise definition might be the following: soul food draws on ingredients, cooking methods, and dishes that originated in Africa, were brought to the New World by slaves, and were modified or supplemented in the Caribbean and the American South.

Note A complete sentence *after* a colon may begin with a capital letter or a small letter (as in the preceding example). Just be consistent throughout an essay.

Series

At least three soul food dishes are familiar to most Americans: fried chicken, barbecued spareribs, and sweet potatoes.

Appositive

Soul food has only one disadvantage: fat.

Namely, that is, and other expressions that introduce appositives *follow* the colon: *Soul food has only one disadvantage: namely, fat.*

Quotation

One soul food chef has a solution: "Soul food doesn't have to be greasy to taste good. Instead of using ham hocks to flavor beans, I use smoked turkey wings. The soulful, smoky taste remains, but without all the fat of pork."

Use a colon before a quotation when the introduction is a complete sentence.

41b Use a colon after the salutation of a business letter, between a title and subtitle, and between divisions of time.

Salutation of business letter
Dear Ms. Burak:

Title and subtitle
Charles Dickens: An Introduction to His Novels

Time
12:26 AM   6:00 PM

Key term

appositive A noun or noun substitute that renames another noun immediately before it: *my brother, Jack.* (See **4** p. 190.)

41c Delete or replace unneeded colons.

Use the colon only at the end of a main clause, not in the following situations:

- ■ **Delete a colon after a verb.**

  Not The best-known soul food dish is: fried chicken.

  But The best-known soul food dish is fried chicken.

- ■ **Delete a colon after a preposition.**

  Not Soul food recipes can be found in: mainstream cookbooks as well as specialized references.

  But Soul food recipes can be found in mainstream cookbooks as well as specialized references.

- ■ **Delete a colon after *such as* or *including*.**

  Not Many Americans have not tasted delicacies such as: chitlins and black-eyed peas.

  But Many Americans have not tasted delicacies such as chitlins and black-eyed peas.

42 The Apostrophe

The apostrophe (') appears as part of a word to indicate possession (p. 278), the omission of one or more letters (p. 280), or sometimes plural number (p. 281).

Grammar checkers A grammar checker usually has mixed results in recognizing apostrophe errors. For instance, it may flag missing apostrophes in contractions (as in *isnt*) but may not distinguish between *its* and *it's*, *their* and *they're*, *your* and *you're*, *whose* and *who's*. A checker may identify some apostrophe errors in possessives but overlook others, and it may flag correct plurals. Instead of relying on your checker, try using your computer's Search or Find function to hunt for all words you have ended in *-s*. Then check them to ensure that apostrophes are used correctly.

Video tutorial

Video tutorial

Key term

preposition *In, on, outside,* or another word that takes a noun or pronoun as its object: *in the house.* (See 4 p. 182.)
---

mycomplab

Visit *mycomplab.com* for the eText and for resources and exercises on the apostrophe.

42a | Use the apostrophe to show possession.

Exercise

A noun or indefinite pronoun shows possession with an apostrophe and, usually, an *-s*: *the dog's hair, everyone's hope*. Only certain

---

Uses and misuses of the apostrophe

Uses of the apostrophe

■ **Use an apostrophe to form the possessives of nouns and indefinite pronouns** (this page and opposite).

Singular	Plural
Ms. Park's	the Parks'
lawyer's	lawyers'
everyone's	two weeks'

■ **Use an apostrophe to form contractions** (p. 280).

it's a girl	shouldn't
you're	won't

■ **The apostrophe is optional for plurals of abbreviations, dates, and words or characters named as words** (p. 281).

MAs or MA's	Cs or C's
1960s or 1960's	*if*s or *if*'s

Misuses of the apostrophe

■ **Do not use an apostrophe plus *-s* to form the possessives of plural nouns** (next page). Instead, first form the plural with *-s* and *then* add an apostrophe.

Not	But
the Kim's car	the Kims' car
boy's fathers	boys' fathers
babie's care	babies' care

■ **Do not use an apostrophe to form plurals of nouns** (p. 280).

Not	But
book's are	books are
the Freed's	the Freeds

■ **Do not use an apostrophe with verbs ending in *-s*** (p. 280).

Not	But
swim's	swims

■ **Do not use an apostrophe to form the possessives of personal pronouns** (p. 280).

Not	But
it's toes	its toes
your's	yours

pronouns do not use apostrophes for possession: *mine, yours, his, hers, its, ours, theirs,* and *whose*.

Note Apostrophes are easy to misuse. Always check your drafts to be sure that all words ending in *-s* neither omit needed apostrophes nor add unneeded ones. Also, remember that the apostrophe or apostrophe-plus-*s* is an *addition*. Before this addition, always spell the name of the owner or owners without dropping or adding letters.

1 **Singular words: Add -'s.**

Bill Boughton**'s** skillful card tricks amaze children.

Some of the earth**'s** forests are regenerating.

Everyone**'s** fitness can be improved through exercise.

The *-'s* ending for singular words pertains also to singular words ending in *-s*, as the next examples show.

Henry James**'s** novels reward the patient reader.

The business**'s** customers filed suit.

Exception An apostrophe alone may be added to a singular word ending in *-s* when another *s* would make the word difficult to say: *Moses' mother, Joan Rivers' jokes*. But the added *-s* is never wrong (*Moses's, Rivers's*).

Podcast

2 **Plural words ending in -s: Add -' only.**

Workers**'** incomes have fallen slightly over the past year.

Many students benefit from several years**'** work after high school.

The Jameses**'** talents are extraordinary.

Note the difference in the possessives of singular and plural words ending in *-s*. The singular form usually takes the apostrophe plus *-s*: *James's*. The plural takes only the apostrophe: *Jameses'*.

3 **Plural words not ending in -s: Add -'s.**

Children**'s** educations are at stake.

We need to attract the media**'s** attention.

Podcast

4 **Compound words: Add -'s only to the last word.**

The brother-in-law**'s** business failed.

Taxes are always somebody else**'s** fault.

Key term

indefinite pronoun A pronoun that does not refer to a specific person or thing, such as *anyone, each, everybody, no one,* or *something*. (See **4** p. 226.)

5 Two or more owners: Add -'s depending on possession.

Individual possession

Zimbale**'s** and Mason**'s** comedy techniques are similar. [Each comedian has his own technique.]

Joint possession

The child recovered despite her mother and father**'s** neglect. [The mother and father were jointly neglectful.]

42b Delete or replace any apostrophe in a plural noun, a singular verb, or a possessive personal pronoun.

1 Plural nouns

The plurals of nouns are generally formed by adding -*s* or -*es*: *boys, families, Joneses, Murphys*. An apostrophe is never used to form a plural:

Not   The Jones' controlled the firm's until 2010.
But   The Joneses controlled the firms until 2010.

2 Singular verbs

Verbs ending in -*s* never take an apostrophe:

Not   The subway break's down less often now.
But   The subway breaks down less often now.

3 Possessives of personal pronouns

His, hers, its, ours, yours, theirs, and *whose* are possessive forms of *he, she, it, we, you, they,* and *who*. These personal pronouns do not take apostrophes:

Not   The house is her's. It's roof leaks.
But   The house is hers. Its roof leaks.

Don't confuse possessive pronouns with contractions. See below.

42c Use the apostrophe to form contractions.

A **contraction** replaces one or more letters, numbers, or words with an apostrophe, as in the following examples:

it is, it has	it's	cannot	can't
they are	they're	does not	doesn't
you are	you're	were not	weren't
who is, who has	who's	class of 2012	class of '12

Note Don't confuse contractions with personal pronouns:

Contractions	Personal pronouns
It's a book.	Its cover is green.
They're coming.	Their car broke down.
You're right.	Your idea is good.
Who's coming?	Whose party is it?

Podcast

Exercise

42d The apostrophe is optional to mark plural abbreviations, dates, and words or characters named as words.

You'll sometimes see apostrophes used to form the plurals of abbreviations (BA's), dates (1900's), and words or characters named as words (*but*'s). However, most current style guides recommend against the apostrophe in these cases.

BAs   PhDs
1990s   2000s

The sentence has too many *but*s.
Two *3*s end the zip code.

Note Italicize or underline a word or character named as a word (see **6** p. 304), but not the added -*s*.

43 Quotation Marks

Quotation marks—either double (" ") or single (' ')—mainly enclose direct quotations from speech or writing, enclose certain titles, and highlight words used in a special sense. These are the uses covered in this chapter, along with placing quotation marks outside or inside other punctuation marks. Additional information on using quotations appears elsewhere in this book:

Video tutorial

- **Using commas with signal phrases introducing quotations.** See pp. 269–70.
- **Using the ellipsis mark and brackets to indicate changes in quotations.** See pp. 287–89.
- **Quoting sources versus paraphrasing or summarizing them.** See **7** pp. 352–56.
- **Integrating quotations into your text.** See **7** pp. 356–59.

- Acknowledging the sources of quotations to avoid plagiarism. See 7 pp. 367–68.
- Formatting long prose quotations and poetry quotations. See **MLA** pp. 447–48 and **APA** p. 482.

Note Always use quotation marks in pairs, one at the beginning of a quotation and one at the end.

Grammar checkers A grammar checker will help you use quotation marks in pairs by flagging a lone mark. It may also look for punctuation inside or outside quotation marks, but it may not detect errors when punctuation should fall outside quotation marks.

43a Use double quotation marks to enclose direct quotations.

A **direct quotation** reports what someone said or wrote, in the exact words of the original:

> "Life," said the psychoanalyst Karen Horney, "remains a very efficient therapist."

Note Do not use quotation marks with a direct quotation that is set off from your text. See **MLA** pp. 447–48 and **APA** p. 482. Also do not use quotation marks with an **indirect quotation**, which reports what someone said or wrote but not in the exact words.

> The psychoanalyst Karen Horney claimed that life is a good therapist.

43b Use single quotation marks to enclose a quotation within a quotation.

> "In formulating any philosophy," Woody Allen writes, "the first consideration must always be: What can we know? Descartes hinted at the problem when he wrote, 'My mind can never know my body, although it has become quite friendly with my leg.'"

Notice that two different quotation marks appear at the end of the sentence—one single (to finish the interior quotation) and one double (to finish the main quotation).

43c Set off quotations of dialog according to standard practice.

When quoting conversations, begin a new paragraph for each speaker.

> "What shall I call you? Your name?" Andrews whispered rapidly, as with a high squeak the latch of the door rose.
>
> "Elizabeth," she said. "Elizabeth."
>
> —Graham Greene, *The Man Within*

When you quote a single speaker for more than one paragraph, put quotation marks at the beginning of each paragraph but at the end of only the last paragraph.

Note Quotation marks are optional for quoting unspoken thoughts or imagined dialog:

I asked myself, "How can we solve this?"
I asked myself, How can we solve this?

43d | **Put quotation marks around the titles of works that are parts of other works.**

Use quotation marks to enclose the titles of works that are published or released within larger works. (See the following box.) Use single quotation marks for a quotation within a quoted title, as in the article title and essay title in the box. And enclose all punctuation in the title within the quotation marks, as in the article title.

Exercise

Titles to be enclosed in quotation marks

Other titles should be italicized or underlined. (See **6** pp. 302–03.)

Song
"The Star-Spangled Banner"

Short poem
"Mending Wall"

Short story
"The Gift of the Magi"

Article in periodical
"Does 'Scaring' Work?"

Essay
"Joey: A 'Mechanical Boy'"

Page or document on a Web site
"Readers' Page" (on the site *Friends of Prufrock*)

Episode of a television or radio program
"The Mexican Connection" (on *60 Minutes*)

Subdivision of a book
"The Mast Head" (Chapter 35 of *Moby-Dick*)

Note Some academic disciplines do not require quotation marks for titles within source citations. See **APA** p. 466 and **CSE** p. 503.

43e | **Quotation marks may enclose words being used in a special sense.**

On film sets, movable "wild walls" make a one-walled room seem four-walled on film.

Note Use italics or underlining for defined words. (See **6** p. 304.)

43f Delete quotation marks where they are not required.

Title of your paper

Not "The Death Wish in One Poem by Robert Frost"

But The Death Wish in One Poem by Robert Frost

Or The Death Wish in "Stopping by Woods on a Snowy Evening"

Common nickname

Not As President, "Jimmy" Carter preferred to use his nickname.

But As President, Jimmy Carter preferred to use his nickname.

Slang or trite expression

Quotation marks will not excuse slang or a trite expression that is inappropriate to your writing. If slang is appropriate, use it without quotation marks.

Not We should support the President in his "hour of need" rather than "wimp out on him."

But We should give the President the support he needs rather than turn away like cowards.

43g Place other punctuation marks inside or outside quotation marks according to standard practice.

Podcast

1 **Commas and periods: Inside quotation marks**

Swift uses irony in his essay "A Modest Proposal."

Many first-time readers are shocked to see infants described as "delicious."

"'A Modest Proposal,'" writes one critic, "is so outrageous that it cannot be believed."

Exception When a parenthetical source citation immediately follows a quotation, place any period or comma *after* the citation:

One critic calls the essay "outrageous" (Olms 26).

Partly because of "the cool calculation of its delivery" (Olms 27), Swift's satire still chills a modern reader.

2 **Colons and semicolons: Outside quotation marks**

A few years ago the slogan in elementary education was "learning by playing"; now educators are concerned with basic skills.

We all know what is meant by "inflation": more money buys less.

3 | **Dashes, question marks, and exclamation points: Inside quotation marks only if part of the quotation**

When a dash, question mark, or exclamation point is part of the quotation, place it *inside* quotation marks. Don't use any other punctuation, such as a period or comma:

"But must you——" Marcia hesitated, afraid of the answer.

"Go away!" I yelled.

Did you say, "Who is she?" [When both your sentence and the quotation would end in a question mark or exclamation point, use only the mark in the quotation.]

When a dash, question mark, or exclamation point applies only to the larger sentence, not to the quotation, place it *outside* quotation marks—again, with no other punctuation:

One evocative line in English poetry—"After many a summer dies the swan"—comes from Alfred, Lord Tennyson.

Who said, "Now cracks a noble heart"?

The woman called me "stupid"!

44 Other Marks

The other marks of punctuation are the dash, parentheses, the ellipsis mark, brackets, and the slash.

Video tutorial

Exercise

Grammar checkers A grammar checker may flag a lone parenthesis or bracket so that you can match it with another parenthesis or bracket. But most checkers cannot recognize other misuses of the marks covered here and instead simply ignore the marks.

44a | **Use the dash or dashes to indicate shifts and to set off some sentence elements.**

The dash (—) is mainly a mark of interruption: it signals a shift, insertion, or break. Form a dash with two hyphens (--), or use the character called an em dash on your word processor. Do not add extra space around or between the hyphens or around the em dash.

Note When an interrupting element starting with a dash falls in the middle of a sentence, be sure to add the closing dash to signal the end of the interruption. See the first example on the next page.

mycomplab

Visit *mycomplab.com* for the eText and for resources and exercises on the dash, parentheses, the ellipsis mark, brackets, and the slash.

1 Shifts in tone or thought

The novel—if one can call it that—appeared in 2010.
If the book had a plot—but a plot would be conventional.

2 Nonessential elements

Dashes may be used instead of commas to set off and emphasize modifiers, parenthetical expressions, and other nonessential elements, especially when these elements are internally punctuated:

The qualities Monet painted—sunlight, rich shadows, deep colors—abounded near the rivers and gardens he used as subjects.

Though they are close together—separated by only a few blocks—the two neighborhoods could be in different countries.

3 Introductory series and concluding series and explanations

Shortness of breath, skin discoloration or the sudden appearance of moles, persistent indigestion, the presence of small lumps—all these may signify cancer. [Introductory series.]

The patient undergoes a battery of tests—MRI, bronchoscopy, perhaps even biopsy. [Concluding series.]

Many patients are disturbed by the MRI—by the need to keep still for long periods in an exceedingly small and noisy space. [Concluding explanation.]

A colon could be used instead of a dash in the last two examples. The dash is more informal.

4 Overuse

Too many dashes can make writing jumpy or breathy.

Not   In all his life—eighty-seven years—my great-grandfather never allowed his picture to be taken—not even once. He claimed the "black box"—the camera—would steal his soul.

But   In all his eighty-seven years, my great-grandfather did not allow his picture to be taken even once. He claimed the "black box"—the camera—would steal his soul.

44b Use parentheses to enclose parenthetical expressions and labels for lists within sentences.

Note Parentheses *always* come in pairs, one before and one after the punctuated material.

Key term

nonessential element Gives added information but does not limit the word it refers to. (See pp. 264–67.)

1 Parenthetical expressions

Parenthetical expressions include explanations, facts, digressions, and examples that may be helpful or interesting but are not essential to meaning. Parentheses de-emphasize parenthetical expressions. (Commas emphasize them more than parentheses do, and dashes emphasize them still more.)

The population of Philadelphia (now about 1.5 million) has declined since 1950.

Note Don't put a comma before a parenthetical expression enclosed in parentheses. Punctuation after the parenthetical expression should be placed outside the closing parenthesis.

Not The population of Philadelphia compares with that of Phoenix, (just under 1.5 million.)

But The population of Philadelphia compares with that of Phoenix (just under 1.5 million).

If you enclose a complete sentence in parentheses, capitalize the sentence and place the closing period *inside* the closing parenthesis:

In general, coaches will tell you that scouts are just guys who can't coach. (But then, so are brain surgeons.) —Roy Blount

2 Labels for lists within sentences

Outside the Middle East, the countries with the largest oil reserves are (1) Venezuela (63 billion barrels), (2) Russia (57 billion barrels), and (3) Mexico (51 billion barrels).

When you set a list off from your text, do not enclose such labels in parentheses.

44c Use the ellipsis mark to indicate omissions from quotations.

Exercise

The ellipsis mark, consisting of three periods separated by space (. . .), generally indicates an omission from a quotation. All the following examples quote from this passage about environmentalism:

Original quotation

"At the heart of the environmentalist world view is the conviction that human physical and spiritual health depends on sustaining the planet in a relatively unaltered state. Earth is our home in the full, genetic sense, where humanity and its ancestors existed for all the millions of years of their evolution. Natural ecosystems—forests, coral reefs, marine blue waters—maintain the world exactly as we would wish it to be maintained. When we debase the global environment and extinguish the variety of life, we are dismantling a support system that is too complex to understand, let alone replace, in the foreseeable future."

—Edward O. Wilson, "Is Humanity Suicidal?"

1. Omission of the middle of a sentence

"Natural ecosystems . . . maintain the world exactly as we would wish it to be maintained."

2. Omission of the end of a sentence, without source citation

"Earth is our home . . . ." [The sentence period, closed up to the last word, precedes the ellipsis mark.]

3. Omission of the end of a sentence, with source citation

"Earth is our home . . ." (Wilson 27). [The sentence period follows the source citation.]

4. Omission of parts of two or more sentences

Wilson writes, "At the heart of the environmentalist world view is the conviction that human physical and spiritual health depends on sustaining the planet . . . where humanity and its ancestors existed for all the millions of years of their evolution."

5. Omission of one or more sentences

As Wilson puts it, "At the heart of the environmentalist world view is the conviction that human physical and spiritual health depends on sustaining the planet in a relatively unaltered state. . . . When we debase the global environment and extinguish the variety of life, we are dismantling a support system that is too complex to understand, let alone replace, in the foreseeable future."

6. Omission from the middle of a sentence through the end of another sentence

"Earth is our home. . . . When we debase the global environment and extinguish the variety of life, we are dismantling a support system that is too complex to understand, let alone replace, in the foreseeable future."

7. Omission of the beginning of a sentence, leaving a complete sentence

a. Bracketed capital letter

"[H]uman physical and spiritual health," Wilson writes, "depends on sustaining the planet in a relatively unaltered state." [No ellipsis mark is needed because the brackets around the *H* indicate that the letter was not capitalized originally and thus that the beginning of the sentence has been omitted.]

b. Small letter

According to Wilson, "human physical and spiritual health depends on sustaining the planet in a relatively unaltered state." [No ellipsis mark is needed because the small *h* indicates that the beginning of the sentence has been omitted.]

c. Capital letter from the original

One reviewer comments, ". . . Wilson argues eloquently for the environmentalist world view" (Hami 28). [An ellipsis mark *is* needed because the quoted part of the sentence begins with a capital letter and it is otherwise not clear that the beginning of the original sentence has been omitted.]

8. Use of a word or phrase

Wilson describes the earth as "our home." [No ellipsis mark needed.]

Note these features of the examples:

- **Use an ellipsis mark when it is not otherwise clear that you have left out material from the source,** as when you omit one or more sentences (examples 5 and 6) or when the words you quote form a complete sentence that is different in the original (examples 1–4 and 7c).

- **You don't need an ellipsis mark when it is obvious that you have omitted something,** such as when a bracketed capital letter or a small letter indicates omission (examples 7a and 7b) or when a phrase clearly comes from a larger sentence (example 8).

- **Place an ellipsis mark after any sentence period** *except* **when a parenthetical source citation follows the quotation,** as in example 3. Then the sentence period falls after the citation.

If you omit one or more lines of poetry or paragraphs of prose from a quotation, use a separate line of ellipsis marks across the full width of the quotation to show the omission.

In "Song: Love Armed" from 1676, Aphra Behn contrasts two lovers' experiences of a romance:

> Love in fantastic triumph sate,
>> Whilst bleeding hearts around him flowed,
> . . . .
> But my poor heart alone is harmed,
>> Whilst thine the victor is, and free. (lines 1-2, 15-16)

(See **MLA** pp. 447–48 for the format of displayed quotations like this one.)

44d Use brackets to indicate changes in quotations.

Brackets have specialized uses in mathematical equations, but their main use for all kinds of writing is to indicate that you have altered a quotation to explain, clarify, or correct it.

"That Chevron station [just outside Dallas] is one of the busiest in the nation," said a company spokesperson.

The word *sic* (Latin for "in this manner") in brackets indicates that an error in the quotation appeared in the original and was not made by you. Do not underline or italicize *sic* in brackets.

According to the newspaper report, "The car slammed thru [sic] the railing and into oncoming traffic."

Do not use *sic* to make fun of a writer or to note errors in a passage that is clearly nonstandard.

44e Use the slash between options and between lines of poetry run into the text.

Option

Some teachers oppose pass/fail courses.

Poetry

Many readers have sensed a reluctant turn away from death in Frost's lines "The woods are lovely, dark and deep, / But I have promises to keep" (13–14).

When separating lines of poetry in this way, leave a space before and after the slash. (See **MLA** pp. 447–48 for more on quoting poetry.)

PART 6

Spelling and Mechanics

PART 6

Spelling and Mechanics

45 Spelling and the Hyphen

Video
tutorial

You can train yourself to spell better, and this chapter will tell you how. But you can improve instantly by acquiring three habits:

- **Carefully proofread your writing.**
- **Cultivate a healthy suspicion of your spellings.**
- **Check a dictionary *every time* you doubt a spelling.**

Spelling checkers A spelling checker can help you find and track spelling errors in your papers. But its usefulness is limited, mainly because it can't spot the confusion of words with similar spellings, such as *now/not, to/too,* and *their/they're/there.* See **1** p. 32 for more on spelling checkers.

45a Anticipate typical spelling problems.

Certain situations, such as misleading pronunciation, commonly lead to misspelling.

1 Pronunciation

In English, pronunciation of words is an unreliable guide to how they are spelled. Pronunciation is especially misleading with **homonyms,** words pronounced the same but spelled differently. Some homonyms and near-homonyms appear in the following box.

Video
tutorial

Words commonly confused

accept (to receive)
except (other than)

affect (to have an influence on)
effect (a result)

all ready (prepared)
already (by this time)

allusion (an indirect reference)
illusion (an erroneous belief or
  perception)

ascent (a movement up)
assent (to agree, or an agreement)

bare (unclothed)
bear (to carry, or an animal)

board (a plane of wood)
bored (uninterested)

brake (to stop)
break (to smash)

buy (to purchase)
by (next to)

cite (to quote an authority)
sight (the ability to see)
site (a place)

(continued)

Podcast

Words commonly confused
(continued)

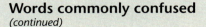

Podcast

desert (to abandon)
dessert (after-dinner course)

discreet (reserved, respectful)
discrete (individual, distinct)

fair (average, or lovely)
fare (a fee for transportation)

forth (forward)
fourth (after *third*)

hear (to perceive by ear)
here (in this place)

heard (past tense of *hear*)
herd (a group of animals)

hole (an opening)
whole (complete)

its (possessive of *it*)
it's (contraction of *it is* or *it has*)

know (to be certain)
no (the opposite of *yes*)

loose (not attached)
lose (to misplace)

meat (flesh)
meet (to encounter, or a competition)

passed (past tense of *pass*)
past (after, or a time gone by)

patience (forbearance)
patients (persons under medical care)

peace (the absence of war)
piece (a portion of something)

plain (clear)
plane (a carpenter's tool, or an airborne vehicle)

presence (the state of being at hand)
presents (gifts)

principal (most important, or the head of a school)
principle (a basic truth or law)

rain (precipitation)
reign (to rule)
rein (a strap for an animal)

right (correct)
rite (a religious ceremony)
write (to make letters)

road (a surface for driving)
rode (past tense of *ride*)

scene (where an action occurs)
seen (past participle of *see*)

stationary (unmoving)
stationery (writing paper)

their (possessive of *they*)
there (opposite of *here*)
they're (contraction of *they are*)

to (toward)
too (also)
two (following *one*)

waist (the middle of the body)
waste (discarded material)

weak (not strong)
week (Sunday through Saturday)

weather (climate)
whether (*if*, or introducing a choice)

which (one of a group)
witch (a sorcerer)

who's (contraction of *who is* or *who has*)
whose (possessive of *who*)

your (possessive of *you*)
you're (contraction of *you are*)

2 Different forms of the same word

Often, the noun form and the verb form of the same word are spelled differently: for example, *advice* (noun) and *advise* (verb).

Sometimes the noun and the adjective forms of the same word differ: <u>height</u> and <u>high</u>. Similar changes occur in the parts of some irregular verbs (<u>kn</u>ow, <u>kn</u>ew, <u>kn</u>own) and the plurals of irregular nouns (m<u>a</u>n, m<u>e</u>n).

3 American vs. British spellings CULTURE LANGUAGE

When writing for an American audience, use American spellings instead of their British equivalents. An American dictionary will show a British spelling as a variant or give it a label such as *chiefly British*.

American	British
color, humor	colour, humour
theater, center	theatre, centre
canceled, traveled	cancelled, travelled
judgment	judgement
realize, civilize	realise, civilise
connection	connexion

45b Follow spelling rules.

1 *ie* vs. *ei*

To distinguish between *ie* and *ei*, use the familiar jingle:

I before *e*, except after *c*, or when pronounced "ay" as in *neighbor* and *weigh*.

Exercise

i before *e*	believe	thief	hygiene
	grief	bier	friend
ei after *c*	ceiling	conceive	perceive
	deceit	receive	conceit
ei sounded as "ay"	sleigh	eight	beige
	vein	freight	neighbor

Exceptions For some exceptions, remember this sentence:

The w<u>ei</u>rd for<u>ei</u>gner n<u>ei</u>ther s<u>ei</u>zes l<u>ei</u>sure nor forf<u>ei</u>ts h<u>ei</u>ght.

2 Final *e*

When adding an ending to a word with a final *e*, drop the *e* if the ending begins with a vowel:

Video tutorial

advis<u>e</u> + able = advisable   surpris<u>e</u> + ing = surprising

Keep the *e* if the ending begins with a consonant:

care + ful = careful   like + ly = likely

Exceptions Retain the *e* after a soft *c* or *g*, to keep the sound of the consonant soft rather than hard: *courag<u>e</u>ous, chang<u>e</u>able*. And drop the *e* before a consonant when the *e* is preceded by another vowel: *argue + ment = argument, true + ly = truly.*

3 Final *y*

When adding an ending to a word with a final *y*, change the *y* to *i* if it follows a consonant:

beauty, beauties   worry, worried   supply, supplies

But keep the *y* if it follows a vowel, if it ends a proper name, or if the added ending is *ing*:

day, days   Minsky, Minskys   cry, crying

4 Final consonants

When adding an ending to a one-syllable word ending in a consonant, double the final consonant when it follows a single vowel. Otherwise, don't double the consonant.

slap, slapping   park, parking   pair, paired

In words of more than one syllable, double the final consonant when it follows a single vowel *and* when it ends a stressed syllable once the new ending is added. Otherwise, don't double the consonant.

refer, referring   refer, reference   relent, relented

5 Prefixes

When adding a prefix, do not drop a letter from or add a letter to the original word:

unnecessary   disappoint   misspell

6 Plurals

Most nouns form plurals by adding *s* to the singular form. Add *es* for the plural of nouns ending in *s, sh, ch,* or *x.*

boy, boys   kiss, kisses   church, churches

Nouns ending in *o* preceded by a vowel usually form the plural with *s.* Those ending in *o* preceded by a consonant usually form the plural with *es.*

ratio, ratios   hero, heroes

Video
tutorial

Some very common nouns form irregular plurals.

child, children   woman, women   mouse, mice

Some English nouns that were originally Italian, Greek, Latin, or French form the plural according to their original language:

analysis, analyses	criterion, criteria	piano, pianos
basis, bases	datum, data	thesis, theses
crisis, crises	medium, media	

A few such nouns may form irregular *or* regular plurals: for instance, *index, indices, indexes*; *curriculum, curricula, curriculums*. The regular plural is more contemporary.

With compound nouns, add *s* to the main word of the compound. Sometimes this main word is not the last word.

city-states   fathers-in-law   passersby

CULTURE LANGUAGE Noncount nouns do not form plurals, either regularly (with an added *s*) or irregularly. Examples of noncount nouns include *equipment, intelligence,* and *wealth.* See **4** p. 236.

45c | Use the hyphen to form or divide words.

The hyphen is used either to form compound words or to divide words at the ends of lines.

Podcast

Exercise

1 Compound adjectives

When two or more words serve together as a single modifier before a noun, a hyphen forms the modifying words clearly into a unit.

She is a well-known actor.
Some Spanish-speaking students work as translators.

When such a compound adjective follows the noun, the hyphen is unnecessary.

The actor is well known.
Many students are Spanish speaking.

The hyphen is also unnecessary in a compound modifier containing an *-ly* adverb, even before the noun: *clearly defined terms.*

When part of a compound adjective appears only once in two or more parallel compound adjectives, hyphens indicate which words the reader should mentally join with the missing part.

School-age children should have eight- or nine-o'clock bedtimes.

2 Fractions and compound numbers

Hyphens join the numerator and denominator of fractions: *one-half, three-fourths.* Hyphens also join the parts of the whole numbers *twenty-one* to *ninety-nine.*

When a hyphenated number is part of a compound adjective before a noun, join all parts of the modifier with hyphens: *sixty-three-foot wall.*

3 Prefixes and suffixes

Do not use hyphens with prefixes except as follows:

■ **With the prefixes *self-*, *all-*, and *ex-*:** *self-control, all-inclusive, ex-student.*

■ **With a prefix before a capitalized word:** *un-American.*

■ **With a capital letter before a word:** *T-shirt.*

■ **To prevent misreading:** *de-emphasize, re-create a story.*

The only suffix that regularly requires a hyphen is *-elect,* as in *president-elect.*

4 Words at the ends of lines

You can avoid occasional short lines in your documents by setting your word processor to divide words automatically at appropriate breaks. To divide words manually, follow these guidelines:

■ **Divide words only between syllables**—for instance, *win-dows,* not *wi-ndows.* Check a dictionary for correct syllable breaks.

■ **Never divide a one-syllable word.**

■ **Leave at least two letters on the first line and three on the second line.** If a word cannot be divided to follow this rule (for instance, *a-bus-er*), don't divide it.

■ **Do not use a hyphen in breaking a URL** because readers may perceive any added hyphens as part of the electronic address. The documentation styles differ in where they allow breaks in URLs. For example, MLA style allows a break only after a slash, while APA style allows a break before a slash and most other punctuation marks.

46 Capital Letters

Video tutorial

Exercise

Generally, capitalize a word only when a dictionary or conventional use says you must. Consult one of the style guides listed in **8** pp. 393 and 397 for special uses of capitals in the social, natural, and applied sciences.

Grammar checkers A grammar checker will flag overused capital letters and missing capitals at the beginnings of sentences. It will also spot missing capitals at the beginnings of proper nouns and adjectives—*if* the nouns and adjectives are in the checker's dictionary. For example, a checker caught *christianity* and *europe* but not *china* (for the country) or *Stephen king*.

CULTURE LANGUAGE Conventions of capitalization vary from language to language. English, for instance, is the only language to capitalize the first-person singular pronoun (*I*), and its practice of capitalizing proper nouns but not most common nouns also distinguishes it from some other languages.

common   proper
noun   noun   pronoun

My friend Nathaniel and I both play the drums.

46a Capitalize the first word of every sentence.

No one expected the outcome.

When quoting other writers, you should reproduce the capital letters beginning their sentences or indicate that you have altered the source's capitalization. Whenever possible, integrate the quotation into your own sentence so that its capitalization coincides with yours:

> "Psychotherapists often overlook the benefits of self-deception," the author argues.

> The author argues that "the benefits of self-deception" are not always recognized by psychotherapists.

If you need to alter the capitalization in the source, indicate the change with brackets:

> "[T]he benefits of self-deception" are not always recognized by psychotherapists, the author argues.

> The author argues that "[p]sychotherapists often overlook the benefits of self-deception."

Note Capitalization of questions in a series is optional. Both of the following examples are correct:

> Is the population a hundred? Two hundred? More?
> Is the population a hundred? two hundred? more?

Also optional is capitalization of the first word in a complete sentence after a colon.

46b Capitalize proper nouns, proper adjectives, and words used as essential parts of proper nouns.

1 Proper nouns and proper adjectives

Proper nouns name specific persons, places, and things: *Shakespeare, California, World War I.* **Proper adjectives** are formed from some proper nouns: *Shakespearean, Californian.* Capitalize all proper

Video tutorial

nouns and proper adjectives but not the articles (*a, an, the*) that precede them:

Proper nouns and adjectives to be capitalized

Specific persons and things
Stephen King
Napoleon Bonaparte

Boulder Dam
the Empire State Building

Specific places and geographical regions
New York City
China

the Mediterranean Sea
the Northeast, the South

But: northeast of the city, going south

Days of the week, months, holidays
Monday
May

Yom Kippur
Christmas

Historical events, documents, periods, movements
the Vietnam War
the Constitution

the Renaissance
the Romantic Movement

Government offices, departments, and institutions
House of Representatives
Department of Defense

Polk Municipal Court
Sequoia Hospital

Academic institutions and departments
University of Kansas
Santa Monica College

Department of Nursing
Haven High School

But: the university, college course, high school diploma

Political, social, athletic, and other organizations and associations and their members
Democratic Party, Democrats
Sierra Club
B'nai B'rith

League of Women Voters
Boston Celtics
Chicago Symphony Orchestra

Races, nationalities, and their languages
Native American
African American
Caucasian

Germans
Swahili
Italian

But: blacks, whites

Religions, their followers, and terms for the sacred
Christianity, Christians
Catholicism, Catholics
Judaism, Orthodox Jews
Islam, Muslims

God
Allah
the Bible [**but** biblical]
the Koran, the Qur'an

2 Common nouns used as essential parts of proper nouns

Capitalize the common nouns *street, avenue, park, river, ocean, lake, company, college, county,* and *memorial* when they are part of proper nouns naming specific places or institutions:

Main Street	Lake Superior
Central Park	Ford Motor Company
Mississippi River	Madison College
Pacific Ocean	George Washington Memorial

3 Compass directions

Capitalize compass directions only when they name a specific region instead of a general direction:

Students from the West often melt in eastern humidity.

4 Relationships

Capitalize the names of relationships only when they precede or replace proper names:

Our aunt scolded us for disrespecting Father and Uncle Jake.

5 Titles with persons' names

Before a person's name, capitalize his or her title. After or apart from the name, do not capitalize the title.

Professor Otto Osborne	Otto Osborne, a professor
Doctor Jane Covington	Jane Covington, a doctor
Governor Ella Moore	Ella Moore, the governor

Note Many writers capitalize a title denoting very high rank even when it follows a name or is used alone: *Ronald Reagan, past President of the United States.*

46c Capitalize most words in titles and subtitles of works.

Within your text, capitalize all the words in a title *except* the following: articles (*a, an, the*), *to* in infinitives, coordinating conjunctions (*and, but,* etc.), and prepositions (*with, between,* etc.). Capitalize even these words when they are the first or last word in a title or when they fall after a colon or semicolon.

"Courtship through the Ages"	*Management: A New Theory*
A Diamond Is Forever	"Once More to the Lake"
"Knowing Whom to Ask"	*An End to Live For*
Learning from Las Vegas	*File under Architecture*

Note The style guides of the academic disciplines have their own rules for capitals in titles. For instance, the preceding guidelines reflect MLA style for English and some other humanities. In contrast, APA style for the social sciences and CSE style for the sciences capitalize only the first word and proper names in book and article titles within source citations (see **APA** p. 466 and **CSE** p. 503).

46d   Use capitals according to convention in online communication.

Online messages written in all-capital letters or with no capital letters are difficult to read. Further, messages in all-capital letters may be taken as rude (see also **2** p. 78). Use capital letters according to rules 46a–46c in all your online communication.

47   Italics or Underlining

Exercise

Italic type and underlining indicate the same thing: the word or words are being distinguished or emphasized. Italic type is now used almost universally in academic and business writing. Some instructors do recommend underlining, so ask your instructor for his or her preference.

Always use either italics or underlining consistently throughout a document in both text and source citations. If you are using italics, make sure that the italic characters are clearly distinct from the regular type. If you are using underlining and you underline two or more words in a row, underline the space between the words, too: Criminal Statistics: Misuses of Numbers.

Grammar checkers A grammar checker cannot recognize problems with italics or underlining. Check your work to ensure that you have used highlighting appropriately.

47a   Italicize or underline the titles of works that appear independently.

Within your text, underline or italicize the titles of works that are published, released, or produced separately from other works. (See the box on the facing page.) Use quotation marks for all other titles. (See **5** p. 283.)

my**comp**lab

Visit *mycomplab.com* for the eText and for resources and exercises on italics or underlining.

Titles to be italicized or underlined

Other titles should be placed in quotation marks. (See **5** p. 283.)

Books

War and Peace
And the Band Played On

Plays

Hamlet
The Phantom of the Opera

Periodicals

Time
Philadelphia Inquirer

Television and radio programs

NBC Sports Hour
Radio Lab

Movies, DVDs, and videos

Schindler's List
How to Relax

Pamphlets

The Truth about Alcoholism

Long poems

Beowulf
Paradise Lost

Long musical works

Tchaikovsky's *Swan Lake*
But: Symphony in C

Works of visual art

Michelangelo's *David*
Picasso's *Guernica*

Computer software

Microsoft Internet Explorer
Google

Web sites

YouTube
Friends of Prufrock

Published speeches

Lincoln's *Gettysburg Address*

Exceptions Legal documents, the Bible, the Koran, and their parts are generally not italicized or underlined:

Not   We studied the *Book of Revelation* in the *Bible*.

But   We studied the Book of Revelation in the Bible.

47b Italicize or underline the names of ships, aircraft, spacecraft, and trains.

Challenger	*Orient Express*	*Queen Mary 2*
Apollo XI	*Montrealer*	*Spirit of St. Louis*

47c Italicize or underline foreign words that are not part of the English language.

Italicize or underline a foreign expression that has not been absorbed into English. A dictionary will say whether a word is still considered foreign to English.

The scientific name for the brown trout is *Salmo trutta*. [The Latin scientific names for plants and animals are always italicized or underlined.]

The Latin *De gustibus non est disputandum* translates roughly as "There's no accounting for taste."

47d   Italicize or underline words or characters named as words.

Use italics or underlining to indicate that you are citing a character or word as a word rather than using it for its meaning. Words you are defining fall under this convention.

> The word *syzygy* refers to a straight line formed by three celestial bodies, as in the alignment of the earth, sun, and moon.
>
> Some people say *th*, as in *thought*, with a faint *s* or *f* sound.

47e   Occasionally, italics or underlining may be used for emphasis.

Italics or underlining can stress an important word or phrase, especially in reporting how someone said something. But use such emphasis very rarely, or your writing may sound immature or hysterical.

47f   In online communication, use alternatives for italics or underlining.

Some forms of online communication do not allow conventional highlighting such as italics or underlining for the purposes described in this chapter. If you can't use italics or underlining to distinguish book titles and other elements that usually require highlighting, type an underscore before and after the element: *Measurements coincide with those in _Joule's Handbook_*. You can also emphasize words with asterisks before and after: *I *will not* be able to attend*.

Don't use all-capital letters for emphasis; they yell too loudly. (See also p. 302.)

48   Abbreviations

Video
tutorial

Exercise

The following guidelines on abbreviations pertain to the text of a nontechnical document. All academic disciplines use abbreviations in source citations, and much technical writing, such as in the sciences and engineering, uses many abbreviations in the document text. For the in-text requirements of the discipline you are writing in, consult one of the style guides listed in **8** pp. 389 (humanities), 393 (social sciences), and 397 (natural and applied sciences).

---

mycomplab

Visit *mycomplab.com* for the eText and for resources and exercises on abbreviations.

Usage varies, but writers increasingly omit periods from abbreviations that consist of or end in capital letters: *US, BA, USMC, PhD.* See 5 p. 259 on punctuating abbreviations.

Grammar and spelling checkers A grammar checker may flag some abbreviations, such as *ft.* (for *foot*) and *st.* (for *street*). A spelling checker will flag abbreviations it does not recognize. But neither checker can tell you whether an abbreviation is appropriate for your writing situation or will be clear to your readers.

48a Use standard abbreviations for titles immediately before and after proper names.

Before the name	After the name
Dr. James Hsu	James Hsu, MD
Mr., Mrs., Ms., Hon.,	DDS, DVM, PhD,
St., Rev., Msgr., Gen.	EdD, OSB, SJ, Sr., Jr.

Do not use abbreviations such as *Rev., Hon., Prof., Rep., Sen., Dr.,* and *St.* (for *Saint*) unless they appear before a proper name.

48b Familiar abbreviations and acronyms are acceptable in most writing.

An **acronym** is an abbreviation that spells a pronounceable word, such as WHO, NATO, and AIDS. These and other abbreviations using initials are acceptable in most writing as long as they are familiar to readers.

Institutions	LSU, UCLA, TCU
Organizations	CIA, FBI, YMCA, AFL-CIO
Corporations	IBM, CBS, ITT
People	JFK, LBJ, FDR
Countries	US, USA

Note If a name or term (such as *operating room*) appears often in a piece of writing, then its abbreviation (*OR*) can cut down on extra words. Spell out the full term at its first appearance, indicate its abbreviation in parentheses, and then use the abbreviation.

48c Use *BC, BCE, AD, CE, AM, PM, no.,* and *$* only with specific dates and numbers.

44 BC	AD 1492	11:26 AM (*or* a.m.)	no. 36 (*or* No. 36)
44 BCE	1492 CE	8:05 PM (*or* p.m.)	$7.41

The abbreviations BC ("before Christ"), BCE ("before the common era"), and CE ("common era") always follow a date. In contrast, AD (*anno Domini*, Latin for "in the year of the Lord") precedes a date.

48d Generally reserve Latin abbreviations for source citations and comments in parentheses.

Latin abbreviations are generally not italicized or underlined.

i.e.	*id est:* that is
cf.	*confer:* compare
e.g.	*exempli gratia:* for example
et al.	*et alii:* and others
etc.	*et cetera:* and so forth
NB	*nota bene:* note well

He said he would be gone a fortnight (i.e., two weeks).
Bloom et al., editors, *Anthology of Light Verse*
Trees, too, are susceptible to disease (e.g., Dutch elm disease).

Some writers avoid these abbreviations in formal writing, even within parentheses.

48e Use *Inc., Bros., Co.,* or & (for *and*) only in official names of business firms.

Not The Santini <u>bros.</u> operate a large moving firm in New York City <u>&</u> environs.

But The Santini <u>brothers</u> operate a large moving firm in New York City <u>and</u> environs.

Or Santini <u>Bros.</u> is a large moving firm in New York City <u>and</u> environs.

48f Generally spell out units of measurement and names of places, calendar designations, people, and courses.

In most academic, general, and business writing, the following types of words should always be spelled out. (In source citations and technical writing, however, these words are more often abbreviated.)

Units of measurement
The dog is thirty <u>inches</u> [not <u>in.</u>] high.

Geographical names
The publisher is in <u>Massachusetts</u> [not <u>Mass.</u> or <u>MA</u>].

Names of days, months, and holidays
The truce was signed on <u>Tuesday</u> [not <u>Tues.</u>], <u>April</u> [not <u>Apr.</u>] 16.

Names of people
<u>Robert</u> [not <u>Robt.</u>] Frost wrote accessible poems.

Courses of instruction
I'm majoring in <u>political science</u> [not <u>poli. sci.</u>].

49 Numbers

This chapter addresses the use of numbers (numerals versus words) in the text of a document. All disciplines use many more numerals in source citations.

Video tutorial

Grammar checkers A grammar checker will flag numerals beginning sentences and can be customized to ignore or to look for numerals. But it can't tell you whether numerals or spelled-out numbers are appropriate for your writing situation.

49a Use numerals according to standard practice in the field you are writing in.

Always use numerals for numbers that require more than two words to spell out:

Exercise

> The leap year has <u>366</u> days.
> The population of Minot, North Dakota, is about <u>32,800</u>.

In nontechnical academic writing, spell out numbers of one or two words. A hyphenated number may be considered one word.

> <u>Twelve</u> nations signed the treaty.
> The ball game drew <u>forty-two thousand</u> people.
> Jenson lived to be <u>ninety-nine</u> or <u>one hundred</u>.

In much business writing, use numerals for all numbers over ten: *five reasons, 11 participants*. In technical academic and business writing, such as in science and engineering, use numerals for all numbers over ten, and use numerals for zero through nine when they refer to exact measurements: *2 liters, 1 hour*. (Consult one of the style guides listed in **8** pp. 393 and 397 for more details.)

Notes Use a combination of numerals and words for round numbers over a million: *26 million, 2.45 billion*. Use either all numerals or all words when several numbers appear together in a passage, even if convention would require a mixture. And avoid using two numbers in a row, which can be confusing:

> **Confusing**   Out of 530 101 children caught the virus.
> **Clear**   Out of 530 <u>children</u> 101 caught the virus.

CULTURE LANGUAGE In standard American English, a comma separates the numerals in long numbers (*26,000*), and a period functions as a decimal point (*2.06*).

49b Use numerals according to convention for dates, addresses, and other information.

Days and years

June 18, 1985 AD 12
456 BCE 2010

The time of day

9:00 AM 3:45 PM

Addresses

355 Clinton Avenue
Washington, DC 20036

Exact amounts of money

$3.5 million $4.50

Decimals, percentages, and fractions

22.5 3½
48% (*or* 48 percent)

Scores and statistics

21 to 7 a ratio of 8 to 1
a mean of 26

Pages, chapters, volumes, acts, scenes, lines

Chapter 9, page 123
Hamlet, act 5, scene 3

Exceptions Round dollar or cent amounts of only a few words may be expressed in words: *seventeen dollars*; *sixty cents*. When the word *o'clock* is used for the time of day, also express the number in words: *two o'clock* (not *2 o'clock*).

49c Spell out numbers that begin sentences.

For clarity, spell out any number that begins a sentence. If the number requires more than two words, reword the sentence so that the number falls later and can be expressed as a numeral.

Not 3.9 billion people live in Asia.
But The population of Asia is 3.9 billion.

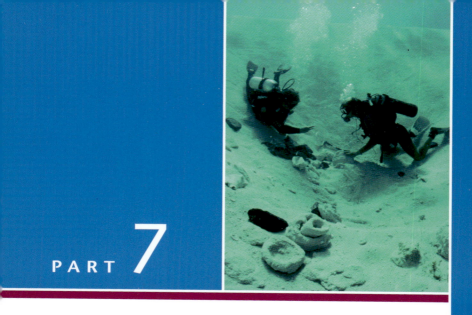

Research Writing

50 Research Strategy

Research writing gives you a chance to work like a detective solving a case. The mystery is the answer to a question you care about. The search for the answer leads you to consider what others think about your subject, but you do more than simply report their views. You build on them to develop and support your own opinion, and ultimately you become an expert in your own right.

Your investigation will be more productive and enjoyable if you take some steps described in this chapter: plan your work (below), keep a research journal (p. 312), find an appropriate subject and research question (p. 312), set goals for your sources (p. 314), and keep a working, annotated bibliography (p. 317).

50a Planning your work

Research writing is a *writing* process:

- ■ **You work within a particular situation of subject, purpose, audience, genre, and other factors** (see **1** pp. 3–9).
- ■ **You gather ideas and information about your subject** (**1** pp. 9–14).
- ■ **You focus and arrange your ideas** (**1** pp. 14–22).
- ■ **You draft to explore your meaning** (**1** pp. 22–23).
- ■ **You revise and edit to develop, shape, and polish** (**1** pp. 25–34).

Although the process seems neatly sequential in this list, you know from experience that the stages overlap—that, for instance, you may begin drafting before you've gathered all the information you expect to find, and then while drafting you may discover a source that causes you to rethink your approach. Anticipating the process of research writing can free you to be flexible in your search and open to discoveries.

A thoughtful plan and systematic procedures can help you follow through on the diverse activities of research writing. One step is to make a schedule like the one on the next page that apportions the available time to the necessary work. You can estimate that each segment marked off by a horizontal line will occupy *roughly* one-quarter of the total time—for example, a week in a four-week assignment or two weeks in an eight-week assignment. The most unpredictable segments are the first two, so get started early enough to accommodate the unexpected.

mycomplab

Visit *mycomplab.com* for the eText and for resources and exercises on research strategy.

311

Complete
by:

_____	1.	Setting a schedule and beginning a research journal (here and below)
_____	2.	Finding a researchable subject and question (below and facing page)
_____	3.	Setting goals for sources (p. 314)
_____	4.	Finding print and electronic sources (p. 319), and making a working, annotated bibliography (p. 317)
_____	5.	Evaluating and synthesizing sources (pp. 338, 350)
_____	6.	Gathering information from sources (p. 351), often using summary, paraphrase, and direct quotation (p. 352)
_____	7.	Taking steps to avoid plagiarism (p. 360)
_____	8.	Developing a thesis statement and creating a structure (p. 369)
_____	9.	Drafting the paper (p. 370), integrating summaries, paraphrases, and direct quotations into your ideas (p. 356)
_____	10.	Revising and editing the paper (p. 370)
_____	11.	Citing sources in your text (p. 367)
_____	12.	Preparing the list of works cited or references (p. 367)
_____	13.	Preparing the final manuscript (p. 371)
_____		Final paper due

50b Keeping a research journal

While working on a research project, carry a notebook or a computer with you at all times to use as a **research journal,** a place to record your activities and ideas. (See **1** p. 9 on journal keeping.) In the journal's dated entries, you can write about the sources you consult, the leads you want to pursue, and any difficulties you encounter. Most important, you can record your thoughts about sources, leads, dead ends, new directions, relationships, and anything else that strikes you. The very act of writing in the journal can expand and clarify your thinking.

Note The research journal is the place to track and develop your own ideas. To avoid mixing up your thoughts and those of others, keep separate notes on what your sources actually say, using one of the methods discussed on pp. 351–52.

50c Finding a researchable subject and question

Video
tutorial

Before reading this section, review the suggestions given in Chapter 1 for finding and narrowing a writing subject (**1** pp. 5–6).

Generally, the same procedure applies to writing any kind of research paper. However, selecting and limiting a subject for a research paper can present special opportunities and problems. And before you proceed with your subject, you'll want to transform it into a question that can guide your search for sources.

1 Appropriate subject

Seek a research subject that you want to explore and learn more about. (It may be a subject you've already written about without the benefit of research.) Starting with your own views will motivate you, and you will be a participant in a dialog when you begin examining sources.

Exercise

When you settle on a subject, ask the following questions about it. For each requirement, there are corresponding pitfalls.

■ **Are ample sources of information available on the subject?**

Avoid very recent subjects, such as a newly announced medical discovery or a breaking story in today's news.

■ **Does the subject encourage research in the kinds and number of sources required by the assignment?**

Avoid (*a*) subjects that depend entirely on personal opinion and experience, such as the virtues of your hobby, and (*b*) subjects that require research in only one source, such as a straight factual biography.

■ **Will the subject lead you to an objective assessment of sources and to defensible conclusions?**

Avoid subjects that rest entirely on belief or prejudice, such as when human life begins or why women (or men) are superior. Your readers are unlikely to be swayed from their own beliefs.

■ **Does the subject suit the length of paper assigned and the time given for research and writing?**

Avoid broad subjects that have too many sources to survey adequately, such as a major event in history.

2 Research question

Asking a question or questions about your subject opens avenues of inquiry. In asking questions, you can consider what you already know about the subject, explore what you don't know, and begin to develop your own perspective. (See the next page for suggestions on using your own knowledge.)

Try to narrow your research question so that you can answer it in the time and space you have available. The question *How does human activity affect the environment?* is very broad, encompassing issues as diverse as pollution, distribution of resources, climate change, population growth, land use, biodiversity, and the ozone layer. In contrast, the question *How can buying environmentally friendly products help the environment?* or *How, if at all, should carbon emissions be taxed?* is much narrower. Each question also requires more than a simple *yes* or *no* answer, so that answering, even tentatively, demands thought about pros and cons, causes and effects.

As you read and write, your question will probably evolve to reflect your increasing knowledge of the subject, and eventually its answer will become your main idea, or thesis statement (see p. 369).

50d Setting goals for sources

Before you start looking for sources, consider what you already know about your subject and where you are likely to find information on it.

1 Your own knowledge

Discovering what you already know about your topic will guide you in discovering what you don't know. Take some time at the start to write down everything you know about the subject: facts you have learned, opinions you have heard or read elsewhere, and of course your own opinions. Use one of the discovery techniques discussed in **1** pp. 9–14 to explore and develop your ideas: keeping a journal, observing your surroundings, freewriting, brainstorming, drawing, and asking questions.

When you've explored your thoughts, make a list of questions for which you don't have answers, whether factual (*How much do Americans spend on green products?*) or more open-ended (*Are green products worth the higher prices?*). These questions will give you clues about the sources you need to look for first.

2 Kinds of sources

For many research projects, you'll want to consult a mix of sources, as described on the next two pages. You may start by seeking the outlines of your topic—the range and depth of opinions about it—in reference works and articles in popular periodicals or through a Web search. Then, as you refine your views and your research question, you'll move on to more specialized sources, such as scholarly books and periodicals and your own interviews or surveys. (See pp. 319–38 for more on each kind of source.)

The mix of sources you choose depends heavily on your subject. For example, a paper on green consumerism would require the use of very recent sources because environmentally friendly products are fairly new to the marketplace. Your mix of sources may also be specified by your instructor or limited by the requirements of your assignment.

Library and Internet sources

The print and electronic sources available at your library or through its Web site—mainly reference works, books, and periodicals—have two big advantages over most of what you'll find on the open Web: library sources are cataloged and indexed for easy retrieval; and they are generally reliable, having been screened first by their publishers and then by the library's staff. In contrast, the Internet's retrieval systems are more difficult to use effectively, and Internet sources tend to be less reliable because most do not pass through any screening before being posted. (There are many exceptions, such as online scholarly journals and reference works. But these sources are generally available through your library's Web site as well.)

Most instructors expect research writers to consult library sources. But they'll accept Internet sources, too, if you have used them judiciously. Even with its disadvantages, the Internet can be a valuable resource for primary sources, current information, and a diversity of views. For guidelines on evaluating both library and Internet sources, see pp. 338–49.

Primary and secondary sources

Use **primary sources** when they are available or are required by your assignment. These sources are firsthand accounts, such as works of literature, historical documents (letters, speeches, and so on), eyewitness reports (including articles by journalists who are on location), reports on experiments or surveys conducted by the writer, and sources you originate (interviews, experiments, observations, or correspondence).

Many assignments will allow you to use **secondary sources,** which report and analyze information drawn from other sources, often primary ones. Examples include a reporter's summary of a controversial issue, a historian's account of a battle, a critic's reading of a poem, and a psychologist's evaluation of several studies. Secondary sources may contain helpful summaries and interpretations that direct, support, and extend your own thinking. However, most research-writing assignments expect your own ideas to go beyond those in such sources.

Scholarly and popular sources

The scholarship of acknowledged experts is essential for depth, authority, and specificity. Most instructors expect students to emphasize scholarly sources in their research. But the general-interest views and information of popular sources can help you apply more scholarly approaches to daily life.

- **Check the title.** Is it technical, or does it use a general vocabulary?
- **Check the publisher.** Is it a scholarly journal (such as *Cultural Geographies*) or a publisher of scholarly books (such as Harvard University Press), or is it a popular magazine (such as *Consumer Reports* or *Newsweek*) or a publisher of popular books (such as Little, Brown)? For more on the distinction between scholarly and popular sources, see pp. 325 and 339.
- **Check the length of periodical articles.** Scholarly articles are generally much longer than magazine and newspaper articles.
- **Check the author.** Have you seen the name elsewhere, which might suggest that the author is an expert?
- **Check the URL.** A Web site's URL, or electronic address, includes an abbreviation that can tell you something about the origin of the source: scholarly sources usually end in *edu*, *org*, or *gov*, while popular sources usually end in *com*. (See pp. 329–33 for more on types of online sources.)

Older and newer sources

Check the publication date. For most subjects a combination of older, established sources (such as books) and current sources (such as newspaper articles, interviews, or Web sites) will provide both background and up-to-date information. Only historical subjects or very current subjects require an emphasis on one extreme or another.

Impartial and biased sources

Seek a range of viewpoints. Sources that attempt to be impartial can offer an overview of your subject and trustworthy facts. Sources with clear biases can offer a diversity of opinion. Of course, to discover bias, you may have to read the source carefully (see pp. 338–49); but you can infer quite a bit just from a bibliographical listing.

- **Check the author.** You may have heard of the author as a respected researcher (thus more likely to be objective) or as a leading proponent of a certain view (less likely to be objective).
- **Check the title.** It may reveal something about point of view. (Consider these contrasting titles: "Go for the Green" versus "Green Consumerism and the Struggle for Northern Maine.")

Note Sources you find on the Internet must be approached with particular care. See pp. 342–49.

Sources with helpful features

Depending on your topic and how far along your research is, you may want to look for sources with features such as illustrations (which can clarify important concepts), bibliographies (which can direct you to other sources), and indexes (which can help you develop keywords for electronic searches; see pp. 320–23).

50e | Keeping a working, annotated bibliography

To track where sources are, compile a **working bibliography** as you uncover possibilities. When you have a substantial file—say, ten to thirty sources—you can decide which ones seem most promising and look them up first.

1 | Source information

When you turn in your paper, you will be expected to attach a list of the sources you have used. So that readers can check or follow up on your sources, your list must include all the information needed to find the sources, in a format readers can understand. (See pp. 367–68.) The box on the next page shows the information you should record for each type of source so that you will not have to retrace your steps later.

Note Recording source information meticulously will help you avoid accidental plagiarism because you will be less likely to omit the information in your paper. Careful records will also help you avoid omitting or mixing up numbers, dates, and other data when it's time to write your citations. This book describes four documentation styles: MLA (see **MLA** p. 402), APA (see **APA** p. 461), Chicago (see **Chic** p. 489), and CSE (see **CSE** p. 501). For other styles, consult one of the guides listed in **8** pp. 393 and 397.

2 | Annotations

Creating annotations for your bibliography converts it from a simple list into a tool for assessing sources. As you discover and evaluate each source, record not only its publication information but also the following:

Student
paper

- **What you know about the content of the source.** Periodical databases and book catalogs generally include abstracts, or summaries, of sources that can help with this part of the annotation.
- **How you think the source may be helpful in your research.** Does it offer expert opinion, statistics, an important example, or a range of views? Does it place your subject in a historical, social, or economic context?
- **Your assessment of the source.** Consider how reliable the source is and how it might fit into your research. (See pp. 338–51 for more on evaluating and synthesizing sources.)

Taking the time with your annotations can help you discover gaps that may remain in your sources and will help you decide which sources to pursue in depth. The entry from an annotated bibliography on p. 319 shows one student's annotation of a source, including a summary, a note on the source features the student thought would be helpful, and an assessment of the source's strength and weakness for his purposes.

Information for a working bibliography

For books

Library call number
Name(s) of author(s), editor(s), translator(s), or others listed
Title and subtitle
Publication data:
  Place of publication
  Publisher's name
  Date of publication
Other important data, such as edition or volume number
Medium (print, Web, etc.)

For periodical articles

Name(s) of author(s)
Title and subtitle of article
Title of periodical
Publication data:
  Volume number and issue number (if any) in which article appears
  Date of issue
  Page numbers on which article appears
Medium (print, Web, etc.)

For electronic sources

Name(s) of author(s)
Title and subtitle of source
Title of Web site, periodical, or other larger work
Publication data, such as data listed above for a book or article; the publisher or sponsor of a Web site; and the date of release, revision, or online posting

Any publication data for the source in another medium (print, film, etc.)
Format of online source (Web site or page, podcast, e-mail, etc.)
Date you consulted the source
Title of any database used to reach the source
Complete URL (see the note below)
Digital Object Identifier, if any (see the note below)
Medium (Web, online database, CD-ROM, etc.)

For other sources

Name(s) of author(s), creator(s), or others listed, such as a government department, recording artist, or photographer
Title of work
Format, such as unpublished letter, live performance, or photograph
Publication or production data:
  Publication title
  Publisher's or producer's name
  Date of publication, release, or production
Identifying numbers (if any)
Medium (print, typescript, etc.)

Note Documentation styles vary in requiring URLs and DOIs (Digital Object Identifiers) for citations of electronic sources. (See **APA** p. 466 for more on DOIs.) For instance, MLA style generally does not require URLs or DOIs, APA style generally requires DOIs if available or just home-page URLs, and some other styles always require complete URLs. Even if you don't need the complete URL or DOI in your final citation of a source, record it anyway so that you'll be able to track the source down if you want to consult it again. For a source you reach through a library database, record just a DOI if one is available because database URLs generally cannot be used to locate sources.

Annotated bibliography entry with assessment

Gore, Al. *Our Choice: A Plan to Solve the Climate Crisis.* Emmaus: Rodale, 2009. Print. — Publication information for source

A sequel to Gore's *An Inconvenient Truth* that emphasizes solutions to global warming. Expands on the argument that global warming is a serious threat, with recent examples of natural disasters. Proposes ways that governments, businesses, and individuals can reduce or reverse the risks of global warming. Includes helpful summaries of scientific studies, short essays on various subjects, and dozens of images, tables, charts, and graphs. — Summary of source / Helpful features

Compelling overview of possible solutions, with lots of data that seem thorough and convincing. But the book is aimed at a general audience and doesn't have formal source citations. Can use it for broad concepts, but for data I'll have to track down Gore's scholarly sources. — Assessment of source

51 Finding Sources

This chapter discusses conducting electronic searches (next page) and taking advantage of the range of sources, both print and electronic, that you have access to: reference works (p. 323); books (p. 324); periodicals (p. 324); the Web (p. 329); social media (p. 332); government publications (p. 333); visuals, audio, and video (p. 334); and your own interviews, surveys, and other primary sources (p. 336).

Note As you look for sources, avoid the temptation to seek a "silver bullet"—that is, to locate two or three perfect sources that already say everything you want to say about your subject. Instead of merely repeating others' ideas, read and synthesize many sources so that you enter into a dialog with them and develop your own ideas. For more on synthesis, see pp. 350–51.

51a Starting with your library's Web site

As you conduct academic research, your library's Web site will be your gateway to ideas and information. Always start with your

Video tutorial

mycomplab

Visit *mycomplab.com* for the eText and for resources and exercises on finding sources.

library's Web site, not with a public search engine such as *Google*. The library site will lead you to vast resources, including books, periodical articles, and reference works that aren't available on the open Web. More important, unlike many sources on the open Web, every source you find on the library site will have passed through filters to ensure its value. A scholarly journal article, for instance, undergoes at least three successive reviews: subject-matter experts first deem it worth publishing in the journal; then a database vendor deems the journal worth including in the database; and finally your school's librarians deem the database worth subscribing to.

Google and other search engines may seem more user-friendly than the library's Web site and may seem to return plenty of sources for you to work with. Many of the sources may indeed be reliable and relevant to your research, but many more will not be. In the end, a library Web search will be more efficient and more effective than a direct Web search. (For help with evaluating sources from any resource, see pp. 338–49.)

Note Start with the library's Web site, but don't stop there. Many books, periodicals, and other excellent sources are available only on library shelves, not online, and most instructors expect research papers to be built to some extent on these resources. When you spot promising print sources while browsing the library's online databases, make records of them and then look them up at the library.

51b Searching electronically

The way you reach your library's resources will vary depending on the way the Web site is set up. Many libraries offer separate searches of their catalogs of physical holdings (such as print books and periodicals) and of individual databases for articles. Other libraries provide a centralized search page that allows a simultaneous search of all the library's resources, including print books and e-books, print and electronic articles, and so on.

In either situation, an electronic search requires planning. A too-casual search can miss helpful sources while returning hundreds, even thousands, of irrelevant sources. Become familiar with the kinds of electronic sources available to you and with the different search strategies for each (below). And take time early in your research to develop **keywords** that name your subject for databases and Web search engines (p. 322).

1 Kinds of electronic sources

Your library's Web site will lead you to many kinds of electronic resources suitable for academic research.

- **The catalog of holdings,** searchable from the library's Web site, is a database that lists all the resources that the library owns or

Video
tutorial

A tip for researchers

Take advantage of two valuable resources offered by your library:

- **An orientation,** which introduces the library's resources and explains how to reach and use the Web site and the print holdings.
- **Reference librarians,** whose job it is to help you and others navigate the library's resources. All libraries offer face-to-face consultations, and many offer e-mail and chat services. Even very experienced researchers often consult reference librarians.

subscribes to. Depending on the library, the catalog may include print and electronic books, journals, magazines, newspapers, reference works, and more. It may also include the holdings of other school libraries nearby or in your state.

- **Online databases** include indexes, bibliographies, and other reference works. They are your main route to articles in periodicals, providing publication information, summaries, and often full text. Your library subscribes to the databases and makes them available through its Web site, either on its main search page or on a separate database page. (You may also discover databases directly on the Web, but, again, the library is the more productive starting place.)
- **Research guides,** available through some libraries, provide points of access to the library's resources on particular subjects, such as twentieth-century English literature or developmental psychology.
- **Databases on CD-ROM** include the same information as online databases, but they must be read at a library computer terminal. Increasingly, libraries have moved away from CD-ROMs in favor of online databases.

2 Databases and search engines

To develop effective keywords it helps to understand how library databases, library search engines, and public search engines work:

Exercise

- **A database matches your keywords to its index of authors, titles, and subject headings.** The subject headings reflect the database's directory of terms and are assigned by people who have read the sources. You can find these subject headings by using your own keywords until you locate a promising source. The information for the source will list the headings under which the database indexes the source and others like it. (See p. 327 for an illustration.) You can then use those headings for further searches.
- **A library's centralized search engine seeks your keywords among all the library's physical holdings and online offerings.** After your initial keyword search, the engine will provide options to limit

or expand your search within the library's available resources. The search engine will not return content from the open Web.

■ **A Web search engine seeks your keywords in the titles and texts of sites on the public Web.** The results will depend on how well your keywords describe your subject and anticipate the words used in sources. If you describe your subject too broadly or describe it specifically but don't match the vocabulary in relevant sources, your search will turn up few relevant sources and probably many that aren't relevant.

Exercise

3 Keyword refinement

Every database and search engine provides a system that you can use to refine your keywords for a productive search. The basic operations appear in the following box, but resources do differ. For instance, some assume that *AND* should link keywords, while others provide options specifying "Must contain all the words" and other equivalents for the operations in the box. You can learn a search engine's system by consulting its Advanced Search page.

Ways to refine keywords

Video
tutorial

Most databases and many search engines work with **Boolean operators,** terms or symbols that allow you to expand or limit your keywords and thus your search.

■ **Use *AND* or + to narrow the search** by including only sources that use all the given words. The keywords *green AND products* request only the sources in the shaded area.

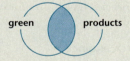

■ **Use *NOT* or − ("minus") to narrow the search** by excluding irrelevant words. The keywords *green AND products NOT guide* exclude sources that use the word *guide*:

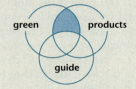

■ **Use *OR* to broaden the search** by giving alternative keywords. The keywords *green AND products OR goods* allow for sources that use a synonym for *products*:

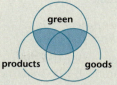

- **Use parentheses or quotation marks to form search phrases.** For instance, *(green products)* requests the exact phrase, not the separate words. Only sources using *green products* would turn up.
- **Use wild cards to permit different versions of the same word.** In *consum**, for instance, the wild card * indicates that sources may include *consume, consumer, consumerism,* and *consumption* as well as *consumptive, consumedly,* and *consummate.* The example suggests that you have to consider all the variations allowed by a wild card and whether it opens up your search too much. If you seek only two or three from many variations, you may be better off using *OR*: *consumption OR consumerism.* (Note that some systems use ?, :, or + for a wild card instead of *.)
- **Be sure to spell your keywords correctly.** Some search tools will look for close matches or approximations, but correct spelling gives you the best chance of finding relevant sources.

Note You will probably have to use trial and error in developing your keywords, sometimes running dry (turning up few or no sources) and sometimes hitting uncontrollable gushers (turning up thousands or millions of mostly irrelevant sources). But the process is not busywork—far from it. Besides leading you eventually to worthwhile sources, it can also teach you a great deal about your subject: how you can or should narrow it, how it is and is not described by others, what others consider interesting or debatable about it, and what the major arguments are. See pp. 331–32 for an example of a student's keyword search of the Web.

51c Finding reference works

Reference works, often available online, include encyclopedias, dictionaries, digests, bibliographies, indexes, atlases, almanacs, and handbooks. Your research *must* go beyond these sources, but they can help you decide whether your topic really interests you and whether it meets the requirements for a research paper (p. 313). Preliminary research in reference works can also help you develop keywords for electronic searches and can direct you to more detailed sources on your topic.

You'll find many reference works through your library and directly on the Web. The following list gives general Web references for all disciplines:

INFOMINE (infomine.ucr.edu)
ipl2 (*ipl.org*)
Library of Congress (lcweb.loc.gov)
World Wide Web Virtual Library (vlib.org)

For Web sites in specific academic disciplines, see **8** pp. 383 (literature), 388–89 (other humanities), 392 (social sciences), and 396 (natural and applied sciences).

Note The Web-based encyclopedia *Wikipedia* (found at *wikipedia .org*) is one of the largest reference sites on the Internet. Like any encyclopedia, *Wikipedia* can provide background information for research on a topic. But unlike other encyclopedias, *Wikipedia* is a **wiki,** a kind of Web site that can be contributed to or edited by anyone. Ask your instructor whether *Wikipedia* is an acceptable source before you use it. If you do use it, you must carefully evaluate any information you find, following the guidelines on pp. 342–49.

51d Finding books

Your library's catalog is searchable at computers in the library and via the library's Web site. You can search the catalog by author or title, of course, and by your own keywords or the headings found in *Library of Congress Subject Headings* (*LCSH*). The screen shot below shows the complete record for a book, including the *LCSH* headings that can be used to find similar sources.

Book catalog full record

Building the green economy : success stories from the grassroots

Title and subtitle

Author: Kevin Danaher 1950-
Shannon Biggs ; Jason Mark — Authors

Subjects: Sustainable development -- Citizen participation ; Environmentalism -- Economic aspects ; Green products — Subject headings for book

Publisher: Sausalito, CA : PoliPointPress : Distributed by Ingram Publisher Services

Creation Date: c2007 — Publisher and date

Description: 282 p. ; 24 cm..

Language: English

Format: Book

Identifier: ISBN9780977825363 (alk. paper);ISBN0977825361 : — Library call number

Available {HC79.E5 D3252 2007) (Get It)

51e Finding periodicals

Periodicals include newspapers, academic journals, and magazines, either print or online. Newspapers are useful for detailed accounts of past and current events. Journals and magazines can be harder to distinguish, but their differences are important. Most college instructors expect students' research to rely more on journals than on magazines.

Journals	Magazines
Examples	
American Anthropologist, Journal of Black Studies, Journal of Chemical Education	*The New Yorker, Time, Rolling Stone, People*
Availability	
Mainly college and university libraries, either on library shelves or in online databases	Public libraries, newsstands, bookstores, the open Web, and online databases
Purpose	
Advance knowledge in a particular field	Express opinion, inform, or entertain
Authors	
Specialists in the field	May or may not be specialists in their subjects
Readers	
Often specialists in the field	Members of the general public or a subgroup with a particular interest
Source citations	
Source citations always included	Source citations rarely included
Length of articles	
Usually long, ten pages or more	Usually short, fewer than ten pages
Frequency of publication	
Quarterly or less often	Weekly, biweekly, or monthly
Pagination of issues	
May be paged separately (like a magazine) or may be paged sequentially throughout an annual volume, so that issue number 3 (the third issue of the year) could open on page 373	Paged separately, each beginning on page 1

1 Indexes to periodicals

How indexes work

Periodical databases index the articles in journals, magazines, and newspapers. Often these databases include abstracts, or summaries, of the articles, and they may offer the full text of the articles as well. Your library subscribes to many periodical databases and to services that offer multiple databases. (See p. 328 for a list.) Most databases and services will be searchable through the library's Web site.

Video tutorial

Note The search engine *Google* is developing *Google Scholar*, a search engine at *scholar.google.com* that seeks out scholarly articles. It is particularly useful for subjects that range across disciplines, for which discipline-specific databases can be too limited. *Google Scholar* can connect to your library's holdings if you tell it to do so under Scholar Preferences. Keep in mind, however, that *Google Scholar*'s searches are not as yet exhaustive, and they may list articles that you cannot obtain in full text. Your library is the best source for articles that are available to you, so begin there.

Selection of databases

To decide which databases to consult, you'll need to consider what you're looking for:

- **Does your research subject span more than one discipline?** Then start with a broad database such as *Academic Search Complete, JSTOR, Lexis Nexis Academic Universe,* or *CQ Researcher.* A broad database covers many subjects and disciplines but does not index the full range of periodicals in each subject.

- **Does your research subject focus on a single discipline?** Then start with a discipline-specific database such as *Historical Abstracts, MLA International Bibliography, Biological Abstracts,* or *Education Search Complete.* A specific database covers few subjects but includes most of the available periodicals in each subject. If you don't know the name of an appropriate database, the library's Web site probably lists possibilities by discipline.

- **Which databases most likely include the kinds of resources you need?** The Web sites of most libraries allow you to narrow a database search to a particular discipline. Some libraries also provide research guides, which list potentially helpful databases for your search terms. You can then discover each database's focus by checking the description of the database (sometimes labeled "Help" or "Guide") or the list of indexed resources (sometimes labeled "Publications" or "Index"). The description will also tell you the time period the database covers, so you'll know whether you also need to consult older print indexes at the library.

Database searches

When you first search a database, use your own keywords to locate sources. The procedure is illustrated in the three screen shots shown opposite and on p. 328. Your goal is to find at least one source that seems just right for your subject, so that you can see what subject headings the database itself uses for such sources. Using one or more of those headings will focus and speed your search.

Note Many databases allow you to limit your search to so-called peer-reviewed or refereed journals—that is, scholarly journals whose articles have been reviewed before publication by experts in the field and then revised by the author. Limiting your search to peer-reviewed journals can help you navigate huge databases that might otherwise return scores of unusable articles.

1. Initial keyword search of a periodical database

Database

Searching: Academic Search Complete | Choose Databases »

green

AND products

AND shopping

Keywords

Limit your results

Search limited to peer-reviewed journals

2. Partial keyword search results

1. Going **Green** to Be Seen: Status, Reputation, and Conspicuous Conservation.

   By: Griskevicius, Vladas; Tybur, Joshua M.; Van den Bergh, Bram. Journal of Personality & Social Psychology, Mar2010, Vol. 98 Issue 3, p392-404, 13p

   Subjects: CONSUMER behavior; GREEN products; ALTRUISM; LUXURIES; MOTIVATION (Psychology); ECONOMIC status; SHOPPING; SOCIAL aspects

   Database: Academic Search Complete

   Article title

   Authors

   Journal and publication information

   Available full text

2. Can you calculate the carbon cost of your **shopping**?

   By: Cervi, B.. Engineering & Technology (17509631), 11/22/2008, Vol. 3 Issue 20, p18-21, 4p, 6 Color Photographs, 1 Diagram; DOI: 10.1049/et:20082000

   Subjects: GREEN products; ECOLOGICAL impact; ENVIRONMENTAL economics; SUSTAINABLE development; ENVIRONMENTAL policy; CARBON -- Environmental aspects; GREAT Britain; Administration of Air and Water Resource and Solid Waste Management Programs; Administration of General Economic Programs

   Database: Academic Search Complete

The use of abstracts

In screen 3 on the next page, the full article record shows a key feature of many databases' periodical listings: an **abstract** that summarizes the article. By describing research methods, conclusions, and other information, an abstract can tell you whether you want to pursue an article and thus save you time. However, the abstract cannot replace the actual article. If you want to use the work as a source, you must consult the full text.

3. Full article record with abstract

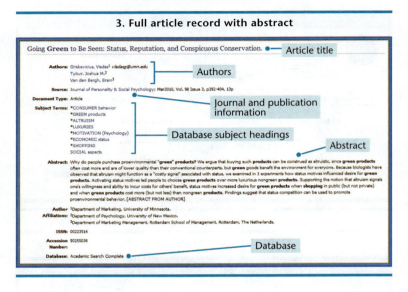

Helpful databases

The following list includes databases to which academic libraries commonly subscribe. Some of these databases cover much the same material, so your library may not subscribe to all of them.

> *EBSCOhost Academic Search.* A periodical index covering magazines and journals in the social sciences, sciences, arts, and humanities. Many articles are available full-text.
>
> *InfoTrac Expanded Academic.* The Gale Group's general periodical index covering the social sciences, sciences, arts, and humanities as well as national news periodicals. It includes full-text articles.
>
> *LexisNexis Academic.* An index of news and business, legal, and reference information, with full-text articles. *LexisNexis* includes international, national, and regional newspapers, news magazines, legal and business publications, and court cases.
>
> *ProQuest Research Library.* A periodical index covering the sciences, social sciences, arts, and humanities, including many full-text articles.

2 Locations of periodicals

If an index listing does not include or link directly to the full text of an article, you'll need to consult the periodical itself. Recent issues of periodicals are probably held in the library's periodical room. Back issues are usually stored elsewhere, either in bound volumes or on film that requires a special machine to read. A librarian will show you how to operate the machine.

51f Finding sources on the Web

As an academic researcher, you enter the Web in two ways: through your library's Web site, and through public search engines such as *Bing* and *Google*. The library entrance, covered in the preceding sections, is your main path to the books and periodicals that, for most subjects, should make up most of your sources. The public entrance, discussed here, can lead to a wealth of information and ideas, but it also has disadvantages that limit its usefulness for academic research:

- **The Web is a wide-open network.** Anyone with the right tools can place information on the Internet, and even a carefully conceived search can turn up sources with widely varying reliability: journal articles, government documents, scholarly data, term papers written by high school students, sales pitches masked as objective reports, wild theories. You must be especially diligent about evaluating Internet sources (see pp. 342–49).
- **The Web changes constantly.** No search engine can keep up with the Web's daily additions and deletions, and a source you find today may be different or gone tomorrow. You should not put off consulting an online source that you think you may want to use.
- **The Web is not all-inclusive.** Most books and many periodicals are available only via the library, not directly via the Web.

Clearly, the Web warrants cautious use. It should not be the only resource you work with.

1 Search engines

To find sources on the Web, you use a **search engine** that catalogs Web sites in a series of directories and conducts keyword searches. Generally, use a directory when you haven't yet refined your topic or you want a general overview. Use keywords when you have refined your topic and you seek specific information.

Current search engines

The box on the next page lists popular search engines. To reach any one of them, enter its address in the Address or Location field of your Web browser.

Note For a good range of sources, try out more than a single search engine, perhaps as many as four or five. No search engine can catalog the entire Web—indeed, even the most powerful engine may not include half the sites available at any given time, and most

Web search engines

The features of search engines change often, and new ones appear constantly. For the latest on search engines, see the links collected by *Easy Searcher* at *easysearcher.com*.

Directories that review sites
INFOMINE (*infomine.ucr.edu*)
ipl2 (*ipl.org*)
Internet Scout Project (*scout.wisc.edu/archives*)

Search engines
AlltheWeb (*alltheweb.com*)
AltaVista (*altavista.com*)
Ask.com (*ask.com*)
Bing (*bing.com*)
Dogpile (*dogpile.com*)
Google (*google.com*)
MetaCrawler (*metacrawler.com*)
Yahoo! (*yahoo.com*)

engines include only a fifth or less. In addition, most search engines accept paid placements, giving higher billing to sites that pay a fee. These so-called sponsored links are usually marked as such, but they can compromise a search engine's method for arranging sites in response to your keywords.

Customized searches

The home page of a search engine includes a field for you to type your keywords into. Generally, it will also include an Advanced Search link that you can use to customize your search. For instance, you may be able to select a range of dates, a language, or a number of results to see. Advanced Search will also explain how to use operators such as *AND, OR,* and *NOT* to limit or expand your search.

Search records

No matter which search engine you use, your Web browser includes functions that allow you to keep track of Web sources and your search:

- Use *Favorites* or *Bookmarks* **to save site addresses as links.** Click one of these terms near the top of the browser screen to add a site you want to return to. A favorite or bookmark remains on file until you delete it.
- Use *History* **to locate sites you have visited before.** The browser records visited sites for a certain period, such as a single online session or a week's sessions. (After that period, the history is

deleted.) If you forgot to bookmark a site, you can click History or Go to locate your search history and recover the site.

2 A sample search

The following sample Web search illustrates how the refinement of keywords can narrow a search to maximize the relevant hits and minimize the irrelevant ones. Justin Malik, a student researching the environmental effects of green consumer products, first used the keywords *green products* on *Google*. But, as shown on screen 1 below, the search produced more than 53 million items, with the first page consisting entirely of sites selling products, including sponsored sites and other advertisers.

1. First *Google* search results

Malik realized he had to alter his strategy to get more useful results. He experimented with combinations of synonyms and narrower terms and arrived at *"green consumerism"* and *products*, which refined the search but still produced 130,000 results. Adding *site:.gov* limited the results to government sites, whose URLs end in *.gov*. With *"green consumerism" products site:.gov*, Malik received 197 results (see screen 2 on the next page). He continued to limit the search by replacing *site:.gov* with *site:.org* (nonprofit organizations), *site:.edu* (educational institutions), and *site:.com* (commercial organizations).

2. *Google* **results with refined keywords**

51g Finding sources using social media

Online sources that you reach through interactive media can put you directly in touch with experts and others whose ideas and information may inform your research. These social media include e-mail, blogs, social-networking sites, and discussion groups. Like Web sites, they are unfiltered, so you must always evaluate them carefully. (See pp. 348–49.)

Note If your paper includes social-media correspondence that is not already public—for instance, an e-mail or a discussion-group posting—ask the author for permission to use it. Doing so advises the author that his or her ideas are about to be distributed more widely and lets the author verify that you have not misrepresented the ideas. (See also pp. 336–37 on interviews.)

1 E-mail

As a research tool, e-mail allows you to communicate with others who are interested in your topic. You might, for instance, carry on an e-mail conversation with a teacher at your school or interview an expert in another state to follow up on a scholarly article he or she published.

2 Blogs and social-networking sites

Blogs (Web logs) are Web sites on which an author or authors post time-stamped comments, generally centering on a common theme, in a format that allows readers to respond to the writer or to one another. You can find directories of blogs at *blogcatalog.com*.

Somewhat similar to blogs, pages on social-networking sites such as *Facebook* are increasingly being used by organizations, businesses, individuals, and even scholars to communicate with others.

Like all other social media discussed in this section, blogs and pages on social-networking sites must be evaluated carefully as potential sources. Some are reliable sources of opinion and evolving scholarship, and many refer to worthy books, articles, Web sites, and other resources. But just as many are little more than outlets for their authors' gripes or self-marketing. See pp. 348–49 for tips on telling the good from the bad.

3 Discussion lists

A **discussion list** (sometimes called a **listserv** or just a **list**) uses e-mail to connect individuals who are interested in a common subject, often with a scholarly or technical focus. By sending a question to an appropriate list, you may be able to reach scores of people who know something about your topic. For an index of discussion lists, see *tile.net/lists*.

Begin research on a discussion list by consulting the list's archive to ensure that the discussion is relevant to your topic and to see whether your question has already been answered. When you write to the list, follow the guidelines for writing e-mail in **2** pp. 77–78. And always evaluate messages you receive, following the guidelines on pp. 348–49. Although many contributors are reliable experts, almost anyone with an Internet connection can post a message.

4 Web forums and newsgroups

Web forums and newsgroups are more open and less scholarly than discussion lists, so their messages require even more diligent evaluation. **Web forums** allow participants to join a conversation simply by selecting a link on a Web page. For a directory of forums, see *delphiforums.com*. **Newsgroups** are organized under subject headings such as *soc* for social issues and *biz* for business. For a directory of newsgroups, see *groups.google.com*.

51h Using government publications

Government publications provide a vast array of data, reports, policy statements, public records, and other historical and contemporary information. For US government publications, consult the Government Printing Office's *GPO Access* at *www.gpoaccess.gov*. Also helpful is *Google US Government Search* (*google.com/unclesam*) because it returns *.gov* (government) and *.mil* (military) documents and its ranking system emphasizes the most useful documents. Many federal, state, and local government agencies post important publications—legislation, reports, press releases—on their own Web sites. You can find lists of sites for various federal agencies by using the keywords *United States federal government* with a search engine. Use the name of a state, city, or town with *government* for state and local information.

51i Finding visuals, audio, and video

Visuals, audio, and video can be used as both primary and secondary sources in a research project. A painting, an advertisement, or a video of a speech might be the subject of your writing and thus a primary source. A podcast of a radio interview with an expert on your subject or a college lecture might serve as a secondary source. Because many of these sources are unfiltered—they can be posted by anyone—you must always evaluate them as carefully as you would any source you find on the open Web. (See pp. 342–49.)

Caution You must also cite every visual, audio, and video source fully in your paper, just as you cite text sources, with author, title, and publication information. In addition, some sources will require that you seek permission from the copyright holder, either the source itself or a third party such as a photographer or the creator of a video. Permission is especially likely to be required if you are submitting your project on the public Web. (See pp. 366–67 for more about online publication.) To avoid having to seek permission, you can search for visuals, audio, and video that are not protected by copyright. On *Google*, for instance, go to Advanced Search and select "Labeled for reuse." Consult a librarian at your school if you have questions.

1 Visuals

The use of visuals to support your writing is discussed in **1** pp. 58–64 and **2** pp. 112–16. To find visuals, you have a number of options:

- **Scout for visuals while reading print or online sources.** Your sources may include charts, graphs, photographs, and other visuals that can support your ideas. When you find a visual you may want to use, photocopy or download it so you'll have it available later.
- **Create your own visuals,** such as photographs or charts. See **1** pp. 58–62 for suggestions on creating visuals.
- **Use an image search engine.** *Google, Yahoo!, AlltheWeb,* and some other search engines can be set to search for visuals, and they allow you to restrict your search to visuals that don't require reuse permission. Although search engines can find scores of visuals, the results may be inaccurate or incomplete because the sources surveyed often do not include descriptions of the visuals. (The engines search file names and any text accompanying the visuals.)

■ **Use a public image database.** The following sites generally conduct accurate searches because their images are filed with information such as a description of the visual, the artist's name, and
the visual's date:

Duke University, *Ad*Access* (*library.duke.edu/digitalcollections/adaccess*).
Print advertisements spanning 1911–55.
Library of Congress, *American Memory* (*memory.loc.gov/ammem*). Maps,
photographs, prints, and advertisements documenting the American
experience.
Library of Congress, *Prints and Photographs Online Catalog* (*loc.gov/
pictures*). Visuals from the library's collection, including those available through *American Memory*.
New York Public Library Digital Gallery (*digitalgallery.nypl.org/nypldigital*).
Maps, drawings, photographs, and paintings from the library's collection.
Political Cartoons (*politicalcartoons.com*). Cartoons on contemporary issues and events.

■ **Use a public image directory.** The following sites collect links to
image sources:

Art Project (*googleartproject.com*). Selections of fine art from major museums in the United States and Europe.
Art Source (*ilpi.com/artsource/general.html*). Sources on art and architecture.
MuseumLink's Museum of Museums (*museumlink.com*). Links to museums
all over the world.
Cultural Politics: Resources for Critical Analysis (*culturalpolitics.net*). Sources
on advertising, fashion, magazines, toys, and other artifacts of popular
culture.
Yale University Arts Library, *Image Resources* (*www.library.yale.edu/arts*).
Sources on the visual and performing arts.

■ **Use a subscription database.** Your library may subscribe to the
following resources:

ARTstor. Museum collections and a database of images typically used in
art history courses.
Associated Press, *AccuNet/AP Multimedia Archives.* Historical and contemporary news images.
Grove Art Online. Art images and links to museum sites.

Many visuals you find will be available at no charge for copying
or downloading, but some sources do charge a fee for use. Before
paying for a visual, check with a librarian to see if it is available
elsewhere for free.

2 **Audio and video**

Audio and video, widely available on the Web and on disc, can
provide your readers with the experience of "being there." For example, if you are researching the media response to Martin Luther

King's famous *I Have a Dream* speech and you are publishing your paper electronically, you might insert links to the speech and to TV and radio coverage of it.

- **Audio files** such as podcasts, Webcasts, and CDs record radio programs, interviews, speeches, lectures, and music. They are available on the Web and through your library. Online sources of audio include the Library of Congress's *American Memory* (see the previous page) and podcasts at *www.podcastdirectory.com*.
- **Video files** capture performances, speeches and public presentations, news events, and other activities. They are available on the Web and on DVD or Blu-ray disc from your library. Online sources of video include the Library of Congress's *American Memory* (see the previous page); *YouTube*, which includes commercials, historical footage, current events, and much more (*youtube.com*); and search engines such as *Google* (*video.google.com*).

51j Generating your own sources

Academic writing will often require you to conduct primary research for information of your own. For instance, you may need to analyze a poem, conduct an experiment, or interview an expert. Three common forms of primary research are observation, personal interviews, and surveys.

1 Personal interviews

An interview can be especially helpful for a research project because it allows you to ask questions precisely geared to your topic. You can conduct an interview in person, over the telephone, or online. A personal interview is preferable if you can arrange it, because you can see the person's expressions and gestures as well as hear his or her tone.

Here are a few guidelines for interviews:

- **Call or write for an appointment.** Tell the person exactly why you are calling, what you want to discuss, and how long you expect the interview to take. Be true to your word on all points.
- **Prepare a list of open-ended questions to ask**—perhaps ten or twelve for a one-hour interview. Do some research on these questions before the interview to discover background on the issues and your subject's published views on the issues.
- **Pay attention to your subject's answers** so that you can ask appropriate follow-up questions. Take care in interpreting answers, especially if you are online and thus can't depend on facial expressions, gestures, and tone of voice to convey the subject's attitudes.
- **Keep thorough notes.** Take notes during an in-person or telephone interview, or record the interview if you have the equipment and

your subject agrees. For online interviews, save the discussion in a file of its own.

■ **Verify quotations.** Before you quote your subject in your paper, check with him or her to ensure that the quotations are accurate.

■ **Send a thank-you note immediately after the interview.** Promise your subject a copy of your finished paper, and send the paper promptly.

2 | Surveys

Asking questions of a defined group of people can provide information about respondents' attitudes, behavior, backgrounds, and expectations. Use the following tips to plan and conduct a survey:

■ **Decide what you want to find out.** The questions you ask should be dictated by your purpose. Formulating a **hypothesis** about your subject—a generalization that can be tested—will help you refine your purpose.

■ **Define your population.** Think about the kinds of people your hypothesis is about—for instance, college men or preschool children. Plan to sample this population so that your findings will be representative.

■ **Write your questions.** Surveys may contain closed questions that direct the respondent's answers (checklists and multiple-choice, true/false, or yes/no questions) or open-ended questions that allow brief, descriptive answers. Avoid loaded questions that reveal your own biases or make assumptions about subjects' answers.

■ **Test your questions.** Use a few respondents with whom you can discuss the answers. Eliminate or recast questions that respondents find unclear, discomforting, or unanswerable.

■ **Tally the results.** Count the actual numbers of answers, including any nonanswers.

■ **Seek patterns in the raw data.** Such patterns may confirm or contradict your hypothesis. Revise the hypothesis or conduct additional research if necessary.

3 | Observing

Observation can be an effective way to gather fresh information on your subject. You may observe in a controlled setting—for instance, watching children at play in a child-development lab. Or you may observe in a more open setting—for instance, watching the interactions among students at a cafeteria on your campus. Use these guidelines for planning and gathering information through observation:

■ **Be sure that what you want to learn *can* be observed.** You can observe people's choices and interactions, but you would need an interview or a survey to discover people's attitudes or opinions.

- ■ **Allow ample time.** Observation requires several sessions of several hours in order to be reliable.
- ■ **Record your impressions.** Throughout the observation sessions, take careful notes on paper, a computer, or a mobile device. Always record the date, time, and location for each session.
- ■ **Be aware of your own bias.** Such awareness will help you avoid the common pitfall of seeing only what you expect or want to see.

52   Working with Sources

Research writing is much more than finding sources and reporting their contents. The challenge and interest come from interacting with and synthesizing sources: reading them critically to discover their meanings, judge their relevance and reliability, and create relationships among them; and using them to extend and support your own ideas so that you make your subject your own.

CULTURE LANGUAGE Making a subject your own requires thinking critically about sources and developing independent ideas. These goals may at first be uncomfortable if your native culture emphasizes understanding and respecting established authority more than questioning and enlarging it. The information here will help you work with sources so that you can become an expert in your own right and convincingly convey your expertise to others.

52a   Evaluating sources

Video tutorial

Before you gather information and ideas from sources, scan them to evaluate what they have to offer and how you might use them. As you evaluate each source, add an assessment of it to your annotated bibliography, as discussed and illustrated on pp. 317 and 319.

Note In evaluating sources, you need to consider how they come to you. The sources you find through the library, both in print and on the Web, have been previewed for you by their publishers and by the library's staff. They still require your critical reading, but you can have some confidence in the information they contain. With online sources you reach directly, however, you can't assume similar previewing, so your critical reading must be especially rigorous. Special tips for evaluating Web sites and other online sources begin on p. 342.

mycomp**lab**

Visit *mycomplab.com* for the eText and for resources and exercises on working with sources.

1 Relevance and reliability

Not all the sources you find will prove worthwhile: some may be irrelevant to your project, and others may be unreliable. Gauging the relevance and reliability of sources is the essential task of evaluating them. If you haven't already done so, read this book's chapter on critical thinking and reading (**2** pp. 79–87). It provides a foundation for answering the questions in the following box.

Video tutorial

Exercise

Questions for evaluating sources

For online sources, supplement these questions with those on pp. 343 and 348.

Checklist

Relevance

- **Does the source devote some attention to your subject?** Does it focus on your subject or cover it marginally? How does it compare to other sources you've found?
- **Is the source appropriately specialized for your needs?** Check the source's treatment of a topic you know something about, to ensure that it is neither too superficial nor too technical.
- **Is the source up to date enough for your subject?** When was it published? If your subject is current, your sources should be, too.

Reliability

- **Where does the source come from?** Did you find it through your library or directly through the Internet? (If the latter, see pp. 342–49.) Is the source popular or scholarly?
- **Is the author an expert in the field?** Check the author's credentials in a biography (if the source includes one), in a biographical reference, or by a keyword search of the Web.
- **What is the bias of the source?** How do the author's ideas relate to those in other sources? What areas does the author emphasize, ignore, or dismiss?
- **Is the source fair, reasonable, and well written?** Does it provide sound reasoning and a fair picture of opposing views? Is the tone calm and objective? Is the source logically organized and error-free?
- **Are the author's claims well supported?** Does the author provide accurate, relevant, representative, and adequate evidence to back up his or her claims? Does the author cite sources, and if so are they reliable?

---

2 Evaluating library sources

To evaluate sources you find through your library—either in print or on the library's Web site—look at dates, titles, summaries, introductions, headings, author biographies, and any source citations. The criteria on p. 342 expand on the most important tips in the preceding box. On the next two pages you can see how Justin Malik applied these criteria to two print sources, a magazine article and a journal article, that he consulted while researching green consumerism.

(continued on p. 342)

Evaluating library sources

Opposite are sample pages from two library sources that Justin Malik considered for his paper on green consumerism. Malik evaluated the sources using the questions and the guidelines on pp. 339 and 342.

Makower

Origin

Interview with Joel Makower published in *Vegetarian Times*, a popular magazine.

Author

Gives Makower's credentials at the beginning of the interview: the author of a book on green products and of a monthly newsletter on green businesses. Quotes another source that calls Makower the "guru of green business practice."

Bias

Describes and promotes green products. Concludes with an endorsement of a for-profit Web site that tracks and sells green products.

Reasonableness and writing

Presents Makower's data and perspective on distinguishing good from bad green products, using conversational writing in an informal presentation.

Source citations

Lacks source citations for claims and data.

Assessment

Probably unreliable: Despite Makower's reputation, the article comes from a nonscholarly source, takes a one-sided approach to consumption, and depends on statistics credited only to Makower.

Jackson

Article by Tim Jackson published in *Journal of Industrial Ecology,* a scholarly journal sponsored by two reputable universities: MIT and Yale.

Includes a biography at the end of the article that describes Jackson as a professor at the University of Surrey (UK) and lists his professional activities related to the environment.

Presents multiple views of green consumerism. Argues that a solution to environmental problems will involve green products and less consumption but in different ways than currently proposed.

Presents and cites opposing views objectively, using formal academic writing.

Includes more than three pages of source citations, many of scholarly and government sources and all cited within the article.

Probably reliable: The article comes from a scholarly journal, the author is an expert in the field, he discusses many views and concedes some, and his source citations confirm evidence from reliable sources.

First and last pages of an interview with Joel Makower, published in *Vegetarian Times*

Largest manufacturer of renewable energy equipment in the United States?	Largest buyer of green energy in the United States?	Largest buyer of fair-trade coffee in the world?
General Electric	**Johnson & Johnson**	**Starbucks**

a greater capacity than they did 10 years ago because landfill operators are more sophisticated about compacting.

The problem with landfills is the energy and resources used to make the stuff that goes into them. Over 95 percent of the things we buy—disposable razors, single-use water bottles—have a useful life of less than six weeks, and sometimes less than a day. Almost every environmental problem we face is a result of our own wastefulness. We pay a high price for being a consumer society, and not just at the checkout counter. The premise of green consumerism is that we won't have to do without things we want or need. But that means demanding that manufacturers find better ways to make these things and rewarding the companies that do by buying their products.

q: What are they?

q: Can we really do much in our own homes?

a: Sure. I live in the house where I grew up. We've made a series of eco-friendly renovations, using wood that is harvested in a sustainable way, paints that don't emit harmful chemicals, energy-efficient appliances and windows. We also asked that the contractor recycle all of the waste from the work they did. Because we live in California, which is a pretty eco-conscious state, contractors got asked to do that quite a lot. But you have to ask. That's what creates a demand for the service.

Being a green consumer isn't just passively selecting the right item at your supermarket. It involves complaining when complaining is warranted, demanding new products and services when they don't exist and buying them when they exist. It means taking action. ●

go for the green
interview by alan pell crawford

**buying beer? sneakers? a car?
the most eco-conscious companies
aren't always the most obvious**

It isn't easy being green. No fewer than 137 eco-labels appear on consumer products these days, reports Consumers Union, and that's not counting stickers such as "everything free." This explosion of claims comes from companies eager to meet the demand for healthful, environmentally friendly products—or at least to cash in on it. Figuring out which products really are green and which are mere hype can be overwhelming.

Fortunately, there's help. To find out more about the current state of green consumerism, *VT* interviewed Joel Makower, who has spent the past 20 years helping consumers become savvier shoppers and getting

corporations to become more responsible corporate citizens. The author of *The Green Consumer* and editor of *The Green Business Letter*—a monthly publication that offers information to companies working to integrate environmental thinking into their operations—Makower is the "guru of green business practices," according to the Associated Press.

If anybody knows how corporations have responded to this demand for environmentally responsible products, it's Makower. General Electric, General Motors, Hewlett-Packard, Levi Strauss & Co., Nike and Procter & Gamble have all had the benefit of his counsel. Now it's your turn.

green-rated products

…onovo.com—from the Latin *ala novo* for "nurturing change"—is an online eco-shopping service that's associated with Amazon.com. Find a product on …onovo, and in addition to the description, reviews and …ce, you'll also see a five-dot rating for the company …d produced it. Better still, Alonovo allows you to …hance the ratings that product and companies receive …y weighting the values most important to you—Healthy …ironment, Business Ethics and so forth. Best of all, …u can buy products through Alonovo at Amazon prices. …last 20 percent of revenues are sent to a nonprofit …at you specify. Alonovo processes the transaction and …ps the goods.

…Launched in August 2005, Alonovo [a for-profit …mpany] is one of a number of new services designed …help consumers make smart choices. Similar in concept …Buildswitch [ideetwork.com], which allows you to put …more emphasis on a company's animal-welfare policies, …r example, than on its concern for workplace equity— …vice versa.

…How good will Alonovo be? "If it catches on," says Joel …akower, "it could be one of the most powerful social …ange tools ever put into consumers' hands."

STATE OF THE DEBATE

Live Better by Consuming Less?

Is There a "Double Dividend" in Sustainable Consumption?

Tim Jackson

…nster Publishing.

UNDP (United Nations Development Programme) 1998. *Human development report 1998.* Oxford, UK: Oxford University Press.

UNEP (United Nations Environment Programme) 2001. *Consumption opportunities: Strategies for change.* Paris: UNEP.

Van den Bergh, J. C. J. M., A. Ferrer-i-Carbonell, and G. Munda. 2000. Alternative models of individual behaviour and implications for environmental policy. *Ecological Economics* 32(1): 43–61.

About the Author

Tim Jackson is Professor of Sustainable Development at the Centre for Environmental Strategy (CES) in the University of Surrey, Guildford, United Kingdom. He currently holds a research fellowship in sustainable consumption funded by the Economic and Social Research Council and leads the Ecological Economics Research Group at CES. He is also chair of the Ecosystems Steering Group of the UK Sustainable Development Commission and sits on the UK Round Table on Sustainable Consumption.

Keywords

consumer behavior
consumer choice
consumer culture
evolutionary psychology
industrial ecology
symbolic interactionism

Summary

Industrial … the offici… tion is at… ment. Th… this. But … really be… debates…
self. This article explores some of these wider debates. In particular, it draws attention to a fundamental disagreement that runs through the literature on consumption and haunts the debate on sustainable consumption: the question of whether, or to what extent, consumption can be taken as "good for us." Some approaches assume that increasing consumption is more or less synonymous with improved well-being: the more we consume the better off we are. Others argue, just as vehemently, that the scale of consumption in modern society is both environmentally and psychologically damaging, and that we could reduce consumption significantly without threatening the quality of our lives. This second viewpoint suggests that a kind of 'double dividend' is inherent in sustainable consumption: the ability to live better by consuming less and reduce our impact on the environment in the process. In the final analysis, this article argues, such "win win" solutions may exist but will require a concerted societal effort to realize.

First and last pages of an article by Tim Jackson, published in the *Journal of Industrial Ecology*

(continued from p. 339)

Identify the origin of the source.

Check whether a library source is popular or scholarly. Scholarly sources, such as refereed journals and university press books, are generally deeper and more reliable. But some popular sources, such as first-hand newspaper accounts and books for a general audience, are often appropriate for research projects.

Check the author's expertise.

The authors of scholarly publications tend to be experts whose authority can be verified. Check the source to see whether it contains a biographical note about the author, check a biographical reference, or check the author's name in a keyword search of the Web. Look for other publications by the author and for his or her job and any affiliation, such as teacher at a university, researcher with a nonprofit organization, or writer for popular magazines.

Identify the author's bias.

Every author has a point of view that influences the selection and interpretation of evidence. You may be able to learn about an author's bias from biographies, citation indexes, and review indexes. But also look at the source itself. How do the author's ideas relate to those in other sources? What areas does the author emphasize, ignore, or dismiss? When you're aware of sources' biases, you can acknowledge them in your writing and try to balance them.

Determine whether the source is fair, reasonable, and well written.

Even a strongly biased work should present solid reasoning and give balanced coverage to opposing views—all in an objective tone. Any source should be organized logically and should be written in clear, error-free sentences. The absence of any of these qualities should raise a warning flag.

Analyze support for the author's claims.

Evidence should be accurate, relevant to the argument, representative of its context, and adequate for the point being made (see **2** p. 106). The author's sources should themselves be reliable.

3 Evaluating Web sites

Video tutorial

The same critical reading that helps you evaluate library sources will help you evaluate Web sites that you reach directly. Just as you would not use a popular magazine such as *People* for academic research, you would not use a celebrity's Web site, a fan site, or a gossip site as a source. But Web sites that might seem worthy pose extra challenges for evaluation because they have not undergone prior screening by editors and librarians. On your own, you must distinguish scholarship from corporate promotion, valid data from invented statistics, well-founded opinion from clever propaganda.

The strategy summarized in the following box can help you make such distinctions. On the next two pages you can see how Justin Malik applied this strategy to two Web sites that he consulted while researching green consumerism.

Questions for evaluating Web sites

Supplement these questions with those on pp. 339 and 348.

- **What type of site are you viewing?** What does the type lead you to expect about the site's purpose and content?
- **Who is the author or sponsor?** How credible is the person or group responsible for the site?
- **What is the purpose and bias of the site?** What does the site's author or sponsor intend to achieve? What bias do you detect?
- **What does context tell you?** What do you already know about the site's subject that can inform your evaluation? What kinds of support or other information do the site's links provide?
- **What does presentation tell you?** Is the site's design well thought out and effective? Is the writing clear and error-free?
- **How worthwhile is the content?** Are the site's claims well supported by evidence from reliable sources? When was the site last updated?

Checklist

Note To evaluate a Web document, you'll often need to travel to the site's home page to discover the author or sponsor, date of publication, and other relevant information. The page you're reading may include a link to the home page. If it doesn't, you can find it by editing the URL in the Address or Location field of your browser. Working backward, delete the end of the URL up to the last slash and hit Enter. Repeat this step until you reach the home page. There you may also find a menu option, often labeled "About," that will lead you to a description of the site's author or sponsor.

Determine the type of site.

When you search the Web, you're likely to encounter various types of sites. Although they sometimes overlap, the types can usually be identified by their content and purposes. Here are the main types of Web sites you will find using a search engine:

Video tutorial

- **Scholarly sites:** These sites have a knowledge-building interest, and they are likely to be reliable. They include research reports with supporting data and extensive documentation of scholarly sources. For such sites originating in the United States, the URLs generally end in *edu* (originating from a college or university), *org* (a nonprofit organization), or *gov* (a government department or agency). Sites originating in other countries will end differently, usually with a country code such as *uk* (United Kingdom), *de* (Germany), or *kr* (South Korea).

(continued on p. 346)

Evaluating Web sites

Video tutorial

Opposite are screen shots from two Web sites that Justin Malik consulted for his paper on green consumerism. Malik evaluated the sources using the questions in the boxes on pp. 339 and 343.

Allianz Knowledge Partnersite	*Nature Climate Change*
Author and sponsor	
Site sponsor is the Allianz Group, a global insurance company partnering with well-known organizations to provide information on a variety of issues. Author of article is identified as an editor, not a scientist.	Listed author is a scientist, an expert on climate science. (Biography appears at the end of the article.) Site sponsor is the Nature Publishing Group, which also publishes the reputable science journal *Nature*.
Purpose and bias	
Educational page on a corporate-sponsored Web site with the self-stated purpose of gathering information about global issues and making it available to an international audience.	Informational site with the self-stated purpose of "publishing the most significant and cutting-edge research on the impacts of global climate change." Article expresses bias toward reducing pollution to stop climate change.
Context	
One of many sites publishing current information on climate issues.	One of many sites publishing current research on climate issues.
Presentation	
Clean, professionally designed site with mostly error-free writing.	Clean, professionally designed site with error-free writing.
Content	
Article gives basic information about climate change and provides links to other pages that expand on its claims. Probably because of the intended general (nonscientist) audience, the pages do not include citations of scholarly research.	Article is current (date below the author's name) and clearly explains an effect of climate change with references and links to scholarly sources. Other links connect to hundreds of articles elsewhere on the site about climate-related topics.
Assessment	
Probably unreliable: Despite the wealth of information in the article and its links, the material lacks the scholarly source citations necessary for its use as evidence in an academic paper.	**Probably reliable:** The article has an explicit bias toward stopping climate change, but the site sponsor has a scholarly reputation, the author is a climate expert, and the references cite scholarly and government sources.

Article published on the Web site *Allianz Knowledge Partnersite*

Article published on the Web site *Nature Climate Change*

(continued from p. 343)

- **Informational sites:** Individuals, nonprofit organizations, corporations, schools, and government bodies all produce sites intended to centralize information on subjects as diverse as astronomy, hip-hop music, and zoo design. The sites' URLs may end in *edu, org, gov,* or *com* (originating from a commercial organization). Such sites generally do not have the knowledge-building focus of scholarly sites and may omit supporting data and documentation, but they can provide useful information and sometimes include links to scholarly and other sources.

- **Advocacy sites:** Many sites present the views of individuals or organizations that promote certain policies or actions, such as the National Rifle Association or People for the Ethical Treatment of Animals. Their URLs usually end in *org*, but they may end in *edu* or *com*. Most advocacy sites have a strong bias. Some sites include serious, well-documented research to support their positions, but others select or distort evidence.

- **Commercial sites:** Corporations and other businesses such as automakers, electronics manufacturers, and booksellers maintain Web sites to explain themselves, promote themselves, or sell goods and services. URLs of commercial sites usually end in *com*; however, some end in *biz,* and those of businesses based outside the United States often end in the country code. Although business sites intend to further the sponsors' profit-making purposes, they can include reliable data.

- **Personal sites:** The sites maintained by individuals range from diaries of a family's travels to opinions on political issues to reports on evolving scholarship. The sites' URLs usually end in *com* or *edu*. Personal sites are only as reliable as their authors, but some do provide valuable eyewitness accounts, links to worthy sources, and other usable information. Personal sites are often blogs or social-networking pages, discussed on pp. 348–49.

Note Informational sites called wikis allow anyone to contribute and edit information on the site. Older entries on reputable wikis, such as *Wikipedia,* tend to be reliable because they have been reviewed and edited by experts, but recent entries may contain errors and even misinformation. Ask your instructor whether wikis are acceptable sources. If so, evaluate them carefully against other, more reliable sources using the following guidelines.

Identify the author and sponsor.

A reputable site lists its authors, names the group responsible for the site, and provides information or a link for contacting the author and the sponsor. If none of this information is provided, you should not use the source. If you have only the author's or the sponsor's name, you may be able to discover more in a biographical dictionary, through a keyword search, or in your other sources. Make sure the author and the sponsor have expertise on the subject they're presenting: if an author is a doctor, for instance, what is he or she a doctor of?

Gauge purpose and bias.

A Web site's purpose determines what ideas and information it offers. Inferring that purpose tells you how to interpret what you see on the site. If a site is intended to sell a product or advocate a particular position, it may emphasize favorable ideas and information while ignoring or even distorting unfavorable information or opposing views. In contrast, if a site is intended to build knowledge—for instance, a scholarly project or journal—it will likely acknowledge diverse views and evidence.

Determining the purpose and bias of a site often requires looking beyond the first page and beneath the surface of words and images. To start, read critically what the site says about itself, usually on a page labeled "About." Be suspicious of any site that doesn't provide information about itself and its goals.

Consider context.

Your evaluation of a Web site should be informed by considerations outside the site itself. Chief among these considerations is your own knowledge. What do you already know about the site's subject and the prevailing views of it? Where does this site seem to fit into that picture? What can you learn from this site that you don't already know?

In addition, you can follow some of the site's links to see how they support, or don't support, the site's credibility. For instance, links to scholarly sources lend authority to a site—but *only* if the scholarly sources actually relate to and back up the site's claims.

Look at presentation.

Considering both the look of a site and the way it's written can illuminate its intentions and reliability. Do the site's elements all support its purpose, or is the site cluttered with irrelevant material and graphics? Is the text clearly written and focused on the purpose? Is it relatively error-free, or does it contain typos and grammatical errors? Does the site seem carefully constructed and well maintained, or is it sloppy? How intrusive are any pop-up advertisements?

Analyze content.

With information about a site's author, purpose, and context, you're in a position to evaluate its content. Are the ideas and information current, or are they dated? (Check the publication date.) Are they slanted and, if so, in what direction? Are the views and data authoritative, or do you need to balance them—or even reject them? Are claims made on the site supported by evidence drawn from reliable sources? These questions require close reading of both the text and its sources.

4 | Evaluating other online sources

Social media and multimedia require the same critical scrutiny as Web sites do. Social media—including e-mail, blogs, discussion groups, *Facebook* pages, and wikis—can be sources of reliable data and opinions, but they can also contain wrong or misleading data and skewed opinions. Multimedia—visuals, audio, and video—can provide valuable support for your ideas, but they can also mislead or distort. For example, a *YouTube* search using "I have a dream" brings up videos of Martin Luther King, Jr., delivering his famous speech as well as videos of people speaking hatefully about King and the speech.

Answer the following questions when evaluating social media and multimedia.

Checklist

Video
tutorial

> ## Questions for evaluating social media and multimedia
>
> Supplement these questions with those on pp. 339 and 343.
>
> - **Who is the author or creator?** How credible is he or she?
> - **What is the author's or creator's purpose?** What can you tell about why the author or creator is publishing the work?
> - **What does the context reveal?** What do responses to the work, such as responses to a blog posting or the other messages in a discussion thread, indicate about the source's balance and reliability?
> - **How worthwhile is the content?** Are the claims made by the author or creator supported by evidence? Is the evidence from reliable sources?
> - **How does the source compare with other sources?** Do the claims made by the author or creator seem accurate and fair given what you've seen in sources you know to be reliable?

Identify the author or creator.

Checking out the author or creator of a potential source can help you judge its reliability. You may be able to learn about the background of an author or creator with a keyword search of the Web or in a biographical dictionary. If you can't identify the author or creator at all, you can't use the source.

You can also get a sense of the interests and biases of an author or creator by tracking down his or her other work. For instance, you might check whether a blog author cites or links to other publications, look for other postings by the same author in a discussion-group archive, or try to gain an overview of a photographer's work.

Analyze the author's or creator's purpose.

What can you tell about *why* the author or creator is publishing the work? Look for claims, the use (or lack) of evidence, and the treatment of opposing views. All these factors convey the person's stand on the subject and general fairness, and they will help you position the source among your other sources.

Consider the context.

Social media and multimedia are often difficult to evaluate in isolation. Looking beyond a particular contribution to the responses of others can give you a sense of context by indicating how the author or creator is regarded. On a blog or *Facebook* page, for example, look at the comments others have posted. If you discover negative or angry responses, try to understand why: sometimes online anonymity encourages hateful responses to even quite reasonable postings.

Analyze content.

A reliable source will offer evidence for claims and sources for evidence. If you don't see such support, then you probably shouldn't use the source. However, when the source is important to you and biographical information or context indicates that the author or creator is serious and reliable, you might ask him or her to direct you to supporting information.

The tone of writing can also be a clue to its purpose and reliability. In most social media, the writing tends to be more informal and may be more heated than in other kinds of sources; but look askance at writing that's contemptuous, dismissive, or shrill.

Compare with other sources.

Always consider social-media and multimedia sources in comparison to other sources so that you can distinguish singular, untested views from more mainstream views that have been subject to verification. Don't assume that a blog author's information and opinions are mainstream just because you see them on other blogs. The technology allows content to be picked up instantly by other blogs, so widespread distribution indicates only popular interest, not reliability.

Be wary of blogs that reproduce periodical articles, reports, or other publications. Try to locate the original version of the publication to be sure it has been reproduced fully and accurately, not quoted selectively or distorted. If you can't locate the original version, don't use the publication as a source.

52b Synthesizing sources

Video tutorial

When you begin to see the differences and similarities among sources, you move into the most significant part of research writing: forging relationships for your own purpose. This **synthesis** is an essential step in reading sources critically, and it continues through the drafting and revision of a research paper. As you infer connections—say, between one writer's opinions and another's or between two works by the same author—you shape your own perspective on your subject and create new knowledge.

Your synthesis of sources will grow more detailed and sophisticated as you proceed through the process of working with sources described in the balance of this chapter: gathering information from sources (opposite); deciding whether to summarize, paraphrase, or quote directly from sources (pp. 352–56); and integrating sources into your sentences (pp. 356–60). Unless you are analyzing primary sources such as the works of a poet, at first read your sources quickly and selectively to obtain an overview of your subject and a sense of how the sources approach it. Don't get bogged down in gathering detailed information, but *do* record your ideas about sources in your research journal (p. 312) or your annotated bibliography (p. 317).

Respond to sources.

One way to find your own perspective on a topic is to write down what your sources make you think. Do you agree or disagree with the author? Do you find his or her views narrow, or do they open up new approaches for you? Is there anything in the source that you need to research further before you can understand it? Does the source prompt questions that you should keep in mind while reading other sources?

Connect sources.

When you notice a link between sources, write about it. Do two sources differ in their theories or their interpretations of facts? Does one source illuminate another—perhaps commenting or clarifying or supplying additional data? Do two or more sources report studies that support a theory you've read about or an idea of your own?

Heed your insights.

Apart from ideas prompted by your sources, you are sure to come up with independent thoughts: a conviction, a point of confusion that suddenly becomes clear, a question you haven't seen anyone else ask. These insights may occur at unexpected times, so it's good practice to keep a notebook or computer handy to record them.

Draw your own conclusions.

As your research proceeds, the responses, connections, and insights you form through synthesis will lead you to answer your starting research question with a statement of your thesis (see p. 369). They will also lead you to the main ideas supporting your thesis—conclusions you have drawn from your synthesis of sources, forming the main divisions of your paper. Be sure to write them down as they occur to you.

Use sources to support your conclusions.

Effective synthesis requires careful handling of evidence from sources so that it meshes smoothly into your sentences and yet is clearly distinct from your own ideas. When drafting your paper, make sure that each paragraph focuses on an idea of your own, with the support for the idea coming from your sources. Generally, open each paragraph with your idea, provide evidence from a source or sources with appropriate citations, and close with an interpretation of the evidence. (Avoid ending a paragraph with a source citation; instead, end with your own idea.) In this way, your paper will synthesize others' work into something wholly your own. For more on structuring paragraphs in academic writing, see **2** pp. 97–98.

52c Gathering information from sources

You can accomplish a great deal of synthesis while gathering information from your sources. This information gathering is not a mechanical process. Rather, as you read you assess and organize the information in your sources.

Video tutorial

Exercise

Researchers vary in their methods for working with sources, but all methods share the same goals:

- **Keep accurate records of what sources say.** Accuracy helps prevent misrepresentation and plagiarism.
- **Keep accurate records of how to find sources.** These records are essential for retracing steps and for citing sources in the final paper. (See pp. 317–19 on keeping a working bibliography.)
- **Synthesize sources.** Information gathering is a critical process, leading to an understanding of sources, the relationships among them and your own ideas, and their support for your ideas.

To achieve these goals, you can take handwritten notes, type notes into your computer or mobile device, annotate photocopies or printouts of sources, or annotate downloaded documents. On any given project, you may use all the methods. Each has advantages and disadvantages.

- **Handwritten notes:** Taking notes by hand is especially useful if you come across a source with no computer or photocopier handy. But handwritten notes can be risky. It's easy to introduce errors as you work from source to paper. And it's possible to copy source language and then later mistake and use it as your own, thus plagiarizing the source. Always take care to make accurate notes and to place big quotation marks around any passage you quote.

- **Electronic notes:** Taking notes on a computer or mobile device can streamline the path of source to note to paper because you can import the notes into your draft as you write. However, electronic notes have the same disadvantages as handwritten notes: the risk of introducing errors and the risk of plagiarizing. As with handwritten notes, be a stickler for accuracy and use quotation marks for quotations.

- **Photocopies and printouts:** Photocopying from print sources or printing out online sources each has the distinct advantages of convenience and reduction in the risks of error and plagiarism during information gathering. But each method has disadvantages, too. The busywork of copying or printing can distract you from the crucial work of synthesizing sources. And you have to make a special effort to annotate copies and printouts with the publication information for sources. If you don't have this information for your final paper, you can't use the source.

- **Downloads:** Researching online, you can usually download full-text articles, Web pages, discussion-group messages, and other materials onto your computer. While drafting, you can import source information from one file into another. Like photocopies and printouts, though, downloads can distract you from interacting with sources and can easily become separated from the publication information you must have in order to use the sources. Even more important, directly importing source material creates a high risk of plagiarism. You must keep clear boundaries between your own ideas and words and those of others.

52d Using summary, paraphrase, and quotation

Video tutorial

Deciding whether to summarize, paraphrase, or quote directly from a source is an important step in synthesizing the source's ideas and your own. You engage in synthesis when you use your own words to summarize an author's argument or paraphrase a significant example or when you select a significant passage to quote. Choosing summary, paraphrase, or quotation should depend on why you are using a source.

Caution Summaries, paraphrases, and quotations all require source citations. A summary or paraphrase without a source citation or a quotation without quotation marks and a source citation is plagiarism. (See pp. 360–66 for more on plagiarism.)

1 Summary

When you **summarize,** you condense an extended idea or argument into a sentence or more in your own words. (See **2** pp. 83–85 for tips.) **Summary** is most useful when you want to record the gist of an author's idea without the background or supporting evidence. Following is a passage from a scholarly essay about consumption and its impact on the environment. Then a sample computer note shows a summary of the passage.

Video
tutorial

Original quotation

Such intuition is even making its way, albeit slowly, into scholarly circles, where recognition is mounting that ever-increasing pressures on ecosystems, life-supporting environmental services, and critical natural cycles are driven not only by the sheer number of resource users and the inefficiencies of their resource use, but also by the patterns of resource use themselves. In global environmental policymaking arenas, it is becoming more and more difficult to ignore the fact that the overdeveloped North must restrain its consumption if it expects the underdeveloped South to embrace a more sustainable trajectory.

—Thomas Princen, Michael Maniates, and Ken Conca,
Confronting Consumption, p. 4

Summary of source

Environmental consequences of consumption

Princen, Maniates, and Conca 4

Overconsumption may be a more significant cause of environmental problems than increasing population is.

2 Paraphrase

When you **paraphrase,** you follow much more closely the author's original presentation, but you restate it using your own words and sentence structures. Paraphrase is most useful when you want to present or examine an author's line of reasoning but you don't feel the original words merit direct quotation. The next page shows a paraphrase of the quotation from *Confronting Consumption*.

Video
tutorial

Notice that the paraphrase follows the original but uses different words and different sentence structures. In contrast, an unsuccessful

Paraphrase of source

Environmental consequences of consumption

Princen, Maniates, and Conca 4

Scholars are coming to believe that consumption is partly to blame for changes in ecosystems, reduction of essential natural resources, and changes in natural cycles. Policy makers increasingly see that developing nations will not adopt practices that reduce pollution and waste unless wealthy nations consume less. Rising population around the world does cause significant stress on the environment, but consumption is increasing even more rapidly than population.

paraphrase—one that plagiarizes—copies the author's words or sentence structures or both *without quotation marks*. (See pp. 365–66 for examples.)

Paraphrasing a source

■ **Read the relevant material several times to be sure you understand it.**

■ **Restate the source's ideas in your own words and sentence structures.** You need not put down in new words the whole passage or all the details. Select what is relevant to your topic, and restate only that. If complete sentences seem too detailed or cumbersome, use phrases.

■ **Be careful not to distort meaning.** Don't change the source's emphasis or omit connecting words, qualifiers, and other material whose absence will confuse you later or cause you to misrepresent the source.

CULTURE LANGUAGE If English is not your native language and you have difficulty paraphrasing the ideas in sources, try this. Before attempting a paraphrase, read the original passage several times. Then, instead of "translating" line by line, try to state the gist of the passage without looking at it. Check your effort against the original to be sure you have captured the source author's meaning and emphasis without using his or her words and sentence structures. If you need a synonym for a word, look it up in a dictionary.

3 **Direct quotation**

Video tutorial

Your notes from sources may include many quotations, especially if you rely on photocopies, printouts, or downloads. Whether to use a quotation in your draft, instead of a summary or paraphrase, depends on how important the exact words are and on whether the source is primary or secondary (p. 315):

- **Quote extensively when you are analyzing primary sources—** firsthand accounts such as works of literature, eyewitness reports, and historical documents. The quotations will generally be both the target of your analysis and the chief support for your ideas.
- **Quote selectively when you are drawing on secondary sources—** reports or analyses of other sources, such as a critic's view of a poem or a historian's synthesis of several eyewitness reports. Favor summaries and paraphrases over quotations, and put every quotation to both tests in the box below. Most papers of ten or so pages should not need more than two or three quotations that are longer than a few lines each.

Video
tutorial

Tests for direct quotations from secondary sources

The author's original satisfies one of these requirements:

- The language is unusually vivid, bold, or inventive.
- The quotation cannot be paraphrased without distortion or loss of meaning.
- The words themselves are at issue in your interpretation.
- The quotation represents and emphasizes a body of opinion or the view of an important expert.
- The quotation emphatically reinforces your own idea.
- The quotation is an illustration, such as a graph, diagram, or table.

The quotation is as short as possible:

- It includes only material relevant to your point.
- It is edited to eliminate examples and other unneeded material, using ellipsis marks and brackets (**5** pp. 287–89).

When you quote a source, either in your notes or in your draft, take precautions to avoid plagiarism or misrepresentation of the source:

- **Copy the material carefully.** Take down the author's exact wording, spelling, capitalization, and punctuation.
- **Proofread every direct quotation at least twice.**
- **Use quotation marks around the quotation** so that later you won't confuse it with a paraphrase or summary. Be sure to transfer the quotation marks into your draft as well, unless the quotation is long and is set off from your text. For advice on handling long quotations, see **MLA** pp. 447–48 and **APA** p. 482.

- **Use brackets** to add words for clarity or to change the capitalization of letters (see **5** p. 289 and **6** p. 299).
- **Use ellipsis marks** to omit material that is irrelevant to your point (see **5** pp. 287–89).
- **Cite the source of the quotation in your draft.** See pp. 367–68 on documentation.

52e Integrating sources into your text

Video tutorial

Integrating source material into your sentences is key to synthesizing others' ideas and information with your own. Evidence drawn from sources should *back up* your conclusions, not *be* your conclusions: you don't want to let your evidence overwhelm your own point of view. To keep your ideas in the forefront, you do more than merely present borrowed material; you introduce and interpret it as well.

Note The examples in this section use the MLA style of source documentation and also present-tense verbs (such as *disagrees* and *claims*). See pp. 359–60 for specific variations in documentation style and verb tense within the academic disciplines. Several other conventions governing quotations are discussed elsewhere in this book:

- **Using commas to punctuate signal phrases** (**5** pp. 269–70).
- **Placing other punctuation marks with quotation marks** (**5** pp. 284–85).
- **Using brackets and the ellipsis mark to indicate changes in quotations** (**5** pp. 287–89).
- **Punctuating and placing parenthetical citations** (**MLA** pp. 408–10).
- **Formatting long prose quotations and poetry quotations** (**MLA** pp. 447–48 and **APA** p. 482).

1 Introduction of borrowed material

Always introduce a summary, a paraphrase, or a quotation by identifying it and by providing a smooth transition between your words and ideas and those of your source. In the passage below, the writer has not meshed the structures of her own and her source's sentences:

Awkward One editor disagrees with this view and "a good reporter does not fail to separate opinions from facts" (Lyman 52).

In the following revision the writer adds words to integrate the quotation into her sentence:

Revised One editor disagrees with this view, maintaining that "a good reporter does not fail to separate opinions from facts" (Lyman 52).

To mesh your own and your source's words, you may sometimes need to make a substitution or addition to the quotation, signaling your change with brackets:

Words added	"The tabloids [of England] are a journalistic case study in bad reporting," claims Lyman (52).
Verb form changed	A bad reporter, Lyman implies, is one who "[fails] to separate opinions from facts" (52). [The bracketed verb replaces *fail* in the original.]
Capitalization changed	"[T]o separate opinions from facts" is the work of a good reporter (Lyman 52). [In the original, *to* is not capitalized.]
Noun supplied for pronoun	The reliability of a news organization "depends on [reporters'] trustworthiness," says Lyman (52). [The bracketed noun replaces *their* in the original.]

2 Interpretation of borrowed material

You need to work borrowed material into your sentences so that readers see without effort how it contributes to the points you are making. If you merely dump source material into your paper without explaining how you intend it to be interpreted, readers will have to struggle to understand your sentences and the relationships you are trying to establish. For example, the following passage forces us to figure out for ourselves that the writer's sentence and the quotation state opposite points of view:

Dumped	Many news editors and reporters maintain that it is impossible to keep personal opinions from influencing the selection and presentation of facts. "True, news reporters, like everyone else, form impressions of what they see and hear. However, a good reporter does not fail to separate opinions from facts" (Lyman 52).

In the revision, the underlined additions tell us how to interpret the quotation:

Revised	Many news editors and reporters maintain that it is impossible to keep personal opinions from influencing the selection and presentation of facts. Yet not all authorities agree with this view. One editor grants that "news reporters, like everyone else, form impressions of what they see and hear." But, he insists, "a good reporter does not fail to separate opinions from facts" (Lyman 52).

Signal phrases

The words *One editor grants* and *he insists* in the revised passage above are **signal phrases**: they tell readers who the source is and what to expect in the quotations that follow. Signal phrases usually contain (1) the source author's name (or a substitute for it, such as *One editor* and *he*) and (2) a verb that indicates the source author's attitude or approach to what he or she says.

Some verbs for signal phrases appear in the following list. These verbs are in the present tense, which is typical of writing in the humanities. In the social and natural sciences, the past tense (*noted*) or present perfect tense (*has noted*) is more common. See p. 360.

Author is neutral	Author infers or suggests	Author argues	Author is uneasy or disparaging
comments	analyzes	claims	belittles
describes	asks	contends	bemoans
explains	assesses	defends	complains
illustrates	concludes	holds	condemns
notes	considers	insists	deplores
observes	finds	maintains	deprecates
points out	predicts		derides
records	proposes	**Author agrees**	disagrees
relates	reveals		laments
reports	shows	admits	warns
says	speculates	agrees	
sees	suggests	concedes	
thinks	supposes	concurs	
writes		grants	

Vary your signal phrases to suit your interpretation of borrowed material and also to keep readers' interest. A signal phrase may precede, interrupt, or follow the borrowed material:

Precedes Lyman insists that "a good reporter does not fail to separate opinions from facts" (52).

Interrupts "However," Lyman insists, "a good reporter does not fail to separate opinions from facts" (52).

Follows "[A] good reporter does not fail to separate opinions from facts," Lyman insists (52).

Background information

You can add information to a quotation to integrate it into your text and to inform readers why you are using it. In most cases, provide the author's name in the text, especially if the author is an expert or if readers will recognize the name:

Author named Harold Lyman grants that "news reporters, like everyone else, form impressions of what they see and hear." But, Lyman insists, "a good reporter does not fail to separate opinions from facts" (52).

If the source title contributes information about the author or the context of the quotation, you can provide it in the text:

Title given Harold Lyman, in his book *The Conscience of the Journalist*, grants that "news reporters, like everyone else, form impressions of what they see and hear." But, Lyman insists, "a good reporter does not fail to separate opinions from facts" (52).

If the quoted author's background and experience reinforce or clarify the quotation, you can provide those credentials in the text:

> **Credentials** Harold Lyman, <u>a newspaper editor for more than forty</u>
> **given** <u>years</u>, grants that "news reporters, like everyone else, form impressions of what they see and hear." But, Lyman insists, "a good reporter does not fail to separate opinions from facts" (52).

You need not name the author, source, or credentials in your text when you are simply establishing facts or weaving together facts and opinions from varied sources. In the following passage, the information is more important than the source, so the name of the source is confined to a parenthetical acknowledgment:

> To end the abuses of the British, many colonists were urging three actions: forming a united front, seceding from Britain, and taking control of their own international relations (Wills 325–36).

3 Discipline styles for integrating sources

The preceding guidelines for introducing and interpreting borrowed material apply generally across academic disciplines, but there are differences in verb tenses and documentation style.

English and some other humanities

Writers in English, foreign languages, and related disciplines use MLA style for documenting sources and generally use the present tense of verbs in signal phrases. In discussing sources other than works of literature, the present perfect tense is also sometimes appropriate:

> Lyman <u>insists</u> . . . [present]
> Lyman <u>has insisted</u> . . . [present perfect]

In discussing works of literature, use only the present tense to describe both the work of the author and the action in the work:

> Kate Chopin <u>builds</u> irony into every turn of "The Story of an Hour." For example, Mrs. Mallard, the central character, <u>finds</u> joy in the death of her husband, whom she <u>loves</u>, because she <u>anticipates</u> "the long procession of years that would <u>belong</u> to her absolutely" (23).

Avoid shifting tenses in writing about literature. You can, for instance, shorten quotations to avoid their past-tense verbs.

> **Shift** Her freedom <u>elevates</u> her, so that "she <u>carried</u> herself unwittingly like a goddess of victory" (24).

No shift　Her freedom <u>elevates</u> her, so that she <u>walks</u> "unwittingly like a goddess of victory" (24).

History and other humanities

Writers in history, art history, philosophy, and related disciplines generally use the present perfect tense or present tense of verbs in signal phrases.

> Lincoln persisted, as Haworth <u>has noted</u>, in "feeling that events controlled him."[3]

> What Miller <u>calls</u> Lincoln's "severe self-doubt"[6] undermined his effectiveness on at least two occasions.

The raised numbers after the quotations are part of the Chicago documentation style, used in history and other disciplines.

Social and natural sciences

Writers in the sciences generally use a verb's present tense just for reporting the results of a study (*The data suggest* . . .). Otherwise, they use a verb's past tense or present perfect tense in a signal phrase, as when introducing an explanation, interpretation, or other commentary. (Thus when you are writing for the sciences, generally convert the list of signal-phrase verbs on p. 358 from the present to the present perfect tense or past tense.)

> Lin (1999) <u>has suggested</u> that preschooling may significantly affect children's academic performance through high school (pp. 22–23).

> In an exhaustive survey of the literature published between 1990 and 2000, Walker (2001) <u>found</u> "no proof, merely a weak correlation, linking place of residence and rate of illness" (p. 121).

These passages conform to APA documentation style. APA style, or one quite similar to it, is also used in sociology, education, nursing, biology, and many other sciences.

53　Avoiding Plagiarism and Documenting Sources

The knowledge building that is the focus of academic writing rests on the integrity of everyone who participates, including students, in using and crediting sources. The work of a writer or creator is his or her intellectual property. You and others may borrow the work's ideas and even its words or an image, but you *must* acknowledge that what you borrowed came from someone else.

When you acknowledge sources in your writing, you are doing more than giving credit to the writer or creator of the work you consulted. You are also showing what your own writing is based on, which in turn adds to your integrity as a researcher and writer. Acknowledging sources creates the trust among scholars, students, writers, and readers that knowledge building requires.

Plagiarism (from a Latin word for "kidnapper") is the presentation of someone else's work as your own. Whether deliberate or accidental, plagiarism is a serious offense. It breaks trust, and it undermines or even destroys your credibility as a researcher and writer. In most colleges, a code of academic honesty calls for severe consequences for plagiarism: a reduced or failing grade, suspension from school, or expulsion. The way to avoid plagiarism is to

Video
tutorial

Exercise

Checklist for avoiding plagiarism

Know your source.

Are you using

- your own experience,
- common knowledge, or
- someone else's material?

You must acknowledge someone else's material.

Quote carefully.

- Check that every quotation exactly matches its source.
- Insert quotation marks around every quotation that you run into your text. (A quotation set off from the text does not need quotation marks. See **MLA** pp. 447–48 and **APA** p. 482.)
- Indicate any omission from a quotation with an ellipsis mark and any addition with brackets.
- Acknowledge the source of every quotation.

Paraphrase and summarize carefully.

- Use your own words and sentence structures for every paraphrase and summary. If you have used the author's words, add quotation marks around them.
- Acknowledge the source of the idea(s) in every paraphrase or summary.

Cite sources responsibly.

- Acknowledge every use of someone else's material in each place you use it.
- Include all your sources in your list of works cited. See **MLA** pp. 441–46, **APA** pp. 465–79, **Chic** pp. 489–500, and **CSE** pp. 501–07 for citing sources in the most common documentation styles.

Checklist

acknowledge your sources: keep track of the ones you consult for each paper you write, and document them within the paper and in a list of works cited.

This chapter distinguishes between deliberate and accidental plagiarism (below), shows how to distinguish what doesn't require acknowledgment from what does (opposite and p. 364), discusses copyright issues if your project will be published or posted on the Web (p. 366), and provides an overview of source documentation (p. 367).

CULTURE LANGUAGE The concepts of originality, intellectual property, and plagiarism are not universal. In some other cultures, for instance, students may be encouraged to copy the words of scholars without acknowledgment, in order to demonstrate their mastery of or respect for the scholars' work. In the United States, however, using an author's work without a source citation is a serious offense, whether it is accidental or intentional. When in doubt about the guidelines in this chapter, ask your instructor for advice.

53a Distinguishing deliberate from accidental plagiarism

Instructors usually distinguish between deliberate plagiarism, which is cheating, and accidental plagiarism, which often stems from a writer's inexperience with managing sources.

1 Deliberate plagiarism

Deliberate plagiarism is intentional: the writer chooses to cheat by turning in someone else's work as his or her own. Students who deliberately plagiarize deprive themselves of an education in honest research. When their cheating is detected, the students often face stiff penalties, including expulsion.

Following are examples of deliberate plagiarism:

Copying a phrase, a sentence, or a longer passage from a source and passing it off as your own by not adding quotation marks and a source citation.

Summarizing or paraphrasing someone else's ideas without acknowledging the source in a citation.

Handing in as your own work a paper you have copied off the Web, had a friend write, or accepted from another student.

Handing in as your own work a paper you have purchased from a paper-writing service. **Paying for research or a paper does not make it your work.**

2 Accidental plagiarism

Accidental plagiarism is unintentional: grappling with complicated information and ideas in sources, the writer neglects to put quotation marks around a source's exact words or neglects to include a source citation for a quotation, paraphrase, or summary. Most instructors and schools do not permit accidental plagiarism, but they treat it less harshly than deliberate plagiarism—at least the first time it occurs.

Here are examples of accidental plagiarism:

Reading sources without taking notes on them and then not distinguishing what you recently learned from what you already knew.

Copying and pasting material from a source into your document without placing quotation marks around the other writer's work.

Forgetting to add a source citation for a paraphrase. Even though a paraphrase casts another person's idea in your own words, you still need to cite the source of the idea.

Omitting a source citation for another's idea because you are unaware of the need to acknowledge the idea.

Plagiarism and the Internet

The Internet has made it easier to plagiarize than ever before: with just a few clicks, you can copy and paste passages or whole documents into your own files. If you do so without quoting and acknowledging your source, you plagiarize.

Video tutorial

The Internet has also made plagiarism easier to detect. Instructors can use search engines to find specific phrases or sentences anywhere on the Web, including among scholarly publications, all kinds of Web sites, and term-paper collections. They can search term-paper sites as easily as students can, looking for similarities with papers they've received. They can also use detection software—such as *Turnitin, PlagiServe,* and *Glatt Plagiarism Services*—which compares students' work with other work anywhere on the Internet, seeking matches as short as a few words.

Some instructors suggest that their students use plagiarism-detection programs to verify that their own work does not include accidental plagiarism, at least not from the Internet.

53b Knowing what you need not acknowledge

1 Your independent material

Your own observations, thoughts, compilations of facts, or experimental results—expressed in your words and format—do not require acknowledgment. You should describe the basis for your conclusions so that readers can evaluate your thinking, but you need not cite sources for them.

2 Common knowledge

Common knowledge consists of the standard information on a subject as well as folk literature and commonsense observations.

- **Standard information** includes the major facts of history, such as the dates during which Charlemagne ruled as emperor of Rome (800–14). It does *not* include interpretations of facts, such as a historian's opinion that Charlemagne was sometimes needlessly cruel in extending his power.

- **Folk literature,** such as the fairy tale "Snow White," is popularly known and cannot be traced to a particular writer. Literature traceable to a writer is *not* folk literature, even if it is very familiar.

- **Commonsense observations** are things most people know, such as that inflation is most troublesome for people with low and fixed incomes. However, a particular economist's argument about the effects of inflation on Chinese immigrants is *not* a commonsense observation.

If you do not know a subject well enough to determine whether a piece of information is common knowledge, make a record of the source as you would for any other quotation, paraphrase, or summary. As you read more about the subject, the information may come up repeatedly without acknowledgment, in which case it is probably common knowledge. But if you are still in doubt when you finish your research, always acknowledge the source.

53c Knowing what you *must* acknowledge

Video tutorial

You must always acknowledge other people's independent material—that is, any facts, ideas, or opinions that are not common knowledge or your own. The source may be a formal publication or release, such as a book, an article, a movie, an interview, an artwork, a comic strip, a map, a Web page, or a blog posting. The source may also be informal, such as a tweet, a posting on a *Facebook* page, an opinion you heard on the radio, or a comment by your instructor or a classmate that substantially shaped your argument. You must acknowledge summaries or paraphrases of ideas or facts as well as quotations of the language and format in which ideas or facts appear: wording, sentence structures, arrangement, and special graphics (such as a diagram). You must acknowledge another's material no matter how you use it, how much of it you use, or how often you use it.

1 Copied language: Quotation marks and a source citation

The following example baldly plagiarizes the original quotation from Jessica Mitford's *Kind and Usual Punishment*, p. 9. Without quotation marks or a source citation, the example matches Mitford's wording (underlined) and closely parallels her sentence structure:

Original quotation	"The character and mentality of the keepers may be of more importance in understanding prisons than the character and mentality of the kept."
Plagiarism	But the character of prison officials (the keepers) is of more importance in understanding prisons than the character of prisoners (the kept).

To avoid plagiarism, the writer can paraphrase and cite the source (see the examples below and on the next page) or use Mitford's actual words *in quotation marks* and *with a source citation* (here, in MLA style):

| Revision (quotation) | According to one critic of the penal system, "The character and mentality of the keepers may be of more importance in understanding prisons than the character and mentality of the kept" (Mitford 9). |

Even with a source citation and with a different sentence structure, the next example is still plagiarism because it uses some of Mitford's words (underlined) without quotation marks:

| Plagiarism | According to one critic of the penal system, the psychology of the kept may say less about prisons than the psychology of the keepers (Mitford 9). |
| Revision (quotation) | According to one critic of the penal system, the psychology of "the kept" may say less about prisons than the psychology of "the keepers" (Mitford 9). |

2 Paraphrase or summary: Your own words and sentence structure and a source citation

The example below changes the sentence structure of the original Mitford quotation above, but it still uses Mitford's words (underlined) without quotation marks and without a source citation:

| Plagiarism | In understanding prisons, we should know more about the character and mentality of the keepers than of the kept. |

To avoid plagiarism, the writer can use quotation marks and cite the source (see the revised examples above) or *use his or her own words* and still *cite the source* (because the idea is Mitford's, not the writer's):

| Revision (paraphrase) | Mitford holds that we may be able to learn more about prisons from the psychology of the prison officials than from that of the prisoners (9). |
| Revision (paraphrase) | We may understand prisons better if we focus on the personalities and attitudes of the prison workers rather than those of the inmates (Mitford 9). |

In the next example, the writer cites Mitford and does not use her words but still plagiarizes her sentence structure. The revision changes the sentence structure as well as the words.

Plagiarism   One critic of the penal system maintains that the psychology of prison officials may be more informative about prisons than the psychology of prisoners (Mitford 9).

Revision (paraphrase)   One critic of the penal system maintains that we may be able to learn less from the psychology of prisoners than from the psychology of prison officials (Mitford 9).

3 | Using online sources

Online sources are so accessible and so easy to copy into your own documents that it may seem they are freely available, exempting you from the obligation to acknowledge them. They are not. Acknowledging online sources is somewhat trickier than acknowledging print sources, but it is no less essential: when you use someone else's independent material from an online source, whether in a print or an online document, you must acknowledge the source.

Citing online sources is easier when you keep track of them as you work:

- **Record complete publication information each time you consult an online source.** Online sources may change from one day to the next or even disappear entirely. See p. 318 for the information to record, such as the publication date. Without the proper information, you *may not* use the source.

- **Immediately put quotation marks around any text that you copy and paste into your document.** If you don't add quotation marks right away, you risk forgetting which words belong to the source and which are yours. If you don't know whose words you are using, recheck the source or *do not* use them.

- **Acknowledge linked sites.** If you use not only a Web site but also one or more of its linked sites, you must acknowledge the linked sites as well. The fact that one person has used a second person's work does not release you from the responsibility to cite the second work.

53d   Obtaining permission when publishing your work

When you use material from print or online sources in a project that will be published, you must not only acknowledge your sources but also take care to observe copyright restrictions.

Publication means that your work will circulate outside the limited circle of a class or other group. It may appear in print media, such as magazines and newspapers, or it may appear on the Web, which is a publication medium as well. (The exception is a password-protected Web site, such as a course site, which many copyright holders regard as private.) Whether you are publishing in print or online, borrowing certain kinds or amounts of material requires you to obtain the permission of the copyright holders. You can find information about copyright holders and permissions on the copyright page of a print publication (following the title page) and on a page labeled something like "Terms of Use" on a Web site. If you don't see an explicit release for student use or publication on private Web sites, assume that you must seek permission.

The legal convention of **fair use** allows an author to use a small portion of copyrighted material without obtaining the copyright holder's permission, as long as the author acknowledges the source. The standards of fair use differ for print and online sources and are not fixed in either case. The guidelines below are conservative:

- **Text from print sources:** Quote without permission fewer than fifty words from an article or fewer than three hundred words from a book. You'll need permission to use any longer quotation from an article or a book or any quotation at all from a play, poem, or song.
- **Text from online sources:** Quote without permission text that represents just a small portion of the whole—say, up to forty words out of three hundred. As with print texts, seek permission for any use of a play, poem, or song that you find online.
- **Visuals, audio, and video:** Seek permission to use any copyrighted media from either print or online sources: photographs, charts, maps, cartoons, paintings, audio files, video files, and so on.
- **Links:** You may need to seek permission to link your site to another one—for instance, if the linked site provides substantial evidence for your claims or if it supplies you with a multimedia element (an image or a sound or video clip).

Note Although most online sources are copyrighted, much valuable material is not: either the creator does not claim copyright, or the copyright has lapsed so that the work is in the public domain. The first category includes most government documents as well as material labeled for reuse. (You can find such multimedia sources by setting your search engine to screen for them. See p. 334.) Public-domain sources include most works by authors who have been dead at least fifty years. You do not need permission to reprint from an uncopyrighted source, but *you still must cite the source.*

53e Documenting sources

Every time you borrow the words, facts, or ideas of others, you must **document** the source—that is, supply a reference (or document) telling readers that you borrowed the material and where you borrowed it from.

Editors and teachers in most academic disciplines require special documentation formats (or styles) in their scholarly journals and in students' papers. All the styles use a citation in the text that serves two purposes: it signals that material is borrowed, and it refers readers to detailed information about the source so that they can locate both the source and the place in the source where the borrowed material appears. The detailed source information appears either in footnotes or at the end of the paper.

Aside from these essential similarities, the disciplines' documentation styles differ markedly in citation form, arrangement of source information, and other particulars. Each discipline's style reflects the needs of its practitioners for certain kinds of information presented in certain ways. For instance, the currency of a source is important in the social sciences, where studies build on and correct each other; thus in-text citations in the social sciences include a source's year of publication. In the humanities, however, currency is less important, so in-text citations do not include the date of publication.

The disciplines' documentation formats are described in style guides listed in **8** pp. 389 (literature and other humanities), 393 (social sciences), and 397 (natural and applied sciences). This book also discusses and illustrates four common documentation styles:

Video tutorial

- MLA style, used in English, foreign languages, and some other humanities (**MLA** p. 402).

Video tutorial

- APA style, used in psychology and some other social sciences (**APA** p. 461).
- Chicago style, used in history, art history, philosophy, religion, and some other humanities (**Chic** p. 489).
- CSE style, used in the biological and some other sciences (**CSE** p. 501).

Always ask your instructor which documentation style you should use. If your instructor does not require a particular style, use the one in this book that's most appropriate for the discipline in which you're writing. Do follow a single system for citing sources so that you provide all the necessary information in a consistent format.

Note Bibliography software—*Zotero, Refworks, Endnote, Knightcite,* and others—can help you format your source citations in the style of your choice. Always ask your instructors if you may use such software for your papers. The programs prompt you for needed information (author's name, book title, publication date, and so on) and then arrange, capitalize, italicize, and punctuate the information as required by the style. But no program can anticipate all the varieties of source information, nor can it substitute for your own care and attention in giving your sources complete acknowledgment using the required form.

54 Writing the Paper

This chapter complements and extends the detailed discussion of the writing situation and the writing process in Chapters 1–5 (**1** pp. 3–34). If you haven't already done so, you may want to read those chapters before this one.

54a Focusing and organizing the paper

Before you begin using your source notes in a draft, give some thought to your main idea and your organization.

👁 Video tutorial

1 Thesis statement

You began research with a question about your subject (see pp. 313–14). Though that question may have evolved during research, you should be able to answer it once you've consulted most of your sources. Try to state that answer in a **thesis statement**, a claim that narrows your subject to a single idea. Here, for example, are the research question and thesis statement of Justin Malik, whose final paper appears later in this book (**MLA** pp. 445–58):

Research question

How can green consumerism help the environment?

Thesis statement

Although green consumerism can help the environment, consumerism itself is the root of some of the most pressing ecological problems we face. To make a real difference, we must consume less.

(Malik's thesis statement consists of two sentences, the first setting up the second. Many instructors allow statements of two or more sentences as long as they build a single idea and the final sentence presents the key assertion of the paper. However, other instructors require thesis statements of a single sentence. Ask your instructor for his or her preference.)

A precise thesis statement will give you a focus as you organize and draft your paper. For more on thesis statements, see **1** pp. 14–17.

2 Organization

To structure your paper, you'll need to synthesize, or forge relationships among ideas (see pp. 350–51). The next page gives one approach.

- **Arrange source information in categories.** Each group should correspond to a main section of your paper: a key idea of your own that supports the thesis.
- **Review your research journal** for connections between sources and other thoughts that can help you organize your paper.
- **Look objectively at your categories.** If some are skimpy, with little information, consider whether you should drop the categories or conduct more research to fill them out. If most of your information falls into one or two categories, consider whether they are too broad and should be divided. (If any of this rethinking affects your thesis statement, revise it accordingly.)
- **Within each group, distinguish between the main idea and the supporting ideas and evidence.** Only the support should come from your sources. The main idea should be your own.

See **1** pp. 18–22 for more on organizing a paper, including samples of both informal and formal outlines.

54b Drafting, revising, editing, and formatting the paper

1 First draft

Video
tutorial

In drafting your paper, you do not have to proceed methodically from introduction to conclusion. Instead, draft in sections, beginning with the one you feel most confident about. Each section should center on a principal idea contributing to your thesis, a conclusion you have drawn from reading and responding to sources. Start the section by stating the idea; then support it with information, summaries, paraphrases, and quotations from your notes. Remember to insert source information from your notes as well.

2 Revision

Always revise your draft first, satisfying yourself with the content and shape of the whole before trying to edit sentences and words. Begin with the advice and checklist in **1** pp. 25–27, and supplement them with the following checklist.

Checklist

Checklist for revising a research paper

Assignment
How does the draft satisfy all of the criteria stated in your instructor's assignment?

Thesis statement
How well does your thesis statement describe your subject and your perspective as they emerged during drafting?

Structure

(Outlining your draft can help you see structure at a glance. See **1** p. 26.)

How consistently does borrowed material illuminate and support—not lead and dominate—your own ideas? How well is the importance of ideas reflected in the emphasis they receive? Will the arrangement of ideas be clear to readers?

Evidence

Where might evidence seem weak or irrelevant to readers?

Reasonableness and clarity

How reasonable will readers find your argument? (See **2** pp. 107–11.) Where do you need to define terms or concepts that readers may not know or may dispute?

3 Editing

For editing, consult the advice and checklist in **1** pp. 29–33. Try to read your work from the point of view of someone who has not spent hours planning and researching but instead has come fresh to the paper. Look for lapses in sense, awkward passages, wordiness, poor transitions between ideas and evidence, unnecessary repetition, wrong or misspelled words, errors in grammar, punctuation, or mechanics—in short, anything that is likely to interfere with a reader's understanding of your meaning.

4 Format

The final draft of your paper should conform to the document format recommended by your instructor or by the style guide of the discipline in which you are writing. This book details two common formats: Modern Language Association (**MLA** pp. 446–48) and American Psychological Association (**APA** pp. 480–82).

Student
paper

In any discipline you can use a word processor to present your ideas effectively and attractively with readable typefonts, headings, illustrations, and other elements. See **1** pp. 55–64 for ideas.

Writing in the Disciplines

PART 8

Writing in the Disciplines

55 Working with the Goals and Requirements of the Disciplines

Chapter 10 (**2** p. 93) outlines the general concerns of subject, purpose, and audience that figure in most academic writing situations. The disciplines have more in common as well: methods of gathering evidence, genres for writing (kinds of assignments), scholarly tools, language conventions, and styles for source citations and document format. This chapter introduces these common goals and requirements. The following chapters then distinguish the disciplines along the same lines, focusing on literature (Chapter 56) and on other humanities, the social sciences, and the natural and applied sciences (Chapter 57).

55a   Using methods and evidence

The **methodology** of a discipline is the way its practitioners study their subjects—that is, how they proceed when investigating the answers to questions. Methodology relates to the way practitioners analyze evidence and ideas. For instance, a literary critic and a social historian would probably approach Shakespeare's *Hamlet* quite differently: the literary critic might study the play for a theme among its poetic images; the historian might examine the play's relation to Shakespeare's context—England at the turn of the seventeenth century.

Exercise

Whatever their approach, academic writers do not compose entirely out of their personal experience. Rather, they combine the evidence of their experience with that appropriate to the discipline, drawing well-supported conclusions about their subjects. The evidence of the discipline comes from research using primary or secondary sources.

- **Primary sources** are firsthand or original accounts, such as historical documents, works of art, and reports on experiments that the writer has conducted. When you use primary sources, you conduct original research and generate your own evidence. You might use your analysis of a painting as evidence for an interpretation of the painting. Or you might use data from your own survey of students to support your conclusions about students' attitudes.

- **Secondary sources** are books and articles written *about* primary sources. Much academic writing requires that you use such sources to spark, extend, or support your own ideas, as when

mycomplab

Visit *mycomplab.com* for the eText and for resources and exercises on writing in the disciplines.

375

Guidelines for academic writers

Video
tutorial

- ■ **Become familiar with the methodology and the kinds of evidence appropriate for the discipline in which you are writing.**
- ■ **Analyze the special demands of each assignment.** The genre of the assignment, the questions you set out to answer, and the assertions you wish to support will govern how you choose your sources and evidence.
- ■ **Become familiar with the specialized tools and language of the discipline.**
- ■ **Use the discipline's style for source citations and document format.**

you review the published opinions on your subject before contributing conclusions from your original research.

55b Understanding writing assignments

For most academic writing, your primary purpose will be either to explain something to your readers or to persuade them to accept your conclusions. To achieve your purpose, you will adapt your writing process to the writing situation, particularly to your reader's likely expectations for evidence and how you use it.

Many assignments will specify or suggest the genre in which you are to write. Some genres, such as the social science report in **APA** pp. 483–86, are fairly standard in their content and format. Other assignments contain key words that imply the expectations of the genre—words such as *compare*, *define*, *analyze*, and *illustrate* that express customary ways of thinking about and organizing a vast range of subjects. (See **1** pp. 45–49 for more on the so-called patterns of development.) To be aware of the expectations of the genre in which you are writing, study the wording of each assignment carefully.

55c Using tools and language

When you write in an academic discipline, you use the scholarly tools of that discipline, particularly the research findings published as articles in the scholarly journals of the discipline. In addition, you may use the aids developed by practitioners of the discipline for efficiently and effectively approaching research, conducting it, and recording the findings. Many of these aids, such as a system for recording evidence from sources, are discussed in **7** pp. 311–68 and can be adapted to any discipline. Other aids are discussed in the next two chapters.

Pay close attention to the texts assigned in a course and any materials given out in class, for these items may introduce you to valuable references and other research aids, and they will use the specialized language of the discipline. This specialized language allows practitioners to write to each other both efficiently and precisely. It also furthers certain concerns of the discipline, such as accuracy and objectivity. Scientists, for example, try to interpret their data objectively, so they avoid *undoubtedly, obviously,* and other words that slant conclusions. Some of the language conventions like this one are discussed in the following chapters. As you gain experience in a particular discipline, keep alert for such conventions and train yourself to follow them.

55d Following styles for source citations and document format

Most disciplines publish journals that require authors to use a certain style for source citations and a certain format for documents. In turn, most instructors in a discipline require the same of students writing papers for their courses.

When you cite your sources, you tell readers which ideas and information you borrowed and where they can find your sources. Thus source citations indicate how much knowledge you have and how broad and deep your research was. They also help you avoid **plagiarism,** the serious offense of presenting the words, ideas, and data of others as if they were your own. (See **7** pp. 360–66 on avoiding plagiarism.)

Document format specifies such features as margins and the placement of the title. But it also extends to special elements of the manuscript, such as tables or an abstract, that may be required by the discipline.

The style guides for various disciplines are listed on pp. 389 (humanities), 393 (social sciences), and 397 (natural and applied sciences). If your instructor does not require a particular style, use that of the Modern Language Association, which is described and illustrated at length in **MLA** pp. 402–48.

56 Reading and Writing about Literature

By Sylvan Barnet

Writers of literature—stories, novels, poems, and plays—are concerned with presenting human experience concretely, with *showing* rather than *telling*, with giving a sense of the feel of life. Reading

Exercise

mycomplab

Visit *mycomplab.com* for the eText and for resources and exercises on reading and writing about literature.

and writing about literature thus require extremely close attention to the feel of the words. For instance, the word *woods* in Robert Frost's "Stopping by Woods on a Snowy Evening" has a rural, folksy quality that *forest* doesn't have, and many such small distinctions contribute to the poem's effect.

When you read literature, you interpret distinctions like these, forming an idea of the work. When you write about literature, you state your idea as your thesis, and you support the thesis with evidence from the work. (See **1** pp. 14–17 for more on thesis statements.)

Note Writing about literature is not merely summarizing literature. Your thesis is a claim about the meaning or effect of the literary work, not a statement of its plot. And your paper is a demonstration of your thesis, not a retelling of the work's changes or events.

56a Using the methods and evidence of literary analysis

1 Reading literature

Reading literature critically involves interacting with a text, not in order to make negative judgments but in order to understand the work and evaluate its significance or quality. Such interaction is not passive, like scanning a newspaper or watching television. Instead, it is a process of engagement, of diving into the words themselves.

You will become more engaged if you write while you read. If you own the book you're reading, don't hesitate to underline or highlight passages that especially interest you. Don't hesitate to annotate the margins, indicating your pleasures, displeasures, and uncertainties with remarks such as *Nice detail* or *Do we need this long description?* or *Not believable*. If you don't own the book, make these notes on separate sheets or on your computer.

An effective way to interact with a text is to keep a **reading journal**. A journal is not a diary in which you record your doings; instead, it is a place to develop and store your reflections on what you read, such as an answer to a question you may have posed in the margin of the text or a response to something said in class. You may, for instance, want to reflect on why your opinion is so different from that of another student. You may even make an entry in the form of a letter to the author or from one character to another. (See **1** pp. 9–11 for more on journal keeping.)

2 Meaning in literature

In analyzing literature, you face right off the question of *meaning*. Readers disagree all the time over the meanings of works of literature, partly because (as noted earlier) literature *shows* rather than *tells*: it gives concrete images of imagined human experiences, but it usually does not say how we ought to understand these images.

Further, readers bring different experiences to their reading and thus understand images differently. In writing about literature, then, we can offer only our *interpretation* of the meaning rather than *the* meaning. Still, most people agree that there are limits to interpretation: it must be supported by evidence that a reasonable person finds at least plausible if not totally convincing.

3 Questions for a literary analysis

One reason interpretations of meaning differ is that readers approach literary works differently, focusing on certain elements and interpreting those elements distinctively. For instance, some critics look at a literary work mainly as an artifact of the particular time and culture in which it was created, while other critics stress the work's effect on its readers.

This chapter emphasizes so-called formalist criticism, which sees a literary work primarily as something to be understood in itself. This critical framework engages the reader immediately in the work of literature, without requiring extensive historical or cultural background, and it introduces the conventional elements of literature that all critical approaches discuss, even though they view the elements differently. The following list poses questions for each element that can help you think constructively and imaginatively about what you read.

- *Plot:* **the relationships and patterns of events.** Even a poem has a plot—for instance, a change in mood from grief to resignation.

  What actions happen?
  What conflicts occur?
  How do the events connect to each other and to the whole?

- *Characters:* **the people the author creates,** including the narrator of a story or the speaker of a poem.

  Who are the principal people in the work?
  How do they interact?
  What do their actions, words, and thoughts reveal about their personalities and the personalities of others?
  Do the characters stay the same, or do they change? Why?

- *Point of view:* **the perspective or attitude of the speaker in a poem or the voice who tells a story.** The point of view may be **first person** (a participant, using *I*) or **third person** (an outsider, using *he, she, it, they*). A first-person narrator may be a major or a minor character in the narrative and may be **reliable** or **unreliable** (unable to report events wholly or accurately). A third-person narrator may be **omniscient** (knows what goes on in all characters' minds), **limited** (knows what goes on in the mind of only one or two characters), or **objective** (knows only what is external to the characters).

Who is the narrator (or the speaker of a poem)?
How does the narrator's point of view affect the narrative?

■ *Tone:* **the narrator's or speaker's attitude,** perceived through the words (for instance, joyful, bitter, or confident).

What tone (or tones) do you hear? If there is a change, how do you account for it?
Is there an ironic contrast between the narrator's tone (for instance, confidence) and what you take to be the author's attitude (for instance, pity for human overconfidence)?

■ *Imagery:* **word pictures or details involving the senses of sight, sound, touch, smell, and taste.**

What images does the writer use? What senses do they draw on?
What patterns are evident in the images (for instance, religious or commercial images)?
What is the significance of the imagery?

■ *Symbolism:* **concrete things standing for larger and more abstract ideas.** For instance, the American flag may symbolize freedom, or a dead flower may symbolize mortality.

What symbols does the author use? What do they seem to signify?
How does the symbolism relate to the theme of the work?

■ *Setting:* **the place where the action happens.**

What does the locale contribute to the work?
Are scene shifts significant?

■ *Form:* **the shape or structure of the work.**

What *is* the form? (For example, a story might divide sharply in the middle, moving from happiness to sorrow.)
What parts of the work does the form emphasize, and why?

■ *Themes:* **the main ideas about human experience suggested by the work as a whole.** A theme is neither a plot (what happens) nor a subject (such as mourning or marriage). Rather it is what the author says with that plot about that subject.

Can you state each theme in a sentence? Avoid mentioning specific characters or actions; instead, write an observation applicable to humanity in general. For instance, you might state the following about Agha Shahid Ali's poem "Postcard from Kashmir" (p. 384): *The poem explores feelings of having more than one home.*
Do certain words, passages of dialog or description, or situations seem to represent a theme most clearly?
How do the work's elements combine to develop a theme?

■ *Appeal:* **the degree to which the work pleases you.**

What do you especially like or dislike about the work? Why?
Do you think your responses are unique, or would they be common to most readers? Why?

4 Using evidence in writing about literature

The evidence for a literary analysis always comes from at least one primary source (the work or works being discussed) and may come from secondary sources (critical and historical works). For example, in the paper on pp. 384–86 about Agha Shahid Ali's "Postcard from Kashmir," the primary material is the poem itself, and the secondary material includes two critical studies of the poem and a published interview with the poet. The bulk of the evidence in a literary analysis is usually quotations from the work, although summaries and paraphrases can be useful as well.

Your instructor will probably tell you if you are expected to consult secondary sources for an assignment. They can help you understand a writer's work, but your primary concern should always be the work itself, not what critics A, B, and C say about it. In general, then, quote or summarize secondary material sparingly. And always cite your sources.

56b Understanding writing assignments in literature

A literature instructor may ask you to write papers in one or more of the following genres. The first two are the most common.

Student
paper

■ **A literary analysis paper:** your ideas about a work of literature—your interpretation of its meaning, context, or representations based on specific words, passages, characters, and events.
■ **A literary research paper:** analysis of a literary work combined with research about the work and perhaps about the life of its author. A literary research paper draws on both primary and secondary sources.
■ **A personal response or reaction paper:** your thoughts and feelings about a work of literature.
■ **A book review:** a summary of a book and a judgment about the book's value.
■ **A theater review:** your reactions to and opinions about a theatrical performance.

Key terms

primary source A firsthand account: for instance, a historical document, a work of literature, or your own observations. (See also p. 375.)

secondary source A report on or analysis of other sources, often primary ones: for instance, a historian's account of a battle or a critic's view of a poem. (See also pp. 375–76.)

56c Using the tools and language of literary analysis

1 Writing tools

The fundamental tool for writing about literature is reading critically. Asking analytical questions such as those on pp. 379–81 can help you focus your ideas. In addition, keeping a reading journal can help you develop your thoughts. Make careful, well-organized notes on any research materials. Finally, discuss the work with others who have read it. They may offer reactions and insights that will help you shape your own ideas.

2 Language considerations

Video
tutorial

Use the present tense of verbs to describe both the action in a literary work and the writing of an author: *The poem's speaker imagines his home in Kashmir. Ali compares memory to a photograph. The critic Jahan Ramazani interprets the poem's subject as loss of one's homeland.* Use the past tense to describe events that actually occurred in the past: *Ali moved to the United States in 1976.*

Some instructors discourage students from using the first-person *I* (as in *I felt sorry for the character*) in writing about literature. At least use *I* sparingly to avoid sounding egotistical. Rephrase sentences to avoid using *I* unnecessarily—for instance, *The character evokes the reader's sympathy.*

3 Research sources

In addition to the following resources on literature, you may also want to consult some on other humanities (pp. 388–89).

Specialized encyclopedias, dictionaries, and bibliographies

Cambridge Bibliography of English Literature
Cambridge Encyclopedia of Language
Cambridge Guide to Literature in English
Dictionary of Literary Biography
Handbook to Literature
Literary Criticism Index
McGraw-Hill Encyclopedia of World Drama
MLA International Bibliography
New Princeton Encyclopedia of Poetry and Poetics
Oxford Companion to American Literature
Oxford Companion to the Theatre
Oxford Dictionary of National Biography
Schomburg Center Guide to Black Literature from the Eighteenth Century to the Present

Library databases and indexes

Abstracts of Folklore Studies
Access World News

Dissertation Abstracts International (doctoral dissertations)
Early English Books Online
Eighteenth Century Collections Online
Gale Literary Resource Center
Hathi Trust
Humanities Index
LexisNexis Academic
Literary Criticism Index
Literary Index
Literature Online
MLA International Bibliography
ProQuest Historical Newspapers
World Shakespeare Bibliography

Book reviews

Book Review Digest
Book Review Index

Sources on the open Web

Alex Catalog of Electronic Texts (*infomotions.com/alex*)
EServer (*eserver.org*)
ipl2 (*ipl.org*)
Literary Resources on the Net (*ethnicity.rutgers.edu/~jlynch/Lit*)
Mr. William Shakespeare and the Internet (*Shakespeare.palomar.edu*)
NINES: Nineteenth-Century Scholarship Online (*www.nines.org*)
Online Books Page (*onlinebooks.library.upenn.edu/books*)
Voice of the Shuttle (*vos.ucsb.edu*)

56d Documenting sources and formatting papers in literary analysis

Unless your instructor specifies otherwise, use the documentation style of the Modern Language Association, detailed in **MLA** pp. 402–46. In MLA style, parenthetical citations in the text of the paper refer to a list of works cited at the end. Sample papers illustrating this style appear on the following pages, in **2** pp. 102–04 and 116–19, and in **MLA** pp. 449–58.

Use MLA format for headings, margins, long quotations, and other elements, as detailed in **MLA** pp. 446–48.

56e Examining a sample literary analysis

A poem and a student paper on the work appear on the following pages. The student, Jessie Glenn, makes an argument for a particular interpretation of the poem, not only analyzing the poem itself but also drawing on secondary sources—that is, critical works *about* the poem. In the opening paragraph, for instance, Glenn uses a brief quotation from a secondary source to establish how her interpretation differs from those made by other readers. This quotation and the three later uses of secondary sources are support for Glenn's points.

●
Video
tutorial

Note the following features of the student's paper:

- **The writer does not merely summarize the literary work.** She summarizes briefly to make her meaning clear, but her essay consists mostly of her own analysis.
- **The writer uses many quotations from the literary work.** The quotations provide evidence for her ideas and let readers hear the voice of the work.
- **The writer integrates quotations smoothly into her own sentences.** See **7** pp. 356–59.
- **The writer uses the present tense of verbs** to describe both the author's work and the action in the work.

Poem

Agha Shahid Ali

Postcard from Kashmir

Kashmir shrinks into my mailbox,
my home a neat four by six inches.
I always loved neatness. Now I hold
the half-inch Himalayas in my hand.

This is home. And this the closest   5
I'll ever be to home. When I return,
the colors won't be so brilliant,
the Jhelum's waters so clean,
so ultramarine. My love
so overexposed.   10

And my memory will be a little
out of focus, in it
a giant negative, black
and white, still undeveloped.

An essay on poetry with secondary sources

Past and Future in

Agha Shahid Ali's "Postcard from Kashmir"

Most literary critics interpret Agha Shahid Ali's "Postcard from Kashmir" as a longing for a lost home, a poetic expression of the heartbreak of exile. For instance, Maimuna Dali Islam describes the speaker's futile effort "to capture his homeland" (262). However, such a reading of the poem seems too narrow. "Postcard from Kashmir" does evoke the experience of being displaced from a beloved home, but the speaker does not seem to feel an intense loss. Instead, he seems to reflect on his position of having more than one home.

Ali's brief poem consists of three stanzas and divides into two parts. In the first half, the speaker examines a postcard he has received from his former home of

Kashmir (lines 1-6). In the second half, the speaker looks forward, imagining how Kashmir will look the next time he sees it and assuming that the place will be different from the idealized view of the postcard and his memory (6-14). The geography is significant. Kashmir has been in the news for many years as the focus of territorial conflict, often violent, among the bordering nations of India, Pakistan, and China. Many residents of the region have been killed, and many have left the region. One of the exiles was Ali: he moved to the United States in 1976 and lived here until his death in 2001, but he also regularly visited his family in Kashmir (Benvenuto 261, 263).

In the context of Kashmir, the literary theorist Jahan Ramazani concludes that the poem "dramatizes the . . . condition" of losing one's homeland to political turmoil (12). Yet several lines in the poem suggest that the speaker is not mourning a loss but musing about having a sense of home both in Kashmir and in the United States. This sense is evident in the opening stanza: "Kashmir shrinks into my mailbox, / my home a neat four by six inches" (1-2), with "my mailbox" conveying his current residence as home and "my home" referring to Kashmir. The dual sense of home is even more evident in the lines "This is home. And this is the closest / I'll ever be to home" (5-6). Although Maimuna Dali Islam assumes that "This" in these lines refers to the Kashmir pictured on the postcard (262), it could also or instead refer to the home attached to the mailbox.

The speaker also seems to perceive that his dual sense of home will continue into the future. The critics do not mention that the second half of the poem is written in the future tense. Beginning with "When I return" (6), the speaker makes it clear that he expects to find himself in Kashmir again, and he imagines how things will be, not how they were. Islam takes the image on the postcard as proof that "there is a place that *can* be captured in a snapshot" (263), but the speaker compares photography to memory, characterizing both as flawed and deceptive with terms such as "overexposed" (10) and "out of focus" (12). He acknowledges that the place won't be like the photograph: "the colors won't be so brilliant, / the Jhelum's waters so clean, / so ultramarine" (7-9). Kashmir still exists, but not as any photograph or memory has recorded it. And the speaker's relationship to his original home, his "love" (9), is changing with the place itself.

In "Postcard from Kashmir" the speaker reflects on home and displacement as he gazes into a representation of his past and considers the future. If the poem mourns a loss, as the critics suggest, it is a loss that has not happened yet, at least not completely. More convincingly, the poem captures a moment when the two homes and the past, present, and future all meet.

Works Cited

Ali, Agha Shahid. "Postcard from Kashmir." *The Half-Inch Himalayas*. Middletown: Wesleyan UP, 1987. 1. Print.

Benvenuto, Christine. "Agha Shahid Ali." *Massachusetts Review* 43.1 (2002): 261-73.
  Web. 7 Mar. 2011.

Islam, Maimuna Dali. "A Way in the World of an Asian American Existence: Agha
  Shahid Ali's Transimmigrant Spacing of North America and India and Kashmir."
  Transnational Asian American Literature: Sites and Transits. Ed. Shirley Lim
  et al. Philadelphia: Temple UP, 2006. 257-73. Print.

Ramazani, Jahan. *The Hybrid Muse: Postcolonial Poetry in English*. Chicago: U of
  Chicago P, 2001. Print.

—Jessie Glenn (student)

57 Writing in Other Disciplines

57a Writing in the humanities

Exercise

   The humanities include literature, the visual arts, music, film,
dance, history, philosophy, and religion. The preceding chapter discusses the particular requirements of reading and writing about
literature. This section concentrates on history. Although the arts,
religion, and other humanities have their own concerns, they share
many important goals and methods with literature and history.

1 Methods and evidence in the humanities

   Writers in the humanities record and speculate about the
growth, ideas, and emotions of human beings. Based on the evidence
of written words, artworks, and other human traces and creations,
humanities writers explain, interpret, analyze, and reconstruct the
human experience.

   The discipline of history focuses particularly on reconstructing
the past. In Greek the word for history means "to inquire": historians inquire into the past to understand the events of the past. Then
they report, explain, analyze, and evaluate those events in their context, asking such questions as what happened before or after the
events or how the events related to political and social structures.

   Historians' reconstructions of the past—their conclusions about
what happened and why—are always supported with references to the
written record. The evidence of history is mainly primary sources,
such as eyewitness accounts and contemporary documents, letters,
commercial records, and the like. For history papers, you might also
be asked to support your conclusions with those in secondary sources.

---

mycomplab

Visit *mycomplab.com* for the eText and for resources and
exercises on writing in the disciplines.

In reading historical sources, you need to weigh and evaluate their evidence. If, for example, you find conflicting accounts of the same event, you need to consider the possible biases of the authors. In general, the more a historian's conclusions are supported by public records such as deeds, marriage licenses, and newspaper accounts, the more reliable the conclusions are likely to be.

2 Writing assignments in the humanities

Writing assignments in the humanities often require traditional academic essays that follow the conventional pattern of introduction, thesis statement, supporting paragraphs, and conclusion. An assignment may further refine the genre with one or more of the following words:

Student
paper

- **Explain:** for instance, show how a painter developed a particular technique or clarify a general's role in a historical battle.
- **Argue:** assert and defend an opinion—for instance, about the meaning of a poem or the causes of a historical event.
- **Analyze:** examine the elements of a philosophical argument or break down the causes of a historical event.
- **Interpret:** infer the meaning of a film from its images or the significance of a historical event from contemporary accounts of it.
- **Synthesize:** find a pattern in a composer's works or in a historical period.
- **Evaluate:** judge the quality of an architect's design or a historian's conclusions.

See **2** pp. 85–87 for discussion of these words.

3 Tools and language in the humanities

The tools and language of the humanities vary according to the discipline. Major reference works in each field, available through the library, can clarify specific tools you need and the language you should use.

Writing tools

A useful tool for the arts is to ask a series of questions to analyze and evaluate a work. (A list of such questions for reading literature appears on pp. 379–81.) In any humanities discipline, a journal—a log of questions, reactions, and insights—can help you discover and record your thoughts.

In history the tools are those of any thorough and efficient researcher: a system for finding and tracking sources; a methodical examination of sources, including evaluating and synthesizing them; a system for gathering source information; and a separate system, such as a research journal, for tracking one's own evolving thoughts.

Language considerations

Historians strive for precision and logic. They do not guess about what happened or speculate about "what if." They avoid trying to influence readers' opinions with words having strongly negative or positive connotations, such as *stupid* or *brilliant*. Instead, historians show the evidence and draw conclusions from that. Generally, they avoid using *I* because it tends to draw attention away from the evidence and toward the writer.

Writing about history demands some attention to the tenses of verbs. To refer to events that occurred in the past, historians generally use the past tense, the present perfect tense, or the past perfect tense. They reserve the present tense only for statements about the present or statements of general truths. For example:

Franklin Delano Roosevelt <u>died</u> in 1945. [Simple past.]

He <u>had contracted</u> polio at age thirty-nine. [Past perfect.]

Many historians <u>have praised</u> Roosevelt as President. [Present perfect.]

Some of his economic reforms <u>persist</u> today, such as Social Security and unemployment compensation. [Present.]

See **4** pp. 205–10 for more on verb tenses.

Research sources on the open Web

The following lists give resources in the humanities. (Resources for literature appear on pp. 382–83.)

General
EDSITEment (edsitement.neh.gov)
INFOMINE (infomine.ucr.edu)
ipl2 (ipl.org)
Library of Congress: Performing Arts Reading Room (www.loc.gov/rr/ performi/new.internet.resources.html)
Voice of the Shuttle (vos.ucsb.edu)

Art
Artnet (artnet.com)
World Wide Arts Resources (wwar.com/browse.html)

Dance
Artslynx International Dance Resources (www.artslynx.org/dance)
Society of Dance History Scholars (www.sdhs.org)

Film
Film Studies on the Internet (guides.library.ualberta.ca/filmstudies)
Internet Movie Database (imdb.com)

History
American Memory (memory.loc.gov)
Best of History Web Sites (besthistorysites.net)
National Women's History Project (nwhp.org)

Music
MusicMoz (musicmoz.org)
*Society for American Music (american-music.org/resources/
ResourcesOnWeb.php)*

Philosophy
PhilPapers (philpapers.org)
Stanford Encyclopedia of Philosophy (plato.stanford.edu)

Religion
Academic Info: Religion Gateway (academicinfo.net/religion.html)
Religious Studies Web Guide (people.ucalgary.ca/~lipton)

Theater
*McCoy's Brief Guide to Internet Resources in Theatre and Performance
Studies (www2.stetson.edu/csata/thr_guid.html)*
TheatreHistory.com (theatrehistory.com)

4 Documentation and format in the humanities

Writers in the humanities generally rely on one of the following
guides for source-citation style:

The Chicago Manual of Style, 16th ed., 2010
A Manual for Writers of Research Papers, Theses, and Dissertations, by Kate
L. Turabian, 7th ed., rev. Wayne C. Booth, Gregory G. Colomb, and
Joseph M. Williams, 2007
MLA Handbook for Writers of Research Papers, 7th ed., 2009

See **MLA** pp. 402–48 for the recommendations of the *MLA
Handbook.* Unless your instructor specifies otherwise, use these recommendations for papers in English and foreign languages. In history, art history, and many other disciplines, however, writers rely
on *The Chicago Manual of Style* or the student reference adapted
from it, *A Manual for Writers.* Both books detail two documentation
styles. One, used mainly by scientists and social scientists, closely
resembles the style of the American Psychological Association (see
APA pp. 461–82). The other style, used more in the humanities, calls
for footnotes or endnotes and an optional bibliography. This style is
described in **Chic** pp. 489–500.

57b Writing in the social sciences

The social sciences—including anthropology, economics, education, management, political science, psychology, and sociology—
focus on the study of human behavior. As the name implies, the social sciences examine the way human beings relate to themselves, to
their environment, and to one another.

Exercise

1 Methods and evidence in the social sciences

Researchers in the social sciences systematically pose a question, formulate a **hypothesis** (a generalization that can be tested),

collect data, analyze those data, and draw conclusions to support, refine, or disprove their hypothesis. This is the scientific method developed in the natural sciences (see p. 393).

Social scientists gather data in several ways:

- **They interview subjects about their attitudes and behavior,** recording responses in writing or electronically. (See **7** pp. 336–37 for guidelines on conducting an interview.)
- **They conduct broader surveys using questionnaires,** asking people about their attitudes and behavior. (See **7** p. 337 for guidelines on conducting a survey.)
- **They make firsthand observations of human behavior,** recording the observations in writing or electronically. (See **7** pp. 337–38 for guidelines on conducting an observation.)
- **They conduct controlled experiments,** structuring an environment in which to encourage and measure a specific behavior.

In their writing, social scientists explain their own research or analyze and evaluate others' research.

The research methods of social science generate two kinds of data:

- *Quantitative data* **are numerical,** such as statistical evidence based on surveys, polls, tests, and experiments. When public-opinion pollsters announce that 47% of US citizens polled approve of the President's leadership, they are offering quantitative data gained from a survey. Social science writers present quantitative data in graphs, charts, and other illustrations that accompany their text.
- *Qualitative data* **are not numerical but more subjective:** they are based on interviews, firsthand observations, and inferences, taking into account the subjective nature of human experience. Examples of qualitative data include an anthropologist's description of the initiation ceremonies in a culture she is studying or a psychologist's interpretation of interviews he conducted with a group of adolescents.

Student
paper

2 Writing assignments in the social sciences

Depending on what social science courses you take, you may be asked to write in a variety of genres:

- **A summary or review of research** reports on the available research literature on a subject, such as infants' perception of color.
- **A case analysis** explains the components of a phenomenon, such as a factory closing.
- **A problem-solving analysis** explains the elements of a problem, such as unreported child abuse, and suggests ways to solve it.

- **A research paper** interprets and sometimes analyzes and evaluates the writings of other social scientists about a subject, such as the effect of national appeals in advertising.
- **A research report** explains the author's own original research or the author's attempt to replicate someone else's research. (See **APA** pp. 483–86 for an example of a research report.)

Many social science disciplines have special requirements for the content and organization of each kind of assignment. The requirements appear in the style guides of the disciplines, listed on p. 393. For instance, the American Psychological Association specifies the outline for research reports that is illustrated in **APA** pp. 480–82. Because of the differences among disciplines and even among different kinds of papers in the same discipline, you should always ask your instructor what he or she requires for an assignment.

3 | Tools and language in the social sciences

The following guidelines for tools and language apply to most social sciences. The particular discipline you are writing in, or an instructor in a particular course, may have additional requirements.

Writing tools

Many social scientists rely on a **research journal** or **log**, in which they record their ideas throughout the research-writing process. Even if a research journal is not required in your courses, you may want to use one. As you begin formulating a hypothesis, you can record preliminary questions. Then when you are in the field conducting research, you can use the journal to react to the evidence you are collecting, to record changes in your perceptions and ideas, and to assess your progress.

To avoid confusing your reflections on the evidence with the evidence itself, keep records of actual data—notes from interviews, observations, surveys, and experiments—separately from the journal.

Language considerations

Each social science discipline has specialized terminology for concepts basic to the discipline. In sociology, for example, the words *mechanism, identity,* and *deviance* have specific meanings different from those of everyday usage. And *identity* means something different in sociology, where it applies to groups of people, than in psychology, where it applies to the individual. Social scientists also use precise terms to describe or interpret research. For instance, they say *The subject expressed a feeling of* rather than *The subject felt* because human feelings are not knowable for certain; or they say *These studies indicate* rather than *These studies prove* because conclusions are only tentative.

Just as social scientists strive for objectivity in their research, they also strive to demonstrate their objectivity through language in their writing. They avoid expressions such as *I think* in order to focus attention on what the evidence shows rather than on the researcher's opinions. For the same reason, they also generally use the passive voice of verbs to describe their methods and results, as in *The subjects' responses were recorded.* (However, many social scientists prefer *I* to the artificial *the researcher* when they refer to their own actions, as in *I recorded the subjects' responses.* Ask your instructor for his or her preferences.) Social scientists also avoid direct or indirect expression of their personal biases or emotions, either in discussions of other researchers' work or in descriptions of research subjects. Thus one social scientist does not call another's work *sloppy* or *immaculate* and does not refer to his or her own subjects as *drunks* or *innocent victims.* Instead, the writer uses neutral language and ties conclusions strictly to the data.

Research sources on the open Web

General
INFOMINE (infomine.ucr.edu)
ipl2 (ipl.org)
WWW Virtual Library (vlib.org)

Anthropology
American Folklife Center (loc.gov/folklife)
National Anthropological Archives (www.nmnh.si.edu/naa)

Business and economics
Biz/ed (www.bized.co.uk/learn/index.html)
Resources for Economics on the Internet (rfe.org)

Education
Educator's Reference Desk (eduref.org)
US Department of Education (ed.gov)

Ethnic and gender studies
Internet Resources for Ethnic Studies (www2.lib.udel.edu/subj/ethst/internet.htm)
Voice of the Shuttle: Gender Studies (vos.ucsb.edu)

Political science and law
Political Science Resources (politicsresources.net)
Ultimate Political Science Links (upslinks.net)

Psychology
PsychCentral (psychcentral.com)
Psych Web (psywww.com)

Sociology
SocioSite (sociosite.net)
SocioWeb (socioweb.com)

4 Documentation and format in the social sciences

Some of the social sciences publish style guides that advise practitioners how to organize, document, and type papers. The following is a partial list:

American Anthropological Association, *AAA Style Guide,* 2009 (*www.aaanet .org/publications/guidelines.cfm*)

American Political Science Association, *Style Manual for Political Science,* 2006 (*www.ipsonet.org/data/files/APSAStyleManual2006.pdf*)

American Psychological Association, *Publication Manual of the American Psychological Association,* 6th ed., 2010

American Sociological Association, *ASA Style Guide,* 4th ed., 2010

Linguistic Society of America, "LSA Style Sheet," published every December in *LSA Bulletin*

A Uniform System of Citation (law), 19th ed., 2010

By far the most widely used style is that of the American Psychological Association, detailed in **APA** pp. 461–82. Always ask your instructor in any discipline what style you should use.

57c Writing in the natural and applied sciences

Exercise

The natural and applied sciences include biology, chemistry, physics, mathematics, engineering, computer science, and their branches. Their purpose is to understand natural and technological phenomena. (A *phenomenon* is a fact or event that can be known by the senses.) Scientists conduct experiments and write to explain the step-by-step processes in their methods of inquiry and discovery.

1 Methods and evidence in the sciences

Scientists investigate phenomena by the **scientific method,** a process of continual testing and refinement. The box below outlines this method.

Video tutorial

The scientific method

- **Observe carefully.** Accurately note all details of the phenomenon being researched.
- **Ask questions about the observations.**
- **Formulate a** *hypothesis,* or preliminary generalization, that explains the observed facts.
- **Test the hypothesis** with additional observations or controlled experiments.
- **If the hypothesis proves accurate, formulate a** *theory,* or unified model, that explains *why.*
- **If the hypothesis is disproved, revise it or start anew.**

Scientific evidence is almost always quantitative—that is, it consists of numerical data obtained from the measurement of phenomena. These data are called **empirical** (from a Greek word for "experience"): they result from observation and experience, generally in a controlled laboratory setting but also (as sometimes in astronomy or biology) in the natural world. Often the empirical evidence for scientific writing comes from library research into other people's reports of their investigations. Surveys of known data or existing literature are common in scientific writing.

Student
paper

2 | Writing assignments in the sciences

No matter what your assignment, you will be expected to document and explain your evidence carefully so that anyone reading can check your sources and replicate your research. It is important for your reader to know the context of your research—both the previous experimentation and research on your particular subject (acknowledged in the survey of the literature) and the physical conditions and other variables surrounding your own work.

Assignments in the natural and applied sciences include the following genres:

- **A summary** distills a research article to its essence in brief, concise form. (Summary is discussed in detail in **2** pp. 83–85.)
- **A critique** summarizes and critically evaluates a scientific report.
- **A laboratory report** explains the procedure and results of an experiment conducted by the writer.
- **A research report** explains the experimental research of other scientists and the writer's own methods, findings, and conclusions.
- **A research proposal** reviews the relevant literature and explains a plan for further research.

A laboratory report has four or five major sections:

1. **"Abstract":** a summary of the report.
2. **"Introduction" or "Objective":** a review of why the study was undertaken, a summary of the background of the study, and a statement of the problem being studied.
3. **"Method" or "Procedure":** a detailed explanation of how the study was conducted, including any statistical analysis.
4. **"Results":** an explanation of the major findings (including unexpected results) and a summary of the data presented in graphs and tables.
5. **"Discussion":** an interpretation of the results and an explanation of how they relate to the goals of the experiment. This section also describes new hypotheses that might be tested as a result of the experiment. If the discussion is brief, it may be combined with the results in a single section labeled "Conclusions."

In addition, laboratory or research reports may include a list of references (if other sources were consulted). They almost always include tables and figures (graphs and charts) containing the data from the research.

3 Tools and language in the sciences

Tools and language concerns vary from discipline to discipline in the sciences. Consult your instructor for specifics about the field in which you are writing.

Writing tools

In the sciences a **lab notebook** or **scientific journal** is almost indispensable for accurately recording the empirical data from observations and experiments. Use such a notebook or journal for these purposes:

- **Record observations** from reading, from class, or from the lab.
- **Ask questions and refine hypotheses.**
- **Record procedures.**
- **Record results.**
- **Keep an ongoing record of ideas and findings** and how they change as data accumulate.
- **Sequence and organize your material** as you compile your findings and write your report.

Make sure that your records of data are clearly separate from your reflections on the data so that you don't mistakenly confuse the two in drawing your conclusions.

Language considerations

Science writers use objective language that removes the writer as a character in the situation and events being explained, except as the impersonal agent of change, the experimenter. Although usage is evolving, scientists still rarely use *I* in their reports and evaluations, and they often resort to the passive voice of verbs, as in *The mixture was then subjected to centrifugal force.* This conscious objectivity focuses attention (including the writer's) on the empirical data and what they show. It discourages the writer from, say, ascribing motives and will to animals and plants. For instance, instead of asserting that the sea tortoise *developed* its hard shell *to protect* its body, a scientist would write only what could be observed: that the hard shell *covers and thus protects* the tortoise's body.

Science writers typically change verb tenses to distinguish between established information and their own research. For established information, such as that found in journals and other reliable sources, use the present tense: *Baroreceptors monitor blood pressure.* For your own and others' research, use the past tense: *The bacteria died within three hours. Marti reported some success.*

Each discipline in the natural and applied sciences has a specialized vocabulary that permits precise, accurate, and efficient communication. Some of these terms, such as *pressure* in physics, have different meanings in the common language and must be handled carefully in science writing. Others, such as *enthalpy* in chemistry, have no meanings in the common language and must simply be learned and used correctly.

Research sources on the open Web

General
Google Directory: Science Links (*directory.google.com/Top/Science*)
INFOMINE (*infomine.ucr.edu*)
ipl2 (*ipl.org/div/subject*)
WWW Virtual Library: Natural Sciences and Mathematics (*vlib.org*)

Biology
Biology Online (*biology-online.org*)
National Biological Information Infrastructure (*www.nbii.gov*)

Chemistry
American Chemical Society (*chemistry.org/portal/a/c/s/1/home.html*)
Chemspy (*chemspy.com*)

Computer science
Computer Science: A Guide to Web Resources
    (*libguides.library.albany.edu/csci*)
IEEE Computer Society (*computer.org*)

Engineering
National Academy of Engineering (*nae.edu*)
TechXtra: Engineering, Mathematics, and Computing
    (*www.techxtra.ac.uk*)

Environmental science
EnviroLink (*envirolink.org*)
Environment Directory (*webdirectory.com*)

Geology
American Geological Institute (*www.agiweb.org*)
US Geological Survey Library (*library.usgs.gov*)

Health sciences
Hardin MD (*lib.uiowa.edu/hardinmd*)
World Health Organization (*who.int/en*)

Mathematics
Internet Mathematics Library (*mathforum.org/library*)
Mathematical Atlas (*math-atlas.org*)

Physics and astronomy
American Institute of Physics (*aip.org*)
Science@NASA (*science.nasa.gov*)

4 Documentation and format in the sciences

Within the natural and applied sciences, practitioners use one of two styles of documentation, varying slightly from discipline to discipline. Following are some of the style guides most often consulted:

American Chemical Society, *ACS Style Guide: A Manual for Authors and Editors,* 3rd ed., 2006

American Institute of Physics, *Style Manual for Guidance in the Preparation of Papers,* 4th ed., 1997 (*www.aip.org/pubservs/style/4thed/AIP_Style_4thed.pdf*)

American Medical Association Manual of Style, 10th ed., 2007

Council of Science Editors, *Scientific Style and Format: The CSE Manual for Authors, Editors, and Publishers,* 7th ed., 2006

The most thorough and widely used of these guides is the last one, *Scientific Style and Format*. See **CSE** pp. 501–07 for a description of the style.

MLA Documentation
and Format

MLA Documentation and Format

MLA parenthetical text citations

MLA works-cited models

(continued)

58 MLA Documentation and Format

Video tutorial

English, foreign languages, and some other humanities use the documentation style of the Modern Language Association, described in the *MLA Handbook for Writers of Research Papers* (7th ed., 2009).

In MLA style, you twice acknowledge the sources of borrowed material:

■ **In your text, a brief parenthetical citation adjacent to the borrowed material directs readers to a complete list of all the works you cite.**

■ **At the end of your paper, the list of works cited includes complete bibliographical information for every source.**

Every entry in the list of works cited has at least one corresponding citation in the text, and every in-text citation has a corresponding entry in the list of works cited.

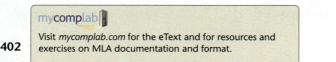

This chapter describes MLA documentation: writing text citations (below), placing and punctuating citations (p. 408), using supplementary notes (p. 410), and preparing the list of works cited (p. 411). A detailed discussion of MLA document format (p. 446) and a sample research paper showing MLA style (p. 448) conclude the chapter.

58a Writing parenthetical text citations

1 Citation formats

In-text citations of sources must include just enough information for the reader to locate the following:

- The *source* in your list of works cited.
- The *place* in the source where the borrowed material appears.

For any kind of source, you can usually meet both these requirements by providing the author's last name and (if the source uses them) the page numbers where the material appears. The reader can find the source in your list of works cited and find the borrowed material in the source itself.

The following models illustrate the basic text-citation forms and also forms for more unusual sources, such as those with no named author or no page numbers. See the **MLA** divider for an index to all the models.

Note Models 1 and 2 show the direct relationship between what you include in your text and what you include in a parenthetical citation. If you do *not* name the author in your text, you include the name in parentheses before the page reference (model 1). If you *do* name the author in your text, you do not include the name in parentheses (model 2).

1. Author not named in your text

When you have not already named the author in your sentence, provide the author's last name and the page number(s), with no punctuation between them, in parentheses.

> One researcher concludes that "women impose a distinctive construction on moral problems, seeing moral dilemmas in terms of conflicting responsibilities" (Gilligan 105-06).

See model 6 for the form to use when the source does not have an author. And see models 10 and 11 for the forms to use when the source does not provide page numbers.

2. Author named in your text

When you have already given the author's name with the material you're citing, do not repeat it in the parenthetical citation. Give just the page number(s).

> Carol Gilligan concludes that "women impose a distinctive construction on moral problems, seeing moral dilemmas in terms of conflicting responsibilities" (105-06).

See model 6 for the form to use when the source does not list an author. And see models 10 and 11 for the forms to use when the source does not provide page numbers.

3. A work with two or three authors

If the source has two or three authors, give all their last names in the text or in the citation. Separate two authors' names with and:

> As Frieden and Sagalyn observe, "The poor and the minorities were the leading victims of highway and renewal programs" (29).

> According to one study, "The poor and the minorities were the leading victims of highway and renewal programs" (Frieden and Sagalyn 29).

With three authors, add commas and also and before the final name:

> The textbook by Wilcox, Ault, and Agee discusses the "ethical dilemmas in public relations practice" (125).

> One textbook discusses the "ethical dilemmas in public relations practice" (Wilcox, Ault, and Agee 125).

4. A work with more than three authors

If the source has more than three authors, you may list all their last names or give only the first author's name followed by et al. (the abbreviation for the Latin *et alii,* "and others"). The choice depends on what you do in your list of works cited (see p. 412).

> Increased competition means that employees of public relations firms may find their loyalty stretched in more than one direction (Wilcox et al. 417).

> Increased competition means that employees of public relations firms may find their loyalty stretched in more than one direction (Wilcox, Cameron, Reber, and Shin 417).

5. A work by an author of two or more cited works

If your list of works cited includes two or more works by the same author, then your citation must tell the reader which of the author's works you are referring to. Give the title either in the text or in a par-

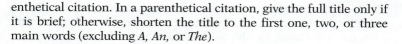

enthetical citation. In a parenthetical citation, give the full title only if it is brief; otherwise, shorten the title to the first one, two, or three main words (excluding *A, An,* or *The*).

> At about age seven, children begin to use appropriate gestures with their stories (Gardner, *Arts* 144-45).

The full title of Gardner's book is *The Arts and Human Development* (see the works-cited entry on p. 413). This shortened title is italicized because the source is a book.

6. An anonymous work

For a work with no named author or editor (whether an individual or an organization), use a full or shortened version of the title, as explained above. In your list of works cited, you alphabetize an anonymous work by the first main word of the title (see p. 413), so the first word of a shortened title should be the same. The following citations refer to an unsigned source titled "The Right to Die." The title appears in quotation marks because the source is a periodical article.

> One article notes that a death-row inmate may demand his own execution to achieve a fleeting notoriety ("Right" 16).

> "The Right to Die" notes that a death-row inmate may demand execution to achieve a fleeting notoriety (16).

If two or more anonymous works have the same title, distinguish them with additional information in the text citation, such as the publication date.

7. A work with a corporate author

Some works list as author a government body, association, committee, company, or other group. Cite such a work by the organization's name. If the name is long, work it into the text to avoid an intrusive parenthetical citation.

> A 2011 report by the Nevada Department of Education provides evidence of an increase in graduation rates (12).

8. A nonprint source

Cite a nonprint source such as a Web page or a DVD just as you would any other source. If your works-cited entry lists the source under the name of an author or other contributor, use that name in the text citation. The following example cites an authored source that has page numbers.

> Business forecasts for the fourth quarter tended to be optimistic (White 4).

If your works-cited entry lists the work under its title, cite the work by title in your text, as explained in model 6. The next example cites an entire work (a film on DVD) and gives the title in the text, so it omits a parenthetical citation (see model 10).

Many decades after its release, *Citizen Kane* is still remarkable for its rich black-and-white photography.

9. A multivolume work

If you consulted only one volume of a multivolume work, your list of works cited will say so (see model 30 on p. 424), and you can treat the volume as you would any book.

If you consulted more than one volume of a multivolume work, give the appropriate volume before the page number (here volume 5):

After issuing the Emancipation Proclamation, Lincoln said, "What I did, I did after very full deliberations, and under a very heavy and solemn sense of responsibility" (5: 438).

The number 5 indicates the volume from which the quotation was taken; the number 438 indicates the page number in that volume. When the author's name appears in such a citation, place it before the volume number with no punctuation: (Lincoln 5: 438).

If you are referring generally to an entire volume of a multivolume work and are not citing specific page numbers, add the abbreviation vol. before the volume number, as in (vol. 5) or (Lincoln, vol. 5) (note the comma after the author's name). Then readers will not misinterpret the volume number as a page number.

10. A one-page work, an entire work, or a work with no page or other reference numbers

When you cite a work that's only a page long or an entire work rather than a part of it, you may omit any page or other reference number. If the work you cite has an author, try to give the author's name in your text. You will not need a parenthetical citation then, but the source must still appear in your list of works cited.

Boyd deals with the need to acknowledge and come to terms with our fear of nuclear technology.

Use the same format when you cite a specific passage from a work with no page, paragraph, or other reference numbers, such as a Web source.

If the author's name does not appear in your text, put it in a parenthetical citation.

Almost 20 percent of commercial banks have been audited for the practice (Friis).

11. A work with numbered paragraphs or sections instead of pages

Some electronic sources number each paragraph or section instead of each page. In citing passages in these sources, give the paragraph or section number(s) and distinguish them from page numbers: after the author's name, put a comma, a space, and par. (one paragraph), pars. (more than one paragraph), sec., or secs.

Twins reared apart report similar feelings (Palfrey, pars. 6-7).

12. A source referred to by another source (indirect source)

When you want to use a quotation that is already in quotation marks—indicating that the author you are reading is quoting someone else—try to find the original source and quote directly from it. If you can't find the original source, then your citation must indicate that your quotation of it is indirect. In the following citation, qtd. in ("quoted in") says that Davino was quoted by Boyd.

George Davino maintains that "even small children have vivid ideas about nuclear energy" (qtd. in Boyd 22).

The list of works cited then includes only Boyd (the work consulted), not Davino.

13. A literary work

Novels, plays, and poems are often available in many editions, so your instructor may ask you to provide information that will help readers find the passage you cite no matter what edition they consult.

- **Novels:** The page number comes first, followed by a semicolon and then information on the appropriate part or chapter of the work.

  Toward the end of James's novel, Maggie suddenly feels "the thick breath of the definite—which was the intimate, the immediate, the familiar, as she hadn't had them for so long" (535; pt. 6, ch. 41).

- **Poems that are not divided into parts:** You may omit the page number and supply the line number(s) for the quotation. To prevent confusion with page numbers, precede the numbers with line or lines in the first citation; then use just the numbers.

  In Shakespeare's Sonnet 73 the speaker identifies with the trees of late autumn, "Bare ruined choirs, where late the sweet birds sang" (line 4). "In me," Shakespeare writes, "thou seest the glowing of such fire / That on the ashes of his youth doth lie . . ." (9-10).

(See **8** pp. 384–86 for a sample paper on a poem.)

- **Verse plays and poems that are divided into parts:** Omit a page number and cite the appropriate part—act (and scene, if any), canto, book, and so on—plus the line number(s). Use Arabic numerals for parts, including acts and scenes (3.4), unless your instructor specifies Roman numerals (III.iv).

  Later in Shakespeare's *King Lear* the disguised Edgar says, "The prince of darkness is a gentleman" (3.4.147).

- **Prose plays:** Provide the page number followed by the act and scene, if any. See the reference to *Death of a Salesman* on p. 410.

14. The Bible

When you cite passages of the Bible in parentheses, abbreviate the title of any book longer than four letters—for instance, Gen. (Genesis), 1 Sam. (1 Samuel), Ps. (Psalms), Prov. (Proverbs), Matt. (Matthew), Rom. (Romans). Then give the chapter and verse(s) in Arabic numerals.

  According to the Bible, at Babel God "did . . . confound the language of all the earth" (Gen. 11.9).

15. Two or more works in the same citation

When you refer to more than one work in a single parenthetical citation, separate the references with a semicolon.

  Two recent articles point out that a computer badly used can be less efficient than no computer at all (Gough and Hall 201; Richards 162).

Since long citations in the text can distract the reader, you may choose to cite several or more works in an endnote or footnote rather than in the text. See pp. 410–11.

2 Placement and punctuation of parenthetical citations

The following guidelines will help you place and punctuate text citations to distinguish between your own and your sources' ideas and to make your own text readable. See also 7 pp. 356–59 on editing quotations and using signal phrases to integrate source material into your sentences.

Where to place citations

Position text citations to accomplish two goals:

- **Make it clear exactly where your borrowing begins and ends.**
- **Keep the citation as unobtrusive as possible.**

You can accomplish both goals by placing the parenthetical citation at the end of the sentence element containing the borrowed material.

This sentence element may be a phrase or a clause, and it may begin, interrupt, or conclude the sentence. Usually, as in the following examples, the element ends with a punctuation mark.

> The inflation rate might climb as high as 30 percent (Kim 164), an increase that could threaten the small nation's stability.

> The inflation rate, which might climb as high as 30 percent (Kim 164), could threaten the small nation's stability.

> The small nation's stability could be threatened by its inflation rate, which, one source predicts, might climb as high as 30 percent (Kim 164).

In the last example the addition of one source predicts clarifies that Kim is responsible only for the inflation-rate prediction, not for the statement about stability.

When your paraphrase or summary of a source runs longer than a sentence, clarify the boundaries by using the author's name in the first sentence and placing the parenthetical citation at the end of the last sentence.

> Juliette Kim studied the effects of acutely high inflation in several South American and African countries since World War II. She discovered that a major change in government accompanied or followed the inflationary period in 56 percent of cases (22-23).

When you cite two or more sources in the same paragraph, position authors' names and parenthetical citations so that readers can see who said what. In the following example, the beginnings and ends of sentences clearly mark the different sources.

> Schools use computers extensively for drill-and-practice exercises, in which students repeat specific skills such as spelling words, using the multiplication facts, or, at a higher level, doing chemistry problems. But many education experts criticize such exercises for boring students and failing to engage their critical thinking and creativity. Jane M. Healy, a noted educational psychologist and teacher, takes issue with "interactive" software for children as well as drill-and-practice software, arguing that "some of the most popular 'educational' software . . . may be damaging to independent thinking, attention, and motivation" (20). Another education expert, Harold Wenglinsky of the Educational Testing Service, found in a well-regarded study that fourth and eighth graders who used computers frequently, including for drill and practice, actually did worse on tests than their peers who used computers less often (*Does It Compute?* 21). In a later article, Wenglinsky concludes that "the quantity of use matters far less than the quality of use." In schools, he says, high-quality computer work, involving critical thinking, is still rare ("In Search" 17).

How to punctuate citations

Generally place a parenthetical citation *before* any punctuation required by your sentence. If the borrowed material is a quotation, place the citation *between* the closing quotation mark and the punctuation:

> Spelling argues that during the 1970s American automobile manufacturers met consumer needs "as well as could be expected" (26), but not everyone agrees with him.

The exception is a quotation ending in a question mark or exclamation point. Then use the appropriate punctuation inside the closing quotation mark, and follow the quotation with the text citation and a period.

> "Of what use is genius," Emerson asks, "if the organ . . . cannot find a focal distance within the actual horizon of human life?" ("Experience" 60). Mad genius is no genius.

When a citation appears at the end of a quotation set off from the text, place it one space *after* the punctuation ending the quotation. Do not use additional punctuation with the citation or quotation marks around the quotation.

> In Arthur Miller's *Death of a Salesman*, the most poignant defense of Willie Loman comes from his wife, Linda:
>
> > He's not the finest character that ever lived. But he's a human being, and a terrible thing is happening to him. So attention must be paid. He's not to be allowed to fall into his grave like an old dog. Attention, attention must finally be paid to such a person. (56; act 1)

(This citation of a play includes the act number as well as the page number. See p. 408.)

See the sample research paper starting on p. 450 for further examples of placing parenthetical references in relation to summaries, paraphrases, and quotations.

3 Footnotes or endnotes in special circumstances

Occasionally you may want to use footnotes or endnotes in place of parenthetical citations. If you need to refer to several sources at once, listing them in a long parenthetical citation could be intrusive. Signal the citation with a numeral raised above the appropriate line. Then write a note beginning with the same numeral:

Text   At least five studies have confirmed these results.[1]

Note   1. Abbott and Winger 266-68; Casner 27; Hoyenga 78-79; Marino 36; Tripp, Tripp, and Walk 179-83.

You may also use a footnote or endnote to comment on a source or to provide information that does not fit easily in the text:

Text   So far, no one has confirmed these results.[2]

Note   2. Manter tried repeatedly to replicate the experiment, but he was never able to produce the high temperatures (616).

Indent a note one-half inch, type the numeral on the text line, and follow the numeral with a period and a space. If the note appears as a footnote, place it at the bottom of the page on which the citation appears, set it off from the text with quadruple spacing, and double-space the note itself. If the note appears as an endnote, place it in numerical order with the other endnotes on a page between the text and the list of works cited. Double-space all the endnotes.

58b Preparing the MLA list of works cited

Exercise

At the end of your paper, a list titled Works Cited includes all the sources you quoted, paraphrased, or summarized in your paper. (If your instructor asks you to include sources you examined but did not cite, title the list Works Consulted.)

Follow this format for the list of works cited:

■ **Arrange your sources in alphabetical order** by the last name of the author. If an author is not given in the source, alphabetize the source by the first main word of the title (excluding *A*, *An*, or *The*).

■ **Type the entire list double-spaced,** both within and between entries.

■ **Indent the second and subsequent lines of each entry one-half inch from the left.** Your word processor can format this so-called hanging indent automatically.

MLA works-cited page

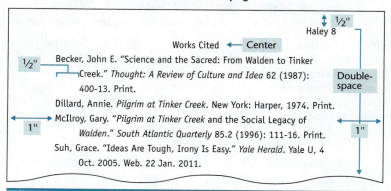

Haley 8

½"

Works Cited ← Center

½"   Becker, John E. "Science and the Sacred: From Walden to Tinker
          Creek." *Thought: A Review of Culture and Idea* 62 (1987):
          400-13. Print.

Double-
space

        Dillard, Annie. *Pilgrim at Tinker Creek*. New York: Harper, 1974. Print.

        McIlroy, Gary. "*Pilgrim at Tinker Creek* and the Social Legacy of
1"   *Walden.*" *South Atlantic Quarterly* 85.2 (1996): 111-16. Print.

1"

        Suh, Grace. "Ideas Are Tough, Irony Is Easy." *Yale Herald*. Yale U, 4
          Oct. 2005. Web. 22 Jan. 2011.

For a complete list of works cited, see the paper by Justin Malik on pp. 457–58.

An index to all the following models appears at the **MLA** divider. Use your best judgment in adapting the models to your particular sources. If you can't find a model that exactly matches a source you used, locate and follow the closest possible match. You will certainly need to combine formats—for instance, drawing on model 2 ("Two or three authors") and model 21 ("A book with an editor") for a book with three editors.

Note MLA style requires the publication medium for every source, such as print, Web, DVD, or television. For example, if you consulted an article in a print magazine, list the medium as Print. If you consulted a book on the Web, list the medium as Web. The models here all conform to this standard.

1 │ Listing authors

The following models show how to handle authors' names in citing any kind of source.

1. One author

Ehrenreich, Barbara. *Dancing in the Streets: A History of Collective Joy*. New
York: Metropolitan-Holt, 2006. Print.

Give the author's full name—last name first, a comma, first name, and any middle name or initial. Omit any title, such as *Dr.* or *PhD*. End the name with a period. If your source lists an editor as author, see model 21, p. 419.

2. Two or three authors

Lifton, Robert Jay, and Greg Mitchell. *Who Owns Death: Capital Punishment,
the American Conscience, and the End of Executions*. New York: Morrow,
2000. Print.

Simpson, Dick, James Nowlan, and Elizabeth O'Shaughnessy. *The Struggle for
Power and Influence in Cities and States*. New York: Longman, 2011. Print.

Give the authors' names in the order provided on the title page. Reverse the first and last names of the first author *only,* not of any other authors. Separate two authors' names with a comma and and; separate three authors' names with commas and with and before the third name. If your source lists two or three editors as authors, see model 21, p. 419.

3. More than three authors

Wilcox, Dennis L., Glen T. Cameron, Bryan H. Reber, and Jae-Hwa Shin. *Think
Public Relations*. Boston: Allyn, 2010. Print.

Wilcox, Dennis L., et al. *Think Public Relations*. Boston: Allyn, 2010. Print.

You may, but need not, give all authors' names if the work has more than three authors. If you choose not to give all names, provide the name of the first author only, and follow the name with a comma and the abbreviation et al. (for the Latin *et alii*, meaning "and others"). If your source lists more than three editors as authors, see model 21, p. 419.

4. The same author(s) for two or more works

Gardner, Howard. *The Arts and Human Development*. New York: Wiley, 1973.
    Print.

---. *Five Minds for the Future*. Boston: Harvard Business School P, 2007.
    Print.

Give the author's name only in the first entry. For the second and any subsequent works by the same author, substitute three hyphens for the author's name, followed by a period. Note that the three hyphens may substitute only for *exactly* the same name or names. If the second Gardner source were by Gardner and somebody else, both names would have to be given in full.

Place an entry or entries using three hyphens immediately after the entry that names the author. Within the set of entries by the same author, arrange the sources alphabetically by the first main word of the title, as in the Gardner examples (*Arts*, then *Five*).

If you cite two or more sources that list as author(s) exactly the same editor(s), follow the hyphens with a comma and ed. or eds. as appropriate. (See model 21, p. 419.)

5. A corporate author

Vault Technologies. *Turnkey Parking Solutions*. Salt Lake City: Mills, 2011.
    Print.

Corporate authors include associations, committees, institutions, government bodies, companies, and other groups. List the name of the group as author when a source gives only that name and not an individual's name.

6. Author not named (anonymous)

The Dorling Kindersley World Atlas. London: Dorling, 2010. Print.

List a work that names no author—neither an individual nor a group—by its full title. If the work is a book, italicize the title. If the work is a periodical article or other short work, enclose the title in quotation marks:

"Leaping the Wall." *Economist* 26 Mar. 2011: 51. Print.

Alphabetize the work by the title's first main word, excluding *A, An,* or *The* (*Dorling* in the first example and Leaping in the second).

2 Listing periodical print sources

Print periodicals include scholarly journals, newspapers, and magazines that are published at regular intervals (quarterly, monthly, weekly, or daily). The following list, adapted from the *MLA Handbook*, itemizes the possible elements in print periodicals, in order of their appearance in a works-cited entry.

- **Author.** Give the author's last name, first name, and any middle name or initial. To cite more than one author, two articles by the same author, a corporate author, or an article with no named author, see models 2–6.
- **Title of the article,** in quotation marks. Give the title and any subtitle. End the title with a period inside the final quotation mark.
- **Title of the periodical,** in italics. Omit any *A*, *An*, or *The* from the beginning of the title. Do not end with a period.
- **Publication information.** The treatment of volume and issue numbers and publication dates varies depending on the kind of periodical you are citing, as shown in models 7–18. (For the distinction between journals and magazines, see **7** p. 325.) If you include the month of publication, abbreviate it unless it is May, June, or July.
- **Page numbers of the article,** without "pp."
- **Medium of publication:** Print, followed by a period.

Articles in scholarly journals

7. An article in a journal with volume and issue numbers (print)

Bee, Robert. "The Importance of Preserving Paper-Based Artifacts in a Digital Age." *Library Quarterly* 78.2 (2008): 174-94. Print.

See pp. 416–17 for the basic format for an article in a print periodical (a journal) and the location of the required information in the journal.

8. An article in a journal with only issue numbers (print)

Rae, Ian. "The Case for Digital Poetics." *Canadian Literature* 204 (2010): 134-37. Print.

If a scholarly journal numbers only issues, not volumes, give the issue number alone after the journal title.

9. An abstract of a journal article or a dissertation (print)

Lever, Janet. "Sex Differences in the Games Children Play." *Social Problems* 23.2 (1996): 478-87. *Psychological Abstracts* 63.5 (1996): item 1431. Print.

For an abstract of a journal article, first provide the publication information for the article, following model 7. Then give the information for the abstract. If the abstract publisher lists abstracts by item rather than page number, add item before the number. Add Abstract after the original publication information if the title of the abstracts journal does not indicate that your source is an abstract. See model 65, p. 439.

For an abstract appearing in *Dissertation Abstracts* (*DA*) or *Dissertation Abstracts International* (*DAI*), give the author's name and the title, Diss. (for "Dissertation"), the institution granting the author's degree, the date of the dissertation, and the publication information.

> Steciw, Steven K. "Alterations to the Pessac Project of Le Corbusier." Diss.
>
> U of Cambridge, England, 1986. *DAI* 46.10 (1986): 565C. Print.

See also model 40 on p. 426 (entire dissertation), model 63 on p. 437 (abstract on the Web), and model 65 on p. 439 (abstract in an online database).

Note Most instructors expect you to consult and cite full articles, not abstracts. See **7** pp. 327–28.

Articles in newspapers

10. An article in a national newspaper (print)

> Harmanci, Reyhan. "Literary Journals Thrive, on Paper and Otherwise." *New York Times* 8 Apr. 2011, natl. ed.: A23+. Print.

Give the author, the title of the article, and then the title of the newspaper as it appears on the first page (but without any *A*, *An*, or *The*). Follow the newspaper title with the day, the month, and the year of publication. (Abbreviate all months except May, June, and July.) If the newspaper lists an edition at the top of the first page, include it after the date (see natl. ed. above). If the newspaper is divided into sections that are lettered, provide the section designation before the page number when the newspaper does the same: A23+ above. (The plus sign indicates that the article continues on a later page.) If the newspaper is divided into numbered or titled sections, provide the section designation before the colon—for instance, sec. 1: 3 or Business Day sec.: 4+. End with the medium, Print.

11. An article in a local newspaper (print)

> Perera, Dilshanie. "Health Department Elaborates on Latest Sharing of Services." *Town Topics* [Princeton] 16 Mar. 2011: 1+. Print.

If the city of publication does not appear in the title of a local newspaper, follow the title with the city name, not italicized, in brackets.

Format for a print journal article

Journal cover

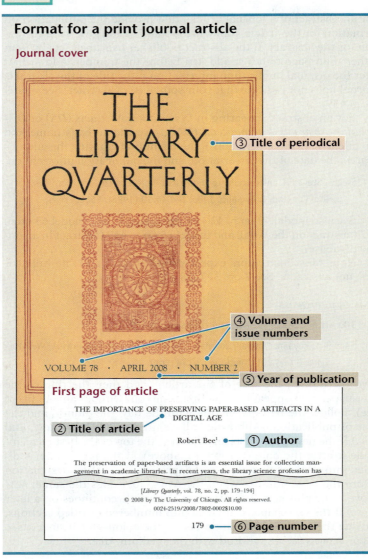

THE LIBRARY QVARTERLY

③ **Title of periodical**

④ **Volume and issue numbers**

VOLUME 78 · APRIL 2008 · NUMBER 2

⑤ **Year of publication**

First page of article

THE IMPORTANCE OF PRESERVING PAPER-BASED ARTIFACTS IN A DIGITAL AGE

② **Title of article**

Robert Bee[1]   ● ① **Author**

The preservation of paper-based artifacts is an essential issue for collection management in academic libraries. In recent years, the library science profession has

[*Library Quarterly*, vol. 78, no. 2, pp. 179–194]
© 2008 by The University of Chicago. All rights reserved.
0024-2519/2008/7802-0002$10.00

179   ● ⑥ **Page number**

Articles in magazines

12. An article in a weekly or biweekly magazine (print)

Danticat, Edwidge. "A Year and a Day." *New Yorker* 17 Jan. 2011: 19-20. Print.

Give the author, title of the article, and title of the magazine. Follow the magazine title with the day, the month, and the year of publication. (Abbreviate all months except May, June, and July.) Don't place

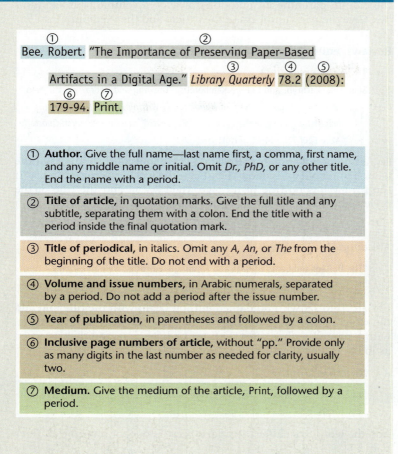

① ②
Bee, Robert. "The Importance of Preserving Paper-Based
③ ④ ⑤
Artifacts in a Digital Age." *Library Quarterly* 78.2 (2008):
⑥ ⑦
179-94. Print.

① **Author.** Give the full name—last name first, a comma, first name, and any middle name or initial. Omit *Dr., PhD,* or any other title. End the name with a period.

② **Title of article,** in quotation marks. Give the full title and any subtitle, separating them with a colon. End the title with a period inside the final quotation mark.

③ **Title of periodical,** in italics. Omit any *A, An,* or *The* from the beginning of the title. Do not end with a period.

④ **Volume and issue numbers,** in Arabic numerals, separated by a period. Do not add a period after the issue number.

⑤ **Year of publication,** in parentheses and followed by a colon.

⑥ **Inclusive page numbers of article,** without "pp." Provide only as many digits in the last number as needed for clarity, usually two.

⑦ **Medium.** Give the medium of the article, Print, followed by a period.

the date in parentheses, and don't provide a volume or issue number. Give the page numbers of the article and the medium, Print.

13. An article in a monthly or bimonthly magazine (print)

Hall, Stephen S. "Diseases in a Dish." *Scientific American* Mar. 2011: 40-45. Print.

Follow the magazine title with the month and the year of publication. (Abbreviate all months except May, June, and July.) Don't place the date in parentheses, and don't provide a volume or issue number. Give the page numbers of the article and the medium, Print.

Reviews, editorials, letters to the editor, interviews

14. A review (print)

Glasswell, Kathryn, and George Kamberelis. "Drawing and Redrawing the Map of Writing Studies." Rev. of *Handbook of Writing Research*, by Charles A. MacArthur, Steve Graham, and Jill Fitzgerald. *Reading Research Quarterly* 42.2 (2007): 304-23. Print.

Rev. is an abbreviation for "Review." The names of the authors of the work being reviewed follow the title of the work, a comma, and by. If the review has no title of its own, then Rev. of and the title of the reviewed work immediately follow the name of the reviewer.

15. An editorial or a letter to the editor (print)

An editorial:

"The Dollars and Cents of Bats and Farming." Editorial. *New York Times* 4 Apr. 2011, natl. ed.: A18. Print.

For an editorial with no named author, begin with the title and add the word Editorial after the title, as in the example. For an editorial with a named author, start with his or her name and then proceed as in the example.

A letter to the editor:

Stasi, Dom. "Climate and Heresy." Letter. *Scientific American* Mar. 2011: 8. Print.

Add the word Letter after the title, if there is one, or after the author's name.

16. An interview (print)

Aloni, Shulamit. Interview. *Palestine-Israel Journal of Politics, Economics, and Culture* 14.4 (2007): 63-68. Print.

Begin with the name of the person interviewed. If the interview does not have a title (as in the example), add Interview after the name. (Replace this description with the title if there is one.) You may also add the name of the interviewer if you know it—for example, Interview by Benson Wright. See model 75 (p. 443) to cite a broadcast interview or an interview you conduct yourself.

Articles in series or in special issues

17. An article in a series (print)

Kleinfeld, N. R. "Living at an Epicenter of Diabetes, Defiance, and Despair."

New York Times 10 Jan. 2006, natl. ed.: A1+. Print. Pt. 2 of a series, Bad Blood, begun 9 Jan. 2006.

Cite an article in a series following a model on pp. 414–18 (scholarly journal, newspaper, or magazine). If you wish, end the entry with a description to indicate that the article is part of a series.

18. An article in a special issue (print)

Rubini, Monica, and Michela Menegatti. "Linguistic Bias in Personnel Selection." *Celebrating Two Decades of Linguistic Bias Research.* Ed. Robbie M. Sutton and Karen M. Douglas. Spec. issue of *Journal of Language and Social Psychology* 27.2 (2008): 168-81. Print.

Cite an article in a special issue of a periodical by starting with the author and title of the article. Follow with the title of the special issue, Ed., and the names of the issue's editor(s). Add Spec. issue of before the periodical title. Conclude with publication information, using the appropriate model on p. 414 or pp. 416–18 for a journal or magazine.

3 Listing nonperiodical print sources

Nonperiodical print sources are works that are not published at regular intervals, such as books, government publications, and pamphlets. To cite one author, more than one author, and other variations, see models 1–6.

Books

19. Basic format for a book (print)

Shteir, Rachel. *The Steal: A Cultural History of Shoplifting.* New York: Penguin, 2011. Print.

The next two pages show the basic format for a book and the location of the required information in the book. To cite electronic books, see also model 44 (a book published only on the Web), model 57 (a scan of a print book), and model 72 (a book formatted for an electronic reader.)

20. A second or subsequent edition (print)

Bolinger, Dwight L. *Aspects of Language.* 3rd ed. New York: Harcourt, 1981. Print.

For any edition after the first, place the edition number after the title. (If an editor's name follows the title, place the edition number after the name. See model 25.) Use the appropriate designation for editions that are named or dated rather than numbered—for instance, Rev. ed. for "Revised edition."

21. A book with an editor (print)

Holland, Merlin, and Rupert Hart-Davis, eds. *The Complete Letters of Oscar Wilde.* New York: Holt, 2000. Print.

Format for a print book

Title page

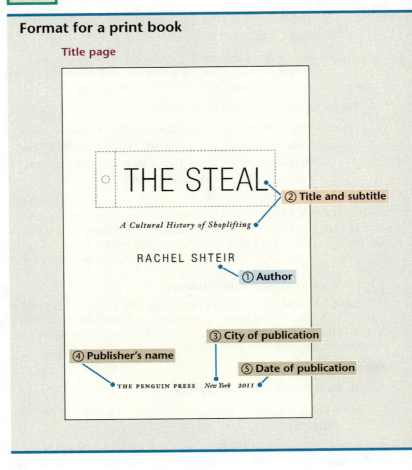

THE STEAL

② **Title and subtitle**

A Cultural History of Shoplifting

RACHEL SHTEIR

① **Author**

③ **City of publication**

④ **Publisher's name**

⑤ **Date of publication**

THE PENGUIN PRESS   *New York*   *2011*

Handle editors' names like authors' names (models 1–4), but add a comma and the abbreviation ed. (one editor) or eds. (two or more editors) after the last editor's name.

22. A book with an author and an editor (print)

Mumford, Lewis. *The City in History*. Ed. Donald L. Miller. New York: Pantheon,

1986. Print.

When citing the work of the author, give his or her name first, and give the editor's name after the title, preceded by Ed. (singular only, meaning "Edited by"). When citing the work of the editor, use model 21 for a book with an editor, adding By and the author's name after the title:

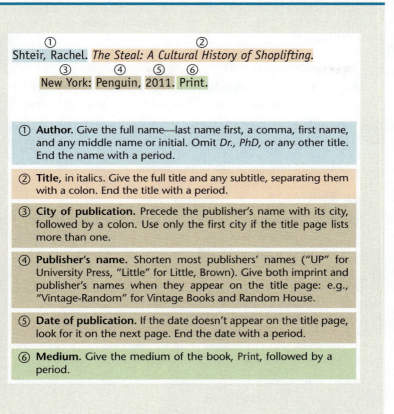

① ②
Shteir, Rachel. *The Steal: A Cultural History of Shoplifting.*
③ ④ ⑤ ⑥
New York: Penguin, 2011. Print.

① **Author.** Give the full name—last name first, a comma, first name, and any middle name or initial. Omit *Dr., PhD,* or any other title. End the name with a period.

② **Title,** in italics. Give the full title and any subtitle, separating them with a colon. End the title with a period.

③ **City of publication.** Precede the publisher's name with its city, followed by a colon. Use only the first city if the title page lists more than one.

④ **Publisher's name.** Shorten most publishers' names ("UP" for University Press, "Little" for Little, Brown). Give both imprint and publisher's names when they appear on the title page: e.g., "Vintage-Random" for Vintage Books and Random House.

⑤ **Date of publication.** If the date doesn't appear on the title page, look for it on the next page. End the date with a period.

⑥ **Medium.** Give the medium of the book, Print, followed by a period.

Miller, Donald L., ed. *The City in History.* By Lewis Mumford. New York: Pantheon, 1986. Print.

23. A book with a translator (print)

Alighieri, Dante. *The Inferno.* Trans. John Ciardi. New York: NAL, 1971. Print.

When citing the work of the author, as in the preceding example, give his or her name first, and give the translator's name after the title, preceded by Trans. ("Translated by").

When citing the work of the translator, give his or her name first, followed by a comma and trans. Follow the title with By and the author's name:

Ciardi, John, trans. *The Inferno.* By Dante Alighieri. New York: NAL, 1971. Print.

When a book you cite by author has a translator *and* an editor, give the translator's and editor's names in the order used on the book's title page.

24. An anthology (print)

Kennedy, X. J., and Dana Gioia, eds. *Literature: An Introduction to Fiction, Poetry, Drama, and Writing.* 11th ed. New York: Longman, 2010. Print.

Cite an entire anthology only when citing the work of the editor or editors or when your instructor permits cross-referencing like that shown in model 26. Give the name of the editor or editors (followed by ed. or eds.) and then the title of the anthology.

25. A selection from an anthology (print)

Mason, Bobbie Ann. "Shiloh." *Literature: An Introduction to Fiction, Poetry, Drama, and Writing.* Ed. X. J. Kennedy and Dana Gioia. 11th ed. New York: Longman, 2010. 569-78. Print.

This listing adds the following to the anthology entry in model 24: author of selection, title of selection (in quotation marks), and inclusive page numbers for the selection (without the abbreviation "pp."). If you wish, you may also supply the original date of publication for the work you are citing, after its title. See model 32 on p. 424.

If the work you cite comes from a collection of works by one author that has no editor, use the following form:

Auden, W. H. "Family Ghosts." *The Collected Poetry of W. H. Auden.* New York: Random, 1945. 132-33. Print.

26. Two or more selections from the same anthology (print)

Bradstreet, Anne. "The Author to Her Book." Kennedy and Gioia 647.

Kennedy, X. J., and Dana Gioia, eds. *Literature: An Introduction to Fiction, Poetry, Drama, and Writing.* 11th ed. New York: Longman, 2010. Print.

Merwin, W. S. "For the Anniversary of My Death." Kennedy and Gioia 834-35.

Stevens, Wallace. "Thirteen Ways of Looking at a Blackbird." Kennedy and Gioia 838-39.

When you are citing more than one selection from the same anthology, your instructor may allow you to avoid repetition by giving the anthology information in full (the Kennedy and Gioia entry) and then simply cross-referencing it in entries for the works you used. Thus the Bradstreet, Merwin, and Stevens examples replace full publication information with Kennedy and Gioia and the appropriate pages in that book. Note that each entry appears in its proper alphabetical place among other works cited. Because the specific

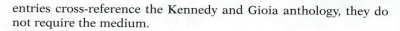

entries cross-reference the Kennedy and Gioia anthology, they do not require the medium.

27. A scholarly article reprinted in a collection (print)

Molloy, Francis C. "The Suburban Vision in John O'Hara's Short Stories." *Critique: Studies in Modern Fiction* 25.2 (1984): 101-13. Rpt. in *Short Story Criticism: Excerpts from Criticism of the Works of Short Fiction Writers*. Ed. David Segal. Vol. 15. Detroit: Gale, 1989. 287-92. Print.

If the work you are citing is a scholarly article that was previously printed elsewhere—for instance, in a scholarly journal—provide the complete information for the earlier publication of the piece. Follow this information with Rpt. in ("Reprinted in") and the information for the source in which you found the piece.

28. An article in a reference work (print)

"Reckon." *Merriam-Webster's Collegiate Dictionary*. 11th ed. 2008. Print.

Wenner, Manfred W. "Arabia." *The New Encyclopaedia Britannica: Macropaedia*. 15th ed. 2007. Print.

List an article in a reference work by its title (first example) unless the article is signed (second example). For works with entries arranged alphabetically, you need not include volume or page numbers. For works that are widely used and often revised, like those above, you may omit the editors' names and all publication information except any edition number, the publication year, and the medium.

For works that are specialized, give full publication information. Such works may have narrow subjects and audiences and may appear in only one edition.

"Fortune." *Encyclopedia of Indo-European Culture*. Ed. J. P. Mallory and Douglas Q. Adams. London: Fitzroy, 1997. Print.

See also models 48 (p. 432) and 68 (p. 440), respectively, to cite reference works appearing on the Web or on a **CD-ROM** or **DVD-ROM**.

29. An illustrated book or graphic narrative (print)

Wilson, G. Willow. *Cairo*. Illus. M. K. Perker. New York: Vertigo-DC Comics, 2005. Print.

When citing the work of the writer of a graphic narrative or illustrated book, follow the example above: author's name, title, Illus. ("Illustrated by"), and the illustrator's name. When citing the work of an illustrator, list his or her name first, followed by a comma and illus. ("illustrator"). After the title and By, list the author's name.

Williams, Garth, illus. *Charlotte's Web*. By E. B. White. 1952. New York: Harper,

1999. Print.

30. A multivolume work (print)

Lincoln, Abraham. *The Collected Works of Abraham Lincoln*. Ed. Roy P. Basler.

Vol. 5. New Brunswick: Rutgers UP, 1953. Print. 8 vols.

If you use only one volume of a multivolume work, give that volume number before the publication information (Vol. 5 in the preceding example). You may add the total number of volumes at the end of the entry (8 vols. in the example).

If you use two or more volumes of a multivolume work, give the work's total number of volumes before the publication information (8 vols. in the following example). Your text citation will indicate which volume you are citing (see p. 406).

Lincoln, Abraham. *The Collected Works of Abraham Lincoln*. Ed. Roy P. Basler.

8 vols. New Brunswick: Rutgers UP, 1953. Print.

If you cite a multivolume work published over a period of years, give the inclusive years as the publication date: for instance, Cambridge: Harvard UP, 1978-90.

31. A series (print)

Bergman, Ingmar. *The Seventh Seal*. New York: Simon, 1995. Print. Mod. Film

Scripts Ser. 12.

Place the name of the series (not quoted or italicized) at the end of the entry, followed by the series number (if any) and a period. Abbreviate common words such as *modern* and *series*.

32. A republished book (print)

James, Henry. *The Bostonians*. 1886. New York: Penguin, 2001. Print.

Republished books include books reissued under new titles and paperbound editions of books originally released in hard covers. Place the original publication date after the title, and then provide the full publication information for the source you are using. If the book originally had a different title, add this title and its publication date after Rpt. of ("Reprint of") at the end of the entry—for example, Rpt. of *Thomas Hardy: A Life*. 1941.

33. The Bible (print)

The Bible. Print. King James Vers.

The Holy Bible. Trans. Ronald Youngblood et al. Grand Rapids: Zondervan,

1984. Print. New Intl. Vers.

When citing a standard version of the Bible (first example), do not italicize the title or the name of the version. You need not provide publication information. For an edition of the Bible (second example), italicize the title, provide editors' and/or translators' names, give full publication information, and add the version name at the end.

34. A book with a title in its title (print)

Eco, Umberto. *Postscript to* The Name of the Rose. Trans. William Weaver.

New York: Harcourt, 1983. Print.

When a book's title contains another book title (here *The Name of the Rose*), do not italicize the second title. When a book's title contains a quotation or the title of a work normally placed in quotation marks, keep the quotation marks and italicize both titles: *Critical Response to Henry James's "The Beast in the Jungle."*

35. Published proceedings of a conference (print)

Stimpson, Bill, ed. *2007 AWEA Annual Conference and Exhibition.* Proc. of

Amer. Wind Energy Assn. Conf., 3-6 June 2007, New York. Red Hook:

Curran, 2008. Print.

To cite the published proceedings of a conference, use a book model—here, an edited book (model 21). Between the title and the publication data, add information about the conference, such as its name, date, and location. You may omit any of this information that already appears in the source title. Treat a particular presentation at the conference like a selection from an anthology (model 25).

36. An introduction, preface, foreword, or afterword (print)

Donaldson, Norman. Introduction. *The Claverings.* By Anthony Trollope. New

York: Dover, 1977. vii-xv. Print.

An introduction, foreword, or afterword is often written by someone other than the book's author. When citing such a piece, give its name without quotation marks or italics, as with Introduction above. (If the piece has a title of its own, provide it, in quotation marks, between the name of the author and the name of the book.) Follow the title of the book with By and the book author's name. Give the inclusive page numbers of the part you cite. (In the example above, the small Roman numerals refer to the front matter of the book, before page 1.)

When the author of a preface or introduction is the same as the author of the book, give only the last name after the title:

Gould, Stephen Jay. Prologue. *The Flamingo's Smile: Reflections in Natural*

History. By Gould. New York: Norton, 1985. 13-20. Print.

37. A book lacking publication information or pagination (print)

Carle, Eric. *The Very Busy Spider.* New York: Philomel, 1984. N. pag. Print.

Some books are not paginated or do not list a publisher or a place of publication. To cite such a book, provide as much information as you can and indicate the missing information with an abbreviation: N.p. if no city of publication, n.p. if no publisher, n.d. if no publication date, and N. pag. if no page numbers.

Other nonperiodical print sources

38. A government publication (print)

United Nations. Dept. of Economic and Social Affairs. *World Youth Report 2010: Youth and Climate Change*. New York: United Nations, 2011. Print.

United States. Cong. House. Committee on Agriculture, Nutrition, and Forestry. *Food and Energy Act of 2008*. 110th Cong., 2nd sess. Washington: GPO, 2008. Print.

Wisconsin. Dept. of Public Instruction. *Bullying Prevention Program*. Madison: Wisconsin Dept. of Public Instruction, 2010. Print.

If a government publication does not list a person as author or editor, give the appropriate agency as author, as in the above examples. Provide information in the order illustrated, separating elements with periods: the name of the government, the name of the agency (which may be abbreviated), and the title and publication information. For a congressional publication (second example), give the house and committee involved before the title, and give the number and session of Congress after the title. In this example, GPO stands for the US Government Printing Office.

If a government publication lists a person as author or editor, treat the source as an authored or edited book:

Kim, Jiyul. *Cultural Dimensions of Strategy and Policy*. Carlisle: US Army War Coll., Strategic Studies Inst., 2009. Print.

See model 47 (p. 431) to cite a government publication you find on the Web.

39. A pamphlet or brochure (print)

Understanding Childhood Obesity. Tampa: Obesity Action Coalition, 2011. Print.

Most pamphlets and brochures can be treated as books. In this example, the pamphlet has no listed author, so the title comes first. If your source has an author, give his or her name first, followed by the title and publication information.

40. A dissertation (print)

McFaddin, Marie Oliver. *Adaptive Reuse: An Architectural Solution for Poverty and Homelessness*. Diss. U of Maryland, 2007. Ann Arbor: UMI, 2007. Print.

Treat a published dissertation like a book, but after the title insert Diss. ("Dissertation"), the institution granting the degree, and the year.

For an unpublished dissertation, use quotation marks rather than italics for the title and omit publication information.

> Wilson, Stuart M. "John Stuart Mill as a Literary Critic." Diss. U of Michigan, 1990. Print.

41. A letter (print)

> Buttolph, Mrs. Laura E. Letter to Rev. and Mrs. C. C. Jones. 20 June 1857. *The Children of Pride: A True Story of Georgia and the Civil War*. Ed. Robert Manson Myers. New Haven: Yale UP, 1972. 334-35. Print.

List a published letter under the writer's name. Specify that the source is a letter and to whom it was addressed, and give the date on which it was written. Treat the remaining information as with a selection from an anthology (model 25, p. 422). (See also model 15, p. 418, for the format of a letter to the editor of a periodical.)

For an unpublished letter in the collection of a library or archive, specify the writer, recipient, and date, as for a published letter. Then provide the medium, either MS ("manuscript") or TS ("typescript"). End with the name and location of the archive.

> James, Jonathan E. Letter to his sister. 16 Apr. 1970. MS. Jonathan E. James Papers. South Dakota State Archive, Pierre.

For a letter you received, give the name of the writer, specify yourself as the recipient, provide the date, and add the medium, MS or TS.

> Silva, Elizabeth. Letter to the author. 6 Apr. 2011. MS.

To cite an e-mail message or a discussion-group posting, see models 70–71 (p. 442).

4 | Listing nonperiodical Web sources

This section shows how to cite nonperiodical sources that you find on the Web. These sources may be published only once or occasionally, or they may be updated frequently but not regularly. (Most online magazines and newspapers fall into the latter category. See pp. 429–30.) Some nonperiodical Web sources are available only on the Web (next page); others are available in other media as well (pp. 434–36). See models 62–67 (pp. 437–41) to cite a scholarly journal that you find on the Web and any periodical that you find in an online database.

Video tutorial

The MLA does not require a URL (electronic address) in Web source citations unless a source is hard to find without it or could be confused with another source. See model 61 (p. 436) for the form to use when citing a URL.

Note The *MLA Handbook* does not label its examples of nonperiodical Web sources as particular types. For ease of reference, the following models identify and illustrate common Web sources. If you don't see just what you need, consult the index of models on the **MLA** tabbed divider for a similar source type whose format you can adapt. If your source does not include all of the information needed for a complete citation, find and list what you can.

Nonperiodical sources available only on the Web

Many nonperiodical Web sources are available only online. The following list, adapted from the *MLA Handbook,* itemizes the possible elements in a nonperiodical Web publication, in order of their appearance in a works-cited entry:

- **Name of the author or other person responsible for the source,** such as an editor, translator, or performer. See models 1–6 (pp. 412–13) for the handling of authors' names. For other kinds of contributors, see models 21–23 (editors and translators) and models 74, 76–77, and 83 (performers, directors, and so on).
- **Title of the cited work.** Use quotation marks for titles of articles, blog entries, and other sources that are parts of larger works. Use italics for books, plays, and other sources that are published independently.
- **Title of the Web site,** in italics.
- **Version or edition cited,** if any, following model 20 (p. 419)—for example, *Index of History Periodicals.* 2nd ed.
- **Publisher or sponsor of the site,** followed by a comma. If you cannot find a publisher or sponsor, use N.p. ("No publisher") instead. (See the Corbett example opposite.)
- **Date of electronic publication, latest revision, or posting.** If the date includes the month, abbreviate it unless it is May, June, or July. If no date is available, use n.d. ("no date") instead. (See the Corbett example opposite.)
- **Medium of publication:** Web.
- **Date of your access:** day, month, year. Abbreviate all months except May, June, and July.

For some Web sources, you may want to include information that is not on this list, such as the names of both the writer and the performers in a *YouTube* video.

42. A short work with a title (Web)

Murray, Amanda. "The Birth of Hip-Hop: Innovation against the Odds." *The Lemelson Center for the Study of Invention and Innovation.* Smithsonian Inst., Natl. Museum of Amer. Hist., Oct. 2010. Web. 11 Apr. 2011.

See pp. 430–31 for an analysis of this entry and the location of the required information on the Web site. If the short work you are citing lacks an author, follow model 6 (p. 413) for an anonymous source, starting with the title as in the following example.

"Clean Energy." *Union of Concerned Scientists: Citizens and Scientists for Environ-*
mental Solutions. Union of Concerned Scientists, 2010. Web. 11 Mar. 2011.

To cite a short Web source that also appears in another medium
(such as print), see models 56–60 (pp. 434–36). To cite an article
from a Web journal or from an online database, see models 62–67
(pp. 437–41).

43. A short work without a title (Web)

Cyberbullying Research Center. Home page. Cyberbullying Research Center,
2010. Web. 15 May 2011.

If you are citing an untitled short work from a Web site, such as the
home page of a site or a posting to a blog, insert Home page, Online posting, or another descriptive label in place of the title. Do not use quotation marks or italics for this label.

44. An entire site (Web)

Crane, Gregory, ed. *The Perseus Digital Library.* Dept. of Classics, Tufts U,
14 Mar. 2011. Web. 21 July 2011.

When citing an entire Web site—for instance, a Web-only book or a
foundation site—include the name of the editor, author, or compiler
(if available); the title of the site; the sponsor; the date of publication
or most recent update; the medium (Web); and your date of access.
    If your source lacks a named author or editor, begin with the
site title:

Union of Concerned Scientists: Citizens and Scientists for Environmental Solutions.
Union of Concerned Scientists, 2011. Web. 11 Mar. 2011.

If your source lacks a sponsor, use the abbreviation N.p. ("No publisher"). If it lacks a publication date, use the abbreviation n.d. The
source below lacks both a sponsor and a publication date:

Corbett, John. *STARN: Scots Teaching and Resource Network.* N.p., n.d. Web. 26
Nov. 2010.

45. An article in a newspaper (Web)

Broad, William J. "Black Market Trinkets from Space." *New York Times.* New
York Times, 4 Apr. 2011. Web. 8 May 2011.

Even when an online newspaper relates to a printed version, it is
treated as a nonperiodical source because the online content can
change often and unpredictably. List the author, article title, and
newspaper title as in model 10 or 11 (p. 415). Then give the publisher's name and the date. End with the medium of publication
(Web) and the date of your access. Use this format to adapt the models for print periodicals if you need to cite a Web newspaper review,

Format for a short work on the Web

Top of page

Bottom of page

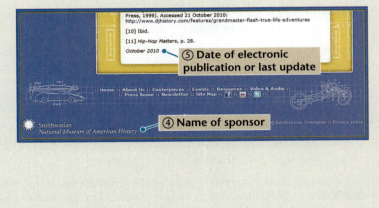

editorial, letter to the editor, interview, or article in a series (models 14–17, p. 418).

See model 66 to cite a newspaper article in an online database.

46. An article in a magazine (Web)

Yabroff, Jennie. "Autism Finds Its Voice." *Newsweek*. Newsweek, 16 Jan. 2011. Web. 15 Mar. 2011.

Even when an online magazine relates to a printed version, it is treated as a nonperiodical source because the online content can change often and unpredictably. List the author, article title, and

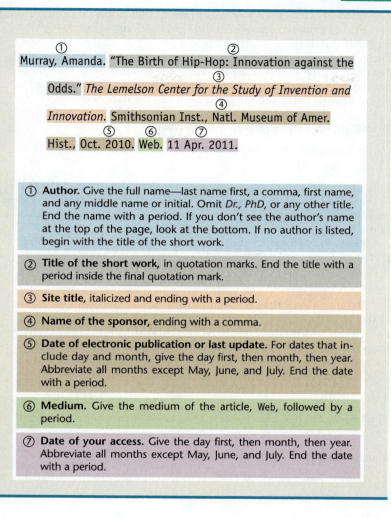

① ②
Murray, Amanda. "The Birth of Hip-Hop: Innovation against the
③
Odds." *The Lemelson Center for the Study of Invention and*
④
Innovation. Smithsonian Inst., Natl. Museum of Amer.
⑤ ⑥ ⑦
Hist., Oct. 2010. Web. 11 Apr. 2011.

① **Author.** Give the full name—last name first, a comma, first name, and any middle name or initial. Omit *Dr., PhD,* or any other title. End the name with a period. If you don't see the author's name at the top of the page, look at the bottom. If no author is listed, begin with the title of the short work.

② **Title of the short work,** in quotation marks. End the title with a period inside the final quotation mark.

③ **Site title,** italicized and ending with a period.

④ **Name of the sponsor,** ending with a comma.

⑤ **Date of electronic publication or last update.** For dates that include day and month, give the day first, then month, then year. Abbreviate all months except May, June, and July. End the date with a period.

⑥ **Medium.** Give the medium of the article, Web, followed by a period.

⑦ **Date of your access.** Give the day first, then month, then year. Abbreviate all months except May, June, and July. End the date with a period.

magazine title as in model 12 or 13 (pp. 416–18). Then give the publisher's name and the date. End with the medium (Web) and the date of your access. Use this format to adapt the models for print periodicals if you need to cite a Web magazine review, editorial, letter to the editor, interview, or article in a series or special issue (models 14–18, pp. 418–19).

See model 67 to cite a magazine article in an online database.

47. A government publication (Web)

United States. Dept. of Education. "Why Teach." *Teach.* US Dept. of
Education, n.d. Web. 1 Mar. 2011.

See model 38 for examples of government publications in print. Provide the same information for online publications, substituting Web for print publication information and adding your date of access. The preceding example includes the names of the government and department; the title of the source, in quotation marks; the title of the Web site, in italics; the name of the sponsor; n.d. (because there is no publication date); the medium (Web); and the date of access.

48. An article in a reference work (Web)

"Yi Dynasty." *Encyclopaedia Britannica Online*. Encyclopaedia Britannica, 2011.

    Web. 7 Apr. 2011.

This source does not list an author, so the entry begins with the title of the article and then proceeds as for other Web sources. If a reference article has an author, place the name before the article title, as in model 42.

For reference works that you find in print or on CD-ROM or DVD-ROM, see models 28 (p. 423) and 68 (p. 440), respectively.

49. A visual (Web)

To cite a visual that is available only on the Web, give the name of the artist or creator, the title of the work, the date of the work (if any), a word describing the type of visual (if not otherwise clear from the title of the visual or the site), the title of the Web site, the sponsor, the date of the site, the medium (Web), and your date of access. The following examples show a range of possibilities.

A work of art:

Simpson, Rick. *Overload. Museum of Computer Art*. Museum of Computer Art,

    2008. Web. 1 Apr. 2011.

A photograph:

Touboul, Jean. *Desert 1*. 2002. Photograph. *Artmuse.net*. Jean Touboul, 2007.

    Web. 14 Nov. 2010.

An advertisement:

FreeCreditReport.com. Advertisement. *Facebook*. Facebook, 2011. Web. 6 May

    2011.

A map, chart, graph, or diagram:

"Greenhouse Effect." Diagram. *Earthguide*. Scripps Inst. of Oceanography,

    2008. Web. 17 July 2011.

See also model 60 (p. 435) to cite a visual that appears both on a computer and in another medium; model 73 (p. 443) to cite a visual in a digital file; and models 78–82 (pp. 444–45) to cite a visual that isn't on the Web.

50. A television or radio program (Web)

Norris, Michele, host. *All Things Considered*. Natl. Public Radio, 6 Apr. 2011.
Web. 21 Apr. 2011.

The Web sites of television and radio networks and programs often include both content that was broadcast as part of a show and content that is unique to the site. Cite either kind of source by its title or by the name of the person whose work you are citing. Identify the role of anyone but an author (host in the example). Give the site title, the sponsor, the date, the medium (Web), and the date of your access. You may also cite other contributors (and their roles) after the title, as in model 52.

See also model 74 (p. 443) to cite a television or radio program that isn't on the Web.

51. A video recording (Web)

CBS News, prod. "1968 King Assassination Report." *YouTube*. YouTube, 3 Apr.
2008. Web. 22 Feb. 2011.

Cite a video on the Web either by its title or by the name of the person whose work you are citing—in this example, the organization that produced the video. Identify the role of anyone but an author (prod. in the example). Give the video title, the site title, the sponsor, the date, the medium (Web), and the date of your access. You may also cite other contributors (and their roles) after the title, as in model 52.

See also model 53 to cite a podcast of a video recording; model 59 (p. 435) to cite a video recording or film that appears both on the Web and in another medium (such as DVD); and model 77 (p. 444) to cite a film, DVD, or video recording that isn't on the Web.

52. A sound recording (Web)

Beglarian, Eve. *Five Things*. Perf. Beglarian et al. *Earbud Music: Eve Beglarian*.
N.p., 23 Oct. 2001. Web. 8 Mar. 2011.

Cite a musical sound recording by its title or by the name of the person whose work you are citing—in this example, the composer. (If the composer's name comes after the title, precede it with By. See the next example.) The preceding example also gives the work title, the performers of the work, the site title, the sponsor (here unknown, so replaced with N.p.), the date, the medium (Web), and the date of access.

The same format may be used for a spoken-word recording that you find on the Web:

Wasserstein, Wendy, narr. "Afternoon of a Faun." By Wasserstein. *The Borzoi Reader Online*. Knopf, 2001. Web. 14 Feb. 2011.

See also the next model to cite a sound podcast; model 58 to cite a sound recording that appears both on the Web and in another medium (such as CD); and model 76 (p. 444) to cite a sound recording that isn't on the Web.

53. A podcast (Web)

Glass, Ira. "Very Tough Love." *This American Life.* Chicago Public Media, 25 Mar. 2011. Web. 14 Apr. 2011.

This podcast from a radio program lists the author of a story on the show, the title of the story (in quotation marks), and the program (italicized) as well as the site title, sponsor, date, medium (Web), and access date. If a podcast does not list an author or other creator, begin with the title.

54. A blog entry (Web)

Marshall, Joshua Micah. "Explosion at Nuclear Plant." *Talking Points Memo.* TPM Media, 12 Mar. 2011. Web. 21 May 2011.

For a blog entry, give the author, the title of the entry, the title of the blog or site, the name of the sponsor (or N.p. if no sponsor is named), the publication date, the medium (Web), and the date of your access. See model 43 (p. 429) to cite a blog entry without a title.

55. A wiki (Web)

"Podcast." *Wikipedia.* Wikimedia, n.d. Web. 20 Nov. 2010.

For a wiki entry, follow the example: entry title, site title, sponsor, publication date (here n.d. because the wiki entry is undated), medium (Web), and date of access. Begin with the site title if you are citing the entire wiki.

Nonperiodical Web sources also available in print

Some sources you find on the Web may be books, poems, short stories, and other works that have been scanned from print versions. To cite such a source, generally provide the information for original print publication as well as that for Web publication. Begin your entry as if you were citing the print work, consulting models 19–41 for an appropriate format. Then, instead of giving "Print" as the medium, provide the title of the Web site you used, any version or edition number, the medium you used (Web), and the date of your access.

56. A short work with print publication information (Web)

Wheatley, Phillis. "On Virtue." *Poems on Various Subjects, Religious and Moral.* London, 1773. N. pag. *American Verse Project.* Web. 21 July 2011.

The print information for this poem follows model 25 (p. 422) for a selection from an anthology, but it omits the publisher's name because the anthology was published before 1900. The print information ends with N. pag. because the original source has no page numbers.

57. A book with print publication information (Web)

James, Henry. *The Ambassadors*. 1903. New York: Scribner's, 1909. *Oxford Text Archive*. Web. 5 May 2011.

The print information for this novel follows model 32 (p. 424) for a republished book, so it includes both the original date of publication (1903) and the publication information for the scanned book.

Nonperiodical Web sources also available in other media

Some visuals, films, and sound recordings that you find on the Web may have been published before in other media and then scanned or digitized for the Web. To cite such a source, generally provide the information for original publication as well as that for Web publication. Begin your entry as if you were citing the original, consulting models 74–84 (pp. 443–46) for an appropriate format. Then, instead of giving the original medium of publication, provide the title of the Web site you used, the medium you used (Web), and your date of access.

58. A sound recording with other publication information (Web)

"Rioting in Pittsburgh." CBS Radio, 1968. *Vincent Voice Library*. Web. 7 Dec. 2011.

For Web sound recordings with original publication information, base citations on model 76 (p. 444), adding the information for Web publication.

59. A film or video recording with other publication information (Web)

Coca-Cola. Advertisement. Dir. Haskell Wexler. 1971. *American Memory*. Lib. of Cong. Web. 8 Apr. 2011.

For Web films or videos with original publication information, base citations on model 77 (p. 444), adding the information for Web publication.

60. A visual with other publication information (Web)

Pollock, Jackson. *Lavender Mist: Number 1*. 1950. Natl. Gallery of Art, Washington. *WebMuseum*. Web. 7 Apr. 2011.

Keefe, Mike. "World Education Rankings." Cartoon. *Denver Post* 5 Apr. 2011. *PoliticalCartoons.com*. Web. 9 May 2011.

For Web visuals with original publication information, base citations on models 78–82 (pp. 444–45), adding the information for Web publication.

Citation of a URL

61. A source requiring citation of the URL (Web)

Joss, Rich. "Dispatches from the Ice: The Second Season Begins." *Antarctic Expeditions*. Smithsonian Natl. Zoo and Friends of the Natl. Zoo, 26 Oct. 2007. Web. 26 Sept. 2011. <http://nationalzoo.si.edu/ ConservationAndScience/AquaticEcosystems/Antarctica/Expedition/ FieldNew/2-FieldNews.cfm>.

The MLA does not require URLs in works-cited entries. However, you should include URLs when your instructor requires them. You should also give a URL when readers may not be able to locate a source without one. For example, using a search engine to find "Dispatches from the Ice" (the title in the example) yields more than ten hits, one of which links to the correct site but the wrong document.

If you need to include a URL, ensure accuracy by using Copy and Paste to duplicate it in a file or an e-mail to yourself. In your list of works cited, give the URL after your date of access and a period. Put angle brackets on both ends of the URL, and end with a period. Break URLs *only* after slashes—do not hyphenate.

5 | Listing journals on the Web and periodicals in online databases

This section covers two kinds of periodicals: scholarly journals that you reach directly on the Web (facing page) and journals, newspapers, and magazines that you reach through online databases (p. 439). Newspapers and magazines that you reach directly on the Web are typically not periodicals (because their content changes often and unpredictably), so they are covered in models 45 and 46 (pp. 429–30).

Citations for Web journals and for periodicals in online databases resemble those for print periodicals, with some changes for the different medium. The following list, adapted from the *MLA Handbook*, itemizes the possible elements in the online periodicals, in order of their appearance in a works-cited entry.

- **Author.** Give the author's last name, first name, and any middle name or initial. To cite more than one author, two articles by the same author, a corporate author, or an article with no named author, see models 2–6.
- **Title of the article,** in quotation marks. Give the title and any subtitle. End the title with a period inside the final quotation mark.

- **Title of the periodical,** in italics. Omit any *A, An,* or *The* from the beginning of the title. Do not end with a period.
- **Publication information.** The treatment of volume and issue numbers and publication dates varies depending on the kind of periodical you are citing, as shown in the following models and explained with the corresponding print models on pp. 414–17. If you include the month of publication, abbreviate it unless it is May, June, or July. For the distinction between journals and magazines, see **7** p. 325.
- **Page numbers of the article,** without "pp." If the article is unpaged, give n. pag. instead.
- **Name of the database,** in italics, if you found the source through an online database.
- **Medium of publication:** Web, followed by a period.
- **Date of your access:** day, month, year. Abbreviate all months except May, June, and July.

Web journals consulted directly

The journals you find directly on the Web may be published only online or may be published in print versions as well. The citation format is the same in either case: begin with an appropriate print model (pp. 414–17), but replace "Print" with Web and add your access date. Because many Web journals are unpaged, you may have to substitute n. pag. for page numbers, as in the entry illustrated on the next page.

62. An article in a scholarly journal (Web)

Polletta, Francesca. "Just Talk: Public Deliberation after 9/11." *Journal of Public Deliberation* 4.1 (2008): n. pag. Web. 7 Apr. 2011.

See the next page for an analysis of this entry and the location of the required information in the Web journal. Use the same format to adapt the models for print periodicals if you need to cite a Web journal review, editorial, letter to the editor, interview, article in a series, or special issue (models 14–18, pp. 418–19).

For a journal article reached in an online database, see model 64.

63. An abstract of a journal article (Web)

Polletta, Francesca. "Just Talk: Public Deliberation after 9/11." *Journal of Public Deliberation* 4.1 (2008): n. pag. Abstract. Web. 7 Apr. 2011.

Treat a Web abstract like a Web journal article, but add Abstract between the publication information and the medium. (You may omit this label if the journal title clearly indicates that the cited work is an abstract.) See model 65 to cite an abstract in an online database.

Format for a journal article on the Web

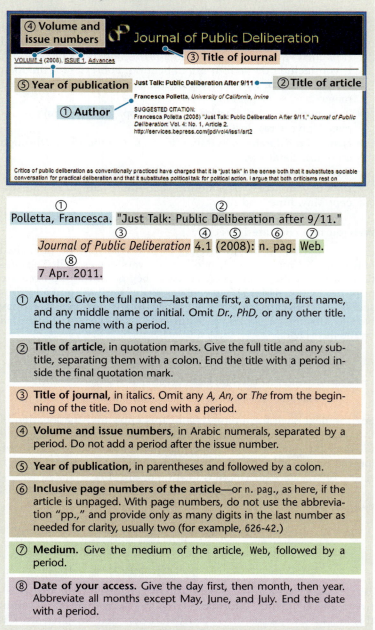

④ **Volume and issue numbers**

Journal of Public Deliberation

VOLUME 4 (2008), ISSUE 1, Advances

③ **Title of journal**

⑤ **Year of publication**

Just Talk: Public Deliberation After 9/11 ● ② **Title of article**

Francesca Polletta, *University of California, Irvine*

① **Author**

SUGGESTED CITATION:
Francesca Polletta (2008) "Just Talk: Public Deliberation After 9/11," *Journal of Public Deliberation:* Vol. 4: No. 1, Article 2.
http://services.bepress.com/jpd/vol4/iss1/art2

Critics of public deliberation as conventionally practiced have charged that it is "just talk" in the sense both that it substitutes sociable conversation for practical deliberation and that it substitutes political talk for political action. I argue that both criticisms rest on

① ②
Polletta, Francesca. "Just Talk: Public Deliberation after 9/11."
③ ④ ⑤ ⑥ ⑦
Journal of Public Deliberation 4.1 (2008): n. pag. Web.
⑧
7 Apr. 2011.

① **Author.** Give the full name—last name first, a comma, first name, and any middle name or initial. Omit *Dr., PhD,* or any other title. End the name with a period.

② **Title of article,** in quotation marks. Give the full title and any sub-title, separating them with a colon. End the title with a period inside the final quotation mark.

③ **Title of journal,** in italics. Omit any *A, An,* or *The* from the beginning of the title. Do not end with a period.

④ **Volume and issue numbers,** in Arabic numerals, separated by a period. Do not add a period after the issue number.

⑤ **Year of publication,** in parentheses and followed by a colon.

⑥ **Inclusive page numbers of the article**—or n. pag., as here, if the article is unpaged. With page numbers, do not use the abbreviation "pp.," and provide only as many digits in the last number as needed for clarity, usually two (for example, 626-42.)

⑦ **Medium.** Give the medium of the article, Web, followed by a period.

⑧ **Date of your access.** Give the day first, then month, then year. Abbreviate all months except May, June, and July. End the date with a period.

Web periodicals consulted in online databases

Many articles in journals, newspapers, and magazines are available in online databases that you reach through your library's Web site, such as *Academic Search Complete, ProQuest,* and *Project Muse.* Follow models 7–18 (pp. 414–19) for print periodicals, but replace "Print" with the title of the database you consulted, the medium (Web), and the date of your access.

64. An article in a scholarly journal (online database)

Penuel, Suzanne. "Missing Fathers: *Twelfth Night* and the Reformation of
   Mourning." *Studies in Philology* 107.1 (2010): 74-96. *Academic Search
   Complete.* Web. 10 Apr. 2011.

See the next two pages for an analysis of the preceding entry and the location of the required information in the database.

65. An abstract of a journal article (online database)

Penuel, Suzanne. "Missing Fathers: *Twelfth Night* and the Reformation of
   Mourning." *Studies in Philology* 107.1 (2010): 74-96. Abstract. *Academic
   Search Complete.* Web. 10 Apr. 2011.

Treat an abstract in an online database like a journal article in a database, but add Abstract between the publication information and the database title. (You may omit this label if the journal title clearly indicates that the cited work is an abstract.)

66. An article in a newspaper (online database)

Ball, Jeffrey. "Wind Power Hits a Trough." *Wall Street Journal* 5 Apr. 2011,
   eastern ed.: B1+. *LexisNexis Academic.* Web. 10 Sept. 2011.

Follow model 10 or 11 (p. 415) for citing author, title of article, title of newspaper, publication date, edition (if any), and page numbers. Add the title of the database, the medium (Web), and the date of your access.

67. An article in a magazine (online database)

Katz, Jamie. "The Painting in the Cellar." *Smithsonian* Apr. 2011: 60-65.
   ProQuest Research Library. Web. 3 Aug. 2011.

Follow model 12 or 13 (pp. 416–18) for citing author, title of article, title of magazine, publication date, and page numbers. Add the title of the database, the medium (Web), and the date of your access.

Format for a journal article in an online database

② **Title of article**

Missing Fathers: Twelfth Night and the Reformation of Mourning.

① **Author**   ⑤ **Year of publication**   ④ **Volume and issue numbers**

Authors: Penuel, Suzanne[1]

Source: Studies in Philology; Winter2010, Vol. 107 Issue 1, p74-96, 23p

Document Type: Literary Criticism   ③ **Title of journal**   ⑥ **Inclusive page numbers**

Subject Terms: *CRITICISM
*FATHERS & daughters
*INTERGENERATIONAL relations

Reviews & Products: TWELFTH Night (Theatrical production)

People: SHAKESPEARE, William, 1564-1616 -- Criticism & interpretation

Abstract: A literary criticism is presented of the play "Twelfth Night," by William Shakespeare, in which the absence of fathers and what that may mean is discussed. It notes that no older generation exists in the play to hover over the young and tamp down their sexuality, yet this does not result in celebration. Instead, a feeling of loss prevails. Various passages in the verse are analyzed to shed light on mourning rituals, doubling and gender changes in some of the characters.

Author Affiliations: [1]University of South Carolina Lancaster

ISSN: 00393738

Accession Number: 46990801

Database: Academic Search Complete   ⑦ **Name of database**

---

6 | Listing other electronic sources

Publications on CD-ROM or DVD-ROM

68. A nonperiodical CD-ROM or DVD-ROM

Nunberg, Geoffrey. "Usage in the Dictionary." *The American Heritage Dictionary of the English Language*. 4th ed. Boston: Houghton, 2000. CD-ROM.

Penuel, Suzanne. "Missing Fathers: *Twelfth Night* and the
Reformation of Mourning." *Studies in Philology* 107.1
(2010): 74-96. *Academic Search Complete.* Web.
10 Apr. 2011.

① **Author.** Give the full name—last name first, a comma, first name, and any middle name or initial. Omit *Dr., PhD,* or any other title. End the name with a period.

② **Title of the article,** in quotation marks. End the title with a period inside the final quotation mark. (Note that the play title *Twelfth Night* is italicized within the quoted article title.)

③ **Title of journal,** in italics. Omit any *A, An,* or *The* from the beginning of the title. Do not end with a period.

④ **Volume and issue numbers,** in Arabic numerals, separated by a period. Do not add a period after the issue number.

⑤ **Year of publication,** in parentheses and followed by a colon.

⑥ **Inclusive page numbers** of article, without "pp." Provide only as many digits in the last number as needed for clarity, usually two. Use n. pag. if the article is unpaged.

⑦ **Name of the database,** in italics, ending with a period.

⑧ **Medium.** Give the medium of the article, Web, followed by a period.

⑨ **Date of your access.** Give the day first, then month, then year. Abbreviate all months except May, June, and July. End the date with a period.

Single-issue CD-ROMs may be encyclopedias, dictionaries, books, and other resources that are published just once, like print books. Follow models 19–37 for print books (pp. 419–26), but replace "Print" with CD-ROM or DVD-ROM. If the disc has a vendor that differs from the publisher of the work, add the vendor's place of publication, name, and publication date after the medium—for instance, Oklahoma City: Soquest, 2010.

See also models 28 (p. 423) and 48 (p. 432) to cite reference works in print and on the Web.

69. A periodical CD-ROM or DVD-ROM

Kolata, Gina. "Gauging Body Mass Index in a Changing Body." *New York Times* 28 June 2005, natl. ed.: D1+. CD-ROM. *New York Times Ondisc*. UMI-ProQuest. Sept. 2005.

Databases on CD-ROM or DVD-ROM are issued periodically—for instance, every six months or every year. The journals, newspapers, and other publications included in such a database are generally available in print as well, so your works-cited entry should give the information for both formats. Start with information for the print version, following models 7–18 (pp. 414–19). (The article here appeared in the *New York Times*.) Then replace "Print" with the medium (CD-ROM or DVD-ROM), the database title, the vendor's name (UMI-ProQuest in the example), and the database publication date.

E-mail and discussion-group postings

70. An e-mail message

Bailey, Natasha. "Re: Cairo." Message to the author. 27 Mar. 2011. E-mail.

For e-mail, give the writer's name; the title, if any, from the e-mail's subject heading, in quotation marks; Message to the author (or the name of a recipient besides you); the date of the message; and the medium, E-mail. You do not need to include the date of your access to the e-mail.

71. A posting to a discussion group

Williams, Frederick. "Circles as Primitive." *The Math Forum @ Drexel*. Drexel U, 28 Feb. 2008. E-mail.

Cite a posting to a discussion group like a blog entry (model 54, p. 434). This example for a discussion-list posting includes the author's name, the title of the posting, the title of the discussion list, the name of the sponsor, the date of the posting, and the medium (E-mail). If the posting is untitled, give Online posting instead. You need not add the date of your access.

Digital files

You may want to cite a digital file that is not on the Web or on a disc, such as an electronic book, a PDF document, a JPEG image, or an MP3 sound recording that you downloaded onto your computer. Use the appropriate model for your kind of source (for instance, model 79 for a personal photograph), but replace the medium with the file format you're using. If you don't know the file format, use Digital file for the medium.

72. A text file (digital)

Berg, John K. "Estimates of Persons Driving While Intoxicated." *Law Enforcement Today* 22 Apr. 2011. PDF file.

Packer, George. *Interesting Times: Writings from a Turbulent Decade*. New York: Farrar, 2010. Kindle file.

73. A media file (digital)

Springsteen, Bruce. "This Life." *Working on a Dream*. Columbia, 2009. MP3 file.

Girls playing basketball. Personal photograph by Granger Goetz. 2011. JPEG file.

7 | Listing other print and nonprint sources

The source types covered in this section are not on a computer or, generally, in printed sources. Most of them have parallel citation formats elsewhere in this chapter when you reach them through electronic and print media. See model 16 (p. 418) to cite an interview in print. See models 49–52 (pp. 432–33) to cite visuals, television and radio programs, video recordings, and sound recordings that are available only on the Web. See models 58–60 (p. 435) to cite such sources when they are available on the Web and in other media. And see model 73 to cite such sources in digital files.

74. A television or radio program

"The Time Warp." By Zoanne Clark. Dir. Rob Corn. *Grey's Anatomy*. ABC. KGO, San Francisco, 18 Feb. 2010. Television.

Start with the title unless you are citing the work of a person or persons. The example here cites an episode title (in quotation marks) and the names of the episode's writer and director: By and Dir. identify their roles. Then the entry gives the program title (in italics), the name of the network, the call letters and city of the local station, the date, and the medium (Television). If you list individuals who worked on the entire program rather than an episode, put their names after the program title.

75. A personal or broadcast interview

Wang, Charlotte. Personal interview. 12 Mar. 2011.

Filkins, Dexter. Interview by Terry Gross. *Fresh Air*. Natl. Public Radio. WGBH, Boston, 6 Apr. 2011. Radio.

Begin with the name of the person interviewed. For an interview you conducted, specify Personal interview or the medium (such as Telephone interview or E-mail interview), and then give the date. For an interview you heard or saw, provide the title if any or Interview if there is no title. Add the name of the interviewer if he or she is identified. Then follow an appropriate model for the kind of source (here, a radio program), and end with the medium (here, Radio).

76. A sound recording

Rubenstein, Artur, perf. Piano Concerto no. 2 in B-flat. By Johannes Brahms. Cond. Eugene Ormandy. Philadelphia Orch. RCA, 1972. LP.

Springsteen, Bruce. "This Life." *Working on a Dream*. Columbia, 2009. CD.

Begin with the name of the individual whose work you are citing. Unless this person is the composer, identify his or her role, as with perf. ("performer") in the first example. If you're citing a work identified by form, number, and key (first example), do not use quotation marks or italics for the title. If you're citing a song or song lyrics (second example), give the title in quotation marks; then provide the title of the recording in italics. Following the title, identify the composer or author if you haven't already, after By, and name and identify other participants you want to mention. Then provide the manufacturer of the recording, the date of release, and the medium: LP in the first example, CD in the second.

77. A film, DVD, or video recording

The Joneses. Screenplay by Chris Tyrrell and Stacey Cruwys. Dir. Chris Tyrrell. Bjort, 2010. Film.

Start with the title of the work unless you are citing the work of a person (see the next example). Generally, identify and name the director. You may list other participants (writer, lead performers, and so on) as you judge appropriate. For a film, end with the distributor, date, and medium (Film).

For a DVD or videocassette, include the original release date (if any), the distributor's name and release date, and the medium (DVD or Videocassette).

Balanchine, George, chor. *Serenade*. Perf. San Francisco Ballet. Dir. Hilary Bean. 1991. PBS Video, 2006. DVD.

78. A painting, photograph, or other work of visual art

Arnold, Leslie. *Seated Woman*. N.d. Oil on canvas. DeYoung Museum, San Francisco.

Sugimoto, Hiroshi. *Pacific Ocean, Mount Tamalpais*. 1994. Photograph. Private collection.

To cite an actual work of art, name the artist and give the title (in italics) and the date of creation (or N.d. if the date is unknown). Then provide the medium of the work (such as Oil on canvas or Photograph) and the name and location of the owner, if known. (Use Private collection if not.)

For a work you see only in a reproduction, provide the complete publication information for the source you used. Omit the medium of the work itself, and replace it with the medium of the reproduction (Print in the following example). Omit such information only if you examined the actual work.

> Hockney, David. *Place Furstenberg, Paris*. 1985. Coll. Art Gallery, New Paltz. *David Hockney: A Retrospective*. Ed. Maurice Tuchman and Stephanie Barron. Los Angeles: Los Angeles County Museum of Art, 1988. 247. Print.

79. A personal photograph

> American white pelicans on Lake Winnebago. Personal photograph by the author. 3 Apr. 2011.

For a personal photograph by you or by someone else, give the subject (without quotation marks or italics), the photographer, and the date. (The current edition of the *MLA Handbook* does not cover personal photographs, so this format comes from the previous edition.)

80. A map, chart, graph, or diagram

> "The Sonoran Desert." Map. *Sonoran Desert: An American Deserts Handbook*. By Rose Houk. Tucson: Western Natl. Parks Assn., 2000. 12. Print.

Unless the creator of an illustration is given on the source, list the illustration by its title. Put the title in quotation marks if it comes from another publication or in italics if it is published independently. Then add a description (Map, Chart, and so on), the publication information, and the medium (here, Print).

81. A cartoon or comic strip

> Trudeau, Garry. "Doonesbury." Comic strip. *San Francisco Chronicle* 1 Sept. 2011: E6. Print.

Cite a cartoon or comic strip with the artist's name, the title (in quotation marks), the description Cartoon or Comic strip, the publication information, and the medium (here, Print).

82. An advertisement

> Fusion Hybrid by Ford. Advertisement. *New Yorker* 11 Apr. 2011: 91. Print.

Cite an advertisement with the name of the product or company advertised, the description Advertisement, the publication information, and the medium (Print, Television, Radio, and so on).

83. A performance

Levine, James, cond. Boston Symphony Orch. Symphony Hall, Boston. 2 May
2010. Performance.

The New Century. By Paul Rudnick. Dir. Nicholas Martin. Mitzi E. Newhouse
Theater, New York. 6 May 2009. Performance.

For a live performance, generally base your citation on film citations (model 77). Place the title first (second example) unless you are citing the work of an individual (first example). After the title, provide relevant information about participants as well as the theater, city, and performance date. Conclude with the medium (Performance).

84. A lecture, speech, address, or reading

Fontaine, Claire. "Economics." Museum of Contemporary Art. North Miami.
5 June 2010. Address.

Give the speaker's name, the title if any (in quotation marks), the title of the meeting if any, the name of the sponsoring organization, the location of the presentation, and the date. End with a description of the type of presentation (Lecture, Speech, Address, Reading).

Although the MLA does not provide a specific style for citing classroom lectures in your courses, you can adapt the preceding format for this purpose.

Cavanaugh, Carol. Class lecture on teaching mentors. Lesley U. 4 Apr. 2011.
Lecture.

58c Using MLA paper format

Video tutorial

The *MLA Handbook* provides guidelines for a fairly simple document format, with just a few elements. For guidelines on type fonts, headings, lists, visuals, and other features that MLA style does not specify, see **1** pp. 55–62.

The samples on the next page show the formats for the first page and a later page of a paper. For the format of the list of works cited, see pp. 411–12.

Margins Use one-inch margins on all sides of every page.

Spacing and indentions Double-space throughout. Indent the first lines of paragraphs one-half inch. (See opposite for treatment of poetry and long prose quotations.)

Paging Begin numbering on the first page, and number consecutively through the end (including the list of works cited). Use Arabic numerals (1, 2, 3) positioned in the upper right, about one-half inch from the top. Place your last name before the page number in case the pages later become separated.

First page of MLA paper

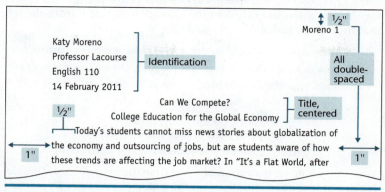

↕ ½"
Moreno 1

Katy Moreno
Professor Lacourse
English 110
14 February 2011

— Identification

All double-spaced

½"

Can We Compete?
College Education for the Global Economy

Title, centered

Today's students cannot miss news stories about globalization of the economy and outsourcing of jobs, but are students aware of how these trends are affecting the job market? In "It's a Flat World, after

1"   1"

Later page of MLA paper

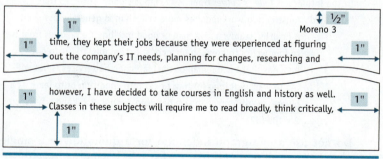

↕ ½"
Moreno 3

1"

1" time, they kept their jobs because they were experienced at figuring out the company's IT needs, planning for changes, researching and 1"

1" however, I have decided to take courses in English and history as well. Classes in these subjects will require me to read broadly, think critically, 1"

1"

Identification and title MLA style does not require a title page for a paper. Instead, give your name, your instructor's name, the course title, and the date on separate lines. Place this identification an inch from the top of the page, aligned with the left margin and double-spaced.

Double-space again, and center the title. Do not highlight the title with italics, underlining, boldface, larger type, or quotation marks. Capitalize the words in the title according to the guidelines in **6** p. 301. Double-space the lines of the title and between the title and the text.

Poetry and long prose quotations Treat a single line of poetry like any other quotation, running it into your text and enclosing it in quotation marks. You may run in two or three lines of poetry as well, separating the lines with a slash surrounded by space.

An example of Robert Frost's incisiveness is in two lines from "Death of the Hired Man": **"**Home is the place where, when you have to go there **/** They have to take you in**"** (119-20).

Always set off from your text a poetry quotation of more than three lines. Use double spacing above and below the quotation and for the quotation itself. Indent the quotation one inch from the left margin. *Do not add quotation marks.*

> In "The Author to Her Book," written in 1678, Anne Bradstreet characterizes her book as a child. In these lines from the poem, she captures a parent's and a writer's frustration with the imperfections of her offspring:
>
> > I washed thy face, but more defects I saw,
> >
> > and rubbing off a spot, still made a flaw.
> >
> > I stretched thy joints to make thee even feet,
> >
> > Yet still thou run'st more hobbling that is meet. (13-16)

Also set off a prose quotation of more than four typed lines. Double-space and indent as with the preceding poetry example. *Do not add quotation marks.*

> In the influential *Talley's Corner* from 1967, Elliot Liebow observes that "unskilled" construction work requires more skill than is generally assumed:
>
> > A healthy, sturdy, active man of good intelligence requires from two to four weeks to break in on a construction job. . . . It frequently happens that his foreman or the craftsman he services is not will-ing to wait that long for him to get into condition or to learn at a glance the difference in size between a rough 2 x 8 and a finished 2 x 10. (62)

Do not use a paragraph indention for a quotation of a single complete paragraph or a part of a paragraph. Use paragraph inden-tions of one-quarter inch only for a quotation of two or more com-plete paragraphs.

58d Examining a sample paper in MLA style

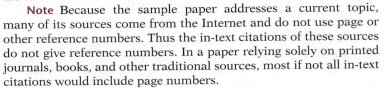

Student paper

Exercise

The sample paper beginning on p. 450 follows MLA guidelines for overall format, parenthetical citations, and the list of works cited. Annotations in the margins highlight features of the paper, such as the structure and the format of citations.

Note Because the sample paper addresses a current topic, many of its sources come from the Internet and do not use page or other reference numbers. Thus the in-text citations of these sources do not give reference numbers. In a paper relying solely on printed journals, books, and other traditional sources, most if not all in-text citations would include page numbers.

A note on outlines

Some instructors ask students to submit an outline of the final paper. For advice on constructing a formal or topic outline, see

1 pp. 20–21. Below is an outline of the sample paper following, written in complete sentences. Note that the thesis statement precedes either a topic or a sentence outline.

> *Thesis statement:* Although green consumerism can help the environment, consumerism itself is the root of some of the most pressing ecological problems we face. To make a real difference, we must consume less.

  I. Green products claiming to help the environment both appeal to and confuse consumers.

    A. The market for ecologically sound products is enormous.

    B. Determining whether or not a product is as green as advertised can be a challenge.

  II. Green products don't solve the high rate of consumption that truly threatens the environment.

    A. Overconsumption is a significant cause of three of the most serious environmental problems.

      1. It depletes natural resources.

      2. It contributes to pollution, particularly from the greenhouse gases responsible for global warming.

      3. It produces a huge amount of solid waste.

    B. The availability of greener products has not reduced the environmental effects of consumption.

III. Since buying green products does not reduce consumption, other solutions must be found for environmental problems.

    A. Experts have proposed many far-reaching solutions, but they require concerted government action and could take decades to implement.

    B. For shorter-term solutions, individuals can change their own behavior as consumers.

      1. Precycling may be the greenest behavior that individuals can adopt.

        a. Precycling means avoiding purchase of products that use raw materials and excessive packaging.

        b. More important, precycling means avoiding purchases of new products whenever possible.

      2. For unavoidable purchases, individuals can buy green products and influence businesses to embrace ecological goals.

Malik 1

Justin Malik

Ms. Rossi

English 112-02

18 April 2011

The False Promise of Green Consumerism

They line the aisles of just about any store. They seem to dominate television and print advertising. Chances are that at least a few of them belong to you. From organic jeans to household cleaners to hybrid cars, products advertised as environmentally friendly are readily available and are so popular they're trendy. It's easy to see why Americans are buying these things in record numbers. The new wave of "green" consumer goods makes an almost irresistible promise: we can save the planet by shopping.

Saving the planet does seem to be urgent. Thanks partly to former vice president Al Gore, who sounded the alarm in 2006 with *An Inconvenient Truth* and again in 2009 with *Our Choice,* the threat of global warming has become a regular feature in the news media and a recurring theme in popular culture. Unfortunately, as Gore himself points out, climate change is just one of many environmental problems competing for our attention: the rainforests are vanishing, our air and our water are dangerously polluted, alarming numbers of species are facing extinction, and landfills are overflowing (*Our Choice* 32). All the bad news can be overwhelming, and most people feel powerless to halt the damage. Thus it is reassuring that we may be able to help by making small changes in what we buy—but that is not entirely true. Although green consumerism can help the environment, consumerism itself is the root of some of the most pressing ecological problems we face. To make a real difference, we must consume less.

The market for items perceived as ecologically sound is enormous. Experts estimate that spending on green products already approaches $500 billion a year in the United States (Bhanoo). Shoppers respond well to new options, whether the purchase is as minor as a bottle of chemical-free dish soap or as major as a front-loading washing machine. Not surprisingly,

Identification: writer's name, instructor's name, course title, date.

Title centered.

Double-space throughout.

Introduction: establishes the issue with examples (first paragraph) and background (second paragraph).

Citation form: no parenthetical citation because author and titles are named in the text and discussion cites entire works.

Citation form: title for one of two works by the same author.

Thesis statement.

Background on green products (next two paragraphs).

Citation form: source with no page number because online source is unnumbered.

many businesses are responding by offering as many new eco-products as they can. Jack Neff reports in *Advertising Age* that the recent growth of green products is a "revolution" in market-ing. He cites a market research report by Datamonitor: between 2007 and 2009, the number of new packaged goods labeled as green increased by 600%, and sales of organic food and bever-ages outpaced other options despite the higher costs (1). These new products are offered for sale at supermarkets and at stores like Walmart, Target, Home Depot, Starbucks, and Pottery Barn. It seems clear that green consumerism has grown into a main-stream interest.

Determining whether or not a product is as green as ad-vertised can be a challenge. Claims vary: a product might be labeled as organic, biodegradable, energy efficient, recycled, carbon neutral, renewable, or just about anything that sounds environmentally positive. However, none of these terms carries a universally accepted meaning, and no enforce-able labeling regulations exist (Dahl A248). Some of the new product options offer clear environmental benefits: for in-stance, LED lightbulbs last fifty times longer than regular bulbs and draw about 15% of the electricity ("Lightbulbs" 26, 27), and paper made from recycled fibers saves many trees. But other "green" products just as clearly do little or nothing to help the environment: a disposable razor made with less plastic is still a disposable razor, destined for a landfill after only a few uses.

Distinguishing truly green products from those that are not so green merely scratches the surface of a much larger is-sue. The products aren't the problem; it's our high rate of con-sumption that poses the real threat to the environment. We seek what's newer and better—whether cars, clothes, phones, computers, televisions, shoes, or gadgets—and they all re-quire resources to make, ship, and use them. Political scien-tists Thomas Princen, Michael Maniates, and Ken Conca main-tain that overconsumption is a leading force behind several ecological crises, warning that

> ever-increasing pressures on ecosystems, life-
> supporting environmental services, and critical

Source author named in text, so not named in parenthetical citation.

Common-knowledge examples of stores and products do not require source citations.

Citation form: author not named in the text.

Citation form: shortened title for anonymous source.

Environmental effects of consumption (next four paragraphs). Writer synthesizes information from half a dozen sources to develop his own ideas.

Quotation over four lines set off without quotation marks. See pp. 447–48.

Ellipsis mark signals omission from quotation.

Citation form with displayed quotation: follows sentence period. Authors named in text, so not named in parenthetical citation.

Text refers to and discusses figure.

natural cycles are driven not only by the sheer
number of resource users . . . but also by the patterns of resource use themselves. (4)

Those patterns of resource use are disturbing. In just the last century, gross world product (the global output of consumer goods) grew at five times the rate of population growth—a difference explained by a huge rise in consumption per person. (See fig. 1.) Such growth might be good for the economy, but it is bad for the environment. As fig. 1 shows, it is accompanied by the depletion of natural resources, increases in the carbon emissions that cause global warming, and increases in the amount of solid waste disposal.

Figure presents numerical data visually.

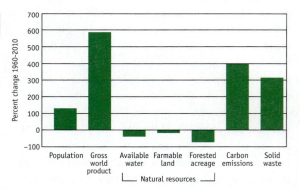

Figure caption explains the chart and gives complete source information.

Fig. 1. Global population, consumption, and environmental impacts, 1960-2010. Data from United Nations Development Programme; *Human Development Report: Changing Today's Consumption Patterns—For Tomorrow's Human Development* (New York: Oxford UP, 1998; print; 4); and from Earth Policy Inst.; "Data Center"; *Earth Policy Institute*; EPI, 12 Jan. 2011; Web; 16 Mar. 2011.

Brackets signal capitalization changed to integrate quotation with writer's sentence.

The first negative effect of overconsumption, the depletion of resources, occurs because the manufacture and distribution of any consumer product depends on the use of water, land, and raw materials such as wood, metal, and oil. Paul Hawken, a respected environmentalist, explains that just in the United States "[i]ndustry moves, mines, extracts, shovels, burns, wastes, pumps, and disposes of *4 million pounds of material* in order to provide one average . . . family's needs for a year" (qtd. in DeGraaf, Wann, and Naylor 85; emphasis added). The United Nations Development Programme's 1998 *Human Development Report* (still the most comprehensive study of the environmental impacts of consumerism) warns that many regions in the world don't have enough water, productive soil, or forests to meet the basic needs of their populations (4). More recent data from the Earth Policy Institute show that as manufacturing and per-person consumption continue to rise, the supply of resources needed for survival continues to decline. Thus heavy consumption poses a threat not only to the environment but also to the well-being of the human race.

In addition to using up scarce natural resources, manufacturing and distributing products harm the earth by spewing pollution into the water, soil, and air. The most worrisome aspect of that pollution may be its link to global warming. As Al Gore explains, the energy needed to power manufacturing and distribution comes primarily from burning fossil fuels, a process that releases carbon dioxide and other greenhouse gases into the air. Those gases build up and trap heat in the earth's atmosphere. The result, most scientists now believe, is increasing global temperatures that will raise sea levels, expand deserts, and cause more frequent floods and hurricanes (*Inconvenient* 26-27, 81, 118-19, 184). As the bar chart in fig. 1 shows, carbon emissions, like production of consumer goods in general, are rising at rates out of proportion with population growth. The more we consume, the more we contribute to global warming.

As harmful as they are, gradual global warming and the depletion of resources half a world away can be difficult to comprehend or appreciate. A more immediate environmental effect of our buying habits can be seen in the volumes of trash those habits create. The US Environmental Protection Agency found that in a single year (2009), US residents, corporations, and institutions produced 243 million tons of municipal solid waste, amounting to "4.34 pounds per person

Citation form: source with three authors; "qtd. in" indicates indirect source (Hawken quoted by DeGraaf, Wann, and Naylor); "emphasis added" indicates italics were not in original quotation.

Citation form: corporate author is named in the text, so page number only.

Citation form: no parenthetical citation because author is named in the text and online source has no page or other reference numbers.

Summary reduces six pages in the source to three sentences. Signal phrase and parenthetical citation mark boundaries of the summary.

Citation form: shortened title for one of two works by the same author; page numbers indicate exact locations of information in source.

Writer's own conclusion from preceding data.

Citation form: author (a US government body) named in text.

Malik 5

per day" (1). Nearly a third of that trash came just from the wrappers, cans, bottles, and boxes used for shipping consumer goods. Yet the mountains of trash left over from consumption are only a part of the problem. In industrial countries overall, 90 percent of waste comes not from what gets thrown out, but from the manufacturing processes of converting natural resources into consumer products (DeGraaf, Wann, and Naylor 198). Nearly everything we buy creates waste in production, comes in packaging that gets discarded immediately, and ultimately ends up in landfills that are already overflowing.

Unfortunately, the growing popularity of green products has not reduced the environmental effects of consumption. A study conducted by economists Jeff Rubin and Benjamin Tal found that while eco-friendly and energy-efficient products have become more available, "consumption is growing by ever-increasing amounts." The authors give the example of automobiles: in the last generation, cars have become much more energy efficient, but the average American now drives 2500 more miles a year, for a net gain in energy use (4-5). At the same time, per-person waste production in the United States has risen by more than 20% (United States 2). Greener products may reduce our cost of consumption and even reduce our guilt about consumption, but they do not reduce consumption and its effects.

If buying green won't solve the problems caused by overconsumption, what will? Politicians, environmentalists, and economists have proposed an array of far-reaching ideas, including creating a financial market for carbon credits and offsets, aggressively taxing consumption and pollution, offering financial incentives for environmentally positive behaviors, and even abandoning market capitalism altogether (de Blas). However, all of these are "top-down" solutions that require concerted government action. Gaining support for any one of them, putting it into practice, and getting results could take decades. In the meantime, the environment would continue to deteriorate. Clearly, short-term solutions are also essential.

Annotations (margin notes):

Citation form: source with three authors; authors not named in text.

Environmental effects of green consumption.

Citation form: authors are named in the text, so page numbers only.

Citation form: US government source not named in text.

Writer's own conclusion from preceding data.

Solutions to problem of consumption (next three paragraphs).

Citation form: author's name only, because scholarly article on the Web has no page or other reference numbers.

Malik 6

    The most promising short-term solution is for individuals to change their own behavior as consumers. The greenest behavior that individuals can adopt may be precycling, the term widely used for avoiding purchases of products that involve the use of raw materials. Precycling includes choosing eco-friendly products made of recycled or nontoxic materials (such as aluminum-free deodorants and fleece made from soda bottles) and avoiding items wrapped in excessive packaging (such as kitchen tools strapped to cardboard and printer cartridges sealed in plastic clamshells). More important, though, precycling means not buying new things in the first place. Renting and borrowing, when possible, save money and resources; so do keeping possessions in good repair and not replacing them until absolutely necessary. Good-quality used items, from clothing to furniture to electronics, can be obtained for free, or very cheaply, through online communities like *Craigslist* and *Freecycle,* from thrift stores and yard sales, or by trading with friends and relatives. When consumers choose used goods over new, they can help to reduce demand for manufactured products that waste energy and resources, and they can help to keep unwanted items out of the waste stream.

    Avoiding unnecessary purchases brings personal benefits as well. Brenda Lin, an environmental activist, explained in an e-mail interview that frugal living not only saves money but also provides pleasure:

> You'd be amazed at what people throw out or give away: perfectly good computers, oriental rugs, barely used sports equipment, designer clothes, you name it. . . . It's a game for me to find what I need in other people's trash or at Goodwill. You should see the shock on people's faces when I tell them where I got my stuff. I get almost as much enjoyment from that as from saving money and helping the environment at the same time.

Lin's experience relates to a study of the personal and social consequences of consumerism by the sociologist Juliet B. Schor. Schor found that the more people buy, the less happy they tend to feel because of the stress of working longer hours

Common-knowledge definition and writer's own examples do not require source citations.

Primary source: personal interview by e-mail.

Quotation of over four lines set off without quotation marks. See pp. 447–48.

Ellipsis mark signals omission from quotation.

Citation form: no parenthetical citation because author is named in the text and interview has no page or other reference numbers.

to afford their purchases (11-12). Researching the opposite effect, Schor conducted interviews with hundreds of Americans who had drastically reduced their spending so that they would be less dependent on paid work. For these people, she discovered, a deliberately lower standard of living improved quality of life by leaving more time to spend with family and pursue personal interests (136-42). Reducing consumption, it turns out, does not have to translate into sacrifice.

For unavoidable purchases like food and light bulbs, buying green can make a difference by influencing corporate decisions. Some ecologists and economists believe that as more shoppers choose earth-friendly products over their traditional counterparts—or boycott products that are clearly harmful to the environment—more manufacturers and retailers will look for ways to limit the environmental effects of their industrial practices and the goods they sell (de Blas; Gore, *Inconvenient* 314). Indeed, as environmental business consultant Joel Makower and his coauthors point out, Coca-Cola, Walmart, Proctor and Gamble, Dell, and other major companies have already taken up sustainability initiatives in response to market pressure. In the process, the companies have discovered that environmentally minded practices tend to raise profits and strengthen customer loyalty (5-6). By giving industry solid, bottom-line reasons to embrace ecological goals, consumer demand for earth-friendly products can magnify the effects of individual action.

Careful shopping can help the environment, but green doesn't necessarily mean "Go." All consumption depletes resources, increases the likelihood of global warming, and creates waste, so even eco-friendly products must be used in moderation. As individuals, we can each play a small role in helping the environment—and help ourselves at the same time—by not buying anything we don't really need, even if it seems environmentally sound. Reducing our personal impact on the earth is a small price to pay for preserving a livable planet for future generations.

Writer's own conclusion from two sources.

Benefits of green consumerism.

Citation form: two works in the same citation; shortened title for one of two works by the same author.

Citation form: authors are named in the text, so page numbers only.

Conclusion: summary and a call for action.

Malik 8

Works Cited

New page, double-spaced. Sources alphabetized by authors' last names.

Bhanoo, Sindya N. "Products That Are Earth-and-Profit Friendly." *New York Times*. New York Times, 11 June 2010. Web. 23 Mar. 2011.

Article in a newspaper online.

Dahl, Richard. "Green Washing: Do You Know What You're Buying?" *Environmental Health Perspectives* 18.6 (2010): A246-52. *Academic Search Complete*. Web. 23 Mar. 2011.

Article in a scholarly journal that numbers volumes and issues, consulted in an online database.

de Blas, Alexandra. "Making the Shift: From Consumerism to Sustainability." *Ecos* 153 (2010): n. pag. Web. 25 Mar. 2011.

Article in a Web scholarly journal that numbers only issues and does not use page numbers.

DeGraaf, John, David Wann, and Thomas H. Naylor. *Affluenza: The All-Consuming Epidemic*. 2nd ed. San Francisco: Berrett-Koehler, 2005. Print.

Print book with three authors.

Earth Policy Inst. "Data Center." *Earth Policy Institute*. EPI, 12 Jan. 2011. Web. 16 Mar. 2011.

Short, titled work on a Web site, with a corporate author.

Gore, Al. *An Inconvenient Truth: The Planetary Emergency of Global Warming and What We Can Do about It*. Emmaus: Rodale, 2006. Print.

Print book with one author.

---. *Our Choice: A Plan to Solve the Climate Crisis*. Emmaus: Rodale, 2009. Print

Second source by author of two cited works: three hyphens replace author's name.

"Lightbulbs." *Consumer Reports* Oct. 2010: 26-28. Print.

Anonymous article listed and alphabetized by title.

Lin, Brenda. Message to the author. 21 Mar. 2011. E-mail.

Personal interview by e-mail.

Makower, Joel, et al. *State of Green Business 2011*. GreenBiz.com. GreenBiz Group, 2011. Web. 25 Mar. 2011.

Source with more than three authors.

Neff, Jack. "Green-Marketing Revolution Defies Economic Turndown." *Advertising Age* 20 Apr. 2009: 1+. *Academic Search Complete*. Web. 25 Mar. 2011.

Article in a weekly magazine consulted in an online database.

Princen, Thomas, Michael Maniates, and Ken Conca. Introduction. *Confronting Consumption*. Ed. Princen, Maniates, and Conca. Cambridge: MIT P, 2002. 1-20. Print.

Introduction to a print anthology.

Rubin, Jeff, and Benjamin Tal. "Does Energy Efficiency Save Energy?" *StrategEcon*. CIBC World Markets, 27 Nov. 2007. Web. 23 Apr. 2011.

A short, titled work on a Web site, by two authors.

Schor, Juliet B. *The Overspent American: Upscaling, Downshifting, and the New Consumer*. New York: Basic, 1998. Print.

Print book with one author.

United Nations Development Programme. *Human Development Report: Changing Today's Consumption Patterns—For*

Print book with a corporate author.

Tomorrow's Human Development. New York: Oxford UP, 1998. Print.

United States. Environmental Protection Agency. Solid Waste and Emergency Response. *Municipal Solid Waste Generation, Recycling, and Disposal in the United States: Facts and Figures for 2009*. US Environmental Protection Agency, Dec. 2010. Web. 4 Apr. 2011.

US government source with no named author, so government body given as author.

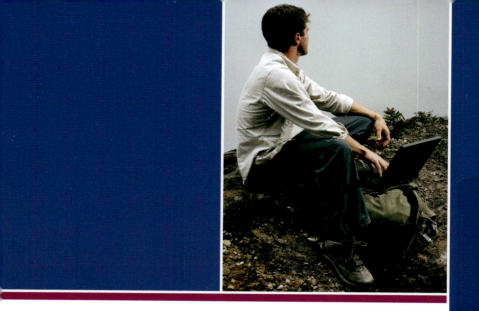

APA Documentation and Format

APA Documentation and Format

APA parenthetical text citations

APA references

Authors

Print periodicals

Print books

Web and other electronic sources

59 APA Documentation and Format

The style guide for psychology and some other social sciences is the *Publication Manual of the American Psychological Association* (6th ed., 2010). The APA provides answers to frequently asked questions at *www.apastyle.org/learn/faqs/index.aspx*.

In APA documentation style, you acknowledge each of your sources twice:

■ **In your text, a brief parenthetical citation adjacent to the borrowed material directs readers to a complete list of all the works you refer to.**

■ **At the end of your paper, the list of references includes complete bibliographical information for every source.**

Every entry in the list of references has at least one corresponding citation in the text, and every in-text citation has a corresponding entry in the list of references.

This chapter describes APA text citations (next page) and references (p. 465), details APA document format (p. 480), and concludes with a sample APA paper (p. 482).

mycomplab

Visit *mycomplab.com* for the eText and for resources and exercises on APA documentation and format.

59a   Writing APA parenthetical text citations

In APA documentation style, parenthetical citations within the body of the text refer the reader to a list of sources at the end of the text. See the **APA** divider for an index to the models for various kinds of sources.

Note   When you cite the same source more than once in a paragraph, APA style does not require you to repeat the date beyond the first citation as long as it's clear what source you refer to. Do give the date in every citation if your source list includes more than one work by the same author(s).

1. Author not named in your text

One critic of Milgram's experiments questions whether the researchers behaved morally toward their subjects (Baumrind, 1988).

When you do not name the author in your text, place in parentheses the author's last name, the date of the source, and sometimes the page number as explained below. Separate the elements with commas. Position the reference so that it is clear what material is being documented *and* so that the reference fits as smoothly as possible into your sentence structure. (See **MLA** pp. 408–09 for guidelines.)

Unless none is available, the APA requires a page or other identifying number for a direct quotation and recommends an identifying number for a paraphrase:

In the view of one critic of Milgram's experiments (Baumrind, 1988), the subjects "should have been fully informed of the possible effects on them" (p. 34).

Use an appropriate abbreviation before the number—for instance, p. for *page* and para. for *paragraph*. The identifying number may fall by itself in parentheses, as in the preceding example, or it may fall with the author and date: (Baumrind, 1988, p. 34). See also model 11, p. 464.

2. Author named in your text

Baumrind (1988) insisted that the subjects in Milgram's study "should have been fully informed of the possible effects on them" (p. 34).

When you use the author's name in the text, do not repeat it in the reference. Place the source date in parentheses after the author's name. Place any page or paragraph reference either after the borrowed material (as in the example) or with the date: (1988, p. 34).

3. A work with two authors

Bunning and Ellis (2010) revealed significant communication differences between teachers and students.

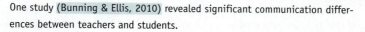

One study (Bunning & Ellis, 2010) revealed significant communication differences between teachers and students.

When given in the text, two authors' names are connected by and. In a parenthetical citation, they are connected by an ampersand, &.

4. A work with three to five authors

Pepinsky, Dunn, Rentl, and Corson (1999) demonstrated the biases evident in gestures.

In the first citation of a work with three to five authors, name all the authors.

In the second and subsequent references to a work with three to five authors, generally give only the first author's name, followed by et al. (Latin abbreviation for "and others"):

In the work of Pepinsky et al. (1999), the loaded gestures included head shakes and eye contact.

However, two or more sources published in the same year could shorten to the same form—for instance, two references shortening to Pepinsky et al., 1999. In that case, cite the last names of as many authors as you need to distinguish the sources, and then give et al.: for instance, (Pepinsky, Dunn, et al., 1999) and (Pepinsky, Bradley, et al., 1999).

5. A work with six or more authors

One study (McCormack et al., 2010) explored children's day-to-day experience of living with a speech impairment.

For six or more authors, even in the first citation of the work, give only the first author's name, followed by et al. If two or more sources published in the same year shorten to the same form, give additional names as explained with model 4.

6. A work with a group author

The students' later work improved significantly (Lenschow Research, 2009).

For a work that lists an institution, agency, corporation, or other group as author, treat the name of the group as if it were one person's name. If the name is long and has a familiar abbreviation, you may use the abbreviation in the second and subsequent citations. For example, you might abbreviate American Psychological Association as APA.

7. A work with no author or an anonymous work

One article ("Leaping the Wall," 2011) examines Internet freedom and censorship in China.

For a work with no named author, use the first two or three words of the title in place of an author's name, excluding an initial *The, A,* or *An.* Italicize book and journal titles, place quotation marks around article titles, and capitalize the significant words in all titles cited in the text. (In the reference list, however, do not use quotation marks for article titles, and capitalize only the first word in all but periodical titles. See p. 466.)

For a work that lists "Anonymous" as the author, use that word in the citation: (Anonymous, 2011).

8. One of two or more works by the same author(s)

At about age seven, most children begin to use appropriate gestures to reinforce their stories (Gardner, 1973a).

When you cite one of two or more works by the same author(s), the date will tell readers which source you mean—as long as your reference list includes only one source published by the author(s) in that year. If your reference list includes two or more works published by the same author(s) *in the same year,* the works should be lettered in the reference list (see p. 468). Then your text citation should include the appropriate letter with the date: 1973a above.

9. Two or more works by different authors

Two studies (Marconi & Hamblen, 1999; Torrence, 2007) found that monthly safety meetings can dramatically reduce workplace injuries.

List the sources in alphabetical order by their authors' names. Insert a semicolon between sources.

10. An indirect source

Supporting data appeared in a study by Wong (as cited in Gallivan, 2011).

The phrase as cited in indicates that the reference to Wong's study was found in Gallivan. Only Gallivan then appears in the list of references.

11. An electronic source

Ferguson and Hawkins (2006) did not anticipate the "evident hostility" of participants (para. 6).

Electronic sources can be cited like printed sources, usually with the author's last name and the publication date. When quoting or paraphrasing electronic sources that number paragraphs instead of pages, provide the paragraph number preceded by para. If the source does not number pages or paragraphs but does include headings, list the heading under which the quotation appears and then (counting paragraphs yourself) the number of the paragraph in which the quotation appears—for example, (Endter & Decker, 2010,

Method section, para. 3). When the source does not number pages or paragraphs or provide frequent headings, omit any reference number.

59b Preparing the APA reference list

In APA style, the in-text parenthetical citations refer readers to the list of sources at the end of the text. Title this list References and include in it the full publication information for every source you cited in your paper. Place the list at the end of the paper, and number its page(s) in sequence with the preceding pages.

The following sample shows the format of the first page of the APA reference list:

APA reference list

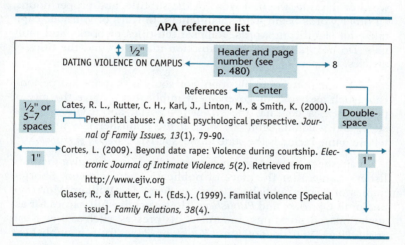

Arrangement Arrange sources alphabetically by the author's last name. If there is no author, alphabetize by the first main word of the title.

Spacing Double-space everything in the references, as shown in the sample, unless your instructor requests single spacing. (If you do single-space the entries themselves, always double-space *between* them.)

Indention As illustrated in the sample, begin each entry at the left margin, and indent the second and subsequent lines five to seven spaces or one-half inch. Your word processor can create this so-called hanging indent automatically.

Punctuation Separate the parts of the reference (author, date, title, and publication information) with a period and one space. Do not use a final period in references that conclude with a DOI or URL (see p. 472).

Authors For works with up to seven authors, list all authors with last name first, separating names and parts of names with commas. Use initials for first and middle names even when names are listed fully on the source itself. Use an ampersand (&) before the last author's name. See model 3 (opposite) for the treatment of eight or more authors.

Publication date Place the publication date in parentheses after the author's or authors' names, followed by a period. Generally, this date is the year only, though for some sources (such as magazine and newspaper articles) it includes the month and sometimes the day as well.

Titles In titles of books and articles, capitalize only the first word of the title, the first word of the subtitle, and proper nouns; all other words begin with small letters. In titles of journals, capitalize all significant words. Italicize the titles of books and journals. Do not italicize or use quotation marks around the titles of articles.

City and state of publication For sources that are not periodicals (such as books or government publications), give the city of publication, a comma, the two-letter postal abbreviation of the state, and a colon. Omit the state if the publisher is a university whose name includes the state name, such as University of Arizona.

Publisher's name Also for nonperiodical sources, give the publisher's name after the place of publication and a colon. Shorten names of many publishers (such as Morrow for William Morrow), and omit *Co.*, *Inc.*, and *Publishers*. However, give full names for associations, corporations, and university presses (such as Harvard University Press), and do not omit *Books* or *Press* from a publisher's name.

Page numbers Use the abbreviation p. or pp. before page numbers in books and in newspapers. Do *not* use the abbreviation for journals and magazines. For inclusive page numbers, include all figures: 667-668.

Digital Object Identifier (DOI) Many publishers assign a DOI to journal articles and other documents. A DOI functions as a unique identifier and link to the text. When a DOI is available, include it in your citation of any print or electronic source. (For example, see model 18, p. 472.) Do not add a period at the end of a DOI.

An index to the following models appears at the **APA** divider. If you don't see a model for the kind of source you used, try to find one that comes close, and provide ample information so that readers can trace the source. Often you will have to combine models to cite a source accurately.

1 | Listing authors

1. One author

Rodriguez, R. (1982). *A hunger of memory: The education of Richard Rodriguez.* Boston, MA: Godine.

The initial R. appears instead of the author's first name, even though the author's full first name appears on the source. In this book title, only the first words of the title and subtitle and the proper name are capitalized.

2. Two to seven authors

Nesselroade, J. R., & Baltes, P. B. (1999). *Longitudinal research in behavioral studies.* New York, NY: Academic Press.

With two to seven authors, separate authors' names with commas and use an ampersand (&) before the last author's name.

3. Eight or more authors

Wimple, P. B., Van Eijk, M., Potts, C. A., Hayes, J., Obergau, W. R., Smith, H., . . . Zimmer, S. (2001). *Case studies in moral decision making among adolescents.* San Francisco, CA: Jossey-Bass.

For a work by eight or more authors, list the first six authors' names, insert an ellipsis mark (three spaced periods), and then give the last author's name.

4. A group author

Lenschow Research. (2009). *Trends in secondary curriculum.* Baltimore, MD: Arrow Books.

For a work with a group author—such as a research group, a committee, a government agency, or a corporation—begin the entry with the group name. In the reference list, alphabetize the work as if the first main word (excluding any *The, A,* or *An*) were an author's last name.

5. Author not named (anonymous)

Merriam-Webster's collegiate dictionary (11th ed.). (2008). Springfield, MA: Merriam-Webster.

The Conversation. (2011, April 11). *Time, 177*(14), 4.

When no author is named, list the work under its title and alphabetize it by the first main word (excluding any *The, A, An*).

For a work whose author is actually given as "Anonymous," use that word in place of the author's name and alphabetize it as if it were a name:

Anonymous. (2006). *Teaching research, researching teaching.* New York, NY: Alpine Press.

6. Two or more works by the same author(s) published in the same year

Gardner, H. (1973a). *The arts and human development.* New York, NY: Wiley.

Gardner, H. (1973b). *The quest for mind: Piaget, Lévi-Strauss, and the structuralist movement.* New York, NY: Knopf.

When citing two or more works by exactly the same author(s), published in the same year, arrange them alphabetically by the first main word of the title and distinguish the sources by adding a letter to the date. Both the date and the letter are used in citing the source in your text (see p. 464).

When citing two or more works by exactly the same author(s) but *not* published in the same year, arrange the sources in order of their publication dates, earliest first.

2 Listing print periodicals: Journals, newspapers, magazines

7. An article in a journal (print)

Hirsh, A. T., Gallegos, J. C., Gertz, K. J., Engel, J. M., & Jensen, M. P. (2010). Symptom burden in individuals with cerebral palsy. *Journal of Rehabilitation Research & Development, 47,* 863-876.

See the illustration on pp. 470–71 for the basic format for a print journal article and the location of the required information in the journal.

Note Some journals number the pages of issues consecutively throughout a year, so that each issue after the first begins numbering where the previous issue left off—say, at page 132 or 416. For this kind of journal, give the volume number after the title, as above. The page numbers are enough to guide readers to the issue you used. Other journals and most magazines start each issue with page 1. For these journals and magazines, place the issue number in parentheses and not italicized immediately after the volume number. See model 10.

8. An abstract of a journal article (print)

Emery, R. E. (2006). Marital turmoil: Interpersonal conflict and the children of discord and divorce. *Psychological Bulletin, 92,* 310-330. Abstract obtained from *Psychological Abstracts*, 2007, *69,* Item 1320.

When you cite the abstract of an article rather than the article itself, give full publication information for the article, followed by Abstract obtained from and the information for the collection of abstracts, including title, date, volume and issue numbers, and either page number or other reference number (Item 1320 in the example).

9. An article in a newspaper (print)

Wade, N. (2011, April 15). Ancient clicks hint language is Africa-born. *The New York Times,* pp. A1, A3.

Give month *and* day along with year of publication. Use *The* in the newspaper name if the paper itself does. Precede the page number(s) with p. or pp.

10. An article in a magazine (print)

Walsh, B. (2011, April 11). The gas dilemma. *Time, 177*(14), 40-48.

Give the full date of the issue: year, followed by a comma, month, and day (if any). Give all page numbers even when the article appears on discontinuous pages, without "pp." If a magazine has volume and issue numbers, provide both because magazine issues are paginated separately. (See the note in model 7.)

11. A review (print)

Dinnage, R. (1987, November 29). Against the master and his men [Review of the book *A mind of her own: The life of Karen Horney,* by S. Quinn]. *The New York Times Book Review,* 10-11.

If the review is not titled, use the bracketed information as the title, keeping the brackets.

3 | Listing print books

12. Basic format for a book (print)

Ehrenreich, B. (2007). *Dancing in the streets: A history of collective joy.* New York, NY: Holt.

Give the author's or authors' names, following models 1–4. Then give the complete title, including any subtitle. Italicize the title, and capitalize only the first words of the title and subtitle. End the entry with the city and state of publication and the publisher's name. (See p. 466 for how to treat these elements.)

13. A book with an editor (print)

Dohrenwend, B. S., & Dohrenwend, B. P. (Eds.). (1999). *Stressful life events: Their nature and effects.* New York, NY: Wiley.

List the names of the editors as if they were authors, but follow the last name with (Eds.).—or (Ed.). with only one editor. Note the periods inside and outside the final parenthesis.

14. A book with a translator (print)

Trajan, P. D. (1927). *Psychology of animals* (H. Simone, Trans.). Washington, DC: Halperin.

Format for a print journal article

Journal cover

⑤ **Volume number**

Volume 47 • Number 9 • 2010

② **Year of publication**

JRRD
Journal of Rehabilitation Research & Development
www.rehab.research.va.gov/jrrd

④ **Title of periodical**

First page of article

Department of Veterans Affairs

JRRD — Volume 47, Number 9, 2010
Pages 863–876 ●

⑥ **Page numbers**

Journal of Rehabilitation Research & Development

③ **Title of article**

Symptom burden in individuals with cerebral palsy

① **Authors**

Adam T. Hirsh, PhD;[1] Juan C. Gallegos, BA;[1] Kevin J. Gertz, BA;[1] Joyce M. Engel, PhD;[2] Mark P. Jensen, PhD[1]
[1]Department of Rehabilitation Medicine, University of Washington School of Medicine, Seattle, WA; [2]Department of Occupational Science and Technology, University of Wisconsin-Milwaukee, Milwaukee, WI

Abstract—The current study sought to (1) determine the relative frequency and severity of eight symptoms in adults with cerebral palsy (CP), (2) examine the perceived course of these eight symptoms over time, and (3) determine the associations between the severity of these symptoms and psychosocial functioning. Eighty-three adults with CP completed a measure assessing the frequency, severity, and perceived course of eight ... gressive disorder, research over the past several years has highlighted a number of health conditions and functional declines experienced by individuals with CP as they age [2–5]. This is an important line of research since the vast majority of individuals with this condition survive until at least early adulthood [6–7]. In fact, the number of adults ...

The name of the translator appears in parentheses after the title, followed by a comma, Trans., a closing parenthesis, and a final period.

15. A later edition (print)

Bolinger, D. L. (1981). *Aspects of language* (3rd ed.). New York, NY: Harcourt Brace Jovanovich.

The edition number in parentheses follows the title and is followed by a period.

16. A work in more than one volume (print)

Lincoln, A. (1953). *The collected works of Abraham Lincoln* (R. P. Basler, Ed.). (Vol. 5). New Brunswick, NJ: Rutgers University Press.

Hirsh, A. T., Gallegos, J. C., Gertz, K. J., Engel, J. M., & Jensen, ①

M. P. (2010). Symptom burden in individuals with cerebral ② ③

palsy. *Journal of Rehabilitation Research & Development,* ④

47, 863-876. ⑤ ⑥

① **Authors.** Give each author's last name, first initial, and any middle initial. Separate names from initials with commas, and use & before the last author's name. Omit *Dr., PhD,* or any other title. See models 1–6 (pp. 467–68) for how to cite various numbers and kinds of authors.

② **Year of publication,** in parentheses and followed by a period.

③ **Title of article.** Give the full article title and any subtitle, separating them with a colon. Capitalize only the first words of the title and subtitle, and do not place the title in quotation marks.

④ **Title of periodical,** in italics. Capitalize all significant words and end with a comma.

⑤ **Volume number,** italicized and followed by a comma. Include just the volume number when all the issues in each annual volume are paginated in one sequence. Include the issue number only when the issues are paginated separately.

⑥ **Inclusive page numbers of article,** without "pp." Do not omit any numerals.

Lincoln, A. (1953). *The collected works of Abraham Lincoln* (R. P. Basler, Ed.). (Vols. 1-8). New Brunswick, NJ: Rutgers University Press.

The entry on the previous page cites a single volume (5) in the eight-volume set. The entry above cites all eight volumes. Use Vol. or Vols. in parentheses and follow the closing parenthesis with a period. In the absence of an editor's name, this description would follow the title directly: *The collected works of Abraham Lincoln* (Vol. 5).

17. An article or a chapter in an edited book (print)

Paykel, E. S. (1999). Life stress and psychiatric disorder: Applications of the clinical approach. In B. S. Dohrenwend & B. P. Dohrenwend (Eds.), *Stressful life events: Their nature and effects* (pp. 239-264). New York, NY: Wiley.

Give the publication date of the collection (1999 in the example) as the publication date of the article or chapter. After the article or chapter title and a period, say In and then provide the editors' names (in normal order), (Eds.) and a comma, the title of the collection, and the page numbers of the article in parentheses.

4 | Listing Web and other electronic sources

In APA style, most electronic references begin as those for print references do: author, date, title. Then you add information on how to retrieve the source.

- **Give a source's Digital Object Identifier (DOI), not the URL, when a DOI is available.** You may find the DOI on the source or by clicking on "Article" or "Cross-Ref." See models 18, 23, and 25 for examples of DOIs.
- **Give the URL when a DOI is not available.** Provide the URL in a statement beginning Retrieved from. For most sources, use the home page URL of the Web site where your source can be found. (See models 19 and 22.) Use the complete URL only if the source is hard to find from the home page. (See model 32.)
- **Do not add a period after a DOI or a URL.**
- **Break a DOI or URL from one line to the next only before punctuation,** such as a period or a slash. (But break after the two slashes in http://.) Do not hyphenate a URL or a DOI.
- **Generally, do not provide the date of your access.** Give the date only if the source is likely to change or if it lacks a publication date or version number. See model 29 for use of an access date.

If you don't see a model for your particular source, consult the index of models at the **APA** divider for a similar source type whose format you can adapt. If your source does not include all of the information needed for a complete citation, find and list what you can.

18. A journal article with a Digital Object Identifier (DOI) (Web)

Cunningham, J. A., & Selby, P. (2007). Relighting cigarettes: How common is it? *Nicotine and Tobacco Research, 9,* 621-623. doi:10.1080 /14622200701239688

See pp. 474–75 for the basic format for a periodical article that you access either directly online or through an online database, as well as the location of the required information on the source.

19. A journal article without a DOI (Web)

Polletta, F. (2008). Just talk: Public deliberation after 9/11. *Journal of Public Deliberation, 4*(1). Retrieved from http://services.bepress.com/jpd

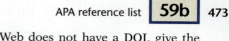

When a journal article on the Web does not have a DOI, give the URL of the journal's home page in a statement beginning Retrieved from. Do not add a period at the end of the URL.

20. A periodical article in an online database (Web)

Rosen, I. M., Maurer, D. M., & Darnall, C. R. (2008). Reducing tobacco use in adolescents. *American Family Physician, 77*, 483-490. Retrieved from http://www.aafp.org/online/en/home/publications/journals/afp.html

Generally, do not give the name of the database in which you found your source, because readers may not be able to find the source the same way you did. Instead, use a search engine to find the home page of the periodical and give the home page URL, as above.

If you don't find the home page of the periodical, then give the database name in your retrieval statement, as in the next example:

Smith, E. M. (1926, March). Equal rights—internationally! *Life and Labor Bulletin, 4,* 1-2. Retrieved from Women and Social Movements in the United States, 1600-2000, database.

21. An abstract of a journal article (Web)

Polletta, F. (2008). Just talk: Public deliberation after 9/11. *Journal of Public Deliberation, 4*(1). Abstract retrieved from http://services.bepress.com/jpd

22. An article in a newspaper (Web)

Broad, W. J. (2011, April 4). Black market trinkets from space. *The New York Times.* Retrieved from http://www.nytimes.com

Give the URL of the newspaper's home page in the retrieval statement. If you found the article in an online database, see model 20.

23. An article in a magazine (Web)

Hamzelou, J. (2011, April 17). How antidepressants boost growth of new brain cells. *New Scientist, 203*(24), 15. doi:10.1038/mp.2011.26

If the magazine article includes a DOI, give it as here. Otherwise, give the URL of the magazine's home page in a retrieval statement like the one for a newspaper article in model 22. If you found the article in an online database, see model 20.

24. Periodical content that appears only online (Web)

Osnos, E. (2011, April 11). Journey to the west [Supplemental material]. *The New Yorker.* Retrieved from http://www.newyorker.com

If you cite material from a periodical's Web site that is not included in the print version of the publication, add [Supplemental material] after the title and give the URL of the publication's home page.

Format for a journal article on the Web

Top of page

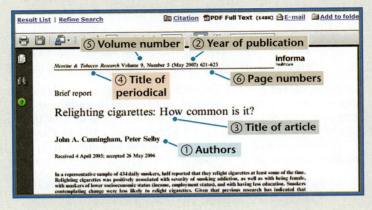

Bottom of page

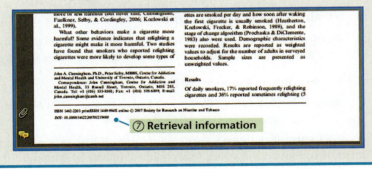

25. A review (Web)

Bond, M. (2008, December 18). Does genius breed success? [Review of the book *Outliers: The story of success,* by M. Gladwell]. *Nature, 456,* 785. doi:10.1038/456874a

Cite an online review like a print review (model 11, p. 469), concluding with retrieval information (here, a DOI).

26. A report or other material from the Web site of an organization or government (Web)

Greene, D. L., & Plotkin, S. E. (2011, January). *Reducing greenhouse gas emissions from U.S. transportation.* Retrieved from the Pew Center on Global Climate Change website: http://www.pewclimate.org

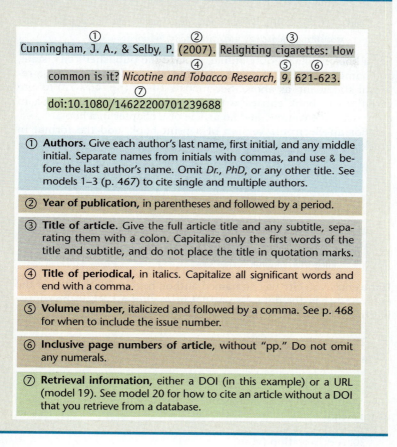

① **Authors.** Give each author's last name, first initial, and any middle initial. Separate names from initials with commas, and use & before the last author's name. Omit *Dr., PhD,* or any other title. See models 1–3 (p. 467) to cite single and multiple authors.

② **Year of publication,** in parentheses and followed by a period.

③ **Title of article.** Give the full article title and any subtitle, separating them with a colon. Capitalize only the first words of the title and subtitle, and do not place the title in quotation marks.

④ **Title of periodical,** in italics. Capitalize all significant words and end with a comma.

⑤ **Volume number,** italicized and followed by a comma. See p. 468 for when to include the issue number.

⑥ **Inclusive page numbers of article,** without "pp." Do not omit any numerals.

⑦ **Retrieval information,** either a DOI (in this example) or a URL (model 19). See model 20 for how to cite an article without a DOI that you retrieve from a database.

Treat the title of an independent Web document like the title of a book. Provide the name of the publishing organization as part of the retrieval statement when the publisher is not listed as the author, as in the Greene and Plotkin example.

If the document you cite is difficult to locate from the organization's home page, give the complete URL in the retrieval statement:

Union of Concerned Scientists. (2010). *Clean vehicles.* Retrieved from http://www.ucsusa.org/clean_vehicles

If the document you cite is undated, use the abbreviation n.d. in place of the publication date and give the date of your access in the retrieval statement:

U.S. Department of Education. (n.d.). *Teach.* Retrieved April 23, 2011, from http://www.teach.gov

27. A book (Web)

Reuter, P. (Ed.). (2010). *Understanding the demand for illegal drugs*. Retrieved from http://books.nap.edu/catalog.php?record_id=12976

For a book available only online, replace the publisher's city, state, and name with a DOI if one is available (see model 18) or with a retrieval statement, as above. See models 14–17 (pp. 469–72) to cite variations in book entries: a translator, a later edition, a book in more than one volume, and an article or a chapter in a book.

For an electronic version of a print book, add the format in brackets:

Freud, S. (1920). *Dream psychology: Psychoanalysis for beginners* (M. D. Eder, Trans.). [iPad version]. Retrieved from http://www.apple.com/itunes

28. An article in a reference work (Web)

Wood, R. (1998). Community organization. In W. A. Swatos, Jr. (Ed.), *Encyclopedia of religion and society*. Retrieved from http://hirr.hartsem.edu/ency/commorg.htm

If the entry you cite has no named author, begin with the title of the entry and then the date. Use a DOI instead of a URL if the source has one.

29. An article in a wiki (Web)

Clinical neuropsychology. (2010, November 12). Retrieved April 15, 2011, from Wikipedia: http://en.wikipedia.org/wiki/Clinical_neuropsychology

Give your date of retrieval for sources that are likely to change, such as this wiki.

30. A dissertation (Web)

A dissertation in a commercial database:

McFaddin, M. O. (2007). *Adaptive reuse: An architectural solution for poverty and homelessness* (Doctoral dissertation). Available from ProQuest Dissertations and Theses database. (ATT 1378764)

If a dissertation is from a commercial database, give the name of the database in the retrieval statement, followed by the accession or order number in parentheses.

A dissertation in an institutional database:

Chang, J. K. (2003). *Therapeutic intervention in treatment of injuries to the hand and wrist* (Doctoral dissertation). Retrieved from http://medsci.archive.liasu.edu/61724

If a dissertation is from an institution's database, give the URL in the retrieval statement.

See also model 38 (p. 478) for examples of print dissertations.

31. A podcast (Web)

Glass, I. (Producer). (2011, March 25). Very tough love [Audio podcast]. *This American life*. Retrieved from http://thisamericanlife.org

32. A film or video recording (Web)

CBS News (Producer). (1968, April 4). *1968 King assassination report* [Video file]. Retrieved from http://www.youtube.com/watch?v=cm0BbxgxKvo

If the film or video you cite is difficult to locate from the home page of the Web site, give the complete URL in the retrieval statement, as in the example.

33. A visual (Web)

United Nations Population Fund (Cartographer). (2005). *Percent of population living on less than $1/day* [Demographic map]. Retrieved from http://www.unfpa.org

34. A message posted to a blog or discussion group (Web)

Sharma, A. (2011, April 15). How effective is lifestyle management of obesity? [Web log post]. Retrieved from http://www.drsharma.ca

Include postings to blogs and discussion groups in your list of references only if they are retrievable by others. (The source above is retrievable by a search of the home page URL.) Follow the message title with [Web log post], [Electronic mailing list message], or [Online forum comment]. Include the name of the blog or discussion group in the retrieval statement if it isn't part of the URL.

35. A personal communication (text citation)

At least one member of the research team has expressed reservations about the design of the study (L. Kogod, personal communication, February 6, 2011).

Personal e-mail and other online postings that are not retrievable by others should be cited only in the text, not in the list of references.

5 Listing other sources

36. A report (print)

Gerald, K. (2003). *Medico-moral problems in obstetric care* (Report No. NP-71). St. Louis, MO: Catholic Hospital Association.

Treat a printed report like a book, but provide any report number in parentheses after the title, with no punctuation between them.

For a report from the Educational Resources Information Center (ERIC), provide the ERIC document number in parentheses at the end of the entry:

> Jolson, M. K. (2001). *Music education for preschoolers* (Report No. TC-622). New York, NY: Teachers College, Columbia University. (ERIC Document Reproduction Service No. ED264488)

37. A government publication (print)

> Hawaii. Department of Education. (2011). *Kauai district schools, profile 2010-11.* Honolulu, HI: Author.

> Stiller, A. (2010). *Historic preservation and tax incentives.* Washington, DC: U.S. Department of the Interior.

If no person is named as the author, list the publication under the name of the sponsoring agency. When the agency is both the author and the publisher, use Author in place of the publisher's name, as in the first example.

For legal materials such as court decisions, laws, and testimony at hearings, the APA recommends formats that correspond to conventional legal citations. The following example of a congressional hearing includes the full title, the number of the Congress, the page number where the hearing transcript starts in the official publication, and the date of the hearing.

> *Medicare payment for outpatient physical and occupational therapy services: Hearing before the Committee on Ways and Means, House of Representatives,* 110th Cong. 3 (2007).

38. A dissertation (print)

A dissertation abstracted in DAI:

> Steciw, S. K. (1986). Alterations to the Pessac project of Le Corbusier. *Dissertation Abstracts International, 46*(6), 565C.

An unpublished dissertation:

> Hernandez, A. J. (2005). *Persistent poverty: Transient work and workers in today's labor market* (Unpublished doctoral dissertation). University of Illinois, Urbana-Champaign.

39. An interview (print)

> Schenker, H. (2007). No peace without third-party intervention [Interview with Shulamit Aloni]. *Palestine-Israel Journal of Politics, Economics, and Culture, 14*(4), 63-68.

List a published interview under the interviewer's name, and provide the title, if any, without italics or quotation marks. If there is no title, or if the title does not indicate the interview format or the interviewee (as in the example), add a bracketed explanation. End with the publication information for the kind of source the interview appears in (here, a journal).

An interview you conduct yourself should not be included in the list of references. Instead, use an in-text parenthetical citation, as shown in model 35 (p. 477) for a personal communication.

40. A motion picture

American Psychological Association (Producer). (2001). *Ethnocultural psychotherapy* [DVD]. Available from http://www.apa.org/videos

Tyrrell, C. (Director). (2010). *The Joneses* [Motion picture]. United States: Bjort Productions.

Begin with the name of the group or person whose work you are citing, followed by the function in parentheses. (The second example would begin with the producer's name if you were citing the motion picture as a whole, not specifically the work of the director.) Add the medium in brackets after the title: [Motion picture] (for film), [DVD], or [Videocassette]. For a work in wide circulation (second example), give the country of origin and the studio that released the picture. For a work that is not widely circulated (first example), give the distributor's address or URL.

41. A musical recording

Springsteen, B. (2002). Empty sky. On *The rising* [CD]. New York, NY: Columbia.

Begin with the name of the writer or composer. (If you cite another artist's recording of the work, provide this information after the title of the work—for example, [Recorded by E. Davila].) Give the medium in brackets ([CD], [LP], and so on). Finish with the city, state, and name of the recording label.

42. A television series or episode

Rhimes, S. (Executive producer). (2011). *Grey's anatomy* [Television series]. New York, NY: ABC.

Cahn, D. (Writer), & Allen, D. (Director). (2011). Not responsible [Television series episode]. In S. Rhimes (Executive producer), *Grey's anatomy*. New York, NY: ABC.

For a television series, begin with the producer's name and identify his or her function in parentheses. Add [Television series] after the series title, and give the city and name of the network. For an episode, begin with the writer and then the director, identifying the function of each in parentheses, and add [Television series episode] after the episode title. Then provide the series information, beginning with In and the producer's name and function, giving the series title, and ending with the city and name of the network.

59c Formatting a paper in APA style

Use the following guidelines and samples to prepare documents in APA format. Check with your instructor for any modifications to this format.

Note See pp. 465–66 for the APA format of a reference list. And see **1** pp. 55–62 for guidelines on type fonts, lists, tables and figures, and other elements of document design.

Margins Use one-inch margins on the top, bottom, and both sides.

Spacing and indentions Double-space everywhere. (The only exception is tables and figures, where related data, labels, and other elements may be single-spaced.) Indent paragraphs and displayed quotations one-half inch or five to seven spaces.

Paging Begin numbering on the title page, and number consecutively through the end (including the reference list). Provide a header about one-half inch from the top of every page, as shown in the samples on these pages. The header consists of the page number on the far right and your full or shortened title on the far left. Type the title in all-capital letters. On the title page only, precede the title with the label Running head and a colon. Omit this label on all other pages.

Title page Include the full title, your name, the course title, the instructor's name, and the date. (See below.) Type the title on the top half of the page, followed by the identifying information, all centered horizontally and double-spaced.

APA title page

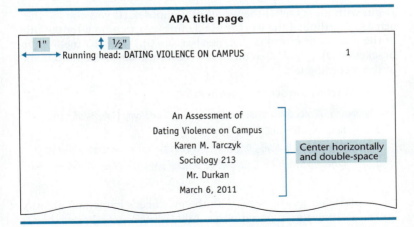

```
1"              ↕ ½"
      ←──→ Running head: DATING VIOLENCE ON CAMPUS            1



                        An Assessment of
                    Dating Violence on Campus
                        Karen M. Tarczyk        ⎤  Center horizontally
                         Sociology 213          ⎥  and double-space
                           Mr. Durkan           ⎦
                         March 6, 2011
```

Abstract Summarize (in a maximum of 120 words) your subject, research method, findings, and conclusions. (See opposite.) Put the abstract on a page by itself.

Body Begin with a restatement of the paper's title and then an introduction (not labeled). (See opposite.) The introduction presents

APA abstract

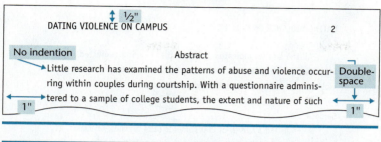

½"
DATING VIOLENCE ON CAMPUS   2

No indention   Abstract

Little research has examined the patterns of abuse and violence occur-   Double-space
ring within couples during courtship. With a questionnaire administered to a sample of college students, the extent and nature of such
1"   1"

First page of APA body

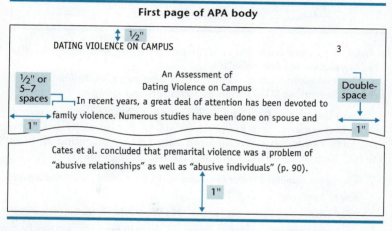

½"
DATING VIOLENCE ON CAMPUS   3

An Assessment of
Dating Violence on Campus

½" or 5–7 spaces
In recent years, a great deal of attention has been devoted to   Double-space
family violence. Numerous studies have been done on spouse and
1"   1"

Cates et al. concluded that premarital violence was a problem of
"abusive relationships" as well as "abusive individuals" (p. 90).
1"

the problem you researched, your method, the relevant background (such as related studies), and the purpose of your research.

After the introduction, a section labeled **Method** provides a detailed discussion of how you conducted your research, including a description of the research subjects, any materials or tools you used (such as questionnaires), and the procedure you followed. In the illustration on the next page, the label **Method** is a first-level heading and the label **Sample** is a second-level heading.

Format headings (including a third level, if needed) as follows:

First-Level Heading

Second-Level Heading

    Third-level heading. Run this heading into the text paragraph with a standard paragraph indention.

The **Results** section (labeled with a first-level heading) summarizes the data you collected, explains how you analyzed them, and presents them in detail, often in tables, graphs, or charts.

The **Discussion** section (labeled with a first-level heading) interprets the data and presents your conclusions. (When the discussion

Later page of APA body

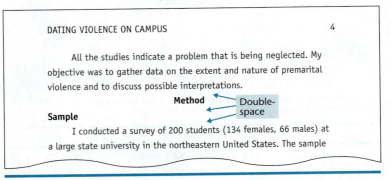

DATING VIOLENCE ON CAMPUS   4

    All the studies indicate a problem that is being neglected. My objective was to gather data on the extent and nature of premarital violence and to discuss possible interpretations.

Method ← Double-space

Sample

    I conducted a survey of 200 students (134 females, 66 males) at a large state university in the northeastern United States. The sample

is brief, you may combine it with the previous section under the heading **Results and Discussion**.)

    The References section, beginning a new page, includes all your sources. See pp. 465–66 for an explanation and sample.

    Long quotations Run into your text all quotations of forty words or less, and enclose them in quotation marks. For quotations of more than forty words, set them off from your text by indenting all lines one-half inch or five spaces, double-spacing throughout.

> Echoing the opinions of other Europeans at the time, Freud (1961) had a poor view of Americans:
>
> > The Americans are really too bad. . . . Competition is much more pungent with them, not succeeding means civil death to every one, and they have no private resources apart from their profession, no hobby, games, love or other interests of a cultured person. And success means money. (p. 86)

Do not use quotation marks around a quotation displayed in this way.

    Illustrations Present data in tables, graphs, or charts, as appropriate. (See the sample on p. 485 for a clear table format to follow.) Begin each illustration on a separate page. Number each kind of illustration consecutively and separately from the other (Table 1, Table 2, etc., and Figure 1, Figure 2, etc.). Refer to all illustrations in your text—for instance, (see Figure 3). Generally, place illustrations immediately after the text references to them. (See **1** pp. 58–64 for more on illustrations.)

59d Examining a sample paper in APA style

    The following excerpts from a sociology paper illustrate elements of a research paper using the APA style of documentation and format.

Student paper

[Title page.]

> Shortened title and page number.

An Assessment of

Dating Violence on Campus

Karen M. Tarczyk

Sociology 213

Mr. Durkan

March 6, 2011

> Double-space all information: title, name, course title, instructor, date.

[New page.]

Abstract

Little research has examined the patterns of abuse and violence occurring within couples during courtship. With a questionnaire administered to a sample of college students, the extent and nature of such abuse and violence were investigated. The results, interpretations, and implications for further research are discussed.

> Abstract: summary of subject, research method, conclusions.

> Double-space throughout.

[New page.]

An Assessment of

Dating Violence on Campus

In recent years, a great deal of attention has been devoted to family violence. Numerous studies have been done on spouse and child abuse. However, violent behavior occurs in dating relationships as well, yet the problem of dating violence has been relatively ignored by sociological research. It should be examined further because the premarital relationship is one context in which individuals learn and adopt behaviors that surface in marriage.

The sociologist James Makepeace (1989) contended that courtship violence is a "potential mediating link" between violence in one's family of orientation and violence in one's later family of procreation (p. 103). Studying dating behaviors at Bemidji State University in Minnesota, Makepeace reported that one-fifth of the respondents had had at least one encounter with dating violence. He then extended these percentages to students nationwide, suggesting the existence of a major hidden social problem.

> Title repeated on first text page.

> Introduction: presentation of the problem researched by the writer.

> Citation form: author named in the text.

> Citation form: page number given for quotation.

Citation form: source with five authors, named in the text.

Citation form: author not named in the text.

More recent research supports Makepeace's. Cates, Rutter, Karl, Linton, and Smith (2000) found that 22.3% of respondents at Oregon State University had been either the victim or the perpetrator of premarital violence. Another study (Cortes, 2005) found that so-called date rape, while much more publicized and discussed, was reported by many fewer woman respondents (2%) than was other violence during courtship (21%). [The introduction continues.]

All these studies indicate a problem that is being neglected. My objective was to gather data on the extent and nature of premarital violence and to discuss possible interpretations.

Method

First- and second-level headings.

"Method" section: discussion of how research was conducted.

Sample

I conducted a survey of 200 students (134 females, 66 males) at a large state university in the northeastern United States. The sample consisted of students enrolled in an introductory sociology course. [The explanation of method continues.]

The Questionnaire

A questionnaire exploring the personal dynamics of relationships was distributed during regularly scheduled class. The survey had three sections. [The explanation of method continues.]

Section 3 required participants to provide information about their current dating relationships. Levels of stress and frustration, communication between partners, and patterns of decision making were examined. These variables were expected to influence the amount of violence in a relationship. The next part of the survey was adopted from Murray Strauss's Conflict Tactics Scales (1992). These scales contain 19 items designed to measure conflict and the means of conflict resolution, including reasoning, verbal aggression, and actual violence. The final page of the questionnaire contained general questions on the couple's use of alcohol, sexual activity, and overall satisfaction with the relationship.

Results

"Results" section: summary and presentation of data.

The questionnaire revealed significant levels of verbal aggression and threatened and actual violence among dating couples. A high number of students, 50% (62 of 123 subjects), reported that they had been the victim of verbal abuse, either being insulted or sworn at. In addition, almost 14% of respondents (17 of 123) admitted being threatened with some type of violence, and more than 14% (18 of 123) reported

Reference to table.

being pushed, grabbed, or shoved. (See Table 1.) [The explanation of results continues.]

[Table on a page by itself.]

Table 1

Incidence of Courtship Violence

Type of violence	Number of students reporting	Percentage of sample
Insulted or swore	62	50.4
Threatened to hit or throw something	17	13.8
Threw something	8	6.5
Pushed, grabbed, or shoved	18	14.6
Slapped	8	6.5
Kicked, bit, or hit with fist	7	5.7
Hit or tried to hit with something	2	1.6
Threatened with a knife or gun	1	0.8
Used a knife or gun	1	0.8

Table presents data in clear format.

Discussion

Violence within premarital relationships has been relatively ignored. The results of the present study indicate that abuse and force do
occur in dating relationships. Although the percentages are small, so
was the sample. Extending them to the entire campus population of
5,000 would mean significant numbers. For example, if the nearly 6%
incidence of being kicked, bitten, or hit with a fist is typical, then 300
students might have experienced this type of violence.
[The discussion continues.]

If the courtship period is characterized by abuse and violence,
what accounts for it? The other sections of the survey examined some
variables that appear to influence the relationship. Level of stress and
frustration, both within the relationship and in the respondent's life, was
one such variable. The communication level between partners, both the
frequency of discussion and the frequency of agreement, was another.
[The discussion continues.]

The method of analyzing the data in this study, utilizing frequency distributions, provided a clear overview. However, more tests of
significance and correlation and a closer look at the social and individual variables affecting the relationship are warranted. The courtship
period may set the stage for patterns of married life. It merits more
attention.

"Discussion" section: interpretation of data and presentation of conclusions.

[New page.]

New page for reference list.

References

An article in a print journal.

Cates, R. L., Rutter, C. H., Karl, J., Linton, M., & Smith, K. (2000). Pre-marital abuse: A social psychological perspective. *Journal of Family Issues, 13*, 79-90.

An article in an online journal without a Digital Object Identifier.

Cortes, L. (2009). Beyond date rape: Violence during courtship. *Electronic Journal of Intimate Violence, 5*(2). Retrieved from http://www.ejiv.org

Glaser, R., & Rutter, C. H. (Eds.). (1999). Familial violence [Special issue]. *Family Relations, 38*(4).

Makepeace, J. M. (1989). Courtship violence among college students. *Family Relations, 28*(6), 97-103.

A book. ("Tactics Scales" is capitalized because it is part of a proper name.)

Strauss, M. L. (1992). *Conflict Tactics Scales.* New York, NY: Sociological Tests.

Chicago and CSE Documentation

Chicago and CSE Documentation

Chicago note and bibliography models

60 Chicago Documentation

History, art history, philosophy, and some other humanities use endnotes or footnotes to document sources, following one style recommended by *The Chicago Manual of Style* (16th ed., 2010) and the student guide adapted from it, Kate L. Turabian's *A Manual for Writers of Research Papers, Theses, and Dissertations* (7th ed., revised by Wayne C. Booth, Gregory G. Colomb, and Joseph M. Williams, 2007).

Student paper

60a Using Chicago notes and bibliography entries

In the Chicago note style, raised numerals in the text refer to footnotes (bottoms of pages) or endnotes (end of paper). These

Video tutorial

notes contain complete source information. A separate bibliography is optional: ask your instructor for his or her preference.

For both footnotes and endnotes, use single spacing for each note and double spacing between notes, as shown in the samples below. (This is the spacing recommended by *A Manual for Writers*, the student guide.) For manuscripts that will be published, *The Chicago Manual* recommends double spacing throughout.) Separate footnotes from the text with a short line. Place endnotes directly after the text, beginning on a new page. For a bibliography at the end of the paper, use the format on the facing page. Arrange the sources alphabetically by the authors' last names.

Chicago footnotes

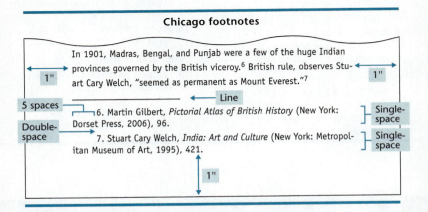

Chicago endnotes

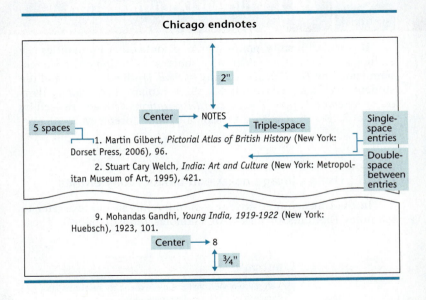

Chicago bibliography

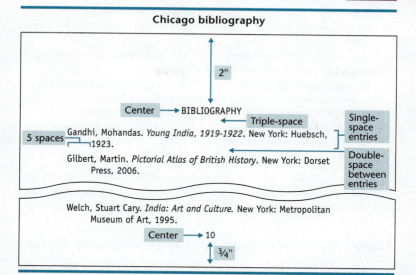

The examples below illustrate the essentials of a note and a bibliography entry.

Note

6. Martin Gilbert, *Pictorial Atlas of British History* (New York: Dorset Press, 2006), 96.

Bibliography entry

Gilbert, Martin. *Pictorial Atlas of British History*. New York: Dorset Press, 2006.

Treat some features of notes and bibliography entries the same:

- Unless your instructor requests otherwise, single-space each note or entry, and double-space between them.
- Italicize the titles of books and periodicals.
- Enclose in quotation marks the titles of parts of books or articles in periodicals.
- Do not abbreviate publishers' names, but omit "Inc.," "Co.," and similar abbreviations.
- Do not use "p." or "pp." before page numbers.

Treat other features of notes and bibliography entries differently:

Note	**Bibliography entry**
Start with a number that corresponds to the note number in the text.	Do not begin with a number.
Indent the first line five spaces.	Indent the second and subsequent lines five spaces.

Note	Bibliography entry
Give the author's name in normal order.	Begin with the author's last name.
Use commas between elements such as author's name and title.	Use periods between elements.
Enclose a book's publication information in parentheses, with no preceding punctuation.	Precede a book's publication information with a period, and don't use parentheses.
Include the specific page number(s) you borrowed from, omitting "p." or "pp."	Omit page numbers except for parts of books or articles in periodicals.

You can instruct your computer to position footnotes at the bottoms of appropriate pages. It will also automatically number notes and renumber them if you add or delete one or more.

60b   Models of Chicago notes and bibliography entries

An index to the following Chicago models appears on the **Chicago** divider. The models show notes and bibliography entries together for easy reference. Be sure to use the numbered note form for notes and the unnumbered bibliography form for bibliography entries.

1   Listing authors

1. One, two, or three authors

1. Carol Gilligan, *In a Different Voice: Psychological Theory and Women's Development* (Cambridge: Harvard University Press, 1982), 27.

Gilligan, Carol. *In a Different Voice: Psychological Theory and Women's Development*. Cambridge: Harvard University Press, 1982.

1. Dennis L. Wilcox, Phillip H. Ault, and Warren K. Agee, *Public Relations: Strategies and Tactics,* 6th ed. (New York: Irwin, 2005), 182.

Wilcox, Dennis L., Phillip H. Ault, and Warren K. Agee. *Public Relations: Strategies and Tactics*. 6th ed. New York: Irwin, 2005.

2. More than three authors

2. Geraldo Lopez et al., *China and the West* (Boston: Little, Brown, 2004), 461.

Lopez, Geraldo, Judith P. Salt, Anne Ming, and Henry Reisen. *China and the West*. Boston: Little, Brown, 2004.

The Latin abbreviation et al. in the note means "and others."

3. Author not named (anonymous)

3. *The Dorling Kindersley World Atlas* (London: Dorling Kindersley, 2010), 150-51.

The Dorling Kindersley World Atlas. London: Dorling Kindersley, 2010.

2 | Listing print periodicals: Journals, newspapers, magazines

4. An article in a journal (print)

4. Janet Lever, "Sex Differences in the Games Children Play," *Social Problems* 23 (Spring 1996): 482.

Lever, Janet. "Sex Differences in the Games Children Play." *Social Problems* 23 (Spring 1996): 478-87.

For journals that are paginated continuously throughout an annual volume, include just the volume number or, for greater clarity, add the issue number, if any, or the month or season of publication. The month or season precedes the year of publication in parentheses, as above. The issue number follows the volume number:

4. Robert Bee, "The Importance of Preserving Paper-Based Artifacts in a Digital Age," *Library Quarterly* 78, no. 2 (2008): 176.

Bee, Robert. "The Importance of Preserving Paper-Based Artifacts in a Digital Age." *Library Quarterly* 78, no. 2 (2008): 174-94.

Note that the issue number and/or the month or season is required for any journal that pages issues separately or that numbers only issues, not volumes.

5. An article in a newspaper (print)

5. Reyhan Harmanci, "Literary Journals Thrive, on Paper and Otherwise," *New York Times*, April 8, 2011, national edition, A23.

Harmanci, Reyhan. "Literary Journals Thrive, on Paper and Otherwise." *New York Times*, April 8, 2011, national edition, A23.

Chicago style does not require page numbers for newspaper articles, whether in notes or in bibliography entries. Thus A23 could be omitted from the above examples.

6. An article in a magazine (print)

6. Edwidge Danticat, "A Year and a Day," *New Yorker*, January 17, 2011, 19.

Danticat, Edwidge. "A Year and a Day." *New Yorker*, January 17, 2011, 19-20.

Chicago bibliography style does not require inclusive page numbers for magazine articles, so 19-20 could be omitted from the preceding example.

7. A review (print)

7. John Gregory Dunne, "The Secret of Danny Santiago," review of *Famous All over Town*, by Danny Santiago, *New York Review of Books*, August 16, 1994, 25.

Dunne, John Gregory. "The Secret of Danny Santiago." Review of *Famous All over Town*, by Danny Santiago. *New York Review of Books*, August 16, 1994, 17-27.

3 | Listing print books

8. Basic format for a book (print)

8. Barbara Ehrenreich, *Dancing in the Streets: A History of Collective Joy* (New York: Henry Holt, 2006), 97-117.

Ehrenreich, Barbara. *Dancing in the Streets: A History of Collective Joy*. New York: Henry Holt, 2006.

9. A book with an editor (print)

9. Hendrick Ruitenbeek, ed., *Freud as We Knew Him* (Detroit: Wayne State University Press, 1973), 64.

Ruitenbeek, Hendrick, ed. *Freud as We Knew Him*. Detroit: Wayne State University Press, 1973.

10. A book with an author and an editor (print)

10. Lewis Mumford, *The City in History,* ed. Donald L. Miller (New York: Pantheon, 1986), 216-17.

Mumford, Lewis. *The City in History*. Edited by Donald L. Miller. New York: Pantheon, 1986.

11. A translation (print)

11. Dante Alighieri, *The Inferno,* trans. John Ciardi (New York: New American Library, 1971), 51.

Alighieri, Dante. *The Inferno*. Translated by John Ciardi. New York: New American Library, 1971.

12. A later edition (print)

12. Dwight L. Bolinger, *Aspects of Language,* 3rd ed. (New York: Harcourt Brace Jovanovich, 1981), 20.

Bolinger, Dwight L. *Aspects of Language*. 3rd ed. New York: Harcourt Brace Jovanovich, 1981.

13. A work in more than one volume (print)

Citation of one volume without a title:

13. Abraham Lincoln, *The Collected Works of Abraham Lincoln,* ed. Roy P. Basler (New Brunswick: Rutgers University Press, 1953), 5:426-28.

Lincoln, Abraham. *The Collected Works of Abraham Lincoln*. Edited by Roy P. Basler. Vol. 5. New Brunswick: Rutgers University Press, 1953.

Citation of one volume with a title:

13. Linda B. Welkin, *The Age of Balanchine,* vol. 3 of *The History of Ballet* (New York: Columbia University Press, 1999), 56.

Welkin, Linda B. *The Age of Balanchine*. Vol. 3 of *The History of Ballet*. New York: Columbia University Press, 1999.

14. A selection from an anthology (print)

14. Rosetta Brooks, "Streetwise," in *The New Urban Landscape,* ed. Richard Martin (New York: Rizzoli, 2005), 38-39.

Brooks, Rosetta. "Streetwise." In *The New Urban Landscape,* edited by Richard Martin, 37-60. New York: Rizzoli, 2005.

15. A work in a series (print)

15. Ingmar Bergman, *The Seventh Seal,* Modern Film Scripts 12 (New York: Simon and Schuster, 1995), 27.

Bergman, Ingmar. *The Seventh Seal.* Modern Film Scripts 12. New York: Simon and Schuster, 1995.

16. An article in a reference work (print)

16. *Merriam-Webster's Collegiate Dictionary,* 11th ed., s.v. "reckon."

Merriam-Webster's Collegiate Dictionary. 11th ed. S.v. "reckon."

As in the example, use the abbreviation s.v. (Latin *sub verbo,* "under the word") for reference works that are alphabetically arranged. Well-known works like the one listed in the example do not need publication information except for edition number. Chicago style generally recommends notes only, not bibliography entries, for reference works; a bibliography model is given here in case your instructor requires such entries.

4 Listing Web and other electronic sources

The Chicago Manual's models for documenting electronic sources mostly begin as those for print sources do. Then you add electronic publication information that will help readers locate the source. If one is available, give the Digital Object Identifier (DOI) for the source—a unique identifier that many publishers assign to periodical articles and other documents. (See model 17.) If no DOI is available, give the URL, as shown in models 18 and 19. If you retrieve an article from an online database, see model 20.

For Web pages and other electronic sources that are likely to change, *The Chicago Manual* suggests including the date of the most recent update in a statement beginning last modified (see model 22). If no date is available, give the date of your access (see model 23).

Note Chicago style allows many ways to break DOIs and URLs at the ends of lines: after a colon or double slash and before a single slash, period, comma, hyphen, and most other marks. *Do not* break after a hyphen or add any hyphens.

17. An article in a journal (Web)

17. Joseph J. Campos et al., "Reconceptualizing Emotion Regulation," *Emotion Review* 3, no. 1 (2011): 32, doi:10.1177/1754073910380975.

Campos, Joseph J., Eric A. Walle, Audun Dahl, and Alexandra Main. "Reconceptualizing Emotion Regulation." *Emotion Review* 3, no. 1 (2011): 26-35. doi:10.1177/1754073910380975.

Give a DOI if one is available (as here) or a URL if not (next two models).

18. An article in a magazine (Web)

18. Jan Swafford, "The Elusive Maestro," *Slate*, April 12, 2011, http://www.slate.com/id/2291008.

Swafford, Jan. "The Elusive Maestro." *Slate*, April 12, 2011. http://www.slate.com/id/2291008.

19. An article in a newspaper (Web)

19. Elisabetta Povoledo, "The Little-Known Racing Legend underneath the Logo," *New York Times*, April 8, 2011, http://www.nytimes.com/2011/04/09/business/global/09iht-dallara09.html?hpw.

Povoledo, Elisabetta. "The Little-Known Racing Legend underneath the Logo." *New York Times*, April 8, 2011. http://www.nytimes.com/2011/04/09/business/global/09iht-dallara09.html?hpw.

20. An article in an online database (Web)

20. Jonathan Dickens, "Social Policy Approaches to Intercountry Adoption," *International Social Work* 52 (September 2009): 600, doi:10.1177/0020872809337678.

Dickens, Jonathan. "Social Policy Approaches to Intercountry Adoption." *International Social Work* 52 (September 2009): 595-607. doi:10.1177/0020872809337678.

If a database article has neither a DOI nor a URL that takes readers directly to the source, end with the name of the database:

20. Suzanne Penuel, "Missing Fathers: *Twelfth Night* and the Reformation of Mourning," *Studies in Philology* 107, no. 1 (2010): 82, Academic Search Complete.

Penuel, Suzanne. "Missing Fathers: *Twelfth Night* and the Reformation of Mourning." *Studies in Philology* 107, no. 1 (2010): 74-96. Academic Search Complete.

21. A book (Web)

21. Jane Austen, *Emma*, ed. R. W. Chapman (1816; Oxford: Clarendon, 1926; Oxford Text Archive, 2004), chap. 1, http://ota.ahds.ac.uk/Austen/Emma.1519.

Austen, Jane. *Emma*. Edited by R. W. Chapman. 1816. Oxford: Clarendon, 1926. Oxford Text Archive, 2004. http://ota.ahds.ac.uk/Austen/Emma.1519.

Provide print publication information, if any.

22. An article in a reference work (Web)

22. *Wikipedia*, s.v. "Wuhan," last modified March 31, 2011, http://en.wikipedia.org/wiki/Wuhan.

Wikipedia. S.v. "Wuhan." Last modified March 31, 2011. http://en.wikipedia.org/wiki/Wuhan.

Use the abbreviation s.v. (Latin *sub verbo*, "under the word") for reference works that are alphabetically arranged.

23. A Web page

23. "Toyota Safety," Toyota Motor Sales, accessed July 23, 2011, http://www.toyota.com/safety.

Toyota Motor Sales. "Toyota Safety." Accessed July 23, 2011. http://www.toyota.com/safety.

24. A message posted to a blog or discussion group (Web)

24. Sharyn Stein, "CFLs: Get the Whole Story," *Climate 411* (blog), January 31, 2011, http://blogs.edf.org/climate411/2011/01.

Stein, Sharyn. "CFLs: Get the Whole Story." *Climate 411* (blog). January 31, 2011. http://blogs.edf.org/climate411/2011/01.

24. Michael Tourville, "European Currency Reform," e-mail to International Finance discussion list, January 6, 2011, http://www.weg.isu.edu/finance-dl/archive/46732.

Tourville, Michael. "European Currency Reform." E-mail to International Finance discussion list. January 6, 2011. http://www.weg.isu.edu/finance-dl/archive/46732.

25. An audio or visual source (Web)

A work of art:

25. Jackson Pollock, *Shimmering Substance,* 1946, Museum of Modern Art, New York, http://moma.org/collection/conservation/pollock/shimmering_substance.html.

Pollock, Jackson. *Shimmering Substance*. 1946. Museum of Modern Art, New York. http://moma.org/collection/conservation/pollock/shimmering_substance.html.

See also model 33 to cite a work of art that you view in person.

A sound recording:

25. Ronald W. Reagan, "State of the Union Address," January 26, 1982, Vincent Voice Library, Digital and Multimedia Center, Michigan State University, http://www.lib.msu.edu/vincent/presidents/reagan.html.

Reagan, Ronald W. "State of the Union Address." January 26, 1982. Vincent Voice Library. Digital and Multimedia Center, Michigan State University. http://www.lib.msu.edu/vincent/presidents/reagan.html.

A film or film clip:

25. Leslie J. Stewart, *96 Ranch Rodeo and Barbecue* (1951), 16mm, from Library of Congress, *Buckaroos in Paradise: Ranching Culture in Northern Nevada, 1945-1982,* MPEG, http://memory.loc.gov/cgi-bin/query.

Stewart, Leslie J. 96 *Ranch Rodeo and Barbecue*. 1951. 16 mm. From Library of Congress, *Buckaroos in Paradise: Ranching Culture in Northern Nevada, 1945-1982*. MPEG. http://memory.loc.gov/cgi-bin/query.

26. A podcast (Web)

26. Ira Glass, "Very Tough Love," *This American Life*, podcast audio, March 25, 2011, http://www.thisamericanlife.org/radio-archives/episode/430 /very-tough-love.

Glass, Ira. "Very Tough Love." *This American Life*. Podcast audio. March 25, 2011. http://www.thisamericanlife.org/radio-archives/episode/430 /very-tough-love.

27. E-mail

25. Naomi Lee, "Re: Cairo," e-mail message to author, May 16, 2011.

Lee, Naomi. "Re: Cairo." E-mail message to author. May 16, 2011.

Chicago style generally recommends notes only, not bibliography entries, for personal communication. A bibliography model is given here in case your instructor requires such entries.

28. A work on CD-ROM or DVD-ROM

28. *The American Heritage Dictionary of the English Language,* 4th ed. (Boston: Houghton Mifflin, 2006), CD-ROM.

The American Heritage Dictionary of the English Language. 4th ed. Boston: Houghton Mifflin, 2006. CD-ROM.

5 Listing other sources

29. A government publication (print)

29. House Comm. on Agriculture, Nutrition, and Forestry, *Food and Energy Act of 2008,* 110th Cong., 2nd Sess., H.R. Doc. No. 884, at 21-22 (2008).

House Comm. on Agriculture, Nutrition, and Forestry. *Food and Energy Act of 2008*. 110th Cong. 2nd Sess., H.R. Doc. No. 884 (2008).

29. Hawaii Department of Education, *Kauai District Schools, Profile 2010-11* (Honolulu, 2011), 38.

Hawaii Department of Education. *Kauai District Schools, Profile 2010-11*. Honolulu, 2011.

30. A published letter (print)

30. Mrs. Laura E. Buttolph to Rev. and Mrs. C. C. Jones, June 20, 1857, in *The Children of Pride: A True Story of Georgia and the Civil War,* ed. Robert Manson Myers (New Haven, CT: Yale University Press, 1972), 334.

Buttolph, Laura E. Mrs. Laura E. Buttolph to Rev. and Mrs. C. C. Jones, June 20, 1857. In *The Children of Pride: A True Story of Georgia and the Civil War,* edited by Robert Manson Myers. New Haven, CT: Yale University Press, 1972.

31. A published or broadcast interview

31. Dexter Filkins, interview by Terry Gross, *Fresh Air,* NPR, April 6, 2011.

Filkins, Dexter. Interview by Terry Gross. *Fresh Air*. NPR. April 6, 2011.

32. A personal letter or interview

32. Ann E. Packer, letter to author, June 15, 2011.

Packer, Ann E. Letter to author. June 15, 2011.

32. Janelle White, interview by author, December 19, 2010.

White, Janelle. Interview by author. December 19, 2010.

33. A work of art

33. John Singer Sargent, *In Switzerland,* 1908, Metropolitan Museum of Art, New York.

Sargent, John Singer. *In Switzerland*. 1908. Metropolitan Museum of Art, New York.

34. A film, DVD, or video recording

34. George Balanchine, *Serenade,* San Francisco Ballet, performed February 2, 2000 (New York: PBS Video, 2006), DVD.

Balanchine, George. *Serenade*. San Francisco Ballet. Performed February 2, 2000. New York: PBS Video, 2006, DVD.

35. A sound recording

35. Philip Glass, *String Quartet no. 5,* with Kronos Quartet, recorded 1991, Nonesuch 79356-2, 1995, compact disc.

Glass, Philip. *String Quartet no. 5*. Kronos Quartet. Recorded 1991. Nonesuch 79356-2, 1995, compact disc.

6 Using shortened notes

To streamline documentation, Chicago style recommends shortened notes for sources that are fully cited elsewhere, either in a bibliography or in previous notes. Ask your instructor whether your paper should include a bibliography and, if so, whether you may use shortened notes for first references to sources as well as for subsequent references.

A shortened note contains the author's last name, the work's title (minus any initial *A, An,* or *The*), and the page number. Reduce long titles to four or fewer key words.

Complete note

4. Janet Lever, "Sex Differences in the Games Children Play," *Social Problems* 23 (Spring 1996): 482.

Complete bibliography entry

Lever, Janet. "Sex Differences in the Games Children Play." *Social Problems* 23 (Spring 1996): 478-87.

Shortened note

12. Lever, "Sex Differences," 483.

You may use the Latin abbreviation ibid. (meaning "in the same place") to refer to the same source cited in the preceding note. Give a page number if it differs from that in the preceding note.

12. Lever, "Sex Differences," 483.

13. Gilligan, *In a Different Voice,* 92.

14. Ibid., 93.

15. Lever, "Sex Differences," 483.

Chicago style allows for in-text parenthetical citations when you cite one or more works repeatedly. In the following example, the raised number 2 refers to the source information in a note; the number in parentheses is a page number in the same source.

British rule, observes Stuart Cary Welch, "seemed as permanent as Mount Everest."[2] Most Indians submitted, willingly or not, to British influence in every facet of life (42).

61 CSE Documentation

Writers in the life sciences, physical sciences, and mathematics rely for documentation style on *Scientific Style and Format: The CSE Manual for Authors, Editors, and Publishers* (7th ed., 2006), published by the Council of Science Editors.

Student paper

Scientific Style and Format details both styles of scientific documentation: one using author and date and one using numbers. Both types of text citation refer to a list of references at the end of the paper. Ask your instructor which style you should use.

61a Writing CSE name-year text citations

In the CSE name-year style, parenthetical text citations provide the last name of the author being cited and the source's year of publication. At the end of the paper, a list of references, arranged alphabetically by authors' last names, provides complete information on each source. (See opposite.)

The CSE name-year style closely resembles the APA name-year style detailed in **APA** pp. 462–65. You can follow the APA examples for in-text citations, making several notable changes for CSE:

- **Do not use a comma to separate the author's name and the date:** (Baumrind 1968, p. 34).
- **Separate two authors' names with and (not "&"):** (Pepinsky and DeStefano 1997).
- **For sources with three or more authors, use et al. (Latin abbreviation for "and others") after the first author's name:** (Rutter et al. 1996).

61b Writing CSE numbered text citations

In the CSE number style, raised numbers in the text refer to a numbered list of references at the end of the paper.

Two standard references [1,2] use this term.

These forms of immunity have been extensively researched [3].

Hepburn and Tatin [2] do not discuss this project.

Assignment of numbers The number for each source is based on the order in which you cite the source in the text: the first cited source is 1, the second is 2, and so on.

mycomplab

Visit *mycomplab.com* for the eText and for resources on CSE documentation.

501

Reuse of numbers When you cite a source you have already cited and numbered, use the original number again (see the last example on the previous page, which reuses the number 2 from the first example).

This reuse is the key difference between the CSE numbered citations and numbered references to footnotes or endnotes. In the CSE style, each source has only one number, determined by the order in which the source is cited. With notes, in contrast, the numbering proceeds in sequence, so that each source has as many numbers as it has citations in the text.

Citation of two or more sources When you cite two or more sources at once, arrange their numbers in sequence and separate them with a comma and no space, as in the first example on the previous page.

61c Preparing the CSE reference list

Video
tutorial

For both the name-year and the number styles of in-text citation, provide a list, titled References, of all sources you have cited. Center this heading about an inch from the top of the page, and double-space beneath it.

The following examples show the differences and similarities between the name-year and number styles:

Name-year style

Hepburn PX, Tatin JM. 2005. Human physiology. New York (NY): Columbia University Press.

Number style

2. Hepburn PX, Tatin JM. Human physiology. New York (NY): Columbia University Press; 2005.

Spacing In both styles, single-space each entry and double-space between entries.

Arrangement In the name-year style, arrange entries alphabetically by authors' last names. In the number style, arrange entries in numerical order—that is, in order of their citation in the text.

Format In the name-year style, type all lines of entries at the left margin—do not indent. In the number style, begin the first line of each entry at the left margin and indent subsequent lines.

Authors In both styles, list each author's name with the last name first, followed by initials for first and middle names. Do not use a comma between an author's last name and initials, and do not use periods or spaces with the initials. Do use a comma to separate authors' names.

Placement of dates In the name-year style, the date follows the author's or authors' names. In the number style, the date follows the publication information (for a book) or the periodical title (for a journal, magazine, or newspaper).

Journal titles In both styles, do not italicize or underline journal titles. For titles of two or more words, abbreviate words of six or more letters (without periods) and omit most prepositions, articles, and conjunctions. Capitalize each word. For example, *Journal of Chemical and Biochemical Studies* becomes J Chem Biochem Stud, and *Hospital Practice* becomes Hosp Pract.

Book and article titles In both styles, do not italicize, underline, or use quotation marks around a book or an article title. Capitalize only the first word and any proper nouns.

Publication information for journal articles The name-year and number styles differ in the placement of the publication date (see opposite). However, after the journal title both styles give the journal's volume number, any issue number in parentheses, a colon, and the inclusive page numbers of the article, run together without space: 28:329-30 or 62(2):26-40. See model 6 on the next page.

The following examples show both a name-year reference and a number reference for each type of source. An index to all the models appears opposite the **CSE** divider (p. 489).

1 Listing authors

1. One author

Gould SJ. 1987. Time's arrow, time's cycle. Cambridge (MA): Harvard University Press.

1. Gould SJ. Time's arrow, time's cycle. Cambridge (MA): Harvard University Press; 1987.

2. Two to ten authors

Hepburn PX, Tatin JM, Tatin JP. 2008. Human physiology. New York (NY): Columbia University Press.

2. Hepburn PX, Tatin JM, Tatin JP. Human physiology. New York (NY): Columbia University Press; 2008.

3. More than ten authors

Evans RW, Bowditch L, Dana KL, Drumond A, Wildovitch WP, Young SL, Mills P, Mills RR, Livak SR, Lisi OL, et al. 2004. Organ transplants: ethical issues. Ann Arbor (MI): University of Michigan Press.

3. Evans RW, Bowditch L, Dana KL, Drummond A, Wildovitch WP, Young SL, Mills P, Mills RR, Livak SR, Lisi OL, et al. Organ transplants: ethical issues. Ann Arbor (MI): University of Michigan Press; 2004.

4. Author not named

Health care for children with diabetes. 2011. New York (NY): US Health Care.

4. Health care for children with diabetes. New York (NY): US Health Care; 2011.

5. Two or more cited works by the same author(s) published in the same year

Gardner H. 1973a. The arts and human development. New York (NY): Wiley.

Gardner H. 1973b. The quest for mind: Piaget, Lévi-Strauss, and the structuralist movement. New York (NY): Knopf.

(The number style does not require such forms.)

2 | Listing print periodicals: Journals, newspapers, magazines

6. An article in a journal (print)

Campos JJ, Walle EA, Dahl A, Main A. 2011. Reconceptualizing emotion regulation. Emotion Rev. 3(1):26-35. doi:10.1177/1754073910380975

6. Campos JJ, Walle EA, Dahl A, Main A. Reconceptualizing emotion regulation. Emotion Rev. 2011;3(1):26-35. doi:10.1177/1754073910380975

If a journal article has a Digital Object Identifier (DOI), include the number at the end of the entry, as here. (See **APA** p. 466 for more on DOIs.)

7. An article in a newspaper (print)

Wade N. 2011 Apr 15. Ancient clicks hint language is Africa-born. New York Times (National Ed.). Sect. A:1 (col. 3).

7. Wade N. Ancient clicks hint language is Africa-born. New York Times (National Ed.). 2011 Apr 15;Sect. A:1 (col. 3).

8. An article in a magazine (print)

Hall S. 2011 Mar. Diseases in a dish. Scientific American. 40-45.

8. Hall S. Diseases in a dish. Scientific American. 2011 Mar:40-45.

3 | Listing print books

9. Basic format for a book (print)

Wilson EO. 2004. On human nature. Cambridge (MA): Harvard University Press.

9. Wilson EO. On human nature. Cambridge (MA): Harvard University Press; 2004.

10. A book with an editor (print)

Jonson P, editor. 2008. Anatomy yearbook 2008. Los Angeles (CA): Anatco.

10. Jonson P, editor. Anatomy yearbook 2008. Los Angeles (CA): Anatco; 2008.

11. A selection from a book (print)

Kriegel R, Laubenstein L, Muggia F. 2005. Kaposi's sarcoma. In: Ebbeson P, Biggar RS, Melbye M, editors. AIDS: a basic guide for clinicians. 2nd ed. Philadelphia (PA): Saunders. p. 100-26.

11. Kriegel R, Laubenstein L, Muggia F. Kaposi's sarcoma. In: Ebbeson P, Biggar RS, Melbye M, editors. AIDS: a basic guide for clinicians. 2nd ed. Philadelphia (PA): Saunders; 2005. p. 100-26.

4 | **Listing Web and other electronic sources**

CSE references to electronic sources require additions to the basic print formats:

- **Give the medium you used to find the source**, in brackets: [Internet], [DVD], and so on.
- **Give the date you accessed the source preceded by cited,** in brackets: [cited 2009 Dec 7].
- **Give the URL of an Internet source.** Use an availability statement that starts with Available from: and ends with the URL. If you must break a URL from one line to the next, do so only before punctuation such as a period or a slash and do not hyphenate. Do not add a period at the end of a URL.
- **Give the DOI (Digital Object Identifier) of the source if one is available.** Add it at the end of the entry after a space, as in model 12. (See **APA** p. 466 for more on DOIs.)

12. An article in a journal (Web)

Grady GF. 2010. The here and now of hepatitis B immunization. Today's Med [Internet]. [cited 2010 Dec 7]; 6(2):39-41. Available from: http://www.fmrt .org/todaysmedicine/Grady050293.pdf6 doi:10.1076/262543668

12. Grady GF. The here and now of hepatitis B immunization. Today's Med [Internet]. 2010 [cited 2010 Dec 7]; 6(2):39-41. Available from: http://www .fmrt.org/todaysmedicine/Grady050293.pdf6 doi:10.1076/262543668

Give the date of your access, preceded by "cited," in brackets: [cited 2010 Dec 7] in the examples. If the article has no reference numbers (pages, paragraphs, and so on), give your calculation of its length in brackets—for instance, [about 15 p.] or [20 paragraphs].

13. An article in a database (Web)

McAskill MR, Anderson TJ, Jones RD. 2005. Saccadic adaptation in neurological disorders. Prog Brain Res. 140:417-431. PubMed [Internet]. Bethesda (MD): National Library of Medicine; [cited 2011 Mar 6]. Available from: http://www.ncbi .nlm.nih.gov/PubMed

13. McAskill MR, Anderson TJ, Jones RD. Saccadic adaptation in neurological disorders. Prog Brain Res. 2005;140:417-431. PubMed [Internet]. Bethesda (MD): National Library of Medicine; [cited 2011 Mar 6]. Available from: http://www.ncbi.nlm.nih.gov/PubMed

Provide information on the database: title, [Internet], place of publication, and publisher. (If the database author is different from the publisher, give the author's name before the title.) If you see a date of publication or a copyright date for the database, give it after the publisher's name.

14. A book (Web)

Ruch BJ, Ruch DB. 2009. Homeopathy and medicine: resolving the conflict [Internet]. New York (NY): Albert Einstein College of Medicine [cited 2011 Jan 28]. Available from: http://www.einstein.edu/medicine/books/ruch.html

14. Ruch BJ, Ruch DB. Homeopathy and medicine: resolving the conflict [Internet]. New York (NY): Albert Einstein College of Medicine; 2009 [cited 2011 Jan 28]. Available from: http://www.einstein.edu/medicine/books/ruch.html

15. A Web site

American Medical Association [Internet]. 2011. Chicago (IL): American Medical Association; [cited 2011 Nov 26]. Available from: http://ama-assn.org

15. American Medical Association [Internet]. Chicago (IL): American Medical Association; 2011 [cited 2011 Nov 26]. Available from: http://ama-assn.org

16. A message posted to a discussion list

Stalinsky Q. 2011 Aug 16. More studies about hormone-replacement therapy. Woman Physicians Congress [discussion list on the Internet]. Chicago (IL): American Medical Association; [cited 2011 Aug 17]. Available from: ama-wpc@ama-assn.org

16. Stalinsky Q. More studies about hormone-replacement therapy. Woman Physicians Congress [discussion list on the Internet]. Chicago (IL): American Medical Association; 2011 Aug 16 [cited 2011 Aug 17]. Available from: ama-wpc@ama-assn.org

17. A personal online communication (text citation)

One member of the research team has expressed reservation about the study design (personal communication from L. Kogod, 2011 Feb 6; unreferenced).

A personal letter or e-mail message should be cited in your text, not in your reference list. The format is the same for both the name-year and the number styles.

18. A document on CD-ROM or DVD-ROM

Reich WT, editor. 2011. Encyclopedia of bioethics [DVD-ROM]. New York (NY): Co-Health.

18. Reich WT editor. Encyclopedia of bioethics [DVD-ROM]. New York (NY): Co-Health; 2011.

5 Listing other sources

19. A report written and published by the same organization

Warnock M. 2006. Report of the Committee on Fertilization and Embryology. Waco (TX): Baylor University Department of Embryology. Report No.: BU/DE.4261.

19. Warnock M. Report of the Committee on Fertilization and Embryology. Waco (TX): Baylor University Department of Embryology; 2006. Report No.: BU/DE.4261.

20. A report written and published by different organizations

Hackney, JD (Rancho Los Amigos Hospital, Downey, CA). 2007. Effect of atmospheric pollutants on human physiologic function. Washington (DC): Environmental Protection Agency (US). Report No.: R-801396.

20. Hackney, JD (Rancho Los Amigos Hospital, Downey, CA). Effect of atmospheric pollutants on human physiologic function. Washington (DC): Environmental Protection Agency (US); 2007. Report No.: R-801396.

21. An audio or visual recording

Cell mitosis [DVD–ROM]. 2011. White Plains (NY): Teaching Media.

21. Cell mitosis [DVD-ROM]. White Plains (NY): Teaching Media; 2011.

Glossary of Usage

This glossary provides notes on words or phrases that often cause problems for writers. The recommendations for standard American English are based on current dictionaries and usage guides. Items labeled **nonstandard** should be avoided in academic and business settings. Those labeled **colloquial** and **slang** occur in speech and in some informal writing but are best avoided in formal college and business writing. (Words and phrases labeled *colloquial* include those labeled by many dictionaries with the equivalent term *informal*.)

a, an   Use *a* before words beginning with consonant sounds, including those spelled with an initial pronounced *h* and those spelled with vowels that are sounded as consonants: *a historian, a one-o'clock class, a university*. Use *an* before words that begin with vowel sounds, including those spelled with an initial silent *h*: *an organism, an L, an honor*.

The article before an abbreviation depends on how the abbreviation is to be read: *She was once an AEC undersecretary* (*AEC* is to be read as three separate letters). *Many Americans opposed a SALT treaty* (*SALT* is to be read as one word, *salt*).

See also **4** pp. 237–38 on the uses of *a/an* versus *the*.

accept, except   *Accept* is a verb meaning "receive." *Except* is usually a preposition or conjunction meaning "but for" or "other than"; when it is used as a verb, it means "leave out." *I can accept all your suggestions except the last one. I'm sorry you excepted my last suggestion from your list.*

advice, advise   *Advice* is a noun, and *advise* is a verb: *Take my advice; do as I advise you.*

affect, effect   Usually *affect* is a verb, meaning "to influence," and *effect* is a noun, meaning "result": *The drug did not affect his driving; in fact, it seemed to have no effect at all.* But *effect* occasionally is used as a verb meaning "to bring about": *Her efforts effected a change.* And *affect* is used in psychology as a noun meaning "feeling or emotion": *One can infer much about affect from behavior.*

agree to, agree with   *Agree to* means "consent to," and *agree with* means "be in accord with": *How can they agree to a treaty when they don't agree with each other about the terms?*

all ready, already   *All ready* means "completely prepared," and *already* means "by now" or "before now": *We were all ready to go to the movie, but it had already started.*

all right   *All right* is always two words. *Alright* is a common error.

all together, altogether   *All together* means "in unison" or "gathered in one place." *Altogether* means "entirely." *It's not altogether true that our family never spends vacations all together.*

allusion, illusion   An *allusion* is an indirect reference, and an *illusion* is a deceptive appearance: *Paul's constant allusions to Shakespeare created the illusion that he was an intellectual.*

almost, most   *Almost* means "nearly"; *most* means "the greater number (or part) of." In formal writing, *most* should not be used as a substitute for *almost*: *We see each other almost* [not *most*] *every day.*

a lot   *A lot* is always two words, used informally to mean "many." *Alot* is a common misspelling.

among, between   In general, use *among* for relationships involving more than two people or for comparing one thing to a group to which it belongs. *The four of them agreed among themselves that the choice was between New York and Los Angeles.*

amount, number   Use *amount* with a singular noun that names something not countable (a noncount noun): *The amount of food varies.* Use *number* with a plural noun that names more than one of something countable (a plural count noun): *The number of calories must stay the same.*

and/or   *And/or* indicates three options: one or the other or both (*The decision is made by the mayor and/or the council*). If you mean all three options, *and/or* is appropriate. Otherwise, use *and* if you mean both; use *or* if you mean either.

ante-, anti-   The prefix *ante-* means "before" (*antedate, antebellum*); *anti-* means "against" (*antiwar, antinuclear*). Before a capital letter or *i*, *anti-* takes a hyphen: *anti-Freudian, anti-isolationist.*

anxious, eager   *Anxious* means "nervous" or "worried" and is usually followed by *about*. *Eager* means "looking forward" and is usually followed by *to*. *I've been anxious about getting blisters. I'm eager* [not *anxious*] *to get new running shoes.*

anybody, any body; anyone, any one   *Anybody* and *anyone* are indefinite pronouns; *any body* is a noun modified by *any*; *any one* is a pronoun or adjective modified by *any*. *How can anybody communicate with any body of government? Can anyone help Amy? She has more work than any one person can handle.*

any more, anymore   *Any more* means "no more"; *anymore* means "now." Both are used in negative constructions. *He doesn't want any more. She doesn't live here anymore.*

apt, liable, likely   *Apt* and *likely* are interchangeable. Strictly speaking, though, *apt* means "having a tendency to": *Horace is apt to forget his lunch in the morning. Likely* means "probably going to": *Horace is leaving so early today that he's likely to catch the first bus.*

   Liable normally means "in danger of" and should be confined to situations with undesirable consequences: *Horace is liable to trip over that hose.* Strictly, *liable* means "responsible" or "exposed": *The owner will be liable for Horace's injuries.*

are, is   Use *are* with a plural subject (*books are*), *is* with a singular subject (*a book is*).

as   *As* may be vague or ambiguous when it substitutes for *because*, *since*, or *while*: *As the researchers asked more questions, their money ran out.* (Does *as* mean "while" or "because"?) *As* should never be used as a substitute for *whether* or *who*. *I'm not sure whether* [not *as*] *we can make it. That's the man who* [not *as*] *gave me directions.*

as, like   In formal speech and writing, *like* should not introduce a full clause (with a subject and a verb) because it is a preposition. The preferred choice is *as* or *as if*: *The plan succeeded as* [not *like*] *we hoped. It seemed as if* [not *like*] *it might fail. Other plans like it have failed.*

as, than   In comparisons, *as* and *than* precede a subjective-case pronoun when the pronoun is a subject: *I love you more than he* [*loves you*]. *As* and *than* precede an objective-case pronoun when the pronoun is an object: *I love you as much as* [*I love*] *him.* (See also **4** p. 224.)

assure, ensure, insure   *Assure* means "to promise": *He assured us that we would miss the traffic. Ensure* and *insure* are often used interchangeably to mean "make certain," but some reserve *insure* for matters of legal and financial protection and use *ensure* for more general meanings: *We left early to ensure that we would miss the traffic. It's expensive to insure yourself against floods.*

at   The use of *at* after *where* is wordy and should be avoided: *Where are you meeting him?* is preferable to *Where are you meeting him at?*

awful, awfully   Strictly speaking, *awful* means "awe-inspiring." As intensifiers meaning "very" or "extremely" (*He tried awfully hard*), *awful* and *awfully* should be avoided in formal speech or writing.

a while, awhile   *Awhile* is an adverb; *a while* is an article and a noun. *I will be gone awhile* [not *a while*]. *I will be gone for a while* [not *awhile*].

bad, badly   In formal speech and writing, *bad* should be used only as an adjective; the adverb is *badly*. *He felt bad because his tooth ached badly.* In *He felt bad*, the verb *felt* is a linking verb and the adjective *bad* describes the subject. See also **4** p. 233.

being as, being that   Colloquial for *because*, the preferable word in formal speech or writing: *Because* [not *Being as*] *the world is round, Columbus never did fall off the edge.*

beside, besides   *Beside* is a preposition meaning "next to." *Besides* is a preposition meaning "except" or "in addition to" as well as an adverb meaning "in addition." *Besides, several other people besides you want to sit beside Dr. Christensen.*

better, had better   *Had better* (meaning "ought to") is a verb modified by an adverb. The verb is necessary and should not be omitted: *You had better* [not just *better*] *go.*

between, among   See *among, between.*

bring, take   Use *bring* only for movement from a farther place to a nearer one and *take* for any other movement. *First take these books to the library for renewal; then take them to Mr. Daniels. Bring them back to me when he's finished.*

but, hardly, scarcely   These words are negative in their own right; using *not* with any of them produces a double negative (see **4** p. 235). *We have but* [not *haven't got but*] *an hour before our plane leaves. I could hardly* [not *couldn't hardly*] *make out her face.*

but, however, yet   Each of these words is adequate to express contrast. Don't combine them. *He had finished, yet* [not *but yet*] *he continued.*

can, may   Strictly, *can* indicates capacity or ability, and *may* indicates permission or possibility: *If I may talk with you a moment, I believe I can solve your problem.*

censor, censure   To *censor* is to edit or remove from public view on moral or some other grounds; to *censure* is to give a formal scolding. *The lieutenant was censured by Major Taylor for censoring the letters her soldiers wrote home from boot camp.*

center around   *Center on* is more logical than, and preferable to, *center around.*

cite, sight, site   *Cite* is a verb usually meaning "quote," "commend," or "acknowledge": *You must cite your sources. Sight* is both a noun meaning "the ability to see" or "a view" and a verb meaning "perceive" or "observe": *What a sight you see when you sight Venus through a strong telescope. Site* is a noun meaning "place" or "location" or a verb meaning "situate": *The builder sited the house on an unlikely site.*

climatic, climactic   *Climatic* comes from *climate* and refers to the weather: *Recent droughts may indicate a climatic change. Climactic* comes from *climax* and refers to a dramatic high point: *During the climactic duel between Hamlet and Laertes, Gertrude drinks poisoned wine.*

complement, compliment   To *complement* something is to add to, complete, or reinforce it: *Her yellow blouse complemented her black hair.* To *compliment* something is to make a flattering remark about it: *He complimented her on her hair. Complimentary* can also mean "free": *complimentary tickets.*

conscience, conscious   *Conscience* is a noun meaning "a sense of right and wrong"; *conscious* is an adjective meaning "aware" or "awake." *Though I was barely conscious, my conscience nagged me.*

contact   Often used imprecisely as a verb instead of a more exact word such as *consult, talk with, telephone,* or *write to.*

continual, continuous   *Continual* means "constantly recurring": *Most movies on television are continually interrupted by commercials. Continuous* means "unceasing": *Some cable channels present movies continuously without commercials.*

could of   See *have, of.*

credible, creditable, credulous   *Credible* means "believable": *It's a strange story, but it seems credible to me. Creditable* means "deserving of credit" or "worthy": *Steve gave a creditable performance. Credulous* means "gullible": *The credulous Claire believed Tim's lies.* See also *incredible, incredulous.*

criteria The plural of *criterion* (meaning "standard for judgment"): *Our criteria are strict. The most important criterion is a sense of humor.*

data The plural of *datum* (meaning "fact"). Though *data* is often used as a singular noun, most careful writers still treat it as plural: *The data fail* [not *fails*] *to support the hypothesis.*

device, devise *Device* is the noun, and *devise* is the verb: *Can you devise some device for getting his attention?*

different from, different than *Different from* is preferred: *His purpose is different from mine.* But *different than* is widely accepted when a construction using *from* would be wordy: *I'm a different person now than I used to be* is preferable to *I'm a different person now from the person I used to be.*

differ from, differ with To *differ from* is to be unlike: *The twins differ from each other only in their hairstyles.* To *differ with* is to disagree with: *I have to differ with you on that point.*

discreet, discrete *Discreet* (noun form *discretion*) means "tactful": *What's a discreet way of telling Maud to be quiet? Discrete* (noun form *discreteness*) means "separate and distinct": *Within a computer's memory are millions of discrete bits of information.*

disinterested, uninterested *Disinterested* means "impartial": *We chose Pete, as a disinterested third party, to decide who was right. Uninterested* means "bored" or "lacking interest": *Unfortunately, Pete was completely uninterested in the question.*

don't *Don't* is the contraction for *do not*, not for *does not*: *I don't care, you don't care,* and *he doesn't* [not *don't*] *care.*

due to the fact that Wordy for *because.*

eager, anxious See *anxious, eager.*

effect See *affect, effect.*

elicit, illicit *Elicit* is a verb meaning "bring out" or "call forth." *Illicit* is an adjective meaning "unlawful." *The crime elicited an outcry against illicit drugs.*

emigrate, immigrate *Emigrate* means "to leave one place and move to another": *The Chus emigrated from Korea. Immigrate* means "to move into a place where one was not born": *They immigrated to the United States.*

ensure See *assure, ensure, insure.*

enthused Used colloquially as an adjective meaning "showing enthusiasm." The preferred adjective is *enthusiastic*: *The coach was enthusiastic* [not *enthused*] *about the team's prospects.*

et al., etc. Use *et al.*, the Latin abbreviation for "and other people," only in source citations: *Jones et al.* Avoid *etc.*, the Latin abbreviation for "and other things," in formal writing, and do not use it to refer to people or to substitute for precision, as in *The government provides health care, etc.*

everybody, every body; everyone, every one *Everybody* and *everyone* are indefinite pronouns: *Everybody* [*everyone*] *knows Tom steals. Every one* is a pronoun modified by *every*, and *every body* a noun modified by *every*. Both refer to each thing or person of a specific group and are typically followed by *of*: *The game commissioner has stocked every body of fresh water in the state with fish, and now every one of our rivers is a potential trout stream.*

everyday, every day *Everyday* is an adjective meaning "used daily" or "common"; *every day* is a noun modified by *every*: *Everyday problems tend to arise every day.*

everywheres Nonstandard for *everywhere*.

except See *accept, except*.

except for the fact that Wordy for *except that*.

explicit, implicit *Explicit* means "stated outright": *I left explicit instructions. Implicit* means "implied, unstated": *We had an implicit understanding.*

farther, further *Farther* refers to additional distance (*How much farther is it to the beach?*), and *further* refers to additional time, amount, or other abstract matters (*I don't want to discuss this any further*).

fewer, less *Fewer* refers to individual countable items (a plural count noun), *less* to general amounts (a noncount noun, always singular). *Skim milk has fewer calories than whole milk. We have less milk left than I thought.*

flaunt, flout *Flaunt* means "show off": *If you have style, flaunt it. Flout* means "scorn" or "defy": *Hester Prynne flouted convention and paid the price.*

flunk A colloquial substitute for *fail*.

fun As an adjective, *fun* is colloquial and should be avoided in most writing: *It was a pleasurable* [not *fun*] *evening.*

further See *farther, further*.

get This common verb is used in many slang and colloquial expressions: *get lost, that really gets me, getting on. Get* is easy to overuse: watch out for it in expressions such as *it's getting better* (substitute *improving*) and *we got done* (substitute *finished*).

good, well *Good* is an adjective, and *well* is nearly always an adverb: *Larry's a good dancer. He and Linda dance well together. Well* is properly used as an adjective only to refer to health: *You look well.* (*You look good*, in contrast, means "Your appearance is pleasing.")

good and Colloquial for "very": *I was very* [not *good and*] *tired.*

had better See *better, had better*.

had ought The *had* is unnecessary and should be omitted: *He ought* [not *had ought*] *to listen to his mother.*

hanged, hung Though both are past-tense forms of *hang*, *hanged* is used to refer to executions and *hung* is used for all other meanings: *Tom*

Dooley was hanged [not hung] *from a white oak tree. I* hung [not hanged] *the picture you gave me.*

hardly   See *but, hardly, scarcely.*

have, of   Use *have,* not *of,* after helping verbs such as *could, should, would, may, must,* and *might: You* should have [not should of] *told me.*

he, she; he/she   Convention has allowed the use of *he* to mean "he or she": *After the infant learns to creep,* he *progresses to crawling.* However, many writers today consider this usage inaccurate and unfair because it seems to exclude females. The construction *he/she,* one substitute for *he,* is awkward and objectionable to most readers. The better choice is to make the pronoun plural, to rephrase, or, sparingly, to use *he or she.* For instance: *After* infants *learn to creep,* they *progress to crawling. After learning to creep,* the infant *progresses to crawling. After the infant learns to creep,* he or she *progresses to crawling.* See also **3** p. 160 and **4** pp. 227–28.

herself, himself   See *myself, herself, himself, yourself.*

hisself   Nonstandard for *himself.*

hopefully   *Hopefully* means "with hope": *Freddy waited* hopefully *for a glimpse of Eliza.* The use of *hopefully* to mean "it is to be hoped," "I hope," or "let's hope" is now very common; but try to avoid it in writing because many readers continue to object strongly to the usage. *I* hope [not Hopefully] *the law will pass.*

idea, ideal   An *idea* is a thought or conception. An *ideal* (noun) is a model of perfection or a goal. *Ideal* should not be used in place of *idea: The* idea [not ideal] *of the play is that our* ideals *often sustain us.*

if, whether   For clarity, use *whether* rather than *if* when you are expressing an alternative: *If I laugh hard, people can't tell* whether *I'm crying.*

illicit   See *elicit, illicit.*

illusion   See *allusion, illusion.*

immigrate, emigrate   See *emigrate, immigrate.*

implicit   See *explicit, implicit.*

imply, infer   Writers or speakers *imply,* meaning "suggest": *Jim's letter* implies *he's having a good time.* Readers or listeners *infer,* meaning "conclude": *From Jim's letter I* infer *he's having a good time.*

incredible, incredulous   *Incredible* means "unbelievable"; *incredulous* means "unbelieving": *When Nancy heard Dennis's* incredible *story, she was frankly* incredulous. See also *credible, creditable, credulous.*

individual, person, party   *Individual* should refer to a single human being in contrast to a group or should stress uniqueness: *The US Constitution places strong emphasis on the rights of the* individual. For other meanings *person* is preferable: *What* person [not individual] *wouldn't want the security promised in that advertisement? Party* means "group" (*Can you seat a* party *of four for dinner?*) and should not be used to refer to an individual except in legal documents. See also *people, persons.*

infer   See *imply, infer.*

in regards to   Nonstandard for *in regard to, as regards,* or *regarding.*

inside of, outside of   The *of* is unnecessary when *inside* and *outside* are used as prepositions: *Stay inside* [not *inside of*] *the house. The decision is outside* [not *outside of*] *my authority. Inside of* may refer colloquially to time, though in formal English *within* is preferred: *The law was passed within* [not *inside of*] *a year.*

insure   See *assure, ensure, insure.*

irregardless   Nonstandard for *regardless.*

is, are   See *are, is.*

is because   See *reason is because.*

is when, is where   These are faulty constructions in sentences that de-fine: *Adolescence is a stage* [not *is when a person is*] *between childhood and adulthood. Socialism is a system in which* [not *is where*] *government owns the means of production.* See also **4** p. 253.

its, it's   *Its* is the pronoun *it* in the possessive case: *That plant is losing its leaves. It's* is a contraction for *it is* or *it has*: *It's* [*It is*] *likely to die. It's* [*It has*] *got a fungus.* Many people confuse *it's* and *its* because posses-sives are most often formed with *-'s*; but the possessive *its*, like *his* and *hers*, never takes an apostrophe.

-ize, -wise   The suffix *-ize* changes a noun or an adjective into a verb: *revolutionize, immunize.* The suffix *-wise* changes a noun or adjective into an adverb: *clockwise, otherwise, likewise.* Avoid the two suffixes except in established words: *I'm highly sensitive* [not *sensitized*] *to that kind of criticism. Financially* [not *Moneywise*], *it's a good time to buy real estate.*

kind of, sort of, type of   In formal speech and writing, avoid using *kind of* or *sort of* to mean "somewhat": *He was rather* [not *kind of*] *tall.*
   Kind, sort, and *type* are singular and take singular modifiers and verbs: *This kind of dog is easily trained.* Agreement errors often occur when these singular nouns are combined with the plural adjectives *these* and *those*: *These kinds* [not *kind*] *of dogs are easily trained. Kind, sort,* and *type* should be followed by *of* but not by *a*: *I don't know what type of* [not *type* or *type of a*] *dog that is.*
   Use *kind of, sort of,* or *type of* only when the word *kind, sort,* or *type* is important: *That was a strange* [not *strange sort of*] *statement.*

lay, lie   *Lay* means "put" or "place" and takes a direct object: *We could lay the tablecloth in the sun.* Its main forms are *lay, laid, laid. Lie* means "recline" or "be situated" and does not take an object: *I lie awake at night. The town lies east of the river.* Its main forms are *lie, lay, lain.* (See also **4** p. 196.)

leave, let   *Leave* and *let* are interchangeable only when followed by *alone*: *leave me alone* is the same as *let me alone.* Otherwise, *leave* means "depart" and *let* means "allow": *Jill would not let Sue leave.*

less   See *fewer, less.*

liable See *apt, liable, likely.*

lie, lay See *lay, lie.*

like, as See *as, like.*

like, such as Strictly, *such as* precedes an example that represents a larger subject, whereas *like* indicates that two subjects are comparable. *Steve has recordings of many great saxophonists such as Ben Webster and Lee Konitz. Steve wants to be a great jazz saxophonist like Ben Webster and Lee Konitz.*

likely See *apt, liable, likely.*

literally This word means "actually" or "just as the words say," and it should not be used to qualify or intensify expressions whose words are not to be taken at face value. The sentence *He was literally climbing the walls* describes a person behaving like an insect, not a person who is restless or anxious. For the latter meaning, *literally* should be omitted.

lose, loose *Lose* means "mislay": *Did you lose a brown glove? Loose* means "unrestrained" or "not tight": *Ann's canary got loose. Loose* also can function as a verb meaning "let loose": *They loose the dogs as soon as they spot the bear.*

lots, lots of Colloquial substitutes for *very many, a great many,* or *much.* Avoid *lots* and *lots of* in college or business writing.

may, can See *can, may.*

may be, maybe *May be* is a verb, and *maybe* is an adverb meaning "perhaps": *Tuesday may be a legal holiday. Maybe we won't have classes.*

may of See *have, of.*

media *Media* is the plural of *medium* and takes a plural verb: *All the news media are increasingly visual.* The singular verb is common, even in the media, but many readers prefer the plural verb and it is always correct.

might of See *have, of.*

moral, morale As a noun, *moral* means "ethical conclusion" or "lesson": *The moral of the story escapes me. Morale* means "spirit" or "state of mind": *Victory improved the team's morale.*

most, almost See *almost, most.*

must of See *have, of.*

myself, herself, himself, yourself The *-self* pronouns refer to or intensify another word or words: *Paul helped himself; Jill herself said so.* The *-self* pronouns are often used colloquially in place of personal pronouns, but that use should be avoided in formal speech and writing: *No one except me* [not *myself*] *saw the accident. Our delegates will be Susan and you* [not *yourself*]. See also **4** p. 221 on the unchanging forms of the *-self* pronouns in standard American English.

nowheres Nonstandard for *nowhere.*

number See *amount, number.*

of, have See *have, of.*

off of *Of* is unnecessary. Use *off* or *from* rather than *off of*: *He jumped off* [or *from*, not *off of*] *the roof.*

OK, O.K., okay All three spellings are acceptable, but avoid this colloquial term in formal speech and writing.

on account of Wordy for *because of.*

on the other hand This transitional expression of contrast should be preceded by its mate, *on the one hand*: *On the one hand, we hoped for snow. On the other hand, we worried that it would harm the animals.* However, the two combined can be unwieldy, and a simple *but, however, yet,* or *in contrast* often suffices: *We hoped for snow. Yet we worried that it would harm the animals.*

outside of See *inside of, outside of.*

owing to the fact that Wordy for *because.*

party See *individual, person, party.*

people, persons In formal usage, *people* refers to a general group: *We the people of the United States. . . . Persons* refers to a collection of individuals: *Will the person or persons who saw the accident please notify. . . .* Except when emphasizing individuals, prefer *people* to *persons.* See also *individual, person, party.*

per Except in technical writing, an English equivalent is usually preferable to the Latin *per*: *$10 an* [not *per*] *hour; sent by* [not *per*] *parcel post; requested in* [not *per* or *as per*] *your letter.*

percent (per cent), percentage Both these terms refer to fractions of one hundred. *Percent* always follows a number (*40 percent of the voters*), and the word is often used instead of the symbol (%) in nontechnical writing. *Percentage* stands alone (*the percentage of voters*) or follows an adjective (*a high percentage*).

person See *individual, person, party.*

persons See *people, persons.*

phenomena The plural of *phenomenon* (meaning "perceivable fact" or "unusual occurrence"): *Many phenomena are not recorded. One phenomenon is attracting attention.*

plenty A colloquial substitute for *very*: *The reaction occurred very* [not *plenty*] *fast.*

plus *Plus* is standard as a preposition meaning "in addition to": *His income plus mine is sufficient.* But *plus* is colloquial as a conjunctive adverb: *Our organization is larger than theirs; moreover* [not *plus*], *we have more money.*

precede, proceed The verb *precede* means "come before": *My name precedes yours in the alphabet.* The verb *proceed* means "move on": *We were told to proceed to the waiting room.*

prejudice, prejudiced   *Prejudice* is a noun; *prejudiced* is an adjective. Do not drop the -*d* from *prejudiced*: *I was fortunate that my parents were not prejudiced* [not *prejudice*].

pretty   Overworked as an adverb meaning "rather" or "somewhat": *He was somewhat* [not *pretty*] *irked at the suggestion.*

previous to, prior to   Wordy for *before*.

principal, principle   *Principal* is an adjective meaning "foremost" or "major," a noun meaning "chief official," or, in finance, a noun meaning "capital sum." *Principle* is a noun only, meaning "rule" or "axiom." *Her principal reasons for confessing were her principles of right and wrong.*

proceed, precede   See *precede, proceed*.

question of whether, question as to whether   Wordy substitutes for *whether*.

raise, rise   *Raise* means "lift" or "bring up" and takes a direct object: *The Kirks raise cattle*. Its main forms are *raise, raised, raised*. *Rise* means "get up" and does not take an object: *They must rise at dawn*. Its main forms are *rise, rose, risen*. (See also **4** p. 196.)

real, really   In formal speech and writing, *real* should not be used as an adverb; *really* is the adverb and *real* an adjective. *Popular reaction to the announcement was really* [not *real*] *enthusiastic.*

reason is because   Although colloquially common, this expression should be avoided in formal speech and writing. Use a *that* clause after *reason is*: *The reason he is absent is that* [not *is because*] *he is sick.* Or: *He is absent because he is sick.* (See also **4** p. 254.)

respectful, respective   *Respectful* means "full of (or showing) respect": *Be respectful of other people*. *Respective* means "separate": *The French and the Germans occupied their respective trenches.*

rise, raise   See *raise, rise*.

scarcely   See *but, hardly, scarcely*.

sensual, sensuous   *Sensual* suggests sexuality; *sensuous* means "pleasing to the senses." *Stirred by the sensuous scent of meadow grass and flowers, Cheryl and Paul found their thoughts growing increasingly sensual.*

set, sit   *Set* means "put" or "place" and takes a direct object: *He sets the pitcher down*. Its main forms are *set, set, set*. *Sit* means "be seated" and does not take an object: *She sits on the sofa*. Its main forms are *sit, sat, sat*. (See also **4** p. 196.)

shall, will   *Will* is the future-tense helping verb for all persons: *I will go, you will go, they will go*. The main use of *shall* is for first-person questions requesting an opinion or consent: *Shall I order a pizza? Shall we dance?* *Shall* can also be used for the first person when a formal effect is desired (*I shall expect you around three*), and it is occasionally used with the second or third person to express the speaker's determination (*You shall do as I say*).

should of   See *have, of*.

sight, site, cite   See *cite, sight, site.*

since   *Since* mainly relates to time: *I've been waiting since noon.* But *since* is also often used to mean "because": *Since you ask, I'll tell you.* Revise sentences in which the word could have either meaning, such as *Since I studied physics, I have been planning to major in engineering.*

sit, set   See *set, sit.*

site, cite, sight   See *cite, sight, site.*

so   Avoid using *so* alone or as a vague intensifier: *He was so late. So* needs to be followed by *that* and a clause that states a result: *He was so late that I left without him.*

somebody, some body; someone, some one   *Somebody* and *someone* are indefinite pronouns; *some body* is a noun modified by *some*; and *some one* is a pronoun or an adjective modified by *some. Somebody ought to invent a shampoo that will give hair some body. Someone told Janine she should choose some one plan and stick with it.*

sometime, sometimes, some time   *Sometime* means "at an indefinite time in the future": *Why don't you come up and see me sometime? Sometimes* means "now and then": *I still see my old friend Joe sometimes. Some time* means "a span of time": *I need some time to make the payments.*

somewheres   Nonstandard for *somewhere.*

sort of, sort of a   See *kind of, sort of, type of.*

such   Avoid using *such* as a vague intensifier: *It was such a cold winter. Such* should be followed by *that* and a clause that states a result: *It was such a cold winter that Napoleon's troops had to turn back.*

such as   See *like, such as.*

supposed to, used to   In both these expressions, the *-d* is essential: *I used to* [not *use to*] *think so. He's supposed to* [not *suppose to*] *meet us.*

sure   Colloquial when used as an adverb meaning *surely: James Madison sure was right about the need for the Bill of Rights.* If you merely want to be emphatic, use *certainly: Madison certainly was right.* If your goal is to convince a possibly reluctant reader, use *surely: Madison surely was right.*

sure and, sure to; try and, try to   *Sure to* and *try to* are the correct forms: *Be sure to* [not *sure and*] *buy milk. Try to* [not *Try and*] *find some decent tomatoes.*

take, bring   See *bring, take.*

than, as   See *as, than.*

than, then   *Than* is a conjunction used in comparisons, *then* an adverb indicating time: *Holmes knew then that Moriarty was wilier than he had thought.*

that, which   *That* introduces an essential clause: *We should use the lettuce that Susan bought* (*that Susan bought* limits the lettuce to a particular lettuce). *Which* can introduce both essential and nonessential clauses, but many writers reserve *which* only for nonessential clauses:

The leftover lettuce, which is in the refrigerator, would make a good salad (*which is in the refrigerator* simply provides more information about the lettuce we already know of). Essential clauses (with *that* or *which*) are not set off by commas; nonessential clauses (with *which*) are. See also **5** pp. 264–65.

that, which, who   Use *that* for animals, things, and sometimes collective or anonymous people: *The rocket that failed cost millions. Infants that walk need constant tending.* Use *which* only for animals and things: *The river, which flows south, divides two countries.* Use *who* only for people and for animals with names: *Dorothy is the girl who visits Oz. Her dog, Toto, who accompanies her, gives her courage.*

their, there, they're   *Their* is the possessive form of *they*: *Give them their money. There* indicates place (*I saw her standing there*) or functions as an expletive (*There is a hole behind you*). *They're* is a contraction for *they are*: *They're going fast.*

theirselves   Nonstandard for *themselves*.

them   In standard American English, *them* does not serve as an adjective: *Those* [not *them*] *people want to know.*

then, than   See *than, then.*

these kind, these sort, these type, those kind   See *kind of, sort of, type of.*

this, these   *This* is singular: *this car* or *This is the reason I left. These* is plural: *these cars* or *These are not valid reasons.*

thru   A colloquial spelling of *through* that should be avoided in all academic and business writing.

to, too, two   *To* is a preposition; *too* is an adverb meaning "also" or "excessively"; and *two* is a number. *I too have been to Europe two times.*

too   Avoid using *too* as a vague intensifier: *Monkeys are too mean.* If you do use *too*, explain the consequences of the excessive quality: *Monkeys are too mean to make good pets.*

toward, towards   Both are acceptable, though *toward* is preferred. Use one or the other consistently.

try and, try to   See *sure and, sure to; try and, try to.*

type of   See *kind of, sort of, type of.* Don't use *type* without *of*: *It was a family type of* [not *type*] *restaurant.* Or better: *It was a family restaurant.*

uninterested   See *disinterested, uninterested.*

unique   *Unique* means "the only one of its kind" and so cannot sensibly be modified with words such as *very* or *most*: *That was a unique* [not *a very unique* or *the most unique*] *movie.*

usage, use   *Usage* refers to conventions, most often those of a language: *Is "hadn't ought" proper usage? Usage* is often misused in place of the noun *use*: *Wise use* [not *usage*] *of insulation can save fuel.*

use, utilize   *Utilize* can be used to mean "make good use of": *Many teachers utilize computers for instruction.* But for all other senses of "place in service" or "employ," prefer *use.*

used to   See *supposed to, used to.*

wait for, wait on In formal speech and writing, *wait for* means "await" (*I'm waiting for Paul*) and *wait on* means "serve" (*The owner of the store herself waited on us*).

ways Colloquial as a substitute for *way*: *We have only a little way* [not *ways*] *to go.*

well See *good, well.*

whether, if See *if, whether.*

which, that See *that, which.*

which, who, that See *that, which, who.*

who's, whose *Who's* is the contraction of *who is* or *who has*: *Who's* [*Who is*] *at the door? Jim is the only one who's* [*who has*] *passed. Whose* is the possessive form of *who*: *Whose book is that?*

will, shall See *shall, will.*

-wise See *-ize, -wise.*

would be Often used instead of *is* or *are* to soften statements needlessly: *One example is* [not *would be*] *gun-control laws. Would* can combine with other verbs for the same unassertive effect: *would ask, would seem, would suggest,* and so on.

would have Avoid this construction in place of *had* in clauses that begin *if* and state a condition contrary to fact: *If the tree had* [not *would have*] *withstood the fire, it would have been the oldest in town.* See also **4** pp. 212–13.

would of See *have, of.*

you In all but very formal writing, *you* is generally appropriate as long as it means "you, the reader." In all writing, avoid indefinite uses of *you*, such as *In one ancient tribe your first loyalty was to your parents.* See also **4** pp. 230–31.

your, you're *Your* is the possessive form of *you*: *Your dinner is ready. You're* is the contraction of *you are*: *You're bound to be late.*

yourself See *myself, herself, himself, yourself.*

Credits

Text and Illustrations

Ali, Agha Shahid. "Postcard from Kashmir," *The Veiled Suite: The Collected Poems*. © 2009 by Agha Shahid Ali. Reprinted by permission of Wesleyan University Press.

Campbell, Neil A., and Jane B. Reece. *Biology*, 7th edition. Glenview: Benjamin Cummings, 2005, p. 47.

Cunningham, John A., and Peter Selby. "Relighting Cigarettes: How Common Is It?" by John A. Cunningham and Peter Selby, *Nicotine and Tobacco Research*, 9 (5), 621–623, 2007, reprinted by permission of Taylor & Francis Ltd., *www.tandf.co.uk/journals*.

Dyson, Freeman J. From *Disturbing the Universe* by Freeman J. Dyson. Copyright © 1979 by Freeman J. Dyson. Reprinted by permission of Basic Books, a member of Perseus Books Group.

Mayer, Lawrence. "The Confounding Enemy of Sleep." *Fortune*, June, 1974.

Ouchi, William G. *Theory Z*. Addison-Wesley, 1981.

Rosen, Ruth. "Search for Yesterday" by Ruth Rosen, from *Watching Television*, edited by Todd Gitlin. Pantheon Books, 1986.

Sale, Kirkpatrick. "The Environmental Crisis Is Not Our Fault" from *The Nation*, April 30, 1990. Reprinted with permission. For subscription information, call 1-800-333-8536. Portions of each week's *Nation* magazine can be accessed at *http://www.thenation.com*.

Shteir, Rachel. *The Steal: A Cultural History of Shoplifting*. © 2011 by Rachel Shteir. Used by permission of The Penguin Press, a division of Penguin Group (USA) Inc.

Sowell, Thomas. "Student Loans" from *"Is Reality Optional?" and Other Essays* by Thomas Sowell. Copyright © 1993 by Thomas Sowell. Reprinted by permission of Creators Syndicate.

Tuchman, Barbara. "The Decline of Quality" by Barbara Tuchman, *The New York Times*, November 2, 1980. Copyright © 1980 by Barbara Tuchman. Reprinted by the permission of Russell & Volkening as agents for the author.

UNFPA. "AIDS Clock" from the UNFPA Web site, *www.unfpa.org*, 2011. Produced by UNFPA, the United Nations Population Fund, using data provided by UNAIDS. Design by Allysson Lucca. Reprinted by permission.

Woodward, Kenneth L. "Life after Death?" by Kenneth L. Woodward. From *Newsweek*, July 12, 1976. © 1976 Newsweek Inc. All rights reserved. Used by permission and protected by the copyright laws of the United States. The printing, copying, redistribution, or retransmission of the material without express written permission is prohibited.

Woolf, Virginia. *The Waves*. Harcourt, 1931.

Photos

Courtesy AB Electrolux. **67:** Bill Aron/PhotoEdit. **68:** Cartoon provided by the author. **71:** David Fischer/Getty Images. **89:** *BoostUp.org*. **92:** UNFPA, the UN Population Fund. **113:** Army materials courtesy of the US government. **115:** Image courtesy of the National Highway Traffic Safety Administration and the Ad Council. **139:** Steve Cole/Getty Images. **175:** Sabah Arar/AFP/Getty Images. **257:** Steven Hunt/Getty Images. **291:** Paul Taylor/ Getty Images. **309:** Shinya Sasaki/NeoVision/Getty Images. **327, 328:** Reproduced with permission of EBSCO Publishing, Inc. All rights reserved. **345 top:** Allianz SE. **345 bottom:** Reprinted by permission from Macmillan Publishers Ltd: *Nature Climate Change* 1, 29–31, copyright 2011. **373:** Exactostock/SuperStock. **430:** "The Birth of Hip-Hop: Innovation against the Odds," by Amanda Murray, Lemelson Center, National Museum of American History, Smithsonian Institution. **438:** Reproduced with permission of Dr. Ted Becker/*Journal of Public Deliberation*. **440:** Reproduced with permission of EBSCO Publishing, Inc. All rights reserved.

Index

Pretentious writing, **3** 157–58
pretty, **Gl** 520
Previewing, for critical reading or viewing
 of text, **2** 79–81
 of visuals, **2** 88
previous to, prior to, **Gl** 520
Primary sources
 defined, **7** 315, **8** 375
 one's own knowledge as, **7** 314
 one's own research as, **7** 336–38
 for research, **7** 315, 334, **8** 375
 vs. secondary sources, **7** 315, **8** 375–76
principal, principle, **6** 294, **Gl** 520
Principal parts of verbs, **4** 193
Printing out research sources, pros and cons, **7** 352
Prints and Photographs Online Catalog, **7** 335
Print sources, documenting
 APA style, **APA** 469–72, 477–79
 Chicago style, **Chic** 493–95, 498–99
 CSE style, **CSE** 504–05, 506–07
 MLA style, **MLA** 414–27, 445
prior to, **3** 165
prior to, previous to, **Gl** 520
Privacy issues, electronic communication, **2** 78
Problem-solution organization, **1** 19
Problem-solving analysis, **8** 390
proceed, precede, **Gl** 520
Proceedings, MLA style, **MLA** 425
Process
 critical reading and viewing, **2** 79–93
 research writing, **7** 369–71
 writing, **1** 3–70
Process analysis
 in essay development, **1** 14
 in paragraph development, **1** 49
Progressive tenses
 defined, **4** 199
 formation of, **4** 199–200, 208
 uses of, **4** 208
Pronoun-antecedent agreement. *See* Agreement of pronouns and antecedents
Pronouns, **4** 220–31

 adjectives to modify, **4** 232
 agreement with antecedents, **4** 225–28
 apostrophes misused with possessives, **5** 280
 cases of, **4** 221
 consistency in, **4** 231
 defined, **4** 179, 220
 demonstrative, **4** 179
 gender of, **4** 225
 grammar checkers for, **4** 229
 indefinite. *See* Indefinite pronouns
 intensive, **4** 179
 interrogative, **4** 179
 for paragraph coherence, **1** 43
 personal. *See* Personal pronouns
 reference of, **4** 228–31
 reflexive, **4** 179
 relative. *See* Relative pronouns
 as subject complements, **4** 220
 types of, **4** 179
Pronunciation, spelling and, **6** 293–94
Proofreading
 of direct quotations, **7** 355
 for online communications, **2** 78, **3** 156
 as part of writing process, **1** 33–34, **3** 169
Proper adjectives, capitalization of, **6** 299–300
Proper nouns
 articles with, **4** 238
 capitalization of, **6** 299–300
 common nouns as essential parts of, **6** 301
 defined, **4** 178, 236, **6** 299
Proposals. *See* Reports
ProQuest, **7** 328, 338
Prose, formatting long quotations from
 APA style, **APA** 482
 MLA style, **MLA** 448
proud of, **3** 165
Psychology, research sources on, **8** 393
Publication Manual of the American Psychological Association. *See* APA style

Throughout this handbook, the symbol **CULTURE LANGUAGE** signals topics for students whose first language or dialect is not standard American English. These topics can be tricky because they arise from rules in standard English that are quite different in other languages and dialects. Many of the topics involve significant cultural assumptions as well.

Whatever your language background, as a college student you are learning the culture of US higher education and the language that is used and shaped by that culture. The process is challenging, even for native speakers of standard American English. It requires not just writing clearly and correctly but also mastering conventions of developing, presenting, and supporting ideas. The challenge is greater if, in addition, you are trying to learn standard American English and are accustomed to other conventions. Several habits can help you succeed:

- **Read.** Besides course assignments, read newspapers, magazines, and books in English. The more you read, the more fluently and accurately you'll write.
- **Write.** Keep a journal in which you practice writing in English every day.
- **Talk and listen.** Take advantage of opportunities to hear and use English.
- **Ask questions.** Your instructors, tutors in the writing lab, and fellow students can clarify assignments and help you identify and solve writing problems.
- **Don't try for perfection.** No one writes perfectly, and the effort to do so can prevent you from expressing yourself fluently. View mistakes not as failures but as opportunities to learn.
- **Revise first; then edit.** Focus on each essay's ideas, support, and organization before attending to grammar and vocabulary. See the revision and editing checklists in **1** pp. 27 and 31.
- **Set editing priorities.** Concentrate first on any errors that interfere with clarity, such as problems with word order or subject-verb agreement.

The following index leads you to text discussions of topics that you may need help with.

Contents

CULTURE LANGUAGE **Guide on reverse**